Using Language

The Structures of Speech Acts

SUNY Series in Philosophy
Robert C. Neville, Editor

Using Language

The Structures of Speech Acts

John T. Kearns

State University of New York, Buffalo

State University of New York Press
Albany

Published by
State University of New York Press, Albany

Printed in the United States of America

For information, address State University of New York Press, State University Plaza, Albany, N.Y., 12246

Library of Congress Cataloging in Publication Data

Kearns, John T., 1936–
Using language.

1. Speech acts (Linguistics) I. Title.
P95.55.K42 1984 401′.9 83-14491
ISBN 0–87395–808–1
ISBN 0–87395–809–8 (pbk.)

10 9 8 7 6 5 4 3 2 1

Contents

Acknowledgements

I have been engaged in the specific project of this book for the last seven years. The pursuit of this project has been the occasion for many surprises. I discovered things about language and about human action that were news to me. I had to change my mind about various issues on innumerable occasions. And the final product of my labors amazes me. I hadn't initially thought that things would be this complicated—though the complicated account exhibits an underlying simplicity. I wouldn't have believed that I was capable of developing such an elaborate account.

I have contracted many intellectual debts in working out the views of the present book. There is an enormous debt to Wilfrid Sellars, who taught me in graduate school and who has influenced me since then. This debt may be obscured by the criticisms I aim in his direction, but what I have learned, and borrowed, from him is more important than those aspects of his views that I reject. My work has also benefitted from the presence of many colleagues over the years. They haven't commented on, or criticized, the present book, but I have learned a great deal from being around them. I have found it especially helpful to have been around John Pollock, William T. Parry, and John Corcoran. John Pollock has had a lot to say about logic and epistemology. What he says isn't always right, but it is nearly always thought provoking. Bill Parry and John Corcoran have helped me to get clear about logic, although they may not agree that I am clear about it. I have also learned a lot from talking with John Searle, and from reading his work.

While I am expressing gratitude, I should include many graduate students over the course of several years. These students haven't very often told me things I needed to know. But the efforts required to organize the material for use in several courses, and the actual presentation of the material, have been enormously useful in clarifying many topics and issues. It is one thing to put something down in writing. It is something quite different, and more difficult, to talk about it in class. Although most of the graduate students who have been helpful to me have provided an occasion for talking about the issues I discuss in the book, there is one who has helped by telling me things I needed to know. A recent graduate seminar was graced by the presence of Stanley Ziewacz. His background in mathematics and linguistics, and his talents, enabled him to understand what I was up to, to ask just the right questions, and to make useful suggestions. The book and I have both gained from his presence in that seminar.

Introduction

1. A Speech-Act Theory

In this book, I develop a speech-act theory of language. In my conception, the primary linguistic reality is the linguistic acts and activity of human beings. Expressions are instruments that people use to perform these acts. There are rules for using these expressions. But linguistic acts are primary. We make an abstraction—we proceed abstractly—when we consider expressions apart from acts and actors. Such abstraction can be legitimate and helpful. But it must be recognized for what it is. An abstract study won't fully succeed unless it is situated within the framework provided by the concrete reality it is abstracted from.

A speech-act theory investigates acts and their features. For example, we might consider an act done for a certain purpose, and determine how the purpose of this act relates it to another act or acts. In the present setting, we want to use the analyses of acts and their features to shed light on linguistic phenomena more narrowly conceived. For example, if the acts of using expressions in a sentence are related in a certain way, we want to use our understanding of this relation to shed light on the syntactic structure of the sentence. Or we might relate the truth conditions of a sentence to a speaker's intentions in using the sentence.

The present speech-act theory does not displace or replace more traditionally conceived linguistic studies. This theory leaves room for both syntax and semantics. But syntax and semantics are abstract theories, while this speech act theory is not. (It may be safer to claim only that the speech-act theory is less abstract than syntax or semantics.) While the present theory does not abolish syntax and semantics, it does provide a framework within which these studies can be located. To a very considerable extent, the present speech-act theory determines the shapes of acceptable theories of syntax and semantics.

Many articles and books investigate and develop different theories of speech acts. Most studies of speech acts deal with one or another kind of act, and attempt to give its essential characteristics. In the work of John Searle, for example, most attention has been paid to illocutionary acts. Searle has listed the various kinds of conditions and rules which are involved in all illocutionary acts. He has tried to provide the specifics of such illocutionary acts as promising and asserting. Searle has made attempts to similarly characterize referring and predicating, but these have been treated much less fully than illocutionary acts.

What is characteristic of the present theory is its focus on the relations between linguistic acts. Some linguistic acts are complex. The relation between a component act and the complex act it helps constitute is an important relation. Another fundamental relation links one act to another act which it makes possible. The study of such relations is the main concern of the present theory. This study makes possible structural analyses of complex linguistic acts. These analyses provide the basis for an account of syntactic structure and an account of the general semantic features of complex expressions. Without an understanding of the relations between linguistic acts, there can be no comprehensive speech act theory of language. Without such an understanding there can be no satisfactory explanation of language or linguistic activity.

2. The More General Framework

The account of speech acts in this book is developed within the framework of a more general theory of intentional acts. This more general theory is not a well known current theory. So before I can deal with speech acts, I must come up with an account of intentional acts. I will develop the theory of intentional acts in a somewhat sketchy fashion. What I present is the outline of a theory, not a full-blown theory. My strategy is to begin with this outline, and then to flesh out the theory by applying it to a variety of specific topics and problems. The general theory of intentional acts becomes more fully articulated through its applications. But the general theory also provides an understanding of particular phenomena.

I originally intended for this book to include four applications of the general theory:

(1) A treatment of pronouns.
(2) An explanation of proper names, referring, and existential presupposition.

(3) An explanation of talk about fictional and mythical individuals.
(4) An explanation of talk about intentional states and relations—e.g., believing, hoping, and looking for.

Once this project was underway, I realized that it is not possible to include all four applications in a book of reasonable size. I have left the third and fourth applications out of the present book; they will be dealt with on other occasions.

In order to make the strategy of this book clearer to the reader, I will say a few things about theories. I distinguish two kinds of theory, *framework theories* and *nonframework theories*. A framework theory establishes a conceptual scheme; it provides language to be used in describing (and explaining) a class of phenomena. A framework theory cannot be established or supported either by deductive arguments from other knowledge, or by inductive arguments from empirical evidence. A framework theory provides conceptual structure to its phenomena; this renders it immune from outside support. Justified by its success and fruitfulness, such a theory, when successful, provides satisfactory explanations for its phenomena. It promises to provide more explanations in the future. A nonframework theory is developed within the confines of a framework theory. This second kind of theory deals with a subclass of the phenomena covered by the framework theory, and supplements the framework theory. A nonframework theory can be supported by inductive and deductive arguments. The framework theory makes room for the nonframework theory, and provides criteria to be used in evaluating evidence for or against statements of the nonframework theory.

The general theory of intentional acts that is outlined in this book is a framework theory. It provides the resources for describing intentional acts and linguistic acts. These descriptions are explanatory, for they provide understanding of the ways that component acts combine to constitute complex acts. The general theory also describes and explains experience and its relation to language. To develop a framework theory, we must develop new ways of talking and thinking. This does not mean that we shall invent some totally new language. Although it will occasionally prove necessary to introduce new expressions, I will more commonly follow the practice of giving new (technical) meanings to existing expressions. The characteristic expressions of a framework theory cannot be completely defined in terms of expressions available prior to the theory's formulation. To develop a new conceptual scheme, we must explain how to use the new expressions with respect to one another, and also how to use them with respect to previously existing expressions.

We must explain how to use the expressions to describe the phenomena under consideration. We cannot introduce a new expression, or a new meaning for an old expression, and explain it once and for all. We must instead explain these expressions a little at a time. For we are developing a theory, not describing a finished product. The initial explanations of theoretical expressions are partial. These can be modified and supplemented as we proceed. I don't regard the theory developed in this book as a finished product, not even at the end of the book. The theory needs to be further developed, primarily through further applications.

In this book, the theory of intentional acts and the more specific theory of linguistic acts are formulated in response to various problems. I will often describe a problem and then work out a solution to it. I want the reader to take these problems as real problems for herself. She should consider how they might be solved. And then, I hope, see that the solution I give is just what is wanted. It is characteristic of the manner of presentation used in this book that later discussions can correct earlier ones. I may deal with a problem, and work out a solution. Then in a later section I might discover that the original solution is inadequate. It may need to be modified or refined. My practice in this book makes great demands on the reader. For it is left to the reader to distinguish cases where an earlier view is corrected by a later one from cases where I have simply been inconsistent. My method of presentation also allows expressions to be introduced and given partial meanings which are later supplemented or amended. If an expression is given a technical meaning at a certain point, it will generally not be used with this technical sense before the sense has been explained. So we may find an ordinary expression, used in the ordinary way, in an early part of the book. Later, once it is given a technical meaning, it will no longer be used in the ordinary way (unless I make a slip).

3. The Plan of the Book

The general theory of intentional acts is outlined in chapter one. This chapter gives a brief account of the structures of complex acts. Chapter two makes a preliminary application of the theory of intentional acts to linguistic acts. Chapter two is primarily concerned with illocutionary acts and their structures: a notation is developed for representing complex acts.

Chapters three, four, and five deal with the semantic dimensions of language and linguistic acts. In chapter three, two kinds of meaning are discussed: representational meaning and inferential meaning. The representational meaning of an expression is what the expression is used to represent. The inferential meaning is the network of relations tying an expression to other expressions by the inferences it authorizes. The inferential meaning of an expression is claimed to be more fundamental than the representational meaning. But the inferential meaning is based on acts of accepting and rejecting sentences, and on the commitments to accept or reject sentences that are generated by acts of accepting and rejecting.

Chapter four explores the relations between expressions and experience. Their relations to experience are essential to the representational meanings of expressions. But expressions are needed for providing a conceptual structure to experience. In chapter four it proves necessary to outline an epistemological theory. I regard this as the most tentative part of the book. Some such theory is needed to ground the present account of language. Certain fundamental concepts necessary to understand the use of language are uncovered in investigating experience. But the present epistemological theory might be revised in various ways, and still provide an adequate foundation for the theory of language. Chapter five discusses three semantic dimensions of language—representational meaning, inferential meaning, and truth conditions—and the kinds of semantic theory appropriate to them.

Views held by various philosophers and logicians about the relation between grammatical form and logical form, and the status of artificial logical languages, are discussed in chapter six. These views are contrasted with the view of the present book. In this book, logical and grammatical forms are conceived to be different, but not to be opposed. Artificial logical languages are regarded as models of natural languages. The fact that first-order languages are quite different from English or other natural languages is taken to be a disadvantage to the purpose of understanding natural languages and the linguistic acts performed with natural languages. I propose that different artificial languages be developed. To model and help explain selected features of natural languages, artificial languages should be simpler than natural languages, but more like them than first order languages are.

In chapter seven, there is a discussion of transformational theories developed by linguists. These theories are contrasted with the theory of the present book. The speech act theory developed in this book is incompatible with transformational theories. Linguistic acts performed by English speakers are performed with English expressions. The components of the complex acts performed with sentences are acts performed with expressions which are components of sentences. The present view aims at giving a complete explanation of sentences and sentential acts in terms of component expressions and component acts, together with the organization of the components to constitute the complexes. Chapter seven is intended to make clear the differences between the present approach and the linguists' approach, as well as to convey the style of the speech act analyses of expressions and linguistic acts.

Chapters eight and nine explain the artificial language $\mathscr{L}$ that is the basic artificial language used to model portions of English. The language $\mathscr{L}$ is designed to be more similar to English than is a first-order language. This makes it possible to treat $\mathscr{L}$ as if it were a language that people actually used, and to develop speech act syntactic and semantic theories for $\mathscr{L}$. This treatment of $\mathscr{L}$ sheds light on corresponding English expressions, and their syntactic and semantic features. Chapter eight presents the language $\mathscr{L}$ in isolation from speech act considerations. This makes it easier to compare $\mathscr{L}$ to standard logical languages. A set-theoretic semantic account is given for $\mathscr{L}$, a deductive system is developed, and soundness and completeness results are obtained. Chapter nine deals with $\mathscr{L}$ as if it were a language spoken by people, and explains the speech acts performed by users of $\mathscr{L}$.

The first ten chapters are preliminary chapters. They present general theories of intentional and linguistic acts, present a general theory of language in its relation to experience, contrast the approach of this book to other familiar approaches, and prepare the language $\mathscr{L}$ to serve as an instrument in dealing with various specific topics and problems. Chapters ten, eleven and twelve apply the general theories to the case of pronouns. The language $\mathscr{L}$ is extended to $\overline{\mathscr{L}}$, which contains pronouns (or expressions like pronouns). The speech act account of $\overline{\mathscr{L}}$ helps us to understand the use of pronouns in English. Chapters thirteen and fourteen deal with names, referring, and existential presupposition. The language $\mathscr{L}$ is extended to form $(\mathscr{L})$, which allows for referring and non-referring uses of certain expressions.

The concluding chapter, fifteen, covers a variety of topics. This chapter touches on some of the limits of a speech-act theory—some syntactic features are not based on speech-act structure. The chapter also provides a characterization of specifically logical expressions, and gives an explanation of the close connection these expressions have to inference. This discussion is linked to the claim that there is an important difference between logical form and what might be called *semantic structure*. Logic is and will remain an "autonomous" subject matter; it will not yield its place to a more fully developed semantic theory.

At the end of each chapter is a brief bibliography and list of references. The bibliography lists articles and books that provide the background for the discussion in the chapter. The references are the works actually cited in the body of the chapter.

4. Some Other Views

The present book offers new and unfamiliar conceptions of language and linguistic acts. Even though the conceptions are novel, they owe a great deal to the work of other philosophers and linguistic theorists. My account is unusual in trying to combine insights of speech act theories with techniques borrowed from formal logic. It is also unusual in the details of the speech act theory developed and the details of the treatment of formal logic. I have borrowed from many sources, but what I have borrowed has been arranged in a novel way.

Views associated with logicians usually see a language as built-up in layers. First comes the syntactic level. Next comes semantics. Finally we add contextual factors to get the utterances that are actually produced. Instead of conceiving language as built-up in this way, I take linguistic activity to be the primary linguistic reality. Semantic and syntactic features are what we have left when we abstract from, or ignore, certain features of linguistic activity (including the actors). In my conception, there is no reason why, say, syntax should constitute an independent and autonomous field of study. And, in fact, it doesn't. An artificial language can be developed by first describing sentences of the language (giving the syntax), and then explaining the truth conditions of these sentences. These two steps do not reflect the make-up of a natural language. Once an artificial language is available, it can be treated as if it were a language actually used for communication—as if it were a natural language. This is the way an artificial language can model a natural one. Treating the artificial language as if it were used for communication leads to a different syntactic account than that provided in setting up the language. For the syntactic account appropriate for a model must reflect the structures of acts of using sentences. This is what enables the artificial language to shed light on the natural one.

The use of artificial languages to model a natural one distinguishes my approach from that of Montague (as illustrated in the essays in [*1*]). He treats a natural language, or part of it, as if it were an artificial formal language—the clearest example of this approach is seen in [*2*]. We might say that instead of developing a portion of English, Montague is actually developing a formal language very similar to a portion of English, which formal language models that portion. But Montague's formal language does not model English in my sense of 'model.' For he does not consider how the formal language, or the corresponding portion of English, is actually used. He takes his rules for assembling sentences to provide a sufficient syntactic account, and his statement of truth conditions with the help of mathematical functions to provide a sufficient semantic account. This provides no understanding of the way that people actually use language; it makes it difficult to understand how people could use language. The semantic account that I am trying to provide is intended to explain how real people use and understand language.

To develop a realistic semantic account, it is necessary to develop the account within the framework of a theory of linguistic intentional acts. People who use language are *doing* something when they speak and write. They are performing intentional acts with the expressions they produce. To understand how complex expressions are constituted, we must understand how the complex acts of using the expressions are constituted. To understand what expressions mean, we must understand how people use expressions to perform meaningful acts. Speech-act theorists don't, at least they need not, conceive of language as built-up in layers, starting with syntax. But speech act theorists generally don't have a fully developed conception of language, for they ordinarily concentrate on one or another variety of linguistic acts. These theorists don't account for the structures of complex expressions or complex acts. Antipathy between logically-oriented philosophers and speech-act philosophers has worked to the detriment of both camps. Logically-oriented theorists are unable to connect the languages they study to the languages people actually use, as they use them. Logically-oriented philosophers frequently fail to understand the importance of connecting their artificial languages to natural ones, and speech act theorists overlook or ignore structure because they have no convenient way to represent it.

This failing is especially prominent in the work of John Searle. He has been primarily concerned to identify and characterize certain kinds of acts; his most enlightening work deals with illocutionary acts. Searle provides rules and conditions that must be satisfied by a fully successful performance of one kind of act. His detailed discussions of illocutionary acts provide a useful understanding of these acts. But he has been less successful in his account of referring and predicating. An adequate account of these acts must explain the structures of illocutionary acts, and the roles of referring and predicating in these structures. Searle does not provide such explanations. Instead he seems content for his accounts of illocutionary and other acts to be supplemented by the work of linguists. It is the linguist's task to deal with structures, deep or otherwise. The philosopher's work merely complements that of the linguist.

Searle fails to understand that a speech act theory is not compatible with the transformational theories that are common in linguistics. Speech acts are intentional acts. A speech act theory must deal with states, events, and acts that a language user is aware of, if only implicitly. If the language we speak is simply a code for deeper, unspoken, structures, then acts of speaking and writing won't reward analysis in their own terms. Speech acts would need to be translated, not explained by giving various rules and conditions for their performance. The speech-act theorist must recognize that his view has consequences outside of philosophy. It is not appropriate in this case for the philosopher to try to stay out of the way of the empirical scientist. A line drawn between philosophy of language and linguistics would be arbitrary and artificial. The philosopher of language and the linguist are in many cases developing theories to explain the same phenomena. These theories can conflict. The speech-act theory presented in this book claims to overthrow many current theories in linguistics—while providing the resources to salvage what is valuable in those theories.

Bibliography and References

1. Richard Montague. *Formal Philosophy, Selected Papers of Richard Montague*, edited by Richmond H. Thomason. New Haven: Yale University Press, 1974.
2. Richard Montague. "English as a Formal Language," in [1], pp. 188–221.
3. John R. Searle. *Speech Acts, An Essay in the Philosophy of Language*. Cambridge: Cambridge University Press, 1969.

Chapter 1
Intentional Acts

1. Introduction

A natural language must ultimately be identified with the linguistic activity (talking, writing, listening, reading) and the linguistic skills of a community over a period of time. A linguistic study which does not deal with speech acts is marked by that very fact as a partial study. It is also an abstract study in the sense that it ignores an important feature of the concrete reality of language. It is no criticism to say of a study, or a subject matter, that it is abstract and partial. Most systematic bodies of knowledge are abstract and partial. But the tables are sometimes turned against theories which aim at being comprehensive and concrete. Speech act theories have been criticized for being (or trying to be) too comprehensive. Katz, for example, objects to speech act theories for including both material that belongs to semantics and material that belongs to pragmatics. (He makes this criticism in chapter 1 of [1].) Katz's criticism is misguided. A speech-act theory should be at once comprehensive and concrete. It should provide a framework within which we can situate more abstract studies of language, as well as provide the resources for integrating the various studies of language.

Before dealing with speech acts, I will develop a preliminary account of intentional acts. This account will then be applied to speech acts. The theory developed in the present chapter will be somewhat sketchy. It constitutes a framework that needs "filling in." The filling in will be accomplished by means of various applications of the basic theory.

2. Acts for a Purpose

An intentional act is one which is done on purpose. The actor is aware of what he is doing, and intends to be doing it. An act can be done *on* purpose without being done *for* a purpose. Such acts appear to be idle. I will restrict my attention here to those intentional acts which do have purposes. These include acts which are ends in themselves. Intentional acts done for a purpose are either acts of commission or acts of omission. Since the speech acts which are my ultimate concern are acts of commission, I will pretty much ignore acts of omission. But it is not difficult to adapt the present discussion so that the result also covers acts of omission.

Any intentional act can be described, or regarded, in two ways. The first way takes account of the intentional character of the act; to describe an act in this way, one must use expressions suited to its intentional character. But an intentional act can also be considered as stripped of its intentional character. If my neighbor is digging behind his garage for worms, which he wants to use for fishing, his behavior is intentional. And my description of what he is doing has characterized his behavior as intentional. Even if I said that he is digging, but didn't say why, I would be characterizing his behavior as intentional. For digging is something that a person does for some purpose or other, and we take it for granted that he has a purpose. To strip my neighbor's activity of its intentional character, I must describe what is going on behind the garage without placing that phenomenon in an intentional context. To do this, I might describe the position of my neighbor's body and the physical relation of his body to the shovel, and then describe the motions that are taking place. If I knew enough, I could indicate the physiological states and events involved. But my description cannot mention (or presuppose) that my neighbor is acting for an end, or even that what is going on is the kind of thing that generally constitutes intentional behavior. Normally, to say a person is acting in some way, or doing something, is sufficient to locate his behavior in an intentional framework.

Let us call the two sorts of descriptions of an intentional act *intentional descriptions* and *brute fact* descriptions. It is possible that a single description might combine elements of both sorts of description, and there may also be other kinds of borderline cases, but the distinction between intentional and brute fact descriptions is clear enough. For any act which gets an intentional description, we can also frame a brute fact description. The two descriptions describe the same state of affairs, but they are not equivalent, and neither is reducible to the other. For most purposes of daily life, intentional descriptions are more adequate than brute fact descriptions. When we ask what is going on in some situation where people are involved, we normally don't want an explanation in terms of motions and muscles. Intentional explanations, or descriptions, are needed for a satisfactory account of language, because the use of language by human beings is intentional behavior.

There is some intentional behavior for which it is awkward to use the term 'act.' Such behavior is typically complicated. Suppose Allan hits a nail several times to drive it into a board (or boards). If we want to describe, or label, what he is doing in such a way as to cover more than one hit, we will not speak of his act of hitting the nail. We might instead speak of his act*s* of hitting the nail. But we can also naturally describe him as engaged in the *activity* of hitting the nail. His intentional activity of hitting the nail may include distinct individual acts of hitting the nail. Again, suppose Jones is building a house. It is inappropriate to speak of his act of building a house. Nor would we speak of his acts of building a house. But we can speak quite naturally of the activity of building a house. I will use 'activity' for cases of complicated intentional behavior where it seems inappropriate to use the word 'act.' I will regard both acts and activities in roughly the same way, and attribute the same kinds of intentional features to both.

I will concentrate on intentional acts or activities performed by one person. To begin with, I will devise standard locutions for describing intentional acts done for a purpose. So long as we consider acts which aren't ends in themselves, the following sentence forms are probably sufficient:

(1) *X* does *Y* in order to obtain *Z*.
(2) *X* does *Y* in order to accomplish *Z*.

With a little forcing, we might be able to make do with either (1) or (2). But each form fits certain acts better than does the other. Form (1) works best when it is having something after the act that matters. Form (2) is appropriate when it is doing (or being done) that is most important. In (1) and (2), *X* is the person who acts, and *doing Y* is the action. In (1), the purpose is *to obtain Z*. In (2), it is *to accomplish Z*. The expression 'in order' will serve as "a purpose introducing" expression; it functions to indicate that the phrase which follows designates purpose. The purpose for performing an act is not the same as the end or goal of the act. For the act has its purpose while it is being performed; its purpose is a feature of the act. *Aiming at* a certain goal is also a feature of the act, but the goal itself does not exist unless the act succeeds. However, we can describe a successful act both as achieving its purpose and as achieving its goal. The purpose for doing something is *to reach* the goal. If *X* does *Y* in order to obtain *Z*, the purpose is *to obtain Z*. The goal is *X*'s obtaining *Z* (by doing *Y*). (We sometimes describe *Z* by itself as the goal. But it is understood that *Z* is *X*'s goal, so that *X* really aims at *X*'s getting *Z*.)

If act *Y* is an end in itself, there are also two standard forms for describing it:

(3) *X* does *Y* in order to be doing *Y*.
(4) *X* does *Y* in order to have done *Y*.

Form (3) is appropriate for acts that *X* enjoys—acts that give *X* pleasure. Form (4) fits acts which satisfy an obligation.

In describing specific acts, I will not limit myself to the standard forms above. It is useful to consider the standard forms for dealing with intentional acts (for a purpose) in general. They prove awkward for specific cases. So I might describe Allan as striking the nail (with the hammer) in order to fasten two boards together. Allan's act is *striking the nail*, his purpose is *to fasten the two boards together*. Whether this is a case of obtaining or accomplishing depends on what Allan is up to. If he is making something, then the fastening is obtaining. If he is trying to show someone that he *can* drive a nail, then the fastening is accomplishing.

3. Completable and Completing Acts

We can distinguish two kinds of intentional acts which have a purpose. If the difference between these two kinds of acts (activities) is overlooked, characteristics proper to one kind may be attributed to all acts with purposes. We can approach the distinction between these two kinds of acts by contrasting acts and activities which take some time with certain acts which do not. My activity of walking to work takes some time, because I am walking to work from the time I start until the time I arrive. The activity of building a house takes time. Some acts and activities that take time have a definite goal such that the agent gets closer and closer to this goal, until she finally achieves it. Other acts which take time are not like this. If Jane walks in the park to get fresh air, her activity takes time. But there is no amount of walking she must accomplish. Whenever she stops she will have gotten fresh air.

An activity which takes time can be interrupted. Jones can be building a house on weekends, and working at his regular job during the week. There are situations in which, during the week, we would not say that Jones is building a house. These are situations where we are concerned with what Jones is doing at the time we are talking. In other situations it is proper, even during the week, to say that Jones is building a house. (We are concerned with Jones' long-term projects.) These two locutions (during the week) do not pose a problem for our account of intentional activities that take time. We understand what is going on (with respect to Jones) perfectly well. It is the speaker's purpose for communicating that determines which locution is appropriate.

The second kind of intentional acts with purposes to which I want to call attention is that of acts which are the successful completion of some preceding intentional act or activity. These acts are the goals of the preceding acts or activities. Not all intentional acts aim at such goals, but many do. Winning the race is the successful completion of running in the race. Reaching London is the successful completion of traveling to London. And finding what one has lost successfully completes looking for what he lost. These *completing acts* are events, but they are events which are counted as intentional acts. For we consider a person to be *doing* something when he wins a race, reaches London, or finds what he was looking for. Completing acts are located in time, but they are not "spread out" in time. A completing act need not be instantaneous, but we wouldn't normally speak of a person as performing the same completing act at recognizably different times.

Completing acts are a special case of *completing events*. We can also have a completing event which is not an act. Suppose Kevin pumps air into a balloon in order to make it explode. The activity of pumping, if successful, is completed by the explosion. The explosion is an event but not an act. A completing event brings a preceding act or activity to a successful conclusion. Bringing about this event is the goal of the act or activity. When a completing event is not an act, we bring it about by performing an act or acts which cause the event. We bring about a completing act by performing it as the conclusion of the act or activity it completes. A completing act can have a purpose, as when Jesse wins the race in order to bring honor to his native land. An event which is not an act does not have a purpose. But the agent can have a purpose for bringing the event about. Kevin's purpose for pumping is *to cause the balloon to explode*. The explosion itself has no purpose. But Kevin might have a purpose for causing the explosion. If he does, we might informally describe this as the purpose of the explosion.

An act which has a completing event for its goal may not be successful. Such an act may be finished (as opposed to being interrupted during its course), but it will not have a completing act or event. At first it might seem that losing a race is perfectly analogous to winning it. But the contestant who tries to win and loses instead is not losing on purpose. The losing is not an intentional act. Nor does losing complete the running in the sense of providing the goal for the running. (But a contestant who tries to lose can have his running completed by losing.)

It was convenient initially to distinguish completing acts from others by focusing on the time they take. Completing acts are short-lived, in contrast to acts which take some time. But not all short-lived acts with purposes are completing acts. Suppose Phil flips the light switch in order to turn on the lights. The lights going on is an event which successfully completes Phil's act of flipping the switch. Phil's act of flipping the switch is very quick, but it is not a completing act. If an act aims at a completing event or act, it may be short-lived or it may take some time. It would be a mistake to identify all short-lived acts with completing acts or to insist that all completing events be short-lived. Completing acts are typically short-lived. But an intentional act might aim at an event of some duration. Some revolutionary might assassinate a political leader in order to cause a war.

I will contrast completing acts and events with *completable* acts and activities. If an intentional act or activity with a purpose aims at a goal which is a completing event, the act or activity is completable. There may be distinct and separate acts with purposes which aim at the same completing event. These are also completable acts. But I will understand completable acts to include more than acts aiming at a completing event. A completable act is not a completing act. A completable act must aim at a goal outside of itself; this is to exclude acts which are their own ends (such acts are neither completing nor completable). A completable act is an act which is not a completing act, which has a purpose, and which is intended to combine with other acts or events to constitute a further act or activity. Kevin's pumping is completable because it is intended to combine with the explosion to constitute the act of destroying the balloon. Jesse's running in the race is completable, because it is intended to combine with the act of winning. But two completable acts might combine with one another.

A completable act has a purpose beyond itself. The competent performance of such an act is always distinct from its successful conclusion. This is so even for those completable acts whose competent performance coincides, or nearly coincides, with their successful conclusion, as happens with some short-lived acts. If a completable act is intended to bring about, or to contribute to bringing about, an event which is its goal, then that event is a completing event. A completing event which is an act is a completing act. We can't distinguish between the performance of the completing act and its successful conclusion. Because it completes a preceding act or activity, the completing act isn't itself completed or concluded. Of course, the completing act may have a purpose of its own, as in the case where Jesse won the race in order to bring honor to his native land. And this purpose may or may not be achieved. But even if it is, we would not consider this achieving to be the successful completion of the winning—the winning *is* a completion; it doesn't *have* one.

4. Complex Acts

Completable acts and activities may not be concluded successfully, even when they are performed competently. Flipping the switch may not get the lights turned on, and constructing competently may not get the house built. Language often provides a distinct label for completable activities brought to a successful conclusion, where the label indicates that the activity was successful. We can say that Phil turned on the lights (by flipping the switch) if we want to make it known that his flipping succeeded. When language provides one label for an act or activity and another for that act or activity brought to a successful conclusion, it appears that there are two acts (activities) rather than one. For Phil can flip the switch in order to turn on the lights without getting them turned on—his act of flipping is the same no matter what its outcome. So flipping the switch is one act, and turning on the lights another. That there are two acts rather than one is a suggestion that I accept, and I will say that the first act is a component of the second. In order to make sense of this claim, to make it plausible, and to understand how it is that one act or activity can contain others, we must consider complex acts and activities.

There are many acts and activities which we ordinarily regard as complex—as containing other acts and activities. When Green carves the roast, his carving includes the act of putting the fork in the roast and various acts of slicing. And when a secretary types a letter, his typing includes various component acts. Acts and activities contained in a complex act or activity are not contained like bundles in a sack or elements in a set. The complex act has a structure. One act must precede another because it prepares the way for the other, or an act may wait on the completion of several other acts. What makes the several components of an act to be parts of one act rather than several ununited acts is that they aim at the same conclusion.

It may help to gain an understanding of complex acts if we consider a complex act with few components. An act is not complex unless it contains more than one component. But a complex act may contain a single component of a given kind. In particular, a complex act might contain a single act-component. Consider this example: Let us suppose that O'Brien wants to blow up a bridge illegally. He plants explosives which are attached to a timing device set to detonate them at a later time; then he leaves. Two acts concern me here: his planting the explosives and his blowing up the bridge. These are distinct acts, and the first is a component of the second. The planting act has as its goal the bridge-destroying explosion. The complex act of blowing up the bridge consists of the completable act of planting the explosives and the completing event of the explosion. (It is probably better to think of the completing event as the whole process triggered by O'Brien, which process culminates in the explosion.)

If I am right that the planting and the blowing up are distinct acts, how can this be demonstrated? We might note that one of these acts can be performed without the other. O'Brien has planted the explosives no matter what happens after he leaves. But if the explosives are discovered and disarmed, or if the timing mechanism or the detonator fails, then he hasn't blown up the bridge. On the other hand, if everything goes right (from O'Brien's point of view) and the explosion wrecks the bridge, then O'Brien has performed the act of blowing it up. The explosion that destroys the bridge is the planting brought to a successful conclusion, just as the lights going on successfully concludes flipping the switch.

If we have two descriptions of acts, and want to know if the descriptions describe two acts or only one, we cannot always decide that the answer is "two" if we can perform one without the other. For one of the two descriptions might be more general than the other. Suppose Peter performs the act of pronouncing 'Constantinople.' This can also be described as an act of making vocal sounds. The description "act of making vocal sounds" is more general than "act of pronouncing 'Constantinople'." The two descriptions describe Peter's one act. But if Peter stutters, or his tongue slips, he might perform an act of producing vocal sounds without pronouncing 'Constantinople.' Peter intended to pronounce 'Constantinople,' but he failed. When Peter succeeds, his one act has two descriptions. When he fails, the more general description still fits what he is doing; the more specific description does not.

However, O'Brien's case is not like Peter's. The planting can be done right without the explosion occurring. The time lapse between the planting and the explosion makes it obvious that the planting and the blowing up are different acts. The time of the planting is not the time of the blowing up. It is even difficult to give the time of the blowing up. If the planting and the explosion both take place on Thursday, we can say that O'Brien blew up the bridge on Thursday. But our conventions do not provide for giving a precise time or temporal period when the blowing up took place. We content ourselves with giving the time of the planting and the time of the explosion.

O'Brien's act of planting the explosives and his act of blowing up the bridge are both done for a purpose, but their purposes are not quite the same. O'Brien planted the explosives in order *to blow up the bridge.* And, if his planting succeeds, his blowing up the bridge has the purpose *to further the Revolution* (or *to get revenge*, or whatever). All the purposes for blowing up the bridge will also be purposes for planting the explosives, but the planting has one purpose which is not a purpose for the blowing up. The purpose for the first act, *to blow up the bridge*, "defines" the second act, *blowing up the bridge.* Purposes are often crucial for determining if we have one act or two. Of course, acts performed at different times, or by different people, are obviously distinct. It becomes a problem to determine if acts are distinct only when the same actors are involved, and the acts take place at roughly the same time. If one act has a different purpose from a second, they are different acts. In those cases that give rise to problems, when we find two acts rather than one, it commonly happens that one act is a component of the second. The structure of the second is due to purposes of its components.

When someone does *Y* for some purpose outside itself, and succeeds, we must recognize two acts: the (competent) doing of *Y* and the successful realization of the agent's purpose (*by* doing *Y*). It may be that acts other than *Y* are also needed to achieve this purpose, so that doing *Y* isn't all that the agent must do; or it may happen that doing *Y* is the only contribution the agent needs to make. In either case, the successful realization of the agent's purpose is a complex act which contains *doing Y* as a component. Some completable acts or activities are successfully completed by events which are not acts, as O'Brien's planting is completed by the explosion. Some are successfully completed by events which are acts, as running in the race is successfully completed by winning it. For those which are completed by non-act events, we commonly have distinct labels for the component act and the component-act-brought-to-a-successful-conclusion (as flipping the switch and turning on the lights). For these acts, the complex act includes both the component act and the completing event. When completable acts or activities are completed by acts, there is frequently no name for the act-brought-to-a-successful-conclusion. We don't seem to have, for example, a special label for successfully running in a race. This is probably because normal conversational demands can be met by talking of running and of winning. But the successful running is a distinct activity which includes as components both the running and the winning. It is acceptable English to say that Jones ran in the race in order to win it. But winning is not the purpose for his running; winning is only the goal. Jones' purpose might be *to accomplish winning*, or *to achieve victory*. Achieving victory is not winning, it is running successfully. The purpose for successful running is also the purpose of winning; in fact the purpose for winning is derivative from the purpose for running successfully. This explains why achieving the purpose for winning the race does not count as the completion of the winning. Winning has no purpose proper to itself; it is the successful running which may be further completed by achieving its purpose.

Now I want to consider slightly more complex acts than O'Brien's. Since I will make use of the next example several times, I will describe it in some detail. Allan needs a wagon to use in delivering the Sunday papers. (He uses a bag for delivering during the week.) So Allan purchases a wagon kit. This contains precut boards for the sides, ends, bottom, and top of the wagon. It also contains six narrower boards; three are to be fastened to each side to facilitate fastening the sides to the ends and the bottom. The kit includes hinges for attaching the top, a rear wheel and axle assembly, and a front wheel, axle, and tongue assembly. There are also nuts and bolts for attaching the hinges and wheel assemblies. The directions in the kit indicate that three narrower boards are to be nailed to each side as follows:

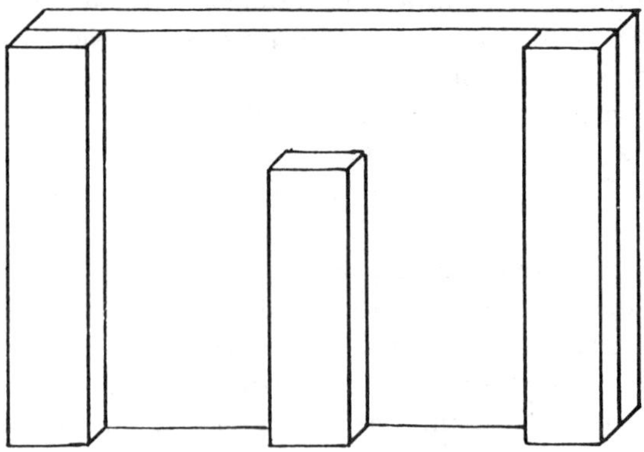

Then the sides and ends are to be nailed together. After this the bottom is nailed on. Holes are drilled and the wheel assemblies attached. Finally, holes are drilled and the hinges attached to one side and the top.

Let us now consider what goes on when Allan attaches one of the narrow boards to one of the sides. This board is attached at the edge of the side, not in the middle. Allan picks up the narrow board, and taps a nail near one end, to start the nail. Then Allan holds the narrow board and the side together—in the desired position—with his left hand; he strikes the nail four times with his hammer. The fourth blow drives the nail all the way in. The acts I want to consider are the act of holding the boards with his left hand, the four acts of striking the nail, and the act of fastening the boards together in the specified position.

One way that Allan's act might be structured is the following. Allan holds the two boards together in order to fasten them in the specified position. Each act of striking the nail has the goal of driving the nail further in. So each act is a completable act which is completed by the nail's becoming further imbedded. The nail's becoming more deeply imbedded is a completing event. I will call each complex consisting of an act of striking together with its completing event an act of driving the nail. The purpose of each act of driving is to fasten the boards together in the specified position. The act of fastening the boards together in this position has five "major" components: one act of holding and four acts of driving. These five major components are completable acts. But they do not aim at a completing event. In a sense, they complete each other. The complex act of fastening the two boards together in this position is constituted by its five completable components. (But it is constituted by them only if they are successful. If one of the boards splits, so that the two do not become fastened, the five acts do not constitute a further intentional act.) Allan's first act of fastening these boards together will be followed by others. The first act fastens the narrow board only at one end—that is the "specified position" for that act. A second act will fasten the narrow board at its other end. Two more nails will be driven in between the ends. The four fastening acts can then constitute a complex act of fastening the two boards securely together in certain relative positions.

The preceding describes one way in which Allan's acts might be structured. There are other ways: how his acts are structured depends on Allan. One way in which the same kind of act might have a different structure is as follows. In describing the first act of fastening, I said that Allan performs four acts of striking the nail, and four acts of driving it. If Allan performs four distinct intentional acts, he must attend separately to each strike. But if Allan is skillful with tools, he may be able to strike the nail all four times as a single, simple intentional act. This single act or activity would be complicated without being complex. The single act would be completed by the event of the nail's becoming fully imbedded. (A more careful statement has it that the single act is completed by the sequence of imbedding events which culminates in the nail's becoming fully imbedded.) The first act of fastening would then have two major components: the act of holding the two boards together and the complicated act of driving the nail in.

5. The Structures of Acts

We must consider the purposes of intentional acts more carefully. The purpose of a component defines the complex act of which it is a component. A complex intentional act is structured by the purposes of its components (and the purposes of their components, and so on). Most acts with purposes have more than one purpose. If intentional act Y_1 is a component of act Y_2, then any purpose for doing Y_2 is also a purpose for doing Y_1. (Similarly, if Y_2 is a component of Y_3, than any purpose of Y_3 is also a purpose of both Y_2 and Y_1.) The purposes of a given intentional act can be distinguished as more and less remote. The least remote purpose of a completable act is its *immediate* purpose. I will not speak of the immediate purpose of a completing act, because the purposes of a completing act are derivative. They are derived from the purposes of the act in which the completing act is a direct component. A completing event is one whose occurrence brings a preceding act, acts, or activity to a successful conclusion. The completing event is the goal of the preceding act, acts, or activity. The immediate purpose of the preceding act, acts, or activity is to bring about the completing event. The immediate purpose of a completable act enables us to distinguish the act from complex acts to which it belongs. For the immediate purpose is the one purpose which it does not share with some complex act which contains it.

It is possible for a single act to have more than one immediate purpose. Suppose Victor turns on the radio in the morning in order to bring in the weather report (in order to bring it about that the radio station's weather report is audible in his room). But he turns the radio on very low in order not to disturb his wife (in order to not disturb his wife). Let the radio be equipped with transistors, so that no warm-up time is required. In normal circumstances, Victor's act of turning on the radio will be the same act as his turning it on very low. The different immediate purposes of his act are located in different sequences of purposes.

We saw before that we can sometimes distinguish one act from another by finding a purpose of one act which is not a purpose of the other. Victor's act raises a different problem. When we have two immediate purposes, how are we to tell if there are two acts or just one? In the present case, we may note that it is possible to turn the radio on without turning it on very low. But Victor's act of turning it on low is not different from his act of turning it on. The same actor is carrying out the same relevant motions to turn it on and to turn it on very low. A single completing event—the radio's producing the weather report at a low volume—completes Victor's act of twisting the dial. In the present case, we can't even describe Victor's act of turning the radio on low without describing his act of turning on the radio. So we don't really have a motivation for looking for two acts, since we don't have two dissimilar descriptions. Victor's act of turning on the radio is an act with a purpose. This act is intentionally given a special character: the low volume. The basic act has one purpose. It is given its special character in order to achieve the second purpose.

Most acts with purposes have immediate and remote purposes. If act Y has purposes Z_1, Z_2, Z_3, . . . , where Z_1 is the immediate purpose, Z_2 is the next least remote purpose, etc., then if Y is successful it is a component of the act of obtaining Z_1. And if the act of obtaining Z_1 is successful, it is a component of the act of obtaining Z_2, etc. But Y might not be successful. In that case, doing Y is trying unsuccessfully to obtain Z_1. It is also trying unsuccessfully to obtain Z_2. And so on. (Of course, even if Y does not succeed, we might later do something else and succeed in obtaining Z_2.) When Y is unsuccessful in achieving its immediate purpose, Y is not a component of a complex intentional act. Y may be a component of some other event—such as competing unsuccessfully in the race—but that event is not an intentional act. (An act with two immediate purposes might achieve one and fail to achieve the other.)

The immediate purpose of an intentional act defines the act of which it is a component (if it succeeds) in the sense that the expression for the purpose of the component can be transformed to yield a label for the complex act which contains the component. (As the purpose expression 'to fasten the boards together' is transformed into the act expression 'fastening the boards together.') In making such a transformation, it is important to understand the difference between the purpose of an act and the end or goal of the act. Our standard form has it that X does Y in order to obtain or accomplish Z. In this formula, the expression, 'in order' signals (that what follows is) the expression for the purpose. In English sentences, this expression does not always indicate the purpose of an act. For example, in the clumsy sentence

> Bill wrote a check to Sears in order to own a refrigerator.

the expression 'to own a refigerator' does not label the purpose of Bill's act. Even if Bill succeeds (his check doesn't bounce), he won't have performed an act of owning a refrigerator. Owning a refrigerator is Bill's goal. The purpose of Bill's act is *to achieve* the goal by performing that act. If we want to adapt our standard form to reveal Bill's purpose, we need a sentence like this:

> Bill wrote a check to Sears in order to obtain a refrigerator.

When a purpose expression is transformed into a complex act expression, it labels the component act or acts *brought to a successful conclusion*. Bill's obtaining the refrigerator is his check-writing brought to a successful conclusion, just as O'Brien's blowing up the bridge is his planting explosives brought to a successful conclusion. The purpose of its components defines the complex act because the complex can be labeled by the purpose of its components. And because the complex is constituted by its components.

Many acts have immediate and remote purposes, but it is plausible that any sequence of purposes must be finite. It might seem that the terminal purpose in such a sequence must define an act or activity which is an end in itself. There can be no doubt that some terminal purposes define such acts. Suppose Michelle is skiing down a hill. In the course of her trip she makes a turn which is a simple intentional act. It may be that she makes the turn in order to ski to a specific place. And she may ski to that place because the place is convenient for performing a certain maneuver. And so on. Her ultimate activity in this case is skiing down the hill. She does not ski down the hill in order to accomplish some further goal. She skis down the hill because she likes doing this.

There are some problems in describing Michelle's ultimate activity. From one point of view, skiing down the hill is an end in itself. So she skis down the hill in order to be skiing down the hill. But we might also say that Michelle skis down the hill in order to obtain a certain kind of pleasure. This locution suggests that skiing down the hill is merely a component of obtaining pleasure. We can support this analysis by noting that it is possible to ski down for pleasure without obtaining pleasure (e.g., if the hill is too steep, too icy, or too easy). However, the earlier account of completing and completable acts does not fit this analysis very well. Skiing down the hill does not seem to be completable. Michelle does not first ski down and then obtain pleasure. There is no pleasure event which completes the exertion of skiing. It is not the case that the skiing is one thing and the pleasure is something else. To say that Michelle obtained pleasure from skiing is just a (pompous) way to say that Michelle liked skiing. Skiing and obtaining pleasure from skiing are the same activity—when Michelle enjoys it.

This example will be better understood if we distinguish a person's intention *for* an act from the intention *of* the act. The intention of the act is what the agent intends to accomplish; the intention of the act is its purpose. The intention for the act is what the agent intends to be doing—what the agent intends for his act to *be*, rather than to accomplish. Suppose that Mark has taken lessons but still can't swim. However, Mark thinks he can swim. So Mark jumps into the water where it is shallow and flails his arms and legs. Mark isn't swimming. But he *intends* to be swimming. Mark's intention *for* his activity is that it constitute swimming. We can describe what Mark is doing in different ways. For example, we can say that Mark is moving his arms and legs. This description describes an intentional activity, for Mark intends to be moving his arms and legs. We can also say that Mark is futilely attempting to swim. The description is correct, but it does not describe what Mark intends to be doing. (However, it is an intentional description, as opposed to a brute fact description.)

When an agent is performing an act that doesn't realize his intentions for the act, we can describe his act in such a way that he intends to be performing the act we describe. We can also describe the act in terms appropriate to his intention for the act. This will give a correct description that does not describe what the agent intends to be doing. If Michelle skis down the hill to enjoy herself, her intention for her skiing activity is that it also be an enjoyed activity. If Michelle fails to enjoy her trip down the hill, the activity of skiing fails to realize her intention. (She intends to be enjoying herself, but isn't.) It is correct to describe her as skiing down the hill and intending to. It is also correct to describe her as skiing down the hill without enjoying it. But it is incorrect to say that she intends this.

If an act is not its own end, the intention for the act is distinct from the intention of the act. The two intentions are the same when an act is its own end. To say that Michelle skis down the hill in order to enjoy skiing down the hill is to give a description which explicitly provides for the possibility that Michelle's skiing won't succeed. When we say that Michelle skis in order to be skiing, our description suggests that Michelle's activity can't miss. So long as she makes it down the hill, she will have accomplished her aim. We have seen that this is not the case. The description which has Michelle skiing in order to be skiing is not mistaken. This description describes Michelle's activity with respect to Michelle's intention. The act is its own end because of Michelle's intention for it (but the description leaves out the specifics of Michelle's intention).

Not every act which is its own end is an act the agent either enjoys doing or hopes that he will enjoy doing. Fulfilling an obligation can also be an end in itself. Bill's repaying Al the ten dollars he borrowed can be done for its own sake, even though Bill hates to part with the money. This kind of case has its own standard form. We can say

X does Y in order to be doing Y.

for those acts that X enjoys doing (or hopes to enjoy doing). And use

X does Y in order to have done Y.

for the cases of duty. In some cases (sexual examples come to mind) one act might be an end in itself in both respects: some compound purpose expression may then be required.

6. Enabling Acts

Many sequences of purposes do not terminate in purposes defining an act which is its own end. Suppose Chuck flips the switch in order to turn on the lights. His reason for turning them on is that he wants to read a certain book. It seems worse than odd to suggest that turning on the lights is part of reading the book. Turning on the lights sets the stage for reading the book, but it isn't a component of the reading. However, it would also be (slightly) odd to say that Chuck turns on the lights in order to read the book. It is more appropriate to say that he turns on the lights to be able to read the book. Here the expression 'to be able to read the book' does not give the purpose of Chuck's act; instead it gives the act's intended outcome. In turning on the lights, Chuck *enables himself to read the book*. Ordinarily, turning on the lights is not the only thing Chuck needs to do. He must also sit down, pick up the book and open it. These different acts all serve to enable him to read the book.

No one of these acts, by itself, is sufficient to enable him to start reading. So, strictly speaking, no one of these acts enables Chuck to read his book; each contributes to enabling him to read the book. Such contributing acts are included among *enabling acts*. Similarly, one act might facilitate another rather than enabling or contributing to enabling the other. There may be enough daylight coming through the windows so that Chuck could read, although with some difficulty. In that case, Chuck's turning on the lights does not contribute to making it possible for him to read the book, but it makes reading more convenient, or easier. Such facilitating acts will also be counted as enabling acts.

Let us consider Chuck's actions in more detail. Having decided to read further in the book he has been reading, Chuck enters his study, turns on the lights, walks to the table and picks up his book, walks to his chair and sits down, opens the book to the place he has marked, and finally starts to read. His act of entering the study is intended to enable himself to read. This act also makes it possible for him to turn on the lights (the switch is by the doorway). However, he didn't intend for his entering to enable him to turn on the lights. Once he found himself inside the doorway, it occurred to him that the lights would be of help, so he turned them on. An act isn't an enabling act just because it makes some other act possible. An enabling act must be intended to enable the further act. Once he is in the study, Chuck is in a position to walk to the table and pick up the book. This was intended when he entered the room. Chuck entered the room with his book in mind. But certain enabling acts prepare the way for other acts, and are intended to do this. Chuck's entering the study was intended to enable him to walk to the table and pick up the book. Doing this enables him to carry the book to the chair and sit down, which, in turn, enables him to open the book to the correct place.

In this example we have a sequence of enabling acts. One act enables the next, though each has the common goal of Chuck's reading his book. The only act that I mentioned which is not a member of the chain is Chuck's act of turning on the lights. Turning on the lights does not prepare the way for some other enabling act. It simply "points" to the reading. (If I had not supposed that there is enough daylight in the room for Chuck to see, and had instead supposed that it was dark in his study, then the lights might be needed for moving around in the study as well as for reading.) Each act in the sequence enables the next one; each contributes to enabling subsequent acts as well. We can distinguish immediate and remote goals for an enabling act, and nearer and more remote enabled acts.

An enabling act is not a component of the act or acts it is intended to enable. An enabling act is neither a completable nor a completing act. We might informally describe Chuck as entering the room in order to enable himself to walk to the table and pick up the book. But entering the room is not a component of enabling himself to walk to the table. If one act is a major component of a second, there must be at least one other major component. (A major component is one whose immediate purpose defines the complex.) There is not another component in this case. The act of entering the room is the same as the act of enabling himself to walk to the table—so long as the act of entering does enable (contribute to enabling) the walking. (For the book might not be on the table; it might not even be in the study.) An enabling act, as such, has no purpose beyond itself. This does not mean that an enabling act is an end in itself; we do not perform it for its own sake. *Enabling acts have no purposes.* If we say that Chuck turned on the lights to enable or to facilitate himself to read, the phrase 'to enable himself to read' does not give the purpose of turning on the lights. Instead the phrase gives Chuck's intention for the act. The use of 'in order' in connection with enabling acts will be regarded as informal. The standard form for describing an enabling act is the following:

X does *Y*, intending to enable (facilitate) the doing of *Z*.

An enabling act might itself be complex, but we can't conclude that two acts which are both intended to enable *Z* are components of a single enabling act. Acts which are components of a further act are acts with purposes. Completable acts which are major components of a further act have a common purpose which defines that further act.

An act with a purpose typically has multiple purposes; it has a sequence, or chain, of purposes. One act can be located in different chains, by virtue of having different immediate purposes, each "leading in a different direction." A chain of purposes can be terminated by a purpose defining an act which is an end in itself. But the terminal purpose in a sequence of purposes can also define an enabling act, which is an act valuable as a means. Although an enabling act has no purpose, it can have a goal. If an act has a purpose and a goal, its purpose can be to obtain the goal. If an act is intended to enable a further act, its goal is performing that further act. An enabling act typically has multiple goals and multiple intentions. (An act with a purpose can also have multiple goals.)

When *X* does *Y* to enable the doing of *Z*, *X* may enable herself to do *Z* or *X* may enable someone else to do *Z*. The doing *Z* that is enabled may be a specific act, but an enabling act may also be intended to enable a (nonspecific) variety of acts and activities. Suppose Stan pays his electric bill. Now Stan may have an obligation to do this. When he had the electricity turned on initially, he in effect agreed to pay for the electricity he would use. But Stan does not take his obligation seriously enough to act on it. If he could get away with not paying, he would. Stan pays his electric bill to keep the electricity from being turned off. Stan pays his bill, intending to enable himself and others to make use of electricity in his apartment. His enabling act contributes to making possible an indefinite number of acts and activities, but Stan has no specific act in mind.

Consider Allan once again, and his wagon. When Allan fastens the narrow boards to each side, his acts are enabling acts. For the narrow boards make it possible, or make it easier, to securely fasten the sides to the ends and to the bottom. Once Allan has fastened the narrow boards to the sides, he proceeds as follows: He fastens one end to one side. Then he fastens the other side to that end, after which he attaches the other end. Next he attaches the bottom. Then he fastens the rear wheel assembly to the bottom. Then the front wheel assembly goes on. And finally the top is attached. Allan thinks about what he is doing, and the order in which the fastening is done. The acts of fastening first one side and then the other to one end are performed in order to constitute the subportion (of the wagon) consisting of those three pieces. The act of constituting this subportion is a distinct act because it is an enabling act. Having the subportion available makes it easier to fasten the other end. As well as being an enabling act, the act of constituting the subportion has as its immediate purpose *to constitute the subportion consisting of both ends and both sides.* (A single act can have two immediate purposes. It can also be both an enabling act in one respect and an act with a purpose in another.) Constituting the subportion with two ends and two sides is an enabling act which facilitates attaching the bottom. It also has as its immediate purpose *to constitute the subportion consisting of sides, ends, and bottom.* The act of fastening the bottom has the same immediate purpose. This last subportion is constructed in order to construct (to constitute) the wagon. Each of the remaining fastening acts has the same immediate purpose.

It isn't necessary that Allan's acts be as just described. I am simply supposing that Allan structures his acts as I have said. The structure that Allan gives to his acts depends on his own conception of what he is doing, and the way that he goes about doing it. Instead of organizing the construction as I have described it, Allan might slavishly follow the directions that came with the kit. Making the various subportions will not constitute distinct acts, and are not enabling acts, for he does not intend for the making of a subportion to facilitate later acts. Each fastening act has as its immediate purpose *to construct the wagon*. With this structure, each fastening act is a major component of the act of constructing the wagon.

An enabling act is not as such a component of the act that it enables. However, I will say that the relation between the enabling and the enabled act is a *structural* relation. So is the relation between a component act and the complex defined by the purpose of the component. An enabling act is not a component of a complex act (unless the enabling act also has a purpose), but the enabling act can be included in an activity. In the first description, Allan's acts of fastening the narrow boards to the sides of the wagon are simply enabling acts. They are not also acts with purposes. But these acts are included in Allan's activity of making the wagon. We have been using 'activity' in two ways, for two sorts of activity. When Allan strikes the nail four times without performing a separate act for each strike, we can say that he performed a single, simple intentional activity. This activity can also be regarded as a simple but complicated act. When we speak of Allan's activity of making the wagon, we are labeling a collection of acts and activities which point to a common goal. There is no single intentional act of which all these acts and activities are components. There is no single purpose which they all share. This second kind of activity has less "unity" than the first. It is appropriate that in the future we confine the use of 'activity' to the second kind of activity. Activities of the first kind can properly be called acts.

7. Trying

This account of complex intentional acts makes it possible to explain what it is to *try* to do something, and it enables us to distinguish between two kinds of trying (between two senses of 'try'). Suppose *X* does *Y* in order to obtain or accomplish *Z*. She may do *Y* and succeed, or she may do *Y* and fail. If she fails, we would commonly say that *X* *tried* to accomplish *Z*. Trying to accomplish *Z* is the same thing as doing *Y*, (plus doing whatever else she does with accomplishing *Z* as its purpose). Trying, in this case, is acting with a purpose. So *X* has tried to accomplish *Z* even if she succeeds. If *Y* is an act (activity) for which we have a name, then we normally speak of trying only if *X* fails, or if we are worried that *X* might fail. We say that Doug tried to find his ring when he didn't find it. And that Michelle is trying to finish typing her paper by eight when we aren't sure she will make it. But if we have no convenient name for *Y*, we might describe *Y* as a case of trying to accomplish *Z*, in which case there need be no suggestion of failure. When a component act is performed as part of a complex act, we can transform the label for the purpose of the component into a label for the complex act. With the use of 'trying,' we can transform the label for the complex act into a label for the component.

The first kind of trying is associated with the intention of an act, its purpose. The second kind of trying is associated with the intention for an act. The performance of an intentional act of a certain kind requires some competence on the part of the agent. To say that someone is doing *Y* (where doing *Y* is an intentional act) is to say he's doing it right, or approximately right. This is so whether he is solving a differential equation, or building a wagon, or tying a shoelace. But suppose that doing *Y* requires a skill that *X* doesn't possess, or depends on certain circumstances that *X* doesn't control and that aren't favorable. Then in attempting to do *Y, X* does something else. Suppose we call it *W*. If *X* wanted to do *Y* in order to obtain *Z*, then his purpose for doing *W* will also be *to obtain Z*. Doing *W* is trying to obtain *Z*, in the first sense of 'trying.' We can also use 'trying' in its second sense to describe what *X* is doing. *X* does *W* by default; he wants to be doing *Y*. Doing *W* is *trying* to do *Y*. Doing *Y* is not the purpose of doing *W*, doing *Y* is *X*'s intention for *W*. Mark flailed his arms and legs in an effort to swim. Mark tried to swim; his intention for what he was doing was swimming. And Michelle tried to enjoy skiing down the hill, but didn't. She knows how to ski, and can enjoy it, but the conditions weren't right.

When we use 'trying' in its second sense to describe what someone is doing, there is a suggestion of failure. This suggestion seems stronger for the second sense than for the first. We wouldn't normally say that someone was trying to swim if the person was swimming. However, it *is* true that someone who is swimming is trying, successfully, to swim.

Very often when the second sort of trying is involved, we have no name for the defective imitation of doing *Y*. When we do have such a name, like *W*, we sometimes say that *X* does *W* to do *Y*. This does not mean that *X* does *W* in order to do *Y*. It is rather that *X* does *W*, intending to do *Y*, as, for example, we might say that a young child is scribbling on a piece of paper, to write a letter to her grandparents.

8. Instrumental Acts

In performing intentional acts we frequently use instruments. When person *X* does *Y* in order to obtain *Z*, he may use instrument *A* in doing *Y*. Instrumental acts are very important kinds of intentional acts, for they are the ones we must understand if we are to understand the use of language. There are many different sorts of instrument and different ways to use them. Some instruments are used on something, or applied to it as a hammer is used on or applied to a nail, and a pencil is used on a piece of paper. But other instruments are not applied to anything. The tightrope walker who uses a pole to balance is not using the pole on something.

If we wish to adequately characterize an instrumental act, we must indicate what instrument is used, and what, if anything, it is used on. When doing *Y* is an instrumental act, and *A* is the instrument, we can replace 'doing *Y*' by 'using *A*.' So that we could write:

X uses *A* (on *B*) in order to obtain *Z*.

as our standard form. The parentheses around 'on *B*' indicate that instruments aren't always used on something. However, this standard form isn't adequate. To completely characterize an instrumental act, we must indicate more than the instrument used and the object it is used on. We need also to indicate the manner in which the instrument is used, because many instruments can be used in different ways. A claw hammer, for example, is designed for use in pounding nails and in pulling them up. And the hammer is used one way to pound and a different way when it is used to pull up.

To completely characterize an instrumental act, we must indicate the instrument(s) used, the object on which it is used (if any), and the manner in which the instrument is used. But we need to be more specific about what manner is intended here, because many different aspects of the performance of an act are part of the manner or manners in which it is performed. If we say that something was done well or poorly, we are evaluating a performance, but we are also characterizing the manner in which the act was performed. So are we when we say that something was done rapidly or slowly, easily or with difficulty. But these manners are clearly distinct from the manner of using an instrument which determines an act to be one kind of intentional act rather than another. To identify such manners as the manner of using a hammer to pound nails, I will speak of the *instrumental manner of use*.

The standard form for describing instrumental intentional acts now looks like:

X uses *A* ϕ-ly (on *B*) in order to obtain or accomplish *Z*.

(We could also build the 'on *B*' into ϕ—as 'Jones uses the hammer nail-poundingly'—which would yield the simpler:

X uses *A* ϕ-ly in order to obtain or accomplish *Z*.)

This form provides a relatively complete analysis of instrumental acts, though sentences which have this form are frequently not very good English. For English doesn't often provide us with convenient adverbs for indicating the instrumental manner in which an instrument is used. If we wish to distinguish the use of hammers to pound nails from the use involved in pulling nails up, we can introduce a clumsy expression and speak of using the hammer *poundingly* on nails (or nail-poundingly). But it is possible to characterize instrumental manners of use without inventing barbarous adverbs. To do this we can label the instrumental act without referring to the instrument used, and then convert this label into a phrase to indicate the instrumental manner of use. If *doing Y* is an instrumental act or activity and *A* is the instrument, we can say that *X* uses *A in doing Y*, or that *X* uses *A to do Y*. So now, instead of saying that Jones used the hammer nail-poundingly, we can say that he used the hammer in pounding nails, or that he used it to pound nails. Of the two locutions, I prefer the 'to do *Y*' locution and will use it as an alternative to the adverbial one.

The two standard forms for characterizing instrumental acts are:

X uses *A* ϕ-ly (on *B*) in order to obtain or accomplish *Z*.
X uses *A* to do *Y* in order to obtain or accomplish *Z*.

The second form gives more natural English sentences than the first, as

The acrobat used the pole to balance in order to walk across the tightrope without falling.

The second form contains two expressions which label the same act. The instrumental act is the act of using *A*. This is the same act as doing *Y*. To say that *X* uses *A* is to describe *X*'s act very generally. We make the description more specific, and indicate how *A* is used, when we add 'to do *Y*.' (But even when we make the description more specific in this way, it may fail to be fully specific. In such a case we will be able to further specify the manner in which the instrument is used.)

An English sentence

(1) *X* uses *A* to obtain or accomplish *Z*.

is a special case of sentences having this form:

(2) *X* does *Y* to obtain or accomplish *Z*.

Such sentences are ambiguous in English. It is possible to use (2) with the sense:

(3) *X* does *Y* in order to obtain or accomplish *Z*.

Here 'to obtain or accomplish *Z*' is the purpose for doing *Y*. It is also possible to use (2) with the sense:

(4) *X* does *Y*, intending to be obtaining or accomplishing *Z*.

where obtaining or accomplishing *Z* is the intention for *Y*, not the intention of *Y*. The sentence

(5) Joe clapped his hands to get Mary's attention.

is most naturally understood as:

(6) Joe clapped his hands in order to get Mary's attention.

But

(7) Mark flailed his arms and legs to swim.

is better construed as

(8) Mark flailed his arms and legs, intending to swim.

In English, we can use the same form of words to indicate both the intention for an act and the intention of an act. Indeed, in English sentences the expression 'in order' is not always sufficient to distinguish the purpose of an act from the intention for the act. It would not be incorrect, in ordinary English, to say that Mark flailed his arms and legs in order to swim. However, in our standard form sentences, 'in order' always signals purpose. We speak of doing *W*, intending to do *Y*, to indicate the intention for the act. When the 'intending' locution is used in a standard form sentence, there is no suggestion of failure—as there is when we use 'trying.' The second standard form for instrumental acts:

X uses A to do Y in order to accomplish Z.

actually involves both the intention for the act and the intention of the act. For we could expand the standard form this way:

X uses A, intending to do Y, in order to accomplish Z.

Ordinarily, we won't employ this expanded form.

The phrase 'to do Y, can indicate both the intention for an act and the intention of an act, depending on whether we use 'intending' or 'in order.' But the very same 'to do Y' phrase could be used on one occasion to indicate the intention for an act, and on another occasion to indicate the intention of an act, in connection with the same situation. For if doing Y is a complex act, then 'to do Y' will be the purpose of the component acts. And if doing Y is also an instrumental act, then 'to do Y' will indicate the manner of using A—it will indicate the agent's intention for using A. It can sometimes prove difficult to translate an ordinary sentence into standard form, since we may need to decide whether a 'to do Y' phrase indicates the intention for an act or the intention of the act. There is no simple rule we can follow in making such translations. We must simply analyze the act or acts in question, and determine what structures they involve.

Consider Bob, who wants to produce a straight line connecting points P and Q on a sheet of paper, and who is using a straightedge and a pencil to produce this line. Bob holds the straightedge in place with his left hand. He presses the pencil against the paper as he moves it along the ruler with his right hand. He attends separately to what he is doing with each hand, so there are two (simple) intentional acts: the holding and the pressing-and-moving. The two acts have the common purpose *to produce a straight line from P to Q*. The act of producing the straight line is constituted by these two component acts together with the completing event of the line's coming to connect P and Q. (Bob's pressing is causally related to the line's appearing; if his pencil had defective lead, he could press it and move it without a line being produced.) Each component act is an instrumental act, with its own instrument. The purpose of these components defines the complex act producing a straight line from P to Q. This complex act is also an instrumental act. We can either describe this as an act with two instruments or as an act with one complex instrument (the pencil and the straightedge together). The complex act can be described as the act of using a straightedge and pencil to produce a straight line from *P* to *Q*. The phrase 'to produce a straight line from *P* to *Q*' gives the purpose of the component acts and the manner of using the straightedge and pencil.

9. Developing a Theory

In this chapter, I have developed a preliminary and sketchy framework theory of intentional acts which have purposes or goals. Further details of the theory are to be filled in when the theory is applied to this or that kind of intentional act. It is important to understand that ordinary terms appearing in the statement of a framework theory need not have their ordinary meanings. Of course, ordinary expressions that do not play special roles in the theory should and do have their ordinary meanings. Those terms which express concepts central to the theory may have one meaning within the theory and a different meaning outside it. For example, consider the word 'purpose.' In the present theory, this word has a specialized meaning. Although there is considerable overlap between the theoretical and the ordinary meanings of 'purpose,' there are many situations where it would ordinarily be correct to use 'purpose,' where 'purpose' with its theoretical sense would be incorrect. Someone looking at a ten-speed bike might ask what is the purpose of the derailleur. The questioner wants to know how the derailleur contributes to the functioning of the bike, to know what is the rationale for incorporating it in the bike's design. The question is appropriate even if no one acted with a relevant purpose in either building or designing the bike. And it would ordinarily be correct to speak of purpose in connection with an enabling act.

To understand a framework theory, we must understand how the central concepts (expressions) are related to one another. We must also understand how to use the theory (how to use the theoretical expressions or concepts) in relation to experience. This may include describing and even conceptually structuring experience. There is no requirement that we should be able to explain the fundamental expressions of the theory in terms of antecedently available expressions with their ordinary meanings. Such a "requirement" could not be met. Nor, as the theory is being developed, is it necessary that each key expression should be capable of being defined within the theory. This may not even be possible for a completely developed theory. But with a completely developed theory, we can probably introduce additional expressions to insure that every theoretical expression is intratheoretically definable.

My understanding of what I am up to in this chapter and this book leads me to proceed in a way that is different from a popular current style of doing philosophy. This style is exemplified by such different philosophers as Roderick Chisholm and John Searle. Someone who employs this style locates fundamental concepts, and then tries to "nail down" these concepts by providing exhaustive lists of conditions under which the concepts apply. Once one philosopher produces such a list, her challengers look for counterexamples where the concept applies but the conditions aren't satisfied. If they come up with such examples, the original listmaker goes "back to the drawing board" to produce a new list. And so on, apparently forever. This style of doing philosophy may be appropriate for someone who is trying to clarify an existing conceptual framework or theory which is completely developed. It is not appropriate here. If I tried to employ that style, I could make no progress in developing a theory. I have not, for example, given exhaustive lists which determine what counts as either a completable or a completing act. I have explained each kind of act with respect to the other, and also with respect to such concepts as purpose. We have an understanding of these acts that is sufficient for the present if we can distinguish one kind from the other, and determine in actual situations when we have a case of one or the other kind.

As well as avoiding this popular style of doing philosophy, I am failing to give much attention to a problem (topic?) of central importance in recent philosophy. This is the problem of identity and conditions for identity. It is felt that in order to legitimately talk about things of a certain kind, we must be able to specify identity conditions for things of that kind. (This can be the same enterprise as nailing down a concept by providing a list of conditions where it applies.) There appears to be no problem about identifying physical objects, but such entities as propositions have strikes against them for not being so readily identifiable. I do not direct much attention toward the identity conditions of intentional acts, nor do I provide rules for determining how, given two descriptions of acts, we can tell whether these are descriptions of one act or two. I *have* made some remarks about identity and identification. But I don't believe it is appropriate to deal with this topic in a general way. The present sketchy theory is to be filled in by applying it to one or another kind of intentional act. In this book, the theory acquires additional flesh by being applied to linguistic acts. Instead of developing a general procedure for determining whether there are two acts or just one, we must consider acts of a kind and learn how to identify them. An understanding of acts of a kind will enable us to analyze acts of that kind, and to determine what structural relations they involve. This knowledge enables us to identify and distinguish these acts.

After all these remarks to justify my sidestepping the problem of identity, I *will* say a few general things about the problem of determining whether two descriptions describe two acts. The first is that there may not be a determinate answer to the question whether one description describes a different act from that labelled by a second description. The descriptions in question may be too vague, or too general, so that one description cannot be tied unambiguously to one act. If this is not a problem, then the general approach for determining the number of acts is to analyze the act or acts involved in the relevant situation, and to determine what are the intentional structures and what are the purposes. Given such an analysis, we try to tie specific descriptions to specific acts. There are certain difficulties, which I have mentioned previously, in locating the act which a description labels. One difficulty is associated with general—as opposed to specific—descriptions. We can call a single act both *opening the window* and *raising the sash*. Both of these descriptions are relatively specific; we would have no difficulty in determining that they fit the same act. When we describe Peter's act of pronouncing 'Constantinople' as an act of producing vocal sounds, the description "act of producing vocal sounds" is more general than "act of pronouncing 'Constantinople'." Since he can produce vocal sounds without pronouncing 'Constantinople,' we might initially think that there are two acts. However, the act of making vocal sounds is not one that Peter attends to separately. It neither enables him to pronounce 'Constantinople' or combines with some other act or event to constitute pronouncing 'Constantinople.' The only sensible analysis has Peter's act of pronouncing 'Constantinople' being a single, simple act. So it must be the same as his act of making vocal sounds. (The description "act of pronouncing 'Constantinople'" is more specific than "act of making vocal sounds." But it is a fairly general description of an act of referring to Constantinople, by using 'Constantinople.') I will call general descriptions *abstract*. We must be careful not to take an abstract description of act *Y* for a description of some component of *Y*.

A second difficulty in counting acts is occasioned by 'to do *Y*' phrases. When these occur in ordinary contexts, we must determine whether they indicate the intention for an act or the intention of an act (in those cases where they do indicate one or the other). If *X* does *W*, intending to do *Y*, then either doing *W* is the same as doing *Y*, or there is no act of doing *Y*. If she does *W in order to do Y*, then if she succeeds, doing *W* is one act, doing *Y* is another.

A third difficulty is due to the complicated character of some simple intentional acts. If an act is complicated, we may be able to divide it into different "parts" where these fail to be different intentional acts. Consider an accomplished skier who turns, bending his body a certain way, moving his skis, and using his poles. If he is truly accomplished, this turn may be a simple intentional act. But we can focus on his use of his poles, and distinguish this from the rest of what he does in turning. Or suppose that Peter's pronouncing 'Constantinople' is a single and simple intentional act. We can isolate each syllable, and consider it apart from the others. When an intentional act can be subdivided into parts which are not themselves intentional acts, I will call these *virtual components* of the intentional act.

The virtual components of an intentional act fail to be intentional acts because they are not separately attended to by the agent and they have no purposes proper to themselves. It isn't always easy to determine whether we have a virtual component of an intentional act or a full-fledged intentional component. This situation is made more difficult by the fact that what counts as a virtual component for one person might be an intentional act for another person, or for the same person at another time. An accomplished skier may perform a complicated maneuver as a single, simple intentional act. A less accomplished skier may be able to perform the same maneuver, but need to give separate attention to the different movements. So the maneuver is a simple intentional act for the accomplished skier and a complex intentional act for the other skier. The same situation arises for language users. A person who speaks deliberately, choosing her words carefully, may perform more intentional acts than the person who speaks the same sentence less self-consciously.

This poses a problem for a theory of language and linguistic acts. We wish to have an account of the acts performed in using language, but we want to ignore the features which distinguish one language user from another. We will solve this problem by developing the theory to fit the relatively deliberate language user. We will recognize as many acts as prove helpful for explaining how an expression is used. This provides a rich and complex theory which gives the right results about the language, even when it is used by an unself-conscious speaker. The speech-act analysis which fits the deliberate language user fails to give us the psychological truth about all language users. But this analysis yields the linguistic understanding we are after.

Reference

1. Jerrold J. Katz. *Propositional Structure and Illocutionary Force.* New York: Thomas Y. Crowell, 1977.

Chapter 2
Linguistic Acts

1. Sentential Acts

Expressions are instruments used in performing a variety of intentional acts. The expressions employed are tokens rather than types. These expressions are real instruments: physical objects employed by human beings. (Even the expressions we use in thinking can probably be identified with physiological objects or events.) Spoken expressions are short-lived instruments; they do not survive the time of their production. Let us consider a speaker's act of producing an expression and her act of using that expression in normal circumstances. Are these two acts or one? She would not produce the expression in order to use it. There is no other act or event which might combine with the producing to constitute using. The act of producing might enable the using. But the producing is not normally attended to separately. The producing and the using must constitute a single act. To call it either an act of producing or an act of using is to describe it abstractly. It is an act of producing-and-using.

Written expressions are longer-lived than spoken ones. And the act of writing an expression seems more complicated than the act of speaking one. The writer must hold the pen or pencil against the paper and move it. This causes the written expression to appear when the holding-and-moving is successful. For some defect in the pen or pencil (including being out of ink) may prevent the expression from appearing. An act of writing could be a complex act. One component is the act of holding and moving the pen or pencil. This is a completable act which aims at the completing event of the expression's appearing. The complex act is the act of producing the expression. However, for a person who knows how to write, the act of writing an expression is normally not complex. She doesn't hold-and-move the pencil in order to produce the expression. Her act of producing is complicated but not complex. If something is wrong with the pencil, so that no expression appears, she has performed an act which she intended to be an act of producing. But she has not succeeded. The situation here is analogous to the case where Jorge raises his arm intentionally. A physiological analysis may inform us that for Jorge to raise his arm, there must first occur an event in his brain. This is followed by signals being transmitted to nerves and muscles. Finally his arm goes up. We do not view Jorge's act of raising his arm as a complex act, because the initial event in the brain is not an intentional act. Jorge is not aware of it, and does not intend to be doing it. Jorge's act of raising his arm is a complex event but not a complex act. Similarly, for the person who is accustomed to writing, her act of producing an expression is a complex event but a simple intentional act. We can make analogous remarks about the skilled typist who composes as he types.

When the writer's act of producing an expression is a simple act, then if she thinks what she writes, her producing and using the expression are a single act. However, once the written expression has been produced, it can then be put to further use. The original use of the written expression is to express the writer's thoughts. But this locution, 'to express thought,' is misleading. A person who speaks, and thinks what he is speaking, is thinking out loud. A person who thinks what he is writing is thinking on paper. It often happens, in writing a formal letter or writing something for publication, that the writer first formulates a sentence in his head, and then puts it down on paper. In my own case, at least, the writing is not simply copying. I rethink the sentence in writing it—I often change the sentence in writing it. Similar remarks apply to someone who types, composing as he does so. So long as the typist is thinking what he types, his producing and using an expression are one act. It is possible for someone to merely copy an expression, either by hand or on a typewriter. The person who merely copies is not thinking with the expression she produces. Her act of producing the expression is not an act of using it. We can also imagine someone who keeps a stock of words typed on pieces of cardboard. When he wants to communicate, he takes them from the box he carries, and assembles them for his audience. That person's acts of producing expressions are different from his acts of using the expressions—he produced them to enable himself to use them. But his acts of assembling sentences will probably be identical with his acts of using them.

Normally, when one person speaks to another, his act of producing an expression is the same act as his using the expression to express his thought—as his act of thinking with the produced expression. The speaker is also using his expression to convey his thought to his audience. The act of using the expression to convey his thought will not be a distinct act. He does not produce-and-use-the-expression-to-express-his-thought in order to convey the thought. And his producing-and-using does not enable the conveying. He produces-and-uses-to-express-and-uses-to convey as a single act.

Things are different when Megan writes a letter. Megan refers to individuals and characterizes individuals when she writes her letter. Her act of producing an expression is the same act as her using that expression to express her thought. Megan's act or activity of writing the letter is an enabling act. Her writing the letter enables her to send it. Whether or not the sending constitutes conveying her thoughts depends on how we understand 'convey' (and 'conveying'). We can understand the sending and conveying to be the same thing. Or we can understand 'convey' to include getting the message to its intended audience. In that case she sends the letter in order to convey her thoughts. (Not all writing involves a gap between expressing thought and conveying thought. The professor who writes on a blackboard may express and convey her thought in a single act.)

Suppose someone uses instrument *A* to perform act *Y*, and that he does *Y* in order to obtain *Z*. We may be able to describe both doing *Y* and obtaining *Z* as instrumental acts, where *A* is the instrument. We may be able to do this even though the agent doesn't use *A* "over again" to perform some act *W* which is also a component of obtaining *Z*. So long as doing *Y* is not itself complex, with one component which is an act of using *Z* (in order to do *Y*), I will say that doing *Y* is the *minimal act performed in using A*—it is the *minimal act of using A*. If we can also describe obtaining *Z* as an act of using *A*, it will not be the minimal act of using *A*. Even if *Y* is itself a complex act, it is the minimal act of using *A* so long as it does not have a component which is an act of using *A*. The concept of a minimal act is important for dealing with linguistic acts. A sentence is a complex instrument; an act of using a sentence is normally a complex intentional act. We can say that a component expression is used to perform a component act. We can also say that the act of using the sentence is in part the act of using the component expression. In this case the component act will be the minimal act of using the component expression. The act of using the sentence is also an act of using the component expression, but it is not the minimal act of using that expression. However, there will also be a minimal act of using the whole sentence. If George used the expression 'the president' in 1939 to refer to Franklin Delano Roosevelt, then the act of referring to FDR was the minimal act that George performed with the definite description. If George referred to FDR in order to assert that FDR was too friendly with Stalin, George used 'the president' in making this assertion. But the assertion was not the minimal act of using the description. A whole sentence can also be used in performing different acts. Jean Pierre might use the sentence 'Le baton est rouge' to assert that the stick is red. He might also use this sentence to persuade us that the stick is red. His assertion can be the minimal act of using the sentence, but his persuading cannot. Jean Pierre asserts in order to persuade.

A *sentential act* is the minimal act performed in using a sentence. A sentential act is normally a complex intentional act. Sentential acts are always complex for the deliberate language user. But a person who must frequently repeat the same sentence may perform a single and simple intentional act of using that sentence—radio operators may often be in this position. We shall only consider complex sentential acts. The immediate purpose for using the major components of the sentence will define the sentential act. Suppose Steve uses the sentence 'Switzerland is mountainous.' Steve uses the name 'Switzerland' to refer to Switzerland. And I will say that Steve uses the predicate 'is mountainous' (or '[is mountainous]'—the predicate is properly regarded as containing a gap) to perform an act of *predicative denoting.* (Such acts will be fully discussed later. Steve's act is one of predicatively denoting mountainous regions or objects.) Steve's act of referring and his act of predicative denoting constitute his sentential act. Each of these acts is a completable act; they complete each other to constitute the sentential act. Steve also asserts that Switzerland is mountainous. We must consider the relation between his sentential act and his assertion. They take place at the same time (or approximately so), and they involve the same instrument—the same sentence. If these are not the same act, then either we must say that the sentential act is performed in order to assert that Switzerland is mountainous, or we must say that the sentential act is intended to enable the assertion. The sentential act is not a component of the assertion, because there is no other act or event which combines with the sentential act to constitute the assertion. The sentential act does not enable the assertion either. Steve does not first say that Switzerland is mountainous, and then assert it. He does not separately attend to the saying and the asserting. Steve's sentential act is his assertion. Steve's act of referring and his act of predicative denoting are both done *in order to assert that Switzerland is mountainous.* These component acts (with their common purpose) constitute Steve's assertion. When we say that Steve uses 'Switzerland' to refer to Switzerland, the phrase 'to refer to Switzerland' indicates Steve's manner of using 'Switzerland.' The phrase 'to assert that Switzerland is mountainous' gives the purpose of the component acts and the manner of using the sentence.

Steve's sentential act might not have been an assertion. Steve might, rhetorically, have pronounced 'Switzerland is mountainous' as a question. And then continued "Yes!" (or "Yes it is!"). In this case, Steve has still asserted that Switzerland is mountainous. But his assertion is more complicated than in the case considered above. For now the sentential act performed with 'Switzerland is mountainous' is an enabling act. It gives him the "material" for his assertion. He asserts that Switzerland is mountainous when he says "Yes!"

A sentential act is the minimal act performed in using a sentence. But the sentential act must be conventional or customary in the sense that this act (this kind of act with this kind of sentence) is "provided for" by the language. I will adapt Austin's terminology, and label a sentential act performed with a complete and separate sentence an *illocutionary act.* (A separate sentence is one which is not a component of a longer sentence.) Steve's act of asserting that Switzerland is mountainous is an illocutionary act. So are acts of supposing, warning, commanding, etc. When a sentence is used to perform an illocutionary act, the illocutionary force of the act is part of the instrumental manner of using the sentence. But the force is only part of the manner. Steve asserted that Switzerland is mountainous. What Steve asserted (the "content" of the assertion) is also part of his instrumental manner of using the sentence. A sentential act need not be an illocutionary act. If the sentence in question is a component of a larger sentence, then the act of using the sentence can be sentential without being illocutionary. When John tells Kevin, "If you think that I am kind, then you are mistaken," he uses the conditional sentence to make an assertion. The antecedent is not asserted, and it is not used to perform an illocutionary act. The sentential act performed with the antecedent is performed in the course of making the assertion.

2. Illocutionary Acts

I have identified one kind of illocutionary act, but I have not defined 'illocutionary act.' The expression 'illocutionary act' expresses (embodies?) a concept that is of fundamental importance to the theory being developed. As the theory now stands, it does not possess sufficient resources to define 'illocutionary act.' We will develop an understanding of illocutionary acts as we develop the theory. There are both linguistic and nonlinguistic illocutionary acts. For we can use a sentence to threaten someone, or we can do it with a gesture. Linguistic illocutionary acts are fundamental. We countenance nonlinguistic illocutionary acts only because they are the same general kind of intentional acts as linguistic illocutionary acts.

My strategy in dealing with illocutionary acts is to identify certain clear cases of such acts; other illocutionary acts are picked out by their resemblance to the clear cases. A sentential act performed with a complete and separate sentence is the paradigm case of an illocutionary act. Such an act can be performed with either a spoken or a written sentence. Steve's saying "Switzerland is mountainous" is an assertion. He could also write the sentence to make an assertion. Since an illocutionary act is a sentential act, and this is the minimal act performed by using a sentence, a person does not do something with the sentence in order to perform the illocutionary act. His using the sentence *is* the illocutionary act. If a man tells his daughter, "Your uncle will take you to the circus tomorrow," he may be performing different acts. Suppose that what he says constitutes an assertion. His assertion is an illocutionary act because he does not do something with the sentence in order to assert. As well as asserting, the father may be reassuring his daughter who feared that her uncle was leaving town that very night. He might reassure her without intending to, for he might be ignorant of his daughter's fears. In that case, reassuring her is not an intentional act. But suppose he reassures her intentionally. This reassuring is an intentional act, but it is not an illocutionary act. The reassuring is not a minimal act performed with the sentence. The father asserts in order to reassure.

It sometimes happens that the kind of act which can be performed with a complete and separate sentence can also be performed with the component of a longer sentence. English is fairly flexible about jamming sentences together to form bigger sentences; the jamming together sometimes allows the components to be used to perform the same acts that could be performed when they stand alone. For example, in presenting a premise-conclusion argument, we can present the premises as separate sentences and the conclusion as a separate sentence. If a person seriously advanced this argument:

> French emperors are always short.
> Napoleon was a French emperor.
> So Napoleon was short.

we would recognize three assertions being made. Essentially the same argument could be made with this single sentence:

> Napoleon must have been short, because he was a French emperor and French emperors are always short.

We can regard this as a one-premise argument, having a compound premise. But we must still recognize at least two assertions, one for the premise, and one for the conclusion. It is because the premise can be asserted with a complete and separate sentence that we are prepared to recognize the assertion made with the premise-as-component. And similarly for the conclusion. If, impossibly, the premises and conclusions could never be presented by separate sentences, we would have no basis for claiming that these component sentences were used to perform illocutionary acts.

As well as admitting that some component sentences are used to perform illocutionary acts, we are also compelled to recognize complex illocutionary acts. Any illocutionary act will be a complex intentional act—when performed by a deliberate language user. A complex illocutionary act is an illocutionary act which contains other illocutionary acts as components. What leads us to recognize complex illocutionary acts is the fact that some kinds of illocutionary act that can be performed with a single sentence can also be performed with several sentences. Consider this example. Suppose Bill tells Lynn, "I apologize for stepping on your foot." His apology is a sentential illocutionary act. But Bill might have apologized by telling Lynn this: "It is very dark here, and I did not see you. I am very sorry I stepped on your foot." Bill's two sentential acts together constitute an apology. But the individual sentential acts are not apologies. When Bill says, "It is very dark here, and I did not see you," his act is an assertion. He makes this assertion in order to apologize to Lynn. The second sentential act is an expression of regret; its purpose is also to apologize.

Apologizing is an illocutionary act. The multi-sentence apology is a complex illocutionary act. Apologies are of optional length, but some illocutionary acts are typically complex illocutionary acts. Premise-conclusion arguments will ordinarily contain at least two assertions. But what leads us to think that arguing, or making an argument, constitutes an illocutionary act? We are led to this position by noting the analogy between the argument and the complex apology. The complex apology contains components which are illocutionary acts, and is constituted by its illocutionary components. The immediate purpose of the premise-assertions and the conclusion-assertion defines the act which is an argument. The argument is constituted by its illocutionary components. The relation between the argument and its illocutionary components is not like the relation between the father's act of reassuring his daughter and his assertion which is a component of the reassuring. The assertion is a completable act which points toward the completing event of his daughter's being reassured. It is not solely up to the father to determine whether his assertion will succeed in reassuring his daughter. It *is* up to the arguer to determine that his premises and conclusion will constitute an argument. He makes an argument whether or not he succeeds in convincing anyone. (The premise-assertions and the conclusion-assertion have a common purpose which defines the argument. But the different acts have different roles to play in the argument. We might mark this by saying that X asserts each premise *as supporting the conclusion,* in order to argue that such and such. And X asserts the conclusion *as supported by the premises,* in order to argue that such and such. We could also say of Bill, in the example above, that he asserted that it was dark and he didn't see Lynn *as explaining his blunder,* in order to apologize.)

As well as having one illocutionary act be a component of a second, we can have one illocutionary act enabling another. Consider Steve's second assertion, where he first pronounces 'Switzerland is mountainous' as a question, and then says "Yes!" The sentential act performed with 'Switzerland is mountainous' is a question—a questioning act. When Steve says "Yes!" he is not uttering a complete and separate sentence. But he uses the expression 'Yes' to (publicly) accept the sentence 'Switzerland is mountainous.' This constitutes an assertion that Switzerland is mountainous. (It is the same kind of act performed by someone who uses 'Switzerland is mountainous' to assert that Switzerland is mountainous.) The question is not a component of Steve's assertion. Instead it prepares the way for his assertion; it makes Steve's assertion possible.

It now seems appropriate to say that the minimal intentional act or activity performed by using a text one or more sentences long is an illocutionary act or activity, so long as it is a conventional or customary linguistic act or activity. This allows assertions, suppositions, apologies, arguments, and even activities like telling a story or giving a speech to count as illocutionary acts or activities. However, not every consecutive sequence of sentences uttered by a person will constitute an illocutionary act. The sequence of sentences must be used to perform a single intentional act or activity. If a speaker performs one illocutionary act at time

t_1, is silent for a while, and then performs a second and unrelated illocutionary act at time t_2, we have no reason to recognize a complex illocutionary act constituted by the two illocutionary acts. Changing the paradigm for illocutionary acts from a sentential act performed with a complete and separate sentence to a minimal act performed with a text consisting of one or more complete and separate sentences still allows us to recognize illocutionary acts performed with the components of sentences. These are illocutionary acts if they are the same kind of acts as the minimal acts performed with texts one or more sentences in length.

Illocutionary acts, especially sentential illocutionary acts, are important to the study of language because knowing how to perform these acts, and being able to recognize them when performed by someone else, are inseparable from the ability to use and understand language. Linguistic acts which are components of illocutionary acts are equally important. But the acts defined by the nonillocutionary purposes of illocutionary acts are less important to the study of language. Many such acts are tied to language in an essential and conventional way; these include acts of informing, persuading, entertaining, etc. Acts like these usually depend on a reaction from the audience of the language producer, and are not within the producer's control. A person would not be said to understand the language if he could not make assertions. But someone can understand the language perfectly in spite of the fact that she is not very good at persuading others to accept her beliefs. Success in persuasion requires more than a knowledge of the language.

3. Audience Participation

It is customary (following Austin) to apply the expression 'illocutionary act' to acts in which a speaker addresses an audience that understands the speaker. If a speaker aims at an audience, but the audience either doesn't hear or doesn't understand the speaker, then no illocutionary act has been performed. The speaker tried to perform the act but didn't succeed. The customary account does not provide a label for the act performed by the speaker whether the audience "gets it" or not. But the speaker has the same thoughts and intentions, he makes the same effort and uses the same muscles, producing the same sounds, when his audience fails to comprehend his message as when the audience does comprehend it. I find it convenient to have a label for the speaker's act considered independently of his audience. So I have changed the Austin-Searle usage to say that the speaker's act is an illocutionary act. Someone who expresses herself in writing also performs illocutionary acts. This includes the person writing a letter and the person writing a book, but not the typist who simply copies a manuscript.

I will use 'consummated illocutionary act' for what are ordinarily called illocutionary acts. If a speaker addresses his assertion to an audience which understands him, the author's assertion is consummated—he has made a consummated assertion. When one person is talking to others, the issue of whether an assertion is consummated depends on what happens at the time he is talking. The events which cause a letter writer's assertion to be consummated may take place considerably later than the time of writing. But an illocutionary act can only be consummated by its intended audience. If the letter never reaches its destination, but is read instead by postal officials, then the writer's assertions are not consummated.

The difference between plain illocutionary acts and consummated illocutionary acts is worth exploring in some detail. But it is not appropriate to begin this investigation by considering acts performed with texts that are one or more sentences long. Sentential acts (those we are considering) are complex acts. The distinction between plain and consummated acts is also found with the components of sentential acts. It seems reasonable to first gain an understanding of plain and consummated component acts, and then turn to the difference between plain and consummated illocutionary acts.

Suppose *X* is addressing *R*, and *X* makes an assertion. In the course of making this assertion, *X* uses expression *A* to refer to *B*. Here 'to refer to *B*' gives the manner of using *A*, not its purpose; the act of using *A* is the same act as referring to *B*. *X* produces-and-uses-*A* to express his thoughts; *X* thinks with *A*. *X*'s act of using *A* to think (out loud) is his referring act. His referring is a kind of thinking. His referring is also an act of conveying his thought to *R*. This is *X*'s *plain* referring act. It is at once an act of expressing thought (an act of thinking out loud) and an act of conveying thought in *R*'s direction. In speaking to *R*, *X* intends that *R* understand him. In this case, *X* intends that *R* will understand his referring. We cannot say that *X* intends for his referring to *cause* *R* to understand him. The connection between his plain referring and her understanding is not that tight. However, *X* does *influence* *R* to understand him. For *X* is not just an automatic talking machine. *X* looks at *R*. He directs his speech and gestures in her direction. Social customs and conventions, which include linguistic customs and conventions, are such that *X*'s act or acts make it clear to *R* what *X* wants and expects her to do. In the present case, *R* is expected to understand *X*'s referring. *X*'s plain referring act influences *R* to understand his use of *A* to refer. *X* performs his plain referring act in order to bring about, or contribute to bringing about, *R*'s understanding. *X*'s plain referring is a completable act; *R*'s understanding is a completing event. The *consummated* referring act is constituted by *X*'s plain referring act and *R*'s understanding.

R's understanding of *X*'s referring is produced in part by (1) *R*'s recognizing what *X* is doing—using *A* to refer to *B*, and (2) *R*'s recognizing what *X* intends for her to do—understand. *X* intends that *R* will understand his referring, by virtue of recognizing his intention. Customary accounts of speech acts have little to say about what *R*'s understanding consists in. In the case of referring, we can follow John Searle and say that *X*'s uttering *A* identifies *B* to *R*. This makes *R*'s understanding consist in having *B* identified to her by *A* (by *X*'s saying *A*). But this is not illuminating—what is it to have *B* identified? When *R* understands *X*, *R* is doing something. Anyone with children is well aware that there is an important difference between hearing what someone says and listening with understanding to that person. Listening with understanding is an intentional act (activity). I propose the following analysis of *R*'s understanding *X*'s referring. *X* uses *A* to refer to *B*, in order to influence *R* to understand this referring. *R's understanding consists in her using A to perform a plain act of referring to B.* This doesn't mean that *R* performs a separate act of producing *A*, either out loud or in her head. Instead she uses the expression (token) that *X* has produced to perform her referring act. A person can think out loud with her own words—words she produces. She can also think (out loud?) with someone else's words.

X uses *A* to refer (plainly) to *B*, in order to influence *R* to use *A* to refer (plainly) to *B*. The influence of *X*'s act is due in part to custom and convention. It is because she knows how to function in this framework of custom and convention that *R* can recognize what *X* is up to, and know what is expected of her. It is a small step from *R*'s recognizing what she is supposed to do, to her actually doing it. This small step is not one that must be taken. The child who hears but doesn't understand doesn't take this step; the child may even be refusing to take this step. *X*'s act of referring is brought to a successful conclusion by *R*'s using *A* to refer to *B*. There are a number of ways in which *X*'s referring might go wrong; these would keep his referring from being consummated. *R* might not hear him. Or *R* might hear *X* but not understand him. Finally, *R* might misunderstand *X*. Instead of using *A* to refer to *B*, she might use *A* to refer to C ($\neq B$). *X*'s consummated act of referring is constituted by *X*'s plain act of referring, with its purpose, and *R*'s plain act of referring. From *X*'s standpoint, *R*'s referring act is a completing event. This completing event is also an act. It is an act with a purpose. But *R*'s purpose does not define *X*'s consummated act of referring. From *X*'s viewpoint, *R*'s referring act is a completing event. From *R*'s viewpoint, her referring act is completable. *R* does not perform the consummated act of referring; *X* does. Since *X* succeeds in performing a consummated act of referring just in case *R* uses his expression *A* to refer to *B*, *X*'s act of producing-and-using-*A*-to-refer is also an enabling act. So *X*'s one act is both an act with a purpose and an enabling act.

Let us suppose that *X* is Steve, *A* is 'Switzerland,' and *B* is Switzerland. Steve's referring act is performed in the course of asserting that Switzerland is mountainous, using the sentence 'Switzerland is mountainous.' Just as Steve's plain referring act is a simple act, let us suppose that his plain act of predicative denoting is a simple act. The difference between the plain act of predicative denoting and the consummated act of predicative denoting is completely analogous to that between the plain and consummated referring. Steve performs the plain act of using '[is mountainous]' to predicatively denote mountainous places in order to influence *R* (Harriet) to perform a similar act. His predicative denoting act is also an enabling act. Steve performs a consummated act of predicative denoting if Harriet performs the appropriate plain act.

Now that we have considered the components of Steve's assertion, we must try to understand Steve's assertion. In performing his plain acts of referring and predicative denoting, Steve aims at communicating—at being understood by Harriet. But he also aims at making an assertion. He doesn't simply want Harriet to understand his referring and his predicative denoting. Steve wants Harriet to understand his assertion. If Harriet is to understand Steve's assertion, she must combine her plain acts of referring and predicative denoting to constitute a sentential act. And if these acts are to be combined in this way, they must have a common purpose. This purpose cannot be *to make an assertion.* Steve is the one who is making an assertion. Harriet's purpose must be something like *to understand Steve's assertion.* So Harriet (plainly) refers to Switzerland in order to understand Steve's assertion. And Harriet predicatively denotes mountainous areas in order to understand Steve's assertion. These two acts combine to constitute Harriet's act of understanding Steve's assertion. Steve's two consummated acts will also combine to constitute his consummated assertion. Steve performs a consummated act of referring to Switzerland in order to make the consummated assertion that Switzerland is mountainous. And Steve performs the consummated act of predicatively denoting mountainous areas in order to make the consummated assertion that Switzerland is mountainous. Harriet's two acts, referring and predicative denoting, are both ingredients of Steve's consummated acts; her sentential act does not appear to be an ingredient of Steve's consummated assertion, though its occurrence is necessary to Steve's consummated assertion.

We must take a closer look at Harriet's acts of referring and predicative denoting. When Steve performs his plain act of referring, he aims at getting Harriet to understand his referring. He also aims at getting her to understand his assertion. It isn't enough to say that Steve's referring is intended to influence Harriet to use 'Switzerland' to refer to Switzerland. Harriet must not only refer to Switzerland, but she must do this for the appropriate purpose. Harriet must refer in order to understand Steve's assertion. Steve's plain act of referring won't be successfully completed if Harriet merely refers to Switzerland. His successful referring requires that her referring have a suitable purpose. The same goes for the successful completion of Steve's predicative denoting. For Steve's two acts to succeed, Harriet's two acts must have a common purpose which unites them to form a complex act.

When we discussed referring above, we remarked that it is not illuminating to describe *R*'s act as an act of understanding *X*'s referring. Our more explanatory account has it that *R*'s act of understanding is the same as *R*'s act of using *A* to refer to *B* (for a suitable purpose). It is similarly not very enlightening to describe Harriet's sentential act as an act of understanding Steve's assertion. I will say in this case that Harriet's act of understanding is an act of using Steve's sentence to *represent* (to represent Switzerland as mountainous). Harriet does not know before Steve says it what Steve is going to say. So it is not appropriate to say that Harriet refers to Switzerland in order to represent Switzerland as mountainous. We can say something like this: Harriet refers to Switzerland in order to represent whatever Steve is saying about Switzerland. By the time she performs the act of predicative denoting, she knows what Steve is saying about Switzerland. So Harriet performs the act of predicatively denoting mountainous areas in order to represent Switzerland as mountainous. The two acts have the common purpose *to represent what Steve asserts (about Switzerland)*. The purpose of the first act, when specifically described, is determinable. The purpose of the second act is determinate; it further determines the purpose of Harriet's referring act. However, it isn't enough to describe Harriet's sentential act as an act of representing Switzerland as mountainous. In describing her act, we need to include the force and the author of the illocutionary act, as well as its "content." We can for the present describe her act as an act of representing Switzerland as mountainous as asserted by Steve.

The analysis of our consummated assertion, as developed to this point, involves a puzzle. The consummated assertion is constituted by the consummated act of referring and the consummated act of predicative denoting. Each consummated component has two components of its own: a plain act performed by Steve and a plain act performed by Harriet. In order for the consummated assertion to come off, Harriet must perform a sentential act. However, Harriet's sentential act does not seem to be a component of the consummated assertion. And Harriet's sentential act is an act of understanding Steve's assertion, but it isn't clear what assertion this is. If Harriet's sentential act is as I have explained it, then Steve needs to make a plain assertion for her to understand. The account so far provides no place for Steve's plain assertion.

When we first considered referring, we said that Steve's (*X*'s) immediate purpose for his plain referring act is *to influence Harriet to perform a referring act.* Later it proved necessary to qualify this. The purpose is *to perform a referring act for the appropriate purpose.* We must similarly complicate Steve's plain act of referring. When Steve performs his plain acts of referring and predicative denoting, he is using expressions to think out loud. But Steve's thinking is sentential. Steve must combine his plain act of referring and his plain act of predicative denoting to constitute a plain sentential act. Steve performs his plain act of referring to Switzerland in order to plainly assert that Switzerland is mountainous. Steve's plain referring act has two purposes: (1) to make a plain assertion, (2) to influence Harriet to understand. The first purpose is more fundamental. Steve's referring act with purpose (1) is the act that has purpose (2). His act with purpose (1) aims at Harriet's act as qualified by an appropriate purpose. Besides having two purposes, Steve's referring act—with purpose (1)—is an enabling act. Steve's act with its sentential purpose enables Harriet to perform her act with its sentential purpose. Steve's plain act of predicative denoting also has two purposes and is an enabling act. Steve's plain act of referring is an ingredient of distinct complex acts. It is a major element of his consummated referring act and of his plain assertion. It is also a component of his consummated assertion, but not a major component.

As we have it so far, the consummated assertion is constituted by the consummated referring act and the consummated act of predicative denoting. In addition to these components, we have Steve's plain assertion and Harriet's sentential act. Our analysis has not made these sentential acts components of the consummated assertion, even though they are necessary to the consummated assertion. But Steve's plain assertion and Harriet's sentential act are both constituted by acts which are also components of the consummated assertion. Indeed, the consummated assertion has no simple component which is not also a component of one of the sentential acts. In order to make sense of all this, we seem to be required to recognize that a consummated assertion and other consummated complex acts have a very special kind of structure. The consummated assertion, constituted by its two consummated components, has two distinct structures. It is also constituted by Steve's plain assertion, together with Harriet's sentential act. Just as Steve's plain referring act is performed in order to influence Harriet to understand it, so Steve's plain assertion is performed in order to influence Harriet to understand it. If she does understand it, then his plain assertion has been brought to a successful conclusion. The consummated assertion is like some kind of intricate puzzle. The components "interlock" in different ways to constitute the whole.

4. Habitual Acts

It is likely to strike some people as odd or worse when I describe Harriet's understanding what Steve says as an intentional act. Listening with understanding is not commonly regarded as an act or activity. But a parent might order his child to listen, or listen carefully. If he can command someone to listen, and the command can be obeyed, then the obeyer must be performing an intentional act. It doesn't sound so odd to describe reading as an intentional activity. A person must choose to read, and she must make some effort. However, there is no essential difference, so far as they are intentional acts or activities, between listening with understanding and reading. In each case, the person "on the receiving end" makes use of expressions produced by someone else (or produced by herself at another time). Using these expressions in the appropriate manner, for suitable purposes, constitutes understanding.

Intentional acts are sometimes understood as involving conscious choices. When Henry accuses Nina of bumping into him on purpose, he conceives her as making a deliberate decision to bump him. Henry accuses Nina because he thinks she could and should have chosen to act differently. Most of the times when one person listens to another, he is not deliberately choosing to do so. I don't make a conscious choice to listen, I just listen. The situation is similar for the person who reads. She may choose to begin reading, but once she has begun, she does not choose to understand this or that sentence. She just does understand them. As I am conceiving an intentional act, it is one that the agent is conscious of performing, and intends to perform. This need not involve a deliberate choice on the part of the agent. Indeed, the agent need not realize that she is performing an intentional act. (She can know that she is listening without knowing that her listening constitutes an intentional act or activity.) Some intentional acts do result from a deliberate choice. In such a situation it can be appropriate to *accuse* someone of acting intentionally. But when I describe Harriet's understanding Steve's assertion as an intentional act, I am not accusing her of acting intentionally. I wouldn't dream of it.

Listening with understanding, and reading, are intentional acts and activities that come very easily. Once we learn how to perform these acts, we perform them with very little effort. We perform them nearly automatically, scarcely ever making a deliberate choice with respect to them. These features of listening and reading are characteristic of *habitual* acts and activities. But an act's being habitual is not opposed to its being intentional.

5. Plain and Consummated Acts

There are some labels for illocutionary acts which seem natural to apply to plain acts. As I understand 'assertion,' a plain assertion is an assertion. And a supposition is a supposition independently of an audience's response. But some illocutionary labels apply only to consummated acts. If Victor tells Carolyn, "I promise to help with the house cleaning tomorrow," but Carolyn does not hear him, then Victor has not promised. A plain promise is not a promise. All promises are consummated promises. And similarly (I think) with commands. With labels that fit only consummated acts, we must be careful to add the adjective 'plain' in talking about the illocutionary constituents of consummated illocutionary acts.

The change from the Austin-Searle usage has some disadvantages when we use expressions that ordinarily label consummated acts. But the change has several advantages. The most prominent advantage is that the changed terminology gives us the resources to accurately describe what goes on when people use language. Using the Austin-Searle terminology, we would have to say that a plain act is an act of trying to perform the consummated act. Frank's plain assertion is Frank's attempt at an assertion from the Austin-Searle viewpoint. It is awkward to describe Frank's assertion this way, because talk of trying is often taken to indicate failure. The Austin-Searle terminology has some problems when we discuss spoken acts; these are compounded when we discuss acts of writing. And, in fact, most discussions of illocutionary acts focus entirely on spoken acts.

It is sometimes difficult to use the Austin-Searle terminology (i.e., their expressions with their meanings) for describing linguistic acts aimed at an audience. But that terminology is totally unable to accommodate acts which are not aimed at any audience. Some illocutionary acts are in no way directed at an audience. I frequently think out loud, and I also write down things just to try them out. I am not looking for an audience when I think out loud; it can even be embarrassing to have one. (My children take such talking to be a sign of weakness, or worse.) But I am definitely making claims, proposals, conjectures, etc. John Searle once told me that such talking should be construed as talking to oneself. And this is just a special case (is it degenerate?) of a two-person conversation. Searle's analysis is not convincing. Thinking out loud is just like thinking "in one's head." I certainly do not *address* my thoughts *to* myself; I just think them. Nor am I really talking *to* myself. Even when I think with language, but not out loud or in writing, I am performing linguistic acts. I believe these acts involve parts of the brain and events in the brain, so that even purely mental linguistic acts are acts of using physical objects. Whether I am right about that or not, it is definitely the case that some acts of thinking are linguistic acts. In my usage, some purely mental acts are illocutionary acts.

A final advantage of my changed terminology primarily concerns acts other than illocutionary acts. This advantage is that the change makes it possible to give a uniform account of the acts performed both by the producer and the receiver of language. The speaker or writer produces a public object. This object, the expression, must be appropriated and used by the audience if there is to be understanding. The person who listens and understands is doing more than hearing sounds. The person who reads with understanding is not simply seeing. The language producer performs intentional instrumental acts. So does the language receiver. When dealing with acts that are nonillocutionary components of illocutionary acts, we can use the same expression for the act of the producer and the act of the receiver. When *X* uses *A* to refer to *B*, he refers in order to assert. But *X* also refers in order to influence *R* to understand him. For *R* to understand *X*, she must also use expression *A*. *R*'s understanding *X*'s referring *is* *R*'s using *A* to refer to *B*.

For most kinds of linguistic acts, the plain act performed by the producer is the same kind of act performed by the receiver. Of course, the producer produces-and-uses as one act, while the receiver simply uses the expression. But it is the same kind of using in each case (it is the same kind of using if the receiver gets the message correctly). But with illocutionary acts, the producer and receiver do not perform the same kind of act. When the producer makes an assertion, the receiver does not. The illocutionary force of the act can only be attributed to the producer of the expressions used. He is the one who asserts, he is the one who promises. The illocutionary force is related to the producer's reason for wanting to get his message across. With sentential illocutionary acts I will distinguish the illocutionary force of the act from what is represented by the act. When Steve asserts that Switzerland is mountainous, the force is asserting (assertive?). What is represented by the act is *Switzerland being mountainous,* or *Switzerland as mountainous.* The same representing can be accomplished by acts with different forces. It is also possible to suggest and to suppose that Switzerland is mountainous. When John promises to take Jane to dinner Saturday, the force is promising; the act represents John taking Jane to dinner. If I command Jesse to shut the door, what is represented is Jesse's shutting the door. A sentential illocutionary act is a representing act, but to describe such an act as a representing act is to describe it abstractly. Such a description abstracts from its force. Other linguistic acts such as referring are also representing acts, but not sentential representing acts. When a language producer performs a sentential representing act with a certain illocutionary force, his audience performs the same kind of representing act, but without the illocutionary force. However, to fully understand the language producer, the audience must recognize the illocutionary force involved.

6. Propositional Acts

My goal is to present an account of language and linguistic acts within the framework of a theory of intentional acts. But in what follows I shall limit the scope of my discussion. I am going to consider less than a whole language, and fewer than all the linguistic acts that can be performed. These limitations are due to the extremely finite amounts of space and time at my disposal. With illocutionary acts, I will focus on sentential acts in which the sentence that is used can appropriately be evaluated in terms of truth and falsity. In these acts, the sentence used may not actually be true or false, it may fail to be either. But questions of truth and falsity must be appropriate. (If a vague expression is predicated of a borderline case for that expression, I have it that the resulting sentence can be asserted. But it is not either true or false.) An illocutionary act in which the sentence used (as used) can appropriately be evaluated in terms of truth and falsity is a *propositional act.* Assertions are propositional acts, whether they are confident or hesitant. So are conjectures and suppositions. There are certain kinds of illocutionary acts which are sometimes propositional and sometimes not. If Bill makes a promise to his children this way: "I promise to take you to the circus," it is not obvious that his act is a propositional act. But if he promises, "I will take you to the circus," then he has certainly performed a propositional act. Similarly, Mary can warn Frank by saying "Watch out!" Her act is not propositional. If she warns him by saying "There is a car coming right at you," then her act is propositional.

When we describe a sentential illocutionary act as a propositional act, this is an abstract description of the act. The propositional act and the illocutionary act are the very same act. To describe the illocutionary act as a propositional act is *less* abstract than describing it as a sentential representing act. I am using these terms so that every sentential illocutionary act is a sentential representing act. But only some sentential illocutionary acts are propositional. If David asks Rosemary, "Is it eight o'clock yet?" he has performed a sentential illocutionary act. His act represents the time of utterance as being eight o'clock. But his is not a propositional act. My terminology here is at odds with that explained by John Searle in [2]. Searle uses 'propositional act' to label acts like those I am calling sentential representing acts and has no term for my propositional acts. When a speaker addresses a propositional illocutionary act to an audience, the audience does not perform an illocutionary act in understanding the speaker. But the audience will perform the same kind of propositional act.

Although I will focus on those illocutionary acts which are propositional acts, I claim that my account of these acts can be extended to all illocutionary acts. My account is a model of a more comprehensive, and lengthy, account. I will occasionally make remarks about other illocutionary acts, but I will not provide a systematic treatment of them.

There are other propositional acts than illocutionary acts. Any act of using a sentence, when the sentence can appropriately be evaluated in terms of truth and falsity, is a propositional act. The component sentences of a compound sentence may be used to perform propositional acts which are not illocutionary acts when the compound is used to perform a propositional illocutionary act. When the teacher announces that the next test will be given on Friday or else it will be given the following Monday, his announcement is an illocutionary act. But he has announced and asserted a disjunction. He has not asserted either disjunct, but he has performed propositional acts with the disjuncts. A propositional act can also be a component of an illocutionary act which is not a propositional act. The antecedent of a conditional command (e.g., If it rains tonight, get up and shut the attic windows) may be used propositionally, even though the command is not a propositional act.

7. Tree Diagrams

We have identified two *structural* relations between intentional acts: (i) the relation between a component act and a complex defined by the purpose of its components, (ii) the relation between an act which enables a further act and that further act. It is convenient to have some uniform way to represent these relations. I will use tree diagrams for this purpose. Suppose *Y* is a complex act, defined by the purpose of its two component acts *A, B; Y* does not contain a completing event. I will represent the structure of *Y* this way:

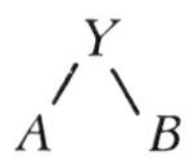

This indicates that both *A* and *B* are performed in order to perform *Y*. The left-to-right order of the components indicates their temporal order, if they occur at distinct times. I have not decided how to diagram a complex act which contains a completing event, for in what follows I won't have a need for such diagrams. But if *A* is an act whose purpose defines the complex act *Y*, and *A* aims at completing event *B*, the following might be a reasonable representation:

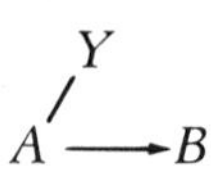

In representing linguistic acts, I will consider only plain acts. It is the study of these acts which is most enlightening with respect to syntax and semantics. We can use the following diagram to represent Steve's (plain) assertion that Switzerland is mountainous—the assertion he makes with the sentence 'Switzerland is mountainous.'

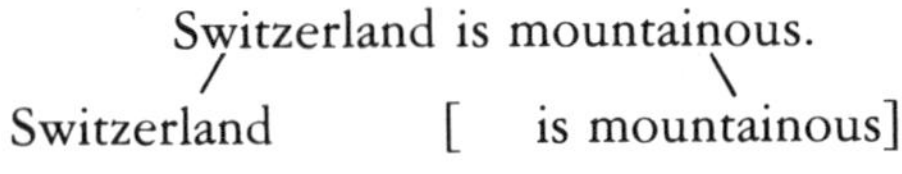

Steve (plainly) refers to Switzerland in order to (plainly) assert that Switzerland is mountainous. He predicatively denotes mountainous places in order to assert that Switzerland is mountainous. These two acts, with their common purpose, constitute Steve's assertion. The above diagram only shows the structure of Steve's act (together with the expressions he used). It does not show the force of his act. The same diagram would be used for a supposition or a suggestion. It would be used for the act performed when the sentence is a component of a larger sentence. (But it is not much trouble to introduce additional notation to signal different forces.)

If *A* and *Y* are acts such that *A* enables *Y*, I don't want to represent their relation with a solid line:

```
Y
|
A
```

Instead I will use a dotted line:

```
Y
⋮
A
```

Recall the case where Steve puts 'Switzerland is mountainous' as a question, and then makes his assertion by saying "Yes!" We can represent that like this:

```
Yes!
 ⋮
Switzerland is mountainous?
```

This diagram does not have an explicit notation to mark illocutionary force, but the punctuation suggests the force.To show the entire structure of this last situation, we could use this diagram:

```
           Yes!
            ⋮
           Switzerland is mountainous?
              /                 \
Switzerland           [    is mountainous]
```

Bibliography and References

If a book or article has been listed at the end of a previous chapter, only the author and the title will be given.

1. J. L. Austin. *How To Do Things With Words,* edited by J. O. Urmson. New York: Oxford University Press, 1965.
2. John R. Searle. "Austin on Locutionary and Illocutionary Acts," *The Philosophical Review* 77 (1968): 405–424.
3. John R. Searle. *Speech Acts, An Essay in the Philosophy of Language.*

Chapter 3
The System of Language

1. Representational Meaning

A linguistic act is an instrumental intentional act. In performing a linguistic act, an expression is used in an instrumental manner which defines the act. When we consider linguistic acts, there seem at first to be two distinct aspects: (i) the kind of act performed, and (ii) the "content" of the act. So that when Steve uses 'Switzerland' to refer to Switzerland, his act is a referring act; Switzerland provides the content of the act. But it is not appropriate to use the metaphor of a container and its contents for this distinction. When we describe an act as being of a certain kind, we have given an abstract description of the act. We describe Steve's act abstractly as a referring act. When we say that Steve's is an act of referring to Switzerland, our specific description tells which kind of referring act it was. We don't have one kind of container and many different contents; we have many different kinds of item which share a general feature.

We make an abstract description of a linguistic act more specific by giving the meaning of the act. It is common to talk of meaning as if it attached to expressions, but to the present view it is linguistic acts that are the primary bearers of meaning. We give meaning to an act by choosing a suitable expression, and using it in an appropriate manner. (But it is a common slip to use the wrong expression in the right manner.) I give the meaning of Steve's assertion when I say he asserted that Switzerland is mountainous. Its meaning is what makes this assertion a different (specific) kind of assertion than, say, the assertion that Switzerland is highly industrialized.

To discuss these matters carefully and thoroughly, I shall distinguish two kinds of meaning, or two senses of 'meaning.' The *representational meaning* of a linguistic act is what the act is used to represent. In a derivative sense, the representational meaning of an expression is the representational meaning of standard acts of using the expression. These statements are easy to misunderstand. Someone might think that representational meaning links an act or an expression to an extra-linguistic item. I would say, for example, that Steve's act of referring to Switzerland represents Switzerland. I would also say that someone's act of using 'Pegasus' represents Pegasus, and that an act of using 'blue' represented a blue object. Representing, as I understand it, is what I call an *intentional* relation. I will have more to say about these later. But if *R* is an intentional relation, and *a* has *R* to *b*, then *b* need not be a real object. Its representational meaning is, strictly speaking, a property of the linguistic act. The second kind of meaning involves relations between linguistic acts (derivatively, relations between expressions). This systematic meaning is the *inferential meaning* of an act or an expression. Linguistic acts and expressions have both kinds of meanings. There are some expressions which, by themselves, are not used to represent anything. But these expressions contribute to the representing done with compound expressions in which they occur. We understand their representational meanings in terms of their contributions.

A linguistic act is the primary bearer of meaning. A complex linguistic act is constituted by component acts, organized in a certain way. The meaning of the complex act must be constituted by the meanings of the components, and the semantic effects of their combination. Some views hold that language primarily serves to express thought which is distinct from, and prior to, language. Such views often hold that there are features of language which are misleading with respect to thought, in that the linguistic features do not perspicuously reflect features of thought. These thought-behind-language views are incompatible with the present approach. For my view is that we think with language; the speech act is also the mental act. To understand linguistic acts, we must understand the relation between simple and complex acts—we must understand how complex acts are constituted by simple acts. The present account of the relation between complex acts and their components requires that these acts themselves be the mental acts "expressed" in language. The representational meaning of linguistic acts does not point backward to mental events; these acts point in the direction of the represented objects. It is very likely that there are mental events and acts which are not linguistic, but a linguistic act is at the same time a mental one. We don't first think and then say. Thinking-and-saying is a single act.

The two kinds of meaning are distinct, but intimately related. It is the inferential meaning of an expression which makes its representational meaning possible—though this must not be taken as a claim that there is inferential meaning before there is representational meaning. At first the relation between the two kinds of meaning seems just the opposite of what I have said. For it is common to attempt to explain *P*'s entailing *Q* by saying that *Q* represents the same situation as *P*, but in a more general way—or, at least, in a no-more-specific way. But if the entailment gives rise to the representing, we cannot use the representing to explain the entailment.

Let us consider representing more carefully. It is a familiar fact that expressions need have no resemblance to the things which they are used to represent. It is also the case that expressions don't function by triggering a process of imagining ideas which do resemble the things represented. Some empiricist accounts suggest that language works this way. We can use expression *A* to represent *B*'s because expression *A* triggers image *I* which actually resembles the *B*'s. I am taking it to be well known that such an account cannot be correct. But how is it, then, that expression *A* is used to represent *B*'s? Expression *A* is related to other expressions in the language. (Strictly, acts of using *A* are related to acts of using the other expressions.) If everything represented by *A* is, as a matter of language, also represented by *C*, then *A* is *included in C*. *A* may also include other expressions. And *A* will be incompatible with some expressions. But a language isn't simply a network of expressions (or acts). The relevant network includes expressions and experiences. Its place in this system is what enables us to use *A* to represent *B*'s.

To use *A* to represent *B*'s is to relate *A* to other expressions and to experience in the appropriate manner. Someone might object that these relations are furnished by the language; they are certainly not established by the language user. This is correct, but we must understand that talk of a system containing expressions and experiences cannot be taken literally. This system is what I call a heuristic model; thinking about the model helps us to understand what is really going on. What actually exists are linguistic acts, linguistic skills, and linguistic conventions—in the language-using community. When someone uses an expression to perform a meaningful act, she is performing a conventional act. Linguistic conventions make her act possible. To use an expression in conformity with linguistic conventions is to use it in the appropriate instrumental manner. This involves knowing what follows from a certain use, what is incompatible with it, and so on.

To understand the inferential meaning of expression *A* is to be able to trace the connections between *A* and other expressions, and the connections tying *A* to experience (to kinds of experience). These connections are what we understand when we use *A* to represent. Of course, this does not mean that we represent the connections. We exploit the connections to represent things we can experience or might experience, or to represent things related to what we experience in ways we can explain.

2. Inferential Meaning

Linguistic acts are the primary bearers of meaning. The representational meaning of a linguistic act is what the act represents. This meaning is not an individual separate from the linguistic act. Representational meaning is a feature of the representing act. To explain representational meaning is to explain how the expression used is being taken for some object or situation. Inferential meaning is constituted by relations linking linguistic acts. But this way of putting it can be misleading. If David makes an assertion, this can commit him to accepting some other sentence. But he is under no obligation to assert that other sentence; he is not even required to think about it. In talking about relations between linguistic acts, I am speaking hypothetically. The acts will be related *if* they happen to be performed. As a heuristic model, we can imagine a realm where all possible linguistic acts are performed, and think of the semantic relations as structuring this realm.

Instead of talking about linguistic acts, it is often convenient to talk about the instruments used to perform these acts. By the representational meaning of an expression we shall understand the representational meaning of acts of using that expression in a certain manner. The inferential meaning of an expression is the inferential meaning that would characterize acts of using that expression. I shall adapt the heuristic model of the preceding paragraph and speak of the *system of language*. This is conceived as containing expressions which are related by such semantic relations as inclusion, incompatibility, and entailment. Semantic relations provide the structure of the system of language. This heuristic model helps us to get a proper perspective on inferential meaning. The model should help us to ask the right questions about this meaning; the model should also help us to answer such questions. Our conception of the system of language requires that the expressions involved be types rather than tokens. But we must not think that these expressions, as related, exist in some platonic conceptual space. What actually exist are people who perform linguistic acts and possess linguistic skills. Groups of these people constitute linguistic communities in which we find linguistic conventions. Talking and thinking about the system of language is a convenient but indirect way of dealing with linguistic acts, linguistic skills, and linguistic conventions.

The system of language being considered here only contains sentences suited for propositional acts, and expressions which are components of such sentences. A complete and thorough account of language and linguistic acts must deal with a more comprehensive system. I won't discuss the more generous system now, but I will say a few things about it at the end of chapter five. It seems natural to think that the system presently under consideration occupies a central place in the more comprehensive system. If we could give a satisfactory explanation of the sense in which our system is central, we would illuminate both the narrower and the broader systems.

When it comes to inferential meaning, sentences are fundamental in the sense that features of sentences (of sentential acts) provide the basis for recognizing features of other expressions. Entailment is a relation between sentences. We understand and explain the relation of inclusion between terms with respect to the relation of entailment. For example, 'scarlet' is included in 'red.' The "cash value" of this inclusion is that a sentence of the form 'α is scarlet' entails one of the form 'α is red.' (This is oversimplified, since we must also consider the relations between other kinds of sentences which contain these words.) Similarly, incompatibility between terms is understood as the relation which causes incompatibility between sentences. We explain the inferential meanings of component expressions by explaining their contributions to the inferential meanings of sentences in which they occur. Inferential meaning is sentence-directed.

From this perspective, a natural-deduction system of propositional logic, in which each rule of inference involves but one connective, is a perspicuous theory (explanation) of the inferential meanings of these connectives. In such a system, the rules for '&' might be:

& Introduction	& Elimination	
$\dfrac{A \quad B}{[A \& B]}$	$\dfrac{[\mathrm{A} \& B]}{A}$	$\dfrac{[A \& B]}{B}$

These rules explain the inferential meaning of '&' by showing how '&' affects the significance of sentences formed with it. Whatever entails both *A*, *B* entails [*A* & *B*]. And [*A* & *B*] entails whatever is entailed by either *A* or *B*.

The inferential meaning of an expression is its place in the system of language. To explain what language users do in terms of the heuristic model of the system of language, it is tempting to say that the language user situates his expression in the system of language. Using an expression in an instrumental manner would be the same as situating the expression in the system. But such a locution would place too great a strain on our heuristic model. The expressions in the system of language are conceived of as types. In linguistic acts it is tokens that get employed. However, we can exploit this difference to signal the difference between linguistic conventions and particular linguistic acts. We conceive of the system of language as existing independent of and prior to the linguistic acts of a particular person. (Just as the linguistic conventions do.) We can say that the language user employs the expression (the token) to *exemplify* the expression (the type) in the system of language. To use the token correctly, in the correct instrumental manner, is to properly reflect the features of the type in the system of language. What the language user really does is use the expression in accordance with the linguistic conventions; concern with inferential meaning requires that the language user recognizes or is aware of at least some of the relations of incompatibility and entailment linking the sentences he uses to other sentences.

Entailment and incompatibility are two of the fundamental relations between sentences suited for propositional acts. These and other semantic features provide its structure to the system of language. Such features have generated considerable problems for twentieth-century philosophers. Quine and others have furnished compelling arguments to show that we can't make clear sense of these features. (Although Quine has directed his attacks chiefly against analyticity and synonymy, it is not difficult to adapt these to yield arguments against entailment and incompatibility.) These arguments have succeeded, to my satisfaction, in showing that we can't give an account of such semantic features by using what I previously called brute fact descriptions. This should not be regarded as a problem for semantic features. These features are intentional features; we require intentional descriptions to give an adequate account of them.

3. Accepting and Rejecting Sentences

We are discussing the system of language in order to achieve an understanding of inferential meaning. The semantic features which provide the structure to the system of language are essentially bound up with inferential meaning. These features make it possible to "locate" an expression in the system of language; its location *is* the inferential meaning of an expression. The semantic features which structure the system of language are derivative from the semantic features of linguistic acts. When we consider linguistic intentional acts, there are certain kinds of acts, and certain features of acts, which are fundamental. We explain other acts and their features in terms of the fundamental acts and features. But we can't explain the latter in terms of anything more fundamental. When it comes to fundamental acts and features, I must imitate Frege and give hints that will enable readers to recognize them. This does not reduce me simply to pointing, for I can also describe connections between the fundamental acts and features, and between them and the less fundamental acts and features.

Two fundamental mental acts involving sentences which can be used propositionally are *accepting* and *rejecting*. I will only speak of accepting and rejecting in cases where a person gives explicit consideration to a sentence, and makes up her mind about it. This can be done out loud, in writing, or in one's head. But it is an event located in time. If Sheila accepted a sentence yesterday, then it is not correct to describe her as accepting it today—unless she thinks about it again. Instead of saying that a person accepts sentences she is not even thinking about, we can say that she is disposed to accept them. But once we start talking about dispositions, we must distinguish *ready* dispositions from others. There are some sentences that a person is readily disposed to accept or reject. If the issues come up, the person will immediately accept or reject these sentences. There are other sentences that a person is disposed to accept or reject after giving the matter some thought. (But I am not allowing her to gather new information.) And, of course, there are many sentences about which a person is not disposed one way or the other.

Acts of accepting and rejecting are mental acts, but they are also linguistic acts or involve linguistic acts. For it isn't possible to think about the sentences involved without using the sentences. Thinking about sentences is not like thinking about other objects. I can certainly think about the moon without making contact with the moon. But to understand a sentence is to use it in a certain way. Thinking about a meaningful sentence—thinking with understanding—involves using the sentence.

Acts of accepting a sentence can be acts of asserting that sentence. Recall that not every assertion is directed at an audience, and not every assertion is a public event. A purely mental assertion—just thinking the sentence—can be an act of accepting the sentence. But there is no reason to limit acts of accepting sentences to purely mental, private acts. A public linguistic act is also a mental act—not in the sense that the public act is preceded by a mental act, but rather in the sense that thinking out loud is thinking.

An assertion can be an act of accepting a sentence. But an audience-directed assertion might fail to be an act of accepting, because the assertion might not be sincere. An act of accepting a sentence is always an act of *really* accepting the sentence. It is not clear to me whether an assertion that is not aimed at an audience can be insincere. We can certainly think a sentence which we don't accept. We can pronounce it out loud in a firm voice. But if we are not aiming at an audience, what we are doing doesn't seem to be asserting. We are just pretending. If this is right, any genuine assertion not aimed at an audience is an act of accepting. And any sincere assertion aimed at an audience is an act of accepting. But accepting is more basic than asserting. So any act of accepting a sentence by using that sentence is an assertion. Any act of using a sentence which is directed at an audience, and which is presented as an act of accepting the sentence, is an assertion.

But not every act of accepting a sentence is an assertion. We might first think about *P*, but in a noncommittal way. Then later say "Yes," or do something analogous to this, to accept the sentence. In the cases that I have in mind, we use the sentence before we accept it. But the using is not an enabling act for the accepting. If the speaker has already decided to accept the sentence when he uses it, and in using intends to enable the subsequent accepting, then that act of accepting the sentence (the act of saying "Yes") is both an assertion and an assent. If the act of using the sentence is not intended to enable the accepting, then the subsequent accepting is an assent but not an assertion. (It is really an arbitrary matter whether we decide to admit assents that are not assertions, or we decide to count such assents as a special kind of assertions.) Just as there are at least two kinds of acts of accepting, so there are two kinds of acts of rejecting a sentence. A rejecting may be a denial, and it may be a dissenting.

In developing his account of language, Quine has been attracted to the public versions of acts of accepting and rejecting sentences. But he has focused on assenting and dissenting rather than on asserting and denying, possibly because he feels that the former are easier to spot. Quine's quasi-empiricist outlook leads him to place reliance on features that are public and observable. Assent and dissent seem to be such features of linguistic behavior, and he exploits them in developing as much as he thinks possible in the way of a "verifiable" substitute for semantic theory. However, public acts of assent and dissent are not really suitable for founding such a theory. Assents and dissents must be sincere if they are to do the job Quine wants done. But even if lie detector tests were completely reliable, the criteria for an act's being one of sincere assent or dissent would not be public and observable. We can only understand and explain an act's sincerity by bringing in nonobservable features of the act and its agent.

Even if all public assents and dissents were sincere, they would not measure up to Quine's methodological requirements. The real trouble with these acts is not that they involve unobservable mental phenomena. It is that these acts are essentially intentional. The criteria that Quine finds acceptable for identifying things in the world are brute fact criteria. He is unwilling to countenance essentially intentional features or objects. This is exactly the status of acts of assent and dissent. Acts of accepting and rejecting are done on purpose and (ordinarily) for some purpose. When these acts are complex, they have components which are also intentional acts. There is no way to make sense of these acts in brute fact terms. Nor is it possible to countenance a "minimal amount" of intentional features, and eschew the rest. Once it is recognized that some intentional features are genuine, fundamental features of real objects, there is no way to keep the whole camel out of the tent.

Public assertions which use the asserted sentences can be made in two forms. Steve can assert that Switzerland is mountainous just by pronouncing the sentence 'Switzerland is mountainous.' But Steve can also say, "I assert that Switzerland is mountainous." In the second case he has uttered a prefix which makes explicit the illocutionary force of his act. In describing Steve's first assertion, I identified two major intentional components: Steve's referring to Switzerland, and his predicatively denoting mountainous places. These two acts constitute Steve's assertion, which can be represented like this:

```
          Switzerland is mountainous.
            /                    \
Switzerland          [     is mountainous]
```

It is not immediately clear how this analysis is to be adapted (or developed) to explain what goes on in Steve's second assertion.

Two possible analyses suggest themselves: (1) Steve might perform his referring act and his act of predicative denoting in order to perform a propositional act which is not an assertion. In this propositional act, the sentence 'Switzerland is mountainous' is used to represent a situation, without any commitment. (This is analogous to considering a sentence before we make up our minds.) Steve uses the sentence propositionally, and then accepts it. In this case we must account for Steve's act of using the force-indicating prefix. What kind of act is this, and what is its purpose? If we tried to use the analysis of Steve's simpler assertion as a model, we might think that both the sentence and the prefix are used to perform acts whose purpose is to assert that Switzerland is mountainous. So the assertion would have two major components, a propositional component and a prefix-uttering component. Their common purpose would define Steve's act of asserting that Switzerland is mountainous. However, this is not a satisfactory analysis. Using the sentence 'Switzerland is mountainous' and some other act can't together constitute Steve's accepting (and asserting) the sentence. A person can accept a sentence in using that sentence. And a person can perform a separate act to accept the sentence. But nothing could prevent an act of using a sentence in order to accept it from being an act of using-and-accepting it. Nothing further is required to accept the sentence. If the propositional act is not an act of accepting the sentence, then the propositional act must be an enabling act. It enables the accepting (the assertion) by providing the material for the accepting. If the propositional act is an enabling act, it might seem that Steve's prefix act couldn't be his act of accepting (asserting) the sentence. For an enabling act should not take place later than the act which it enables. But the speaker who knows what he is going to say could accept the propositional act in advance, by virtue of his knowing what comes next. To the present analysis, Steve's prefix act *is* his act of accepting the sentence (the propositional act). The prefix act is also an act which makes illocutionary force explicit. Steve's making the force explicit gives his accepting a special character. This is similar to the example in which Victor turns on the radio in order to bring in the weather report, but turns it on low in order not to wake Carolyn. As well as having an immediate purpose for making his assertion, Steve can have a different immediate purpose for making the illocutionary force explicit. If he does, it is presumably something like *to facilitate communication*—to influence Harriet to recognize of the assertion that it is an assertion (as opposed to, say, a guess).

The following diagram represents Steve's prefixed assertion, given this first analysis:

```
I assert that:  Switzerland is mountainous.
                            ¦
                Switzerland is mountainous
                   /                    \
           Switzerland          [    is mountainous]
```

The act of using the sentence 'Switzerland is mountainous' is a complex act; it represents Switzerland as mountainous. This propositional act enables the act of accepting, and asserting, that Switzerland is mountainous. In this case, the enabled act is performed with 'I assert that.' (The prefix act has a structure which is being ignored for the present.) The sentence 'Switzerland is mountainous' is written at both ends of the dotted line. This is done so that the top node will contain a complete sentence. But the expression used to perform the act which corresponds to the top node is flanked by colons (unless it occurs at one end, in which case it receives a single colon). The act performed with the sentence 'Switzerland is mountainous' is represented only at the bottom of the dotted line.

(2) The second analysis of Steve's prefixed assertion is (in some ways) simpler than the first. In this analysis, there is no intermediate propositional act. The propositional act of using 'Switzerland is mountainous' is accepted (and asserted) as it is performed. In this case, the act of using the prefix is not the act of accepting the sentence. But then, just what is the prefix act, and how is it related to the propositional act—to the assertion? The act of using the prefix is an act of making illocutionary force explicit. But the prefix act and the propositional act do not have a common purpose which defines the assertion that Switzerland is mountainous. The propositional act, by itself, constitutes that assertion. Nor do the prefix act and the assertion have a common purpose which gives rise to some further act. The purpose for asserting that Switzerland is mountainous is independent of the purpose for making the assertion's force explicit. The purpose for asserting can be *to persuade Harriet* or *to bring about her knowing that Switzerland is mountainous.* The purpose for making the force explicit can be the same as that given in the first analysis.

To account for the relation between the prefix act and the assertion, we must recognize a third structural relation linking intentional acts. In the assertion described in the first analysis (above), the prefix act was an act of asserting. But the asserting had a special explicit character with a purpose of its own. In the present case, the assertion is one act, and the prefix act is a separate act. The prefix act is a new kind of component of the assertion. The prefix act is an act of giving a special explicit character to the assertion. The act does not serve to constitute the assertion, it adds a feature to the assertion. In the example of Victor and his radio, and in Steve's assertion described by analysis (1), there was an act with a special character, which special character had a purpose of its own, but a separate act wasn't required for giving the special character. In the present case, the special character requires a separate act. But the act which gives the special character must be a component of the act which gets the character. The component which gives the special character does not have a purpose which defines the complex. For the complex has one purpose apart from its special character. It has a second (immediate) purpose due to its special character—this purpose can be assigned to the character-giving act.

We need a new convention for our diagrams to represent the third structural relation. If *B* is one act, and *A* is a distinct act which is an act giving *B* a special character, we will represent their relation in one of these ways:

$(A+)\ B \qquad\qquad B\ (+A)$

We can represent the structure of Steve's prefixed assertion in the second analysis like this:

(I assert that+) Switzerland is mountainous.

/ \

Switzerland [is mountainous]

The second analysis of Steve's assertion seems psychologically more plausible than the first. For in the second analysis, Steve's assertion is simpler. Why use the sentence without accepting it, intending to enable its acceptance, when the sentence can simply be accepted as it is used? While it is true that the second analysis is more plausible than the first, there is no basis for saying that it is the correct analysis. Each analysis represents one way in which the explicit assertion might be performed. It is essential to understand that different people might compose the same general kind of act in different ways, where the difference has no effect on the inferential meaning of their results. It is quite unreasonable in a case like this to insist that one analysis is right for all acts of using a given sentence. (But one analysis *will* be the right one for a particular act.)

In dealing with linguistic acts in this book, I will concentrate on plain acts rather than consummated acts. However, it is of some interest to consider Harriet's understanding act performed in response to Steve's prefixed assertion. Harriet can structure her act of understanding in (at least) two ways—these are independent of whether Steve's assertion conforms to the first or second analysis. (1) Harriet might represent Steve as asserting that Switzerland is mountainous. The prefix is used to represent Steve as asserting. Harriet uses Steve's 'I' to refer to Steve. She uses '[assert]' to predicatively denote individuals (people?) that assert. The complex act constituted by these two acts represents Steve as asserting. On this analysis, the propositional act of representing Switzerland as mountainous serves to specify what specific kind of assertion Steve is making. Harriet uses the sentence 'Switzerland is mountainous' to give a special specific character to the act of predicatively denoting individuals that assert. The purpose for the predicative denoting is *to represent Steve as asserting.* The further purpose for the special character is *to represent Steve as asserting that Switzerland is mountainous.* Harriet's act of representing Steve as making this assertion will also normally be an act of accepting this representing. If Harriet has confidence in Steve, she may also accept his assertion (what he asserts).

(ii) In the second analysis, Harriet is focusing more on what Steve asserts than on who is asserting it. Instead of representing Steve as asserting a certain sentence (propositional act), Harriet concentrates on the sentence and takes it to be asserted by Steve. Here the propositional act of representing Switzerland as mountainous is an enabling act. This furnishes the material for Harriet's further act of taking the propositional act to be asserted by Steve. But the propositional act is not represented in order to take it. The propositional act is "right there," it doesn't need to be represented. The act of taking the propositional act to be asserted by Steve is performed by using the prefix—this is also an act of representing Steve as asserting nonspecifically.

So far we have focused pretty exclusively on acts of accepting sentences, which take the form of assertions and assents. Now we shall take a closer look at acts of rejecting sentences. These acts can take the form of denials and dissents. It is sometimes claimed that these "negative" acts are reducible to their positive counterparts. So that instead of denying a sentence, we can assert its negation. And we can assent to the negation of a sentence rather than dissenting to (from?) the sentence. In considering paradoxes of self-reference, I have come to the view that such reduction is not feasible. (A preliminary version of this view is found in [1].) Apart from that, it is clear that there are denials which are not the assertions of negative sentences, and there are dissents which are different from assents to negative sentences. Even if reduction were possible in principle, it does not take place in practice.

Acts of dissent are parallel to acts of assent. They involve saying "No" rather than "Yes." But acts of denial involve certain difficulties. There are different ways to deny a sentence. Let us first consider a public and explicit denial. Suppose Carol says, "I deny that Switzerland is landlocked." We can give her act an analysis exactly parallel to our first analysis of Steve's explicit assertion. That would give Carol's act this structure:

I deny that: Switzerland is landlocked

Switzerland is landlocked

/ \

Switzerland [is landlocked]

The analysis that was implausible for Steve's assertion becomes plausible for Carol's denial. Carol's prefix-using act serves to reject the subsequent propositional act. The prefix act also makes explicit the rejecting force of her act. The rejected propositional act is an enabling act which provides the material for Carol's rejection. To reject a sentence is to reject it as representing things as they are; this is to reject an act of using the sentence to represent. For such an act to be rejected, it must be a separate act from the rejecting act. So the second analysis of Steve's prefixed assertion does not have a parallel for Carol's denial. We can perform a single act of representing-and-accepting. It does not seem possible to perform a single act of representing-and-rejecting.

Carol need not use the prefix 'I deny' in making her denial. She might simply say "Switzerland is not landlocked." There are (at least) two ways in which her act of using this sentence might be composed. The first way does not constitute a denial. Carol might use 'Switzerland' to refer to Switzerland, and use '[is not landlocked]' to predicatively denote (geographical) areas that are not landlocked. Both acts are done in order to assert that Switzerland is not landlocked. The following diagram represents this:

Switzerland is not landlocked.

/ \

Switzerland [is not landlocked]

Carol's act is an assertion rather than a denial; she accepts the sentence as representing things as they are. But her accepting commits her to rejecting that Switzerland is landlocked. And that rejecting would commit her to accepting that Switzerland is not landlocked. Carol might also use 'Switzerland' to refer to Switzerland and '[is. . .landlocked]' to predicatively denote landlocked places. In this case her immediate purpose for doing these things is to deny that Switzerland is landlocked. Instead of combining these two acts to constitute a sentential act which represents Switzerland as landlocked, Carol is blocking this combination. She is keeping Switzerland apart from landlocked places. For this denial, there is no act of representing Switzerland as landlocked. The act of using 'not' serves to block this representing. Carol's denial has three major components: her referring act, her act of predicative denoting, and her blocking act. All are performed in order to deny that Switzerland is landlocked. We might represent this act as follows:

Switzerland is not landlocked.
/ | \
Switzerland not [is . . . landlocked]

Carol's denial (if it is sincere) is a public act of rejecting a propositional act which represents Switzerland as landlocked. She rejects that act by preventing it from occurring. It is not clear whether Carol's denial should be counted as a propositional act, since it is not a representing act. (Not all assertions are propositional acts. Assertions which are assents are not propositional; Steve's first prefixed assertion is not. So we have no reason for thinking that all denials must be propositional acts.) However, the denial is a sentential act. It appears to be true. (My uncertainty is whether 'Switzerland is not landlocked' can be used to perform a nonrepresenting sentential act when used as a component of 'It is true that Switzerland is not landlocked.') I will tentatively classify Carol's denial as a propositional act; a better understanding of "preventing" acts could lead to a reclassification. Carol's second kind of denial that Switzerland is landlocked seems to be what previous philosophers and logicians had in mind when they distinguished judgments of division from judgments of composition. Judgments of division don't put things together, they keep them from being put together.

This discussion of illocutionary acts performed with sentences containing illocutionary prefixes gives us reason to qualify the earlier characterization of the illocutionary paradigm. When I described the paradigm illocutionary act (activity) as a minimal act performed with a text one or more sentences long, I wasn't thinking of sentences which contain illocutionary prefixes. When Steve says "I assert that Switzerland is mountainous," he performs two minimal acts: the assertion and the act of making illocutionary force explicit. It is true that it is the prefix act which contributes the explicit character, but the explicit character "covers" the whole assertion. It is the assertion which is explicit for a purpose. We must now say that the paradigm illocutionary act or activity is the minimal act (activity) performed by using a text one or more sentences in length, which act is not an act of making force explicit.

4. Commitment

Acts of accepting and rejecting sentences should not be construed on the model of a person looking at a physical object, where the object is independent of the person's looking at it. Acts of accepting sentences are either acts of using the sentences, or are acts of assent enabled by acts of using the sentences. Acts of rejecting sentences are either acts of blocking the sentences' being used, or they are acts of dissent enabled by acts of using the sentences. It is true that acts of assent and dissent point toward a further object, but the further object is another act, not an independent sentence. To accept a (simple) sentence in the primary way is to use the sentence to represent, and to be self-consciously committed to this sentence's representing things as they are. The primary way of accepting a sentence is to use-and-accept the sentence. The fundamental way to deny a sentence is to use the sentence with a negative expression which blocks the propositional act performed with the negated sentence (i.e., the act that would be performed with the sentence without the negative expression), and to be self-consciously opposed to the representing of the negated sentence. But accepting and rejecting are fundamental acts; my descriptions are intended to direct attention to these acts, not to analyze the acts.

Acts of accepting and rejecting give rise to the relation of commitment. If we accept these sentences and reject those, then we are committed to accepting this further sentence, and rejecting that one. Commitment is not an act, it is a feature of acts. It is a fundamental feature that we must simply recognize; there are no resources for analyzing it. Accepting and rejecting sentences generate commitments. We only speak of a person's accepting or rejecting a sentence at the time the act is being performed. But we consider commitment to be more enduring. If Allan asserts that today is Friday, and he is sincere, then Allan is committed to accepting that tomorrow is Saturday. Allan remains committed once his asserting, and his accepting, are finished. It is probably most appropriate to link commitment to dispositions to accept and reject. So long as Allan is disposed to accept that today is Friday, he is committed to accepting that tomorrow is Saturday. Once we bring in dispositions in this way, it will be important to distinguish ready dispositions from the rest. But we must not speak of dispositions to commitments, or dispositions to have commitments; for commitments are not acts. (While a person can't be disposed to have a commitment, she can be disposed to recognize one.)

Commitment is objective. A person is committed whether he knows it or not, whether he likes it or not. But the ability to use language is one that essentially involves the ability to recognize commitments. No one can recognize all the commitments of the sentences he is disposed to accept and reject. Everyone must be able to recognize some of these commitments. Commitment is the source of the structure of the system of language. Without an awareness of commitment, we would be unable to use expressions to represent. It isn't possible to learn a language piecemeal. We must master the system in order to have mastered its parts. But, of course, we need not master the whole system in order to master a partial system.

Commitment is a feature essentially tied to intentional acts and activities; it is an essentially intentional feature. But commitment is not characteristic of all intentional acts. When Phil flips the switch in order to turn on the lights, Phil's act generates no commitments. Commitment is constitutive of some kinds of intentional acts—better, commitment is constitutive of some forms of intentional activity. Linguistic activity is one such form.

Although I have used the word "commitment" for a fundamental feature of certain forms of intentional activity, this word has certain drawbacks. The primary disadvantage is that the word "commitment" is often used for moral obligation. We speak of one person making a commitment to another, where this amounts to accepting an obligation to the other. But the commitments that concern me now are not obligations. We can note that obligation is a two-party affair (or a multi-party affair). A person must owe her obligation to a second person. If there is such a thing as an obligation to oneself, this is a degenerate case of a two-party obligation. But commitment is not owed *to* anyone. A person is committed by the sentences he accepts and rejects, and by the sentences he is disposed to accept and reject, regardless of whether anyone else knows about his acts and dispositions. And obligations are specifically ethical (the expression 'moral obligation' is redundant). Indeed, I think the category of obligation is the fundamental ethical category. But commitment is not specifically, or characteristically, ethical. However, commitment is relevant to ethical considerations. If Allan tells Bonnie that today is Friday, and Allan's assertion is consummated, Allan's act generates certain obligations on his part. (Various institutions and practices are such that, by engaging in them one places oneself under obligations.) Allan is obligated to accept what he has asserted. And he is obligated to assent to sentences to which his assertion commits him. (He is obligated to assent to some of them; at least to the ones where the commitment is obvious. And he is obligated to assent only if the question comes up.)

I have been conceiving commitment as a relation between mental acts, or between dispositions and acts. If we accept this sentence, then the relation of commitment links our accepting this to the act of accepting that sentence. But this conception is another heuristic device, not to be taken literally. When we accept *P*, we may be committed to accepting *Q*. But this does not require that we actually perform an act of accepting *Q*. (And, of course, it is not possible to actually accept all the consequences of the sentences we are disposed to accept.) Since there may not be any act of accepting *Q*, commitment can't be a relation. For we are committed to accepting *Q* regardless of whether we ever do accept *Q*. Instead of a single relation of commitment linking a variety of acts, there are a large variety of commitment properties. There is the property of being committed to accepting this sentence, and the property of being committed to accepting that one. There are also properties of being committed to reject sentences. These properties are not properties of acts, but of agents. An act of accepting one sentence can generate a commitment to accept another. But it is the person accepting the sentence who is committed.

Commitment belongs to the category I label 'Intentional Relations.' Other members of this category are hoping, believing, knowing, and representing. The expressions we use to talk about intentional relations have many similarities to the expressions used for genuine relations. There are also important differences. For intentional relations are not really relations. But it is common and convenient to treat them like relations.

5. Semantic Features

The system of language is characterized by the commitment "relations" which are constitutive of its use. These relations are given by (or with) the language. For we can recognize the relations of a sentence that we neither accept nor reject (and that we aren't disposed to accept or reject.) These commitment relations make representing possible, and so are epistemically prior to the representing. We talk about commitment in connection with acts and dispositions to perform acts. When we abstract from acts and actors, and consider expressions by themselves as constituting a system, it is convenient to use some other terminology. I will simply employ the usual terminology for the semantic features of sentences (or propositions). I will talk about the same semantic features as everyone else, but I will provide a new explanation of these features. These semantic features are derivative from commitment.

For example, we can say that A entails B if, and only if, (from now on: iff) accepting A commits a person to accepting B. A is incompatible with B iff accepting A commits a person to rejecting B. And B is analytic iff adopting the language containing B commits a person to accepting B. Two-place entailment and incompatibility, and also analyticity, are special cases of more general features. I will consider two general semantic relations: (1) Accepting sentences $A_1, \ldots, A_n$ and rejecting sentences $B_1, \ldots, B_m$ commit a person to accepting C. In this case I will say that $A_1, \ldots, A_n; B_1, \ldots, B_m$ are related to C by *hyper-entailment*. (In discussing hyper-entailment, it is extremely important to distinguish the accepted "premises" from the rejected ones.) If $m = 0$, we have a case of ordinary entailment. If $n = 0$, we have a relation for which there is no ordinary expression; I will call it *reverse incompatibility*. If $m = n = 0$, we have a case of analyticity.

(2) Accepting sentences $A_1, \ldots, A_n$ and rejecting $B_1, \ldots, B_m$ commits a person to rejecting C. This is the relation of *hyper-incompatibility*. If $m = 0$, we have ordinary incompatibility. If $n = 0$, we have *reverse entailment*. And if $m = n = 0$, we have *anti-analyticity*.

We can easily generalize these two general relations to the cases where we have a set of sentences that are accepted and a set of sentences that are rejected. If either set is infinite, it is probably not possible for a person to accept or reject all its members. But a person can be disposed to accept or reject an infinite number of sentences. In the set versions of the semantic relations, we need to say something like this: If a person is disposed or committed to accept the sentences in set X, and disposed or committed to reject the sentences in set Y, then the person is committed to accepting (rejecting) C.

The preceding definitions concern (expressions for) what might be called *epistemic* semantic features. These are explained in terms of accepting, rejecting, and commitment, rather than in terms of representational meaning or truth and falsity. I believe that these epistemic semantic features are the fundamental semantic features. For they "generate" the inferential meanings of expressions. The inferential meaning of an expression is prior to its representational meaning, because it makes representational meaning possible. The inferential meaning of a sentence is also prior to its truth conditions. In a perfectly constructed language, all epistemically analytic sentences will be true, though this wouldn't make it appropriate to define analyticity in terms of truth. In a natural language, some analytic sentences may turn out to be false. For a language can incorporate a theory, and the theory turn out to be mistaken. An incorrect theoretical sentence may then be analytic for the language. Similar possibilities for error are associated with other semantic features. Sentences $A_1, \ldots, A_n$ might entail *B*, even though $A_1, \ldots, A_n$ were true and *B* false. This possibility that semantically distinguished sentences can come out wrong in terms of truth and falsity is a plus for the present account. The refusal to acknowledge that analytic sentences can be incorrect has led to implausible theories which either deny meanings to natural kind terms, or else deny these terms meanings which are sufficient to provide essential features of the individuals they represent.

The present characterization of semantic features also leaves open the possibility that there might be an instance of a semantic feature that people were unable to find out. *P* might entail *Q* even though some essential limitation of human intellects precludes us from ever finding out this entailment. I don't believe there are any instances of entailment (or other semantic features) that we are in principle unable to discover; but our characterization allows there to be.

As well as defining epistemic semantic features, we could define other, less fundamental features. Given epistemic entailment, for example, a sentence *P* entails (for me) 'I accept *P*.' (But this doesn't make an inference from *P* to 'I accept *P*' legitimate in a proof from hypotheses. Supposing *P* is not the same as supposing that I accept *P*.) We could also define a nonepistemic entailment, where *P* entails 'It is true that *P*' but not 'I accept *P*.' (Metaphysical entailment?) This might be defined in terms of the representational meanings of sentences, or of their truth conditions. These other semantic features are less fundamental than the epistemic ones, for they depend on (presuppose) the epistemic features. But that does not mean that these less fundamental features are unimportant, or that they will prove easy to define.

So far in dealing with semantic features and also in discussing accepting, rejecting, and commitment, I have only dealt with the "deductive" aspect of language. This is another oversimplification. The acts of accepting and rejecting we considered earlier might be called acts of wholehearted accepting and rejecting, or acts of complete accepting and rejecting. In addition to these acts, there are acts of provisional accepting and rejecting. Provisional acts range from highly tentative to fairly confident. We can be committed by such acts and committed to them. Not all inductive considerations are matters of language. I follow Popper in thinking that the premises of an inductive generalization provide no support to its conclusion. But many inductive features are constitutive of linguistic activity. The move from a fairly confident acceptance of *P* to a complete acceptance of 'It is probable that *P*' is one such. I have ignored inductive considerations so far because they are too difficult to handle, and too little understood. We must not think that these considerations have no importance for the understanding of language and linguistic activity.

Bibliography and References

1. John T. Kearns. "Fully Explicit Deductive Systems," *To H. B. Curry: Essays on Combinatory Logic, Lambda Calculus and Formalism,* edited by J. R. Hindley and J. P. Seldin, pp. 35–54. London: Academic Press, 1980.
2. Saul A. Kripke. "Naming and Necessity," *Semantics of Natural Language.* Edited by Donald Davidson and Gilbert Harman, pp. 253–355. Dordrecht-Holland: D. Reidel Publishing Co., 1972.
3. Hilary Putnam. "Is Semantics Possible?," *Naming, Necessity, and Natural Kinds.* Edited by Stephen P. Schwartz, pp. 102–118. Ithaca, New York: Cornell University Press, 1977.
4. Willard Van Orman Quine. "Two Dogmas of Empiricism," *From a Logical Point of View,* pp. 20–46. New York: Harper & Row, 1963.
5. Willard Van Orman Quine. *Word and Object.* Cambridge, Massachusetts: The Massachusetts Institute of Technology Press, 1960.

Chapter 4
The Role of Experience in the System of Language

1. Experience

A language is not a self-contained system of expressions, or of acts performed with them. Language and linguistic acts are essentially tied to experience. The system of language must be conceived as including experiences as well as expressions. We can see this more clearly when we realize that acts of accepting and rejecting sentences are not the only sources of commitments. In a trivial sense, we might accept a map or a picture, and so generate commitments. Sentences are only one kind of symbols. We can also generate commitments without accepting or rejecting any symbols. When I recognize that the fruit on the table is a grapefruit, I am committed to accepting the sentence 'That fruit is a grapefruit,' and to rejecting 'That fruit is an orange.' It is possible to recognize that the fruit is a grapefruit by using a certain sentence. The act of recognizing that the fruit is a grapefruit can be the same act as using-and-accepting the sentence 'That is a grapefruit.' But I can also recognize that the fruit is a grapefruit without using any expression—though the experience of the grapefruit will commit me to performing linguistic acts. (I am only committed to performing them if the occasion arises; I am not committed to performing them come what may.) Making a decision also generates commitments. But if the decision is made in words, then the decision may simply be the act of accepting or rejecting a sentence. In such a case we do not have a nonlinguistic source of commitment. (We can accept a sentence as representing what is the case independently of us. We can also accept a sentence as representing what will be the case because of us.) A nonverbal decision generates linguistic commitments only because we are aware of what we are doing. The awareness that we are deciding to do *M* is an experience; the experience generates the commitments.

Commitments are generated by more things than acts of accepting sentences and acts of rejecting sentences. It should also be noted that we are committed *to* more things than acts of accepting and rejecting. If a sentence has consequences concerning the future, then accepting or rejecting the sentence can commit us to performing certain nonlinguistic acts. These commitments are often more specific than the commitment to accept a sentence if the occasion arises. We are often committed to actions for which we know that the occasion will arise; we often know when and where it will arise. (It is important to distinguish obligations from commitments. An insincere promise obligates the promiser. But he may not be committed to performing the promised action.)

The system of language is structured by relations derived from commitment. This system contains experiences as well as expressions; we must achieve an understanding of the way these are connected. In what follows, I will outline a theory which seems to me the only theory which does the job that is wanted. But I won't try to prove this; I will simply present the theory. This view is derived from Kant's, although it is simpler than Kant's view.

A fundamental principle of my theory is that experience is structured in a sentential or propositional way. Experience is not primarily experience of individuals, or experience of properties and relations. Seeing *that* the grapefruit is yellow is the primary experience. We are only describing this experience in an incomplete way when we say that it is an experience of a grapefruit, or of yellow(ness). It is because sentences and experiences are structured in a similar fashion that there can be commitment relations between them.

2. The Levels of Experience

There are different "levels" of experience. The first level is the most basic; this experience is pre-verbal and pre-conceptual. First-level experience can be attributed to a young child or to a sentient animal that does not use language (or any equivalent substitute). First-level experiences are not organized like sentential acts; I will not use 'that'-clauses to describe these experiences. But first-level experience does have a structure that is built-on by higher-level experience. Even in first-level experience, we don't primarily have experiences of individuals, or of qualities and relations. First-level experience is primarily of individuals *as* qualified (as propertied) and of individuals *as* related. Someone's first-level experience would not be adequately described as an experience of a yellow ball. The person experiences the ball as yellow, or as round. Two objects can be experienced as adjacent to one another.

It is very difficult to accurately describe first-level experience. Any linguistic description tends to distort the experience. When I say that my dog Muppet sees her water dish as adjacent to her food dish, I have used words to describe her experience. But Muppet is unable to employ words. Nor does she possess concepts corresponding to these words. My description suggests that she does. At the first level of experience, the subject experiences individuals as qualified and as related. But the subject does not recognize either that the qualities and relations are instances of universals, or that one individual is qualitatively similar to another. If I say that Muppet experiences this dish as round and experiences that dish as round, I do not intend to say that she recognizes that the objects have a common property or that she recognizes them to be similar with respect to shape. In describing Muppet's experience, I am forced to use my word for the quality involved. And, of course, I recognize both that the two dishes have the same or similar properties, and that the dishes are similar with respect to shape. As well as experiencing the same feature twice without recognizing that it is the same, Muppet experiences the same individual over again without recognizing that it is the same.

In saying that Muppet does not recognize or experience similarity, I don't mean to deny that she can react similarly to similar objects. She can also respond similarly to a single object which she experiences more than once. But there is nothing important about this, for simple mechanisms can be devised to react similarly to similar stimuli. The reason I am denying that Muppet experiences similarity or identity is because I regard such experiences as conceptual. And I don't think Muppet possesses concepts—*as I understand this.* It is conceivable that I am wrong about Muppet. Perhaps she enjoys a richer mental (and experiential) life than I imagine. This does not change the fact that first-level experience is not conceptually organized. It would only show that Muppet has higher-level experience.

Let us consider identity more carefully. We do describe Muppet as recognizing various people; she recognizes me, for example. Taken literally, this description attributes to Muppet possession of concepts. But we only apply this description to Muppet by analogy. We should not take it literally. She can have a suitable response when she sees me, even be happy to see me, without recognizing that I this time am the same person as last time. First-level experience has a structure provided by properties and relations. But it is possible to have a structured experience without recognizing that it is structured—it is possible to have it without being able to recognize that it is structured. When a person employs concepts, he introduces additional structure to his experience. The concept of an identifiable individual enables us to tie together different experiences of one individual; it enables us to recognize that these are different experiences of one individual.

Identity is likely to strike many people as a somewhat abstract concept; it may seem reasonable that identity does not come into first-level experience. But similarity does not seem so abstract. Why isn't a first-level experience of similarity (of individuals as similar) on a par with first-level experiences of spatial relations? I have not ruled out similarity because it is a relation, but because it is the particular relation that it is. If we allow that similarity is on a par with sensible relations, we will be driven to admit many different kinds of similarity. For example, the similarity between two sounds couldn't be the same as the similarity between two shades of color. But this leads to an impossibly complicated view. My own view is that the similarity between two individuals amounts to the sameness of a feature they share. This understanding does not require us to admit a variety of irreducible similarities.

It is difficult to describe first-level experience without distorting that experience. It is easier to say what such experience is not than to say what it is. First-level experience of propertied and related individuals is not conceptually organized. In first-level experience, the subject does not recognize that this individual is the same individual he saw yesterday. He does not recognize that these two individuals are different. And he does not recognize that this individual is similar to that.

The second and third levels of experience are conceptually organized. These different levels don't exist side by side; a person only has one "stream" of experience. First-level experience is everyone's raw material. When a person acquires concepts, these impose additional structure on the raw material. Once this happens, a person no longer has first-level experience as I have described it. First-level experience is transformed into conceptually organized experience. But what is it to have a concept? In what does the transformation consist? In most cases, having a concept, say the concept of redness, is the same as being able to employ a word or longer expression—in this case, 'red.' However, there are other symbols than words. The ability to employ some nonverbal symbol may be counted as the possession of a concept. And once a person has gotten the "hang" of using symbols, she can recognize situations in which an expression might be employed, even when there is no suitable expression. She might notice a shade of color for which she has no name. The person can recognize such a situation without introducing a new expression. This kind of recognition can also be counted as the possession of a concept, though if no symbol is introduced, the concept will probably be possessed for only a short time.

In the present account, to recognize that two objects are similar in a given respect is to realize that one symbol can be used to represent both of them—and also to represent other objects that possess the relevant feature. The ability to use symbols to represent is identical with the ability to recognize similarity. Some sentient animals have this ability, while others don't seem to. The innate possession of such abilities might be described as the possession of innate ideas, though most supporters of innate ideas have probably regarded such ideas as more specific abilities than these. In talking about abilities to use symbols, there are two sorts (or two levels) of ability that we need to distinguish. Before a person has learned a language, she has the ability to use language, because she can learn to do it. Once a person has learned a language, she also has the ability to use it. But this second ability is closer to linguistic activities than the first. When it is important to distinguish the two kinds of ability, I will call the second kind skills. Before our friend learns a language, she is able to use a language but possesses no linguistic skills. After she has learned a language, she is still able to use language; now her ability consists in possessing linguistic skills. The innate idea of similarity is not a skill. It is the ability to acquire skills. (The innate ideas that Descartes accepted were skills rather than abilities to acquire skills, but he didn't regard these skills as linguistic.) When a person learns to use expressions to represent different kinds of things, she has the skills for representing them. We might also describe her position by saying that she possesses the skills for recognizing various specific kinds of similarity, without necessarily possessing the concept of similarity. For she might not have learned to recognize that the different specific similarities are instances of similarity-in-general. All this means is that she might not (yet) have learned to use the word 'similar' or some equivalent expression.

The concept of identity is also tied to a general ability to use symbols. To understand this, we must distinguish two kinds of symbol. One kind of symbol can be used to represent more than one individual or more than one *n*-tuple. A second kind consists of symbols used to represent a single individual. The concept of identity is tied to the ability to use individual symbols. To recognize a single individual is to have acquired the skill of using a single symbol to represent that individual—and to understand that the "same" symbol can be used more than once for this job. To possess the concept of identity in general is to have acquired the skill for recognizing that various individual symbols are or are not used to represent the same individuals. This skill is to be identified with the skills for using words like 'is,' 'same,' and 'identical.'

Second-level experience is structured by concepts of identifiable individuals, and concepts of sensible properties and relations. In second-level experience, I can recognize that this individual is the same one I saw earlier. I can recognize that this individual is different from the one over there. I can also "deal" with colors, shapes, sounds, etc. The words associated with properties and relations label individuals with respect to these properties and relations. The concept *round*, for example, is more fundamental than roundness. 'Round' labels round objects. The properties and relations that are recognized in second-level experience are first-level properties and relations. It is recognizing these properties and relations, or the propertied and related individuals and *n*-tuples, that transforms first-level experience into second-level experience. In using 'that'-clauses to describe second-level experience, it is perfectly natural to use these clauses with verbs for the particular senses. I *see* that this object is yellow. I *hear* that a sound is high pitched. And I *feel* that an object is smooth. If I want to talk about experience more generally, it is awkward to say I *experience* that something is the case. Instead of saying this I will say I *recognize* that something is the case. Seeing that the object is yellow is recognizing that it is yellow. Second-level experience includes experience obtained through the five external senses. It is also a second-level experience when I recognize that one event follows another, or that one event is longer than another. Second-level experience is not exclusively concerned with external objects; my experience is also second-level when I recognize of myself that I am tired or hungry.

Third-level experience may not be sharply distinguished from second-level experience. Some experiences constitute borderline cases for the two levels as I understand them. (But, remember, the two levels are not side by side. A person has only one stream of experience. We distinguish second and third-level components in this single stream.) Third-level concepts are concepts of kinds of individuals, where these kinds have natures carrying causal relations in their train. Third-level experience involves modal features. It is a third-level experience when I recognize that this object is a grapefruit, or that this grapefruit is yellow. It is also a third-level experience when I recognize that that flipping of the switch caused this event of the lights going on. Or when I recognize that flipping that switch would cause the lights to go on. Third-level concepts are not concepts of sensible qualities and relations, nor are they reducible to second-level concepts. (The classical Empiricist program envisioned just this reduction.) We can recognize that one event causes a second, but we can't see this with our eyes, feel it with our hands, etc. The causal structure of third-level experience is brought to it by our concepts; it is not found there. However, the raw material provided by first-level experience must be suited to the employment of the concepts that we employ. If people were constituted differently, many concepts currently employed might have no application.

3. Taking To Be and Taking For

If we are to understand how conceptually organized experience can be sententially structured, we must consider what is involved in applying a concept to the raw material of first-level experience. Consider the experience of seeing that this individual is green. The experience might be constituted by our saying out loud or in our heads "This is green." But we can have the experience without using any words. We can do this only because we have the relevant words (or other symbols) at our disposal.

At this point, I find that I need to call attention to another fundamental kind of act, and to provide some more terminology. I will speak of *taking* an individual to be this or that. We sometimes speak of taking *A* to be *B* when we really mean *mis*taking *A* for *B*. But my talk of taking should not be understood as suggesting error. In first-level experience, we experience an individual as qualified. In second-level experience, we take this to be a specific, identifiable individual—to be *this* individual. We also take it to be an individual of a certain kind. (This kind is not a natural kind, like a dog or a cat. That would involve third-level experience. Here I am thinking of, say, green things as things of a kind.) The two sorts of taking correspond to two kinds of linguistic act. Individual takings are counterparts to referring. Predicative takings involve taking an individual to be of a kind; or taking several individuals in order to be an *n*-tuple of a kind. An act of taking to be may be performed by using an expression. Such an act would be at once a representing act and an act of taking to be. An act of taking to be need not be a linguistic act. In either case, such an act involves dispositions to perform linguistic acts. More than this, an act of taking an individual to be a green object *activates* linguistic dispositions. An activated disposition is one which is brought very close to being "discharged." Some dispositions are such that an individual is disposed to act in a certain way if certain other things are done first. Such a disposition is activated when the preliminary conditions, or some of them, are satisfied. George may be disposed to punch Joe if George sees Joe and remembers that Joe insulted him. Reminding George of Joe's insult when Joe is nearby activates George's disposition. When a person takes an individual to be green, that person's linguistic dispositions are activated with respect to the individual. (She is prepared to accept the sentence 'This is green,' reject 'This is red,' and so on.)

We shall try to use our previous accounts of sentential acts to understand higher-level experience. I perform an act of taking an individual to be this particular individual—one with sufficient status to be reidentified or, at least, referred to at a later time. And I perform an act of taking an individual to be green. Both acts will be performed in order to recognize that this individual is green. Such a description gives prominence to the fact that people have a need, a drive, to make sense of what goes on with them. We are not passive observers of the passing show.

However, several qualifications and clarifications are necessary here. In saying that second-level experience involves sensible features and is conceptually organized, it is necessary to distinguish what we pay attention to in our experience from what we don't. The conceptual organization of experience applies primarily to what we notice, which is always experienced against a background. The background is first-level experience, and is not conceptually organized. But the background of one experience can become the foreground of a subsequent experience. What happens is that we bring our conceptual structures to bear on this experience. It is even possible to close our eyes, and recall the background of the preceding experience. We can bring our conceptual structures to bear on it at a time it is no longer present.

Taking an individual to be a specific identifiable individual, taking an individual to be a kind of individual, and taking *n* individuals to be related in a certain way are fundamental acts. When symbols are used to represent, another kind of fundamental act is being performed. I describe these as acts of *taking* a symbol *for* a specific individual, a kind of individual, or an *n*-tuple. In an act of taking for, we have a symbol we know to be distinct from whatever it is we take it for. It is appropriate to speak of *taking to be* rather than *taking for* when we are dealing with an object we experience directly—an object with which we are acquainted in something like Russell's sense. But I am also speaking of taking to be when

I discuss our experience of objects around us, even though I don't believe we are acquainted with those objects. When we experience external objects, I believe that we are really "operating" on neural intermediaries (states, events) caused by the external objects. (I will have more to say about this later.)

When we consider a single experience, and the things we notice, the experience is often much more complex than anything that can be represented by a sentence of ordinary length. A picture *is* worth a thousand words. Experience embodies knowledge more efficiently than sentences do. This greater efficiency raises some problems for our understanding of the sentential (the sentence-like) structure of experience. In one experience, a person might (1) recognize that this particular individual is green, (2) recognize that this green individual is larger than that red individual, (3) recognize that the green individual and the red individual are both circular, and so on. These examples illustrate that acts of individual taking need not be construed as the takings of "bare," unqualified individuals. We can take an individual to be this identifiable individual, pure and simple. We can also take an individual to be this green individual or this circular individual. Qualities are involved in experience both in acts of predicative taking and as identifying characters in individual takings. The problem posed by multiple recognitions concerns the multiplicity of distinct intentional acts that seem to be required. How can a perceiving subject perform so many acts, and have so many purposes in such a short time? The answer must be that she cannot. Recall that in considering linguistic acts, we have focused on the relatively deliberate language user. That person performs more linguistic acts than is customary for a skilled language user. The deliberate language user performs a distinct act with each denoting expression. An accomplished language user will often use a compound expression to perform a single intentional act, but the deliberate speaker will not.

Focusing on the deliberate language user is not realistic, but doing so provides a greater understanding of language (than being realistic would), and it provides a suitable framework for carrying out various studies of language. The situation is similar with conceptually organized experience. In a single experience a subject may recognize several different things. We don't need to admit a distinct intentional act for each recognition that is correctly described by a sentence. Nor do we need to admit a distinct act for each individual the person notices, or each feature she is aware of. A single experience can consist in a few intentional acts. But these are complicated. To intentionally take individuals to be specific, identifiable individuals, and to intentionally take them to be of a kind is to notice the individuals and their characteristics, to activate linguistic dispositions, and to be aware of being prepared to come up with verbal descriptions. Such experience may also involve acts and dispositions to perform acts that aren't verbal. There is nothing to prevent many dispositions from being activated at once. The experienced experiencer would not normally perform a distinct intentional act for each individual that she notices. Nor does the accomplished skier perform as many intentional acts as he makes movements. Individual and predicative takings will frequently be virtual components of intentional experience rather than being distinct intentional acts. But it is always possible to perform these as distinct intentional acts, if it seems appropriate. We can concentrate on an individual and *really* notice it. We can concentrate on what it is, or how it is related to others. By considering the intentional structure of an experience where what would normally be virtual components are actual intentional components, we can get a better understanding of experience. And a better understanding of the way that experience and language are connected.

4. The Sentential Structure of Experience

Attributing sentential structure to experience helps us to understand and explain how language is related to experience. It also creates problems. For if experience is sententially structured, then experience can be mistaken. In discussing this I will consider two examples. In the first, let us suppose that we take an object to be green. Then we discover that it isn't green, it is yellow. The object was a grapefruit seen in a bluish light. At the time of our experience, we would be willing to say that we see that the object is green. Once we discover our mistake, we will not say that we saw that the object was green. Instead we will say we *thought* the object was green, or that it *looked* green. If we had been a little more alert at first, and recognized that the object looked like a grapefruit except for its color, we might not have initially described ourselves as seeing that the object is green. Being careful, we might only have said that it looks green.

Or suppose we are at a crowded party. Across the room we see our friend Paul. Because of the crowd we never get near him. In this case we are willing to describe ourselves as having recognized Paul, as having recognized that Paul was at the party. Several days later we ask Paul about the party, and find that he wasn't there. We saw someone else who resembles Paul. We will no longer describe ourselves as having recognized Paul. We say instead that we thought we saw Paul.

To accommodate the facts that experience is propositionally structured, and that it can be mistaken, we must recognize a distinction between performing an act of taking to be and accepting that act. This is analogous to the distinction between using a sentence with understanding, and accepting the sentence. We can use a sentence to represent, and accept this representing act. The accepting may coincide with the representing, so that there is a single act of representing-and-accepting. Or the representing can be preliminary to the accepting—it enables the accepting. We can use a sentence to represent without accepting the representing act. We may be uncertain whether the representing is correct. We may reject the representing act. We can also perform acts of taking to be that are and aren't accepted. An act of taking to be can be tentative or provisional. When a detective investigates a crime, he may try to "see" the situation in different lights. He may first take the crime to be one of passion. He may then take it to be a cold-blooded, premeditated affair. These takings are provisional; he is only trying them out. We can take an experience a certain way without accepting this way of taking it. We can also take it a certain way and accept this. A single act can be an act of taking-and-accepting; an act of accepting can also be subsequent to an act of taking to be. Taking this object to be green is not the same as thinking the object is green. It is not the same as seeing that the object is green or recognizing that it is green.

Normally, when we are awake and paying attention to things around us, our sentential acts of taking to be are accepted as they are performed. These acts can be mistaken. An act of taking to be that isn't accepted can't be mistaken, though it might be an act of taking something to be what it isn't. (This is analogous to an act performed with a false sentence.) Mistakes occur when sentential acts are accepted, and the acts either represent what isn't the case, or they take something to be what it isn't. We are having an experience (we are experiencing) when we perform acts of taking to be, whether or not we accept them. When we accept an experience, and are mistaken, we can find this out. If we do find out, we can "reorganize" experience that we have had. Past experience remains accessible to us in the following sense. We can't change what happened, or what we took things to be. We can't change the fact that we accepted certain acts of taking to be. But we can now reject those acts of taking to be. We can reconstrue our past experience, by taking things differently now than we did then. We formerly took, and accepted it, that other person to be our friend Paul. We now take, and accept it, that person to be different from Paul, but to resemble Paul.

The word 'recognize' is used similarly to 'know.' When I have a conceptually structured experience, and perform and accept sentential acts of taking to be, I can describe myself as recognizing that such and such. I would have described myself as recognizing that Paul was at the party. Once I discover my mistake, I do not say I recognized that Paul was at the party. A genuine case of recognizing requires that (1) a person perform a sentential act of taking to be, (2) the person accept the sentential act, (3) the person's sentential act is correct.

To fully understand the difference between trying out an interpretation ("This looks green") and accepting it ("This is green"), we must pay closer attention to the difference between taking to be and taking for. Earlier I suggested that an act of recognition has a structure exactly parallel to that of an assertion. Steve refers to Switzerland and predicatively denotes a mountainous place, both in order to assert that Switzerland is mountainous. I take an individual from first-level experience to be a specific, identifiable individual, and I take it to be a grapefruit, both in order to recognize that it is a grapefruit. However, this second description is not accurate. In the sentential act, the two denoting acts are acts of taking for. These two acts involve two symbols. One symbol is taken for Switzerland, the other for a mountainous place. The single purpose of these two acts unites them to form the assertion. In experience, we "begin" with a first-level experience of an individual as qualified in some way. In conceptually-organized experience, the first-level individual is taken to be an identifiable individual. There is no different individual to serve for the predicative taking. The individual taking takes the first-level individual to be an identifiable individual. This same individual is then taken to be an individual of a kind. The predicative taking is not a taking act alongside the individual taking, which two acts then constitute a sententially structured experience. The predicative taking completes the individual taking, and is itself the counterpart to a sentential act. This object is taken to be a specific, identifiable individual; it is then taken to be a grapefruit. If this predicative taking is accepted, then taking this object to be a grapefruit is the very same act as recognizing that it is a grapefruit. But predicative takings need not be accepted. The locutions 'looks' and 'seems to be' are suited to describe predicative takings that are not accepted. An object which looks green is one we take to be green. It can look green without being recognized as green; it can look green without being green.

It is a disadvantage of the word 'take' that it is ordinarily used to describe interpretations that are accepted. So if we say that Carolyn takes this object to be green, we mean she thinks it *is* green. In the technical sense assigned here, a "sentential" act of taking to be need not be accepted. In the technical sense, to describe Carolyn as taking this object to be green is to provide no information about whether she thinks the object is green. Recognizing that the object is green is only one way of taking it to be green.

Individual takings are preliminary to predicative takings. But they are not component acts whose purposes define the predicative takings. They do not combine with the predicative takings to constitute further acts. And acts of individual taking do not serve to confer special characters on acts of predicative taking. Instead, acts of individual taking to be enable predicative acts of taking to be. For an act to be an enabling act, the agent must intend for it to enable the further act. It will normally be the case that an act of individual taking is an enabling act. But a predicative act of taking to be may itself enable a further predicative act. Suppose I take this to be an identifiable individual, and I take this individual to be a grapefruit and accept this. Taking it to be an identifiable individual is simply to notice it, which activates dispositions, putting me in a condition I am aware of. Taking it to be a grapefruit is noticing what this individual is. I would not have paid it any attention if I were not preparing to see what it is. Suppose I also take that to be an identifiable individual, which individual I take to be a table (and accept that it is a table). Suppose, finally, I take (and accept it) this grapefruit to be on that table. The acts of taking this to be a grapefruit and that to be a table enable the further act of taking the grapefruit to be on the table. But these two predicative acts may not be enabling acts. I have a need to make sense of things. Various acts of taking to be satisfy this need. The predicative acts may simply have been performed to satisfy the need to make sense. (Performing them *is* satisfying the need.) Their enabling the further act would be incidental. However, whether or not they are intended to enable the further act, they do enable it. (An intentional act of taking this to be an identifiable individual does not by itself seem to make sense of anything. So it would not be performed simply to satisfy the need to make sense.) An individual act of taking to be is an enabling act. It makes possible a predicative act of taking to be by providing the material for the predicative act. Predicative takings are the experiential counterparts to sentential linguistic acts; I will even describe them as sentential acts. But predicative acts of taking to be are not complex. (They need not be complex; if they are complex, their components are not individual takings.) Predicative takings to be do not have structures matching the structures of sentences. However, predicative takings and their enabling acts display the same multiplicity as sentential acts; this makes it possible for the one to represent the other.

An individual from first-level experience can be taken to be a specific, identifiable individual. This individual can then be taken to be a grapefruit. Several individuals can be taken to be distinct identifiable individuals. There need not be a distinct taking for each individual; a single act might be an act of taking *n* individuals to be distinct individuals. Such an individual taking does not take the individuals to be related. Even if there are distinct takings, temporally ordered, the order of the takings is not what is taken. But the *n* individuals can then be taken to be related in a certain way. Similarly, a single predicative act of taking to be might be an act of taking several individuals to be grapefruit. We don't need a separate predicative act for each one. A single act can be an act of taking distributively several grapefruit to be on the table. There might even be a single act of taking two individuals to be such that one is a grapefruit and the other an orange.

Second and third-level experiences are propositionally structured. Seeing that the cat is on the mat is more basic than simply seeing the cat (or the mat). But the structure of a second or third-level experience is not quite the same as the structure of a sentential act. A relatively simple sentential act consists of individual and predicative acts whose common purpose unites them to constitute the sentential act. In the case of experience, an individual act only enables a predicative act; the predicative act may in turn enable further predicative acts. This difference in structures does not make it wrong or misleading to say that experience is sententially propositionally structured. But the difference helps us understand why many philosophers have thought that seeing the cat is primary, while seeing that the cat is on the mat is strictly a case of judging rather than seeing. Taking this identifiable individual to be a cat is a predicative and sentential act. The same act is preliminary to the act of taking the cat to be on the mat. Those who regard perception as exclusively individual (of individuals) are focusing on the enabling character of these acts of taking to be. The predicative, sentential character of acts of taking to be is most important. It is the intended completion of acts which enable it.

5. First-Level Experience

I do not use 'that'-clauses to describe first-level experience. First-level experience is not sententially structured, although there is clearly a systematic relation between experiencing an individual as red and experiencing that this individual is red. I don't regard first-level experience as a form of intentional activity. For I believe that in first-level experience we employ our neurological "apparatus" without being consciously aware of this. When we have a first-level experience of an external object, the object causes in our neural system certain effects which are not the first-level experience, they are merely states and events. But we employ these states and events, we employ portions of our neural apparatus, to constitute first-level experience. It seems unlikely that a sentient individual has first-level experience from birth. A sentient individual starts out as the "owner" of a neurological apparatus, which is the subject of various states and events. At some point, the owner becomes able to use his apparatus, with its states and events, to experience individuals as qualified and as related to one another. This skill might be totally innate, but "blossom" at a certain stage of development. Or there might only be innate dispositions to acquire the skill.

If first-level experience were intentional activity, then the subject of such experience should be aware that he is using parts of his body, in certain states or as the subject of certain events, to experience external objects. At least it should be possible to become consciously aware of this. Apparently it is not possible to do so; we seem to be constrained by our nature to treat our "neural representation" as what it represents. One of Descartes' main contributions to Western thought is his realization that our "experiential states" do not guarantee the existence of external objects. A genuine experience of external objects might be exactly copied by what merely seems to be an experience of external objects; from the subject's point of view, there would be no perceptible difference between the two situations. When it seems to the subject that he is experiencing external objects, but there are none, his neural states and events will be like those when he genuinely experiences such objects. The subject employs similar neural items in the same way on both occasions. Let us say that the appropriate neural objects, in certain states or events, *reflect* external objects, but understand this in such a way that they reflect external objects both in cases where there are and cases where there aren't external objects. When it seems that we are directly experiencing external objects, we are really using our neural apparatus which reflects these objects. It is plausible that properties and relations of the reflecting items correspond to properties and relations of the reflected items. (The reflecting property need not be the same as the reflected property.)

An intentional act (activity) is one we intend to be doing, and are aware of doing. For at least some first-level experiences, we can say that we intend to be having them. For we can intentionally look in a certain direction. We can shut our eyes if we don't want to see. (But it is harder to "turn off" our other senses.) And first-level experience involves awareness. We are aware of an individual as qualified. But if I am right that in first-level experience we are using our neural apparatus, we are not aware of doing this. For we are aware of an external object, not of some neural item. We might say that in first-level experience we are not aware of what we are doing, but we are aware of what we have done. The acts of using neural items to experience objects constitute an awareness of the objects.

I have previously considered two kinds of intentional "taking" acts. When we use a symbol to represent, we *take* the symbol *for* whatever it represents. When we are actually presented with an object, we can *take* the object *to be* this or that. The acts performed in first-level experience are not intentional. But we need to be able to talk about these acts; we need some way to understand them. I am going to adapt our talk of taking to be so that we can talk of first-level experience in these terms. I am trying to model acts of first-level experience on intentional acts of taking to be. Better, I am trying to understand acts performed in first-level experience on the model of intentional acts of taking to be. I could instead have adapted talk of taking for so that it is used to describe first-level experience. But in taking for, it is essential that we are aware of the symbol as distinct from what it represents. When we take one thing for another it seems "more essential" that we are aware of what we are doing than it does when we take one thing to be this or that. So instead of saying that in first-level experience we take neural items for the objects they reflect, I will say that we take the items *to be* the objects they reflect.

In extending our talk of taking to be so that first-level acts are acts of taking to be, we are modeling our talk and our understanding of first-level experience on our talk of conceptually organized experience. With such modeling, we do not intend that the item which gets modeled is exactly like the item on which it is modeled. We already know several respects in which first-level experience is unlike higher-level experience. To extend talk of taking to be to first-level experience is to deal with some features of that experience as we deal with features of higher-level experience. We determine the features that are to be dealt with in parallel fashion as we develop the theory.

Some theorists may object to the concept of a nonintentional act. It is clear that we do commonly describe a person as doing something in situations where the doing is not intentional. But it might be claimed that this is merely a loose way of talking that should not be taken seriously. For example, instead of saying that a person did something unintentionally, we might say that she performed an intentional act which had an unintended consequence. Or it could be that the person was causally related to some effect without any intentional act on her part. I don't know how I could prove that we must take nonintentional acts as a fundamental category, but I think this is true. Admitting such acts as fundamental is essential for my understanding of first-level experience. First-level experience is not constituted solely by the occurrence of neural states and events. It is rather our using these states and events which constitutes the experience.

In first-level experience, we take neural items to be qualified and related objects. Doing this constitutes our awareness of the qualified and related objects. The objects we are aware of in first-level experience provide the material for second and third-level experience. In first-level experience, we take this to be an individual as qualified in some way. In second-level experience, we take this to be an identifiable individual, a round, yellow individual. What is taken in first-level experience is some neural item, the same item which is taken in second-level experience. But we are aware of it not as a neural item, but as the object it is taken to be. When we take something to be this identifiable individual of that variety, the individual we take is not an external individual. We take it to be an external individual. An intentional act of taking to be can be performed both on an object we are acquainted with and on an object which we are programmed to treat as if it were the object to which it merely corresponds.

6. Habitual Acts Again

There are some difficulties associated with the claim that a conceptually organized experience is an intentional act or activity. In perception, it is common to think of ourselves as passive. When we open our eyes and look in a certain direction, we have no control over what we will see. Experience "forces itself" on us. This objection depends on our identifying intentional acts with voluntary acts which we choose to perform where we could have chosen otherwise. Such deliberative acts *are* intentional, but they do not exhaust the class of intentional acts. Habitual intentional acts are not deliberative. It is as difficult not to see that this object is a cat as it is to unlearn the skill of riding a bicycle. This difficulty is no sign that the act (activity) is not intentional. We perform the act intentionally, and are aware of what we are doing.

The fact that we cannot control what we will perceive is not a reason for thinking that we are not acting when we perceive. But in many cases when we experience this or that, our experiencing seems even more automatic than it is when we understand what we hear or see (read). I can be thinking of one thing, and still be aware of what is going on around me. Perceptual awareness presses in on me. How can I be hard at work, intending to solve a certain logic problem, and at the same time be intending to take this for a cat, and that for a mat? Some qualification of the account developed so far seems to be needed. Consider an intentional act of taking an individual to be of a kind. Let the act of taking this to be an identifiable individual enable the further act of taking this individual to be a cat. And let the act of taking this identifiable individual to be a cat be performed without words—there are no words in writing, out loud, or in my head. This act of taking to be involves my attending to the individual and its kind. This same act is also an act of activating verbal and other dispositions. The attending doesn't cause the dispositions to be activated. In attending I am also activating dispositions. And I am aware of this. The awareness takes the form of my being aware that I am in a position to use appropriate symbols to represent the cat. It can also include the awareness that I am in a position to perform various other acts. If, further, I take this cat to be the one that has been making all the noise, I am in a position (and readily disposed) to give it a kick. I might even take it to be that cat *by* kicking it.

An act of attending to something is at the same time an act of activating verbal and other dispositions. But dispositions can also be activated by other things than intentional acts. The activating of dispositions can be either intentional or nonintentional, though when the activating is intentional it would not be normal for the agent to conceive of herself as performing an act of activating. Let us consider a nonintentional activating. Suppose that I am trying to solve a logic problem, and that I am concentrating as hard as I can. While I am doing this, there is a cat in front of me. However, I am concentrating so intently on the logic problem that I do not notice the cat. But light reflected by the cat will strike my eyes and cause certain neural events. I am uncertain whether (i) I have first-level experience of the cat, but I am unaware of this. (First-level experience is not intentional activity.) Or (ii) I don't have first-level experience, but just the "makings" for this experience. In either case, verbal and other dispositions will be activated by the neural events, though to a lesser extent than when I attend to the cat. For the neural events are a preliminary condition for my using verbal descriptions and performing the other acts. They are also a preliminary condition for my taking the individual to be a cat; so they activate the dispositions to take this to be an identifiable individual, and to take the identifiable individual to be a cat. Even without noticing the cat, I can subsequently recognize that a cat has been in the room. For my disposition to take the individual to be a cat has been activated, and there are presumably some memory traces that I can recall (this information can be stored without my having been aware of it).

When dispositions are activated, but I am not aware of it, I am not taking anything to be an identifiable individual. I am not taking any identifiable individual to be a cat. I am disposed to perform acts of taking to be, but am not doing so. It also seems possible for dispositions to be activated, and for me to be aware of this, without the activating being intentional. I might be concentrating on the logic problem again, but not so intently as to be unaware of the cat. In this case, there is a first-level experience of the cat. This first-level awareness is not an intentional act or activity. The first-level experience will activate various verbal and other dispositions, although this activating is not intentional. But I can nonetheless be aware of the activated dispositions with respect to the individual; I can be aware that I am disposed to identify the individual as a cat. When my dispositions to describe the cat are activated, though not intentionally, this is not merely something that happens *to* me. I am acting; I am *getting* ready to deal with the individual I experience. The conscious but nonintentional activation of dispositions is a second kind of nonintentional taking to be. This nonintentional taking to be constitutes higher-level experience. First-level experience of external objects is a nonintentional activity. Some higher-level experiences also fail to be intentional.

However, there is a distinction between taking this individual to be a cat and accepting this taking—even though one act can be both a taking and an accepting of the taking. An act of accepting (or rejecting) is a paradigm case of an intentional act. I can nonintentionally take this to be a cat. I cannot nonintentionally accept the taking. So I cannot nonintentionally recognize that this is a cat. I cannot nonintentionally see that it is a cat. I can only be disposed (nonintentionally) to accept an act of taking to be. (In dreaming we seem to be performing nonintentional acts of taking to be. Dream experiences are not accepted or rejected, so long as the dream continues. But I have waked myself by recognizing that some unpleasant experience is not real.)

7. The Structure of the System of Language

When a person has a certain experience (and accepts it), that commits her to accepting some sentences and rejecting others. The relation between her experience and the sentences she is committed to accept is little different from entailment. The relation between her experience and the sentences she is committed to reject is like incompatibility. I will call these relations *quasi*-entailment and quasi-incompatibility. (We can also introduce quasi-hyper-entailment and quasi-hyper-incompatibility.) These quasi-relations properly include the plain relations. A person's experience can quasi-entail a certain sentence, but it does not entail that sentence. Any entailment is also a quasi-entailment.

The system of language contains both sentences and conceptually organized experiences—these are the "sententially structured" experiences which consist in taking identifiable individuals to be this or that. The system of language contains both true and false sentences (and sentences that are neither true nor false). It contains the experiences that a person has and accepts, and experiences that a person has and is readily disposed to accept. But the system contains more than actual experiences. It contains possible and actual experiences. Sentences which describe an actual experience are quasi-entailed by that experience. Possible experiences also quasi-entail the sentences which describe them.

In saying that the system of language contains possible experiences, I don't mean this in the possible-worlds sense. None of my possible experiences is the experience of seeing Sherlock Holmes and Doctor Watson. The possible experiences are possible in this world, not some other. They are experiences that might be had, or might have been had, by doing something or other. What is possible in this sense is much more limited than what is imaginable. But the possibility is epistemic rather than metaphysical. The possible experiences are experiences which are not ruled out by our understanding of what the world is like.

In designing the heuristic model which is the system of language, I have included sentences and whatever can be linked to sentences by the commitment relation. (Actually, the various items are not linked to sentences by themselves, but to acts of accepting and rejecting sentences.) An experience of seeing that an object is a grapefruit will generate the commitment to accept the sentence 'That is a grapefruit.' A decision to go to Florida for spring vacation generates the commitment to accept the sentence 'I am going to Florida for spring vacation.' The awareness that I am putting salt on my scrambled eggs commits me subsequently to accepting the sentence 'I have put salt on my eggs.' However, in the system of language, I have not provided separate categories of decisions and intentional acts. For my decision to go to Florida will be "identified" with my awareness of making the decision. When I make the decision, I am aware of myself as deciding. This is first-level experience. I am also disposed to put my decision in words if I haven't done so, and to describe myself as having decided. This is higher-level experience. I am readily disposed to accept that experience. (When I make the decision, I may not be concentrating on myself as making the decision. So I may not have actually accepted the experience of me as deciding.) The act of seasoning my eggs will also be identified with my experience of performing it. The system of language can safely be limited to sentences and sententially structured experiences. We should note that while having and accepting certain experiences can commit us to accepting and rejecting various sentences, acts of accepting or rejecting sentences can also commit us to having experiences. My accepting the sentence 'The sun will rise at 5:46 tomorrow' commits me to having a certain experience if I get up in time and look out the right window. This is a conditional commitment to have an experience. But my commitment to accept a given sentence is also conditional—I am committed to accepting it if the occasion arises. Accepting the sentence 'I will pick up my wife at the airport at 3:45' commits me both to picking her up and to having the experience of doing so. Since for the heuristic model we have reduced intentional acts to the experiences of performing them, we must allow ourselves to speak of being committed to having, and accepting, various experiences. A nonverbal experience can commit us to accepting a sentence. Accepting a sentence can commit us to having a nonverbal experience. Having one nonverbal experience can commit us to having another.

It isn't possible for the system of language to incorporate everything that is linked by commitment. We can be committed to doing something that is impossible, but we cannot incorporate impossible experiences in the model without destroying the model. As an example, by virtue of our dispositions to accept inconsistent sentences, we might be committed to having an experience which is both ϕ and ψ, where ϕ and ψ are incompatible. And even if our beliefs are consistent, the system of language contains sentences which describe impossible experiences. These sentences would be quasi-entailed by the impossible experiences, if there were such. We can also, because our beliefs are inconsistent, be committed to both accepting and rejecting a sentence A, or to accepting $[A \,\&\, \sim A]$. While we can accept A at one time and reject it at another, we can't do both at once—we are even committed to not doing it. And we can't seriously accept a sentence $[A \,\&\, \sim A]$. (We can say we do, but this isn't the same as doing it.) So the system of language contains sentences which describe impossible experiences, but does not contain those experiences. It contains sentences which cannot be accepted, but does not contain the experiences of accepting them.

Sentences which describe impossible experiences and sentences which would quasi-entail impossible experiences are also linked to actual and possible experiences. A sentence which would either quasi-entail or be quasi-entailed by an impossible experience will be quasi-incompatible with actual and possible experiences. But the expressions in such a sentence will also occur in sentences linked by quasi-entailment to actual and possible experiences. To take a simple example, the sentence 'I see a car which is both silver (all over) and blue' describes an object which is impossible (the car) and an experience which is impossible. The sentence would have been quasi-entailed by the impossible experience. The expressions 'silver' and 'blue' also occur in sentences which describe actual experiences. They owe their representational meanings to the relations such sentences have to actual and possible experiences. They bring these representational meanings to the sentence which describes the impossible car and the impossible experience. We understand that sentence on the basis of various analogies linking it to sentences which describe possible experiences.

8. Systems of Language

A system of language contains expressions and experiences; these are linked by quasi-semantic relations. We also find analogies between sentences. The analogies account for the significance of sentences which describe or require impossible experiences or impossible objects of other kinds. The sentence 'I see a car that is silver (all over) and blue' has analogies with sentences like 'I see a car that is silver and rusty,' 'I see a fork that is silver,' 'I see that the sky is blue,' etc. Such analogies enable us to understand sentences describing what we don't or can't experience on the model of sentences describing what we can and do experience.

The experiences in a system of language have a conceptual organization. Their structures correspond to the structures of sentential acts. The conceptual structure of experience is not confined to the experience of an individual with a sensible property, or the experience of individuals linked by sensible relations. We experience individuals related spatially and temporally. We recognize that this grapefruit is on that table. We recognize that this event occurred before that, or that this one took longer than that one. We recognize that one thing causes something else, and that this event made that one possible. Experience has a conceptual structure. But this structure is spatial and temporal, causal and modal. Some of these structures are found both within an experience and between experiences. We can be aware that two objects are in different places. But different experiences occur in different places. One experience precedes another. One causes another. And a possible experience need not always be possible; it is possible with respect to other experiences. If I am having this experience, then I can do something to have that experience. Some of the experiences that were possible for me yesterday are no longer possible today—some will never be possible again. It is convenient to use a horizontal tree diagram to represent this modal structure:

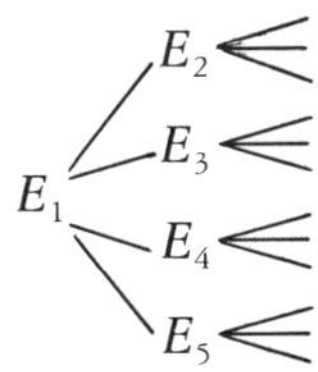

Given a certain experience, a number of further experiences are possible. (From the perspective of experience E_1, the experiences $E_2, \ldots, E_5$ are possible.) Given any one of them, still further experiences are possible. And so on. An experience isn't possible *simpliciter*; it is a relative possibility.

Actual experiences come in great detail that possible but not actual experiences need not have. These experiences enter a system of language through the commitment relation. We can be committed to having a certain experience, but not to a specific, detailed experience. When we are committed, it is to having a kind of experience. A system of language contains expressions, actual conceptually organized experiences, and possible kinds of experiences. Not only does each experience have a conceptual structure, but experience as a whole has such a structure. The commitment relation which links expressions and experiences itself incorporates spatial, temporal, causal, and modal structures.

The actual and possible experiences that have been admitted to the system of language are not impersonal experiences. Every experience is someone's experience. Because we have included experience in the system of language, we are forced to "personalize" this system. There can't be just one system of language, or just one for each language. There must be a different system for each language user. Even though each person has his own system of language, "massive" similarities between the different systems make communication possible.

A person's system of language is organized from his perspective. Many expressions are significant in virtue of locating objects and events with respect to the experiencing subject. These expressions are used to mark relative features, not absolute ones. Such expressions include first and second-person pronouns, words like 'here' and 'there,' 'this' and 'that,' and the tenses of verbs. The quasi-semantic relations are based on spatial, temporal, and modal features. For example, an experience that a certain object is yellow quasi-entails, at the time, the sentence 'I see a yellow object.' At a later time, the same experience quasi-entails 'I saw a yellow object.' One such experience might (at the time) quasi-entail 'This is a yellow ball,' while another quasi-entails 'That is a yellow ball.' The second experience may also quasi-entail 'That ball would look green in a bluish light.' Semantic relations between sentences also incorporate these structures, though it is common to focus attention on the synchronic cases of these relations, from a fixed standpoint. But 'The ball is over here' with respect to one standpoint entails 'The ball is over there,' with respect to a different standpoint. And 'The ball is over here' with respect to a standpoint and a time entails 'The ball was over here' with respect to the same standpoint and a later time.

A system of language is a particular person's system. But one person's system accommodates other language users, and other experiencing subjects. We don't infer the existence of other people, or their inner lives, by reasoning based on their alleged similarity to ourselves. Each language user experiences other language users and their intentional acts. Each language user *recognizes* that the other people's acts are intentional. My system of language makes it possible to recognize that another person is addressing me. Hers allows her to deal with me. When she uses 'you' to refer to me, I also use her 'you' to refer to myself—though I don't do this when I say 'you.' A sentence that does not represent an experience that is possible for me might represent one that is possible for someone else. And I can understand that. But in my system of language it is my experience that counts. I experience other people and their acts. But I understand their experience by analogy with my own. I don't have another person's experience, and I couldn't. Even if it were possible to share bodies, it would not be possible to share conceptually organized experience. Conceptually organized experiencing is acting. Two people might take the same thing to be an identifiable individual; each might take it to be an individual of the same kind. But each person's taking is his own. Each person's accepting is his own.

Chapter 5
Semantics

1. Significance with Respect to Experience

The inferential structure of a system of language is based on commitment. But this incorporates conceptual structure, because commitment involves space and time, causality and modality. The conceptual structure of an experience and the representational meaning of an expression depend on the inferential structure. An experience owes its conceptual structure to expressions which are or can be used to describe it. Although an expression owes its representational meaning to the inferential ties that bind it to experience, representational meaning does not depend solely on ties to experience. Analogy is important for understanding expressions which don't label objects we can experience. But the inferential structure of a system of language is a more fundamental source of representational meaning than is analogy.

An expression is only meaningful as an element of a system of language. Since the basic elements of a system of language are sentences and sententially-structured experiences, the meaning of an expression must somehow be sentence-directed. Let us for now consider predicates and referring expressions, to see how their significance is sentence-directed. (A referring expression is one that is used to represent a specific individual. Both names and descriptions are referring expressions.) The inferential meaning of an expression is defined as the contribution that expression makes to the inferential meanings of sentences which contain it. So we understand the inferential meaning of an expression in terms of the contribution the expression makes to sentences. Similarly, the truth conditions of an expression are understood as the contribution the expression makes to the truth conditions of sentences in which it occurs. But matters are less clear with representational meaning. With representational meaning, there is an important difference between predicates and referring expressions. A referring expression is used to represent a specific individual; this individual can be real or fictitious. Ordinarily, when a referring expression occurs in a sentence, which individual the expression represents is not determined by the sentence. (Unless the sentence supplies a context which enables the audience to determine which of two or more candidates is the referent.) An act of using a referring expression to represent is a little like pointing. The individual "pointed to" is identified by the language user in terms of her knowledge and beliefs. Some of these may be given by the expression's meaning; others will be extralinguistic. The representational significance of a referring expression is not sentence-directed. We can think of the individual it is taken for as the representational significance of a referring expression—more precisely, its significance is *to be taken for that individual*. The referring expression is understood independently of its contribution to sentences; this independent understanding is simply "brought to" sentences in which it occurs. With respect to a referring expression, the most we can say is that an act of using it is sentence-directed. The noncommunicative purpose for using a referring expression is sentential—we refer to the individual in order to sententially say something about it. Apart from a sentential context, referring acts are pointless.

It is also true that acts of predicative denoting are sentence-directed. But for predicates, even representational meaning is sentence-directed. In an act of predicative denoting, we are using a symbol to represent—we are *taking* it *for* something. In an act of predicative denoting, we take a symbol for an arbitrary individual of a kind. (An *n*-place predicate is taken for an arbitrary *n*-tuple of a kind.) We are not able to understand a predicate apart from a sentential context, because a predicate *is* a sentential context. A predicate is significant through its contribution to sentences (sentential acts) in which it occurs. To take the predicate '[is a cow]' for an arbitrary cow is to use the predicate to represent an arbitrary individual *as* a cow. The arbitrary individual "answers to" an empty place in the predicate. A sentence with a referring expression in the argument place of its predicate represents a specific individual as an individual of a certain kind (or it represents *n* specific individuals as related in a certain way). The predicate represents by showing how the individual is qualified (how the individuals are related). A referring act has a kind of autonomy by virtue of "pointing" to a specific individual; but it has no point outside of the sentence. An act of predicative denoting has no such autonomy. It is significant only by virtue of its contribution to the sentence. We see a similar difference between the individual and the predicative in experience. An act of individual taking is autonomous, but pointless in itself. An act of predicative taking is not autonomous; it cannot be performed without an identifiable individual to be taken.

Even though the representational significance of predicates consists in their contributions to sentences (sentential acts), predicates make independent contributions to sentences. The same predicate can make the same contribution to different sentences. At first this seems to be a puzzle. A predicate both gets its significance from sentences and makes an independent contribution to the significance of sentences. How can this be possible? But a predicate does not *get* its significance from sentences. Its representational significance *consists* in its contribution to sentences. There is a puzzle only when predicates are confused with referring expressions. For if predicates were significant as pointing, they could not be significant as contributing. Since a predicate does not get its significance from sentences, where does this significance come from? How can this symbol be used to represent that kind of individual? There is no individual in experience that we can tie the predicate to. And it won't do to drag in abstract individuals like properties and relations. We don't learn to identify such individuals in experience—there is no act of taking an individual to be circularity, for example. When we learn to use a predicate to represent an individual of a kind, we are learning to use this predicate for any and all experiences of the right sort. The significance of the predicate is due to its multiple links with experience—with both actual and possible experiences. But these inferential links come via sentences and sententially structured experiences. The predicate is connected to other expressions via the inferential relations between sentences in which they occur. The predicate is connected to experiences via the quasi-inferential relations connecting sentences to conceptually organized experiences. It is the inferential network of the system of language which makes this symbol suitable for representing those experiences. Each appropriate experience quasi-entails sentences containing a given predicate. (Other experiences are quasi-incompatible with sentences containing that predicate.) Given a predicate and the right number of individual expressions, we can represent an individual of some kind or other; or we can represent *n* individuals related in some way or other. To know just what kind of individual it is, or how the *n* individuals are related, we must understand what the predicate represents. We can only do this by properly situating the predicate in the system of language.

The inferential meanings of even those predicates which are "close" to experience make possible their representational meanings. Without the inferentially structured system of language, there are neither sentences nor conceptually structured experiences. When we consider the system of language as a whole, both the inferential and conceptual structures are equally fundamental. Neither is prior to the other. But the inferential meaning of a single predicate is prior to its representational meaning. Its inferential position "generates" its representing.

There are three important structures in the system of language. The *inferential structure* is based on the relation of commitment. This structure consists of features like entailment, quasi-entailment, incompatibility, and so on. It includes inductive features, and features of expressions which are components of sentences. The *conceptual structure* organizes single experiences. We take objects to be identifiable individuals. We take them to be of this and that kind, and to be related in various ways. The conceptual structure also relates different experiences. In this role, the conceptual structure is incorporated in the inferential structure. The third structure is *analogy*. This enters in various ways. Within an experience we can notice that A is related to B as C is to D. This simply means that a single expression can be used to represent both pairs. The analogy between expressions and experiences is the basis for representing. And the analogy between different complex expressions enables us to understand a sentence which doesn't represent our experience on the model of one which does. The different structures are associated with the different kinds of meanings. Inferential meaning concerns inferential structure. The inferential meaning of a sentence is determined by its inferential relations to other sentences and to experiences. The inferential meaning of a component expression is determined by the inferential meanings of the sentences in which it occurs. The representational meaning of an expression is what it represents. Referring expressions represent specific individuals. For other expressions, their representational meanings are understood in terms of their contributions to sentences. Analogy and conceptual structure account for the representing of sentences, given the representational meanings of their referring components and the inferential meanings of their other components. However, analogy also contributes to the inferential meanings of some expressions. If expressions A, B, and C are used to represent an A^*, a B^*, and a C^* which we can experience, and expression R is used to represent a pair related in a way that is characteristic of pairs $\langle A^*, B^* \rangle$, then we can by analogy introduce an expression D to represent a D^*—where a D^* is related to a C^* as a B^* is to an A^*. But we may either not have experienced a D^*, or even be unable to do so. Expression D is significant by analogy. Some expressions that are significant by analogy have inferential ties to experience. If R represents a causally related pair, then some experiences might quasi-entail a sentence about a D^*. But other expressions significant by analogy may have no such ties.

2. Experiential Connections

We have seen that an experience or kind of experience can be linked to a sentence by various quasi-semantic relations. This raises the question of whether there are quasi-relations linking different experiences. Can one experience quasi-entail another, can one be quasi-incompatible with another? We can also consider quasi-analyticity and quasi-anti-analyticity, and ask whether an experience can have either one of these properties. The answer to the questions about the quasi-relations is "Of course." If I recognize that this individual is a whale, then I am committed to having certain kinds of experience if I examine the animal more closely. And I am committed to not having some other kinds of experience. Such cases of quasi-entailment and quasi-incompatibility are not very interesting. Even though the relations link experiences, these relations are "mediated" by language. It is my knowledge of whales, mammals, and fish—which knowledge is incorporated in my language—that accounts for the quasi-entailments and quasi-incompatibilities. The interesting question is whether there are between experiences quasi-relations which are not mediated by language.

It is not so hard to recognize the difference between a relation mediated by language and one that is not so mediated. But it is difficult to accurately characterize this difference. Conceptually organized experience depends on language; without the language there would be no such experience. But even though language makes experience possible, there are some features of experience which are due to our neural and mental apparatus. Others depend on the linguistic (conceptual) organization we give to experience. There must be something "there" ahead of time to be organized by conceptual structure. A feature of experience which is due to the experiencing subject's apparatus is *native* to experience. A native feature is one of the things that gets organized in experience; it is not contributed by the organization. So even if we were to (even if we could) adopt a different kind of language and give a different kind of structure to experience, we would find the same native features in both experiences. (These features could be described differently in the two languages—they would come in different packages in the two systems.) The perceived quality of a color is an example of a native feature. The look of yellow is not a conceptual contribution to experience.

The question we are asking is whether some quasi-relations between experiences are due to native features of experience. Such quasi-relations cannot themselves be native features. They are relations between sentential items; such items essentially depend on the conceptual organization of experience. A quasi-relation due to native features would be one where the apprehension of native features in their conceptual packages is sufficient for recognizing that accepting one experience commits us to having or not having some other. Our question has some resemblance to earlier questions about the synthetic a priori. Those questions were largely concerned with sentences or judgments rather than sentential experiences. The earlier questioners asked whether there is a substantive knowledge of experience which does not need to be supported by experience. This knowledge would be epistemically prior to experience. To properly relate our question to the earlier questions, we must embark on an historical digression.

We need to compare the present account of the analytic to Kant's account. When Kant discussed analyticity, he was concerned with judgments rather than with sentences. That difference between his view and the present view is not so important. We are not really concerned with sentences, but with sentential acts. Acts of accepting sentences are roughly the same as judgments. (But older views were generally unable to accommodate acts of considering sentences, or acts of supposing that a sentence is true.) A more important difference between Kant's view and the present view is that I have construed analyticity much more broadly than Kant did. Everything that is analytic in Kant's conception is analytic in mine, but not conversely. In linguistic terms, Kant only raises the question of analyticity for certain kinds of sentences (sentential acts): singular and categorical subject-predicate sentences. (Kant may have believed, following Aristotle, that everything important could be stated with such sentences.) Even with respect to this limited class of sentences, some sentences will be analytic in the present conception but not in Kant's. Kant wanted the analytic character of a sentence (judgment) to be intrinsic to that sentence. The analytic character should not be due to relations between the analytic sentence and other sentences. The present conception explains analyticity in terms of the system of language; it is the whole system which determines whether a sentence is analytic or not. This sentence:

> Every triangle whose base is the diameter of a circle, and which is inscribed in the circle, is a right triangle.

is analytic in the present conception but not in Kant's. The subject of the sentence provides enough information to deduce the predicate, but the deduction makes use of the principles of Euclidean geometry. These principles are not represented by the subject.

Kant did not conceive of language as essentially a system, where the various structures are essential. He thought of each expression and each sentence as a self-contained atom or molecule of significance. This is surprising, because Kant was probably the first philosopher to recognize and appreciate our conceptual system—and to understand how important is its systematic character. For him, analytic truths were empty truths. They were true "on the basis of" a rather simple kind of definition, so they were true "as a matter of" language. Substantive a priori truths were not analytic. These were based on the conceptual structure we bring to experience. This conceptual structure is not linguistic. It antedates language; it is built-in to us. We merely use language to give expression to the pre-existing conceptual structure. Given Kant's conception of the analytic, most of the sentences he said were synthetic a priori really were. His conception is not right or wrong, true or false. It is like a system of classification in this respect. But a choice of one conception rather than some other is motivated by views about language and our conceptual system. Kant's views on these matters are mistaken, and give us no reason to adopt his conception of analyticity.

Kant failed to understand that a linguistic system can be fundamental, and not merely the reflection of some antecedent conceptual order. A system of language can incorporate substantive claims about the world in such a way that the claims are both a priori with respect to the system and susceptible of being false. Kant also failed to understand that we can change our linguistic/conceptual system when it proves to be unsatisfactory. In Kant's conception both the content and the structure of experience are native features. Synthetic a priori knowledge is a priori knowledge due to native features of experience. We have separated the conceptual structure of experience from its native features. The structure comes from language, the native features from our physical and mental apparatus. The difference between conceptual structure and native features does not correspond, in the present conception, to the difference between what is analytic and what isn't. Semantic features have been defined in terms of the commitment relation. It is possible that commitment can be based both on linguistic structure and on the apprehension of native features. Everything derived from commitment belongs to the domain of the analytic (or quasi-analytic).

Now let us return to the question whether there are between experiences quasi-relations which are based on native features of the experiences. When we consider experiences of external objects, it does not seem that one such experience (or several) quasi-entails a distinct experience—where this relation is due to native features. Hume seems to have been looking for such a quasi-entailment when he looked for necessary connections in experience. As far as experience of external objects goes, I think Hume must be right. However, it is far more plausible that some such experiences are quasi-incompatible with others, based on native features. Like experiences of shapes and other sensible qualities, an experience of an object being one color excludes a simultaneous experience of that object being another color.

When we consider ourselves as well as external objects, there is a quasi-entailment between a decision to act and the acting, or between the experience of deciding and the experience of acting. This is due to native features of experience. Remember that entailment and quasi-entailment are derived from the commitment relation between intentional acts. So a decision to act can entail the acting without the acting taking place. This failure of the quasi-entailment to guarantee the occurrence of what is entailed cannot be due to the system's incorporating a faulty theory. For the quasi-entailment does not depend on the mediation of language. If there is a time lag between the decision and the action, the agent might change his mind. Since the sentence describing the action is no longer accepted, there is no failure of quasi-entailment. (Perhaps the distant decision should be described as conditional: he decides to-act-if-he-doesn't-change-his-mind-in-the-meantime.) The agent might also decide and then forget his decision, which leads to his not acting. Or he can decide to act, try to act, and find that he is unable to carry out his decision. These are genuinely cases of quasi-entailment for the person who makes the decision (though *we* aren't committed to believing that he will act once we know that he has decided to act). Quasi-entailments based on decisions are chancy affairs.

Let us consider whether, due to native features, an experience can be quasi-analytic or quasi-anti-analytic. An experience which is not (epistemically) possible is one whose description is anti-analytic. The sentence 'I am traveling backward in time' is such a sentence. In such a case we can say that the impossible experience is quasi-anti-analytic. No matter whether or not this is based on native features, it is not so interesting, because the experience does not belong to the system of language. The experience has no basis in reality, and is not strictly the owner of a property. A more interesting case of quasi-anti-analyticity would be a genuine experience of taking things a certain way, which experience could not be accepted. This might be an experience where something looked ϕ but could not be accepted as being ϕ. Some feature of taking the object to be ϕ would have to mark the experience as phony in a way that commits us to rejecting the experience. I do not know whether we have such experiences.

A quasi-analytic experience would not be an experience that we must have; it is an experience that we are committed to accepting once we do have it. It is precisely this status that Descartes attributed to the cogito. He also seems to have felt that it owed its status to native features. Whenever I think, I am in a position to recognize that I exist. I may not recognize this, because it may not occur to me. If I do think about it, I am committed to accepting it. As formulated in these words:

> I think, I exist.

the cogito is a sentence. But I can recognize that I am thinking without saying anything. I can also recognize nonverbally that I exist. I cannot take myself to be thinking without accepting this taking. I cannot take myself to be existing without accepting that (without being committed to accepting that). When I take myself to be anything, I am thinking. So there is an especially important connection between thinking and existing for me. (Even when, following Hobbes, I take myself to be walking, I am thinking.) Thinking and existing are native features of the conceptual and mental apparatus. The cogito has a quasi-analytic character based on native features. So presumably do simple arithmetic experiences. For example, the experience that this square figure has four sides; and the experience that these two individuals and those three individuals together constitute five individuals. But Descartes could imagine that our neural and mental apparatus was improperly designed for the world we live it. A quasi-analytic judgment based on native features might be mistaken—our very make-up might "incorporate" mistaken views about the world. He apparently felt that mathematical experiences could be mistaken. But the cogito is special. That experience has both a quasi-analytic character based on native features, and an additional character which guarantees its truth.

3. Semantics is Possible

We have distinguished three semantic dimensions of a sentence or other expression: (i) its inferential meaning, (ii) its representational meaning, and (iii) its truth conditions. There may be other dimensions than these, but an adequate semantic theory should at least encompass all three. However, such a theory might be formulated as three relatively autonomous subtheories. The inferential meaning of an expression is not ordinarily considered to be a semantic feature of the expression. A theory of representational meaning comes the closest to being a semantic theory as ordinarily understood, although what is called semantics in logic is really an account of truth conditions.

There is some dispute about whether a semantic theory as ordinarily conceived is possible. We can imagine circumstances which would block the development of such a theory. Let us consider some of these. If different people had radically different first-level experiences, this might raise problems. We know that different people's first-level experiences are different in some respects. The experience of a blind or color blind person is different from that of a person with normal vision. These differences are not radical. Two people's experiences would be radically unlike if, in the same situation, each experienced different individuals—even different numbers of individuals—qualified and related in very different ways. If such differences existed, one of two things might happen. The first is that it would prove impossible to develop a language useful for communicating. This possibility is certainly the more likely. The second possibility is that language would be developed. Everyone would understand it and use it to communicate. But each person would understand it differently. So differently in fact that different people would use different parts of the sentences to represent individuals, and to represent how individuals are qualified and related. In this case an objective semantic theory would not be possible.

In a number of places Quine has appealed to considerations like these to argue both that we can't tell whether two people understand the same sentence in the same way, and that because of this there is nothing to tell about. (One of the clearest formulations of this argument is found in [6].) Since it is in principle not possible to tell how Phil understands sentence *p*, there is nothing that counts as understanding *p*. Such an argument would be unanswerable if we were constrained to use only brute fact descriptions of the world, so that even people and linguistic behavior must be described in such terms. Representational meaning is an intentional phenomenon, and so is our understanding of representational meaning. If we were limited to the use of brute fact descriptions, intentional phenomena must escape our notice; such phenomena are invisible from the perspective of brute fact descriptions. From this perspective, we could not even understand what it is for two people to have radically different experiences, because conceptually organized experience is intentional activity. (In describing experience, even first-level experience, we are imposing a conceptual organization on the experience.) However, we have no difficulty in imagining different people having radically different experiences, though it is wildly implausible that they do. I know of no way to prove that everyone has roughly the same kind of first and second-level experience, but it is unreasonable to doubt that they do. The existence of radically different experiences would be more than a barrier to semantic theory. It would effectively block the development of a common language.

Even if people have roughly the same kinds of experiences, there might be systematic differences between the experiences of different people. An example would be for Phil's experience of blue to be qualitatively the same as George's experience of green. Phil uses the word 'blue' to describe what, if he had the same kind of experience, George would call green. But in situations where Phil has his blue experiences, George doesn't have green experiences. Instead George has the kind of experiences for which *he* uses 'blue.' We can imagine similar differences concerning tastes, smells, and other qualities. It is sometimes alleged that such differences are unintelligible because they are not testable. They *might* be testable. Perhaps there is some neural "wiring" we can discover that is different in Phil than it is in George. If we could manipulate the wiring, we might change Phil's experiences in situations where he formerly had the green-experience that he called blue. At first he would describe situations his own way; eventually he would adjust his language to match everyone else's.

Even if there were no differences in neural wiring, we might think that qualitatively different experiences would be revealed by marked differences in aesthetic taste. If Phil's experiences are unlike George's, then Phil should like some decorating schemes that George doesn't. People *do* disagree about taste—we might explain their differences as due to differences in experienced qualities. But this requires us to believe that everyone has basically the same aesthetic sensibility. Anyway, the differences in taste aren't marked enough to support a claim that different people's experiences are very strongly different. If Helen's experience in drinking lemon juice were qualitatively similar to Phil's in drinking Coke, we would expect Helen to drink lemon juice as much as Phil drinks Coke, or else we would expect Phil to shun Coke. But Helen's likes and dislikes might be readjusted as well as her (tongue) tastes. So she dislikes the taste of lemon juice. (She dislikes the taste of juice from lemons, even though *we* would like the experience caused in her by this juice.)

We understand what it would be for people to have qualitatively different experiences. It makes no difference to our understanding whether or not such differences might be detected. To understand this possibly undetectable difference, it is sufficient to understand intentional descriptions as used to describe the connections between language and experience. If there were such systematic differences from one person's experience to the next, these differences would be no barrier to the development of language. Differences in experience would render certain expressions ('blue,' 'green,' 'sweet,' 'sour') systematically ambiguous. They mean one thing for Phil, and something else for George because each person ties his language to his own experience. If the experiences are different, the words have different representational meanings. Systematic differences would not prevent the development of language. Neither would they be a barrier to semantic theory. Such a theory would be systematically ambiguous in just the same way that a sentence 'This is green' would.

We can imagine that there are systematic differences between people's experiences when it comes to secondary qualities. It is much harder to take seriously the possibility of such differences for primary qualities. Shapes and spatial relations, for example, provide the basis for mathematically precise theories, and can be approximately described with mathematical expressions. It is not in the least plausible that different people have experiences of qualitatively different shapes in the same situations. However, if there were undetectable systematic differences, these would prevent neither the development of language nor the development of semantic theories.

It would be silly to take seriously the possibility that different people have wildly different first-level experiences. Systematic differences in their experiences will not affect the transformation of first-level experience into second-level experience. They would make some second-level expressions systematically ambiguous from one person to the next. When it comes to third-level experience and the language that goes with it, the possibilities for differences between people become greater. Such differences might pose a barrier to communication and to semantic theory. Current talk about the incommensurability of different scientific theories is really concerned with the "incommensurability" of the languages which incorporate these theories. A scientific theory can concern the things we experience as well as those we don't; competing theories need not disagree solely about which nonobservable entities there are. Two third-level languages might be such that the sentences in one do not really correspond to sentences in the other, and also such that neither can be expanded to incorporate adequate translations from the other.

Incommensurability can be a problem for scientific languages or sublanguages. It cannot be taken seriously for the language we use to describe our ordinary, nonprofessional experience. It is a reasonable assumption, one we should adopt initially, that everyone, no matter what her language, recognizes roughly the same kinds of objects, with the same properties and relations. One language, and linguistic community, might be more sophisticated than another. Scientific knowledge may have invaded the common sense experience and language of the one community to a much greater extent than it has the other's. But there should ordinarily be little trouble in expanding the less sophisticated language to accommodate the concepts of the more sophisticated. If a language should prove recalcitrant, this could lead us to modify our initial assumption; there is no reason to believe that in such a case we would be unable to discover and explain the problem.

We have considered situations that might seem to pose a barrier to a semantic theory which is correct or incorrect. There is no such barrier; however, these considerations suggest that there might be a genuine problem for a semantic theory. Any semantic theory must be stated in some language. This language, including its expressions significant in terms of theories the language incorporates, must be able to accommodate other languages. For example, a language in which the available number words were 'one,' 'two,' 'three,' and 'many' would not be suitable for describing a language richer in numerical expressions. The language in which a semantic theory is framed might turn out to be inadequate for dealing with some target language. While this would be a problem, it could be overcome by expanding and enriching the language of the theory.

4. Semantic Theories

A complete semantic theory for a natural language would be very complicated. Such a theory must "lay out" the inferential structure of the language. The account of inferential structure must accommodate both experiences and expressions. The complete semantic theory must provide the truth conditions of those sentences which can be used propositionally. The theory for a complete language should provide some analogous conditions for other kinds of sentences. (As, say, the answerability conditions for interrogative sentences. These might determine what would count as the answer to a question.) The semantic theory must provide an account of the representational meanings of both simple and complex expressions.

A complete semantic account of the various semantic dimensions of a natural language must incorporate, or be based on, an analysis of syntactic structure. For a semantic account must be compositional in the sense that semantic features of complex expressions are explained in terms of the semantic features of component expressions, together with the semantic effects of their organization to constitute the complex. The syntactic structure of a complex expression is derived from the structure of the complex linguistic act of using the expression.

It seems reasonable to divide semantic theory into subtheories for the different semantic dimensions of language. So one theory would deal with the inferential meanings of expressions. A different theory would give an account of truth conditions. Still another theory would explain representational meaning. (If there turn out to be more than three semantic dimensions, the additional dimensions would call for still more theories.) Besides the theories for the different dimensions, some comprehensive account is needed to unify them all. For we want to be assured, for example, that the (deductively correct) inferences which are "authorized" by expressions in the premisses will be truth-preserving. Or that the conclusion of such an inference will represent what is already represented by the premises.

At this point we shall give some attention to the different semantic (sub)theories, to develop preliminary notions of what these should be like. We should note that even if we restrict ourselves to one semantic dimension, it is a formidable task to develop a theory of that dimension for a natural language. It is appropriate to work toward such a theory in stages. To begin with, one should develop partial theories, which cover less than the whole language. The initial theories would naturally focus on classes of expressions, and not try to provide an account linking these expressions to experience.

Consider a partial theory of inferential meaning for some language. What would, or should, such a theory be like? It is reasonable to expect that such a theory would deal with some more or less well defined class of expressions, and give the inferential relations between them. Partial theories are likely to be most successful for those expressions which are fairly "distant" from experience. All expressions depend for their significance on the ties linking expressions to experiences. But some expressions are "closer" to experience than others. Color words are intimately bound up with experiences of the associated colors. But a word like 'or' is more circuitously connected to experience. It is unlikely that an interesting theory of the inferential relations among color expressions will not accommodate experience. (There can be such a theory of the inferential meanings of color expressions. It just won't be interesting. It might tell us, for example, that an inference from '*x* is scarlet' to '*x* is red' is a valid inference.)

A partial theory of inferential meaning would most naturally be formulated as a deductive system. There are many different kinds of deductive system that have been developed in modern logic. These provide different kinds of semantic theory for explaining inferential meaning. It is an important feature of logical deductive systems that their basic principles—their axioms and rules of inference—concern one or more expressions in a certain formal context. In an axiomatic deductive system for propositional logic, we might find an axiom like this:

$$[[\sim q \supset \sim p] \supset [p \supset q]]$$

This axiom concerns the relations between '$\sim$' and '$\supset$' in a sentential context. The variables '*p*' and '*q*' can be replaced by any formulas or sentences. In a natural deduction system, we might find a rule like that illustrated here:

$$\frac{[A \;\&\; B]}{B}$$

This rule deals with the role of '&' when it connects two sentences—these are *any* two sentences. The basic principles of deductive systems are presented for specific expressions in sentential contexts. This manner of presentation requires that we have an understanding of the syntax of the language in question. For the axioms, rules, and definitions of a deductive system characterize the inferential meanings of component expressions by showing some of the contributions these expressions make to the inferential meanings of sentences in which they occur. This makes it possible to derive results which give the relations between complex expressions. A semantic deductive system might deal with sentences or sentential formulas of the "target" language. If the results established in the system were also sentences or sentential formulas, the system would be suited to studying analyticity. (Establishing a sentential result shows that it is analytic, or that it has the form of an analytic sentence.) The system would only indirectly provide results about other semantic features. For example, if the sublanguage under consideration contained a conditional expression 'If . . . , then . . . ,' then a result of the form 'If *A*, then *B*' would indirectly establish that *A* entails *B*. (Directly, it establishes that the conditional sentence is analytic.) A deductive system with sentential components might establish two kinds of results: (i) sentential results, (ii) sequences $A_1, \ldots, A_n$ / *B*. The sentential results establish analyticity directly. The sequential results establish entailment directly. (Such a system would still establish other results, like incompatibility, indirectly.) A semantic theory deductive system might also contain both expressions from the target language and semantic functors from the theorist's language. (These functors would be expressions like 'is analytic,' 'entails,' and 'is incompatible with.') The results established in the system would still be sentential, but they would be sentences of the theorist's language. A deductive system of this sort would be suited for dealing directly with component expressions and their semantic features.

It is a surprising consequence of the present conception of language that many deductive systems of modern logic can be construed as semantic theories. This is surprising because it is common to regard deductive systems as the very antithesis of what is semantic. A deductive system is often said to provide a syntactic characterization of expressions which can also be characterized semantically. There is a difference between a deductive system developed for a language that is already a going concern, and a deductive system whose development is part of the work of developing an artificial language. It is most appropriate to speak of a theory when we are concerned with a language that is already a going concern. A genuine theory plays an explanatory role; the going concern gets explained by the theory. But the deductive systems of modern logic do give semantic features of their artificial languages. The deductive systems present the inferential meanings (or part of these) of expressions in the artificial language. It is because inferential meaning is not customarily regarded as meaning that deductive systems are not commonly thought of as semantic. This conception is reinforced by the fact that we can give inferential meaning in isolation from both representational meaning and truth conditions. So long as a partial theory leaves out of account the ties between expressions and experience, we can give the inferential meanings of expressions with respect to one another, without explaining how expressions in the target language correspond to expressions in ours.

In logic, deductive systems are supplemented with what is usually called a semantic account. These accounts present what I shall call the *real world* truth conditions of expressions in the logical languages. Real world truth conditions are not opposed to possible world conditions—if it happens that possible worlds are real. Real world truth conditions are opposed to the truth conditions of sentences in fictional accounts, and to the truth conditions of sentences about fictional characters. (We first learn to use language to describe and otherwise deal with the real world. We subsequently learn to describe what doesn't exist but might exist, and also to tell and understand stories.) Logical accounts of real world truth conditions are compositional. Features of component expressions are used to determine the truth conditions of sentences. But the contributions that logical expressions make to truth conditions are different from those of names and (nonlogical) predicates. It would be odd to speak of the individual it names as the truth condition of a name, for a name has no truth conditions. But the contribution that a name makes to the truth conditions of a sentence is determined by the named individual. And the contribution of a predicate is determined by the individuals or *n*-tuples that it labels. The contributions made by most logical expressions are more evidently part of a theory of truth conditions. We don't pick out something in the world for 'v' to stand for. Instead we explain the wedge by saying that a sentence [*A* v *B*] is true just in case one of *A*, *B* is true.

A theory of truth conditions might also be called a theory of Word-World connections. From the perspective suggested by this title, it is natural to "explain" a name in terms of the named individual, and a predicate in terms of the individuals or *n*-tuples it labels. But instead of giving the truth conditions of a sentence, we might try to find something the sentence stands for. The difference between true and false sentences might come down to differences in the objects they stand for; or it might be that true sentences stand for things, while false ones do not. Frege introduced the True and the False as objects that sentences stand for. Other philosophers have introduced facts and states of affairs. These attempts are not convincing; the philosophers have just "cooked up" items to correspond to sentences. In the accounts developed later in this book, I will provide a correspondence between true sentences and (ordinary) items in the world. As it turns out, this sort of account is what is needed to provide an adequate treatment of pronouns. However, I will continue to speak of this as a theory of truth conditions, rather than as a theory of Word-World connections.

A theory of truth conditions must be based on an adequate syntactic analysis. This is true of any semantic theory which is compositional. But it is essential to understand that the semantic account for a sentence is tied to the speech act structure of acts of using the sentence. This is especially obvious for sentences that are structurally ambiguous. Such sentences can be used to perform (different) acts having different structures. The structural ambiguity of sentences of natural languages is not usually found in sentences belonging to artificial logical languages. The English sentence 'Everyone loves someone' is frequently given as an example of a syntactically ambiguous sentence. This sentence has two unambiguous first-order translations which illustrate its two meanings. We might use the following:

(1) $(\forall x)[P(x) \supset (\exists y)[P(y) \;\&\; L(x, y)]]$
(2) $(\exists y)[P(y) \;\&\; (\forall x)[P(x) \supset L(x, y)]]$

It is common to say that the important differences between (1) and (2) are differences of scope. This is true, but it is not normally understood that scope differences reflect different speech act structures. An act of using (1) might have the structure represented below (this diagram oversimplifies the structure):

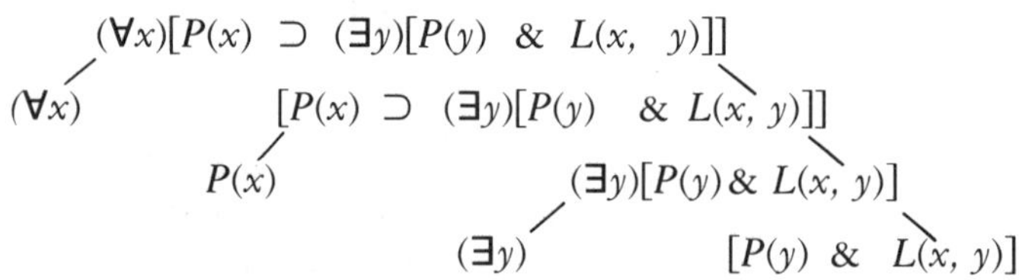

An act of using (2) might be performed like this:

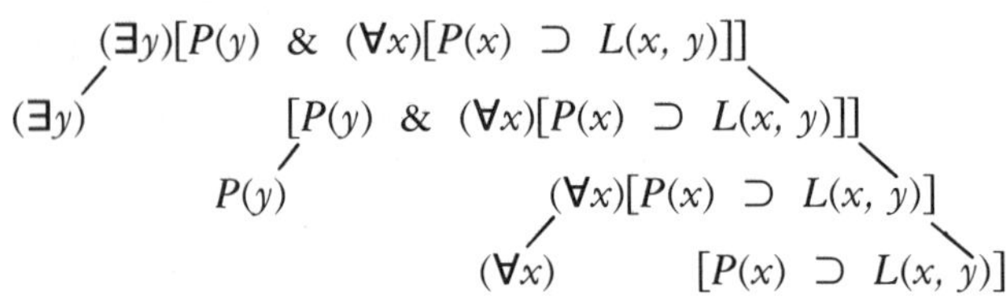

The difference between the scopes of the quantifiers in the two first-order sentences reflects the difference in the "levels" at which the acts of using the quantifiers (the quantified phrases) come into the sentential act. Let us use a temporal metaphor in connection with tree diagrams so that acts represented by lower nodes are *earlier* than acts represented by higher nodes. We can then say that the important difference between the acts of using quantified phrases in acts of using (1) and (2) is that in (1), the act of using the universal phrase is later than the act of using the existential phrase, while in (2) this order is reversed. The scope relations between quantifiers indicates the bottom to top order of using quantified phrases.

We can use tree diagrams to represent the ambiguity of our original English sentence; this saves us from the detour through a first-order language. One understanding is given by an act with this structure:

```
(3)  Everyone loves someone.
       /                 \
Everyone        [  loves someone]
                     /            \
            [  loves  ]        someone
```

The other is given by an act like this:

```
(4)         Everyone loves someone.
              /                 \
     [Everyone loves  ]        someone
        /                \
Everyone           [  loves  ]
```

With the English sentence, it is misleading to describe the ambiguity between (3) and (4) in terms of scope. Scope relations constitute a feature of first-order sentences that indicates the order in which component speech acts of a sentential act are performed. The English sentence is ambiguous precisely because it does not contain such a feature.

5. Theories of Representational Meaning

The representational meanings of expressions depend (in part) on their inferential ties to experience. This is especially true for those expressions used (by deliberate language users) to perform simple linguistic acts. A partial theory of representational meaning which deals only with expressions, omitting an account of experience, must find some way to "assign" representational meanings to simple expressions. The most natural way to do this would be by translating target-language expressions into the language of the semantic theorist. I will describe the theorist's language in this case as a *canonical* language. This might be her natural language, a sublanguage of her natural language, or an artificial language developed for theoretical purposes. (Katz is developing an artificial language for semantic theory. This is described in [3] and [4], among other places. Katz's language is not entirely artificial, for it borrows a lot from English.)

As well as providing canonical translations for simple target-language expressions, a theory of representational meaning might use the same approach for complex expressions. The theory begins by assigning canonical translations to simple expressions of the target language. Given these translations, the theory then gives rules for combining the translations of simple expressions to yield translations of complex expressions. (Katz's semantic theory is like this.) Several problems might be encountered in developing such a theory of representational meaning. For one thing, the canonical language might not be adequate to its task. Just as a language whose numerical expressions were 'one,' 'two,' 'three,' and 'many' would not be adequate for describing a language like ours, so there may be target languages whose expressive possibilities outstrip those of the canonical language. If such a situation were encountered, the obvious move to try would be enriching the canonical language.

A related problem might arise as follows. The target language and the canonical language might have expressions for things of a kind. An expression in the target language might be used for exactly the same things as an expression in the canonical language. But the expressions aren't understood in quite the same ways. In the target language, whales are considered to be fish—and fish are conceived in the same way in both languages. In the canonical language, the fact that whales are mammals is built-in to the meaning of the canonical 'whale' word. In our semantic theory, we can't translate the target 'whale' word by our word. We must instead provide a translation which incorporates an analysis of the target-language understanding of 'whale.' For this to succeed, there must be a stock of simple concepts common to both the target language and the canonical language. There must be a stock of such concepts that is adequate for all human languages; every complex concept must be analyzable in terms of the simple ones. This is plausible when we are concerned with second-level concepts. It is less plausible, but perhaps still plausible, when we are concerned with third-level concepts of familiar medium-sized objects. It is not in the least plausible for scientific concepts. If it happens that in the target language and the canonical language there are simple corresponding concepts which differ as do the two concepts of a whale, then some target expressions will have no adequate canonical translations. If this should happen, we could still discover it, and understand the difficulty. But an adequate semantic theory would have to explain the structures in the target systems of language, and explain meanings in connection with these structures.

A theory of representational meaning which provides canonical translations for simple and complex expressions of the target language must also provide a different canonical translation for every (speech act) structure associated with a target-language sentence. Speech act structures are truly a linguistic universal. Different languages use different means to exemplify the same structures. (Although there might be a language for which, as the language is now constituted, some structures are not possible.) To have a different canonical sentence for each different structure of a target-language sentence would require enormous resources in the canonical language. For most natural-language sentences are representationally ambiguous. And even if we could provide a suitable canonical language, we would need to come up with a semantic theory of the canonical language. A theory which merely provides translations is not sufficiently explanatory. The theory must also analyze speech act structures.

The customary understanding of ambiguity is far too narrow. The difference between a bank which is a depository for money and the bank of a river is counted as an ambiguity of 'bank' (and it is one). The different meanings of 'Everyone loves someone' are rightly taken to show that the sentence is ambiguous. But consider the sentence 'Bob hit Laura.' This may be ambiguous in the ordinary sense because 'hit' is ambiguous. (Bob may be employed by the Mafia, he may have been driving a car, or he may have used his hand or a stick.) But let the meaning of 'hit' be fixed so that we understand Bob to have struck Laura with his hand. The sentence remains representationally ambiguous. An act of using the sentence might have this structure:

```
(1)  Bob hit Laura.
     /    |    \
  Bob  [  hit  ]  Laura
```

The two referring acts and the predicative act are performed in order to assert that Bob hit Laura. This analysis is analogous to our analysis of one of Steve's assertions that Switzerland is mountainous.

The act of using the sentence might have one of these structures:

```
(2)  Bob hit Laura.
    /            \
 Bob        [ hit Laura]
           /          \
      [ hit ]        Laura
```

```
(3)  Bob hit Laura.
    /          \
 [Bob hit ]    Laura
 /       \
Bob     [ hit ]
```

The three different structures do not produce ambiguity as this is ordinarily understood. But the representational meanings of the three acts are not the same. The act represented by (2) gives greater prominence to Bob than to Laura. This structure would be appropriate in an answer to the question 'Who hit Laura?' The structure represented by (3) gives greater prominence to Laura. This could be a suitable answer to 'Who(m) did Bob hit?' Those acts which enter a tree structure "later" receive greater attention than earlier acts. The act represented by (1) gives equal prominence to Bob and Laura (or nearly equal—the subject position is often a position of greater prominence). The differences in the speech act structures represented by diagrams (1), (2), and (3) do not signal differences in inferential meaning or truth conditions. They are solely differences in representational meaning. These differences may not be big, but they are genuine differences which an adequate theory of representational meaning must accommodate. To do so the theory must provide an explicit account of sentential structures, either for the target language or the canonical language. It is not sufficient simply to provide canonical translations.

6. The Broader System of Language

The system of language we have been considering contains only those sentences which (when used) can appropriately be evaluated in terms of truth and falsity. In this section I want to briefly consider the relation of this *propositional* system to the system which contains all sentences and the related experiences. To begin with, we should note that the propositional system does not contain sentences with illocutionary force-indicating prefixes. I have discussed some such prefixes in a previous chapter; but the prefix does not properly belong to the sentence which can be evaluated in terms of truth and falsity. However, the illocutionary prefixes are capable of multiple uses. They can be used to make explicit the force of an illocutionary act. They can also be used in a sentence describing an illocutionary act. If I tell Jane, "I promise that I will wash the car," I might be promising to wash the car. I can also tell someone else about my promising. It is most common to use the past or future tense for this, as when I say, "I promised that I will wash the car," or "I will promise to wash the car." But I might tell Don, "I promise that I will wash the car," when I am only reporting what I have (just) been promising Jane. When an illocutionary prefix is used in a non-force-indicating fashion, it and its sentence belong to the propositional system.

Sentences in the propositional (sub)system are suited for representing what is the case. To simply accept or reject such a sentence *is* to accept or reject it as representing what is the case. But we can distinguish different kinds of acts of accepting a sentence (sentential act) as representing what is the case. I can accept a sentence as representing what is the case because of what I intend to do—I accept it as representing what I intend to bring about. I can also accept a sentence as representing what is the case independently of me. I can accept a sentence as representing what I regret to be the case. I can accept a sentence as representing what I regret to be the case, and take myself to be responsible for. I can similarly accept one as representing what I am delighted is the case, and take myself to be responsible for.

An act of accepting or rejecting a sentence as representing what is the case is a plain illocutionary act. Some such acts are assertions or denials. But some of these acts, when performed publically, are counted as different kinds of illocutionary acts. An act of accepting a sentence as representing what I regret to be the case can be an act of sympathizing. An act of accepting a sentence as representing what I regret to be the case and take myself to be responsible for can be an apology. And an act of accepting a sentence as representing what I am delighted is the case, and take myself to be responsible for can be an act of self-congratulation. When a public act of accepting a sentence as representing what is the case fails to count as an assertion, this is usually due to the purpose of the act with respect to its audience. I can accept the sentence 'I will wash the car tomorrow' as representing what is (will be) the case. But when I use this sentence to make a promise, I am doing more than accepting the sentence. I am also accepting an obligation to my addressee. When I use the sentence 'You will clear the table now' to give a command, I am accepting that sentence as representing what is the case. I am accepting it as representing what I intend to be the case. I am also using the sentence to influence my addressee to make it the case. Some acts of accepting a sentence as representing what is the case are assertions. Others are not. The differences between these different kinds of illocutionary acts can be traced back to different kinds of acts of accepting a sentence as representing what is the case.

The propositional subsystem of language has a structure derived from the commitment relation. The commitment is to accept or reject a sentence as representing what is the case. But since there are different kinds of acts of accepting a sentence as representing what is the case, we can distinguish different commitment relations. We can, for example, distinguish the commitment to accept a sentence as representing what I regret from the commitment to accept a sentence as representing what I celebrate. We can also distinguish "deductive" commitment from "inductive" commitments. For the deductive relation, the commitment is to fully accept or reject a sentence. But there are many degrees of acceptance (rejection). There are hesitant acceptances, tentative acceptances, and confident acceptances. The commitment to accept a sentence hesitantly is different from a commitment to accept the sentence confidently. An act of supposing a sentence to be true is also an illocutionary act. It seems odd to describe an act of supposing as an act of accepting. Though we might say that when we suppose a sentence to be true, we are accepting it temporarily. If we suppose this sentence to be true, then we will be committed to temporarily accepting—to supposing—that sentence. The commitment relations generated by the different kinds (and degrees) of acceptings and rejectings provide a complex structure to the propositional system.

The sentences in the propositional system can be accepted or rejected as representing what is the case. We can also accept or reject them in other ways. Consider some sentence that Henry accepts. I can also accept that sentence, not as representing what is the case, but as representing what Henry believes to be the case. And accepting this sentence as representing what Henry believes to be the case can commit me to accepting that sentence as representing what Henry believes to be the case. However, my accepting a sentence as representing what Henry believes to be the case is not, strictly speaking, an act of accepting a sentence (sentential act). Consider the sentence:

(1) Martinis are a source of Vitamin C.

Suppose this is what Henry believes. I can use sentence (1) to represent—to represent martinis as a source of Vitamin C. If I accept this sentential act, then *I* am the one who believes martinis are a source of Vitamin C. Instead of accepting sentence (1) as representing what is the case, I can perform a representing act which I don't accept. Once this representing act is available, I can perform an act of taking it to be believed by Henry. When I accept this act of taking to be, I am not performing a representing act. Neither is the act of taking to be a representing act. What is informally described as accepting an act of representing martinis as a source of Vitamin C as believed by Henry is really an act of accepting a nonrepresentative act of taking to be.

I might perform a representing act with (1), and take this act to be (the same specific kind of act) believed by Henry without saying (or thinking) anything other than (1). I could also use:

(2) Henry believes martinis are a source of Vitamin C.

to perform an act in which the prefix 'Henry believes' is used to perform an act of taking to be, while the rest of the sentence is used to perform a representing act which enables the act of taking to be. It is possible, for a sentence I accept, to perform an act analogous to what I have done for Henry. I might use sentence (1) to represent, then take this representing act to be believed by me. But this can't be the fundamental act in my case as it can in Henry's. My act of simply accepting the representing act is prior to the act of taking the representing act to be accepted by me. I must be able to use sentence (1) to express my belief before it makes sense to say, "I believe martinis are a source of Vitamin C." Henry must also be able to use (1) to express his belief before it makes sense for me to say (2). But I can't use (1) to express Henry's belief; I can only take (1) to be what Henry believes.

When someone simply accepts a sentential representing act, she accepts the sentence as representing things as they are. This locution can be misleading. For one thing, the locution makes it sound as if there were no simple act of accepting a representing act. We can't just accept the act, we must accept it as this or that. But simply to accept the act *is* to accept it as representing things as they are. The locution also suggests that there are different kinds of representing. We can represent things as they are or we can represent things as Henry believes them to be. But whether it is Henry or I who believes (1), the sentence is used to represent martinis as a source of Vitamin C. There are different ways to employ this sentence, but not different kinds of representings we perform with it.

We can simply accept (or reject) a representing act. We can accept or reject an act of taking to be. But there are still other kinds of accepting and rejecting. We can also accept or reject a sentence as representing what we would like to be the case. Suppose this sentence:

(3) I will inherit a million dollars.

represents what I would like to be the case. There is no special kind of representing involved here. Sentence (3) represents me inheriting a million dollars whether I actually think I will or only wish that I would. And I can't analyze my accepting (3) as representing what I would like to be the case in the same way I analyzed my accepting (1) as representing what Henry believes to be the case. I can use (3) to perform a representing act. But I won't take the representing act to be desirable. What is desirable is what the act represents. It only makes sense to take the representing act to be an act of representing what I would like if there is some more fundamental "liking" situation. I believe we must explain what is going on by recognizing a different, and fundamental, kind of accepting. It is not plain accepting. Acts of accepting and rejecting have different "modalities." Plain acts are the simplest. We can also accept a sentence (sentential act) as representing what we would like to be the case. These acts can be subdivided into groups ranging from those representing what we would like a lot to those representing what we would like a little. Not only can we accept a sentence as representing what we would like, we can accept one as representing what we wouldn't like. (We can reject it as representing what we would like.) The different kinds of accepting and rejecting are fundamental. They are appealed to in giving explanations of various linguistic acts; they are not to be explained by reducing them to multiple real relations linking people and platonic entities.

We have seen that there are different kinds of acts of accepting a sentence (sentential act) as representing things as they are. These find public expression in various kinds of illocutionary acts. The different modes of accepting and rejecting also give rise to different kinds of illocutionary acts. I might give public expression to my million-dollar desire by saying, "Would that I inherited a million dollars!" (That sentence does not belong to the propositional system; its illocutionary force is indicated by its form.) The different kinds of illocutionary act which are constituted by different modes of accepting and rejecting sentences have not always been recognized as illocutionary acts. Suppose I accept sentence (3) as representing what I hope will be the case. And suppose I express this by saying:

(4) I hope I will inherit a million dollars.

This sentence is likely to be construed as an assertion about myself. And the sentence *can* be used to make an assertion about myself. But the sentence can also be used to perform an act with this structure:

I hope: I will inherit a million dollars.
I will inherit a million dollars

The act performed with 'I will inherit a million dollars' represents me as inheriting a million dollars. This sentential act enables the act performed with the prefix. The prefix act is an act of accepting the sentential act as representing what I hope will be the case. This act of accepting is a distinctive kind of illocutionary act. Such acts go unnoticed because sentences like (4) can also be used be make (ordinary) assertions.

The prefix 'I assert' can be used to make illocutionary force explicit. But the assertion made with 'I assert that I will inherit a million dollars' can also be made with 'I will inherit a million dollars.' The hope-expressing act performed with (4) cannot be similarly performed with (3). This is another reason why hope-expressing acts have not been recognized as distinctive kinds of illocutionary act. However, to properly understand and explain illocutionary acts, we must begin with the different kinds of accepting and rejecting. These are fundamental; they "generate" the different kinds of illocutionary acts.

Commitment does not link the different kinds of accepting and rejecting in exactly the same ways. If I accept *A* as representing what is the case, and *A* entails *B*, then I am committed to accepting *B* as representing what is the case. But I might accept *A* as representing what I would like to be the case without being committed to accepting *B* as representing what I would like to be the case. For in addition to wishing that *A* were the case I might also wish that the world were different in such a way that *A* did not entail *B*. (This example marks a difference between what I would like to be the case and what I hope to be the case. If I accept *A* as representing what I hope will be the case, then I am committed to accepting *B* as representing what I hope will be the case.) There is a terminological difficulty in describing this situation. The semantic terminology has been explained in connection with accepting and rejecting sentences as representing what is the case, and the commitment relation based on these acts. But accepting a sentence *A* as representing what I would like to be the case can commit me to accepting *B* as representing what I would like to be the case. It can also commit me to accepting sentence *C* (= I would like that *A*) as representing what is the case. What shall we call the relations between *A* and *B*, and between

A and *C*? If we call them entailment, we are likely to mislead. (*A* can then entail *B* in one sense, and fail to entail *B* in another.) But it is a hopeless task to try to introduce a new term for each different relation. When the semantic expressions are used without qualification, they are understood to signal features derived from the commitment to accept or reject sentences as representing what is the case. These unqualified semantic features are the most basic semantic features. When the commitment between other kinds of accepting fails to match that between accepting as representing what is the case, some kind of explanation is called for. The ordinary semantic terms will be qualified in some way when they are used for relations based on different kinds of accepting and rejecting. (We might, for example, speak of what-I-would-like entailment.)

The propositional system contains sentences which can be used to perform representing acts which can be accepted or rejected as representing what is the case. The propositional system contains sentences which can be used to perform acts of taking (other) sentential acts to be this or that, which acts of taking to be can be accepted or rejected as taking something to be what it really is. Sentences (sentential acts) in the propositional system can also be accepted or rejected in ways that don't involve representing or being what is the case. We can accept or reject a sentence as representing what we would like; we can accept or reject a sentential taking to be as what we would like. (We would like Henry to believe that martinis are a source of Vitamin C.) It is also possible to accept or reject a sentence as representing what we are obligated to see is the case. My obligation to buy the tickets may have been incurred by Jim's command. There will then be a sentence (sentential act) which I take to be the act directed at me by Jim. But this does not reduce my accepting the sentence as representing what I am obligated to do to a case of taking a sentential act to be something or other. (My accepting the sentence as representing what Henry believes *has* been reduced to my taking the sentential act to be one Henry would accept.) My taking a certain sentential act to be Jim's command is different from my accepting an obligation. Accepting a sentence as representing what I am obligated to do is a distinctive modality of accepting. In addition to the different kinds of acts of accepting and rejecting sentences in the propositional system of language, there are acts of accepting incomplete expressions. I can accept 'It is now —— o'clock' as representing incompletely what I would like to know, or as representing incompletely what I have been asked to represent completely and truly.

The propositional system of language contains expressions which provide the "content" for various illocutionary acts. To get the broader system of language from this narrower system, we must consider the different kinds of accepting and rejecting and the commitment relations based on them. We must also add devices for making illocutionary force explicit. Some of these devices are expressions to be prefixed to propositional sentences. Not all of them are. Various syntactic devices also serve to mark illocutionary force. The incomplete expression 'It is now —— o'clock' represents what I would like to know. I make it clear that I am looking for information by using the interrogative sentence 'What time is it?' The expanded system also contains expressions for performing illocutionary acts, where the expressions do not give the sentential content of the act. Examples are 'Watch out!', 'Fore!', 'I agree.' In these cases, the sentential content is either provided by a nearby sentential act, or by sententially structured experience.

The broader system of language contains expressions and experiences. The inferential structure of the system is provided by features derived from commitment. There are various commitment relations, linking different kinds of acceptings and rejectings. The propositional system, with its simpler structure, is fundamental for the broader system. The commitment relation of the propositional system "generates" the other commitment relations. When they fail to match the fundamental commitment relation, it is their deviations that need explaining. The propositional system is also the system that ties expressions to experiences, and provides experience with its conceptual structure. A possible experience may be one that I wish were actual, or that I hope becomes actual. But its status in the system of language is not due to my desires and hopes, and is not affected by them. I can be committed to having an experience. And I can be committed to liking it if I have it. But this is just being committed to having another experience.

An adequate semantic theory must catalogue the various kinds of accepting and rejecting; it must give an account of inferential and representational meanings with respect to all of these. Truth conditions are not affected by the different commitment relations; a sufficient account of truth conditions is provided by a treatment of the propositional system. An adequate semantic theory should also point out and explain those expressions and forms that serve to indicate (to make explicit) illocutionary force. In dealing with devices for indicating illocutionary force, there is a new relation that must be considered. Those features of the system of language that are based on accepting, rejecting, and commitment are *strictly semantic* features. A complete theory of language must give an account of the strictly semantic features. It must also explain the relation that I will call *justification.* This relation "explicitly" involves illocutionary acts. (Strictly semantic relations implicitly involve illocutionary acts. They are generated by acts of accepting and rejecting which are the sources of illocutionary acts.) An illocutionary act is *justified* if it is correctly performed in suitable circumstances. (There are degrees of justification.) Austin and Searle have both explained the various ways in which illocutionary acts can go wrong. From the present perspective, they have explored the justification conditions of (some) illocutionary acts. For example, following Searle ([7], p. 57ff), we might say that *S* is justified in using *T* to promise *H* that he (*S*) will do *A* if

(1) Normal input and output conditions obtain.
(2, 3) *S* can use *T* to represent *S* as doing *A* in the future.
(4) *H* would prefer *S*'s doing *A* to his not doing *A*, and *S* believes this.
(5) It is not obvious to both *S* and *H* that *S* will do *A* in the normal course of events.
(6) *S* intends to do *A*.
(7) *S* can appropriately utter *T* to place *S* under an obligation to do *A*.
(8) *S* could influence *H* to understand that the utterance of *T* counts as placing *S* under an obligation to do *A*. *S* could influence *H* to recognize what he (*S*) is trying to do, and to recognize this through *H*'s understanding of *T*.
(9) *S*'s use of *T* is provided for by the language that *S* and *H* share.

An account of justification for some particular language would omit (9) and reformulate some of the other conditions.

That an illocutionary act is justified for Bob does not mean that Bob is obligated to perform the act. It does not commit him to performing the act of accepting or rejecting that the illocutionary act "expresses." Many situations in which a promise would be justified are not situations in which a promise need be made. It would be possible to use a natural deduction system to explore justification conditions, as well as to investigate strictly semantic features. With strictly semantic features, a proof shows that its hypotheses entail its conclusion. With justification, a proof would show that the premises justify the conclusion. (A justification system would need a device for distinguishing an act which is merely justified from an act which is "in force.") We should note that while, in general, an illocutionary act can be justified for a person without her being committed to performing the act, this is not the case with an assertion about what is the case independently of us. If such an assertion is justified, it need not be made publically; but the person for whom it is justified is committed to accepting the appropriate sentence.

Bibliography and References

1. Rene Descartes. *The Philosophical Works of Descartes,* vols. 1 and 2. Translated by Elizabeth S. Haldane and G. R. T. Ross. Cambridge: Cambridge University Press, 1967.
2. Immanuel Kant. *Critique of Pure Reason.* Translated by Norman Kemp Smith. London: MacMillan & Co. Ltd., 1956.
3. Jerrold J. Katz. *Semantic Theory.* New York: Harper & Row, 1972.
4. Jerrold J. Katz. *Propositional Structure and Illocutionary Force.* New York: Thomas Y. Crowell, 1977.
5. Willard Van Orman Quine. "The Problem of Meaning in Linguistics," *From a Logical Point of View*, pp. 47–64.
6. Willard Van Orman Quine. *Word and Object.*
7. John R. Searle, *Speech Acts, An Essay in the Philosophy of Language.*

Chapter 6
Logical Form and Grammatical Form

1. The Original Distinction

We have been considering the semantic aspects of language and the system of language. It seems appropriate to pay some attention to syntax. I will begin by discussing a distinction that has been philosophically important, the distinction between logical form and grammatical form. This distinction comes to philosophers' attention in the study of language. Either philosophers are concerned to give logical analyses which would enable them to recognize (and characterize) valid arguments, logically true sentences, etc., or they are concerned with some other kind of philosophical analysis, such as trying to account for false beliefs and the objects of these beliefs. In carrying out their analyses, the philosophers have at their disposal certain syntactic, or grammatical, analyses. (I am using 'grammatical' as a synonym for 'syntactic.') This means that they have a classification system assigning expressions to various syntactic categories, and also have some account of the way component expressions are combined to form complex expressions. The grammatical form of a sentence is determined by the categories of its components, and the organization of the components to form the complex. The philosophers have found that, for the purposes of carrying out their analyses, it is not helpful to deal with grammatical form. Expressions which have the same grammatical form exhibit different behavior with respect to the philosophers' analyses. For example, suppose we are concerned with logical analysis. What we find is that arguments which have the same grammatical form can differ in their logically significant properties. One such argument is valid while a second is not. An example of such a pair is supplied by Alonzo Church:

> I have seen a portrait of John Wilkes Booth; John Wilkes Booth assassinated Abraham Lincoln; thus I have seen a portrait of an assassin of Lincoln.
> I have seen a portrait of somebody; somebody invented the wheeled vehicle; thus I have seen a portrait of an inventor of the wheeled vehicle. (p. 2, [1])

A similar situation can arise for other philosophical analyses. For example, it has been alleged that there are philosophers who have been "taken in" by the grammatical resemblance that words like 'nothing' and 'nobody' have to nouns like 'person' and 'table'. Such philosophers would think the world contains nothing, or nothings, in much the same way that it contains tables. If there really are (or have been) such philosophers, they have failed to notice important differences that are relevant to philosophic analysis.

Once philosophers notice that grammatical form is not helpful—and can even be misleading—for the purposes of logical/philosophical analyses, they make different responses. (1) Some philosophers claim that their analyses are concerned with (nonlinguistic) things in the world. Ordinary language does not faithfully reflect the features important for these analyses. Their claim is an ontological one; the shortcoming of ordinary (natural) language is that it does not adequately "capture" ontological features.

(2) Other philosophers maintain that our account of grammatical form is simply the result of one analysis of language. Different analyses are possible; they reveal different features and different kinds of features than grammatical analyses reveal. There may be some linguistic and pedagogical purposes that are well served by attending to grammatical form. Logical and philosophical investigations require a different analysis of language than a grammatical one. This second view has two versions. (2a) The analysis of language that is useful for logical/philosophical purposes (the structures that are uncovered) faithfully reflects ontological features. This fidelity explains the success of the analysis, and enables us to explain the difference between philosophic and grammatical analyses. A philosopher adopting view (2b) holds that linguistic features uncovered by logical/philosophical analysis are ultimate and autonomous. They do not reflect ontological features. (At least, there is no reason to think that they do.)

Different philosophical views have been developed in response to the inadequacy of grammatical analyses for logical/philosophical purposes. The holders of these different views frequently use the same terminology, with different meanings, to present their views. The expression that is contrasted with 'grammatical form' is 'logical form.' The different views give different explanations of logical form. A philosopher adopting view (1) considers logical form to be an ontological feature. Logical form is a structure of things in the world. It might be a structure of propositions, or of facts, or of something else again. In giving a logical/philosophical analysis, we are concerned with the logical forms of things in the world. A philosopher holding view (2) will identify logical form with a structural feature of language. A (2a) philosopher will say that logical forms reflect ontological structures; a (2b) philosopher won't say this.

The different philosophical views about logical form and related issues do not lead to their proponents' engaging in different types of philosophical investigation. Holders of the different views adopt a common strategy. They develop an artificial logical language or make use of one developed by someone else, and use it in making their analyses. In order for this to be a useful strategy, it is essential that the artificial language be perspicuous in ways that natural languages are not. Sentences of the artificial language will have grammatical forms, but these will not be misleading in the way that natural-language grammatical forms are misleading. Artificial sentences which have the same grammatical form will exhibit the same logical behavior. Grammatically similar artificial sentences will behave similarly with respect to philosophical analyses. Exactly how this situation is described will depend on the view that has been adopted. A holder of view (1) will say that the grammatical forms in the artificial language perspicuously reflect the (onto)logical forms in the world. A holder of view (2) will say that in the artificial language, there is no difference between grammatical and logical forms—the two forms coincide in the artificial language.

Let us consider how the artificial logical language is used to carry out logical/philosophical analyses. Ordinary sentences (natural-language sentences) are translated by sentences of the artificial language. These translations do not preserve syntactic features. Nor do they preserve representational meaning. The logical-language sentences do preserve (approximately) inferential meaning and (real world) truth conditions. In making these translations. we rely on our understanding of the two languages. There are no mechanical procedures for moving from an English sentence to its artificial-language counterpart. Philosophers holding the different views we have discussed will conceive of and describe the use of the artificial language in different ways. From viewpoint (1), the artificial language is a perspicuous substitute for a natural language. (But it is only perspicuous for logical and philosophical analyses. It wouldn't be appropriate to adopt the artificial language as the language we speak and write.) The artificial language is perspicuous vis-à-vis the extralinguistic world. Users of natural languages have an intuitive understanding of the world; this enables them to make and recognize valid arguments, and to use natural languages to describe the world. The artificial language is helpful, and perhaps essential, for making careful logical and philosophical analyses.

From viewpoint (1), the artificial language does not help us understand our natural language; it helps us develop a clearer understanding of the world. But for philosophers who hold one of the (2) views, the artificial language makes explicit what is implicit in natural languages. In a natural language, grammatical form is apparent—it is on the "surface." The logical forms of natural language sentences are "hidden deep within" those sentences. The artificial language brings logical form up to the surface, where it coincides with grammatical form.

In considering the role of the artificial language, and the proper description of this role, we can see that a third view, different from (1) and (2), is possible. I don't know if any philosophers have held or now hold this view, but it is a view that might easily be maintained. View (3) holds that the artificial logical language is useful for logical and philosophical analyses. And that this language is perspicuous with respect to these analyses—the language facilitates the analyses. But this view makes no ontological claims; and it makes no claims that the artificial language brings to light hidden features of natural languages. The artificial language is simply a new invention that serves logical and philosophical ends. From this view, it might be misleading to use the expression 'logical form' at all. If it were used, this expression would designate the grammatical form of the artificial language.

From the perspective of all three views, the artificial language serves as a canonical language in a sense similar to that described in the preceding chapter. But this canonical language is useful only for studying inferential meaning and real world truth conditions. It does not provide translations which preserve representational meaning.

2. Some Problems with the Distinction

I have described three (or four) different views about logical form and artificial logical languages. These views have all been developed in response to the same fact: sentences (and arguments) having the same grammatical forms do not exhibit the same behavior with respect to logical and philosophical analyses. Grammatical form is an inadequate guide in carrying out these analyses. And proponents of the different views all employ essentially the same kind of artificial logical language: a first-order language, either with or without identity. One problem common to all these different views is that the examples used to justify the claim about the inadequacy of grammatical form are usually open to criticism. It is always possible to argue that sentences claimed to have the same form do not really have the same form. With many of the examples that have been used, it is more than just possible to claim that they don't have the same form; it is extremely plausible that they don't have the same form. The philosophers who provide examples have never taken the trouble to develop and motivate a systematic syntactic analysis. This needs to be done to justify the claim that two sentences have the same grammatical form. What the philosophers have done instead is to pick examples that seemed to them to be grammatically similar. If we consider the example taken from Church in the preceding section, we can see that in order to hold that the two arguments have the same grammatical form, we must agree that 'somebody' and 'John Wilkes Booth' belong to the same syntactic category. But it seems obvious that an adequate grammatical analysis would recognize fundamental categories that are too narrow to include both expressions. The philosophers' examples don't justify their distinction between grammatical form and logical form. What they show instead is that there is no adequate understanding of grammatical form.

For the moment, let us ignore the weakness of the philosophers' evidence for their distinctions between grammatical form and logical form. Suppose that, after a good understanding of grammatical form was achieved, this form still proved inadequate for logical and philosophical analyses. What sort of philosophical response to this fact would be appropriate? Both views (1) and (2a) seem to be extreme. That a logical/philosophical analysis is successful does not show that it faithfully reflects ontological features. More precisely, that a first-order language proves helpful for logical/philosophical analyses does not show that this language pictures the very make-up of reality. In order to justify such a strong ontological claim, it would be necessary to develop (and justify) techniques for making ontological analyses more directly.

If we ignore ontological claims, both (2a) and (2b) seem extreme. That a first-order language proves helpful for understanding a natural language is not a good reason to say or think that the first-order language brings to light hidden features of the natural language. It might seem that such hidden features provide an explanation for the successful use of first-order languages. But this is a very weak explanation in the absence of analyses which really uncover these features in the natural language.

These criticisms appear to leave (3) as the only reasonable view. But in so far as (3) is developed in response to a nonproblem (in response to a mistaken view about grammatical form), there will be no reason to adopt it. However, regardless of whether philosophers have correctly conceived grammatical form in natural languages, it is definitely the case that they have successfully employed first-order languages in carrying out logical/philosophical analyses. With respect to these successful applications, (3) is the most reasonable view to adopt in the absence of techniques for directly carrying out ontological analyses, and in the absence of a detailed understanding of the actual structures of natural-language sentences.

3. Reformulating the Distinction

The distinction between logical form and grammatical form has been developed on the basis of an unjustified conception of the grammatical forms of natural language sentences. The different philosophical views made unwarranted claims about ontological features of the world and about hidden features of natural languages. But if we consider what the logicians and philosophers actually accomplished, and not what they said they were doing, we find that they achieved considerable success. They developed first-order and other logical languages. They used these in carrying out analyses of natural-language sentences. The analyses proceeded by translating natural-language sentences into the logically perspicuous language, and then "evaluating" the perspicuous translations.

In considering this successful practice, there are two features that I want to remark. The first feature is one that seems to be a limitation of logic. When a first-order language is applied to, say, English, some aspects of English can be "handled," and others can't. If we consider this argument:

> Bill or John has ten dollars.
> Bill doesn't have ten dollars.
> So John has ten dollars.

it is clearly valid. If we translate this argument into a first-order language, the translation will be valid; and we can use the techniques developed for the first-order language to show that it is valid. But the argument:

Bill's car is red.
So Bill's car isn't green.

is also valid. And its first-order translation is valid. But the deductive techniques for first-order languages are inadequate for establishing that the argument is valid. Logical analysis aims at discovering or uncovering certain semantically distinguished items: analytic sentences, valid arguments, incompatible collections of sentences, etc. But logical techniques do not seem adequate for dealing with semantic features in all their generality. For every semantic feature, there is a logical special case of that feature. Logic can't handle all analytic sentences, but restricts its attention to those analytic sentences which are logically true. Instead of dealing with all valid arguments, the logician restricts herself to those which are logically valid. (Analytic sentences in the province of logic are logically true. Anti-analytic sentences which are logical in character are logically false. And I use 'implication' for the logical special case of entailment. For the other semantic features, I designate the logical special case by prefixing 'logical' to the name for the general feature.)

The second feature I want to remark initially concerns artificial logical languages. In such a language, it does not seem that the structure which is logically important is the same as the structure that is appropriately entitled grammatical form. It is most reasonable to say that the grammatical form of a sentence (or other complex expression) is determined by the syntactic categories of its component expressions, together with the way these are combined to form the sentence. But in a first-order language, all two-place sentential connectives should belong to the same syntactic category. So sentences $[A \& B]$, $[A \vee B]$, $[A \supset B]$ would have the same grammatical form. It isn't necessary to conceive grammatical form in this way; my doing so involves a decision on my part. But this seems to me to be the most reasonable conception. Syntax is a very general, abstract study. Why should we adopt some other criterion for membership in a syntactic category than that of combining with the same expressions in the same ways to form the same kinds of complex expressions? Just as sentences having different binary connectives can have the same form, so two sentences $(\exists\alpha)A$ and $(\forall\alpha)A$ will have the same grammatical form.

Even though $[A \& B]$, $[A \vee B]$, $[A \supset B]$ have the same grammatical form, they exhibit different logical behaviors. From a logical perspective it is important to distinguish these sentences. I believe there is no basis for recognizing a logical form which is an ontological feature of propositions, facts, or whatever. There is also no basis for a logical form which is a hidden feature of a natural language. So I propose that we redefine 'logical form' so that the logical form of an artificial-language sentence is determined by (1) the syntactic categories of its component expressions, (2) the distinctively logical expressions it contains, (3) the organization of the components to constitue the sentence. This new conception makes logical form different from grammatical form in logically perspicuous artificial languages. Sentences which have the same grammatical form can have different logical forms. But there is no opposition between the two forms. Grammatical form is not misleading with respect to logical form; logical form is just a further specification of grammatical form.

The grammatical form of a sentence can also be called its syntactic structure. This is not a semantic feature of the sentence. We can describe the grammatical form of a sentence without mentioning meaning or truth conditions. The logical form of a sentence is not a semantic feature either. But it is not appropriate to call logical form a syntactic feature. Those views which have identified logical form with some linguistic feature have frequently described logical form as syntactic. But those views take the syntactic and the semantic to exhaustively divide what is linguistic. In the present conception there is room for a nonsemantic logical form which is not syntactic either. Even though logical form is nonsemantic, our reason for paying attention to logical form is semantic. Logical form provides us with a nonsemantic way to characterize semantically distinguished items. We should note that a sentence has more than one grammatical form. A sentence $[A \& [B \& C]]$ shares a grammatical form with $[A \vee B]$ as well as with $[A \vee [C \supset D]]$. $[A \& [A \& A]]$ also has forms in common with $[A \& [B \& C]]$ and with $[A \vee B]$. The different grammatical forms of a sentence are more and less specific forms; we describe a less specific form by giving less than all the structure of the sentence. As well as having multiple grammatical forms, a sentence has multiple logical forms. When we speak of *the* grammatical form or *the* logical form of a sentence, we ordinarily mean the most specific form (relative to a certain kind of analysis). Not every sentence will contain a distinctively logical expression. For sentences that do not, their grammatical and logical forms coincide. For sentences that do contain distinctively logical expressions, their grammatical forms are included among their less specific logical forms.

Although neither logical nor grammatical form is conceived as a semantic feature, both forms have semantic significance. We can describe a syntactic form in a completely nonsemantic way. We can then ask what are the semantic features common to all sentences which have that form. In order to describe this more carefully, I will distinguish *uninterpreted* logical and grammatical forms from *interpreted* forms. When I speak of these forms without some qualification, I intend the uninterpreted forms. To understand the relation between the two sorts of form, we must understand that the present conception of language is in some ways the reverse of more familiar conceptions. The ordinary logical and linguistic conception has a language built up in "layers." First a syntactic system is obtained. Then meaning is piled on top of this system. Finally we get people talking. In the present conception, the basic linguistic reality is linguistic activity. Language primarily exists in the linguistic acts and linguistic skills of the language-using community. We can abstract from some features of the linguistic reality to concentrate on others. We do this, for example, when we consider expressions apart from acts. Semantics is an abstract study that treats expressions as having meanings and truth values; in reality it is linguistic acts which have these properties. It takes at least one abstraction to get semantics. It takes a further abstraction to move from semantic features to logical and syntactic forms. We ignore meaning and truth conditions in focusing on nonsemantic structure. But a grammatical form still has a meaning, even though we are ignoring it. An interpreted grammatical form is the meaningful structure of a sentence. It is the component of the sentence's meaning that is provided by its organization. (This conception is most appropriate for natural languages. Artificial languages are here being conceived on the model of natural ones.)

Logical semantic features are those which can be traced to interpreted logical forms. Some logical forms are such that a sentence's having the form is sufficient for the sentence's being analytic. A logically true sentence is a sentence which has such a form. Even though it is possible, in my conception of analyticity, for an analytic sentence to be false, this does not seem to possible for logical truths. Controversy surrounding the law of excluded middle does not show that a logically true sentence might be false, or even that we might be led to abandon a previously logically true sentence. The situation is too complicated to discuss thoroughly in this place. Part of the difficulty is caused by confusing truth conditions with justification conditions. Other problems arise from confusion about two truth-valued languages and three truth-valued languages. There are some situations in which we are working with a language (or a sublanguage) in which some sentences are neither true nor false. The law of excluded middle does not hold for those languages. In other situations, we either idealize and treat the language as if every sentence were true or false, or we are working with a language in a context where we know that every sentence is true or false. In those situations the law of excluded middle is acceptable, and logically true.

I have distinguished logical and grammatical forms in artificial logical languages. However, I believe that exactly the same distinction can be drawn for natural languages. It is possible to develop an adequate account of the syntactic structures of natural language sentences. These structures are not misleading with respect to philosophical and logical analyses. Logical forms of natural-language sentences are the further specifications of grammatical forms, which result from taking account of distinctively logical expressions. In subsequent chapters, I will outline an account of grammatical form that is applicable to English. This will not be a detailed syntactic account of the whole English language. I will provide enough details both to make myself understood, and to enable the readers to see that and how further details can be filled in. To do this, I will adopt the artificial language strategy of modern logic. In recent times, first-order languages and related languages have been used as canonical languages for the purpose of carrying out logical analyses. Syllogistic languages were used in the same way in Aristotelian logic. I will develop different artificial languages; these are designed to be syntactically more similar to English than are first-order languages.

The employment of artificial logical languages has in the past reinforced the view that there is an opposition between the logical and grammatical forms of a sentence. The forms that were opposed were the forms of distinct but roughly equivalent sentences—one in the artificial language and one in the natural language. However, there is no reason why an artificial language must be syntactically different from the natural language it is used to analyze. If the two languages are syntactically similar, there will be no temptation to recognize a form that lurks behind deceptive grammatical appearances. An artificial language is well suited for giving syntactic analyses of natural-language sentences. The artificial language is more perspicuous than a natural language by virtue of being much simpler than the natural language. Instead of confronting a natural language in all its complexity, we can study various features of the natural language by incorporating them in the artificial language one or two at a time.

4. Additional Problems

I have proposed a new understanding (a new definition) of the expression 'logical form' and a new distinction between logical form and grammatical form. Objections that have been, and can be, made to this new distinction, were not framed with it in mind, but they do apply to it. The first objection concerns the class of distinctively logical expressions. In order for the new conception of logical form to have an application, there must be such a class. However, some doubts have been raised about the existence (the nonemptiness) of such a class. In [9], Tarski argued that there are no clear criteria for separating distinctively logical expressions from other expressions. Although Tarski's argument was made in 1935, there is still no clear and universally acknowledged criterion for a logical expression. But there are shared intuitions that expressions such as 'or,' 'and,' and 'every' have a common character (or a family resemblance) which other expressions (e.g., 'blue,' 'shrill') clearly lack. The absence of a sharp dividing line would be no argument against the distinction; nor would it be a barrier to the formulation of an adequate account of the distinction. Apart from intuitions, evidence for the distinction is provided by numerous successful and useful logical theories. These theories isolate a relatively small class of expressions, upon which they are based. It is true that these expressions belong to artificial languages, but the meanings of these expressions can be explained in natural languages. Natural-language expressions whose meanings are very close to meanings of artificial logical expressions can lay claim to being distinctively logical expressions. In subsequent chapters, I will provide the resources for characterizing distinctively logical expressions. Even without this, we have good reasons for holding that there are distinctively logical expressions.

A second objection to the new conception of logical form does not deny that there are distinctively logical expressions. This objection admits that sentences have logical forms as I conceive them, and that various semantic features are associated with logical form. This objection claims that logical form has no intrinsic interest. We isolate logical form in order to "get at" the special logical cases of general semantic features. Logically true sentences are the logical special case of analytic sentences; logical implication is the logical special case of entailment. We focus on these logical features by default. If we had a systematic and thorough account of analytic sentences, there would be little interest in singling out those analytic sentences that are logically true. Katz seems to have such an objection in mind when he argues (in [6] and [7]) that his semantic theory is superior to logical theories. He often mixes this argument with different, and erroneous, arguments. But Katz foresees that his semantic theory will attribute no special importance to the class of distinctively logical expressions. Even if sentences have logical forms in my sense, these forms have little theoretical importance. They are not worth noticing.

This second objection raises an important point; the objection is not entirely wrong. If there were a successful semantic theory in which logical expressions played no special role, then logical form would no longer be important. But the greater accessibility of logical semantic features is not simply an historical accident; it will not be eliminated by a successful semantic theory. This greater accessibility is due to the essential character of logical expressions. A proper understanding of the distinctive character of these expressions will yield an explanation of why logical semantic features are more accessible than their more general counterparts. They will retain this greater accessibility after the development of successful semantic theories—elementary classes in logic will not give way to classes in semantic theory. The accessibility and the utility of logical form is surely due to logical expressions being associated with the most general aspects of the system of language (of our conceptual framework). Their general, and fundamental, character is brought out by the fact that any valid argument can be "reduced" to a logically valid argument by supplying additional analytic premises.

Bibliography and References

1. Alonzo Church. *Introduction to Mathematical Logic.* Princeton, New Jersey: Princeton University Press, 1956.
2. Gottlob Frege. "Begriffschrift," *Translations from the Philosophical Writings of Gottlob Frege,* edited by Peter Geach and Max Black, pp. 1–20. Oxford: Basil Blackwell, 1966.
3. Gottlieb Frege. "Function and Concept," *Translations from the Philosophical Writings of Gottlob Frege,* pp. 21–41.
4. Gottlob Frege. "On Concept and Object," *Translations from the Philosophical Writings of Gottlob Frege,* pp. 42–55.
5. Jerrold J. Katz. *Semantic Theory.* New York: Harper & Row, 1972.
6. Jerrold J. Katz. "The Dilemma Between Orthodoxy and Identity," *Language in Focus,* edited by A. Kasher, pp. 165–175. Dordrecht, Holland: D. Reidel Publishing Company, 1976.
7. Jerrold J. Katz. "The Advantage of Semantic Theory Over Predicate Calculus in the Representation of Logical Form in Natural Language," *The Monist* 60 (1977): 380–405.
8. Bertrand Russell. "The Philosophy of Logical Atomism," *Logic and Knowledge,* edited by Robert C. Marsh, pp. 177–281. New York: The MacMillan Company, 1956.
9. Alfred Tarski. "On the Concept of Logical Consequence," *Logic, Semantics, Metamathematics,* pp. 409–420 Oxford: Oxford University Press, 1956.
10. Ludwig Wittgenstein. *Tractatus Logico-Philosophicus.* London: Routledge & Kegan Paul Ltd., 1958.

Chapter 7
Deep Structure, Surface Structure, Semantic Structure

1. Deep and Surface Structure

The linguists' distinction between deep and surface structure is similar in several respects to the philosophers' distinctions between logical and grammatical form. But the linguistic distinction is not associated with the logician's strategy of developing and using artificial languages to analyze natural ones.

The linguist holds that a natural-language sentence has more than one structure. Its most apparent structure is its surface structure. In describing this situation, it is not appropriate to use the philosopher's terminology. We do not want to say that the surface structure is the grammatical or syntactic form of the sentence. From the linguist's perspective, the sentence's different structures are all syntactic; its deep structure is as syntactic as its surface structure. The surface structure of a sentence is not adequate for the purpose of making certain linguistic analyses. These analyses are different from the philosophers' analyses, but there is some overlap between the two kinds. Surface structure does not provide an adequate basis for a semantic account of language. Sentences with the same surface structure display different semantic behavior, which seems to be due to more than differences in meaning of the component expressions. (Logical behavior is semantic behavior. If sentences with the same surface structure behave in logically different ways, this is a semantic difference.) A syntactic account which recognizes only surface structure also seems to be epistemically inadequate. A syntactic theory should render intelligible the fact that people produce and recognize grammatical sentences. An explanation of what it takes for a sentence to be grammatical should not be so complicated that ordinary language users cannot understand it. Apparently it is difficult to formulate a suitably simple syntactic theory based solely on surface structure.

Linguists have introduced deep structures to overcome the shortcomings associated with surface structure analyses. The deep structure of a sentence "belongs" to the sentence, but it is not really in that sentence. Our discussion of deep and surface structures, and a comparison of the linguists' distinction with the philosophers' distinctions, is complicated because there are two meanings of 'structure.' In its first meaning, a structure is the form of an object. Structure-as-form is the way the parts of an object are organized to constitute the object (structure-as-form also "incorporates" the kinds of objects that are organized—a given structure might be one in which an object of kind *a* is related by *R* to an object of kind *b*). In its second meaning, a structure is an object which has a structure in the first sense. In discussing the philosophers' accounts of grammatical form or syntactic structure, we were considering the forms of sentences. The grammatical form of a sentence is determined by the syntactic categories of component expressions, and the organization of the components to constitute the sentence.

The linguists' structures are structures in the second sense. A sentence of a natural language is either a spoken or a written object (either a complex acoustic event or an inscription). We can distinguish types of sentences from tokens. The token is an actual physical object, while the type is an abstract representative of the tokens. Surface structures are ingredients of neither types nor tokens. The surface structure is an object distinct from the sentence. It is like a different expression, with its own form. The picture of linguistic activity that is operative here is the following: a speaker utters a sentence, but before he produces the sentence, he produces a distinct object, the surface structure. The surface structure is the input for the speech-producing device (or algorithm); the surface structure goes in and the spoken sentence comes out. (Actually, we can divide this process still further. The surface structure goes into one device; that device produces a phonetic representation. This representation is the input into the speech-producing device.) Not all linguists think that deep and surface structures have psychological or epistemic reality. Some do—Chomsky does. Regardless of whether such reality is attributed to the surface structure, the picture I have drawn is the one needed to understand the difference between a sentence and its surface structure, as well as the relation between them.

The surface structure of a sentence is not an expression, but it is analogous to one. The form of a surface structure is very important; this makes it convenient to use tree diagrams to represent surface structures. (Someone who denies psychological reality to surface structures could identify surface structures with tree diagrams. For such a person, surface structures would be linguistic objects—but they would belong to an artificial language.) Psychological (or epistemic) considerations aside, it would not be a radical shift to stop thinking of surface structures as objects distinct from sentences, conceiving them instead as the forms of sentences. From this perspective a tree diagram would show how the corresponding sentence is put together. We might do this for the surface structure of a sentence, but we cannot do it for the sentence's deep structure. For the deep structure is like still another sentence, with a different form from that of the surface structure. The deep structure with its form is transformed to yield the surface structure and, ultimately, the sentence.

The deep structure of a sentence is not itself a sentence—at least, it is not supposed to be one. But there is no other way to conceive of deep structures. Linguists talk about deep structures as if they were sentences, and they use sentences to illustrate the operation of transformations. Even when a representation which emphasizes form is used, it is like a two-dimensional sentence. Deep structure in linguistic accounts plays a role analogous to that of logical form in philosophers' accounts. The reason why surface structure is misleading in various ways is that the same surface structure can "cover" different deep structures. The deep structure of a sentence is the level at which meaning is introduced—the semantic behavior of a sentence is determined by its deep structure. (Deep structure itself is syntactic; but it is the deep structure that gets a semantic interpretation.) The linguists' view of deep structure is quite similar to view (3) that was described in connection with the philosophers' distinctions between grammatical form and logical form. In this view, the artificial-language sentence has no form in common with the natural-language sentence that it translates. But the artificial sentence is helpful for dealing with the natural sentence. In the linguists' view, the deep structure has a form it shares with neither the surface structure nor the sentence. We use the deep structure to understand and explain features of the sentence (or sentences) it lies beneath.

The fact that philosophers are concerned with an explicitly artificial language while the linguists aren't is not such an important difference between them. Using roughly the same strategy to solve their various problems, they conceive the relation between the instrument of analysis and the sentence that gets analyzed in much the same way. But the linguists are ahead of the philosophers in an important respect. The philosophers simply rely on their understanding of the natural and artificial languages in making their translations and carrying out their analyses. The linguists have been concerned to present detailed transformation rules for taking deep structures to surface structures (as well as trying to explain how surface structures get turned into sentences). Their accounts aim at giving a much fuller understanding than the philosophers' accounts do.

Original attempts to explain linguistic phenomena in terms of deep structures, surface structures, and transformation rules encountered various difficulties. It was originally thought that semantic interpretation should take place exclusively at the level of deep structure. This requires that transformations taking deep structures to surface structures be meaning-preserving. Subsequently it has been allowed that some transformations can affect the meanings of the transformed objects. This opens the way to new kinds of transformations—but makes the job of giving a semantic account more difficult. Chomsky has also felt the need to introduce still another object with a form intermediate between deep and surface structures. He thinks of this intermediate level as the place where the purely linguistic semantic content of a sentence is fixed. He has proposed that the expression 'logical form' be used for this intermediate object. This is quite a different use from the philosophers' uses, as well as from the use I have adopted. Chomsky has it that the logical form is an object with a form rather than the form of an object. But his logical form is the object that is important for a semantic understanding of the natural-language sentence. The relation between his logical form and his deep structure is at least analogous to the relation I recognize between my logical form and grammatical form. (But it isn't clear that Chomsky thinks there is a class of distinctively logical expressions which helps to distinguish logical form from deep structure.) However, there is no reconciling the two uses of 'logical form.' As I understand the relevant expressions, both grammatical forms and logical forms are forms of natural-language sentences.

2. Abandoning the Linguist's Picture

There are two ways in which someone might construe a linguistic theory admitting deep and surface structures. The first way conceives these structures as having psychological or physiological reality. The different structures either are or represent steps that a speaker goes through in producing his utterances. (But the speaker need not be aware of these steps.) The second conception denies that the various structures have any such reality. Linguistic theories which make use of the structures are simply devices for distinguishing grammatical from ungrammatical expressions. The "stages" in the theory do not correspond to anything that goes on in language users.

I will consider the first conception first. In this view, the sentences we speak and write "front" for what is truly significant. Spoken sentences are like coded messages. There are two sorts of codes. One sort contains codes like Morse Code that just transcribe one medium into another. With this kind of code, it is conceivable that we might use coded messages as our primary language. The second kind of codes is designed to conceal the message. It is not conceivable that coded messages of the second kind could be used as a primary language. We must always have a key to understand these codes; we must always decode the messages in the original language. In the view of deep and surface structures that I am considering, the sentences we speak and write are like messages in a concealing code. Of course, these messages are not intended to conceal their meanings. But we cannot understand them "on their own." We must take them back to their deep structures (or their intermediate structures) to make sense of them.

This view is analogous to the philosophical view that language serves to express thought—where thought is prior to and independent of language. In the philosophical view, language need not perspicuously reflect features of thought. And in the linguistic view, the significant structures may be "camouflaged" in the spoken sentences. The linguistic view is only analogous to the philosophical view, because deep structures need not be mental. However, just as the thought-behind-language view is incompatible with the present speech act theory, so is the significant-structure-beneath-the-finished-sentence view incompatible with the present theory. In the present account, it is the linguistic act which is the primary bearer of meaning. A complex meaningful act is literally constituted by meaningful component acts. A successful semantic theory must explain the meanings of expressions used to perform component acts and the meanings contributed by structures in such a way that we can determine the meanings of complex expressions. This is quite different from the linguist's conception. He thinks the semantically significant item is assembled at a deep level, then tinkered with to produce the actual sentence. Such a conception rules out a compositional semantic account for finished products. (A compositional semantic account for sentences must be based on surface structures. Deep structures have been invoked precisely because surface structures seemed inadequate for this task.)

Suppose we consider a linguistic theory involving deep and surface structures that is not combined with a claim that the structures have psychological reality. Merely an apparatus, this theory enables us to distinguish correct from incorrect expressions. It may provide a framework within which a semantic theory can be developed. I am unable to prove that no successful theory of this sort is possible, although I don't think it is possible. Even if such a theory were possible, and were in fact achieved, it would not be entirely satisfactory. What is wanted is a theory whose entities do have psychological reality. This would be a theory which handles both syntax and semantics, and reflects what people really do. The present speech act theory is intended to be of this kind.

3. Speech-Act Syntactic Structure

The present theory is an alternative to the transformational theories of linguists. I am proposing that syntactic analyses be based on the analyses of acts of using expressions—that syntactic structures be derived from speech act structures. We have recognized three fundamental structural relations between intentional acts:

(1) The relation between a component act and the complex defined by the purpose of its components.
(2) The relation between an enabling act and the act which it enables.
(3) The relation between a component act which gives a special character to a complex act and the complex act which (contains the component and) gets the character.

These relations are represented by tree diagrams. If component acts *A*, *B* have a purpose which defines complex act *Y*, we show this as follows:

(1) 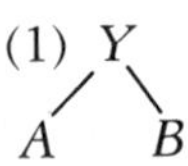

If *A* is an act which enables act *Y*, we use this diagram:

(2) 

And if *A* is a component act which gives a special character to complex act *Y*, we represent their relation as follows: (3) (*A* +) *Y*

A speech act is a meaningful act; the act itself is the bearer of meaning. In semantic studies, we consider expressions apart from acts, and attribute meanings to them. When we consider complex expressions, we analyze their structures. The structures of importance for semantic studies are the abstract versions of the structures of linguistic acts. When we consider interpreted structures, we can call them *speech-act semantic structures*. The (uninterpreted) syntactic structures of a sentence are its *speech-act syntactic structures*. Logical forms are also speech-act structures (*speech-act logical structures*). The same tree diagrams will be used to represent the structures of acts and the corresponding structures of expressions.

If we are concerned solely with the speech-act syntactic structure of a sentence, we might represent this with a tree diagram which contains labels for syntactic categories. The following diagram represents the syntactic structure of a sentence:

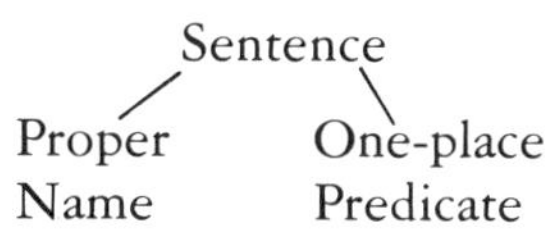

However, tree diagrams with names of categories written for the nodes are not well suited for showing multiple occurrences of a single expression. It is an important feature of this sentence:

(1) Judas killed Judas.

that 'Judas' occurs twice. If we used the following diagram to represent a speech-act syntactic structure of (1):

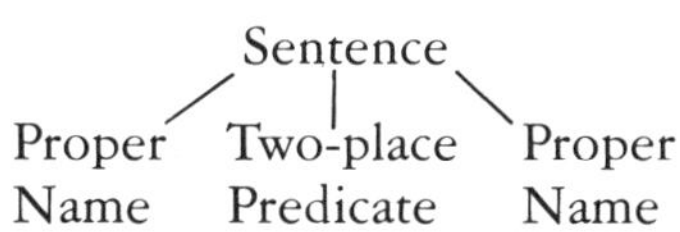

our diagram would not distinguish this structure of (1) from a structure of (2):

(2) Aaron Burr killed Alexander Hamilton.

Instead of combining tree diagrams with labels for syntactic categories, we could instead combine tree diagrams with formulas. We could then show the structure of 'Switzerland is mountainous' with a diagram like this:

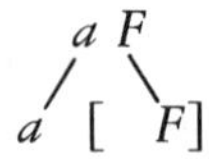

We could also combine labels and formulas:

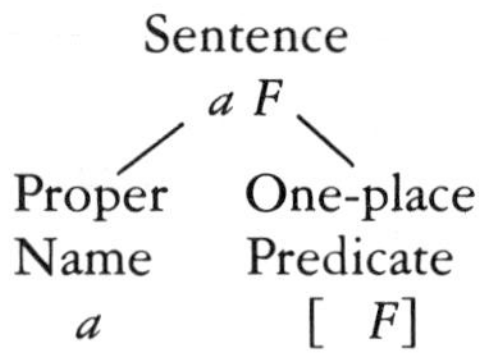

But this is unnecessary. The conventions for using formulas should be devised so that a given formula (or component of a formula) belongs to a uniquely determined category. The different structures of sentences (1) and (2) above can now be represented:

(1)
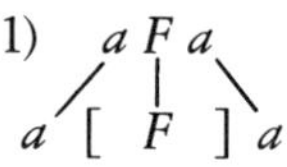

(2)
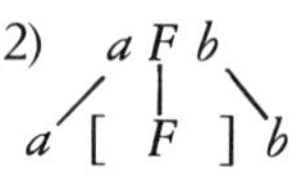

(It should be noted that this speech-act syntactic structure of (2) is also a structure of (1); the structure represented for (1) is not a structure of (2).)

Since we have adopted the logician's formulas for use in tree diagrams showing syntactic structure, I will borrow another logician's device. Instead of marking the empty places in a two-place predicate like this: [*F*], I will mark these with variables: *x F y*. So the diagrams for (1) and (2) will look like:

(1) 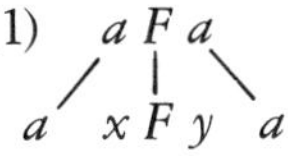

(2) 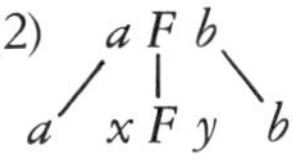

(On the conventions adopted, '*a*' and '*b*' represent names, while '*x*' and '*y*' simply mark empty places.)

The use of formulas in tree diagrams yields diagrams that show the syntactic structures of classes of expressions. We can also show the structure of one specific expression:

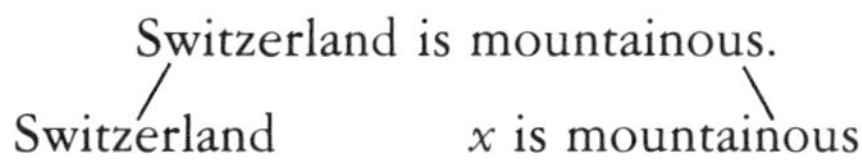

This diagram does more than give a syntactic structure of the sentence. It represents the "complete" speech act structure of the sentence (and the structure of acts of using the sentence). Given such a diagram, it is an easy task to determine the syntactic and logical structures of the sentence. In what follows I will normally employ tree diagrams which contain specific expressions.

A sentence or other expression has more than one syntactic structure. There are three ways in which this is possible. (1) With respect to a single style of structural analysis, and a single way of constituting the sentence (sentential act), the sentence has more and less general structures. In a first-order language, one sentence might be symbolized by all of these formulas: p, $p \phi q$, $p \phi (q \psi r)$. (The Greek letters correspond to connectives.) Using tree diagrams, one sentence (or sentential act) might have a structure represented by all of these:

This multiplicity of structures in a single sentence raises no theoretical problem. The different structures are not opposed to one another; they are simply more and less specific. We generally feel that an analysis which yields the most specific structure of a sentence is the most informative. But on a particular occasion, our reasons for examining a given sentence may allow us to be content with a superficial analysis. It can also happen that the goals of an investigation require that our analysis be carried at least to a certain level of specificity. Such practical considerations can produce an opposition between the different structures of a sentence. Some structures will be inadequate and so misleading with respect to the goals of the investigation. The examples that philosophers use to support their distinctions between grammatical form and logical form are analyzed too superficially to serve the philosophers' ends.

(2) With respect to a single style of structural analysis, a sentence may be constituted in different ways. These reflect the different ways that the sentential act can be performed. For example, we might represent the two acts described earlier in these ways:

```
          Switzerland is not landlocked.
               /                    \
    Switzerland              x is not landlocked

          Switzerland is not landlocked.
               /           |          \
    Switzerland            not  x is landlocked
```

With respect to each way of constituting a complex expression, there will be more and less general structures. There is no theoretical opposition between the structures which represent different ways of constituting the sentence.But a given sentential act can only have one such structure.

(3) A sentence has different forms with respect to a single style of analysis; it also has different forms with respect to different styles of analysis. In this book we shall be concerned with speech-act structures. These are abstract versions of the organizations of linguistic intentional acts. Given a written or spoken sentence, other analyses can lead to different structures. We might, for example, consider a written sentence to be obtained by concatenating the component expressions. We must not think that any one analysis will be correct or incorrect. Like different systems of classification, different styles of analysis can only be judged with respect to the purpose or purposes for which they are carried out. For our purposes, speech-act structures and the analyses which yield them will be most helpful. If important purposes are served by different styles of analysis, yielding different structures, there need be no conflict

between those analyses and mine, or between those structures and speech-act structures. But the other structures will undoubtedly be misleading with respect to the purposes served by considering speech-act structures. If the other structures were regarded as being useful for serving these same purposes, there would be an opposition between the other structures and speech-act structures.

Given the present conception according to which grammatical form is reached by abstracting from the structures of linguistic acts, problems can arise about identifying syntactic categories. We know that a single sentence can have more and less general syntactic structures. In a similar way, an expression can belong to more and less general syntactic categories. For a syntactic category might be subdivided into subcategories. How can we determine which are the "ultimate" syntactic categories (i.e., the narrowest categories)? If we consider English, adjectives are thought to constitute a syntactic category. But adjectives can be subdivided into (i) "absolute" adjectives, (ii) relative adjectives, and (iii) other adjectives. If α is an absolute adjective, a is an αF, and a is also a G, then a is an αG. This principle does not hold for relative adjectives like 'tall.' A tall child is also a person, but probably isn't a tall person. If α is either a class (i) or class (ii) adjective, and a is an αF, then a is an F. But the class (iii) adjectives include 'counterfeit' and 'former.' A counterfeit ten dollar bill is not a ten dollar bill; a former congressman is not a congressman. How can we decide whether the ultimate category is *adjectives*, or whether there are (at least) three ultimate adjective categories? It will not do to reject the three subcategories because they are distinguished on semantic grounds. For we do not begin with syntax and then add semantics; the semantic is prior. In the present conception there can be no definitive answer to a question about ultimate categories. On a given occasion, we stop at categories narrow enough to serve our purposes. For some investigations, we can consider all adjectives together. On other occasions we must recognize different adjective categories. But however narrowly we conceive our categories, they will be syntactic categories. (So logical forms are, after all, syntactic structures; but they aren't the most general syntactic structures. I will ordinarily reserve 'syntactic structure' for structures more general than logical forms.)

4. Speech-Act Structure Instead of Deep Structure

The present speech-act theory is incompatible with theories which recognize deep and surface structures. In order for the present theory to supplant those theories, it should explain why those theories often seem natural and intuitively plausible. For sentences where a deep structure explanation is illuminating, the speech-act explanation should prove equally enlightening. The speech-act theory should also be able to explain why deep structure explanations are useful without being correct. In this section I will discuss some examples that I will use to contrast deep structure and speech-act structure explanations. These examples are no substitute for a comprehensive survey of those sentences where a deep structure analysis is enlightening. But the examples are sufficient to convey the style of speech-act structural analyses. They do make intelligible my claims about the relations between the two kinds of analyses.

Let us first consider a sentence that Chomsky discussed in [1]:

(1) Jorge found the boy studying in the library.

(Chomsky's sentence didn't have 'Jorge' in it.) In [1], Chomsky says that the two meanings of (1) are due to two transformational routes from the same deep structure. It is conceivable that another theorist would explain the ambiguity by locating different deep structures. On the present account we want to explain what is going on with (1) without transforming any sentences into other sentences. Sentence (1) is especially easy to handle in terms of speech-act structures. It can be used to perform an act with this structure:

(2) Jorge found the boy studying in the library.

Jorge   *x* found *y*   the boy studying in the library

(The definite denoting act also has a structure. I am ignoring this structure because it isn't relevant to the ambiguity of (1).) Sentence (1) can also be used to perform an act with this structure:

(3) Jorge found the boy studying in the library.

Jorge   *x* found *y* studying in the library   the boy

(This time the predicative act has a structure which isn't fully explained.) The two kinds of act that can be performed with (1) are more than sufficient to explain the ambiguity.

My second example to illustrate the difference in styles between a deep structure account and a speech act account is rather contrived. This doesn't keep it from illustrating what I want. Consider the two readings which can be given to:

(4) Jesse, Robert shot.

The two readings have each person shooting the other. The one reading would be normal if (4) immediately followed:

(5) Robert stabbed Frank and Billy.

The reading where Jesse shot Robert probably requires that (4) occur in a poem, or some special literary context. Given a deep structure approach, we could explain one reading by deriving (4) from

(6) Jesse shot Robert.

The other reading is due to deriving (4) from

(7) Robert shot Jesse.

Instead of explaining the ambiguity of (4) by different (sentential) starting points and different transformations, we can explain the ambiguity by different ways of combining the same simple acts. We can represent an act which has Robert shooting Jesse this way:

(8) Jesse, Robert shot.
  Robert shot *y* Jesse
Robert *x* shot *y*

Reading up, the act of referring to Robert and the predicative act of using '*x* shot *y*' (or '[shot]') are both performed in order to perform the predicative act of using 'Robert shot *y*.' This predicative act denotes an individual that Robert shot. The predicative act and the act of referring to Jesse are both performed in order to assert that Jesse was shot by Robert. The act represented by (8) has the same basic structure as this act of using 'Robert shot Jesse':

(9) Robert shot Jesse.
  Robert shot *y* Jesse
Robert *x* shot *y*

The difference between (8) and (9) concerns word order. The prefixed position of 'Jesse' in (8) serves to highlight the prominence of the act of referring to Jesse, as compared to the act of referring to Robert.

An act of using (4) which has Jesse shooting Robert might have this structure:

(10) Jesse, Robert shot.

```
      (10)  Jesse, Robert shot.
              /              \
         Jesse shot y       Robert
          /        \
     Jesse       x shot y
```

The two lowest acts are performed in order to perform the predicative act denoting an individual that Jesse shot. This predicative act and the act of referring to Robert are performed in order to assert that Robert was shot by Jesse. Positioning 'Robert' immediately before the verb shows that the act of referring to Robert is more prominent (higher) than the (lower) act of referring to Jesse.

Someone might claim that the difference between deep structure explanations and my kind of speech-act explanations is slight. For we could probably describe a systematic procedure for turning deep structure explanations into speech-act explanations. In the case of (4), instead of starting with different deep structures and using different transformations, we simply incorporate these different deep structures and transformations in the speech-act structures of acts performed with (4). It seems probable that, in those cases where deep structure explanations are most illuminating, there will be a nearly one-to-one correlation between the deep structure explanations and the speech-act explanations. However, a speech-act analysis involves more than a trivial rewriting of a deep structure analysis; for one thing, it represents what is really going on when people use language. The speech-act framework provides a uniform framework for dealing with all aspects of language. Since intentional acts can be studied apart from speech acts, an understanding of these acts is heuristically helpful in dealing with language and linguistic acts. An example of this is provided by the three fundamental structural relations between intentional acts. Knowledge of these relations provides insight into features of language and linguistic acts.

5. English Adjectives

To illustrate how an understanding of intentional acts can be of help in considering syntactic structures, it is useful to (briefly) consider English adjectives and the acts of using them. There are three classes of adjectives in English. We shall begin with absolute adjectives. (If α is an absolute adjective, and β and γ are nouns, then any γ which is an $\alpha\beta$ is also an $\alpha\gamma$.) Consider the adjective 'round' in the phrase 'round barn.' We can suppose that this noun phrase occurs in the following sentence:

(1) George owns a round barn.

We wish to understand how the act of using 'round' is combined with other linguistic acts in using the sentence. It seems clear that the indefinite phrase constitutes a unit which is a component of the sentence. So that we need to understand how 'round' is used in an act of using 'a round barn.' For the present, we will ignore the function of the indefinite article. Its function will be considered later. The phrase 'round barn' is used, by itself, to represent a round barn—an arbitrary round barn. The indefinite article does not contribute to or affect this representing. For the deliberate language user, at least, and probably for many others, the act of using 'round barn' will be complex. The act of using each expression will be a distinct intentional act. We need to understand how these acts are related. It is characteristic of absolute adjectives that they represent "on their own." A round barn is something that is both round and a barn. This suggests that the typical representing act performed with 'round barn' has the following structure:

```
      round barn
      /        \
  round        barn
```

Each expression is used to perform a representing act. The adjective 'round' is used to represent an arbitrary round object (it does not represent the property roundness). And 'barn' is used to represent an arbitrary barn. Neither act represents an object *as* something or other, because neither is a predicative act. And the locution 'representing an individual *as* this or that' is being reserved for predicative acts. Both component acts are performed in order to represent an arbitrary round barn. Again, this is not represented as anything. Even though each component is used to perform a representing act, these two acts don't play the same role in the complex act. For it is the adjective which modifies the noun, not the other way around. When the adjective is combined with the noun to constitute a *nominal* act, the complex nominal act represents a barn *with* the property of being round. (In contrast to representing a barn *as* round.) The role of the adjectival act is to confer a property on the (component) nominal act. The component act, with its property, is the complex act; it represents an object with a property. Both a predicative and a nominal act can represent a propertied individual. The predicative act represents the individual as having the property; the nominal act merely represents the individual with the property. The difference between these two kinds of act is important, for only a complete predicative act can be asserted.

Let us call adjectives in the class which includes 'counterfeit' and 'former' *radical* adjectives. Consider the phrase 'former barn,' which might occur in a sentence like this one:

(2) George's restaurant is a former barn.

The speech-act analysis that works for 'round barn' will not work here. A former barn is not something that is both former and a barn. This means that the act of using 'former barn' does not have this structure:

```
       former barn
         /      \
   former        barn
```

This structure requires independent representing acts which can be combined to constitute a complex representation. In discussing intentional acts, we have recognized three fundamental structural relations between these acts:

(i) The relation between a component act and the complex act defined by the purpose of its components.
(ii) The relation between an enabling act and the act it is intended to enable.
(iii) The relation between an act which gives a special character to a second act and that second act.

Since the first structural relation does not apply to the act of using 'former barn,' we should consider the other two relations. Let us try the third relation. To do this, we might say that 'barn' is used to represent a barn, and 'former' is used to give a special character to this act of representing a barn. In that case the act of using 'barn' is a component of the complex act of using 'former barn.' But if 'former' serves to give a special character to the component act of using 'barn,' this should not prevent the complex act from representing a barn. For we would expect a specially characterized act of representing a barn to represent a special kind of barn.

But the complex act does not represent a kind of barn; a former barn need be a barn no longer.

The remaining possibility for understanding the act of using 'former barn' involves the relation between an enabling act and its enabled act. Trying this, we can say that 'barn' is used to represent a barn. The act of representing a barn enables the act of representing a former barn. It does this by providing material for the act of using 'former' to "work on." The enabled act represents a different individual than the enabling act, but representing a barn is essential to representing a former barn. The expression 'former barn' is not used to perform a complex act. Instead the two expressions are used to perform acts related like this:

```
former: barn
          ¦
         barn
```

Using 'barn' to represent a barn makes it possible to use 'former' to represent a former barn. When one act enables a second, the expression used to perform the enabled act is flanked by colons. If the structure above is imbedded in a larger tree structure, the colon is dropped when 'former barn' is repeated at higher nodes. As, for example, in:

```
        George owns a former barn.
          /        |          \
George     x owns y    a    former: barn
                                      ¦
                                     barn
```

The last class of adjectives consists of relative adjectives. Consider the relative adjective 'small' in the phrase 'small barn.' Now let the sentence be:

(3) George owns a small barn.

It should be completely obvious that I want to use the third structural relation to analyze the act of using 'small barn.' For it is the three structural relations which give rise to the three classes of adjectives. To "apply" the third structural relation, I will say that the act of using 'barn' is a component of the act of using 'small barn.' The act of using 'small' serves to give a special character to the act of using 'barn.' The component act with its special character (furnished by a different component act) *is* the complex act. One difference between the relative and the radical cases is that in the radical case ('former barn'), the representing of the initial nominal act is "wiped out" to give the representing of the enabled act. When we take the relative case, we "begin" with the act of representing a barn. Instead of "wiping out" this act, we modify it: we "cut it down." We end up representing a barn, but a barn that is qualified as opposed to a totally arbitrary barn.

When the speaker uses 'small,' she is not performing a representing act (with 'small' by itself). She performs a representing act with 'barn'—she takes 'barn' for a barn. And she performs a representing act with 'small barn.' She uses 'small,' by itself, to constitute 'small barn'—to constitute the act of representing a small barn. When we perform one act to give a special character to a second, we do not perform the one act in order to give a special character to the second. Performing the one act *is* (and is intended to be) giving the special character. Our speaker's act of representing a barn, with the act's special character, is the act of representing a small barn.

The present case of performing one act to give a special character to a second is unlike the cases we considered previously. In those cases, the "main" act was performed for one purpose; it was given a special character for a different purpose. But it makes no sense to think our speaker represents a barn for one purpose, and represents a small barn for some other purpose. When an act is given a special character on purpose, it can happen that the act, with its character, has two immediate purposes. But this is not required. The act with its special character need not have a purpose apart from its special character. (Alternatively, we might say that in some cases the act alone has the same purpose as the act with its special character.) We represent the use of the relative adjective this way:

(small +) barn

The expression used to give an act a special character is enclosed in parentheses and flanked with plus signs. (When the character-giving expression is at one end, it gets a single '+'.) The parentheses and plus signs are dropped when this expression is repeated at higher nodes of a tree diagram.

Bibliography and References

1. Noam Chomsky. *Syntactic Structures.* The Hague: Mouton & Co., 1957.
2. Noam Chomsky. *Aspects of the Theory of Syntax.* Cambridge, Massachusetts: The Massachusetts Institute of Technology Press, 1965.
3. Noam Chomsky. *Essays on Form and Interpretation.* New York: North-Holland, 1977.
4. Richard Montague. "English as a Formal Language," *Formal Philosophy, Selected Papers of Richard Montague,* pp. 188 – 221.

Chapter 8

The Language $\mathscr{L}$

1. A Simplification

The language $\mathscr{L}$ is an artificial logical language which incorporates some syntactic features of English. $\mathscr{L}$ is syntactically more similar to English than is a first-order language. It is not so similar as to be unduly complicated.

In developing an artificial language and using it in this way, I am following the historical practice of logicians since the time of Aristotle. This practice involves developing a perspicuous artificial language, studying its logical semantic features in great detail (often by means of deductive systems), and applying the artificial language to the analysis of a natural one. One difference between ancient and modern logicians concerns the use of nonverbal symbols. The use of nonverbal symbols is the defining characteristic of symbolic logic, but this difference does not make modern logic essentially different from ancient logic. The artificial-language strategy is the same. (The use of nonverbal symbols is an important contribution to perspicuity. Think what computation would be like if we used number words rather than numerals.) The artificial languages of syllogistic logic do not usually contain nonverbal symbols. But syllogistic logic deals with artificially simple languages, and imposes precise (and unnatural) interpretations on the logical expressions of these languages.

Customary first-order languages are unlike English in many respects. First-order languages have no plural forms, no tenses, no adjectives, no adverbs, etc. These differences can all be regarded as simplifications of first-order languages in comparison to English. The basic language $\mathscr{L}$ will share these simplifications. A difference between first-order languages and English that is a drawback to developing a speech-act account concerns *quantified noun phrases*—or, more simply, *quantified phrases*. In English and some other natural languages, quantified phrases (i) contain nouns and (ii) occur in the same positions in a sentence as proper nouns. For example,

(1) Tom sees Mary.
(2) Tom sees a girl.

are both good English sentences. In a first-order language, these sentences receive very different translations. They might come out as follows:

(3) $S(t, m)$
(4) $(\exists x)\ [G(x)\ \&\ S(t, x)]$

It has been maintained that the difference between (3) and (4) brings out the difference between the logical forms of grammatically similar English sentences. I have already rejected any such view. The fact that there is a bigger difference between (3) and (4) than there is between (1) and (2) shows that first-order languages are unlike English in their handling of quantified phrases. (In a first-order language, '$(\exists x)$' is a quantified phrase.) For many purposes, this difference between English and first-order languages is not so important. For my purposes, it is very important. I need an artificial language which is so constructed that a speech act theory of the artificial language will shed light on speech acts (and speech act structures) performed with English expressions.

In $\mathscr{L}$, I will change the first-order treatment of quantified phrases in two ways. (i) Quantified phrases will incorporate "nouns" (strictly, these are one-place predicate functors). So instead of '$(\forall x)$,' we will have '$\forall\phi x$' for a one-place functor ϕ. (ii) Quantified phrases can occupy the same positions that are occupied by names (by individual constants). But these phrases can also be prefixed in first-order style. Another difference between $\mathscr{L}$ and first-order languages concerns the "functional" style of writing sentences. In place of a first-order sentence $\phi(\alpha_1, \ldots, \alpha_n)$, we find an $\mathscr{L}$ sentence like this: $[\alpha_1\ \phi\ \alpha_2, \ldots, \alpha_n]$, for $n \geq 1$. (When n = 1, we have: $[\alpha_1\ \phi]$.)

In describing $\mathscr{L}$, I will follow the usual logical practice of giving both syntax and (real world) truth conditions. Initially, $\mathscr{L}$ will be interpreted in nonempty domains. Every sentence will be true or false.

2. The Syntax and Truth Conditions of $\mathscr{L}$

In describing $\mathscr{L}$, I will employ some familiar expressions in unorthodox ways. What are ordinarily called formulas, or well-formed formulas, are *predicates* for me. Sentences are a special case of predicates. What are ordinarily called predicates are *predicate functors*. So in the predicate:

$$[x\ F\ y,\ z]$$

'*F*' is the (three-place) predicate functor. I have made these changes to emphasize the difference between free variables and singular terms. Free variables only serve to mark argument places in the predicates of $\mathscr{L}$—they are not at all like names. The number of argument places a predicate has is the number of distinct free variables it contains. Their order is the order of the first free occurrences of the variables.

$\mathscr{L}$ contains the following simple ingredients:

(1) Punctuation: (,), [,], the comma: ,
(2) Individual constants (proper names): $a, b, c, a_1, \ldots$
(3) Individual variables: $x, y, z, x_1, \ldots$
(4) For every $n > 0$, n-place predicate functors: $F^n, G^n, H^n, F^n_1, \ldots$
(5) Two logical predicate functors: $=$ (a two-place functor), T (a one-place functor)
(6) Connectives: $\sim$, &, v, $\supset$
(7) Quantifiers: $\forall$, Λ, η, a, ι
(8) Passive voice symbol: $^{\cup}$
(9) Abstraction symbol: $\ni$

The predicate functors given by (4) and (5) above are *simple* predicate functors. (The predicate '$[x\ T]$' can be read "x is a thing.") If ϕ is a simple n-place predicate functor ($n > 0$), and $\alpha_1, \ldots, \alpha_n$ are distinct individual variables, then $[\alpha_1\ \phi\ \alpha_2, \ldots, \alpha_n]$ is an *atomic* predicate. So

$$[x\ F^1]$$
$$[x = y]$$
$$[y\ F^3\ z,\ x]$$

are atomic predicates, but

$$[a\ F^1]$$
$$[x = x]$$
$$[y\ F^3\ c,\ z]$$

are not.

In describing the syntax of $\mathcal{L}$, I will use *transformations* to generate complex expressions from simpler ones. These transformations are not borrowed from the linguistic theories I have rejected. I am using 'transformation' in its mathematical sense. A transformation is a function *from* certain expressions *to* an expression. I will later discuss the correspondence between these transformations and speech-act syntactic structure. For now they are to be regarded as an abstract device.

$\mathcal{L}$ will be interpreted in nonempty domains. Let $\mathcal{D}$ be nonempty. An *interpreting function of* $\mathcal{L}$ for $\mathcal{D}$ is a function f defined on the individual constants and the simple predicate functors of $\mathcal{L}$ which assigns an individual in $\mathcal{D}$ to each individual constant of $\mathcal{L}$ and assigns a set of n-tuples of individuals in $\mathcal{D}$ to each simple n-place predicate functor of $\mathcal{L}$. An interpreting function must assign $\mathcal{D}$ to 'T' and $\{<\alpha, \alpha>|\ \alpha \in \mathcal{D}\}$ to '='. If β is an individual constant, and $f(\beta) = \gamma$, then β *labels* γ *with respect to* f. If f assigns X to a functor ϕ, then ϕ *labels* each element of X (*with respect to* f). (If ϕ is n-place, then ϕ labels n-tuples. But if X is empty, then ϕ does not label anything.)

Let $[\alpha_1\ \phi\ \alpha_2, \ldots, \alpha_n]$ be an atomic predicate of $\mathcal{L}$. And let $f(\phi) = X$. Then the *value of* $[\alpha_1\ \phi\ \alpha_2, \ldots, \alpha_n]$ *for* f is X. We will also write this: $f[\alpha_1\ \phi\ \alpha_2, \ldots, \alpha_n] = X$. A predicate which has a set as its value for f also *labels* the elements of the set (if there are any) *with respect to* f. (But a sentence does not label.)

In describing transformations, I will first explain the syntactic aspect of a transformation. Then I will give an informal account of its semantic effects. Following this will be a precise and careful statement of the transformation's effect on the value of the transformed expressions (with respect to f). The careful statement will be italicized; the reader can omit these italicized sentences without loss of continuity.

The first three transformations are the simplest. (1) The *reflexive* transformation takes a predicate A into A' by replacing free occurrences of a variable α by occurrences of another variable occurring free in A. This replacement is not allowed if the variable replacing α would become bound at any of the places where α is free. As an example, the atomic predicate '$[x = y]$' is transformed into '$[y = y]$' by the reflexive transformation. This result is not an atomic predicate; it is a one-place predicate where the atomic predicate was two-place. The predicate '$[x = y]$'

labels every pair $< \beta, \beta >$, but '$[y = y]$' does not label pairs at all. The predicate '$[y = y]$' labels every individual in the domain. The reflexive transformation reduces the number of argument places in a predicate by one, but it cannot reduce the number to zero. The significance of the transformation should be clear; it takes a predicate like 'x hit y' into 'x hit x-self.'

The *canonical order* of the distinct individual variables occurring free in a predicate is the order of the first free occurrence of each variable. For transformations (1) - (9a), the initial predicate will be A, and the result of the transformation will be A'. The distinct individual variables occurring free in A, in canonical order, are $\alpha_1, \ldots, \alpha_n$. And $f(A) = V$. (In this case, A labels the members of V.)

Let A' be obtained by the reflexive transformation, by identifying α_i and α_j $(i < j)$. (It doesn't matter whether it is α_i that replaces α_j, or α_j that replaces α_i.) Then $f(A') = V' = \{< d_1, \ldots, d_{n-1}> | < d_1, \ldots, d_{j-1}, d_i, \ldots, d_{n-1}> \in V\}$.

(2) The *individual* transformation takes a constant β and the predicate A into A'. This transformation replaces the free occurrences of individual variable α_i $(1 \leqslant i \leqslant n)$ by occurrences of individual constant β. It reduces the number of free variables in a predicate by one, and can take an open predicate (together with a constant) to a sentence.

Let $f(\beta) = e$. Then if $n > 1$, $f(A') = V' = \{< d_1, \ldots, d_{n-1}> | < d_1, \ldots, d_{i-1}, e, \ldots, d_{n-1} > \in V\}$. If $n = 1$, $f(A') = t(ruth)$ iff $e \in V$. *(Otherwise, $f(A') = f$.)*

(3) The *variable* transformation has no semantic effect. Its only purpose is to make it possible for predicates to contain both free and bound occurrences of a single variable. It is not clear that this is an intrinsically desirable feature, but it is common in formal languages. This transformation takes A into A' by replacing the free occurrences of α_i $(1 \leqslant i \leqslant n)$ by occurrences of an individual variable β which does not occur free in A. This replacement is not allowed if β would become bound at any place where α_i is free. $f(A') = f(A) = V$.

The quantifiers are used to form *quantified phrases*. For each quantifier, there are two kinds of quantified phrase. If Q is a quantifier and ϕ is a one-place predicate functor, then $Q\phi$ is a *plain* quantified phrase. If α is an individual variable, then $Q\phi\alpha$ is an *indexed* quantified phrase.

(a) '$\forall$' is the *universal* quantifier. So $\forall\phi$ and $\forall\phi\alpha$ are *universally* quantified phrases.

(b) 'Λ' is the *mathematician's universal* quantifier. $\Lambda\phi$ and $\Lambda\phi\alpha$ are *mathematically* quantified phrases.

(c) 'η' is the (universal) *negative* quantifier. $\eta\phi$ and $\eta\phi\alpha$ are *negatively* quantified phrases.
(d) 'a' is the *indefinite* quantifier. $a\phi$ and $a\phi\alpha$ are *indefinitely* quantified phrases.
(e) 'ι' is the *definite* quantifier. $\iota\phi$ and $\iota\phi\alpha$ are *definitely* quantified phrases.

The transformation which applies each of these five kinds of quantified phrase to a predicate is subdivided into three transformations. These are exactly parallel for each of the five quantifiers; I will explain them in detail only for the universal quantifier.

(4) Let ϕ be a one-place predicate functor which has no free individual variables in common with A.

(4a) Then $\forall\phi\alpha_i\ A\ (= A')$ is obtained from $\forall\phi, A$ by the *universal* transformation. (For (4a), (4b), (4c), $1 \leqslant i \leqslant n$.)

(4b) If the first free occurrence of α_i in A is within the scope of no operators in A, then A' is obtained from $\forall\phi, A$ by replacing the first free occurrence of α_i in A by $\forall\phi\alpha_i$. A' is obtained from A by the *universal* transformation.

(4c) If there is only one free occurrence of α_i in A, and this is within the scope of no operator in A, then A' is obtained from $\forall\phi, A$ by replacing the single free occurrence of α_i by $\forall\phi$. A' is obtained from A by the *universal* transformation.

It is important to note that quantifiers, connectives, the passive voice symbol, and the abstraction symbol are all operators. So if we have a predicate '$\sim[x\ G]$,' we *cannot* obtain '$\sim[\forall F\ G]$' by the universal transformation. For the single free occurrence of 'x' in '$\sim[x\ G]$' is within the scope of the negation sign. We *can* obtain '$\forall Fx \sim[x\ G]$' from '$\sim[x\ G]$' by the universal transformation. We can also begin with the atomic predicate '$[x\ G]$' (numerical superscripts on predicate functors will normally be omitted by way of abbreviation), and obtain '$[\forall F\ G]$' by the universal transformation. Then we can obtain '$\sim[\forall F\ G]$' by the negation transformation (which is explained below). In $\mathcal{L}$ it is not possible to regard the scope of every operator as a complete expression. Instead we determine when an occurrence of a symbol is *within the scope of* an operator. When a quantified phrase is prefixed to a predicate or inserted within the predicate, every symbol in the predicate which is to the right of the quantifier is within the scope of the (occurrence of the) quantifier. In '$\forall Fx\ [x\ G]$,' even the occurrence of 'F' is within the scope of the universal quantifier.

In an indexed quantified phrase $Q\phi\alpha$, α is the *operator variable.* The displayed occurrence of α in an occurrence of $Q\phi\alpha$ is the *operative occurrence* of α in the quantified phrase. The operative occurrence of the operator variable is bound by the quantifier in a quantified phrase. So are the previously free occurrences of the operator variable that are to the right of the operative occurrence. In '$\forall Fx$ [*x G*],' both occurrences of '*x*' are bound occurrences. In '[$\forall Fx$ *H x*],' both occurrences of '*x*' are also bound occurrences. But if ϕ is a complex one-place functor containing free occurrences of α, those free occurrences are not bound in a predicate $\forall\phi\alpha$ *A*—the free occurrences are within the scope of the quantifier, but not bound by the quantifier. (Complex one-place predicate functors are introduced by the relative clause transformation; this is explained below.) If we begin with atomic predicate '[*x G y, z*],' we can apply the reflexive transformation to obtain '[*x G y, y*].' The universal transformation yields '[*x G* $\forall Fy$, *y*].' Finally the variable transformation gives '[*y G* $\forall Fy$, *y*].' This predicate contains both free and bound occurrences of the variable '*y*.'

When a quantified phrase is applied to a predicate to yield a sentence, all three transformations have the same effect. To illustrate these transformations, I will use capital letters as if they were predicates of $\mathscr{L}$. If '[*x P*]' means *x is a person* and '[*x M*]' means *x is mortal*, we can say that every person is mortal by writing '$\forall Px$ [*x M*].' (The preferred reading for this sentence is "For every person *x*, *x* is mortal.") We can say the same thing by writing '[$\forall Px$ *M*].' ("Every person *x* is mortal.") Even better is '[$\forall P$ *M*].' ("Every person is mortal.") The universal quantifier has existential significance. A sentence $\forall\phi\alpha$ *A* is false if there are no ϕ's. If '[*x K y*]' means *x knows y*, we can say that every person knows himself/herself by writing either '$\forall Px$ [*x K x*]' or '[$\forall Px$ *K x*].' But we cannot use '[$\forall P$ *K x*].' This says that every person knows *x*. Since '*x*' is a free variable in '[$\forall P$ *K x*],' this expression is a one-place predicate—it is not a sentence. (The predicate labels those individuals known by everyone. With any ordinary sense of 'know,' the predicate will not label anything.)

If ϕ is a one-place predicate functor containing free occurrences of individual variable β, and *A* is an *n*-place predicate for $n > 1$, then the quantifier transformations which prefix a quantified phrase can have a different semantic effect than the transformations which insert a quantified phrase. The canonical order of free individual variables is determined by their first free occurrences in a predicate. Suppose ϕ contains free occurrences of a single individual variable '*y*.' Then $\forall\phi z$ [*x F z*] is a two-place predicate. The canonical order is: *y, x*. The predicate [*x F* $\forall\phi$]

is also a two-place predicate. But the canonical order of individual variables is: x, y.

For all the quantifier transformations, let the distinct free individual variables occurring in ϕ, in canonical order, be $\beta_1, \ldots, \beta_m$. (*This means that the predicate* $[\alpha_i \, \phi]$ *is an* $(m + 1)$*-place predicate.*) *Let* $f(A) = V$ *and* $f[\alpha_i \, \phi] = X$.

(4a) *Let* $A' = \forall\phi\alpha_i \, A$. *Then* $f(A') = V' = \{< d_1, \ldots, d_m, e_1, \ldots, e_{n-1}> \mid$ *there is an* $r \in \mathfrak{D}$ *such that* $< r, d_1, \ldots, d_m> \in X$ *and, for every such* r, $< e_1, \ldots, e_{i-1}, r, \ldots, e_{n-1}> \in V\}$. *In case* $m = 0$, $n = 1$, A' *is true iff there is an* $r \in \mathfrak{D}$ *such that* $r \in X$, *and* $X \subset V$.

(4b, c) *Let* A' *be obtained from* A *by replacing the first free occurrence of* α_i *by* $\forall\phi\alpha_i$, *or by replacing the single free occurrence of* α_i *by* $\forall\phi$. *Then* $f(A') = V' = \{< e_1, \ldots, e_{i-1}, d_1, \ldots, d_m, e_i, \ldots, e_{n-1}> \mid$ *there is an* $r \in \mathfrak{D}$ *such that* $< r, d_1, \ldots, d_m> \in X$ *and, for every such* r, $< e_1, \ldots, e_{i-1}, r, \ldots, e_{n-1}> \in V\}$. *In case* $m = 0$, $n = 1$, A' *is true iff* $X \neq \emptyset$ *and* $X \subset V$.

(5) The quantifier 'Λ' differs from '$\forall$' in admitting of vacuous truth. If there are no ϕ's, then $\Lambda\phi\alpha_i \, A$ is vacuously true. If there are ϕ's, then $\Lambda\phi\alpha_i \, A$ is true iff $\forall\phi\alpha_i \, A$ is true.

(5a) *Let* $A' = \Lambda\phi\alpha_i \, A$. *Then* $f(A') = V' = \{< d_1, \ldots, d_m, e_1, \ldots, e_{n-1}> \mid$ *For any* $r \in \mathfrak{D}$ *such that* $< r, d_1, \ldots, d_m> \in X$, *we have* $< e_1, \ldots, e_{i-1}, r, \ldots, e_{n-1}> \in V\}$. (*If there is no suitable* r, *then* V' *contains every* $(m + n - 1)$*-tuple of individuals in* $\mathfrak{D}$.) *If* $m = 0$, $n = 1$, *then* $f(A') = t$ *iff* $X \subset V$.

(5b, c) Let A' *be obtained from* A *by replacing the first free occurrence of* α_i *by* $\Lambda\phi\alpha_i$, *or by replacing the only free occurrence of* α_i *by* $\Lambda\phi$. *Then* $f(A') = V' = \{< e_1, \ldots, e_{i-1}, d_1, \ldots, d_m, \ldots, e_{n-1}> \mid$ *For any* $r \in \mathfrak{D}$ *such that* $< r, d_1, \ldots, d_m> \in X$, we have $< e_1, \ldots, e_{i-1}, r, \ldots, e_{n-1}> \in V\}$. If $m = 0$, $n = 1$, $f(A') = t$ *iff* $X \subset V$.

(6) The negative quantifier 'η' is read "no." So '$[\eta Px \, Kx]$' is "No person x knows x"—i.e., no person knows himself/herself. If 'a' names Alan, then '$[\eta P \, K \, a]$' is "Nobody knows Alan." The negative quantifier has no existential significance. If '$[x \, V]$' means x *is a vampire*, then '$[\eta V \, T]$' is true. (This is "No vampire is a thing"—i.e., no vampire exists.) So is '$[\eta T \, V]$'—"Nothing is a vampire."

(6a) *Let* A' *be* $\eta\phi\alpha_i \, A$. *Then* $f(A') = V' = \{< d_1, \ldots, d_m, e_1, \ldots, e_{n-1}> \mid$ *For any* $r \in \mathfrak{D}$ *such that* $< r, d_1, \ldots, d_m> \in X$, *we have* $< e_1, \ldots, e_{i-1}, r, \ldots, e_{n-1}> \notin V\}$. *If* $m = 0$, $n = 1$, $f(A') = t$ *iff* $X \cap V = \emptyset$.

(6b, c) *Let* A' *be obtained from* A *by replacing the first free occurrence of* α_i *by* $\eta\phi\alpha_i$, *or by replacing the single free occurrence of* α_i *by* $\eta\phi$. *Then* $f(A') = V' = \{< e_1, \ldots, e_{i-1}, d_1, \ldots, d_m, \ldots, e_{n-1}> \mid$ *For any* $r \in \mathfrak{D}$ *such that*

$< r, d_1, \ldots, d_m > \in X$, *we have* $< e_1, \ldots, e_{i-1}, r, \ldots, e_{n-1} > \notin V\}$. *If* $m = 0$, $n = 1$, $f(A') = t$ *iff* $X \cap V = \emptyset$.

(7) The indefinite quantifier 'a ' is read "a," "an," or "some." So 'aPx [x M],' '[aPx M],' and '[aP M]' are different ways to say that some person is mortal. The sentence '[$\forall P$ K aP]' is "Everyone knows someone," while '[aP K $\forall P$]' is "Someone knows everyone." The indefinite quantifier is used to say that at least one individual of the indicated kind has (or does) etc.

(7a) *Let* $A' = a\phi\alpha_i$ A. *Then* $f(A') = V' = \{< d_1, \ldots, d_m, e_1, \ldots, e_{n-1} > \mid$ *There is an* $r \in \mathfrak{D}$ *such that* $< r, d_1, \ldots, d_m > \in X$ *and* $< e_1, \ldots, e_{i-1}, r, \ldots, e_{n-1}, > \in V\}$. *If* $m = 0$, $n = 1$, $f(A') = t$ *iff* $X \cap V \neq \emptyset$.

The reader is left to supply the statement for (7b, c) *for herself.*

(8) The definite quantifier 'ι' is used to say that the one and only individual of the indicated kind is whatever. The (false) sentence '[ιV M]' is "The (sole) vampire is mortal." While '[$\eta P = \iota P$]' truly says that no one is the sole person.

(8a) *Let* $A' = \iota\phi\alpha_i$ A. *Then* $f(A') = V' = \{< d_1, \ldots, d_m, e_1, \ldots, e_{n-1} > \mid$ *There is exactly one* $r \in \mathfrak{D}$ *such that* $< r, d_1, \ldots, d_m > \in X$, *and for this* r *we have* $< e_1, \ldots, e_{i-1}, r, \ldots, e_{n-1} > \in V\}$. *If* $m = 0$, $n = 1$, then $f(A') = t$ *iff* $X = \{r\}$ *and* $r \in V$, *for some* $r \in \mathfrak{D}$.

The statement for (8b, c) *can be supplied by the reader.*

(9) The *negation* transformation is subdivided into two transformations.

(9a) This transforms A into $\sim A$ ($= A'$). Every symbol in A occurs within the scope of '$\sim$' in $\sim A$. Once a predicate $\sim A$ has been obtained by a negation transformation, no subsequent transformation can insert a quantified phrase into an argument place in A. Every free variable occurring in $\sim A$ is within the scope of an operator. $f(A') = V' = \{< e_1, \ldots, e_n > \mid < e_1, \ldots, e_n > \notin V\}$. If $n = 0$, $f(A') = t$ *iff* $f(A) = f$.

(9b) Let $[\alpha_1\ \phi\ \alpha_2, \ldots, \alpha_n]$ ($= A$) be a predicate in which α_1 is an individual symbol (i.e., α_1 is either an individual variable or an individual constant). Then $[\alpha_1 \sim \phi\ \alpha_2, \ldots, \alpha_n]$ ($= A'$) is obtained from A by the negation transformation. Every symbol to the right of the first '$\sim$' in A' is within its scope. This transformation can also be applied to a predicate $[\alpha_1 \sim \ldots \sim \phi\ \alpha_2, \ldots, \alpha_n]$, so long as α_1 is an individual symbol. This transformation puts '$\sim$' to the left of those '$\sim$'s already occurring. So we can iterate '$\sim$' in a sentence like '[$a \sim \sim F$].' If we begin with '[x M],' obtain '[$x \sim M$],' and then get '[$aV \sim M$],' we have "Some vampire is not mortal." This is false, but '$\sim$[a V M]' is true. The *subject* of the sentence is not within the scope of '$\sim$' in $[\alpha_1 \sim \phi\ \alpha_2, \ldots, \alpha_n]$.

Let the distinct free individual variables occurring in A, in canonical order, be $\beta_1, \ldots, \beta_m$. *Let* $f(A) = V$. *Then* $f(A') = V' = \{< e_1, \ldots, e_m > \mid < e_1, \ldots, e_m > \notin V\}$. *If* $m = 0$, *then* $f(A') = t$ *iff* $f(A) = f$.

(10) - (12) If A, B are predicates with no free individual variables in common, then the *disjunction, conjunction,* and *conditional* transformations yield (respectively) $[A \vee B]$, $[A \& B]$, $[A \supset B]$. Symbols occurring within both A and B are within the scope of the infixed connective. So if a predicate $[A \vee B]$, $[A \& B]$, $[A \supset B]$ contains free occurrences of an individual variable, no subsequent transformation can place a quantified phrase where the free variable occurs. Any such free variable occurs within the scope of an operator.

The restriction barring free variables common to both A and B blocks a transformation from '$[x\ F]$' and '$[x\ G]$' to '$[[x\ F] \supset [x\ G]]$.' However, '$[[x\ F] \supset [x\ G]]$' can be obtained by starting with '$[x\ F]$' and '$[y\ G]$,' obtaining '$[[x\ F] \supset [y\ G]]$' by the conditional transformation, and then obtaining '$[[x\ F] \supset [x\ G]]$' by the reflexive transformation. In $\mathcal{L}$, the only way to obtain multiple occurrences of a single free variable in a predicate is by using the reflexive transformation.

In $\mathcal{L}$, *the connectives have their normal truth-table significance.* (i) *Suppose A and B are both sentences. Then* (10) $f[A \vee B] = t$ *iff at least one of* $f(A) = t$, $f(B) = t$. (11) $f[A \& B] = t$ *iff* $f(A) = f(B) = t$. (12) $f[A \supset B] = t$ *iff either* $f(A) = f$ *or* $f(B) = t$. (ii) *Suppose A is a sentence and* $f(B) = \{< e_1, \ldots, e_n> \mid \ldots\}$—*where* $n > 0$. *Then* (10) *if* $f(A) = t$, *then* $f[A \vee B]$ *contains every n-tuple of individuals in* $\mathcal{D}$. *If* $f(A) = f$, *then* $f[A \vee B] = f(B)$. (11) *If* $f(A) = t$, *then* $f[A \& B] = f(B)$. *If* $f(A) = f$, *then* $f[A \& B] = \emptyset$. *(12) If* $f(A) = t$, *then* $f[A \supset B] = f(B)$. *If* $f(A) = f$, *then* $f[A \supset B]$ *contains every n-tuple of individuals in* $\mathcal{D}$. *Case* (iii) *in which B is a sentence and* $f(A) = \{< d_1, \ldots, d_m> \mid \text{---}\}$ *is similar to case* (ii). (iv) *Suppose* $f(A) = \{< d_1, \ldots, d_m> \mid \text{---}\}$ *and* $f(B) = \{< e_1, \ldots, e_n> \mid \ldots\}$. *Then* (10) $f[A \vee B] = \{<d_1, \ldots, d_m, e_1, \ldots, e_n> \mid < d_1, \ldots, d_m> \in f(A)$ *or* $< e_1, \ldots, e_n> \in f(B)\}$. (11) $f[A \& B] = \{< d_1, \ldots, d_m, e_1, \ldots, e_n> \mid < d_1, \ldots, d_m> \in f(A)$ *and* $< e_1, \ldots, e_n> \in f(B)\}$. *(12)* $f[A \supset B] = \{< d_1, \ldots, d_m, e_1, \ldots, e_n> \mid < d_1, \ldots, d_m> \notin f(A)$ *or* $< e_1, \ldots, e_n> \in f(B)\}$.

The sentence '$[\forall P\ K\ aP]$' says that everyone knows someone. '$[a P\ K \forall P]$' says that someone knows everyone. We can say that someone is known by everyone by writing '$aPx\ \forall Py\ [y\ K\ x]$.' This is equivalent to '$aPx\ [\forall P\ K\ x]$.' But we cannot put the indefinite phrase inside the predicate, for the free occurrence of 'x' in '$[\forall P\ K\ x]$' is within the scope of the universal quantifier. In English this problem is "solved" by using the passive voice. We will incorporate that solution in $\mathcal{L}$.

(13) The *passive voice* transformation does not take one predicate to another. Instead this transformation takes one two-place predicate functor to another—the resulting functor is complex. If ψ is a two-place

predicate functor, then $\breve{\psi}$ is obtained from ψ by the passive voice transformation. The passive voice transformation is not applied to a predicate functor within a larger predicate; it is applied only to a predicate functor "in isolation." In constructing a sentence which contains the functor $\breve{\psi}$, $\breve{\psi}$ must be obtained from ψ, and then serve as the functor of a predicate $[\alpha\ \breve{\psi}\ \beta]$ in which α, β are distinct individual variables.

If $f(\psi) = V = \{< d, e > | \ldots\}$, *then* $f(\breve{\psi}) = V' = \{< e, d > | < d, e > \in V\}$. *If* α, β *are distinct individual variables, then* $f[\alpha\ \breve{\psi}\ \beta] = V'$.

Using the passive voice we can say that someone is known by everyone by writing '$[aP\ \breve{K}\ \forall P]$.' This is *not* equivalent to '$[\forall P\ K\ aP]$.' It *is* equivalent to '$aPy\ \forall Px\ [y\ \breve{K}\ x]$,' which is equivalent to '$aPy\ \forall Px\ [x\ K\ y]$.'

For the *relative clause* transformation, we will incorporate the locution 'such that' into $\mathcal{L}$. The reading for '$\ni$' is "such that." This transformation allows us to form a complex one-place functor from a (less complex) one-place functor and a predicate. So we can talk about a ϕ such that whatever.

(14) Let ϕ be a one-place predicate functor. Let A be a predicate which contains no free variables in common with ϕ. Let A contain free occurrences of the distinct individual variables $\alpha_1, \ldots, \alpha_n$ $(n \geqslant 1)$ and no others—this is their canonical order. Let β be an individual variable which does not occur free in ϕ. Then $(\phi\alpha_i \ni A)$ is obtained from $[\beta\ \phi]$, A by the relative clause transformation. (Alternatively, this may be called the *abstraction* transformation.) The expression $(\phi\alpha_i \ni A)$ is a complex one-place predicate functor. Every symbol occurring in $\phi\alpha_i$ or in A occurs within the scope of (the occurrence of) '$\ni$.' In this functor, α_i is the *operator variable*; the displayed occurrence is the *operative occurrence* of α_i in $(\phi\alpha_i \ni A)$. The operative occurrence and every free occurrence of α_i in A are bound in $(\phi\alpha_i \ni A)$. The functor $(\phi\alpha_i \ni A)$ can be used to form a predicate $[\gamma\ (\phi\alpha_i \ni A)]$ in which γ is an individual variable not occurring free in $(\phi\alpha_i \ni A)$; it can be used to form a quantified phrase. (Although the first predicate formed with the functor $(\phi\alpha_i \ni A)$ must be one in which the subject is a variable which does not occur free in the functor, this variable can be replaced in subsequent transformations.)

A predicate $[\beta\ (\phi\alpha \ni A)]$ is read "β is a $\phi\alpha$ such that A." If '*a*' names Alan and '*b*' names Bonnie, then '$[a\ (Px \ni [x\ K\ b])]$' is "Alan is a person x such that x knows Bonnie"—i.e., Alan is a person who knows Bonnie. If '$[x\ L\ y]$' means x *loves* y, then '$[\forall(Px \ni [x\ K\ b])\ L\ b]$' is "Every person x such that x knows Bonnie loves Bonnie."

Let $\gamma_1, \ldots, \gamma_m$ *be the distinct individual variables occurring free in* ϕ, *in canonical order. Let* $f[\beta\ \phi] = X$ *and* $f(A) = V$. *Then* $f(\phi\alpha_i \ni A) = V' = \{< r, d_1, \ldots, d_m, e_1, \ldots, e_{n-1} > | < r, d_1, \ldots, d_m > \in X$ *and* $< e_1, \ldots, e_{i-1}, r, \ldots, e_{n-1} > \in V\}$. (And $f[\beta\ (\phi\alpha_i \ni A)] = V'$ also.)

3. Some Translations

$\mathcal{L}$ is much more convenient for translating English sentences than is a first-order language. $\mathcal{L}$ does not possess the resources for giving a syntactically similar translation for every English sentence, or even for every common English sentence. But $\mathcal{L}$'s translations are usually closer than the best first-order translations. And $\mathcal{L}$ comes naturally to a speaker of English.

Let us consider some examples. The sentence 'Nobody likes everybody' can be translated: $[\eta P\ L\ \forall P]$ where '$[x\ P]$' means *x is a person* and '$[x\ L\ y]$' means *x likes y.*

Suppose we try 'Bill is taller than everyone else in his class.' Then if 'b' names Bill, '$[x\ P]$' means *x is a person,* '$[x\ T\ y]$' means *x is taller than y,* and '$[x\ C\ y]$' means *x is in the same class as y,* we can use this:

$$[b\ T\ \forall(Px \ni [[x\ C\ b]\ \&\ {\sim}[x = b]])]$$

If '$[x\ B]$' means *x is bald,* '$[x\ K\ y]$' means *x is presently a king of y,* '$[x\ P]$' *means x is a person,* and 'c' names France, then

$$[\iota(Px \ni [x\ K\ c])\ B]$$

says that the present king of France is bald. This is false. The sentence

$$[\iota(Px \ni [x\ K\ c])\ {\sim}\ B]$$

says that the present king of France is not bald; this is also false. But

$${\sim}[\iota(Px \ni [x\ K\ c])\ B]$$

is true; this says it is false that the present king of France is bald.

Now let us consider relative clauses which contain free variables. The sentence 'Every man who owns a house must pay taxes on every house he owns,' can be translated with this vocabulary:

$[x\ M]$ - x is a man
$[x\ H]$ - x is a house
$[x\ O\ y]$ - x owns y
$[x\ P\ y]$ - x must pay taxes on y

The following seems to be an adequate translation:

$$[\forall(Mx \ni [x\ O\ \alpha H])x\ P\ \forall(Hy \ni [x\ O\ y])]$$

The variable 'x' in '$\forall(Hy \ni [x\ O\ y])$' is bound by the first universal quantifier.

The sentence 'The owner of some dog will be fined' is, strictly speaking, ambiguous. But one reading is highly unlikely. In the other reading, this sentence says there is a dog whose owner will be fined. If we use this vocabulary:

$[x\ D]$ - x is a dog
$[x\ P]$ - x is a person
$[x\ F]$ - x will be fined
$[x\ O\ y]$ - x owns y

we can translate the sentence:

$$\alpha Dx\ [\iota(Py \ni [y\ O\ x])\ F]$$

One relative clause can be contained in another. Let us try the sentence 'A man who knows a girl who has red hair knows Alan.' Using the obvious vocabulary, we can give this translation:

$$[\alpha(Mx \ni [x\ K\ \alpha(Gy \ni [y\ R])])\ K\ a]$$

Let us consider a case where prefixing a quantified phrase has a different semantic effect than inserting it in the sentence. Let '$(Px \ni [x\ K\ y]])$' be *is a person x such that x knows y.* And let '$[x\ L\ y]$' be *x loves y.* Then the predicate

(1) $\alpha(Px \ni [x\ K\ y])x\ [z\ L\ x]$

labels pairs $< d, e >$ such that e loves a person who knows d. The predicate

(2) $[x\ L\ \alpha(Px \ni [x\ K\ y])]$

labels pairs $< d, e >$ such that d loves a person who knows e. This difference between (1) and (2) is not very important. If the two predicates undergo the same subsequent transformations, they will yield equivalent sentences. (For subsequent transformations to be the "same" they must affect the same variables; if we identified transformations on the basis of their affecting the first or the second variable in canonical order, then the preceding sentence would not be true.)

The predicate functor '=' has its normal logical significance, identity. But '=' is used to make an identity statement only when used to connect two names. E.g., '$[c_1 = c_2]$' means that c_1 is the same individual as c_2. The sentence '$\mathit{a}Px\ [a = x]$' says there is some person with whom Anne is identical. When we move the quantified phrase inside, we get '$[a = \mathit{a}P]$.' This is just "Anne is a person." It happens that '$[a = \mathit{a}P]$' is equivalent to '$[\mathit{a}P = a]$,' but we do not always have such symmetry when quantified phrases flank the identity sign. The sentence '$[\forall P = \mathit{a}P]$' says that every person is a person—which is true. But '$[\mathit{a}P = \forall P]$' is false. This says that some one person is the same as everyone.

The possibility of moving quantified phrases inside predicates gives us sentences of $\mathcal{L}$:

$[a = \mathit{a}P]$
$[\mathit{a}P = \mathit{a}C]$
$[\forall C = \mathit{a}P]$

that closely parallel the corresponding English sentences:

Anne is a person.
Some person is a carpenter.
Every carpenter is a person.

This shows that we do not need different 'is's for predication and identification.

The predicate '$[x\ T]$' is read "x is a thing." So '$\forall T$' is "everything," 'ηT' is "nothing," and '$\mathit{a}T$' is "something." The mathematician's 'everything' is the same as the ordinary 'everything,' so long as the domain is nonempty—i.e., for nonempty domains, we have $[[\forall \mathrm{T}\alpha\ \mathrm{A}] \supset [\Lambda T\alpha\ A]]$ and $[[\Lambda T\alpha\ A] \supset [\forall T\alpha\ A]]$. The difference between using identity between names and between quantified phrases can be emphasized by some examples using 'T.' The sentence

$$[\forall T = \forall T]$$

is false unless the domain contains just one individual, even though identity is reflexive. The sentence

$$[\mathit{a}T = \forall T]$$

is also true only in a one-element domain, although

$$[\forall T = aT]$$

is true in all nonempty domains. And

$$[\Lambda T = aT]$$

is true in all domains, even empty ones. But

$$[aT = \Lambda T]$$

is not true in the empty domain. The sentences

$$[\eta T = \Lambda T]$$
$$[\Lambda T = aT]$$

are true in domains with two or more elements. But

$$[\eta T = aT]$$

is not true in those domains.

To really get a "feeling" for $\mathscr{L}$, readers are invited to pick some English sentences and translate them into this language. It is important in what follows that readers have a better understanding of $\mathscr{L}$ than can be obtained merely by reading my description.

4. Tree Diagrams

In previous chapters, tree diagrams were used to represent structural relations between intentional acts. In some cases a tree diagram represented the structure of a complex act. In others, the tree diagram represented the relation between distinct acts which don't constitute a complex act; instead, one of the distinct acts enables another.

In this chapter, I will use tree diagrams for a different purpose. Tree diagrams will be used to represent the transformational constructions of predicates (and sentences) of $\mathscr{L}$. Tree diagrams are used in this way to represent syntactic structure, but not speech-act syntactic structure. The syntactic account of the present chapter, which generates the predicates and sentences of $\mathscr{L}$, provides a framework on which we can hang accounts of the real world truth conditions of sentences of $\mathscr{L}$ and of the inferential meanings of sentences of $\mathscr{L}$. But this generative syntax does not furnish the basis for an account of representational meaning.

I will later consider how to alter this generative syntactic account to yield an account of the speech-act syntactic structure of sentences of $\mathscr{L}$. I will also consider how to use tree diagrams to represent the acts of using sentences of $\mathscr{L}$. For the present I will use tree diagrams only to represent the transformational constructions of sentences and predicates. And I will use only the kind of tree diagram in which different nodes are connected by solid lines. These tree diagrams begin at the bottom with atomic predicates, names, and quantified phrases, and "work up" toward sentences. The lines leading up to a node represent syntactic transformations. The nodes are the inputs and outputs of the transformations. For example, the sentence '[*a K b*]' might be obtained by this construction:

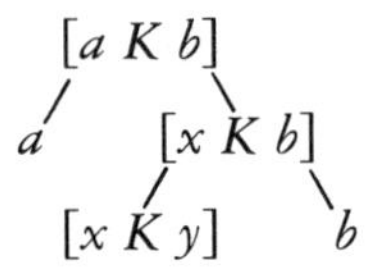

If we modeled the diagrams on proofs in a deductive system, we could label the nodes with the names of the transformations which yield them. But we won't do this; it will always be clear which transformation is involved.

When a transformation has one input, this input is directly below the output. The reflexive transformation is a one-input transformation. We diagram it as follows:

The variable transformation has a single input:

The negation transformations are also one-input transformations:

```
~[a F b]                    ~ ∀Tx [x = x]
    |                              |
 [a F b]                      ∀Tx [x = x]


[x ~ M]                     [a ~ ~ F ∀G]
   |                              |
[x M]                       [a ~ F ∀G]
```

The connective transformations have two inputs. The input which is to the left of the connective in the output is the left node of the input.

```
   [[a F] v [a G]]              [[x F y]  &  [z H]]
     /         \                    /             \
 [a F]        [a G]             [x F y]          [z H]


            [[x = y] ⊃ [y1 = x1]]
                /             \
          [x = y]           [y1 = x1]
```

When a transformation prefixes a quantified phrase, or introduces a name or quantified phrase into the subject position of a predicate, the quantified phrase or the name occupies the left input node.

```
     ∀Px [a L x]                   [∀Px L x]
     /          \                  /        \
  ∀P           [a L x]          ∀P        [x L x]


     [a L x]                       [a L a]
     /      \                      /      \
    a      [y L x]                a      [x L x]
```

When a name or quantified phrase is not introduced into the subject position, but is introduced into a position following the predicate functor, the name or quantified phrase occupies the right input node.

```
       [a L a]                      [a L ∀P]
       /     \                      /      \
  [a L x]     a                [a L x]     ∀P
```

The passive voice transformation will be represented this way:

```
    ∪
 [x F y]
    |
    F
```

This is understood as a transformation taking one predicate functor to another functor—the line connects only the functors. No transformation is required to incorporate a functor in a predicate. Once the transformed functor is available, it can be flanked by variables. The passive voice transformation can be iterated:

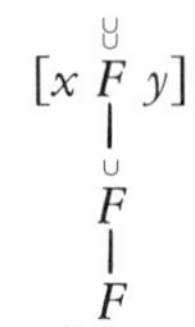

The relative clause transformation also yields a predicate functor rather than a predicate. We can represent it this way:

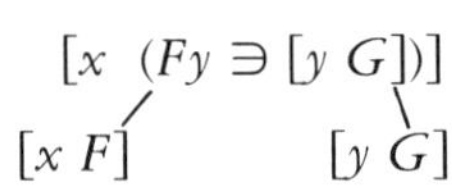

The inputs are to the predicate functor, not the whole predicate. A relative clause functor can also occur in a quantified phrase. We represent this as follows:

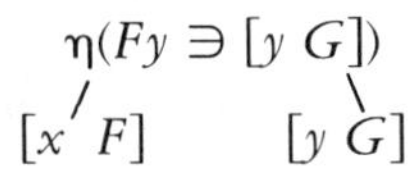

Combining a functor with a quantifier does not require a transformation.

The diagrams of sentences can easily get fairly complicated. Some examples are below:

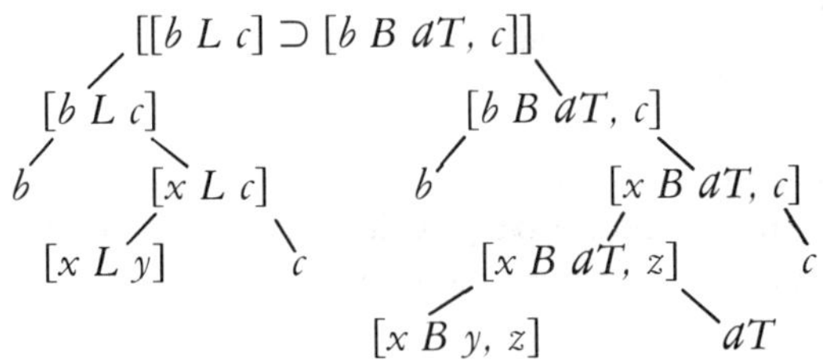

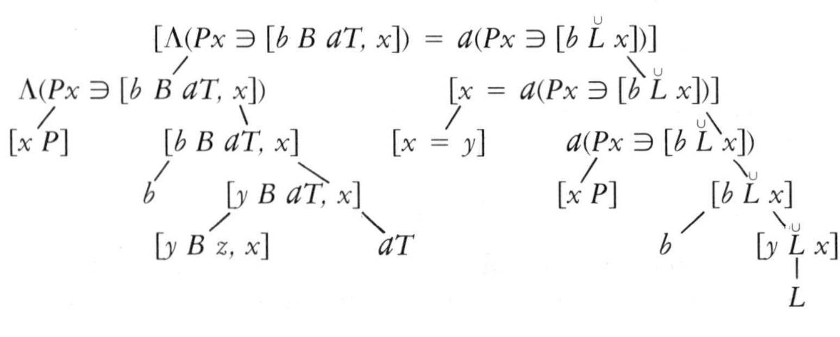

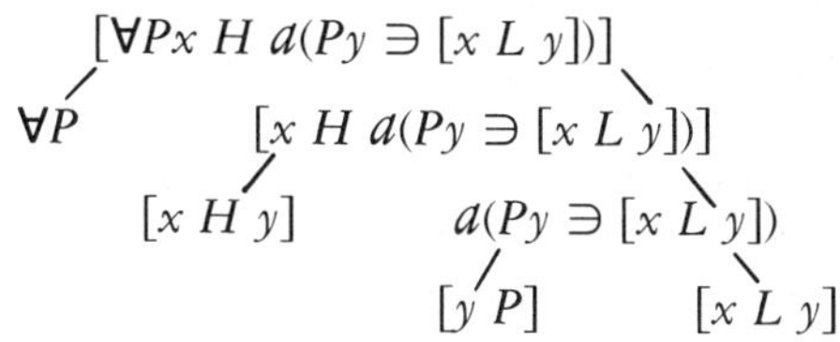

One sentence of $\mathscr{L}$ can be constructed in different ways. Two trivially different constructions of '[*a F a*]' are illustrated:

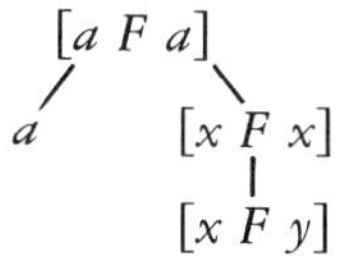

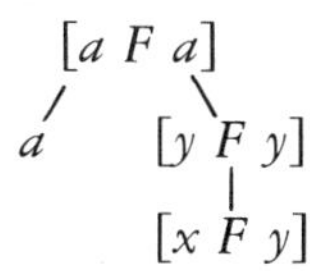

These are only trivially different because each diagram has the same shape, each line represents the same transformation affecting the same argument places, and the same expressions occur at the bottoms of branches. Another trivially different construction of the same sentence is illustrated:

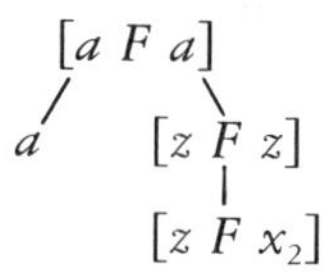

The variables used in the predicates in a tree diagram are not important. Variables are place-holders; it does not matter which ones we use. A construction for '[*a F a*]' that is more than trivially different from the preceding is illustrated:

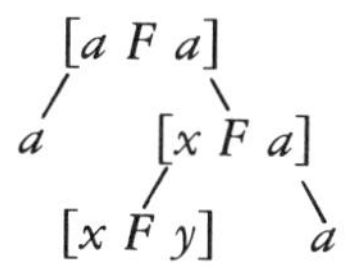

Still another is:

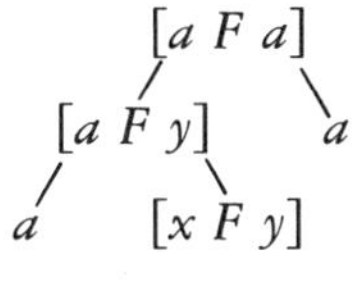

The different constructions of a sentence do not affect the value (the truth conditions) of the finished product. Nor do the different constructions make any difference to inferential meaning.

Even though one sentence can have different constructions, the order in which transformations are performed is not completely free. Scope relations among operators reflect the order of the transformations introducing the operators. Transformations introducing operators with greater scope must follow those introducing operators of lesser scope. The non-trivial alternative constructions are due to those transformations which do not introduce operators. The transformation for which there is the most freedom is the individual transformation. A constant can be introduced at nearly any point in the construction of a sentence, for it is not affected by the operators in a predicate (or sentence).

5. The First-Order Fragment of $\mathscr{L}$

The predicate functor 'T' makes it easy to compare $\mathscr{L}$ to a first-order language. The ordinary first-order quantified phrases $(\forall\alpha)$ and $(\exists\alpha)$ are equivalent to $\forall T\alpha$ and $dT\alpha$ in $\mathscr{L}$. (And $(\forall\alpha)$ is also equivalent to $\Lambda T\alpha$—for nonempty domains.) The comparison of $\mathscr{L}$ with first-order languages is slightly complicated by the different "word" orders in the different languages. A sentence written $\phi(\alpha_1, \ldots, \alpha_n)$ in a first-order language is $[\alpha_1\ \phi\ \alpha_2, \ldots, \alpha_n]$ in $\mathscr{L}$. This difference is more stylistic than anything else; it does not affect syntax or truth conditions in a serious way. In a first-order language, we say that every F is a G by writing this: $(\forall x)[F(x) \supset G(x)]$. This translation fails to capture the existential significance of ordinary uses of 'every.' But we can capture that by writing: $(\forall x)[F(x) \supset G(x)]\ \&\ (\exists x)F(x)$. In $\mathscr{L}$, it is most natural to translate 'Every F is a G' by one of the following: $[\forall F\ G]$ or $[\forall F\ =\ dG]$. With the quantifier '$\forall$,' there is no need for a separate existence clause. If we had in mind a nonexistential sense of 'every' (the mathematical sense), we could write: $[\Lambda F\ G]$ or $[\Lambda F\ =\ dG]$. We can also equip these last translations with existence clauses: $[[\Lambda F\ G]\ \&\ [dT\ F]]$, $[[\Lambda F\ =\ dG]\ \&\ [dT\ F]]$. All of these translations are equivalent to the first-order translations; they have the same truth-conditions as the first-order translations. These $\mathscr{L}$-translations are syntactically more similar to English sentences than to first-order sentences. But $\mathscr{L}$ also possesses the syntactical resources of a first-order language. We can "duplicate" the first-order sentence '$(\forall x)[F(x) \supset G(x)]$' with these: $\forall Tx\ [[x\ F] \supset [x\ G]]$, $\Lambda Tx\ [[x\ F] \supset [x\ G]]$. We can also add existence clauses: $\forall Tx\ [[x\ F] \supset [x\ G]]\ \&$

a $Tx[x\ F]$, $\Lambda Tx\ [[x\ F] \supset [x\ G]]$ & *a*$Tx\ [x\ F]$. These $\mathcal{L}$-sentences have the same make-up and the same truth-conditions as their first-order counterparts.

An English sentence 'Some F is a G' comes out this way in a first-order language: $(\exists x)[F(x)\ \&\ G(x)]$. $\mathcal{L}$ provides these "more natural" translations: [*a*$F\ G$], [*a*F = *a*G]. But in $\mathcal{L}$, we also have the first-order version: *a*$Tx\ [[x\ F]\ \&\ [x\ G]]$. A first-order language can be regarded as an abbreviated sublanguage of $\mathcal{L}$.

The *first-order fragment of* $\mathcal{L}$ is the sublanguage of $\mathcal{L}$ in which:

(1) No quantifiers other than '$\forall$,' '*a*' occur.
(2) Only 'T' occurs in quantified phrases.
(3) Every quantified phrase occurs prefixed to a predicate—i.e., no quantified phrase occurs in an argument place of a predicate.
(4) Every '$\sim$' is prefixed to a predicate.
(5) No predicate contains '$^{\cup}$.'
(6) No predicate contains '$\ni$.'

It is a remarkable fact that every sentence of $\mathcal{L}$ is equivalent to a sentence belonging to the first-order fragment of $\mathcal{L}$. This result will be proved in what follows.

The relation of equivalence (mutual entailment) is based on commitment. In what follows, I will deal with an analogous relation based on the labeling relation and truth values. If sentences are equivalued, they are also equivalent. But it is more convenient to prove that predicates are equivalued.

Let A, B be predicates or predicate functors. Let $\mathcal{D}$ be a nonempty domain, and f be an interpreting function of $\mathcal{L}$ for $\mathcal{D}$. Then A is *equivalued to B with respect to f*, $\mathcal{D}$ iff $f(A) = f(B)$. A is *equivalued to B with respect to* $\mathcal{D}$ iff for every interpreting function $\mathfrak{g}$ of $\mathcal{L}$ for $\mathcal{D}$, $\mathfrak{g}(A) = \mathfrak{g}(B)$. A is *equivalued to* B iff for every nonempty domain $\mathcal{E}$, and every interpreting function $\mathfrak{h}$ of $\mathcal{L}$ for $\mathcal{E}$, $\mathfrak{h}(A) = \mathfrak{h}(B)$.

In what follows, a tree diagram which indicates how a predicate A is constructed will be called a *construction of* A. Let A be an individual constant, binary predicate functor, quantified phrase, or predicate. Let Γ be a construction of A. The *rank* of Γ is the number of transformations represented by Γ. (The rank of an initial element in a tree diagram will be zero. The initial element, by itself, is its own construction. Every expression above the initial elements in a tree diagram is a predicate, except possibly for a binary predicate functor obtained by the passive voice transformation with a diagram like this:

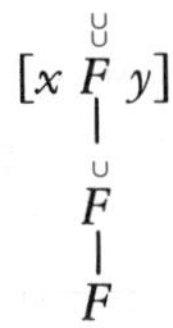

In this case the binary predicate functor '$\overset{\cup}{F}$' has a construction of rank one.)

In what follows, I will adapt Church's substitution notation. If A is a predicate, α is an individual variable, and β is an individual symbol, Then $\overset{\alpha}{\underset{\beta}{S}}\ A|$ is the result of replacing the *free* occurrences of α in A by β.

Proofs of the following results will not be supplied. They are straightforward, and may be furnished by the reader.

LEMMA 1 Let Γ be a construction of predicate A. In Γ, let B' be obtained from B by an application of the variable transformation, by replacing occurrences of α by β. Let γ be an individual variable not occurring in Γ. Let Γ' be obtained from Γ by replacing the occurrence of B' obtained by the variable transformation by $\overset{\alpha}{\underset{\gamma}{S}}\ B|$, and by replacing the occurrences of β which "derive" from the free β introduced in B' by occurrences of γ—this is in transformations subsequent to the application of the variable transformation. Then Γ' is a construction of a predicate A', and A is equivalued to A'.

This is proved by induction on the rank of Γ. (In considering such a construction, the value of a quantified phrase $Q\phi$ occurring as a node is the same as the value of ϕ.)

Suppose Γ is the following:

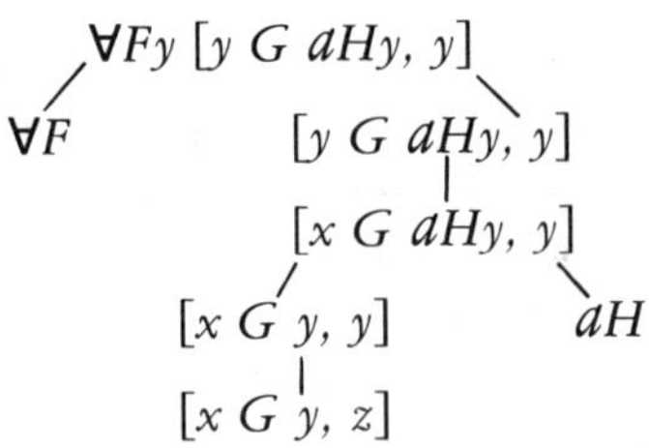

Then Γ' might be:

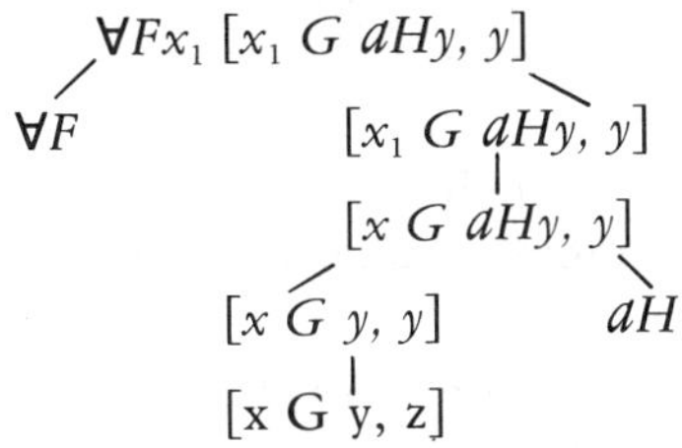

LEMMA 2 Let Γ be a construction of a predicate A. Let Γ contain m applications of the variable transformation, which replace occurrences of $\alpha_1, \ldots, \alpha_m$ by $\beta_1, \ldots, \beta_m$. Let $\gamma_1, \ldots, \gamma_m$ be distinct individual variables not occurring in Γ. Let Γ' be obtained from Γ by replacing the occurrences of $\beta_1, \ldots, \beta_m$ introduced by the variable transformations by $\gamma_1, \ldots, \gamma_m$ (respectively), and making similar replacements of occurrences of $\beta_1, \ldots, \beta_m$ derived from the occurrences introduced by the variable transformations. Then Γ' is a construction of a predicate A', and A is equivalued to A'.

This is proved by induction on m.

Let Γ be a construction of a predicate A. (1) Let Γ' be obtained from Γ as in lemma 2, and let Γ' be a construction of A'. Then (2) we obtain a construction Γ'' from Γ' as follows, working up from the bottom: For each quantifier transformation which inserts a quantified phrase $Q\phi\alpha$ or $Q\phi$ into a predicate C to yield C', we replace C' by $Q\phi\alpha\ C$. This is used as input into subsequent transformations, which then yield new results, and so on. Each transformation which takes $[\alpha_1\ \phi\ \alpha_2, \ldots, \alpha_n]$ to $[\alpha_1 \sim \phi\alpha_2, \ldots, \alpha_n]$ is replaced by the transformation from $[\alpha_1\ \phi\ \alpha_2, \ldots, \alpha_n]$ to $\sim[\alpha_1\ \phi\ \alpha_2, \ldots, \alpha_n]$. Subsequent transformations are modified accordingly.

Let Γ'' be a construction of B. B is a *prefixed predicate corresponding to* A.

LEMMA 3 The procedure described above yields a Γ'' which is a construction of a predicate B. A and B have the same number of distinct individual variables occurring free.

If we modify the construction Γ' given as an illustration above, we get this Γ'':

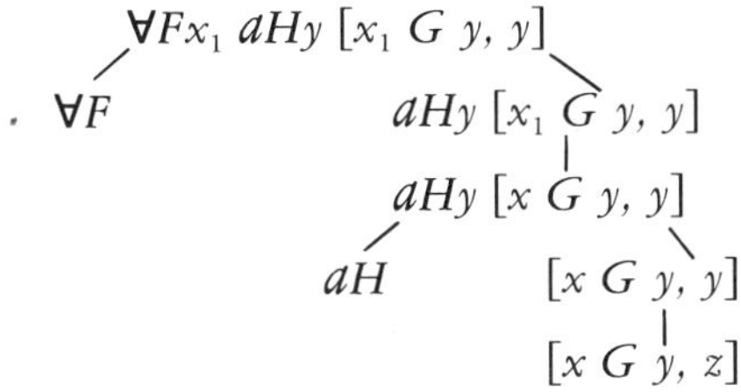

Although the change from Γ' to Γ'' can alter the left-to-right order of certain nodes, this difference is of little importance.

When a predicate A contains free variables, the value of A for an interpreting function f essentially depends on the canonical order of the variables occurring free in A. If we had specified a different canonical order, A would have a different value. This understanding motivates the following definition.

Let A be a predicate whose free individual variables, in canonical order, are $\alpha_1, \ldots, \alpha_n$. Consider the arrangement $\alpha_{i_1}, \ldots, \alpha_{i_n}$ of these variables. Let $\mathcal{D} \neq \emptyset$, and let f be an interpreting function of $\mathcal{L}$ for $\mathcal{D}$ such that $f(A) = V = \{< d_1, \ldots, d_n> | \ldots\}$. Then the *value of A for f with respect to the order* $\alpha_{i_1}, \ldots, \alpha_{i_n}$ is $\{< d_{i_1}, \ldots, d_{i_n}> | < d_1, \ldots, d_n> \in V\}$.

Given this concept, we can say that the value of A for f is the value of A for f with respect to the canonical order of the free variables in A.

Let Γ be a construction of a predicate A. Let Γ'' be obtained as above, yielding a predicate B which is a prefixed predicate corresponding to A. Consider corresponding nodes C and C' in Γ and Γ''. (This correspondence takes account of the switching of nodes which is occasioned by replacing a transformation which inserts a phrase with a transformation which prefixes one.) Let Δ be the (sub)construction of C, and Δ'' be the construction of C''. Let $\alpha_1, \ldots, \alpha_r$ be the distinct individual variables occurring free in C, in canonical order. And let $\beta_1, \ldots, \beta_r$ be the distinct individual variables occurring free in C'', in canonical order. (1) If Δ has rank 0, then $\alpha_1, \ldots, \alpha_r$ in that order correspond to $\beta_1, \ldots, \beta_r$ (in that order). (2) If Δ has rank $n + 1$, and (2a) C is not the output of the variable or relative clause transformation, then $\alpha_1, \ldots, \alpha_r$ correspond to the same variables to which they correspond in the inputs of the transformation yielding C. (2b) If C is $[\gamma\ (\phi\delta \ni D)]$ and the functor is obtained by the relative clause transformation, then $\alpha_1, \ldots, \alpha_r$ correspond to the same variables to which they correspond in the inputs to the relative clause transformation, except that γ corresponds to the individual variable which is the subject of C''. (2c) If Q is a quantifier and C is $Q(\phi\delta \ni D)$, then $\alpha_1, \ldots, \alpha_r$ correspond to the same variables to which they correspond in the inputs to the relative clause transformation. (2d) If C is obtained by the variable transformation which replaces a variable δ by α_i, then the variables $\alpha_1, \ldots, \alpha_r$ correspond to the same variables to which they correspond in the input to the variable transformation, except that α_i corresponds to the β_j which is introduced into C'' by the variable transformation which yields C''.

LEMMA 4 Let Γ be a construction of the predicate A. Let Γ'' be obtained as described above, yielding the predicate B which is a prefixed predicate corresponding to A. Let $\alpha_1, \ldots, \alpha_r$ be the distinct variables occurring free in A, and let these correspond to $\beta_1, \ldots, \beta_r$ in B. Let $\beta_1, \ldots, \beta_r$ be the canonical order of the variables occurring free in B. Let $\mathcal{D} \neq \emptyset$ and let f be an interpreting function of $\mathcal{L}$ for $\mathcal{D}$. Then the value of A for f with respect to the order $\alpha_1, \ldots, \alpha_r$ is $f(B)$.

This is proved by induction on the rank of Γ.

THEOREM 1 Let A be a sentence of $\mathcal{L}$ and let B be a prefixed sentence corresponding to A. Then A is equivalued to B.

This is just the special case of lemma 4 in which $r = 0$.

So every sentence in $\mathcal{L}$ is equivalued (and equivalent) to a sentence in which every quantified phrase and negation sign is in a prefixed position.

LEMMA (The numbering of the lemmas starts over for each theorem. A single lemma is not given a number.) Let A be a predicate in which every quantified phrase and negation sign occurs in prefixed position. Let A' be obtained from A by replacing a single occurrence of $[\alpha_1\ \breve{\phi}\ \alpha_2]$ by $[\alpha_2\ \phi\ \alpha_1]$. Let the distinct individual variables occurring free in A, A' be $\beta_1, \ldots, \beta_r$—this is their canonical order in A'. Let $\mathcal{D} \neq \emptyset$ and let f be an interpreting function of $\mathcal{L}$ for $\mathcal{D}$. Then the value of A for f with respect to the order $\beta_1, \ldots, \beta_r$ is $f(A')$.

THEOREM 2 Let A be a sentence in which all quantified phrases and negation signs occur in prefixed positions. Let A' be obtained from A by replacing every occurrence of a predicate $[\alpha_1\ \breve{\phi}\ \alpha_2]$ by $[\alpha_2\ \phi\ \alpha_1]$, and continuing this process until no functors with the passive voice symbol remain. Then A is equivalued to A'.

LEMMA 1 Let $\forall\phi\alpha\, A$ be a predicate of $\mathcal{L}$. This predicate is equivalued to $\forall T\alpha\ [[\alpha\ \phi] \supset A]\ \&\ \mathit{a}T\alpha\ [\alpha\ \phi]$.

LEMMA 2 A predicate $\Lambda\phi\alpha\, A$ is equivalued to $\forall T\alpha\ [[\alpha\ \phi] \supset A]$.

LEMMA 3 A predicate $\eta\phi\alpha\, A$ is equivalued to $\forall T\alpha\ [[\alpha\ \phi] \supset \sim A]$.

LEMMA 4 A predicate $\mathit{a}\phi\alpha\, A$ is equivalued to $\mathit{a}T\alpha\ [[\alpha\ \phi]\ \&\ A]$.

LEMMA 5 Let $\iota\phi\alpha\, A$ be a predicate of $\mathcal{L}$, and let β be an individual variable not occurring in this predicate. Then $\iota\phi\alpha\, A$ is equivalued to $\mathit{a}T\alpha\ [[[\alpha\ \phi]\ \&\ A]\ \&\ \forall T\beta\ [[\beta\ \phi] \supset [\beta = \alpha]]]$.

LEMMA 6 Let $[\beta\ (\phi\alpha \ni A)]$ be a predicate of $\mathcal{L}$. (1) If no free occurrence of α in A is within the scope of an operator binding occurrences of β and to the right of the operative occurrence of β for this operator, then $[\beta\ (\phi\alpha \ni A)]$ is equivalued to $[[\beta\ \phi]\ \&\ \underset{.}{S}\,{}^{\alpha}_{\beta}\, A|]$. (2) Otherwise let γ be a variable not occurring in $[\beta\ (\phi\alpha \ni A)]$. Let A' result from A by replacing all bound occurrences of β by γ. Then $[\beta\ (\phi\alpha \ni A)]$ is equivalued to $[[\beta\ \phi]\ \&\ \underset{.}{S}\,{}^{\alpha}_{\beta}\, A'|]$.

If α_1, α_2 are individual symbols, then the top occurrence of '∪' is the *main occurrence* of an operator in a predicate $[\alpha_1 \overset{\cup}{\psi} \alpha_2]$. If ϕ is a logical operator other than '∪,' and ϕ occurs in a predicate A, an occurrence of ϕ in A is the *main occurrence* of an operator in A if (1) this is the only occurrence in A of an operator other than '∪,' or (2) every other occurrence of an operator in A, other than occurrences of '∪,' is within the scope of the occurrence of ϕ.

THEOREM 3 Let M, N either both be predicates of $\mathscr{L}$, or both be n-place predicate functors. Let M, N be equivalued. Let A be a predicate or predicate functor of $\mathscr{L}$. And let B be a predicate or predicate functor obtained from A by replacing M by N at zero or more places in A. Then A is equivalued to B.

Proof We first consider the special case where A is the same as M and B is the same as N. In this case the theorem is immediate.

For the remainder of the proof, we argue by induction on the number of occurrences of logical operators in A. (We cannot argue by induction on the rank of a construction of A. For M might occur in A without occurring in the predicate from which A is obtained via a transformation.)

In the base case, A contains 0 occurrences of logical operators. Either (1) we have the special case above, (2) A is a predicate $[\alpha_1\ M\ \alpha_2, \ldots, \alpha_n]$ and B is $[\alpha_1\ N\ \alpha_2, \ldots, \alpha_n]$, or (3) M is replaced at 0 places in A, and B is the same as A. With $\mathscr{L}$ as it now stands, in case (2) M must be the same as N. (M and N must be simple and have the same value for every interpreting function f of $\mathscr{L}$ for every nonempty $\mathscr{D}$.) So in (2) and (3), A is the same as B—and the theorem is immediate.

For the inductive step, we assume the theorem is true when A contains $0, \ldots, m$-1 occurrences of logical operators. And suppose that A contains m occurrences of logical operators. In this step, there is a separate case for each operator whose occurrence might be the main occurrence of an operator in A. I will prove three cases to illustrate the proof. (Once again, the reader is invited to take care of the remaining cases.)

(1) Suppose the main occurrence of an operator in A is an occurrence of '∀.' Then either (a) A is $\forall\phi\alpha\ A_1$, and the displayed occurrence of '∀' is the main occurrence, or (b) A is $[\alpha_1\ \psi\ \alpha_2, \ldots, \alpha_n]$, α_i is $\forall\phi\alpha$ or $\forall\phi$, and the first occurrence of '∀' in α_i is the main occurrence of a logical operator in A.

(1a) A is $\forall\phi\alpha\ A_1$. Either we have the special case above, or B is $\forall\phi'\alpha\ B_1$, where ϕ', B_1 are obtained from ϕ, A_1 by replacing M by N at 0 or more places. By the hypothesis of induction, ϕ and ϕ' are equivalued, and A_1 and B_1 are equivalued. But then A can be obtained from $\forall\phi$, A_1

by the universal transformation. B can be similarly obtained from $\forall\phi'$, B_1. By the account of values and truth conditions in §2, A has the same value as B for every interpreting function f of $\mathscr{L}$ for every nonempty $\mathscr{D}$.

(1b) A is $[\alpha_1\ \psi\ \alpha_2, \ldots, \alpha_n]$, where α_i is either (i) $\forall\phi$ or (ii) $\forall\phi\alpha$. Unless we have the special case above, B is $[\alpha'_1\ \psi'\ \alpha'_2, \ldots, \alpha'_n]$, where $\alpha'_1, \ldots, \alpha'_n, \psi'$ are obtained from $\alpha_1, \ldots, \alpha_n, \psi$ by replacing M by N at 0 or more places. For $j < i$, $\alpha'_j = \alpha_j$. α'_i is either (i) $\forall\phi'$ or (ii) $\forall\phi'\alpha$, where ϕ' is obtained from ϕ by replacing M by N at 0 or more places. Suppose (i) α_i is $\forall\phi$. Let β be an individual variable not occurring in A or B. In A and B replace α_i by β to obtain A', B'. By the hypothesis of induction ϕ and ϕ' are equivalued, and A' and B' are equivalued. But A can be obtained from $\forall\phi$, A' by the universal transformation. B can be similarly obtained from $\forall\phi'$, B'. So A is equivalued to B.

Suppose (ii) α_i is $\forall\phi\alpha$. Let β be an individual variable not occurring in A, B. Replace any free occurrence of α in either A or B by β, yielding A^*, B^*. The same replacement in ϕ, ϕ' yields ϕ^*, ϕ'^*. By the account given earlier of the variable transformation, A^* is equivalued to A, and B^* is equivalued to B. ϕ^* is equivalued to ϕ, and ϕ'^* is equivalued to ϕ'. Let A'' be obtained from A^* by replacing the ith argument by α; let B'' be similarly obtained from B^*. By the hypothesis of induction, ϕ^* and ϕ'^* are equivalued, and A'' and B^* are equivalued. A^* can be obtained from A'', $\forall\phi^*$ by the universal transformation. B^* can be similarly obtained from B'', $\forall\phi'^*$. So A'' is equivalued to B''. But then A is equivalued to B.

(2) Suppose the main occurrence of an operator in A is an occurrence of '$\supset$.' So A is $[A_1 \supset A_2]$. Unless we have the special case above, B is $[B_1 \supset \mathrm{B}_2]$, where B_1, B_2 are obtained from A_1, A_2 by replacing M by N at 0 or more places. By the hypothesis of induction, A_1 and B_1 are equivalued. So are A_2 and B_2. But then A is equivalued to B.

(3) Suppose the main occurrence of an operator in A is an occurrence of '$\cup$.' Then A is $[\alpha_1\ \overset{\cup}{\phi}\ \alpha_2]$. Unless we have the special case above, B is $[\alpha_1\ \psi\ \alpha_2]$, where ψ is obtained from $\overset{\cup}{\phi}$ by replacing M by N at 0 or more places. Let β_1, β_2 be distinct individual variables. Then $[\beta_1\ \overset{\cup}{\phi}\ \beta_2]$ is equivalued to $[\beta_1\ \psi\ \beta_2]$. A and B can be obtained from $[\beta_1\ \overset{\cup}{\phi}\ \beta_2]$ and $[\beta_1\ \psi\ \beta_2]$ (respectively) by the same sequence of variable, constant, and reflexive transformations (affecting the same variables in the same ways). So A is equivalued to B.

THEOREM 4 Let A be a sentence of $\mathscr{L}$. Then there is an effective procedure for finding a sentence B in the first-order fragment of $\mathscr{L}$, where B is equivalued to A.

The first-order fragment is as much of $\mathscr{L}$ as we need for saying things. Whatever we can say with a sentence of $\mathscr{L}$, we can also say with a sentence belonging to the first-order fragment of $\mathscr{L}$. (And, of course, we can also say it in any other first-order language with identity.) This result in no way confers a privileged status on the first-order fragment of $\mathscr{L}$. The equivalence between a sentence of $\mathscr{L}$ and its first-order translation is inferential; they also have the same truth conditions. The two sentences do not have the same speech act structures (and they do not have the same representational meaning). We are developing $\mathscr{L}$ so that we can use it to gain understanding of speech act structures; first-order languages are not helpful for this purpose.

6. The Deductive System $\mathscr{S}$

In this section, I will develop the natural deduction system $\mathscr{S}$ for establishing results about $\mathscr{L}$. These results are *inference sequences*. An inference sequence has zero or more premises and a single conclusion; an inference sequence with premises $A_1, \ldots, A_n$ and conclusion B is written this way: $A_1, \ldots, A_n / B$. An inference sequence $A_1, \ldots, A_n / B$ is (*set-theoretically*) *valid* iff there is no interpreting function f of $\mathscr{L}$ for some nonempty $\mathscr{D}$ such that $f(A_1) = f(A_2) = \ldots = f(A_n) = \mathrm{t}$ but $f(B) = \mathrm{f}$. A sentence B is (*set-theoretically*) *logically true* iff the inference sequence $/ B$ is (set-theoretically) valid. The qualification '(set-theoretically)' inserted in the above definitions serves to distinguish the defined expressions from the unqualified expressions that were defined earlier with respect to the relation of commitment.

The system $\mathscr{S}$ employs tree proofs. This may make $\mathscr{S}$ seem forbidding, but it is extremely easy to develop a facility for constructing these proofs. (However, they are often difficult to fit on a piece of paper.) I find that such systems, and the proofs they contain, are more perspicuous than customary systems and their proofs. For the premises used in obtaining a given conclusion are physically next to the conclusion, and a given conclusion is linked only to those hypotheses (in the proof) to which it is subject. It is left as an exercise for the reader to transform $\mathscr{S}$ into a system with linear proofs.

Only sentences occur as steps in the tree proofs of $\mathscr{S}$. Some of the rules for constructing tree proofs cancel hypotheses used to develop the proof to a certain point. In the following illustration of these rules, canceled hypotheses are enclosed in braces: {, }.

The rules for constructing tree proofs are as follows. (Abbreviations for the names of the rules are in parentheses following the names.)

& *Introduction* (&I)

$$\frac{A \quad B}{[A \,\&\, B]}$$

& *Elimination* (&E)

$$\frac{[A \,\&\, B]}{A} \qquad \frac{[A \,\&\, B]}{B}$$

v *Introduction* (vI)

$$\frac{A}{[A \vee B]} \qquad \frac{B}{[A \vee B]}$$

v *Elimination* (vE)

$$\frac{[A \vee B] \quad \begin{matrix}\{A\} \\ C\end{matrix} \quad \begin{matrix}\{B\} \\ C\end{matrix}}{C}$$

⊃*Introduction* (⊃I)

$$\frac{\begin{matrix}\{A\} \\ B\end{matrix}}{[A \supset B]}$$

⊃ *Elimination* (⊃E)

$$\frac{A \qquad [A \supset B]}{B}$$

~ *Insertion* (~ In)

$$\frac{\sim[\alpha_1 \; \psi \; \alpha_2, \ldots, \alpha_n]}{[\alpha_1 \sim \psi \; \alpha_2, \ldots, \alpha_n]}$$

~ *Extraction* (~ Ex)

$$\frac{[\alpha_1 \sim \psi \; \alpha_2, \ldots, \alpha_n]}{\sim[\alpha_1 \; \psi \; \alpha_2, \ldots, \alpha_n]}$$

For both of these rules, α_1 is a constant.

~ *Elimination* (~ E)

$$\frac{\begin{matrix}\{\sim A\} \\ A\end{matrix}}{A} \qquad \frac{\begin{matrix}\{[\alpha_1 \sim \psi \; \alpha_2, \ldots, \alpha_n]\} \\ [\alpha_1 \; \psi \; \alpha_2, \ldots, \alpha_n]\end{matrix}}{[\alpha_1 \; \psi \; \alpha_2, \ldots, \alpha_n]}$$

α_1 is a constant.

Contradiction Elimination (CE)

$$\frac{A \quad \sim A}{B} \qquad \frac{[\alpha_1 \; \psi \; \alpha_2, \ldots, \alpha_n] \quad [\alpha_1 \sim \psi \; \alpha_2, \ldots, \alpha_n]}{B}$$

α_1 is a constant.

Below are sample proofs to illustrate the workings of $\mathcal{S}$. Each hypothesis of the proof has a numeral written above it. The rules used are identified to the right of the line of an inference figure. The following is a proof of [*A* & *B*] / [*A* v *B*]:

$$\dfrac{\dfrac{\overset{1}{[A \,\&\, B]}}{A}\ \&\text{E}}{[A \text{ v } B]}\ \text{vI}$$

Of course, this is a proof of an inference sequence schema, and not simply of an inference sequence. It becomes an actual proof in $\mathcal{S}$ once *A* and *B* are replaced by actual sentences of $\mathcal{L}$. A proof of [*A* & *B*] / [*B* & *A*]:

$$\dfrac{\dfrac{\overset{1}{[A \,\&\, B]}}{B}\ \&\text{E} \qquad \dfrac{\overset{1}{[A \,\&\, B]}}{A}\ \&\text{E}}{[B \,\&\, A]}\ \&\text{I}$$

When the application of a rule cancels occurrences of an hypothesis, the numeral of the canceled hypothesis (hypotheses) is written to the right of the inference figure that does the canceling. A line is drawn through the numeral(s) of the canceled hypothesis. We can prove $\sim\sim A$ / *A* as follows:

$$\dfrac{\dfrac{\overset{1}{\sim A} \qquad \overset{2}{\sim\sim A}}{A}\ CE}{\text{A}}\ \sim\text{E, 1}$$

A proof of $[A \supset \sim A]$ / $\sim A$:

$$\dfrac{\dfrac{\dfrac{\dfrac{\overset{1}{\sim A} \qquad \overset{2}{\sim\sim A}}{A}\,CE}{A}\sim \mathrm{E}, 1 \qquad [A \supset \sim A]}{\sim A}\supset\mathrm{E}}{\sim A}\sim \mathrm{E}, 2$$

Each quantifier has similar *Insertion* and *Extraction* rules. Let Q be a quantifier. Then the following rules apply to Q.

Q Insertion (QIn)

$\dfrac{Q\phi\alpha\ A}{A'}$ α occurs free in A. The first free occurrence of α in A is within the scope of no operators in A. A' is obtained from A by replacing the first free occurrence of α in A by $Q\phi\alpha$.

$\dfrac{Q\phi\alpha\ A}{A'}$ α has a single free occurrence in A. This free occurrence is within the scope of no operators in A. A' is obtained from A by replacing the free occurrence of α by $Q\phi$.

Q Extraction (QEx)

These are obtained by "turning over" the Insertion rules. The conditions are the same.

Change of Bound Variable$_1$ (CBV)

$\dfrac{A}{A'}$ A' is obtained from A by replacing one occurrence of a quantified phrase $Q\phi\alpha$ by $Q\phi\beta$, and replacing occurrences of α bound by the Q in $Q\phi\alpha$ by occurrences of the variable β. This is allowed only if no occurrence of β that replaces an α becomes bound by a different operator than the Q in the occurrence of $Q\phi\beta$.

The remaining quantifier rules will be illustrated only for initially placed quantified phrases. These rules also apply to an internal occurrence of a quantified phrase in which the occurrence of the quantifier is the main occurrence of an operator in the sentence.

$\forall$ *Elimination* ($\forall$E)

$$\frac{\forall\phi\alpha\ A \qquad [\beta\ \phi]}{\underset{\cdot}{\mathrm{S}}\,{}^{\alpha}_{\beta}\, A|}$$

Subalternation (SubA)

$$\frac{\forall\phi\alpha\ A}{a\phi\alpha\ A}$$

$\forall$ *Introduction* ($\forall$I)

$$\frac{[aT\ \phi] \qquad \begin{array}{c}\{[\beta\ \phi]\}\\ A\end{array}}{\forall\phi\alpha\ \ \mathrm{S}\,{}^{\beta}_{\alpha}\, A|}$$

β is a constant which does not occur in ϕ. β occurs in A but does not occur in any uncancelled hypothesis other than the one in braces in the proof leading to the displayed occurrence of A. No occurrence of β in A is in a position where an occurrence of α would be a bound occurrence. (This notation for substitution is also taken from Church. It labels the result of replacing *every* occurrence of β in A by α.)

a *Introduction* (aI)

$$\frac{[\beta\ \phi] \qquad \underset{\cdot}{\mathrm{S}}\,{}^{\alpha}_{\beta}\, A|}{a\phi\alpha\ A}$$

β is an individual constant.

a *Elimination* (aE)

$$\frac{a\phi\alpha\ A \qquad \begin{array}{c}\{[[\beta\ \phi]\ \&\ \underset{\cdot}{\mathrm{S}}\,{}^{\alpha}_{\beta}\, A|]\}\\ C\end{array}}{C}$$

β is an individual constant which does not occur in ϕ, A, or C, or in any uncancelled hypothesis other than the one in braces leading to the upper occurrence of C.

Λ *Elimination* (ΛE)

$$\frac{\Lambda\phi\alpha\ A \qquad\qquad [\beta\ \phi]}{\underset{\cdot}{\mathrm{S}}{}^{\alpha}_{\beta}\,A|}$$

Λ *Introduction* (ΛI)

$$\frac{\begin{array}{c}\{[\beta\ \phi]\}\\ \\ A\end{array}}{\Lambda\phi\alpha\ \mathrm{S}{}^{\beta}_{\alpha}\,A|}$$

β is a constant which does not occur in ϕ. β occurs in A but does not occur in any uncancelled hypothesis other than the one in braces in the proof leading to the displayed occurrence of A. β does not occur in A in any position where an occurrence of α would be bound.

η *Elimination* (ηE)

$$\frac{\eta\phi\alpha\ A \qquad\qquad [\beta\ \phi]}{\sim \underset{\cdot}{\mathrm{S}}{}^{\alpha}_{\beta}\,A|}$$

η *Introduction* (ηI)

$$\frac{\begin{array}{c}\{[\beta\ \phi]\}\\ \\ \sim A\end{array}}{\eta\phi\alpha\ \mathrm{S}{}^{\beta}_{\alpha}\,A|}$$

The conditions are the same as for ΛI.

ι *Introduction* (ιI)

$$\frac{\forall\phi\gamma\ [\gamma\ =\ \beta] \qquad\qquad \underset{\cdot}{\mathrm{S}}{}^{\alpha}_{\beta}\,A|}{\iota\phi\alpha\ A}$$

α occurs free in A.

ι *Elimination* (ιE)

$$\frac{\iota\phi\alpha\ A \qquad\qquad \begin{array}{c}\{[\forall\phi\gamma\ [\gamma\ =\ \beta]\ \&\ \underset{\cdot}{\mathrm{S}}{}^{\alpha}_{\beta}\,A|]\}\\ \\ C\end{array}}{C}$$

β is an individual constant which does not occur in ϕ, A, or C, or in any uncancelled hypothesis other than the one in braces leading to the upper occurrence of C.

$^{\cup}$ *Introduction* ($^{\cup}$I)

$$\frac{[\alpha\ \ \psi\ \ \beta]}{[\beta\ \ \overset{\cup}{\psi}\ \ \alpha]}$$

α and β are constants.

$^{\cup}$ *Elimination* ($^{\cup}$E)

$$\frac{[\alpha\ \ \overset{\cup}{\psi}\ \ \beta]}{[\beta\ \ \psi\ \ \alpha]}$$

α and β are constants.

$\ni$ *Introduction* ($\ni$I)

$$\frac{[\beta\ \phi] \qquad \underset{\cdot}{S}{}^{\alpha}_{\beta}\, A|}{[\beta\ (\phi\alpha \ni A)]}$$

α occurs free in A.

$\ni$ *Elimination* ($\ni$E)

$$\frac{[\beta\ (\phi\alpha \ni A)]}{[\beta\ \phi]} \qquad \frac{[\beta\ (\phi\alpha \ni A)]}{\underset{\cdot}{S}{}^{\alpha}_{\beta}\, A|}$$

Change of Bound Variable$_2$ (CBV)

$$\frac{A}{A'}$$

A' is obtained from A by replacing $(\phi\alpha \ni B)$ in A by $(\phi\beta \ni \underset{\cdot}{S}{}^{\alpha}_{\beta}\, B|)$, where β is an individual variable and no free occurrence of α in B is in a position in which an occurrence of β would be bound.

$=$ *Introduction* ($=$I)

If β is an individual constant, then $[\beta = \beta]$ can be introduced as a conclusion from no premises (as an axiom).

$=$ *Elimination* ($=$E)

$$\frac{[\alpha = \beta] \qquad A}{A'}$$

A' is obtained from A by replacing some occurrences of α by β, or else A' is obtained from A by replacing some occurrences of β by α.

T Introduction (TI)

If β is an individual constant, then $[\beta\ T]$ can be introduced as a conclusion from no premises.

If B is the conclusion of a tree proof whose uncanceled hypotheses are included among $A_1, \ldots, A_n$, then $A_1, \ldots, A_n / B$ is a *theorem* of $\mathcal{S}$. (In symbols, either $\vdash A_1, \ldots, A_n / B$ or $A_1, \ldots, A_n \vdash B$.) So each tree proof in $\mathcal{S}$ establishes an infinite number of theorems (since a theorem can have premises which do not serve as hypotheses of a proof).

A few proofs involving quantification are below. The following shows $\forall\phi\alpha\, A \vdash \Lambda\phi\alpha\, A$:

Let β be a constant not occurring in ϕ or A.

$$\dfrac{\dfrac{\overset{1}{[\beta\ \phi]} \qquad \overset{2}{\forall\phi\alpha\, A}}{\underset{\cdot}{S}{}^{\alpha}_{\beta}\, A|}\ \forall\text{E}}{\Lambda\phi\alpha\, A}\ \Lambda\text{I, 1}$$

A proof of $\sim a\phi\alpha \sim A\ /\ \Lambda\phi\alpha\ A$:

Let β be a constant not occurring in φ or *A*.

$$\dfrac{\dfrac{\dfrac{\dfrac{\overset{1}{[\beta\ \phi]} \qquad \overset{2}{\underset{\cdot}{S}\,{}^{\alpha}_{\beta} \sim A|}}{a\phi\alpha \sim A}\,a\text{I} \qquad \overset{3}{\sim a\phi\alpha \sim A}}{\underset{\cdot}{S}\,{}^{\alpha}_{\beta}\, A|}\,\text{CE}}{\underset{\cdot}{S}\,{}^{\alpha}_{\beta}\, A|}\,\sim\text{E}, 2}{\Lambda\phi\alpha\ A}\,\Lambda\text{I}, 1$$

A proof that $\vdash [\eta T\ \phi]\ /\ \Lambda\phi\alpha\ A$:

Let β be a constant not occurring in φ or *A*.

Let β be a constant not occurring in φ or *A*.

$$\dfrac{\dfrac{\dfrac{\overset{\text{TI}}{[\beta\ T]} \qquad \overset{1}{[\eta T\ \phi]}}{\sim[\beta\ \phi]}\,\eta\text{E} \qquad \overset{2}{[\beta\ \phi]}}{\underset{\cdot}{S}\,{}^{\alpha}_{\beta}\, A|}\,\text{CE}}{\Lambda\phi\alpha\ A}\,\Lambda\text{I}, 2$$

In $\mathscr{S}$, the universal quantifiers ('∀,' 'Λ,' and 'η') have subproofs for premises in their introduction rules. Proofs in English which establish universal conclusions also have subproof premises. ("Let ABC be a triangle. Then . . . So every triangle . . .") In a first-order system, the introduction rule for the universal quantifier does not need a subproof for a premise—and it does not cancel a hypothesis. Not only does $\mathscr{L}$ do a better job of capturing the syntax of English than does a first-order language, but $\mathscr{S}$ does a better job of illuminating inferences in English than does a first-order system.

7. Soundness and Completeness of $\mathscr{S}$

The system $\mathscr{S}$ is both sound and complete with respect to the set-theoretic statement of the truth conditions of sentences of $\mathscr{L}$. If $A_1, \ldots, A_n\ /\ B$

is a theorem of $\mathcal{S}$, then there is no interpreting function f of $\mathcal{L}$ for a nonempty $\mathcal{D}$ which makes each premise true and the conclusion false. If X is a set of sentences of $\mathcal{L}$, B is a sentence of $\mathcal{L}$, and there is no interpreting function f of $\mathcal{L}$ for a nonempty $\mathcal{D}$ which makes every member of X true and B false, then there is a proof of B from hypotheses in X.

To establish the soundness of $\mathcal{S}$, it is convenient to enlarge the language to form a *pseudo-language.* If $\mathcal{D}$ is a nonempty domain, we obtain *pseudo-predicates* and *pseudo-sentences* by treating individuals in $\mathcal{D}$ as if they were constants (naming themselves), and substituting them for variables in predicates. If A is a predicate containing free occurrences of distinct individual variables $\alpha_1, \ldots, \alpha_n$, and $\rho_1, \ldots, \rho_n$ are individuals, then $A[\alpha_1, \ldots, \alpha_n; \rho_1, \ldots, \rho_n]$ is the result of substituting $\rho_1, \ldots, \rho_n$ for the free occurrences of $\alpha_1, \ldots, \alpha_n$ (resp.).

Let $\mathcal{D}$ be nonempty. The pseudo-language $\mathcal{L}_{\mathcal{D}}$ contains pseudo-predicates obtained as follows: every predicate of $\mathcal{L}$ is a pseudo-predicate of $\mathcal{L}_{\mathcal{D}}$, and the transformations of $\mathcal{L}$ are transformations of $\mathcal{L}_{\mathcal{D}}$. In addition, $\mathcal{L}_{\mathcal{D}}$ contains the following *real* transformation:

(Real) Let A be a pseudo-predicate of $\mathcal{L}_{\mathcal{D}}$ which contains free occurrences of the distinct individual variables $\alpha_1, \ldots, \alpha_n$ and no others; this is their canonical order. Let $\rho \in \mathcal{D}$. Then $A[\alpha_i; \rho]$ $(= A')$ is obtained from ρ, A by the *real* transformation.

Of course, we can't really put an individual in place of a variable in a predicate. In a thoroughly formal treatment, a pseudo-predicate $A[\alpha_1, \ldots, \alpha_n; \rho_1, \ldots, \rho_n]$ might be construed as a $(2n + 1)$-tuple $< A, \alpha_1, \ldots, \alpha_n, \rho_1, \ldots, \rho_n>$. But it does no harm to regard these as expressions; it is heuristically helpful to do so.

If f is an interpreting function of $\mathcal{L}$ for a nonempty $\mathcal{D}$, then f^+ is the extension of f to $\mathcal{L}_{\mathcal{D}}$. If α is an individual constant of $\mathcal{L}$, then $f^+(\alpha) = f(\alpha)$. If ϕ is a simple predicate functor of $\mathcal{L}$, then $f^+(\phi) = f(\phi)$. And if $\rho \in \mathcal{D}$, then $f^+(\rho) = \rho$.

If A is a predicate of $\mathcal{L}$, then $f^+(A) = f(A)$. Now let us consider the semantic effect of the real transformation. Suppose $f^+(A) = V$. If $n > 1$, then $f^+(A') = V' = \{< d_1, \ldots, d_{n-1}> \mid < d_1, \ldots, , d_{i-1}, \rho, \ldots, d_{n-1}> \in V\}$. If $n = 1$, then $f^+(A') = $ t iff $\rho \in V$. Otherwise, $f^+(A') =$ f. (If $n = 1$, then A is a *pseudo-sentence.*)

$\mathcal{S}_{\mathcal{D}}$ is $\mathcal{S}$ extended to accommodate pseudo-sentences of $\mathcal{L}_{\mathcal{D}}$. For most rules, an individual in $\mathcal{D}$ behaves like an individual constant. But in the rules ∀I, aE, ΛI, ηI, and ιE, there is a subproof premiss that contains a constant on which there are special restrictions. For those rules, that constant must be a constant of $\mathscr{L}$. So, for example, in an instance of ∀ Introduction:

$$\frac{[aT\ \phi] \qquad \begin{matrix}\{[\beta\ \phi]\} \\ A\end{matrix}}{\forall\phi\alpha\ S\,{}^{\beta}_{\alpha}\,A|}$$

β must be a constant of $\mathscr{L}$ which does not occur in φ or in any uncanceled hypothesis other than the one in braces in the proof leading to the occurrence of A. (β must also occur in A, and no occurrence of β in A can be at a place in which an occurrence of α would be bound.)

In a proof, an application of ∀ Introduction, *a* Elimination, Λ Introduction, η Introduction, or ι Elimination cancels a hypothesis containing a constant which is displayed in the illustration of the rule. This constant is the *operative* constant for that application of the rule. (The operative constant must be a constant of $\mathscr{L}$.)

Let Γ be a proof of $A_1, \ldots, A_n$ / B. Γ is *normalized with respect to constants* iff each application of ∀I, *a*E, ΛI, ηI, and ιE cancels a hypothesis with a different operative constant, and that constant does not occur in Γ elsewhere than in the subproof leading to the application of the quantifier rule which cancels its hypothesis.

LEMMA 1 If $A_1, \ldots, A_n \vdash B$, then there is a proof Γ of $A_1, \ldots, A_n$ / B which is normalized with respect to constants.

This lemma is similar to one that Gentzen established in proving his Hauptsatz. Any proof can be normalized by starting at the top and working down, introducing new constants to replace the operative constants of the applications of the quantifier rules. This result can be proved by induction on the number of applications of ∀I, *a*E, ΛI, ηI, and ιE in Γ.

Let Γ be a proof in $\mathscr{S}_{\mathscr{D}}$ (or $\mathscr{S}$). The *rank* of Γ is the number of inference figures which it contains. (An inference figure is an instance of one of the rules for constructing tree proofs.)

LEMMA 2 Let Γ be a proof (in $\mathscr{S}_{\mathscr{D}}$) of $A_1, \ldots, A_n$ / B. Γ contains occurrences of an individual constant α of $\mathscr{L}$, but α is not the operative constant of any application of a quantifier rule in Γ. Let $\rho \in \mathscr{D}$, and let Γ′ be obtained from Γ by replacing every occurrence of α by ρ. Then Γ′ is a proof of $A_1[\alpha; \rho], \ldots, A_n[\alpha; \rho]$ / $B[\alpha; \rho]$. (Here the notation for substituting individuals in $\mathscr{D}$ for free variables in a predicate has been extended in the obvious way to indicate the result of substituting an individual for a constant.)

This can be proved by induction on the rank of Γ.

In each section, the theorems are numbered starting with 1. To refer to a theorem in a different section, we prefix the numeral of the theorem with the numeral of its section. So, for example, Theorem 5.3 is Theorem 3 of section 5. We can also prefix numerals with numerals for chapters—Theorem 5.3 is also Theorem 9.5.3.

THEOREM 1 (SOUNDNESS) Let Γ be a proof (of $\mathcal{S}_{\mathcal{D}}$) whose uncanceled hypotheses are $A_1, \ldots, A_n$, and whose conclusion is B. Let f be an interpreting function of $\mathcal{L}$ for $\mathcal{D}$ such that $f^+(A_1) = \ldots = f^+(A_n) = \text{t}$. Then $f^+(B) = \text{t}$.

Proof Since every proof can be replaced by a proof of the same result that is normalized with respect to constants, we may assume without loss of generality that Γ is such a proof. We now argue by induction on the rank of Γ. The base step is that where Γ has rank 0. So $n = 1$, and Γ is just B. Since A_1 is B, it is clear that $f^+(A_1) = f^+(B) = \text{t}$.

For the inductive step, we suppose the theorem true for proofs having rank $0, \ldots, m - 1$. Now suppose that the rank of Γ is m. We need to consider each rule of $\mathcal{S}_{\mathcal{D}}$ that might be used to obtain the conclusion of Γ. I will only consider three cases here, leaving the rest as an exercise for the reader.

Case (i). Suppose that Γ concludes with &I. So B is $[B_1 \,\&\, B_2]$, and Γ concludes:

$$\frac{B_1 \qquad B_2}{[B_1 \,\&\, B_2]}$$

By the hypothesis of induction, $f^+(B_1) = f^+(B_2) = \text{t}$. By the truth conditions for '&,' $f^+(B) = \text{t}$.

Case (ii). Γ concludes with ⊃I. So B is $[B_1 \supset B_2]$, and Γ concludes:

$$\frac{\begin{array}{c}\{B_1\}\\ B_2\end{array}}{[B_1 \supset B_2]}$$

Suppose $f^+(B_1) = \text{t}$. Then by the hypothesis of induction, $f^+(B_2) = \text{t}$. By the truth conditions of '⊃,' $f^+(B) = \text{t}$. If $f^+(B_1) = \text{f}$, then by the truth conditions of '⊃,' $f^+(B) = \text{t}$.

Case (iii). Γ concludes with ∀I. So B is $\forall\phi\alpha\, \mathrm{S}\,^{\beta}_{\alpha}\, A|$. (Or else B is a sentence in which '∀' is the main operator, but in which the quantified phrase occurs in an argument place in *B*. The case of the inserted quantified phrase won't be considered separately. It is essentially the same as the prefixed case.) And Γ concludes:

$$\frac{[\mathit{a}T\ \phi] \qquad \begin{matrix}\{[\beta\ \phi]\}\\ A\end{matrix}}{\forall\phi\alpha\ \mathrm{S}\,{}^{\beta}_{\alpha}\, A|}$$

By the hypothesis of induction, $f^{+}[\mathit{a}T\ \phi] = \mathrm{t}$. By lemma 2, for every $\rho \in \mathscr{D}$ such that $f^{+}[\rho\ \phi] = \mathrm{t}$, we have $f^{+}(A[\alpha;\ \rho]) = \mathrm{t}$. Consequently, $f^{+}(\forall\phi\alpha\ \mathrm{S}\,{}^{\beta}_{\alpha}\, A|) = \mathrm{t}$.

The soundness of $\mathscr{S}$ is a consequence of the soundness of $\mathscr{S}_{\mathscr{D}}$, for $\mathscr{S}$ is a subsystem of every $\mathscr{S}_{\mathscr{D}}$. In proving completeness, we will abandon the practice of dealing with the extensions of $\mathscr{L}$ and $\mathscr{S}$ to $\mathscr{L}_{\mathscr{D}}$ and $\mathscr{S}_{\mathscr{D}}$. Instead we will exploit the equivalence between $\mathscr{L}$ and its first-order fragment.

LEMMA (i) Let *A* be a predicate containing free occurrences of individual variable α, and containing no other free variables. Let ϕ be a one-place predicate functor containing no free variables. Then $\forall\phi\alpha\ A \vdash \mathit{a}T\ \phi$.

(ii) Let *A*, ϕ, α be as in (i). Then $\Lambda\phi\alpha\ A, \mathit{a}T\ \phi \vdash \forall\phi\alpha\ A$.

(iii) Let ϕ, ψ be one-place predicate functors containing no free variables and let α be an individual variable. Then $\Lambda T\alpha\ [[\alpha\ \phi] \supset [\alpha\ \psi]],\ \mathit{a}T\ \phi \vdash \mathit{a}T\ \psi$.

(iv) Let *A* be a predicate containing free occurrences of distinct individual variables $\alpha_1, \ldots, \alpha_n$, and no others. Let $\epsilon_1, \ldots, \epsilon_n$ be individual constants. Then $\Lambda T\alpha_1 \ldots \Lambda T\alpha_n\ A \vdash \mathrm{S}^{\alpha_1}_{\epsilon_1} \cdots {}^{\alpha_n}_{\epsilon_n}\ A|$.

(v) Let *B* be a predicate containing free occurrences of distinct individual variables $\alpha_1, \ldots, \alpha_n$ and no others. Let $A_1, \ldots, A_n$ be sentences. And let $\epsilon_1, \ldots, \epsilon_n$ be distinct individual constants, not occurring in $A_1, \ldots, A_n, B$. Then if $A_1, \ldots, A_n$ $\vdash \mathrm{S}^{\alpha_1}_{\epsilon_1} \cdots {}^{\alpha_n}_{\epsilon_n}\ B|$, then $A_1, \ldots, A_n \vdash \Lambda T\alpha_1 \ldots \Lambda T\alpha_n\ B$.

(vi) Let $\alpha_1, \ldots, \alpha_n$ be distinct individual variables. Let the same variables be rearranged $\alpha_{i_1}, \ldots, \alpha_{i_n}$. Let *A* be a predicate containing free occurrences of $\alpha_1, \ldots, \alpha_n$ and no others. Let ϕ be a one-place predicate functor containing no free variables. Then $\Lambda\phi\alpha_1 \ldots \Lambda\phi\alpha_n\, A \vdash \Lambda\phi\alpha_{i_1} \ldots \Lambda\phi\alpha_{i_n}\, A$.

Let A be a predicate containing free occurrences of distinct individual variables $\alpha_1, \ldots, \alpha_n$, and no others—this is their alphabetical order. Then $\sqcap A$ is an abbreviation of $\Lambda T\alpha_1 \ldots \Lambda T\alpha_n\, A$.

THEOREM 2 (REPLACEMENT) Let M, N either both be predicates of $\mathscr{L}$, or both be one-place predicate functors of $\mathscr{L}$. (i) If M, N are predicates, let $\sqcap[M \supset N]$ and $\sqcap[N \supset M]$ be theorems of $\mathscr{S}$. (A sentence theorem is a sequence theorem $C_1, \ldots, C_n \,/\, D$ where $n = 0$.) (ii) If M, N are predicate functors, then for every individual variable α which occurs free in neither M nor N, let $\sqcap[[\alpha\ M] \supset [\alpha\ N]]$ and $\sqcap[[\alpha\ N] \supset [\alpha\ M]]$ be theorems of $\mathscr{S}$. Let A be a predicate or one-place predicate functor. And let B be a predicate or predicate functor obtained from A by replacing M by N at 0 or more places in A. Then (i) if A is a predicate, then $\sqcap[A \supset B]$ and $\sqcap[B \supset A]$ are theorems of $\mathscr{S}$. (ii) If A is a predicate functor, then for every individual variable α not occurring free in A, B, $\sqcap[[\alpha\ A] \supset [\alpha\ B]]$ and $\sqcap[[\alpha\ B] \supset [\alpha\ A]]$ are theorems of $\mathscr{S}$.

Proof We first consider the special case where M is the same as A and N the same as B. In this case the theorem is immediate.

Now consider the number of occurrences of logical operators in A. We argue by induction on this number. Suppose it is 0. Then either we have the special case above, or M is replaced at 0 occurrences in A, or A is $[\alpha\ M]$ and B is $[\alpha\ N]$ for some individual symbol α. If M is replaced at 0 occurrences in A, then B is the same as A. It is an easy matter to prove $\sqcap[A \supset A]$. Suppose A is $[\alpha\ M]$ and B is $[\alpha\ N]$. Let $\alpha_1, \ldots, \alpha_n$ be the distinct individual variables occurring in M, N. If α is an individual variable distinct from each of $\alpha_1, \ldots, \alpha_n$, we have $\vdash \sqcap[A \supset B]$ and $\vdash \sqcap[B \supset A]$ by the statement of the theorem. Suppose α is α_i. We can construct a proof as follows. (Double lines abbreviate an extended proof. These abbreviations are justified either by the lemma or by the statement of the theorem.)

Let β be an individual variable not occurring in M, N, and let γ be an individual constant not occurring in M, N.

$$\Pi[[\beta\ M] \supset [\beta\ N]]$$

$$\Lambda T\beta\ \Lambda T\alpha_j\ \ \Lambda T\alpha_1 \ldots \Lambda T\alpha_n\ [[\beta\ M] \supset [\beta\ N]] \qquad \overset{1}{[\gamma\ T]}$$

$$\Lambda T\alpha_j\ \Lambda T\alpha_1 \ldots \Lambda T\alpha_n\ [[\gamma\ M] \supset [\gamma\ N]] \qquad \overset{1}{[\gamma\ T]}$$

$$\Lambda T\alpha_1 \ldots \Lambda T\alpha_{j-1}\ \Lambda T\alpha_{j+1} \ldots \Lambda T\alpha_n\ [\mathrm{S}\,{}^{\alpha}_{\gamma}i\ [\gamma\ M]| \supset \mathrm{S}\,{}^{\alpha}_{\gamma}i\ [\gamma\ N]|\,]$$

$$\Lambda T\alpha_j\ \ \Lambda T\alpha_1 \ldots \Lambda T\alpha_n\ [[\alpha\ M] \supset [\alpha\ N]] \qquad \Lambda\mathrm{I},\ 1$$

$$\Pi[[\alpha\ M] \supset [\alpha\ N]]$$

A proof of $\Pi[[\alpha\ N] \supset [\alpha\ M]]$ is similar.

Suppose α is an individual constant. Let β be an individual variable not occurring in M, N. We can construct a proof as follows.

$$\Pi[[\beta\ M] \supset [\beta\ N]]$$

$$\Lambda T\beta\ \Lambda T\alpha_1 \ldots \Lambda T\alpha_n\ [[\beta\ M] \supset [\beta\ N]] \qquad [\alpha\ T]$$

$$\Lambda T\alpha_1 \ldots \Lambda T\alpha_n\ [[\alpha\ M] \supset [\alpha\ N]]$$

$$\Pi[[\alpha\ M] \supset [\alpha\ N]]$$

A proof of $\Pi[[\alpha\ N] \supset [\alpha\ M]]$ is similar.

For the inductive step we assume the theorem is true for $0, \ldots, m - 1$ occurrences of logical operators in A. Now suppose A contains m occurrences. There is a separate case for each operator whose occurrence might be the main occurrence of an operator in A. I will prove only three cases for the sake of illustration. Remaining cases are left for the reader.

(1) Suppose the main occurrence in A is an occurrence of '$\forall$.' There are two cases: (1a) A is $\forall\phi\alpha\ A_1$. (1b) A is $[\sigma_1\ \psi\ \sigma_2, \ldots, \sigma_k]$, where σ_j is $\forall\phi\alpha$ or $\forall\phi$, and the first occurrence of '$\forall$' in α_j is the main occurrence of an operator in A.

(1a) Either we have the special case above, or else B is $\forall\phi'\alpha\, B_1$, where ϕ' is obtained from ϕ and B_1 is obtained from A_1 by replacing M by N at 0 or more places.

Let $\alpha_1, \ldots, \alpha_n$ be the distinct individual variables occurring free in A, B. Let β be an individual variable not occurring in A, B. Let $\gamma_1, \ldots, \gamma_{n+1}$ be distinct individual constants not occurring in A, B. Let ϕ^*, ϕ'^* be obtained from ϕ, ϕ' by replacing free occurrences of $\alpha_1, \ldots, \alpha_n$ by $\gamma_1, \ldots, \gamma_n$. Let A_1^*, B_1^* be similarly obtained from A_1, B_1, EXCEPT that free occurrences of α are not replaced.

By the hypothesis of induction, the following are theorems of $\mathcal{S}$:

(i) $\ulcorner[[\beta\ \phi] \supset [\beta\ \phi']]$
(ii) $\ulcorner[[\beta\ \phi'] \supset [\beta\ \phi]]$
(iii) $\ulcorner[A_1 \supset B_1]$
(iv) $\ulcorner[B_1 \supset A_1]$

We can construct a proof of $\ulcorner[A \supset B]$ as follows. (Abbreviations of extended proofs are justified by the hypothesis of induction and by the lemma.)

SUBPROOF I

$$\dfrac{\dfrac{\overset{1}{\forall\phi^*\alpha\ A_1^*}}{[aT\ \phi^*]} \qquad \dfrac{\dfrac{\overline{\overline{\Pi\ \Lambda T\beta\ [[\beta\ \phi] \supset [\beta\ \phi']]}}}{\Lambda T\beta\ [[\beta\ \phi^*] \supset [\beta\ \phi'^*]]}}{}}{[aT\ \phi'^*]}$$

SUBPROOF II

$$\dfrac{\overset{1}{\forall\phi^*\alpha\ A_1^*} \qquad \dfrac{\dfrac{\overline{\overline{\Pi\ \Lambda T\beta\ [[\beta\ \phi'] \supset [\beta\ \phi]]}}}{[[\gamma_{n+1}\ \phi'^*] \supset [\gamma_{n+1}\ \phi^*]]} \qquad \overset{2}{[\gamma_{n+1}\ \phi'^*]}}{[\gamma_{n+1}\ \phi^*]}}{\mathrm{S}^{\alpha}_{\gamma_{n+1}}\ A_1^*|}$$

SUBPROOF II:

$\Pi[A_1 \supset B_1]$

$[\underset{\cdot}{S}\overset{\alpha}{\gamma_{n+1}} A_1^*| \supset \underset{\cdot}{S}\overset{\alpha}{\gamma_{n+1}} B_1^*|] \quad \underset{\cdot}{S}\overset{\alpha}{\gamma_{n+1}} A_1^*|$

$\underset{\cdot}{S}\overset{\alpha}{\gamma_{n+1}} B_1^*$ ΛI, 2

SUBPROOF I:

$\Lambda\phi'^*\alpha\ B_1^*$

$[aT\ \phi'^*]$

$\forall\phi'^*\alpha\ B_1^*$ $\supset$I, 1

$[\forall\phi^*\alpha\ A_1^* \supset \forall\phi'^*\alpha\ B_1^*]$

$\Pi[\forall\phi\alpha\ A_1 \supset \forall\phi'\alpha\ B_1]$

A proof of $||[B \supset A]$ is similar.

(1b) This can be proved similarly to case (1a). If we do not have the special case treated earlier, we can use the rule $\forall$ Extraction to move the internal quantified phrase to the front of the predicate. We can then reason as above.

(2) The main occurrence of an operator in A is an occurrence of '$\ni$.' There are two cases: (2a) A is $(\phi\alpha \ni A_1)$. (2b) A is $[\beta\ (\phi\alpha \ni A_1)]$.

(2a) Unless we have the special case treated above, B is $(\phi'\alpha \ni B_1)$, where ϕ', B_1 are obtained from ϕ, A_1 by replacing M by N at 0 or more places.

Let $\alpha_1, \ldots, \alpha_n$ be the distinct individual variables occurring free in A, B. Let β be an individual variable not occurring in A, B. Let $\gamma_1, \ldots, \gamma_{n+1}$ be distinct individual constants not occurring in A, B. Let ϕ^*, ϕ'^*, A_1^*, B_1^* be as in case (1a).

By the hypothesis of induction, the following are theorems of $\mathcal{S}$:

(i) $||[[\beta\ \phi] \supset [\beta\ \phi']]$
(ii) $||[[\beta\ \phi'] \supset [\beta\ \phi]]$
(iii) $||[A_1 \supset B_1]$
(iv) $||[B_1 \supset A_1]$

A proof of $||[A \supset B]$ follows.

SUBPROOF I

$$\dfrac{\dfrac{\dfrac{\overset{1}{\Pi[\beta\ (\phi\alpha\ \ni\ A_1)]}}{[\gamma_{n+1}\ (\phi^*\alpha\ \ni\ A_1^*)]}}{[\gamma_{n+1}\ \phi^*]} \qquad \dfrac{\Pi[[\beta\ \phi]\ \supset[\beta\ \phi']]}{[[\gamma_{n+1}\ \phi^*]\ \supset[\gamma_{n+1}\ \phi'^*]]}}{[\gamma_{n+1}\ \phi'^*]}$$

SUBPROOF II

$$\dfrac{\dfrac{\dfrac{\overset{1}{\Pi[\beta\ (\phi\alpha\ \ni A_1)]}}{[\gamma_{n+1}\ (\phi^*\alpha \ni\ A_1^*)]}}{\underset{\cdot}{\mathrm{S}}\,{}^{\alpha}_{\gamma_{n+1}}\ A_1^*|} \qquad \dfrac{\Pi[A_1\ \supset\ B_1]}{[\underset{\cdot}{\mathrm{S}}\,{}^{\alpha}_{\gamma_{n+1}}\ A_1^*|\supset \underset{\cdot}{\mathrm{S}}\,{}^{\alpha}_{\gamma_{n+1}}\ B_1^*|]}}{\underset{\cdot}{\mathrm{S}}\,{}^{\alpha}_{\gamma_{n+1}}\ B_1^*|}$$

$$\dfrac{\dfrac{\dfrac{\dfrac{\dfrac{\begin{matrix}\text{SUBPROOF I:} & \text{SUBPROOF II:} \\ [\gamma_{n+1}\ \phi'^*] & \underset{\cdot}{\mathrm{S}}\,{}^{\alpha}_{\gamma_{n+1}}\ B_1^*|\end{matrix}}{[\gamma_{n+1}\ \phi'^*\ \ni\ B_1^*)]}\ \supset\text{I, } 1}{[[\gamma_{n+1}\ (\phi^*\alpha\ \ni\ A_1^*)]\ \supset[\gamma_{n+1}\ (\phi'^*\alpha\ \ni\ B_1^*)]]}}{\Lambda T\beta\ [[\beta\ (\phi^*\alpha\ \ni\ A_1^*)]\ \supset[\beta\ (\phi'^*\alpha\ \ni\ B_1^*)]]}}{\Pi\Lambda T\beta\ [[\beta\ (\phi\alpha\ \ni\ A_1)]\ \supset[\beta\ (\phi'\alpha\ \ni\ B_1)]]}}{\Pi\ [[\beta\ \ (\phi\alpha\ \ni\ A_1)]\ \supset[\beta\ (\phi'\alpha\ \ni B_1)]]}$$

This works for any variable β not occurring free in A or B. A proof of $\Pi[B \supset A]$ is similar.

(2b) This is proved similarly to (2a).

(3) The main occurrence in A is an occurrence of '$\breve{}$.' Then A is $[\alpha_1 \breve{\psi} \beta_1]$. Either we have the special case treated earlier, or else A is the same as B. The proof for the case where A is the same as B is found in the base case argument.

LEMMA 1 Let $[\sigma_1 \psi \sigma_2, \ldots, \sigma_k]$ be a predicate in which the main occurrence of an operator is an occurrence of the quantifier Q in a phrase $Q\phi$ or $Q\phi\alpha$. The main occurrence is in an occurrence of the quantified phrase as σ_i. Select an individual variable β not occurring in the predicate. Replace σ_i by β. Replace any occurrence of α that was bound by the Q in σ_i by β. Call the result of these replacements A. Then $\vdash \sqcap|[[\sigma_1 \psi \sigma_2, \ldots, \sigma_k] \supset Q\phi\beta\ A]$ and $\vdash \sqcap|[Q\phi\beta\ A \supset [\sigma_1 \psi \sigma_2, \ldots, \sigma_k]]$.

LEMMA 2 Let $[\sigma_1 \sim \psi \sigma_2, \ldots, \sigma_k]$ be a predicate in which the main occurrence of an operator is the displayed occurrence of '$\sim$.' Then
$\vdash \sqcap|[[\sigma_1 \sim \psi \sigma_2, \ldots, \sigma_k] \supset \sim[\sigma_1 \psi \sigma_2, \ldots, \sigma_k]]$ and
$\vdash \sqcap|[\sim[\sigma_1 \psi \sigma_2, \ldots, \sigma_k] \supset [\sigma_1 \sim \psi \sigma_2, \ldots, \sigma_k]]$.

LEMMA 3 Let $\forall\phi\alpha\ A$ be a predicate. Then
$\vdash \sqcap|[\forall\phi\alpha\ A \supset [\forall\ T\alpha\ [[\alpha\ \phi] \supset A]\ \&\ aT\alpha\ [\alpha\ \phi]]]$ and
$\vdash \sqcap|[[\forall T\alpha\ [[\alpha\ \phi] \supset A]\ \&\ aT\alpha\ [\alpha\ \phi]] \supset \forall\phi\alpha\ A]$.

LEMMA 4 Let $\Lambda\phi\alpha\ A$ be a predicate. Then $\vdash \sqcap|[\Lambda\phi\alpha\ A \supset \forall T\alpha\ [[\alpha\ \phi] \supset A]]$ and $\vdash \sqcap|[\forall T\alpha\ [[\alpha\ \phi] \supset A] \supset \Lambda\phi\alpha\ A]$.

LEMMA 5 Let $\eta\phi\alpha\ A$ be a predicate. Then $\vdash \sqcap|[\eta\phi\alpha\ A \supset \forall T\alpha\ [[\alpha\ \phi] \supset \sim A]]$ and $\vdash \sqcap|[\forall T\alpha\ [[\alpha\ \phi] \supset \sim A] \supset \eta\phi\alpha\ A]$.

LEMMA 6 Let $a\phi\alpha\ A$ be a predicate. Then $\vdash \sqcap|[a\phi\alpha\ A \supset aT\alpha\ [[\alpha\ \phi]\ \&\ A]]$ and $\vdash \sqcap|[aT\alpha\ [[\alpha\ \phi]\ \&\ A] \supset a\phi\alpha\ A]$.

LEMMA 7 Let $\iota\phi\alpha\ A$ be a predicate. Let β be an individual variable not occurring in ϕ, A. Then $\vdash \sqcap|[\iota\phi\alpha\ A \supset aT\alpha\ [[[\alpha\ \phi]\ \&\ A]\ \&\ \forall T\beta\ [[\beta\ \phi] \supset [\alpha = \beta]]]]$ and $\vdash \sqcap|[aT\alpha\ [[[\alpha\ \phi]\ \&\ A]\ \&\ \forall T\beta\ [[\beta\ \phi] \supset [\alpha = \beta]]] \supset \iota\phi\alpha\ A]$.

LEMMA 8 Let $[\alpha_1 \breve{\phi} \alpha_2]$ be a predicate in which α_1, α_2 are individual symbols. Then $\vdash \sqcap|[[\alpha_1 \breve{\psi} \alpha_2] \supset [\alpha_2 \psi \alpha_1]]$ and $\vdash \sqcap|[[\alpha_2 \psi \alpha_1] \supset [\alpha_1 \breve{\psi} \alpha_2]]$.

LEMMA 9 Let $[\beta\ (\phi\alpha \ni A)]$ be a predicate such that no free occurrence of α in A is in a position at which an occurrence of β would be bound. Then $\vdash \sqcap|[[\beta\ (\phi\alpha \ni A)] \supset [[\beta\ \phi]\ \&\ \underset{\cdot}{S}{}^{\alpha}_{\beta}\ A|]]$ and $\vdash \sqcap|[[[\beta\ \phi]\ \&\ \underset{\cdot}{S}{}^{\alpha}_{\beta}\ A|] \supset [\beta\ (\phi\alpha \ni A)]]$.

THEOREM 3 Let A be a sentence of $\mathscr{L}$. Then there is a sentence B in the first-order fragment of $\mathscr{L}$ such that $A \vdash B$ and $B \vdash A$.

Let X be a set of sentences of $\mathscr{L}$, and let A be a sentence of $\mathscr{L}$. Then A is a *(set-theoretic) logical consequence of* X ($X \mid\vdash A$), and X *(set-theoretically) (logically) implies* A iff there is no interpreting function f of $\mathscr{L}$ for a nonempty $\mathscr{D}$ which makes every sentence in X true and makes A false.

By virtue of Theorem 3 and Theorem 5.4, in order to prove that $\mathcal{S}$ is complete with respect to logical consequence, it is sufficient to consider proofs which are restricted to the first-order fragment of $\mathcal{L}$. We will show that an "ordinary" system of first-order logic with identity is found within $\mathcal{S}$. Ordinary systems are already known to be complete. So $\mathcal{S}$ is complete.

LEMMA 1 Let Γ be a proof whose conclusion is $\underset{\cdot}{S}\,{}^{\alpha}_{\beta}\,A|$, where α is an individual variable that occurs free in A and β is an individual constant that does not occur in any uncancelled hypothesis of Γ, and does not occur in A. Then Γ can be extended to obtain $\forall T\alpha\ A$.

Proof We can continue Γ as follows:

$$\dfrac{\dfrac{\overset{\text{TI}}{[\beta\ T]} \qquad \overset{\text{TI}}{[\beta\ T]}}{[aT\ T]}\,aI \qquad \dfrac{\dfrac{\overset{1}{[\beta\ T]} \qquad \overset{\Gamma:}{\underset{\cdot}{S}\,{}^{\alpha}_{\beta}\,A|}}{[\beta\ T]\ \&\ \underset{\cdot}{S}\,{}^{\alpha}_{\beta}\,A|}\,\&\text{I}}{\underset{\cdot}{S}\,{}^{\alpha}_{\beta}\,A|}\,\&\text{E}}{\forall T\alpha\ A}\,\forall\text{I},1$$

LEMMA 2 Let Γ be a proof whose conclusion is $\forall T\alpha\ A$. Let β be an individual constant. Then Γ can be extended to obtain $\underset{\cdot}{S}\,{}^{\alpha}_{\beta}\,A|$.

LEMMA 3 Let Γ be a proof whose conclusion is $\underset{\cdot}{S}\,{}^{\alpha}_{\beta}\,A|$, where α is variable that occurs free in A and β is a constant. Then we can extend Γ to obtain $aT\alpha\ A$.

LEMMA 4 Let Γ be a proof whose conclusion is $[\underset{\cdot}{S}\,{}^{\alpha}_{\beta}\,A| \supset C]$, where α is an individual variable that occurs free in A, and β is a constant that does not occur in A, in C or in any uncancelled hypothesis of Γ. Then we can extend Γ to obtain $[aT\alpha\ A \supset C]$.

THEOREM 4 $\mathcal{S}$ is complete with respect to (set-theoretic) logical consequence.

Proof By lemmas 1 – 4, the ordinary first-order rules $\forall$ Introduction, $\forall$ Elimination, $\exists$ Introduction (aT Introduction), and $\exists$ Elimination (a T Elimination) are derived rules of $\mathcal{S}$. But then $\mathcal{S}$ contains a standard deductive system of first-order logic with identity. Such systems are well-known to be complete with respect to logical consequence for first-order languages with identity. Hence, $\mathcal{S}$ is complete with respect to logical consequence for sentences in the first-order fragment of $\mathcal{L}$. So $\mathcal{S}$ is complete with respect to logical consequence.

Bibliography and Reference

1. Alonzo Church. *Introduction to Mathematical Logic.*
2. Haskell B. Curry. *Foundations of Mathematical Logic.* New York: McGraw-Hill, 1963.
3. Gerhard Gentzen. "Investigations into Logical Deduction," *The Collected Papers of Gerhard Gentzen,* edited by M. E. Szabo, pp. 68–131. Amsterdam: North-Holland Publishing Company, 1969.

Chapter 9
Speech-Act Structures

1. Syntax is Part of Semantics

We have previously considered intentional acts and their structures. We have recognized three fundamental structural relations and devised tree diagrams to represent these. In the preceding chapter, I gave a syntactic account which generated the predicates and sentences of $\mathcal{L}$ via transformations. And I used tree diagrams to represent syntactic constructions of predicates of $\mathcal{L}$. Now to treat $\mathcal{L}$ as if it were a language in use, I will provide an account of the structures of acts of using expressions of $\mathcal{L}$. This is an account of the speech-act syntactic structures of $\mathcal{L}$ expressions, which will be treated in ways that are appropriate to the English expressions which they resemble.

When $\mathcal{L}$ is regarded as a language in use, the account of speech-act syntactic structures is not conceived as a generative theory. We are supposing that we begin with the language $\mathcal{L}$, with acts of using expressions of $\mathcal{L}$. We abstract from acts, actors, and meanings to provide structural analyses of complex expressions. But we can only make sense of these structures with respect to the reality they are abstracted from. Recall the adjective + noun phrases we considered earlier. If our only interest was in generating such phrases, we could obtain all of the following by the same procedure:

round barn
former barn
small barn

We simply apply the adjective to the noun (or concatenate the two expressions). These three different diagrams:

```
   round barn
    /      \
round      barn

former:    barn
            ¦
           barn

(small +) barn
```

represent structures whose difference can only be understood with respect to the representational meanings of the connected expressions, or with respect to the representing acts performed with these expressions.

The speech-act syntactic account for $\mathscr{L}$ (or for any language that is actually used) is not an autonomous theory which generates a language that can then be interpreted. Speech-act structures are the abstracted structures of meaningful expressions and (ultimately) meaningful acts. Syntactic theory provides an analysis of complex expressions, but it does not generate these expressions. A syntactic analysis is part of a semantic explanation.

In giving a speech act account of $\mathscr{L}$, I will adapt the techniques of the preceding chapter. When acts are combined to constitute a complex, or acts are performed to enable a further act, I will speak of *transformations* from certain acts to a further act, or transformations from certain expressions to a further expression. We can conceive of these transformations as generating complex expressions from simpler ones. But the expressions which figure in these transformations are not uninterpreted marks or sounds. They are meaningful expressions. A complete explanation of a transformation must (1) explain the speech-act syntactic structure linking the inputs to the output of the transformation, (2) explain the transformation's effect on representational meaning, and (3) explain the transformation's effect on truth conditions (on Word-World connections).

The transformational structure of a complex expression is a semantic structure of that expression—it is a form which links meaningful expressions to constitute (to yield) a meaningful expression. A complex expression has more and less general semantic structures. If we specify the semantic categories of component expressions (we do this by explaining the kinds of meanings they have and the kinds of transformation in which they can figure) and give a transformational derivation of the complex expression, we have described a general semantic structure. If we give the most specific meanings of simple component expressions, and give a transformational derivation of the complex expression, we have given the most specific semantic structure of the complex. (Katz uses the expression 'logical form' for something very close to what I am calling the most specific semantic structure of a sentence.) Syntactic structure is not given prior to semantic structure, and interpreted to yield semantic structure. Semantic structure is prior. Specifically semantic features of this structure are ignored to give syntactic structure.

To explain a transformation, we must explain the transformation's effects on representational meaning and real world truth conditions. We don't explain its effects on inferential meaning. For the outputs of many transformations are not sentences. (Many transformations are such that their outputs are predicates which need not be sentences.) It is most convenient to explain inferential meaning with respect to sentences. However a theory of inferential meaning must incorporate an analysis of speech act structure. The speech act structure of a sentence must be indicated if we are to understand or explain its inferential meaning. To "handle" the inferential ambiguity of a sentence like 'Everyone loves someone' we must either develop an inferential theory for items like these:

(1) Everyone loves someone.
/ \
Everyone — *x* loves someone
/ \
x loves *y* — someone

(2) Everyone loves someone.
/ \
Everyone loves *y* — someone
/ \
Everyone — *x* loves *y*

or else we must use a canonical language whose sentences are not inferentially ambiguous to translate the original sentences, and then develop an inferential theory for canonical translations.

2. Denoting Acts

To give a syntactic-semantic account for $\mathcal{L}$ in terms of transformations, I will consider the transformations that were used in the preceding chapter to generate $\mathcal{L}$. Most of these transformations correspond to transformations which link speech acts (and the abstract versions of these which link meaningful expressions). The original transformations will be altered as needed to constitute speech-act transformations. The altered transformations will have their speech-act structures specified. It is no longer sufficient simply to give inputs and outputs.

As well as the relations which link various acts to form complex acts, the acts that are linked must be better understood. I have so far addressed sentential, propositional, illocutionary, and referring acts, and acts of predicative denoting. We need to recognize more kinds of acts than these and understand what they amount to. I will obtain additional terminology by pressing into service a much abused family of expressions, and adapt 'denote,' 'denoting,' etc. to my purposes. A sentential act is *not* a denoting act. An act of using an open predicate is an act of predicative denoting. An act of using an individual constant is an act of *individual* denoting. An act of using a quantified phrase is an act of *quantificational* denoting; there are several varieties of quantificational denoting. Using a phrase $\forall\phi$ or $\forall\phi\alpha$ is *universal* denoting. Using $\Lambda\phi$ or $\Lambda\phi\alpha$ is *mathematical* denoting. Using $\eta\phi$ or $\eta\phi\alpha$ is *negative* denoting, using $a\phi$ or $a\phi\alpha$ is *indefinite* denoting, and using $\iota\phi$ or $\iota\phi\alpha$ is *definite* denoting. Referring acts will be treated in a later chapter. As it turns out, some acts of individual denoting are referring acts and others aren't. For the present we will limit our attention to sentential acts and denoting acts.

In considering speech act structures of sentences of $\mathcal{L}$ and the different kinds of denoting acts performed with expressions of $\mathcal{L}$, I am treating $\mathcal{L}$ as if it were a language that people actually used for thinking, talking, and writing. I am doing this so that an account developed for $\mathcal{L}$ can fit a natural language. Of course, $\mathcal{L}$ seems much too simple to be useful as a language for communication. It is helpful to treat $\mathcal{L}$ *as if* it were really used. But I am ignoring some questions, important if we actually wanted to use $\mathcal{L}$, such as what to say for various expressions, how to indicate parentheses when speaking, etc. In dealing with acts of using various expressions in $\mathcal{L}$, I will be guided by the consideration of acts of using analogous English expressions.

If Tom uses the individual constant α which is a name of β, then Tom has performed an act of individual denoting. He has denoted individually. I will also say that Tom has denoted β individually. So if Tom uses the sentence '[*a S*]' ("Anne is short"), he has used '*a*' to denote *a* individually—to denote Anne individually. (Acts of using English proper nouns are also acts of individual denoting.) When I describe Tom as using α to denote β individually, I express no commitment to there actually being a β. Nor do I indicate or even suggest that Tom is so committed. Someone who uses 'Pegasus' has denoted Pegasus individually. Similar remarks apply to someone who uses 'Santa Claus' or 'Sherlock Holmes.' To say that Tom denoted Pegasus individually is simply to describe Tom's act in a specific way. An act of denoting Pegasus is one kind of act of individual denoting.

I am using forms of 'denote,' to label certain kinds of intentional acts. My use of these words differs from the standard use, in which 'denote' is used to indicate a relation between an expression and extralinguistic objects. (I always favor giving a new meaning to an old expression, in contrast to coming up with a new expression.) In my usage, though we can speak of denoting expressions—which are used to perform denoting acts—it is people and not expressions that denote. But I am not using 'denote' to signal a relation between a person, an act, or an expression and extralinguistic objects. When I am concerned with such a relation, I use the verb 'label.' When Tom performs a denoting act, he has *labeled* the objects which "answer" to this act (and the expression he used). If Tom says, "George Washington is a U.S. president," he has labeled George Washington in using 'George Washington.' He has labeled U.S. presidents in using '[is a U.S. president].' He has labeled each and every U.S. president, including George Washington.

Although I am using 'denote' to label linguistic acts, I also treat denoting like a relation. I not only say that Tom performed an act of individual denoting, but I say that he denoted Anne individually—in using '*a*' (or 'Anne') to denote Anne. Denoting is what I am calling an *intentional* relation. There are different reasons why this use of 'intentional' is appropriate. It is sufficient at present to note that these "relations" come to our attention in the course of studying intentional (linguistic) acts. Some intentional relations other than denoting are hoping, wanting, believing, expecting, and looking for. Intentional relations are to be contrasted with *real* relations like seeing, being next to, and being older than. (And *labeling*.) We talk about intentional relations in much the same way that we talk about real relations, but there are important differences between the two kinds of talk. Intentional relations aren't really relations. If a real individual α has a real relation *R* to individual β, then β is a real individual. (The restriction to a real individual α is made in order to avoid complications about mythical and fictional individuals.) If a real individual α has a real relation R to every ϕ, and β is a ϕ, then α has R to β. And if a real α has a real relation R to a ϕ, then there is some specific ϕ, say β, that α is related to by R.

It isn't the same for intentional relations. A real person can want an individual that doesn't exist. Dale might want an embrace (or more) from a famous actress. The particular event of her embracing him is the object of his desire—but this event has not, does not, and will not exist. We can also look for what doesn't exist (and never did). We can look for Camelot, or Atlantis. And David can be afraid of every snake without being afraid of each particular snake—without being afraid of them one at a time. For it is necessary to know about a particular snake to be afraid of it. Finally, Henry can want a martini without wanting any particular martini. Jorge can similarly look for a unicorn. Denoting is an intentional relation. If Ted says, "Camelot never existed," he has denoted Camelot (individually). When George says, "Hartford is a city," he has used the predicate '[is a city]' to denote a city predicatively, but he has not denoted a particular city. Similarly, when Jane says "Nobody is a vampire," she has predicatively denoted a vampire without denoting a specific vampire. When I use '$\forall T$' (or 'everything'), I have denoted everything without denoting each particular thing.

Intentional relations are not really relations, but it is convenient to talk about them in much the same way that we talk about genuine relations. A thorough account of intentional relations was intended here, but the initial chapters of this book grew so long that thorough discussion of these relations is being deferred to another occasion. At present I will content myself with giving a very sketchy account of them. A verb that signals an n-place real relation is an n-place functor, used to label n-tuples. A verb that signals an n-place intentional relation is not used to label n-tuples. Suppose we use '[x D y]' to say that x denotes y. Instead of treating 'D' similarly to the two-place functor 'S' for *sees,* I will construe 'D y' as an incomplete one-place functor. When John sees Mary and John sees Sally, we don't have different kinds of seeing in the two cases. The seeing is the same, it is only the objects that are different. When John denotes Mary and John denotes Sally, two kinds of denoting are involved. To describe John's acts as denoting acts, even as acts of individual denoting, is to describe them abstractly and incompletely. We only specify the kinds of acts performed when we say who or what John denoted.

An act of individual denoting is an act of denoting this individual or that individual. If A is a one-place predicate, then an act of using A is an act of predicative denoting. It is an act of denoting an arbitrary individual of a kind. If '[x V]' means *x is a vampire,* then to use this predicate is to denote (predicatively) an arbitrary vampire. This predicate contains a free variable, but it would not be used with a free variable. For in a sentence, the variable is either replaced or bound. Suppose '*c*' names Vlad the Impaler. Then when Jane says "[*c V*]," she hasn't used '[*x V*],' because no '*x*' has passed her lips (or her pen). Instead she has used '[*V*]' with a gap instead of a free variable. Jane has used '[*V*]' to predicatively denote an arbitrary vampire. We only use free variables to mark argument places in written predicates; it is understood that these variables are not there when the predicate is actually used. A one-place predicate is used to denote an arbitrary individual of a kind. An *n*-place predicate is used to denote an arbitrary *n*-tuple of a kind. These *n*-tuples are not set-theoretic constructions. They are simply *n* individuals, in order. We can also say that an *n*-place predicate is used to (predicatively) denote *n* arbitrary individuals, in order.

With quantificational denoting, a greater variety of alternative locutions will be allowed than are allowed for individual and predicative denoting. A speaker who uses $\forall\phi$ or $\forall\phi\alpha$ has denoted the ϕ's universally. He has also denoted an arbitrary ϕ universally. He has *not* denoted a specific ϕ—in case α is a ϕ, he has not denoted α. If he uses $\Lambda\phi$ or $\Lambda\phi\alpha$ he has denoted the ϕ's mathematically, and also denoted an arbitrary ϕ mathematically. With $\eta\phi$ and $\eta\phi\alpha$ he denotes the ϕ's negatively and denotes an arbitrary ϕ negatively. Our speaker uses $a\phi$ and $a\phi\alpha$ to denote ϕ's indefinitely and to denote an arbitrary ϕ indefinitely. Similarly, he uses $\iota\phi$ and $\iota\phi\alpha$ to denote the ϕ's definitely and to denote an arbitrary ϕ definitely.

3. The Individual Transformation

The individual transformation combines an act of individual denoting with an act of predicative denoting. It combines an individual constant (a name) with a predicate. If the predicate contains a single free variable, the output is a sentence. Otherwise, the output is a predicate which contains one less free variable than the predicate input. Suppose '*b*' names Bob and '[*x D*]' means *x is a doctor (x doctors)*. Then Rosemary can assert that Bob is a doctor by performing an act with this structure:

```
    [b D]
   /     \
  b     [x D]
```

Rosemary uses '*b*' to denote Bob individually. She uses '[*D*]' to denote a doctor predicatively. Each of these acts has the same purpose: to assert that Bob is a doctor. Even though the two components have a common purpose which defines the assertion, these components play different roles in the sentential act. An act of using an expression which fills the argument place in a predicate is an act which serves *as a subject* in the act of which it is a component. Using an expression which is the predicate is an act which serves *as the predicate* of the complex act. The same terminology is used for the expressions used to perform the acts. Rosemary's act of denoting Bob individually serves as a subject of her assertion; her act of denoting a doctor serves as the predicate. And '*b*' is a subject and '[*D*]' is the predicate. Every expression in an argument position is *a* subject expression; only the expression in the first argument position is *the* subject of the predicate or sentence. So '*b*' is also the subject of Rosemary's sentence. (We won't speak of *the* subject of a complex act, unless there is only one act serving as a subject. Ordinarily, when we talk about *the* subject we are concerned with an expression rather than an act.)

Rosemary might have used the sentence '[*b D*]' to perform an act which is not an assertion, where the same diagram shows the structure of her act. Nothing in $\mathscr{L}$ or in our diagrams indicates illocutionary force (or the absence of it). From the diagrams, we can only determine part of the purpose for using the components of a sentence.

When diagrams are used to represent speech-act structures, some features are liable to be misunderstood. One such feature is the repetition of expressions in a tree diagram. Component expressions are listed at the bottoms of branches; these same expressions reoccur at higher nodes. But the language user does not produce an expression as many times as it occurs in the diagram. Rosemary, for example, does not say '*b*' once for its occurrence at the bottom of the left branch, and then repeat herself in composing the sentence. The expression at the top of the tree is all that the language user produces—the rest of the tree diagram simply shows the structure of what she says with the top expression. Rosemary uses '*b*' to perform one act, and '[*D*]' to perform a second. By performing these two acts in order, with their common purpose, she manages to make an assertion. She does not do something besides performing the two denoting acts in order to make her assertion. The assertion is constituted by these components.

A second potentially misleading feature of the diagrams is that they contain expressions which are neither spoken nor written by the language user. An example is provided by individual variables, like the '*x*' in the diagram above. Someone might think that such expressions are first supplied, and then deleted by the language user. But the language user does not think, speak, or write the deleted expressions. We use these expressions because they are convenient for our analyses. Individual variables, for instance, are convenient devices for marking argument positions. Rosemary makes no use of '*x*' in asserting that Bob is a doctor. (We must also avoid the mistake of thinking that the language user produces a tree diagram, or some substitute for it, which serves as input into a sound-producing program. *We* use tree diagrams to provide a perspicuous representation of structure. Spatial relations and lines in the diagram represent structural relations which may not be spatial relations. The tree diagrams are instruments of analysis, not instruments employed by language users.)

Let us expand our vocabulary with '*a*,' which names Laura, and '[*x H y*]' which means *x hit y*. We can now translate the sentence 'Bob hit Laura' as '[*b H a*].' We saw earlier that the English sentence can be used to perform acts having different structures. The $\mathscr{L}$ sentence can also be used in different ways. It might be used to perform acts with these structures:

(1)

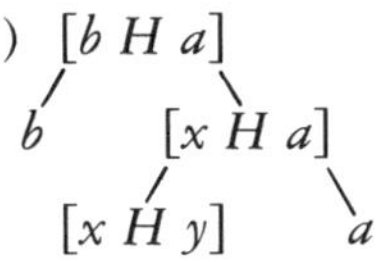

(2)

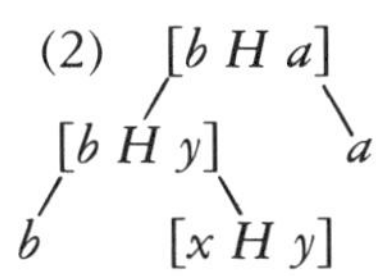

In act (1), Rosemary uses '[*x H y*]' to predicatively denote a pair < hitter, hit > (in the past), and she uses '*a*' to individually denote Laura. She performs both of these acts in order to denote an individual that hit Laura. Predicative denoting is different from individual denoting in that it isn't specific. When Rosemary predicatively denotes a pair < hitter, hit >, she does not denote a specific hitter or a specific victim. To mark the non-specific character of a denoting act, I often use the word 'arbitrary.' Rosemary predicatively denotes an *arbitrary* pair < hitter, hit >.

In (1), Rosemary individually denotes Bob and predicatively denotes an arbitrary individual that hit Laura in order to assert that Bob hit Laura.

If Rosemary performs an act with the structure of (2), she denotes Bob individually and predicatively denotes a pair < hitter, hit >, both in order to denote an arbitrary individual hit by Bob. She predicatively denotes an individual hit by Bob and individually denotes Laura in order to assert that Bob hit Laura. In either case, all that Rosemary says is '[*b H a*].' The differences concern the ways in which the components are assembled.

In discussing the difference between structures (1) and (2), I will continue to use temporal metaphors for the bottom-to-top order of a tree diagram. Lower nodes are earlier, higher nodes are later. I noted before that later nodes, those which are closer to the top, represent acts which are more prominent in the complex acts than are those acts represented by earlier nodes. Act (1) gives greater prominence to the act of denoting Bob than to the act of denoting Laura. Act (1) gives greater prominence to Bob than to Laura. Its structure is appropriate in answer to the question 'Who hit Laura?' Act (2) gives greater prominence to the act of representing Laura, and to Laura. This structure is appropriate for an answer to the question 'Who(m) did Bob hit?' The different tree diagrams show us the different speech-act structures which distinguish the topic or focus of a sentence from other elements in the sentence. In speaking, cues like emphasis and intonation are often used to mark this—what they are marking is speech-act structure. (The same goes for languages which contain expressions to mark the focus.)

In discussing the English sentence 'Bob hit Laura,' I noted three possible structures for acts of using this sentence. In $\mathscr{L}$, the third structure is represented this way:

```
(3)  [b H a]
     /  |  \
    b [x H y] a
```

If we considered the individual transformation of chapter eight, such a structure would not be allowed. The transformations of chapter eight had at most two inputs. This limitation does not hold for transformations based on speech-act structures. Rosemary can make an assertion with the structure of (3), as well as assertions with the structures of (1) and (2). In (3), Rosemary denotes Bob individually, predicatively denotes a pair < hitter, hit >, and denotes Laura individually, all in order to assert that Bob hit Laura. In the speech-act individual transformation, *n* individual constants $\beta_1, \ldots, \beta_n$ can be combined with a predicate *A* to yield *A′*. In practice, *n* will rarely exceed 3—2 is probably the most common upper limit.

4. Representing

We have been considering individual denoting acts, predicative denoting acts, and the sentential acts which are propositional. The only propositional acts considered above are assertions, but propositional acts which are not assertions have the same kinds of structures as assertions.

When someone performs a denoting act, she *takes* an expression *for* a thing. When she performs an individual denoting act, she takes an expression for a specific individual. When she performs a predicative denoting act with a one-place predicate, she takes the predicate for an arbitrary individual of a kind. When she uses an *n*-place predicate, she takes the predicate for an arbitrary *n*-tuple of a kind. This description applies whether the predicate is atomic or not. When Rosemary uses '[*x H y*],' she takes the predicate for an arbitrary pair < hitter, hit > in the past. When she uses '[*x H a*],' she takes this predicate for an arbitrary individual that hit Laura. And it doesn't matter whether anyone or anything did hit Laura—Rosemary can perform a hitter-of-Laura-denoting-act even if nothing hit Laura. Although open predicates are used to perform denoting acts, sentences are not. This is not because there is nothing in the world which answers to a sentence. I am simply stipulating that 'denote' will be used in such a way that sentences don't denote; this is characteristic of the concept of denoting that we shall employ. (But I believe that this concept of denoting is helpful for understanding the usual practice of logicians.)

Denoting acts will also be described as *representing* acts. When Rosemary uses '*b*' to denote Bob individually, she takes the expression '*b*' for Bob. Doing this is using '*b*' to represent Bob. When she uses the name '*b*,' the representational meaning of her act and (derivatively) of the expression '*b*' is *representing Bob.* Representing is another intentional relation. It is possible to represent both real and fictitious individuals. Speaking loosely, we can say that the representational meaning of a name is the individual represented. Strictly speaking, the meaning is *to represent the specific individual.*

The predicate ‘[*x D*]’ can be used to denote an arbitrary doctor; it is taken for an arbitrary doctor. The representing done with the predicate will be described in a slightly different way. For I am using ‘represent’ as a technical term; it has a different job than ‘denote.’ When we use a name, the acts of individual denoting and individual representing are described in the same way. An act of denoting Bob individually is an act of representing Bob. But when we consider the representing done with a predicate, we will distinguish between the individual represented and what the individual is represented as being or doing. I will say that the predicate ‘[*x D*]’ is used to represent an *arbitrary individual as a doctor.* The empty place in the predicate corresponds to the arbitrary individual. (In a natural language, an empty place might correspond to an arbitrary individual of a kind. If, for example, it is a matter of language that only people can have a sense of humor, then the predicate ‘[has a good sense of humor]’ might be used to represent an arbitrary person as having a good sense of humor.) In considering the representing done with a predicate, we distinguish the individual represented and the property it is represented as having. When we talk of denoting, we overlook this distinction. The predicate ‘[*x D*]’ is used to denote an arbitrary doctor even though it is used to represent an arbitrary individual as a doctor. The representational meaning of the predicate is *to represent an arbitrary individual as a doctor.* (The representational meaning of an expression serves to identify the individual or kind of individual that is denoted.)

When the individual act and the predicative act are combined to obtain the propositional act with this structure:

```
   [b D]
   /   \
  b   [x D]
```

the propositional act is not a denoting act. A predicate must contain free variables (or gaps) if it is to denote. But the propositional act is a representing act. It has representational meaning. The propositional act represents *Bob as a doctor.* The predicative act represents an arbitrary individual as a doctor. In the propositional act, the act of representing Bob takes the place of the arbitrary individual—this act (and the expression ‘*b*’) fill the gap in the predicative act.

There is an asymmetry between acts of individual denoting (and representing) and acts of predicative denoting (and representing). The predicative act contains gaps which get filled by individual acts. In describing the two kinds of acts, the asymmetry is marked by speaking of arbitrary individuals. The predicate ‘[*x D*]’ is used to denote an *arbitrary* doctor;

it represents an *arbitrary* individual as a doctor. This use of 'arbitrary' does not mean that some choice function picks some real doctor, but that it doesn't matter which one. Instead 'arbitrary' marks the denoting and representing act as concerned with a kind of individual rather than with a specific individual. When the individual act is combined with the predicative act to yield the propositional act, the individual act has a property conferred on it. This property is the property of being combined with the predicative act. The propositional act *is* the individual act with the property of being combined with the predicative act.

It isn't arbitrary that we describe the propositional act as the individual act with the property of being combined with the predicative act—and not as the predicative act with the property of being combined with the individual act. It is true that the predicative act has this property, but the representing of the propositional act is grounded by the individual act. The propositional act represents an individual with a property—an individual as something or other. The individual act with its property represents the individual with its property. If we tried to construe the propositional act from the "standpoint" of the predicative act, we would have the propositional act representing an arbitrary doctor with the property of being Bob. This isn't how we understand the sentence (act). The asymmetry between individual and predicative acts is sometimes misunderstood by theorists who think that predicates are to properties (or relations) as names are to individuals. These theorists fail to understand how our language works, and what kind of world it represents.

Every denoting act is a representing act, but not conversely. If we consider acts of using names, there is no difference between denoting and representing. If we use α to denote β individually, we are also using α to represent β, an act of taking α for β. When we consider an open predicate, to describe an act of using that predicate as an act of denoting an individual or *n*-tuple of a kind is to describe the act abstractly and incompletely. When we say that Janice used $[x\ \phi]$ to denote an arbitrary ϕ, we have given less information about her act than when we say she used $[x\ \phi]$ to represent an arbitrary individual as ϕ. As well as saying that Janice used $[x\ \phi]$ to denote an arbitrary ϕ, we could say that she represented an arbitrary ϕ. This alternative locution also describes her act abstractly and incompletely; it will usually be avoided, because it may prove confusing. It is convenient to use 'denote' for more abstract descriptions of predicative acts, and 'represent' for more specific descriptions.

A denoting act is an act of taking for. But so is a representing act. When we use α to represent β, we take α for β. When we use '$[x\ D]$' to represent an arbitrary individual as a doctor, we take the predicate for an arbitrary individual, as qualified by being a doctor. A sentential act performed with '[*b D*]' is a representing act, but not a denoting act. This act is constituted by two component acts of taking expressions for things. The complex sentential act will also be described as an act of taking for. The sentence is taken for Bob, as a doctor.

Now let us consider the more complicated propositional act performed with '[*b H a*].' If Rosemary's assertion has this form:

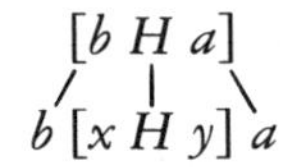

we can treat it as we treated this:

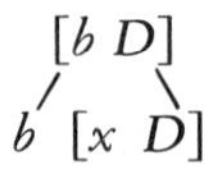

For there are two individual acts, one representing Bob and one representing Laura. The predicative act represents an arbitrary individual as having hit an arbitrary individual; it represents a pair of arbitrary individuals as related by hitting (in the past). The propositional act represents Bob, Laura as related by hitting (in the past). To describe the representational meaning of a predicative or propositional act, we will say which individuals are represented, then say what they are represented as. So we can say that a predicative act represents $\alpha_1, \ldots, \alpha_n$, as such and such.

Suppose we consider a propositional act with this structure:

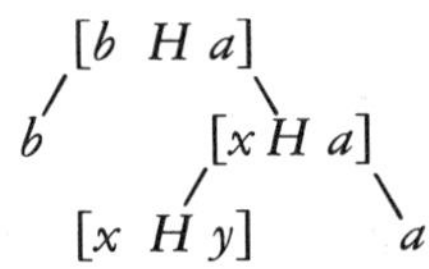

The initial predicative act represents a pair of arbitrary individuals as related by hitting (in the past). We could also say it represents an arbitrary individual *x* and an arbitrary individual *y* as related by hitting (in the past). This predicative act and the act of representing Laura are both performed in order to perform the second predicative act, the act of representing an arbitrary individual, (and) Laura as related by hitting in the past. The act of representing Bob and the intermediate predicative act are both performed in order to represent (as an assertion) Bob as having hit Laura. The propositional act (the assertion) represents both

Bob and Laura, but not on the same level. Bob is given more prominence in the final act. With predicative and propositional acts, I will distinguish *direct* from *indirect* representing. An individual-representing act which is an immediate component of a predicative or propositional act causes the complex act to *directly* represent its individual. The predicate *directly* represents the arbitrary individuals "answering" to its free variables. If a predicate A directly represents a specific individual β, and A is a component of B, then B *indirectly* represents β.

In the propositional act above, the second predicative act directly represents an arbitrary individual and Laura. The propositional act directly represents Bob and indirectly represents Laura. When the free variable (the gap) is replaced by a name, the arbitrary individual is no longer represented—we will not describe the propositional act as indirectly representing an arbitrary individual. In describing the representing of a predicative or propositional act, we will list the individuals that are directly represented, and indicate what they are represented as. Individuals which are indirectly represented are mentioned only in saying what the directly represented individuals are represented as. So the propositional act above represents Bob as having hit Laura.

And this act:

```
            [b H a]
            /      \
      [b H y]       a
      /      \
     b     [x H y]
```

represents Laura as having been hit by Bob.

5. Depicting

When we say that a speaker denoted β, represented β, or represented β as φ, we have not indicated (1) whether β is a real individual, or (2) whether the speaker believes β to be a real individual. It is very often the case that when someone uses language, she intends to be talking about things in the world. We need to have some convenient terminology for discussing the issue of whether she succeeds. I am using the word 'label' in such a way that labeling is a real relation which is a counterpart to the intentional relation denoting. A speaker can denote β whether or not β is real. She can only label a real β. (I also used 'label' in a derivative sense in giving the truth conditions of sentences of $\mathscr{L}$. In the primary sense, it is acts and not expressions that label. What they label is determined not by an interpreting function, but by their representational meanings.) Using 'label' as a technical term, we can replace the second sentence in this paragraph by this: It is very often the case that when someone uses language, she intends to be labeling things in the world.

If Rachel uses the name α to perform an individual-denoting act (which is also an individual-representing act), and α is a name of β, then Rachel has labeled β iff (1) β is real, and (2) Rachel intends to represent a real individual in using α. Rachel can try to perform a labeling act and fail, because the expression she uses is not a name of a real individual. (Rachel thinks Tarzan was a historically real person. When she uses 'Tarzan,' Rachel believes she is making statements about an Englishman who had some wild times in Africa.) Rachel can use a name to perform an act of individual-representing without trying to perform a labeling act. She knows that Sherlock Holmes wasn't real. When Rachel uses 'Sherlock Holmes' to talk about the Arthur Conan Doyle stories, she isn't labeling anyone and she isn't trying to. Rachel can also perform an individual-denoting act with the name of a real individual and not label that individual—if she thinks the name she is using is not the name of a real individual. Rachel thinks Troy was a fictional city and the Trojan War was a fictitious event. When she uses 'Troy' to speak of Troy, she is not labeling the historic city of Troy.

As I am defining 'label,' whether an act labels or not depends in an essential way on the language user's intentions. (This opens the door to the possible situation where a speaker like Rachel uses 'Troy' without labeling, but her audience uses her utterance to label a real city.) My reason for bringing in intentions here is that I have brought them in everywhere else; consistency requires them here as well. The present theory is an account of the intentional structures of linguistic acts. Semantic accounts must be based on intentional structures. It is easy enough to introduce a word for a relation *R* that links Rachel's 'Troy'-acts to the historic city of Troy, because there really is such a relation. But it has not got much interest or importance for the present account.

Given this understanding of labeling, a problem can arise concerning individual-denoting acts performed in the course of discussing fictional situations. Someone talking about Sherlock Holmes says that Holmes lived in London. Has that person, in using 'London,' labeled the real city of London? He has definitely not labeled anyone in denoting Sherlock Holmes. And he has made a true statement in saying that Holmes lived in London. There is no question that there is, and was, a real London. The question is whether the speaker intends to be talking about the real London. This question cannot be decided once and for all, for all language users. On some such occasions a speaker is labeling the real individual involved; on other occasions he is not. The speaker might, for example, be criticizing Arthur Conan Doyle by noting respects in which the London in the Sherlock Holmes stories is unlike the London of Doyle's time. He might say something like "Sherlock Holmes lived in London—allegedly. But I think he must have lived somewhere else. Because in the city where Holmes lived, the following features of nineteenth-century London are absent. Etc." However, if the speaker is simply relating a Sherlock Holmes story, or discussing it "on its own terms," he is not labeling London. Sherlock Holmes lived in London all right, but not the real London.

If Rachel uses an n-place predicate to perform an act of predicative denoting, she has performed a labeling act iff (1) there really are n-tuples answering to the predicate, and (2) Rachel intends to be representing real individuals. When she performs her predicative act, she has denoted an arbitrary n-tuple. She has labeled every n-tuple that answers to her predicate. If Rachel is concerned with the real world, and uses '[x D]' to perform a predicative act, then she has labeled each and every doctor. If '[x V]' means *is a vampire,* then when Rachel uses '[x V]' to perform an act of predicative denoting, she has not labeled anything. She may not have been trying to label anything, for Rachel may believe there are no vampires. Even if she believes there are such, she cannot label them, for she is mistaken. And a predicate which can be used to label need not be. If '[x W]' means x *is a wolf,* and this predicate gets used in telling the story of Red Riding Hood, the narrator need not be labeling wolves—for he is not trying to describe the real world. (The narrator might, however, in the course of telling the story, include factual information about real wolves.)

Whether Rachel performs a labeling act when she performs a predicative act depends in part on her intentions. But if she does perform a labeling act, which individuals or n-tuples she labels do not depend on her intentions. Perhaps Rachel labels the ϕ's. If β is a ϕ, then Rachel has labeled β, even if she happens to believe that β is not a ϕ. Which individuals or n-tuples she labels in using a predicate are determined by the meaning of the predicate she uses—by its place in her system of language. (But Rachel might, by mistake, fail to assign the dictionary meaning to the predicate she uses. Which individuals she labels is determined by the place of the predicate in *her* system of language.)

A linguistic act can be both a labeling and a denoting act. It can be a denoting act without being a labeling act, but it can't be a labeling act and not a denoting act. When learning a language for the first time, it is plausible that we learn to label and to denote simultaneously, for we first learn language in learning (to have and) to structure and describe our experience. Initially, labeling and denoting acts coincide, but once we can use the language, we can become aware of the difference between them. This awareness enables us to understand certain errors. It makes storytelling possible.

It has proved necessary to distinguish the linguistic act of denoting from that of representing, because an account of denoting is not adequate for explaining representational meaning. Labeling is a real relation which is a counterpart to the intentional relation of denoting. We also need to recognize a real relation which is similarly related to the intentional relation of representing. The words I shall use are 'depict' and 'depicting.' Depicting and labeling coincide in certain cases. An act of individual representing, if it labels any individual, labels and depicts the same individual. A predicative act performed with an atomic predicate labels and depicts the same individuals or *n*-tuples, if it labels any. For other predicates, the labeling relation only concerns their free variables (their gaps). A predicate depicts for its free variables and individual constants.

When considering what is depicted by a linguistic act, we are not concerned with representational meaning. So we won't have a distinction between direct and indirect depicting. We shall consider some examples discussed earlier. In the propositional act represented by:

```
    [b D]
    /   \
   b   [x D]
```

we are concerned with a real Bob, who is really a doctor. The individual act of using '*b*,'

(i) denotes Bob,
(ii) represents Bob,
(iii) labels Bob,
(iv) depicts Bob.

The predicative act of using '[*x D*],'

(i) denotes an arbitrary doctor,
(ii) represents an arbitrary individual as a doctor,
(iii) labels every doctor,
(iv) depicts every doctor.

The propositional act

(i) does not denote,
(ii) represents Bob as a doctor,
(iii) does not label,
(iv) depicts Bob—if Bob were not a doctor, the propositional act would depict nothing.

Now consider this propositional act:

```
   [b H a]
   /  |  \
 b [x H y] a
```

where Bob and Laura are real. The account of the individual acts is as before. The predicative act of using '[*x H y*],'

(i) denotes a pair of arbitrary individuals which are related by hitting (in the past),
(ii) represents an arbitrary individual *x*, an arbitrary individual *y*, as related by hitting,
(iii) labels every pair $< \alpha, \beta >$ such that α hit β,
(iv) depicts every pair $< \alpha, \beta >$ such that α hit β.

The propositional act (ii) represents Bob, Laura, as related by hitting (in the past), (iv) depicts < Bob, Laura > just in case < Bob, Laura > is depicted by the predicative act of using '[*x H y*].' Otherwise the propositional act does not depict.

In this propositional act:

```
      [b H a]
      /     \
     b     [x H a]
           /      \
      [x H y]      a
```

the intermediate predicative act

(i) denotes an arbitrary individual that hit Laura,
(ii) represents an arbitrary individual, (and) Laura, as related by hitting (in the past),
(iii) labels every individual that hit Laura,
(iv) depicts every pair $< \alpha$, Laura $>$ such that α hit Laura.

The propositional act (ii) represents Bob as having hit Laura, (iv) depicts < Bob, Laura > iff < Bob, Laura > is depicted by the intermediate predicative act. Otherwise it depicts nothing.

With respect to the propositional acts we have considered, the different speech act structures affect representing and representational meaning. They don't affect depicting. Depicting and labeling are tied to real world truth conditions—the different propositional structures don't affect these. A complete semantic account for a language should explain inferential meaning, representational meaning, and real world truth conditions. A deductive system seems to be the most appropriate device for investigating and explaining inferential meaning. To give an account of representational meaning, we need an account of representing and denoting. But representing is primary. Once we have an account of representing, we can deduce the proper account of denoting. For real world truth conditions, we need an account of depicting and labeling. Here depicting is primary; an account of labeling can be derived from an account of depicting. It is interesting that, in modern logic, artificial languages are usually provided with an explanation of labeling. But depicting has been ignored. This is a shortcoming of logical "semantic" accounts. As we shall see later, there are some phenomena in English that we can't understand without taking account of depicting.

6. Picturing

When intentional acts are components of a complex intentional act, the complex act has a structure. The immediate components are united by their common purpose to constitute the complex. (Some complex acts also contain components which are nonact events.) But there is more to the structure of a complex act than its containing *n* components. For example, all complex acts constituted by three (immediate) component acts don't have the same structure—they have a general structure in common but don't have the same specific structure. The additional structure of a complex act is determined by the roles of its components and by the kinds of its components. In one complex act, different components can play different roles. In different complex acts, the components can play different kinds of roles. We previously considered the example of a complex illocutionary act which is an inference. In such an act, the role of premise-assertions is different from the role of the conclusion-assertion. We can further distinguish the premise roles in inferences where the premises together constitute a single act which supports the conclusion from the premise roles in inferences where each premise provides independent support for the conclusion. (The first case is the normal one for deductively valid inferences.)

When certain component acts are combined to constitute a complex act, each component has the property of being combined with the others. Ordinarily a component with this property does not constitute the complex act. The roles of the various components are not such that one component's role is to confer a property on another component—even though the one component does do this (as if incidentally). In a propositional act in which an individual representing act is combined with a predicative act, the role of the predicative act *is* to confer a property on the individual act. Each component act is a distinct individual; each is an event which is an individual. When they are combined to form a propositional act, the role of the act which represents individually is *to be characterized.* The role of the predicative act is *to characterize.* This general description fits all propositional acts constituted by an individual-representing act combined with a predicative act. Such acts are distinguished from one another in kind by the individual represented and the property conferred. This individual-representing act is combined with that predicative act. The representational meanings of different predicative acts serve to distinguish the property conferred in one case from that conferred in another. The representational meaning of a given predicate (and predicative act) is determined by its place in the system of language.

In this act:

```
  [b H a]
  /  |  \
b [x H y] a
```

it would be misleading to say that the individual acts have a property (or properties) conferred on them. When combined in the propositional act, the two individual-representing acts are related by the predicative act. The predicative act is an individual which is an event. The role that the predicative act plays in the propositional act is to tie together the individual-representing acts. By itself, the predicative act represents a pair of arbitrary individuals (as related). The propositional act does not represent arbitrary individuals; it represents Bob and Laura. The propositional act represents the same individuals as its individual-representing components. It does not represent what its predicative component represents. For in the propositional act, a predicative component serves to characterize or to relate the individual representing components.

If we consider a propositional act like this:

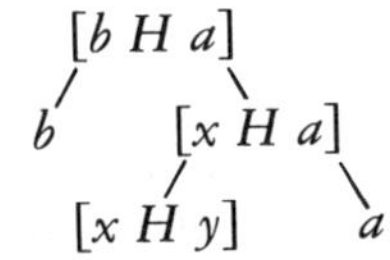

the individual act of representing Laura has an incomplete property conferred on it—it is combined with the act of representing a pair of arbitrary individuals as related by hitting in the past. And it fills the second gap in the predicative act. But the act which represents Laura with the property of being hit by an arbitrary individual is also described as an act which represents an arbitrary individual and Laura as related by hitting. The incomplete character of the predicative act performed with '[*x H a*]' makes the role of '[*x H y*]' in this act more complicated than the role of the (component) predicative act in this sentential act:

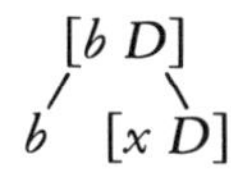

In the act performed with '[*x H a*],' the predicate '[*x H y*]' is used to confer an incomplete property on the act of representing Laura. The role of conferring this incomplete property is more fully described as the role of relating an empty (argument) place to the act of representing Laura. So the predicative act performed with '[*x H a*]' represents two individuals as related. In contrast, the act performed with '[*b H a*]' represents Bob as possessing the relational property of having hit Laura.

The present account of the workings of propositional acts is a picture theory, at least for those propositional acts constituted by individual-representing acts and predicative acts. (We haven't yet considered other propositional acts.) The individual-representing act, with its property, represents an individual with its property. Individual-representing acts, related in a certain way, represent individuals as related.

Frege was moving toward a picture theory when he discussed the distinction between objects and functions, especially concepts, and the distinction between object expressions (names) and function expressions, especially predicates. He did not develop a successful theory, because he could not reconcile the fact that predicate expressions are used to represent with the fact that they serve to characterize individual expressions. The solution to the difficulty is that predicate expressions do not represent properties and relations (Frege's concepts)—instead they represent arbitrary individuals that have the properties and relations. When combined with an individual expression, the result does not represent arbitrary individuals. It shows how the specific individuals are said to be characterized and related.

The picture theory in the *Tractatus* is more nearly satisfactory. But the theory isn't entirely clear, and it is potentially misleading. The *Tractatus* suggests that in some fully analyzed sentences, there are no predicate expressions, but only names. It only *suggests* this. In 3.1432, Wittgenstein gives an essentially correct explanation of a relational sentence. He never gives the corresponding explanation of a sentence with a one-place predicate—my conjecture is that he didn't know what to say about these. The misleading character of the *Tractatus* account is even more prominent in Wilfrid Sellars' many explanations of a picturing language. Sellars thinks he is explaining what Wittgenstein had in mind, when he (Sellars) describes a perspicuous picturing language. Sellars' perspicuous language contains only names. The style of writing these names is what pictures in this language. Several names arranged to form some pattern represent the situation where the named objects are related in some way—perhaps spatially. We can use different type fonts, colored ink, etc. for writing a single name; this pictures the named individual with this or that property.

A language of the sort Sellars describes is a language which could be used to picture things having properties and things being related. But it is easy to get the impression from his descriptions that the language, by itself, does the picturing. This is wrong, because nothing is intrinsically a picture. An object must be taken as, or used as, a picture. The object doesn't picture; the act of using the object pictures. The picturing languages that Sellars describes are especially simple. The sentences which represent individuals as having properties are one-word sentences. When I first descibed predicative acts, like the act of using '[is mountainous],' I called this an act of taking the predicate for an arbitrary mountainous place. Such an act of taking for is an act of representing an arbitrary mountainous place. A more careful and fuller description has it that the predicative act represents an arbitrary individual, or an arbitrary place, as mountainous. If it is possible to perform a single, simple act of representing an arbitrary individual as ϕ, then it is also possible to perform a single, simple act of representing a specific individual as ϕ. We see this in languages like Latin or Spanish in which a verb in the first or second person can be used by itself to constitute a sentential act. The speaker can use a one-word sentence to represent herself as ϕ, or to represent her addressee as ϕ. We can imagine a language in which there aren't just first, second, and third-person endings for verbs. But there is a different ending for every individual that anyone will ever want to talk about. We could then perform a simple act of representing this individual as ϕ, a different simple act of representing that individual as ϕ, and so on. In using this language, we would picture individuals with properties, but we would not exploit speech act structure to do so.

The language whose one-word sentences are distinguished by their different endings is more perspicuous in some respects than a Sellars-style language with different ways of writing names. Not only is it easy to (mistakenly) think that picturing is intrinsic to the expressions of a Sellars-style language, but it is also easy to think that acts of naming (of individual denoting) constitute sentential acts for that language. But an act of individual denoting cannot in ordinary circumstances constitute a sentential act. An act of predicative denoting is essential to a sentential act. Instead of thinking of one-word sentential acts as acts of individual denoting, we must regard them as specific predicative acts—they are specific as opposed to indefinite.

Even in a Sellars-style language, acts of using relational sentences will be complex—at least for the deliberate language user. There will be different acts to denote the different individuals represented as related. No expression will be used to perform an act of predicative denoting, but it will still be necessary to perform an act of taking the individual acts as related, for related individuals. The related individuals acts don't by virtue of being related represent related individuals. The language user must know how to interpret the relation between names, and must actually do so. Even without a predicate expression, a predicative act is required. (It is conceivable but unlikely that an accomplished user of a Sellars-style language would be able to perform a simple act of representing several individuals as related.) A Sellars-style language is simpler in some respects than natural languages. It seems much harder to use than natural languages. And it is potentially misleading in various ways.

7. Multiple Structures

When an act of individual denoting is combined with a predicative act, the resulting act represents an individual as this or that. The individual act with a property represents an individual with a property—it pictures an individual with a property, as do some of the adjectival acts considered earlier. I shall speak of *adjectival transformations* in connection with those acts performed with adjective + noun phrases. We recognize three adjectival transformations: (1) the *absolute* adjectival transformation:

round barn
/ \\
round barn

(2) The *relative* adjectival transformation: (small +) barn
(3) The *radical* adjectival transformation:

former: barn
¦
barn

The acts in the abolute transformation exemplify the same general structure as acts in the individual transformation:

[*b D*]
/ \\
b [*x D*]

The component acts are performed in order to constitute the complex; the complex act is constituted by the components with their common purpose. The difference between the absolute transformation and the individual transformation is due to the differences between component acts, and the different roles the components play in the complexes. In this transformation:

round barn
/ \\
round barn

the adjective input represents an arbitrary round object. The nominal input represents an arbitrary barn. The output represents an arbitrary barn *with* the property of being round. The output is the nominal input characterized by the property of being combined with the adjective input. The output act is an act with a property which pictures an individual with a property. The output of this transformation:

[*b D*]
/ \\
b [*x D*]

is also a complex act which consists of the nominal input characterized by the property of being combined with the other input. The output is a propertied individual act which represents a propertied individual—it represents an individual *as* propertied. It is important to mark the difference between the outputs of the two transformations by different locutions, because in English only a complete predicative act can be accepted or rejected; only a complete predicative act is true or false.

The output of the relative transformation: (small +) barn, is also a nominal act with a property; this represents an arbitrary barn with the property of being small. Both the absolute and the relative transformations use a propertied act to represent a propertied individual. The difference between the two transformations concerns the kind of property that is represented. An absolute property can be understood by itself; a relative property can only be understood with respect to a class of individuals.

With the radical adjectival transformation, we don't represent an individual with a property:

```
former:   barn
           ¦
          barn
```

The input represents one object (an arbitrary barn). The output represents a different object. The individual represented by the output does have a property—in this case, the property of having once been a barn. We can also say that the output act has the property of being enabled by the input act. But this transformation is unlike the other adjectival transformations in not yielding a complex act in which one element gives a property to another. The property of the enabled act is not interpreted as a property of the represented object.

We have noted that a single complex expression can be used to perform acts having different structures. In some cases, the different structures mark ambiguity as this is ordinarily understood. The different structures of acts performed with 'Everyone loves someone':

```
(1) Everyone loves someone.
       /                  \
 Everyone          x loves someone
                     /          \
               x loves y       someone

(2) Everyone loves someone.
        /                  \
  Everyone loves y        someone
      /          \
Everyone       x loves y
```

indicate sentential acts which have

(i) different inferential meanings,
(ii) different truth conditions,
(iii) different representational meanings.

In other cases, the different structures do not mark ambiguity as this is normally conceived. The three structures that we marked for 'Bob hit Laura' (or '[*b H a*]') do signal representational ambiguity. But this is not ordinarily considered to be ambiguity; it is rather a matter of focus, or emphasis. From the perspective of the present theory, such differences in emphasis are instances of the same general phenomena as the ambiguity of 'Everyone loves someone.'

The structural differences (between acts of using a single expression) are allowed for by the transformations we have so far considered. (We have not considered the speech act transformations which generate 'Everyone loves someone.' These would be quantificational transformations. There is a big difference between the quantificational transformations in chapter eight and the speech-act quantificational transformations we shall consider later. However, the quantificational transformations—for English—will provide for the different readings of 'Everyone loves someone.') But some transformations are associated with different structures. There is a typical structure associated with a transformation; this is sufficient for understanding inferential meaning and truth conditions. For certain transformations we also have atypical structures which affect representational meaning. The atypical structures often achieve their effects because of their contrast with the typical structure.

We will consider some atypical structures in connection with the adjectival transformations. If we consider the absolute adjective 'round,' its typical use is illustrated:

```
      round barn
       /      \
  round        barn
```

However, the same noun phrase can be used to perform acts with different structures. It can be used this way: (round +) barn

Here the adjective 'round' is used to give a special character to the act of representing a barn. Such an act would be appropriate in the following situation: Helen says, "George owns a round garage." We correct her by saying, "No, George owns a round barn," (emphasizing 'barn'). We don't represent an arbitrary round object in order to represent a round barn.

Our act "from the start" is one of representing a certain kind of barn. We do this by representing a barn, and giving our act a special character which cuts down the representing to a round barn.

The phrase 'round barn' can also be used this way:

```
round:   barn
          ¦
         barn
```

This would be appropriate if Helen said, "George owns a square barn," and we corrected her, "No, George owns a round barn"—emphasizing 'round.' We are using 'round' to represent a round barn. The act of using 'barn' merely enables this. It is as if our use of 'barn' simply echoed Helen's use, which is the act enabling us to use 'round' to represent a round barn.

An absolute adjective can be used to perform acts having all three structures. A relative adjective like 'small' cannot be used to perform an act with this structure:

```
     small barn
     /        \
 small         barn
```

The relative adjective can be used in both of the following ways:

```
(i)  (small +) barn
(ii) small:    barn
                ¦
               barn
```

The first way is the typical use of a relative adjective. Radical adjectives can only be used in one way:

```
former:   barn
           ¦
          barn
```

(They can only be used in one way by the deliberate language user. The less deliberate speaker can use 'former barn' to perform a simple nominal act.) The fact that all three kinds of adjectives can be used to perform acts with this structure:

```
adjective:   noun
              ¦
             noun
```

is reflected in the semantic account that Montague provides for adjectives in [2]. For adjectives are associated with functions that take the set associated with the modified noun to any other set.

Bibliography and References

1. Gottlob Frege. *Translations from the Philosophical Writings of Gottlob Frege.*
2. Richard Montague. "English as a Formal Language."
3. Wilfrid Sellars. *Science, Perception and Reality.* London: Routledge & Kegan Paul, 1963.
4. Wilfrid Sellars. *Science and Metaphysics, Variations on Kantian Themes.* New York: Humanities Press, 1968.
5. P. F. Strawson. *Individuals, An Essay in Descriptive Metaphysics.* Garden City, New York: Doubleday & Company, Inc., 1963.
6. Ludwig Wittgenstein. *Tractatus Logico-Philosophicus.*

Chapter 10
Pronouns and the Language $\overline{\mathcal{L}}$

1. The Variable Transformation

In the preceding chapter, we began to develop a speech act account for $\mathcal{L}$. This account will be developed by providing an explanation of the speech act structures associated with each of the transformations used in chapter eight to generate $\mathcal{L}$. Explanation of each transformation's effect on truth conditions and representational meaning is also needed. We can provide this by explaining how the depicting and the representing of the output is related to the depicting and representing of the inputs. (We can then determine how the transformation affects labeling and denoting.) In the preceding chapter, we considered the individual transformation, which combines individual constants with a predicate. In discussion of this transformation, it proved necessary to make various distinctions and to introduce new terminology.

Now let us turn our attention to other transformations. Not much needs to be said about the variable transformation. The input and the output of this transformation do not correspond to distinct acts. This transformation only affects free variables, which are not used in performing linguistic acts. If we consider this construction which involves the variable transformation:

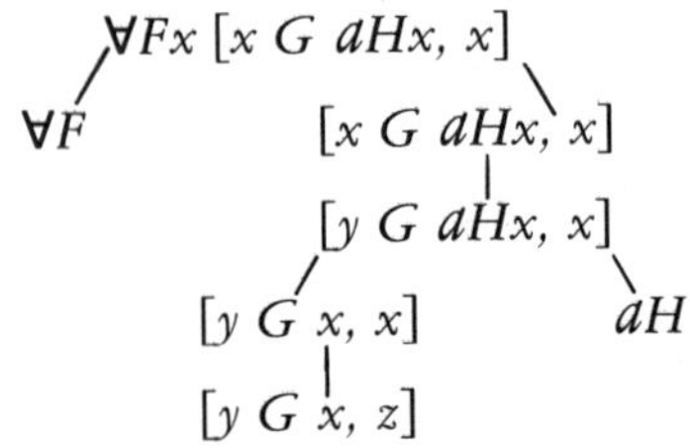

we see that the variable transformation replaces a free '*y*' by a free '*x*.' Since no '*y*'s occur in the final sentence, there cannot be an act corresponding both to '[*y G aHx, x*]' and '[*x G aHx, x*].' In the tree diagrams for speech act structures, the variable transformation will not be shown. Since the effect of this transformation is primarily notational, it will be combined with transformations which introduce variable-binding operators. For example, the above tree diagram can be replaced by this:

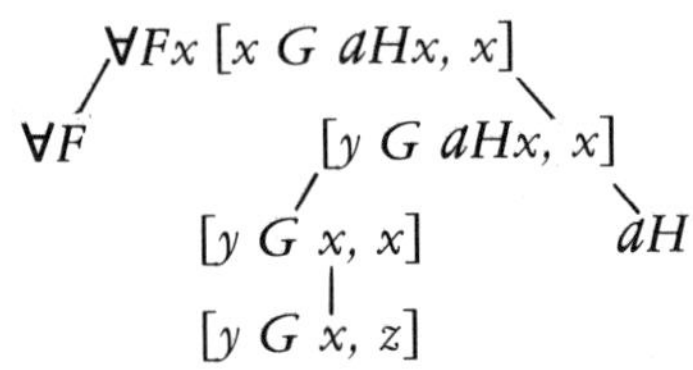

2. The Reflexive Transformation

In describing $\mathscr{L}$, the reflexive transformation was used to "identify" two free variables in a predicate, by replacing occurrences of one by occurrences of the other. Now that we are thinking of transformations as marking relations between linguistic acts, there is no reason to restrict the reflexive transformation to two variables at a time. The reformed reflexive transformation will enable us to identify *n* distinct free variables. So we could have this situation:

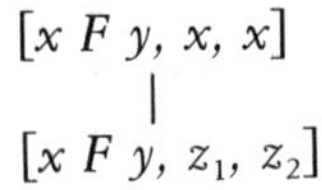

When the reflexive transformation is applied in a language we are actually using, it will be unusual to identify more than two argument places at once.

In order to understand the reflexive transformation, let us consider predicative acts performed with English expressions. Take the verb 'killed' and the predicate '*x* killed *y*' (or '[killed]'). The act of using the predicate is an act of representing a pair < killer, killed >; it is an act of representing arbitrary individuals *x*, *y* as such that *x* killed *y*. If we consider the adverb 'slowly' used in the predicate '*x* killed *y* slowly,' we can see that it is analogous to a relative adjective. A predicative act performed with this predicate would have the structure:

x killed *y* (+ slowly)

Now consider the sentence:

Judas killed himself.

Following our earlier treatment, we might expect this to be used in an act like the following:

```
        Judas killed himself.
       /                \
  Judas            x killed himself
                        |
                   x killed y
```

But this is unsatisfactory. When a complex act is defined by the immediate purpose of its components, and no component is a completing event, then there must be more than one component. With the linguistic acts we are considering, there is no reason to admit completing events. For the reflexive transformation, there is a single input act; this is a predicative act. The output is a different predicative act. The input act is not a component whose purpose defines the output act. We must canvass the remaining two structural relations. Either (ii) the input act enables the output act, or (iii) the output act is the input act equipped (intentionally) with a special character.

There is some analogy between the reflexive transformation and the relative adjective transformation. There is a sense in which the representing done with '*x* killed *y*' is "cut down" rather than "wiped out" to give the representing done with '*x* killed himself.' This reduction in representing is different from the reduction accomplished with the adverb 'slowly.' The predicates '*x* killed *y*' and '*x* killed *y* slowly' both represent pairs; the pair represented by the modified predicate is a more specialized version of the pair represented with the plain predicate. But the predicate '*x* killed himself' does not represent pairs at all. It represents an arbitrary male (possibly an arbitrary male person) as related to himself in the manner represented by '*x* killed *y*.' This reduced representing is nonetheless a qualified form of the representing done with '*x* killed *y*.' The sentence 'Judas killed himself' will typically be used to perform an act like this:

```
        Judas killed himself.
       /                \
  Judas            x killed (+ himself)
```

The reflexive pronoun 'himself' is not used to perform a representing act. It gives a special character to the predicative act. The predicative act with its special character represents an arbitrary male as killing himself. The above representation of the reflexive transformation does not have a separate "entry" for the input and the output of this transformation. In the following:

x killed (+ himself)

the output is '*x* killed (+ himself),' while the input is '*x* killed' without the parenthetical expression. It is sometimes convenient to have input and output on separate lines. An alternative representation of the reflexive transformation will be the following:

x killed (+ himself)
x killed *y*

The input is directly beneath the output. No line connects the input to the output, for the input is the same act as the output. A single act is represented twice, once without its special character, once with it.

The reflexive pronoun cannot be used to perform an act like this:

```
   Judas killed himself.
    /       |        \
Judas   x killed y    himself
```

The pronoun 'himself' is not used to perform an independent representing act; it is not used to perform an independent act whose purpose can define the sentential act. The typical act of using the reflexive pronoun is illustrated in the preceding paragraph, but the reflexive pronoun can also be used to perform an act like this:

```
   Judas killed himself.
    /               \
Judas            x killed   :himself
                     ¦
                 x killed y
```

Here '*x* killed *y*' (or '[killed]') is used to represent a pair $<$ killer, killed $>$ (in the past). This enables the act performed with 'himself'—i.e., the act of representing an arbitrary male as killing himself. Such an act could be appropriate in correcting a person who thought that someone other than Judas had killed Judas.

In English, reflexive pronouns are not the only expressions used to carry out the reflexive transformation. We also find possessive pronouns (possessive adjectives) and plain pronouns associated with the reflexive transformation. Consider the sentence:

(1) Jim hopes he will win the election.

Let us understand that the he in question is Jim. Even with this understanding, the sentence is representationally ambiguous—though it is not inferentially or truth conditionally ambiguous. The ambiguity of (1) can be brought out by considering the more obvious ambiguity of:

(2) Only Jim hopes he will win the election.

Sentence (2) can mean (i) that of all the candidates, Jim is the only one who wants to win. Or (ii) that of all the people interested in the election, only one person hopes Jim will win—and Jim is that person. The same ambiguity infects (1), but with (1) it doesn't make any inferential difference.

In order to represent the different acts of using (1), I need to make some remarks about intentional verbs. These are the verbs which "express" intentional relations; 'hope' is such a verb. Because there is no room for a thorough treatment of intentional verbs in this book, I shall simply and without justification or detailed illustration state principles governing intentional verbs and acts of using these verbs. When a verb like 'hit,' which expresses a real relation, is used, we can have a sentential act like this:

```
     Bob hit Laura.
     /    |      \
  Bob   x hit y   Laura
```

The verb 'denote,' as I am using it, expresses an intentional relation, which is not really a relation. The property of denoting Bob or denoting Laura is not a relational property. Such a property is merely a determinate version of the determinable property of denoting. If we consider this sentence:

Frank's speech act denoted Laura.

the sentence is *not* used to perform an act like the following:

```
        Frank's speech act denoted Laura.
        /                    |         \
Frank's speech act     x denoted y     Laura
```

Instead, the act has this structure:

```
           Frank's speech act denoted Laura.
          /                              \
Frank's speech act                x denoted (+ Laura)
```

A two-place intentional verb is not used in a predicate which represents a pair of individuals as related in some way. The predicate represents an individual as qualified by a determinable property. Another act can be performed which gives a special character to the predicative act; the special character produces a more determinate predicative act. The predicative act

x denoted (+ Laura)

is unlike the nominal act

(small +) barn

in an important respect. When 'small' is used to give a special character to the act of representing a barn, the word 'small,' by itself, is not used to perform a representing act. In the predicative act above, the expression 'Laura' is used to represent and denote Laura. This denoting act gives a special character to the predicative act.

Consider the sentence 'Frank's speech act denoted a man who owns a dog.' This could be used as follows:

```
           Frank's speech act denoted a man who owns a dog.
          /                                            \
Frank's speech act            x denoted (+ a man who owns a dog)
```

In more detail, the act might have this structure:

```
           Frank's speech act denoted a man who owns a dog.
          /                                            \
Frank's speech act            x denoted (+ a man who owns a dog)
                                            /             \
                                          man          x owns a dog
                                                        /        \
                                                   x owns y     a dog
```

However, in using the sentence, we might also have this act:

Frank's speech act denoted a man who owns y

/ \

Frank's speech act x denoted (+ a man who owns y)

/ \

man x owns y

This act would be the input to the transformation whose output is the sentential act. The input act is a predicative act, but it does not denote an arbitrary individual. Neither does it represent Frank's act as related to an arbitrary individual. This speech act *obliquely* represents an arbitrary individual. Directly, it represents Frank's speech act as determinably denoting a man who owns an arbitrary individual. We cannot transform the predicative act to the sentential act in this way:

Frank's speech act denoted a man who owns a dog.

/ \

Frank's speech act denoted a man who owns y a dog

Such an act would represent a dog as having a certain property. For it to be true, there would have to be a dog with that property. Instead, the sentential act will have this structure:

Frank's speech act denoted a man who owns (+ a dog)

/ \

Frank's speech act x denoted (+ a man who owns y)

/ \

man x owns y

To distinguish more clearly between the input and the output of this last transformation, we could also represent the act this way:

Frank's speech act denoted a man who owns (+ a dog)

Frank's speech act denoted a man who owns y

/ \

Frank's speech act x denoted (+ a man who owns y)

/ \

man x owns y

When a representing expression is used in the object of an intentional verb, it is used to perform a representing act. The truth of what is said does not require that the representing expression label any individuals. But sometimes a speaker wishes to acknowledge that a representing expression used in an intentional context does label individuals. One way to do this is to use the representing expression outside of the intentional context:

> George Washington was the first president of the U.S. Frank's speech act denoted George Washington.

Or:

> George Washington was a real person. Frank's speech act denoted George Washington.

We could not use the same strategy with the sentence:

> (3) Frank's speech act denoted a girl.

We should recall that if Frank used 'Laura' to denote Laura, it does not follow that he denoted a girl—even though Laura is a girl. We are talking about the kind of act Frank performed, not about an individual girl which is one term of a real relation. (The inference fails because Frank might not know that Laura is a girl.) The following sentence:

> (4) For some girl, Frank's speech act denoted her.

expresses an indefinite commitment to there being a girl answering to Frank's denoting act. The truth of (4) requires that Frank used a singular term to denote a specific individual, and that the expression he used labels a specific girl. (It would label a specific girl if we used it; Frank's act may not have labeled the girl—if he doesn't believe she is real.) If we use this sentence:

> (5) Laura is a girl, and Frank's speech act denoted her.

we know which girl Frank's expression labels, but not which expression he used. We know in a general way what kind of denoting act Frank performed.

Let us return to sentence (1):

> (1) Jim hopes that he will win the election.

In performing the sentential act, the speaker might perform this act:

(6) *x* hopes (+ (that +) *y* wins the election)
/ \
y wins *z* the election

The expression 'that' is used to give an explicit propositional (or predicative) character to the act of using '*y* wins the election.' The act represented by (6) is neutral between the two (representational) meanings of (1). This act represents an arbitrary individual as hoping that an arbitrary individual wins the election. The first arbitrary individual is represented directly. The second is not; it is represented *obliquely.* In the sentential act performed with 'Judas killed himself,' the predicative act performed with '*x* killed *y*' represents two arbitrary individuals. This predicative act is transformed to the act performed with '*x* killed himself,' which represents one arbitrary individual. The predicative act (6) represents two arbitrary individuals, though in different ways. We can perform a reflexive transformation on the output of (6) to yield '*x* hopes that he wins the election.' I will represent the act this way:

(7) *x* hopes that (+ he +) wins the election

x hopes (+ (that +) *y* wins the election)
/ \
y wins *z* the election

The reflexive transformation "bunches up" argument places in a predicate. It can be used even when one argument place is in an intentional context and the other isn't. The semantic account will be different in such a case than it will when no intentional verbs are present. But I won't give a semantic account for the intentional case here. When (1) is used to perform an act like this:

(8) Jim hopes that he wins the election.
/ \
Jim *x* hopes that (+ he +) wins the election

x hopes (+ (that +) *y* wins the election)
/ \
y wins *z* the election

then (1) has the (approximate) sense of:

(9) Jim hopes to win the election.

(But no reflexive transformation figures in an act of using (9).)

To distinguish the meaning (1) has when used as in (8) from the other meaning we are considering, we must distinguish two uses of pronouns: the reflexive use, and (what I shall call) the *ordinary* use. Reflexive pronouns are normally used reflexively. Plain pronouns can also be used reflexively. In its second meaning, (1) has the sense of:

(10) Jim hopes that Jim wins the election.

An act of using (10) might have this structure:

```
  Jim hopes that (+ Jim +) wins the election.

  Jim hopes that y wins the election
 /                                 \
Jim          x hopes (+ (that +) y wins the election)
                                /              \
                          y wins z        the election
```

To determine whether (1) can be used like (10), we must understand what constitutes the ordinary use of 'he' in (1). One thing we might do is to regard the use of 'he' as a lazy substitute for using 'Jim.' But this use of the pronoun isn't *very* lazy, for there seems to be no energy saving when we say 'he' rather than 'Jim.' Anyway, the idea that 'he' is a kind of abbreviation for 'Jim' is a bad one. For in this sentence:

(11) Some communist hopes that he will win the election.

the pronoun 'he' can be used in the ordinary way. But we can't achieve the effect of (11) by replacing 'he' by 'some communist.'

To understand this use of the pronoun, it is helpful to recall cases in which a single intentional act has two immediate purposes. Earlier we considered Victor's act of turning the radio on softly, and we considered plain and consummated illocutionary acts. Those were cases in which the person performing the act had distinct purposes in mind. Now I want to consider an act which is originally performed with one immediate purpose, and is subsequently "assigned" another purpose.

Suppose that the lights go out in Frank's kitchen. He decides that a fuse has blown, goes downstairs and replaces it. (He is right about the fuse.) When he does this, his daughter Julie accompanies him. Frank's purpose for replacing the fuse is *to restore electricity to the kitchen.* (Of course, there are further purposes as well.) Much later, when Frank is in his office at work, Julie calls up to tell him that the lights and some appliances in the kitchen have gone out. Frank then instructs Julie to remember what he did on the previous occasion, and to do the same. When Frank originally changed the fuse, he did not intend to be teaching or showing Julie anything. She just happened to be there. Now, in retrospect, Frank is "assigning" an educational purpose to his act of changing the fuse.

I believe this example provides a model for understanding how the pronoun 'he' is used when (1) has the sense of (10); it is a model for understanding the ordinary use of a pronoun. The expression 'Jim' is used to represent Jim, for a certain purpose. In this act:

Jim hopes that *y* wins the election
/ \
Jim *x* hopes (+ (that +) *y* wins the election)

the purpose for representing Jim is to represent him as (determinably) hoping that an arbitrary individual wins the election. In this act:

(12) Jim hopes that he wins the election.

Jim hopes that *y* wins the election ←+– he –+→
/ \ \
Jim *x* hopes (+ (that +) *y* wins the election)

the pronoun 'he' is used to give a special character to the antecedent act of using 'Jim.' But 'he' is not used to perform a representing act. The antecedent act with its (new) special character has a new role and a new purpose. The new role is to give a special character to the predicative act. The new purpose of the act of representing Jim is the purpose of the sentential act. The looping arrow leads from the act being assigned a new role and purpose to the act in which the original representing act is a new component. The '+' between 'he' and 'Jim' indicates that 'he' serves to give a special character to the original act. The '+' between 'he' and the sentence indicates that the original act with its new special character gives a special character to the predicative act.

When used ordinarily, a pronoun does not always give a special character to a predicative act. The sentence:

(13) Jim is smart and he is rich.

might be used this way:

(14)

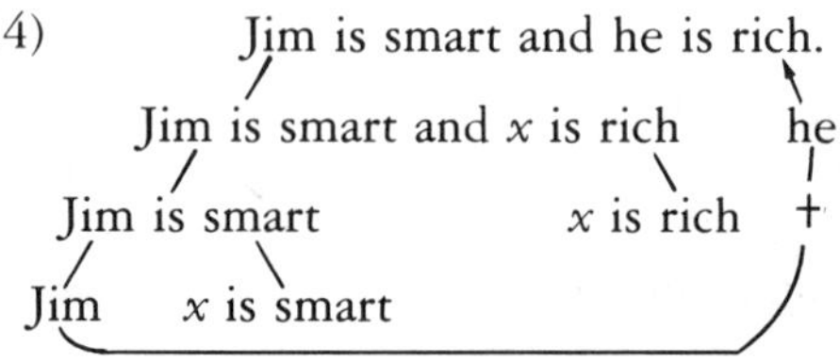

Here, 'Jim' is used in order to represent Jim as smart. The act of representing Jim is assigned the subsequent purpose of representing Jim as such that Jim is smart and rich. The act of using 'he' gives a special character to the act of representing Jim, by way of assigning that act a new purpose. The '+' between 'he' and 'Jim' indicates that (using) 'he' gives a special character to the act of representing Jim. There is no '+' between 'he' and the sentence, because the act of representing Jim is a component whose (new) purpose serves to define the sentential act.

When a pronoun is used reflexively, that pronoun serves to "bunch up" different argument places so that they can be filled "simultaneously." A pronoun used in the ordinary manner does not serve to "identify" different argument places. It serves to "spread out" the antecedent so that it can fill more than one place. (These metaphors will later be cashed in for precise semantic statements.) In customary first-order languages, and in $\mathscr{L}$, individual variables are analogous to pronouns. They are like pronouns used reflexively. Individual variables "tie together" the different argument places that are to be affected by a single (occurrence of an) operator. But there is an important difference between a first-order language (or that portion of $\mathscr{L}$ which is first-order-like) and normal English. For in a first-order language, variable-binding operators precede the predicate expressions to which they apply. In an English sentence, a pronoun used reflexively bunches up argument places by filling the place other than the place where the name or quantified phrase will go. In 'Judas killed himself,' the pronoun 'himself' fills the second argument position so that when 'Judas' goes in the first position, it will count as filling both. In a sentence '$(\forall x)F(x)$' (or '$\forall Tx\ [x\ F]$'), the predicate '$F(x)$' ('$[x\ F]$') has only one argument-place. So different places can't be bunched up. However, the prefixed quantified phrase "fills" or affects the argument place in '$F(x)$' just as 'Judas' fills the second place in 'Judas killed himself.' The essential role of both 'himself' and the second 'x' in '$(\forall x)F(x)$' is to identify the argument place filled (or affected) by an expression located elsewhere. So in '$(\forall x)F(x)$' the second 'x' is behaving like a reflexive pronoun. The 'x' in '$F(x)$' does essentially the same thing as the two '*x*'s in '*F*(*x*, *x*).' (But the '*x*' in '(∀*x*)' is not used in either the reflexive or the ordinary fashion.)

I have previously described the reflexive transformation for $\mathscr{L}$. Now that we have examined the speech act structures associated with the reflexive transformation, we can see that $\mathscr{L}$ is not satisfactory for "carrying out" the reflexive transformation. These problems do not concern quantified phrases. Suppose '[*x D*]' means *x is a doctor* and '[*x L y*]' means *x loves y*. Now consider the sentence '[∀*Dx* L *x*]'("Every doctor loves himself/herself"). In using this sentence, the reflexive transformation takes the predicate '[*x L y*]' to '[*x L x*].' The sentential act might have his structure:

```
        [∀Dx L x]
       /          \
    ∀D             [x L (+ x)]

                   [x L y]
```

The right input to the sentential act is the output of the reflexive transformation. The second occurrence of '*x*' is accompanied with a '+' because this '*x*' is used to give a special character to the predicative act. The left '*x*' gets no plus, because this is not regarded as an expression occurring in the sentential act. Only expressions actually used can serve to give a special character to an act. An act of using '∀*Dx* [*x L x*]' might have this structure:

```
        ∀Dx [x L x]
       /           \
    ∀D              [(x +) L (+ x)]

                    [x L y]
```

Since both '*x*'s occur in the final sentence, they both get '+'s.

Although the reflexive transformation is not used to obtain the sentence '*aPx* [*x D*]' ("For some person *x*, *x* is a doctor"), we can represent the sentential act this way:

```
        aPx [x D]
       /         \
    aP            [(x +) D]
```

Since the (internal) '*x*' occurs in the sentence, it is given a '+' because it gives a special character to the predicative act—marking the place to be affected by the quantifier. (A detailed tree diagram will include '+'s in such cases. Ordinarily I will abbreviate diagrams and leave out the plus signs.)

The problem that the reflexive transformation poses for $\mathscr{L}$ concerns individual constants (and the individual transformation). Suppose we want to say that Bob loves himself. In $\mathscr{L}$, we must use the sentence '[*b L b*].' But in a speech act which has this structure:

```
     [b L b]
     /     \
    b    [x L x]

         [x L y]
```

there is no expression we can use to give a special character to the predicative act. If we were really going to use $\mathscr{L}$ as a language for communication, then we would find that $\mathscr{L}$ lacks the resources for using the reflexive transformation to provide a predicate that can be combined with a name. We can't use $\mathscr{L}$ to say that Bob loves himself. This makes $\mathscr{L}$ unsatisfactory for dealing with the reflexive transformation in English. We will overcome this difficulty by moving from the language $\mathscr{L}$ to $\overline{\mathscr{L}}$. The language $\overline{\mathscr{L}}$ will be used to explore the differences between the reflexive and the ordinary uses of pronouns.

3. The Language $\overline{\mathscr{L}}$

This language does some things differently from our original language $\mathscr{L}$. It also contains additional expressions. The first change we make to $\mathscr{L}$ concerns individual constants. In $\overline{\mathscr{L}}$, a constant can bind occurrences of a variable. Since constants and variables are the same size, the operative occurrence of the operator variable that is bound by a constant will be a subscript. If '*a*' is used to bind occurrences of '*x*,' then '*a*' will have an index: a_x. If α is an individual constant and β is an individual variable, then α_β is an *indexed individual constant*.

The individual transformation for $\mathscr{L}$ must be replaced for $\overline{\mathscr{L}}$. In chapter eight, the statement of the individual transformation gave the inputs and the output of the transformation. There was also a set-theoretic account of the effect of this transformation on truth conditions. The chapter eight account of the individual transformation was not changed in chapter nine; it was merely supplemented. I will continue to provide an initial statement describing the inputs and outputs of transformations in what follows. I will also provide a set-theoretic statement of truth conditions, as well as explanations of speech act structures, depicting, and representing.

The original individual transformation for $\mathcal{L}$ must now be replaced by three individual transformations. (I will explain only the transformations which take a predicate and a single constant to a new predicate. These are extended in a straightforward fashion to obtain transformations which take a predicate and *n* distinct constants to a new predicate.) In describing the new individual transformation, it is convenient to speak of the scope of a free variable. In an atomic predicate (or a predicate $[\alpha \overset{\vee}{\phi} \beta]$ where α, β are distinct variables), any symbol occurring to the right of an occurrence of a variable α is *within the scope of* that occurrence of α. The scope of an occurrence of a free variable remains the same in subsequent transformations. If an occurrence of a variable β is within the scope of an occurrence of a variable α, then any expression (and its components) which replaces the occurrence of β is *within the scope of* the occurrence of α. For example, in '$[x\ F\ a((Gy \ni [z\ H\ y])x_1 \ni [x_1\ M])]$,' every symbol to the right of the first 'x' is within the scope of that occurrence of 'x.' But only 'H' and (the second) 'y' are within the scope of the free occurrence of 'z.'

(2) Let α be an individual constant, and let A be a predicate containing free occurrences of the distinct individual variables $\beta_1, \ldots, \beta_m$ and no others; this is their canonical order.

(2a) Then α_{β_i} A ($= A'$) is obtained from α, A by the *individual* transformation. (Here and in (2b), (2c), $1 \leq i \leq m$.) The expressions occurring in A, as well as the subscript β_i, occur within the scope of the initial occurrence of α.

(2b) Let β_i be such that any free occurrence of β_i other than the first is within the scope of the first free occurrence of β_i in A. Then A' is obtained from α, A by replacing the first free occurrence of β_i in A by α_{β_i}. A' is obtained by the *individual* transformation. The expressions that were within the scope of the first free occurrence of β_i, and the subscripted occurrence of β_i, are within the scope of the occurrence of α introduced by this transformation.

(2c) If there is only one free occurrence of β_i in A then A' is obtained from α, A by replacing the single free occurrence of β_i by α. A' is obtained by the *individual* transformation. Every expression occurring within the scope of the free occurrence of β_i in A occurs within the scope of the occurrence of α introduced by this transformation.

In $\overline{\mathcal{L}}$, individual constants are not operators. But in an indexed constant α_β, β is still called the operator variable. In an occurrence of α_β in a predicate A', the occurrence of β is the *operative occurrence* of the operator variable in this occurrence of α_β. In a predicate $\alpha_\beta A$, the initial occurrence of α binds the operative occurrence of β and every formerly free occurrence of β to the right of the operative occurrence of β. But α_β can only be inserted in place of the first free occurrence of β if the first free occurrence "binds" the remaining free occurrences. This prevents the individual transformation being used to take a predicate

(1) $[[x\ F]\ \mathrm{v}\ [x\ G]]$

to

(2) $[[a_x\ F]\ \mathrm{v}\ [x\ G]]$.

The second free occurrence of '*x*' in (1) is not within the scope of the first.

The change in the individual transformation does not affect the set-theoretic account of truth conditions given in chapter eight. When the individual transformation yields '$a_x\ [[x\ F]\ \mathrm{v}\ [x\ G]]$' rather than '$[[a\ F]\ \mathrm{v}\ [a\ G]]$,' the sentence '$a_x\ [[x\ F]\ \mathrm{v}\ [x\ G]]$' is (still) true just in case *a* is either *F* or *G*. And '$[a_x\ F\ y,\ x]$' will label the same individuals as '$[a\ F\ y,\ a]$.' But in $\mathcal{L}$, '$[a\ F\ y,\ a]$' is representationally ambiguous. It might be obtained either this way:

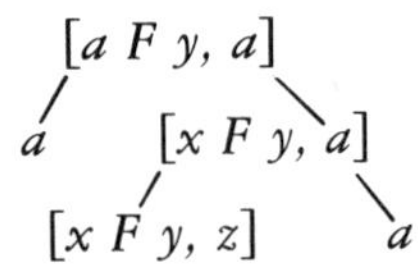

or this way:

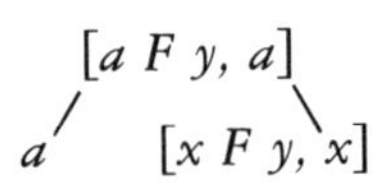

(Still more structures are possible.) In $\overline{\mathcal{L}}$, the predicate '$[a_x\ F\ y,\ x]$' must be obtained essentially like this:

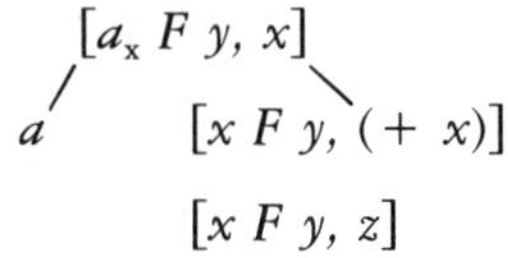

Even though there are three individual transformations for $\overline{\mathcal{L}}$ as compared to one for $\mathcal{L}$, the explanations of speech act structures, depicting, and representing are essentially the same for these transformations as for the individual transformation of $\mathcal{L}$. The chapter eight description of the input and output of the reflexive transformation remains correct for $\overline{\mathcal{L}}$, except that now this transformation can identify n free variables. The set-theoretic statement of truth conditions is unchanged. The speech act structures associated with the reflexive transformation have already been explained. The effect of the reflexive transformation on depicting is similar to its effect on labeling. Suppose A is a predicate containing free occurrences of n distinct free variables $\alpha_1, \ldots, \alpha_n$—this is their canonical order. Let A depict m-tuples $< d_1, \ldots, d_m >$ in which the $i_{1\text{st}}, \ldots, i_{n\text{th}}$ positions answer to the free occurrences of $\alpha_1, \ldots, \alpha_n$. And let A' be obtained from A by the reflexive transformation, by identifying $\alpha_{j1}, \ldots, \alpha_{jr}$ $(j_1 < j_2 < \ldots < j_r)$. Then A' depicts $(m - r + 1)$-tuples $< e_1, \ldots, e_{m-r+1} >$ such that (i) A depicts $< d_1, \ldots, d_m >$, (ii) $d_{i_{j1}} = d_{i_{j2}} = \ldots = d_{i_{jr}}$, and (iii) $< e_1, \ldots, e_{m-r+1} >$ is obtained from $< d_1, \ldots, d_m >$ by deleting $d_{i_{j2}}, \ldots, d_{i_{jr}}$. The output A' directly represents arbitrary individuals answering to its (distinct) free variables. It indirectly represents the other individuals represented by A, other than the arbitrary individuals represented by A.

So if '$[x\ K\ y]$' means x *killed* y, then in this instance of the reflexive transformation:

$$[x\ K\ (+\ x)]$$
$$[x\ K\ y]$$

the input depicts pairs $< d, e >$ such that d killed e. The output depicts individuals d such that $< d, d >$ is depicted by the input. The input represents an arbitrary individual x and an arbitrary individual y as such that x killed y. The output represents an arbitrary individual x as such that x killed x.

In $\overline{\mathcal{L}}$, the reflexive transformation is always marked in sentences—given a sentence A of $\overline{\mathcal{L}}$, either it is obligatory that the reflexive transformation be used to obtain A, or it is obligatory that the reflexive transformation not be used. Let '$[x\ L\ y]$' mean x *loves* y, and let 'a' name Anne. We can say that Anne loves herself by writing either '$a_x\ [x\ L\ x]$' or '$[a_x\ L\ x]$.' These would be used to perform acts like these:

$a_x\ [x\ L\ x]$

/ \

a $\quad$ $[(x\ +)\ L\ (+\ x)]$

$[x\ L\ y]$

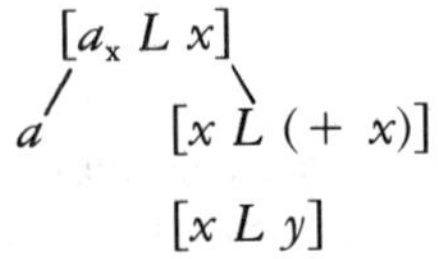

The sentence '[*a L a*]' cannot be obtained using the reflexive transformation. This sentence can be used in an act represented by one of:

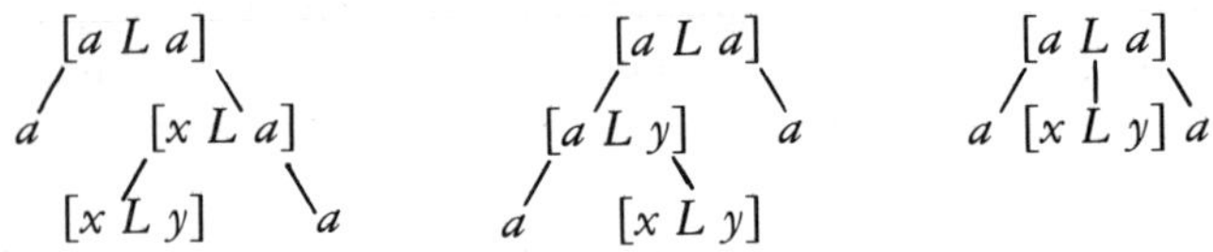

Even though the reflexive transformation is marked in sentences of $\overline{\mathscr{L}}$, the following are valid: [a_x *L x*] / [*a L a*]; [*a L a*] / [a_x *L x*].

The three individual transformations in $\overline{\mathscr{L}}$ have some similarity to the three transformations for each quantifier of $\mathscr{L}$. But there are some differences. A constant is not affected by being in the scope of an operator. So this structure is allowed:

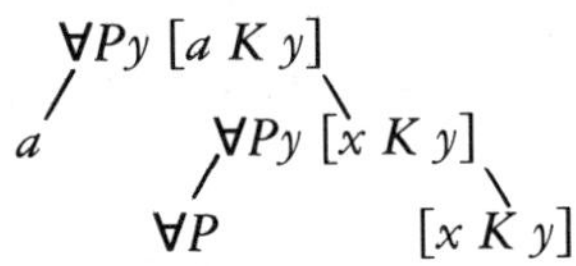

Nothing blocks a constant from being inserted within the scope of an operator.

Even though individual constants bind variables in $\overline{\mathscr{L}}$, they are not counted as operators in $\overline{\mathscr{L}}$. So an operator can be inserted within the scope of a constant. The following structure is allowed:

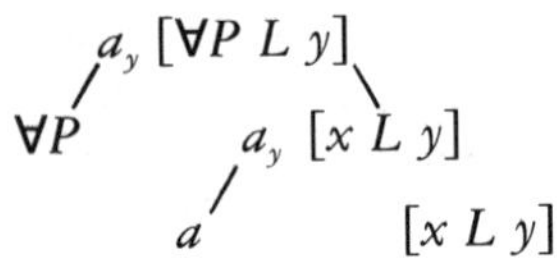

Because of this, the transformations which put a quantified phrase into an argument place in a predicate must be amended. The (b) transformations put a quantified phrase $Q\phi\alpha_i$ in place of the first free occurrence of α_i in *A*, and the (c) transformations put $Q\phi$ in place of the only free occurrence of α_i in *A*. In the original transformations, these replacements were allowed only if the first (or the only) free occurrence of α_i in A was within the scope of no operators in A. Now the restriction must be expanded. Not only must the first free occurrence of α_i be within the scope of no operators in A, but the functor ϕ must contain no free variables that would become bound after replacing the first free occurrence of α_i by $Q\phi\alpha_i$ or $Q\phi$. For example, the following should be blocked:

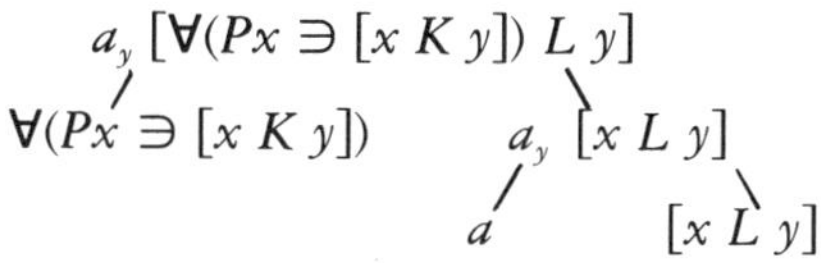

The universally quantified phrase contains a free occurrence of '*y*' that becomes bound by the initial occurrence of '*a*.'

When a constant is prefixed in a sentence, as in 'a_y [$b\,K\,y$],' the preferred reading is "For Anne *y*, Bob knows *y*." (I.e., For Anne, Bob knows her.) As far as the valuation of $\overline{\mathscr{L}}$ for nonempty domains is concerned, a prefixed constant has the same effect as an inserted constant. The same is true for the denoting and labeling done with predicates of $\overline{\mathscr{L}}$, and for the truth conditions of sentences. However, representing and depicting are affected by prefixed constants. If we consider this propositional act:

(1) 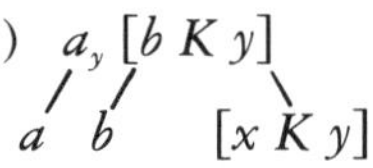

we see that it represents Anne, Bob as related in such a way that Bob knows Anne. The act (and the sentence) depicts < Anne, Bob > iff Bob knows Anne. In this act:

(2) 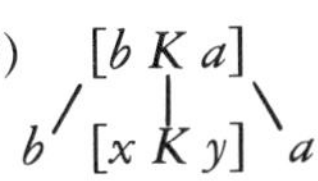

the individuals involved are the same, but their order is different. This act represents Bob, Anne as related by knowing. It depicts < Bob, Anne > iff Bob knows Anne.

In $\overline{\mathscr{L}}$, constants are not treated as operators. This makes the sentences of $\overline{\mathscr{L}}$ representationally ambiguous. There is less representational ambiguity in $\overline{\mathscr{L}}$ than in $\mathscr{L}$, and much less than in English. But many sentences of $\overline{\mathscr{L}}$ can be used to perform acts with importantly different representational meanings. For some purposes, it might be desirable to develop a language which has less representational ambiguity than $\overline{\mathcal{L}}$. If this were done, it might be appropriate to treat individual constants as operators. This would fix the (bottom to top) order of most transformations, including the individual transformations. (However, this would not prevent a sentence '[a F b]' from having these two structures:

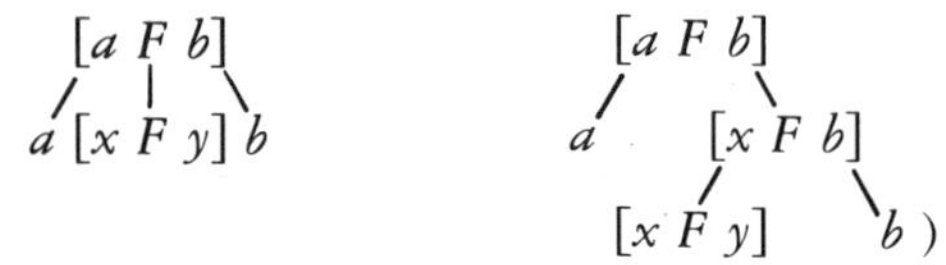

Another innovation in $\overline{\mathcal{L}}$ is a new quantifier: $\mathbb{O}$. This is the *uniqueness* quantifier. This quantifier has the reading "only." The quantifier '$\mathbb{O}$' combines with a constant α to form a quantified phrase $\mathbb{O}\alpha$. If α is a constant and β is a variable, then $\mathbb{O}\alpha$ is a *plain* quantified phrase and $\mathbb{O}\alpha_\beta$ is an *indexed* quantified phrase.

There are three transformations for '$\mathbb{O}$.'

($\mathbb{O}$) Let α be an individual constant. Let A be a predicate containing free occurrences of the distinct individual variables $\beta_1, \ldots, \beta_m$ and no others; this is their canonical order.

($\mathbb{O}$a) Then $\mathbb{O}\alpha_{\beta_i}$ A $(= A')$ is obtained from α, A by the *unique* transformation.

($\mathbb{O}$b) Let the first free occurrence of β_i be within the scope of no operator in A. Then A' is obtained from α, A by replacing the first free occurrence of β_i in A by $\mathbb{O}\alpha_{\beta_i}$. A' is obtained by the *unique* transformation.

($\mathbb{O}$c) Let A contain a single free occurrence of β_i, and let this be within the scope of no operators in A. Then A' is obtained from α, A by replacing the single free occurrence of β_i by $\mathbb{O}\alpha$. A' is obtained by the *unique* transformation.

The quantifier '$\mathbb{O}$' is a logical operator. Its scope is determined like the scopes of other quantifiers.

Let f be an interpreting function of $\overline{\mathcal{L}}$ for a nonempty $\mathcal{D}$. Let $f(\alpha) = d$, $f(A) = V$. Then $f(A') = V' = \{<e_1, \ldots, e_{m-1}> \mid <e_1, \ldots, e_{i-1}, d, \ldots, e_{m-1}> \in V$ and for all $r \in \mathcal{D}$, if *$<e_1, \ldots, e_{i-1}, r, \ldots, e_{m-1}> \in V$, then $[r = d]\}$. If $m = 1$, then $f(A') = t$ iff $\{d\} = V$.*

The quantifier '$\mathbb{O}$' can be used in some of the ways that 'only' is used in English. This quantifier becomes interesting when combined with predicative acts which involve the reflexive transformation. The sentence '[$\mathbb{O}a_x$ L x]' is "Only Anne loves herself." (Not quite: The English translation seems best understood as meaning that Anne is the only female person who loves herself. The $\overline{\mathcal{L}}$ sentence means that Anne is the only individual loving itself.) The sentence '$[\mathbb{O}a_x\ L\ x]$' has quite a different meaning from '$[\mathbb{O}a\ L\ a]$.' For this inference sequence is valid: $[\mathbb{O}a_x\ L\ x]$, $[b_x\ L\ x]$ / $[a = b]$. This one is not: $[\mathbb{O}a_x\ L\ x]$, $[b\ L\ a]$ / $[a = b]$. However, the following is valid: $[\mathbb{O}a\ L\ a]$, $[b\ L\ a]$ / $[a = b]$. While this is not: $[\mathbb{O}a\ L\ a]$, $[b_x\ L\ x]$ / $[a = b]$. (What about the following, is it valid? $[\mathbb{O}a_x\ L\ x]$, $[b\ L\ b]$ / $[a = b]$)

The preceding explanation of the unique transformation is sufficient for a syntactic account which generates $\overline{\mathcal{L}}$. A set-theoretic statement of truth conditions has been provided for the unique transformation. An explanation of the speech act structure associated with this transformation and a fuller semantic explanation are being postponed until later.

4. Ordinary Pronouns

In English, there are at least two uses of pronouns: (1) The reflexive use, and (2) The ordinary use. When a pronoun is used in the ordinary way, it usually follows its antecedent. But it can precede the antecedent, as in this sentence:

> If he has any sense, a boy will get a good education.

In such a sentence, the denoting act is assigned a new purpose before it is performed with its "primary" purpose.

In a way, the ordinary use of a pronoun is the opposite of the reflexive use. Reflexive pronouns (pronouns used reflexively) bunch different argument places together, and in effect reduce the number of argument places in a predicate. Ordinary pronouns "spread out" a denoting act so that it can fill different argument places. In customary first-order languages, bound variables behave like reflexive pronouns. No expressions are used like ordinary pronouns. And, so far, in $\overline{\mathcal{L}}$ (and $\mathcal{L}$), the bound variables all behave like reflexive pronouns. But ordinary pronouns will be incorporated in $\overline{\mathcal{L}}$. Overlined individual variables will be used as ordinary pronouns: $\bar{x}, \bar{y}, \bar{z}, \ldots$

In this section we will consider how individual constants can serve as antecedents of overlined variables. Quantified phrases will be considered in subsequent sections. There is one feature of English pronouns that will not be copied in $\overline{\mathcal{L}}$: an overlined variable cannot precede the expression which serves as its antecedent. In $\overline{\mathcal{L}}$, the expression by which a bound variable is bound must be uniquely determined; the scope of a variable-binding expression must be determined in the same way at all of its occurrences. It seems most convenient to have expressions bind variables only to the right of the operative occurrences of their operator variables. Without this convention, we would need to adopt a rule such as one barring two expressions which can serve as antecedents from having the same operator variable. When constants serve as antecedents to overlined variables, there is no serious loss in requiring them to bind variables only to their right. With quantified phrases, we find sentences like the following that can't effectively be translated in $\overline{\mathcal{L}}$:

The man who deserves it will receive the prize he deserves.

(I got this example from Stan Ziewacz.) Even though such a sentence cannot be translated into $\overline{\mathcal{L}}$, we can use the techniques developed for $\overline{\mathcal{L}}$ to give it a speech act analysis.

When a constant is the antecedent of an overlined variable, the ordinary limitations on the scope of the constant do not apply. When a constant α is introduced into a predicate A to yield A' by the individual transformation, only expressions occurring to the right of α are within its scope. If A' is later used to form $[A' \& B]$, expressions occurring in B are not within the scope of the occurrence of α. But we want a constant in A' to be able to serve as antecedent for an overlined variable in B. For an English sentence like:

John won the race and he was elated.

is perfectly acceptable. For an occurrence of an individual constant, we will distinguish two scopes:

(1) The *ordinary* scope is the scope previously explained.
(2) If α is an individual constant occurring in a predicate (or sentence) A, every expression occurring to the right of the occurrence of α in A occurs within the *extended* scope of the occurrence of α.

(This also applies to an occurrence of α_β. The subscripted β occurs within the extended scope of the occurrence of α—and within the ordinary scope as well.)

In English, reflexive pronouns with the suffix 'self' (or 'selves') only occur in close proximity to their antecedents. These pronouns are used to bunch up places in a predicate determined by a single "predicate functor." So we have:

Judas killed himself.
Bob voted for himself.
Jorge bought a present for himself.

But the following are not correct:

Bob hopes himself will be elected.
If Bob is elected, then himself will be pleased.

(These sentences might be acceptable for an Irishman in a movie. So there is an Anglo-Irish-cinema dialect which allows 'self'-suffix pronouns in subordinate clauses to have antecedents outside the clauses.) However, in the sentence:

Bob hopes he will be elected.

the pronoun 'he' can be used reflexively. It can also be used as an ordinary pronoun. This accounts for the ambiguity of:

Bob hopes he will be elected. So does Jim.

It is not clear to me whether, in a compound sentence where a pronoun in one component has an antecedent in another, it is "natural" for the pronoun to be used reflexively. In the sentence

If Bob is elected, then he will be pleased.

would it be normal for the pronoun to be used reflexively? I think not, for I find that I must strain to regard the second sentence below as ambiguous:

If Bob is elected, then he will be pleased. So will Jim.

My feeling is that the natural reading of the second sentence has Jim being pleased if Bob is elected. If I am right, then the natural understanding of the conditional sentence uses 'he' in the ordinary way. If I am wrong, then the pronoun can naturally be used in either the ordinary or the reflexive way.

In $\mathscr{L}$ a constant can bind a plain variable only in its ordinary scope. So in: $[[b_x\ E] \supset [x\ H]]$ the constant 'b' does not bind the 'x' in the consequent. However, if we wanted the subjects of the two components to be tied together by the reflexive transformation, we could use this: b_x [[x E] ⊃ [x H]]. For to use this sentence, we need to employ the reflexive transformation. The sentence might be used in an act with this structure:

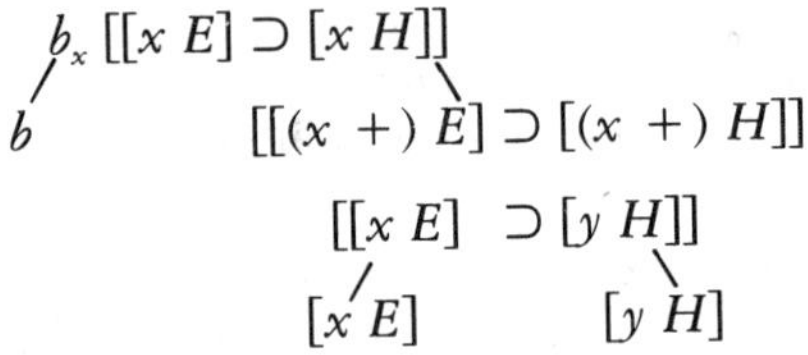

(If the English sentence ‘If Bob is elected, then he will be pleased’ *can* be construed so that ‘he’ is used reflexively, the above sentence would be an appropriate translation in $\overline{\mathscr{L}}$ for the reflexive case.)

A constant can only bind a plain variable in its ordinary scope. It can bind an overlined variable in its extended scope. The first *pronomial* transformation of $\overline{\mathscr{L}}$ is as follows.

(Pro_1) Let α be an individual constant, β be an individual variable, and A be a predicate containing free occurrences of the distinct individual variables $\gamma_1, \ldots, \gamma_n$ and no others—this is their canonical order. Let α_β occur in A, and let every free occurrence of γ_i in A be within the extended scope of this occurrence of α_β. Let no free occurrence of γ_i in A be in a place where an occurrence of $\overline{\beta}$ would be bound by an operator or constant other than the occurrence of α_β. Then A' is obtained from α, A by replacing every free occurrence of γ_i by $\overline{\beta}$. A' is obtained by a *pronomial* transformation. The new occurrences of $\overline{\beta}$ are bound by the occurrence of α in the occurrence of α_β.

Let f be an interpreting function of $\overline{\mathscr{L}}$ for a nonempty $\mathscr{D}$. Let $f(\alpha) = d$ and $f(A) = V$. Then $f(A') = V' = \{< e_1, \ldots, e_{n-1} > \mid < e_1, \ldots, e_{i-1}, d, \ldots, e_{n-1} > \in V\}$. If $n = 1$, then $f(A') = t$ iff $d \in V$.

In $\overline{\mathscr{L}}$ we can say that Bob will be happy if he is elected by using the following sentence: [[b_x E] ⊃ [$\overline{x}$ H]]. We can represent an act of using this sentence like this:

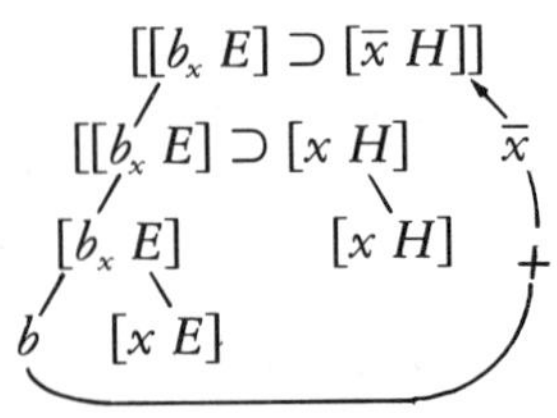

The act of using the overlined variable assigns a new purpose to the act of representing Bob. In doing this, it gives a special character to the act of representing Bob. This act, with its new special character, is performed in order to represent Bob as such that he will be happy if Bob is elected. The above diagram will sometimes be abbreviated like this:

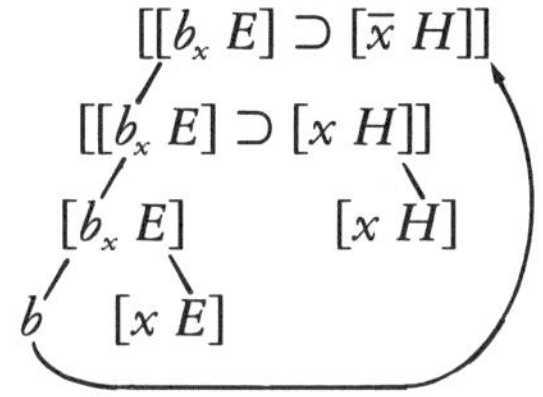

If '[x M y]' means x *is married to* y, '[x P]' means x *is a person,* '[x L y]' means x *loves* y, and 'a' names Anne, then

$$[\iota(Px \ni [x\ M\ a_y])\ L\ \bar{y}]$$

is "The person who is married to Anne loves her." But

$$[\iota(Px \ni [x\ M\ a_y])\ L\ y]$$

is a one-place predicate and not a sentence. The 'y' at the end is not within the ordinary scope of 'a' (of 'a_y').

The reflexive transformation reduces the size of the n-tuple that is denoted by a predicate, the number of individuals that are directly and indirectly represented by a predicate, the size of the n-tuples that are labeled and depicted by a predicate. The pronomial transformation reduces the size of the n-tuple that a predicate denotes, and the size of the n-tuples that it labels. But the pronomial transformation does not reduce the number of individuals that are represented or the size of the n-tuples that are depicted.

In A' (the result of the first pronomial transformation), the individuals represented directly are the arbitrary individuals answering to the free variables in A' and the individual represented by α. The individuals represented indirectly are all the individuals represented directly or indirectly by expressions (other than free variables) in A. So following this pronomial transformation, the individual represented by α will be represented both directly and indirectly. Suppose A depicts m-tuples $< e_1, \ldots, e_m>$ in which the jth position answers to the free occurrences of γ_i in A. Then A' depicts those m-tuples $< e_1, \ldots, e_m>$ depicted by A in which e_j is d. (If A does not depict any m-tuples, then neither does A'. But A' may fail to depict even if A does depict some m-tuples.)

5. Quantified Antecedents

In English some quantified phrases behave very much like names when they serve as antecedents of pronouns. The following are all acceptable English sentences:

> John met Mary, and he asked her for a date.
> John met a girl, and he asked her for a date.
> John met the Queen, and she asked him for a date.
> John asked only Mary to the dance, and she turned him down.

Not all quantified phrases can do this. The following are not acceptable.

> John met every girl in his brother's class, and he asked her for a date.
> John met no girl in his brother's class, and she asked him for a date.

The unacceptability of these examples is due to the quantifiers and the 'and's; it isn't a function of the meanings of the remaining expressions. For the following are all acceptable sentences:

> John met every girl in his brother's class, and he asked every girl in his brother's class for a date.
> For every girl in his brother's class, John met her and he asked her for a date.
> John met no girl in his brother's class, and no girl in his brother's class asked John for a date.
> For no girl in his brother's class, John met her and she asked him for a date.

(This last sentence is certainly awkward, but not, I think, illicit.)

It is clear that every kind of quantified phrase in English can serve as antecedent for a pronoun used reflexively. My conjecture is that indefinite phrases, definite phrases, and unique phrases can serve as antecedents to pronouns used in the ordinary way, but that universal phrases and negative phrases cannot. (Mathematical phrases in English will be like universal phrases in this respect. Both universal and mathematical phrases are formed with 'every' in English—but they are understood differently.) Let us consider another example, to see how this conjecture can explain some phenomena.

Suppose Stacey says, "Some man at the party bought the Hope diamond." Then, as an afterthought, she adds "for his wife." The first part of her statement is perfectly intelligible. The added prepositional phrase has no effect on our understanding of the first part—it simply gives us additional information. But suppose Stacey had said "Every man at the party tried to buy the Hope diamond." This much is perfectly intelligible. If Stacey pauses, and as an afterthought adds "for his wife," the effect is jarring. My initial inclination is to ask "For whose wife?" It seems that we are compelled to go back and "re-think" her original statement if we want to make sense of her total remark, for the sentence 'Every man at the party tried to buy the Hope diamond for his wife' makes good sense if we consider it all at once. My explanation of the difference in the two examples is that the "afterthought" remark involves a pronomial transformation. This is allowed for the indefinite phrase, but not for the universal phrase. When we re-think Stacey's second statement, we are construing the pronoun reflexively.

The speech act structures of Stacey's remarks were not illustrated with tree diagrams, because we have not considered prepositional phrases in English. We can modify the example to give us this as replacement for Stacey's first remark:

(1) Some man at the party bought the Hope diamond, and he bought it for his wife.

This could be used in an act whose structure is similar to this:

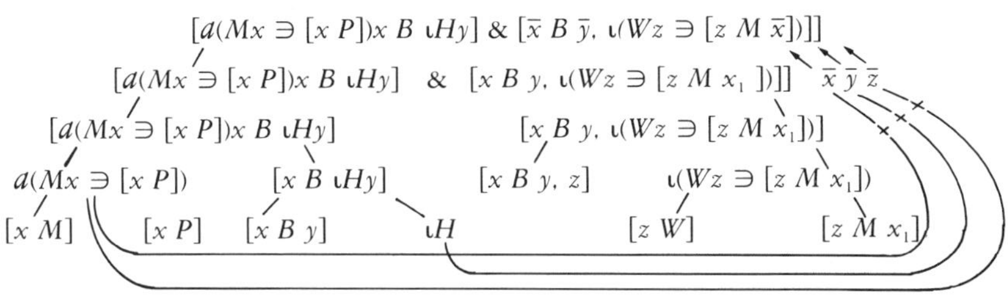

("Some man such that he was at the party bought the Hope diamond and he bought it for the woman such that he is married to her.") Here one quantified phrase ('a(Mx ∋ [x P])') is re-used twice, to "capture" two distinct individual variables.

The following sentence doesn't make good sense in English:

(2) Every man at the party tried to buy the Hope diamond, and he tried to buy it for his wife.

With some straining, we might construe (2) like this sentence of $\overline{\mathcal{L}}$:

$$\forall(Mx \ni [x\ P])x\ [[x\ T\ \iota Hy]\ \&\ [x\ T\ \bar{y},\ \iota(Wz \ni [z\ M\ x])]]$$

In this sentence, the initial universal quantifier is the main operator, binding plain variables rather than overlined ones. The only pronomial transformation required is one to allow 'the Hope diamond' to serve as antecedent in one conjunct to a pronoun (overlined variable) in the second. To use the $\overline{\mathcal{L}}$-sentence, we could perform an act like this:

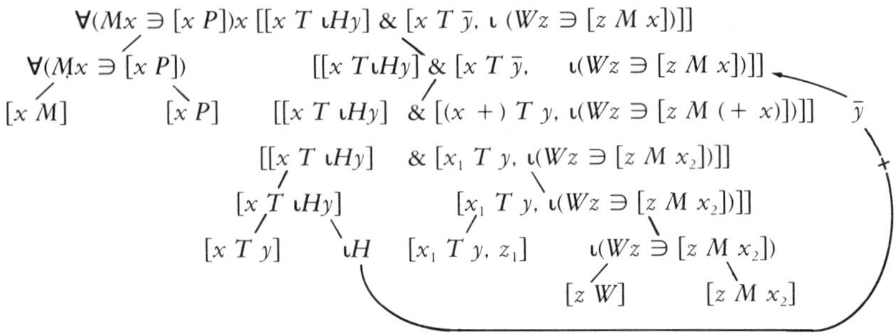

I have made a conjecture about English: that universal and negative quantified phrases do not serve as antecedents of ordinary pronouns. This conjecture about English will be incorporated in $\overline{\mathcal{L}}$ as a stipulation. Indefinite phrases, definite phrases, and unique phrases will serve as antecedents of overlined variables. Other quantified phrases will not. At present my conjecture about English has an empirical character—we can test it by considering a variety of English sentences. In the next chapter, when I develop a semantic account for the various quantifiers, we can check the account to determine whether it supports the conjecture. If it does, the conjecture may seem to be slightly less empirical than it is now. But it will remain a somewhat empirical matter to determine how well the semantic account for $\overline{\mathcal{L}}$ works for English.

The uniqueness quantifier, the definite quantifier, and the indefinite quantifier have both plain and extended scopes. The plain scopes have already been explained; the extended scope of one of these operators reaches to the end of whatever predicate it occurs in. A plain variable which is in the extended scope but not the plain scope of an operator (or constant) cannot be bound by the operator (constant). Only overlined variables can be bound outside the plain scope.

The second pronomial transformation concerns the quantifier '$\mathbb{C}$.' A unique phrase will be allowed to bind variables in the same way that a constant does.

(Pro$_2$) Let α be an individual constant, β be an individual variable, and A be a predicate containing free occurrences of the distinct individual variables $\gamma_1, \ldots, \gamma_n$ and no others—this is their canonical order. Let $\mathbb{O}\alpha_\beta$ occur in A, and let every free occurrence of γ_i in A be within the extended scope of the (selected) occurrence of $\mathbb{O}\alpha_\beta$. Let no free occurrence of γ_i in A be at a position where an occurrence of $\overline{\beta}$ would be bound by an operator or constant other than the occurrence of $\mathbb{O}\alpha_\beta$. Then A' is obtained from A and α by replacing the free occurrences of γ_i by $\overline{\beta}$. A' is obtained by a *pronomial* transformation. The occurrences of $\overline{\beta}$ that are introduced by this transformation are bound by the occurrence of '$\mathbb{O}$' in $\mathbb{O}\alpha_\beta$.

Let f be an interpreting function of $\mathscr{L}$ for a nonempty $\mathscr{D}$. Let $f(\alpha) = d$, $f(A) = V$. Then $f(A') = V' = \{< e_1, \ldots, e_{n-1}> \mid < e_1, \ldots, e_{i-1}, d, \ldots, e_{n-1}> \in V\}$. If $n = 1$, then $f(A') = t$ iff $d \in V$.

When a unique phrase serves as antecedent for an overlined variable, this variable is not included in what the 'only' applies to. In this sentence:

(3) $[[\mathbb{O}b_x\ H\ a]\ \&\ [\overline{x}\ D]]$

("Only Bob hit Laura, and he is a doctor") the '$\mathbb{O}$' indicates that only Bob hit Laura; it does not "involve" Bob's being a doctor. Sentence (3) is equivalent to:

(4) $[[\mathbb{O}b\ H\ a]\ \&\ [b\ D]]$

If 'c' names Judas, and '$[x\ K\ y]$' means x *killed* y, then $[\mathbb{O}c_x\ K\ \overline{x}]$ says that only Judas killed Judas—that no one else had a part in it. This is presumably true. But $[\mathbb{O}c_x\ K\ x]$ says that only Judas killed himself (itself). This is false, for many individuals have killed themselves. (The sentence '$[\mathbb{O}c_x\ K\ \overline{x}]$' does not correspond to an English sentence which employs a pronoun. We cannot say "Only Judas killed him." Various transformations in $\overline{\mathscr{L}}$ are not subject to all the restrictions governing the corresponding transformations in English.)

In A', the individuals represented directly are the arbitrary individuals answering to the free variables in A' and the individual represented by α. The individuals represented indirectly are all the individuals represented directly and indirectly by expressions (other than free variables) in A. If A depicts m-tuples $< e_1, \ldots, e_m>$ in which the jth individual corresponds to the free occurrences of γ_i in A, then A' depicts those m-tuples $< e_1, \ldots, e_m>$ which are depicted by A, in which $e_j = d$.

The introduction of these pronomial transformations requires changes in the individual transformation. For as it stands, the individual transformation could take

(5) $[[a_x\ S]\ \&\ [x\ K\ \overline{x}]]$

to

(6) $[[a_x\ S]\ \&\ [c_x\ K\ \overline{x}]]$.

In (5), the occurrence of '*a*' binds the occurrence of '$\overline{x}$' after '*K*.' But the subject '*x*' of '$[x\ K\ \overline{x}]$' is free; it is not within the plain scope of '*a*' (in 'a_x'). In (6), the constant '*c*' "intercepts" '*a*'s binding. For now it is '*c*' that binds the overlined '$\overline{x}$.' Clause (2b) of the individual transformation needs to be amended as follows.

(2b) Let any free occurrence of β_i in *A*, other than the first, be within the scope of the first free occurrence of β_i in *A*. Let no constant or operator whose operative occurrence of β_i occurs to the left of the first free occurrence of β_i in *A* bind occurrences of $\overline{\beta}_i$ to the right of the first free occurrence of β_i in *A*. Then A' is obtained from α, *A* by replacing the first free occurrence of β_i in *A* by α_{β_i}. A' is obtained by the *individual* transformation. The expressions that were within the scope of the first free occurrence of β_i, and the subscripted occurrence of β_i, are within the scope of the occurrence of α introduced by this transformation.

The unique transformation also requires changes. The (b) clause in this transformation must be replaced as follows.

(©b) Let the first free occurrence of β_i in *A* be within the scope of no operators in *A*. Let no constant or operator whose operative occurrence of β_i occurs to the left of the first free occurrence of β_i in *A* bind occurrences of $\overline{\beta}_i$ to the right of the first free occurrence of β_i in *A*. Then A' is obtained from α, *A* by replacing the first free occurrence of β_i in *A* by ©α_{β_i}. A' is obtained by the *unique* transformation.

Even though indefinite and definite phrases have extended scopes, they can't bind overlined variables within these scopes to the same extent that constants and unique phrases can. We have seen that an indefinite phrase can "reach across" a conjunction in the same way that a name can. Both of the following are acceptable sentences:

John met Mary, and he asked her for a date.
John met a girl, and he asked her for a date.

But now consider these sentences:

(5) John met Mary, or he asked her for a date.
(6) John met a girl, or he asked her for a date.

Sentence (5) is odd, but acceptable. The oddness comes from the situation that is described—how could John ask her for a date if he hadn't met Mary? Sentence (6) is odd and not acceptable. Unless the first disjunct is true, there is no one for John to ask. With the sense of (7):

(7) For some girl, either John met her or he asked her for a date.

(6) would be acceptable. For (7) describes an odd situation, but it is an acceptable and intelligible English sentence. If (6) could naturally be used with the sense of (7), the pronoun 'her' would be used reflexively. The act of using (6) might then have a structure like this:

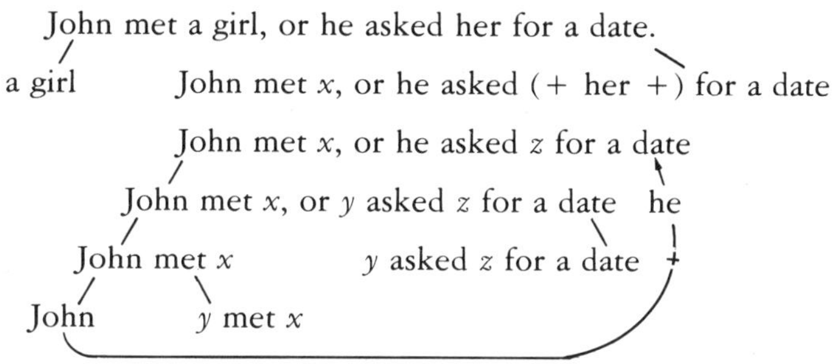

It is unnatural to use (6) in this way. However, the sentence:

(8) John spoke with a girl, or he gave her a note.

is acceptable, though somewhat awkward. Sentence (8) is understood with the sense of (9):

(9) For some girl, either John spoke with her, or he gave her a note.

Sentence (8) could be used with a structure like that illustrated above.

Those cases where a pronoun in one disjunct has an indefinite phrase antecedent in the other seem to be cases where the pronoun is used reflexively. Sentences like (6), for which it is unnatural to use the pronoun reflexively, are not acceptable. So far as the ordinary use of pronouns is concerned, an indefinite phrase can reach across a conjunction, but not across a disjunction. Since '&' and 'v' in $\overline{\mathscr{L}}$ (and $\mathscr{L}$) are being treated as symbolic counterparts to 'and' and 'or,' an indefinite phrase should be allowed to reach across '&' but not 'v.' There is no similar restriction on constants or on unique phrases. However, both of these sometimes give odd results when reaching across a disjunction. Consider this sentence:

John asked only Mary to the dance, or she was not home.

The point of using 'only' is diluted by the disjunction.

To give a careful account of the situations where an indefinite phrase can bind overlined variables, and the situations where it cannot, we will divide logical operators into *radical* and *nonradical* operators. The wedge is radical; '&' is nonradical.

(Pro_3) Let A be a predicate which contains an occurrence of $a\phi\alpha$. Let A contain free occurrences of the distinct individual variables $\beta_1, \ldots, \beta_n$ and no others; this is their canonical order. Let every free occurrence of β_i in A be within the extended scope of the occurrence of 'a' in the occurrence of $a\phi\alpha$, and let every free occurrence be to the right of the operative occurrence of α in (the occurrence of) $a\phi\alpha$. Let no free occurrence of β_i in A be at a place where an occurrence of $\overline{\alpha}$ would be bound by an operator other than the occurrence of 'a' in the occurrence of $a\phi\alpha$. And let the occurrence of $a\phi\alpha$ be within the scope of no radical operator. Then A' is obtained from A and $a\phi$ by replacing the free occurrences of β_i by $\overline{\alpha}$. A' is obtained by a *pronomial* transformation.

The clause about the radical operator sets this pronomial transformation apart from the preceding ones. This transformation allows us to perform the following propositional act:

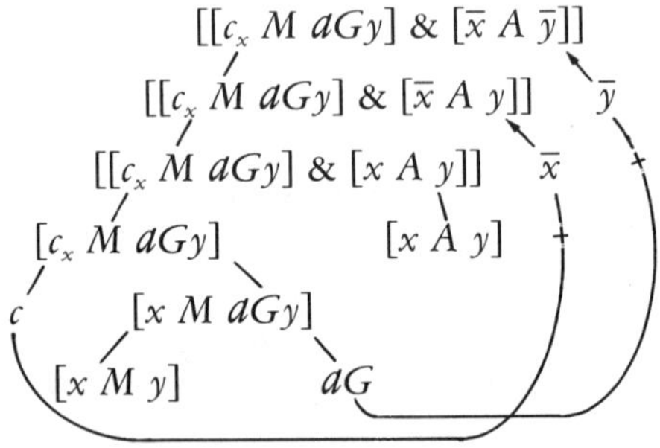

The first pronomial transformation is used to obtain the penultimate predicate. The third pronomial transformation takes this predicate to the sentence. The third is allowed because the occurrence of 'aGy' is not within the scope of a radical operator. However, the following is not allowed:

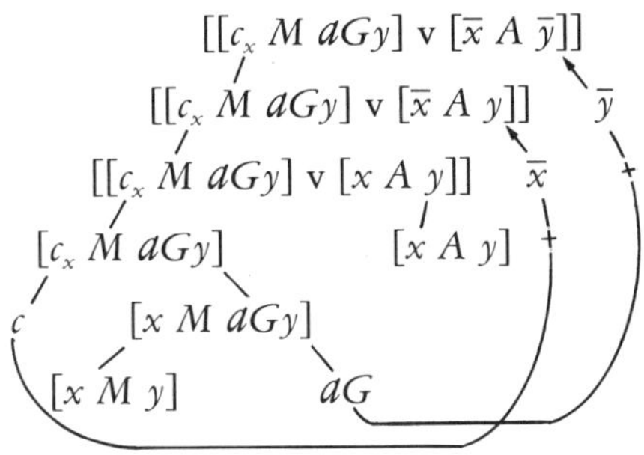

The last move is barred, because the occurrence of '$\mathfrak{a}Gy$' in '[[c_x M $\mathfrak{a}Gy$] v [$\bar{x}$ A y]]' is within the scope of 'v.' And 'v' is a radical operator.

Before we can provide the semantic account of the third pronomial transformation offered in the next chapters, we must have a semantic account for the indefinite quantifier. We also need a better understanding of the difference between radical and nonradical operators.

We will provisionally make the pronomial transformation for the definite quantifier exactly parallel to that for the indefinite quantifier. When we consider the definite transformation and its associated speech act structure, we can determine whether this account is satisfactory.

(Pro_4) Let A be a predicate which contains an occurrence of $\iota\phi\alpha$. Let A contain free occurrences of distinct individual variables $\beta_1, \ldots, \beta_m$ and no others; this is their canonical order. Let every free occurrence of β_i in A be within the extended scope of the occurrence of 'ι' in the occurrence of $\iota\phi\alpha$, and let every free occurrence of β_i be to the right of the operative occurrence of 'α' in (the occurrence of) $\iota\phi\alpha$. Let no free occurrence of β_i in A be at a place where an occurrence of $\bar{\alpha}$ would be bound by an operator other than the 'ι' in the occurrence of $\iota\phi\alpha$. And let the occurrence of $\iota\phi\alpha$ be within the scope of no radical operator. Then A' is obtained from A and $\iota\phi$ by replacing the free occurrences of β_i by $\bar{\alpha}$. A' is obtained by a *pronomial* transformation.

The semantic account for this transformation must also be deferred until later. At present, we need to canvass all the logical operators in $\overline{\mathcal{L}}$, to determine which are radical and which aren't. We will decide this by considering the English expressions which correspond to the logical operators, and seeing how they affect indefinite phrases.

The following:

> Bill doesn't know a girl in the Freshman Class, and he asked her for a date.

is not an acceptable English sentence. The trouble is not due to the 'and,' so it must be traceable to the 'n't.' Anyone who tries out further examples should be able to convince herself that '~' is (should be) a radical operator.

The restriction about radical operators only concerns the antecedent of an overlined variable. We cannot have:

$$[[b_x \sim K\, a(Gy \ni [y\ I\ \iota F])y]\ \&\ [\overline{x}\ A\ \overline{y}]]$$

But we can have this:

$$[[b_x\ K\, a(Gy \ni [y\ I\ \iota F])y]\ \&\ [\overline{x} \sim A\ \overline{y}]]$$

("Bill knows a girl in the Freshman Class, and he didn't ask her for a date.") An indefinite phrase can reach into the scope of a radical operator, so long as the indefinite phrase isn't itself within the scope of such an operator.

As the pronomial transformations now stand, there are some problems in determining the antecedent of an overlined variable. It is our goal that the antecedent be uniquely determined. The predicate:

(1) $[a(Bx \ni [x\ K\ aGy])\ A\ z]$

("Some boy that knows a girl asked z for a date") can be transformed to:

(2) $[a(Bx \ni [x\ K\ aGy])\ A\ \overline{y}]$

and then to:

(3) $\sim[a(Bx \ni [x\ K\ aGy])\ A\ \overline{y}]$

But if (1) is first transformed to:

(4) $\sim[a(Bx \ni [x\ K\ aGy])\ A\ z]$

this cannot be further transformed to (3). The indefinite phrase 'aGy' is in (4) within the scope of a radical operator. But now consider:

(5) $[[c_y\ P]\ \&\ \sim[a(Bx \ni [x\ K\ aGy])\ A\ \overline{y}]$

("Sally is pretty and. . .") What is the antecedent of the overlined '$\overline{y}$'? Is it 'c_y' or 'aGy'?

The statements of the pronomial transformations contain a "safety" clause. This rules out the transformation if any free occurrence of the original variable β_i is in a place where an occurrence of the new variable $\overline{\alpha}$ would be bound by the wrong constant or operator. In the future, instead of saying that the transformations are ruled out if $\overline{\alpha}$ would be bound by the wrong antecedent, we will say they are ruled out if $\overline{\alpha}$ *could* be bound by the wrong antecedent. We will understand that an occurrence of an overlined variable $\overline{\beta}$ could be bound by the closest occurrence on the left of a (plain) constant α or '$\mathbb{C}$,' 'a,' or 'ι' for which (i) the operative occurrence of β is to the left of the occurrence of $\overline{\beta}$, and (ii) there is some sequence of transformations that would lead to the constant's or operator's binding the occurrence of $\overline{\beta}$. (There is some sequence of transformations that would have led to the binding.)

This understanding prevents the predicate:

$$(6)\ [[c_y\ P]\ \&\ {\sim}[a(Bx \ni [x\ K\ aGy])\ A\ z]]$$

from being transformed into (5). The 'c' cannot bind the overlined '$\overline{y}$' in (5). Even so, (5) is likely to prove confusing at first glance. In practice we will avoid giving the appearance of ambiguity by choosing different operator variables for different antecedents.

6. Rethinking the Conditional

The English conditional expression 'If. . . , then . . .' does not seem to be a radical operator. For the following:

(1) If Bill knows a girl in the Freshman Class, then he will ask her for a date.

is a perfectly satisfactory English sentence. The indefinite phrase 'a girl in the Freshman Class' in the 'if'-clause is the antecedent of the pronoun 'her' in the consequent.

It is already well-known that the horseshoe '$\supset$' of material implication does not capture the significance of the English expression 'If . . . , then . . .' But the horseshoe is sometimes described as capturing an "essential part" of the meaning of the English conditional expression. However, if $[A \supset B]$ is understood to mean that either A is false or B is true, we don't seem to be able to capture any of the meaning of sentence (1). For the following:

(2) Either it is false that Bill knows a girl in the Freshman Class, or he will ask her for a date.

is not an acceptable English sentence. It certainly doesn't capture part of the meaning of sentence (1).

In $\overline{\mathcal{L}}$ we would like to use the horseshoe to shed light on some features of English conditional sentences. In particular, we would like to have a unique phrase, a definite phrase, or an indefinite phrase in a sentence A serve as antecedent for occurrences of an overlined variable in the consequent B in a sentence $[A \supset B]$. What is wanted is a new way to understand the horseshoe, so that $[A \supset B]$ doesn't *mean* that either A is false or B is true, but when A and B are independent sentences, $[A \supset B]$ turns out to be equivalent to $[\sim A \vee B]$. And when a quantified phrase in A is antecedent to an overlined variable in B, we can make sense of that too. The task of developing this new understanding will be left until the next chapter.

7. More Radical Operators

We have considered the connectives in $\overline{\mathcal{L}}$, and determined which are radical. Both 'v' and '$\sim$' are radical, while '&' and '$\supset$' are nonradical. We must now consider the remaining operators.

Let us start with '$\forall$.' We shall model our treatment of the universal quantifier on the behavior of 'every' in English. If we consider the left conjunct in:

(1) Every man at the party gave a gift to his wife, and it was a fur coat.

the sentence is ambiguous. It can either be used to perform an act like this:

(2) Every man at the party gave a gift to his wife.
/ \
Every man at the party — x gave a gift to his wife
/ \
x gave y to his wife — a gift

(The diagram can be developed further, but this is enough for the present discussion.) The sentence can be used to perform an act like this:

```
(3)        Every man at the party gave a gift to his wife.
          /                                          \
     Every man at the party gave y to his wife      a gift
    /                                   \
Every man at the party             x gave y to his wife
```

These diagrams don't represent the only acts that can be performed with the sentence. The alternative acts don't affect the point I am concerned with here. The important ambiguity in the sentence concerns the (bottom-to-top) order of the quantified phrases. Sentence (1) could be used to perform an act in which the left conjunct is used as shown by (3). Our knowledge of gift-giving leads us to reject that analysis, for different men can't give the same object to their wives. But if we take the left conjunct as shown in (2), then I find (1) anomalous. With some effort I I can make sense of (1) when the left conjunct is used this way, by construing the right conjunct like a relative clause modifying 'a gift.' As a conjunction, I feel that (1) is ill-formed when the left conjunct is used to perform a propositional act represented by (2).

Let us try another example.

(4) Bob got every one of his friends a date, and he didn't even know her.

The left conjunct of (4) is also ambiguous. The universal phrase or the indefinite phrase can be used to perform the later act. But our knowledge of dates and dating leads us to reject the analysis according to which the indefinite phrase is used to perform the later act. With the other analysis of the left conjunct, sentence (4) strikes me as ill-formed. I will account for this phenomenon by classifying the universal quantifier '∀' as a radical operator.

The mathematician's universal quantifier '⋀' should behave in this respect like '∀.' For the two quantifiers correspond to two senses of 'every.' I will leave to the reader the task of finding examples (using 'no') which justify my classing the negative quantifier as a radical operator.

It is easy to see that the indefinite and definite quantifiers should be regarded as nonradical. The following are all nonproblematic English sentences:

A man met a woman in the evening, and he married her the next day.

Some man met a woman in the evening, and he married her the next day.

The Mayor met a woman in the evening, and he married her the next day.

We need not consider the passive voice operator. The only expressions within the scope of an occurrence of this operator are expressions occurring beneath it. A quantified phrase cannot occur within the scope of the passive voice operator. Let us consider the relative clause (the abstraction) operator. We will look to relative clauses in English to decide the status of '∋.' This sentence:

Jane knows a man who owns a racehorse, and she has ridden it.

is a perfectly satisfactory English sentence. The indefinite phrase 'a racehorse' is a component of the relative clause 'who owns a racehorse.' This indefinite phrase is the antecedent of 'it' in the second conjunct. The following sentence is also acceptable:

Some man who owns a racehorse wants to sell it.

The symbol '∋' is a nonradical operator.

However, there are some problems in this neighborhood. For the following:

(5) Every man who knows a ballerina admires her.

is a perfectly acceptable English sentence. But if we translate (5) with the following sentence of $\overline{\mathcal{L}}$:

(6) $[\forall(Mx \ni [x\ K\ aBy])\ A\ \bar{y}]$

our translation is ill-formed. The indefinite phrase 'aBy' is within the scope of the universal quantifier. And the universal quantifier is a radical operator. An indefinite phrase within the scope of a radical operator is not permitted to bind an overlined variable.

We should note that this restriction on the indefinite phrase only concerns the third pronomial transformation. And an indefinite phrase which already binds an overlined variable can subsequently find itself within the scope of a radical operator. The following is a satisfactory English sentence:

(7) It isn't true both that Bill met a girl, and he asked her to marry him.

The $\overline{\mathscr{L}}$-translation might be:

(8) $\sim[[b_x\ M\ aGy]\ \&\ [\overline{x}\ A\ \overline{y}]]$

This is a well-formed $\overline{\mathscr{L}}$-sentence; it can be used to perform an act like this:

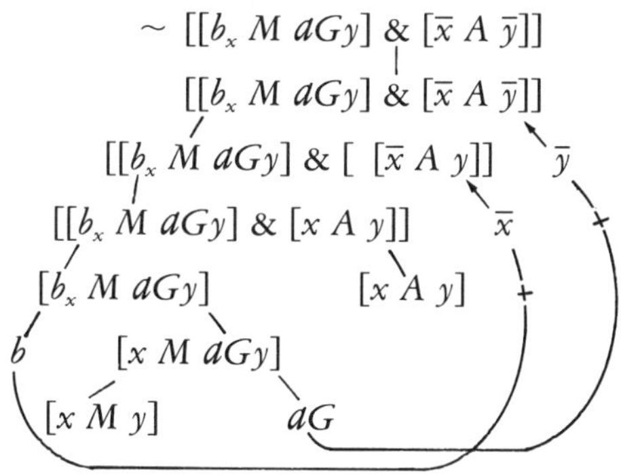

The next to last transformation binds '$\overline{y}$' by the indefinite quantifier of '*aGy*.' The negation transformation introduces a radical operator which includes the indefinite phrase in its scope. This does not affect the variable-binding relations that are already established.

The problem with (6) is that the indefinite phrase '*aBy*' enters the predicate with the universal transformation. It is not there before the universal quantifier enters—if it were, we could handle (6) as we do (8). I will not solve this problem here. For the present, (6) is not a well-formed expression of $\overline{\mathscr{L}}$. In the next chapter, we will find a way to modify $\overline{\mathscr{L}}$ so that (6) is acceptable.

Chapter 11
A Semantic Account for $\overline{\mathscr{L}}$: Part 1

1. A Scaled-Down Model

In the preceding chapter, I indicated how to modify the language $\mathscr{L}$ to obtain $\overline{\mathscr{L}}$. I have, in effect, modified the generative syntactic account of chapter eight to yield a generative syntactic account for $\overline{\mathscr{L}}$. But I have not explained the speech act structures for very many transformations of $\overline{\mathscr{L}}$, and I have not given a semantic account of many transformations. Most of the semantics of $\overline{\mathscr{L}}$ remains to be provided.

In a semantic account of $\mathscr{L}$ and $\overline{\mathscr{L}}$, we don't really give the meanings or truth conditions of individual constants, predicate functors, or predicates. Even though we are treating the artificial languages as if we used them for thinking and talking, we don't really use them for these tasks. The predicates and constants of the artificial languages don't belong to a system that also contains experience—we can't explain how particular expressions fit into the (or a) system of language. What we do is *suppose* that the constants and predicate functors have meanings. Then we explain how these would be affected by the various transformations. This gives us a genuine account of the meanings and truth conditions of the transformations and logical expressions of $\mathscr{L}$ and $\overline{\mathscr{L}}$.

A semantic account for $\mathscr{L}$, $\overline{\mathscr{L}}$, or a language like English is unrestricted. We don't explain meanings or truth conditions with respect to this or that domain. We don't subject genuine expressions to reinterpretation. We use language to talk about the real world. Which things we are talking about are determined by the fixed meanings of the expressions in our language. (These meanings aren't fixed once and for all. They can change over time. But there are no meanings determined with respect to this or that interpreting function.) A general, an unrestricted semantic account does not lend itself to mathematical results such as soundness and completeness results for a deductive system. But the use of set-theoretic definitions and set-theoretic techniques makes it possible to establish such results and gives a way to model an account of real world truth conditions. If an expression in a real language depicts or labels, this is absolute. It depicts or labels individuals or n-tuples in the real world, as determined by its meaning. The set-theoretic model uses an interpreting function (or a valuation) to take the place of meanings. The interpreting function assigns individuals and n-tuples (or sets of them) which are counterparts to the individuals and n-tuples labeled and depicted by expressions in a language we really use. Once the constants, predicate functors, and atomic predicates are taken care of, we can explain how the various transformations yield the individuals and n-tuples labeled or depicted by the resulting expressions. This part of the set-theoretic account is a genuine explanation of truth conditions. Overall, the set-theoretic account provides us with a "scale model" of an account of truth conditions for expressions in $\mathscr{L}$ and $\overline{\mathscr{L}}$. Not only is this useful for proving results, but it helps us get a better understanding of expressions and transformations.

The inferential meanings of expressions in $\mathscr{L}$ or $\overline{\mathscr{L}}$ can be given by developing a deductive system. This is not a model of an account of meaning; it is the real thing. But such a deductive system only deals with logical expressions and logical forms. The representational meanings of expressions in $\mathscr{L}$ or $\overline{\mathscr{L}}$ must also be explained in their own terms; I don't see a useful way to model such an account.

In this chapter, I will outline a semantic account for $\overline{\mathscr{L}}$. To do this, I will consider logical expressions and logical transformations. I will explain the effect of the logical transformations on representational meaning and on truth conditions. No account will be given of inferential meaning for the logical expressions. The reader is left to determine the extent to which the deductive system $\mathscr{S}$ must be modified to constitute $\overline{\mathscr{S}}$.

In considering representational meaning and truth conditions, I will focus on representing rather than denoting, and on depicting rather than labeling. An explanation of denoting and labeling can be derived from an explanation of representing and depicting; the reverse procedure is not always possible. An account in terms of labeling and denoting is inadequate for dealing with pronomial transformations. As well as a general semantic account, I will provide a set-theoretic semantics for $\overline{\mathscr{L}}$.

We should note that sets are a theoretical convenience, but this does not indicate any commitment on the language user's part to the existence of sets. When a predicate ϕ is associated with a set X, the predicate depicts the members of X, not X itself. Set-theoretic concepts are useful for giving truth conditions, and for proving results. This is a convenience for the theoretician, not for the language user. The set-theoretic semantics in this chapter will differ in an important respect from the account provided in chapters eight and ten. Once we are given an interpreting function f which assigns individuals to individual constants and sets of n-tuples to simple predicate functors, we determine the values of predicates for the valuation determined by f. Previously the value of a predicate was the set whose members were labeled by the predicate. *From now on,* the value of a predicate will be the set whose members are *depicted.* This change does not affect the interpreting functions we consider. It also happens that there are cases (such as atomic predicates) where depicting coincides with labeling. But these don't always coincide. Because this account deals with depicting rather than labeling, it will no longer be necessary to distinguish those cases where a transformation yields an open predicate from cases where it yields a sentence. The account of depicting is (relatively) uniform for open predicates and sentences. And a sentence is true iff it depicts. (I.e., if A is a sentence, and $f(A) = V$, then A is true iff V is nonempty.)

A predicate (sentence) A may depict individuals or n-tuples. But A may also fail to depict anything. In this case, there will be a set V such that $f(A) = V$, but $V = \emptyset$. Even if A does not depict anything, it is *suited* to depict n-tuples of a certain size. The size will be determined by the number of argument places (filled or not) in A, together with certain other factors. For example, if '[x V]' means *x is a vampire*, then this predicate does not depict. But it is suited to depict individuals. Similarly, the sentence '[a V]' is suited to depict an individual. And the predicate '[x F y, z]' is suited to depict triples, whether or not it actually depicts them. (Predicates which do and which don't depict are suited to do so.) When a predicate A is suited to depict n-tuples, we must be able to correlate expressions in A with positions in the n-tuples. Initially, the canonical order of free individual variables in an atomic predicate determines which variables are correlated with which positions. If an occurrence of a constant replaces a variable, then the occurrence of the constant is correlated with the same position that the variable was correlated with. For example, the predicate '[x L y]' may depict pairs $< e, d >$ such that e loves d. The occurrence of 'x' is correlated with the first position in these pairs, and 'y' is correlated with the second position. In the predicate '[*a L y*],' the occurrence of '*a*' is correlated with the first position in the pairs depicted. Different occurrences of a single expression might be correlated with different positions. The first occurrence of '*a*' in '[*a L a*]' is correlated with the first position in the pair depicted (in the pair that would be depicted, for the sentence may not depict), and the second occurrence of '*a*' is correlated with the second position. If an occurrence of an expression in *A* is correlated with a position in the *n*-tuples that *A* is suited to depict, then this position *answers to* the occurrence of the expression.

The accounts of the individual and reflexive transformations in the preceding chapters give sufficient information about the speech act structures associated with these transformations. The earlier discussions adequately explain the effect of these transformations on representing and depicting. However, a new set-theoretic account is required for these transformations. Throughout we will suppose that we have an interpreting function f of $\overline{\mathscr{L}}$ for a nonempty $\mathscr{D}$. f assigns individuals in $\mathscr{D}$ to individual constants, and assigns sets of n-tuples of individuals in $\mathscr{D}$ to n-place predicate functors. f is exactly the same kind of interpreting function we considered previously. What is different now is that for a predicate A we are concerned with n-tuples depicted by A (with respect to f) rather than m-tuples labeled by A. If A is a predicate, then we now write $f(A) = V$ to indicate that V is the set of n-tuples depicted by A. f must assign $\{<d, d> \mid d \in \mathscr{D}\}$ to '=' and $\mathscr{D}$ to 'T.' The atomic predicates of $\overline{\mathscr{L}}$ depict and label the same things. So if ϕ is a simple n-place functor, $f(\phi) = V$, and $\alpha_1, \ldots, \alpha_n$ are distinct individual variables, then $f[\alpha_1\ \phi\ \alpha_2, \ldots, \alpha_n] = V$. If $\breve{\phi}$ is obtained by the passive voice transformation, $f(\breve{\phi}) = V$, and α_1, α_2 are distinct individual variables, then $f[\alpha_1\ \breve{\phi}\ \alpha_2] = V$. And if $(\phi\alpha \ni A)$ is obtained by the relative clause transformation, $f(\phi\alpha \ni A) = V$, and β is an individual variable not occurring free in $(\phi\alpha \ni A)$, then $f[\beta\ (\phi\alpha \ni A)] = V$.

For the reflexive transformation, I will explain only the case in which occurrences of one variable are replaced by occurrences of another variable. I won't give the details of a transformation replacing occurrences of n variables by occurrences of a single variable; as far as depicting goes, the same effect can be achieved by n applications of transformations replacing occurrences of a single variable.

(1) Let A' be obtained from A by the reflexive transformation, by replacing free occurrences of β_i by β_j. Let A be suited to depict n-tuples. Let $f(A) = V$. And let the rth and sth positions ($r < s$) in the n-tuples that A is suited to depict answer to the free occurrences of β_i, β_j. (It doesn't matter whether it is the rth or the sth position which answers to

β_i.) Then $f(A') = V' = \{< e_1, \ldots, e_{n-1}> \mid < e_1, \ldots, e_{s-1}, e_r, \ldots, e_{n-1}> \in V\}$. The *r*th position answers to the free occurrences of β_j in A'.

For the individual transformations, I will explain only the case in which one constant replaces or binds occurrences of a single variable.

(2) Let A' be obtained from α, A by the individual transformation. Let A be suited to depict *n*-tuples. Let $f(\alpha) = d$ and $f(A) = V$. Let the *r*th position in the *n*-tuples that A is suited to depict answer to the free occurrences of β_i in A.

(2a) Let $A' = \alpha_{\beta_i} A$. Then $f(A') = V' = \{< d, e_1, \ldots, e_{r-1}, e_{r+1}, \ldots, e_n> \mid < e_1, \ldots, e_{r-1}, d, e_{r+1}, \ldots, e_n> \in V\}$. In these *n*-tuples, the first position answers to the prefixed occurrence of α_{β_i}. For $1 < j \leqslant r$, the *j*th position answers to the same occurrence of an expression that the $j - 1$st position answers to in A. For $r < k \leqslant n$, the *k*th position answers to the same occurrence (or occurrences) of an expression that the *k*th position answers to in A.

(2b, c) Let A' be obtained from A by replacing the first free occurrence of β_i by α_{β_i}, or by replacing the single free occurrence of β_i by α. Then $f(A') = V' = \{< e_1, \ldots, e_n> \mid < e_1, \ldots, e_n> \in V \text{ and } e_r = d\}$. The *r*th position in the *n*-tuples answers to the occurrence of α_{β_i} or α introduced by this transformation—and also to any occurrences of β_i that are bound by α_{β_i}. The remaining positions answer to the same occurrences of expressions that they answered to in A.

2. Sentential Structures

Before we take up the question of representing acts performed with compound sentences of $\overline{\mathscr{L}}$, we will consider various structures that are possible for sentential acts. Between intentional acts are three fundamental structural relations, all of which are found linking adjectives and nouns (linking acts of using these). We need to determine whether all three are found constituting sentential acts. Let the sentence '[*b J*]' be used to represent Bob as jogging. The sentence can be used to perform an act with this structure:

```
  [b J]
  /   \
 b   [x J]
```

The component acts, with their immediate purpose, constitute the sentential act. The purpose defines the sentential act. Can the sentence '[*b J*]' also be used to perform acts incorporating the other structural relations?

Take the relation between one act and a second act which gives a special character to the first. Could we, for example, have an act of representing Bob, and a predicative act which gives a special character to the act of representing Bob? This would give an act with the following structure: [*b* (+ *J*)]. However, such a structure is not consistent with our account of predicative acts. The predicative act performed with '[*J*]' (or '[*x J*]') represents an arbitrary individual as jogging. When combined with the act of representing Bob, the result represents Bob as jogging. The act of representing an arbitrary individual as jogging cannot give a special character to an act of individual representing. The predicative act is incomplete ("gappy"). It is not suited to give an additional character to a complete act.

To represent Bob with a special character is not (by itself) to represent Bob *as* anything. In a sentence like:

> Handsome Bob flirted with Anne.

the phrase 'Handsome Bob' could be used to perform an act with this structure:

> (Handsome +) Bob

This is not a sentential act; it is a special kind of act of representing Bob. When a predicative act is not a sentential act, it is essential to that act that it represent one or more arbitrary individuals as something or other. (Unless its gaps occur in an intentional context.) An act of representing an individual, even when it has a special character, does not represent that the individual has the character.

The fact that a sentential act cannot have this structure: [*b* (+ J)] shows more clearly than ever that Sellars' account of picturing is inadequate. Sellars has it that individual expressions with properties and relations represent individuals with properties and relations. His account of picturing does not concern acts, but only expressions. If it were "translated" in terms of acts, it seems this account should hold that acts of representing individuals, with these acts' special characters, constitute sentential acts. But such an account fails to provide for the feature of sentential acts that makes a sentence (sentential act) assertible. To represent an individual with a character is not to represent the individual as having the character. Acts of individual representing are neither accepted nor rejected. An act must have a predicative character before it can be accepted or rejected.

A sentential act cannot consist of an act of representing a specific individual, even if that act has a special character. But a sentential act might consist of a predicative act with a special character. Our sentence might be used to perform an act like this: [(*b* +) *J*]. The predicative act represents an arbitrary individual as jogging. The act of representing Bob gives a special character to the predicative act; with its special character, the predicative act represents Bob as jogging. We can also represent the act this way:

[(*b* +) *J*]
[*x J*]

The predicative act, by itself, is shown as input to the transformation whose output is the sentential act. Such an act places more emphasis on the jogging than on the person doing the jogging. It might be appropriate in a discourse like this one:

> Everybody jogs. Tom jogs. Bill jogs. Bob jogs.
> Sally jogs. Even Fred jogs.

Such an act is not the typical act of using a sentence containing names, verbs (predicate functors), etc. It may be typical for one-word sentences like some Spanish sentences. Though I am not clear whether using a certain suffix would normally constitute a separate intentional act which gives a special character to the predicative act. (A predicative act can have a special character even when it is not given that character by a separate act.)

A sentential act can have a structure like this:

```
  [b J]              or this:        [(b +) J]
  /   \
 b   [x J]                           [x J]
```

Acts which combine adjectives with nouns can have similar structures, but this doesn't make them sentential. Consider the phrase 'round barn' used in an act like this:

```
    round barn
     /      \
 round      barn
```

The two component acts represent an arbitrary round individual and an arbitrary barn, in order to represent an arbitrary round barn. The complex act is not sentential (or predicative) because neither component is predicative. An arbitrary individual isn't represented as round, or as a barn.

The remaining structural relation links an enabling act to the act it enables. Can this relation give rise to a sentential act like this one:

[*b* :*J*]
⋮
b

Can the act of representing Bob enable the act of representing Bob as jogging? The answer appears to be "Yes." The act of representing Bob doesn't make possible the use of the predicate '[*J*].' What it enables is that the act of using '[*J*]' constitutes an act of representing Bob as jogging. Such an act might be appropriate when attention is directed to Bob to the exclusion of everyone else.

> That Bob! He does everything. Bob plays tennis. Bob swims. Bob jogs. Bob climbs mountains.

Such a discourse could easily be replaced by this one:

> That Bob! He does everything. Plays tennis. Swims. Jogs. Climbs mountains.

Even though the predicates are missing subjects, it is clear that they are used to represent Bob as doing each thing.

The sentence can also be used to perform an act like this:

[*b*: *J*]
⋮
[*x* *J*]

The predicative act of representing an arbitrary individual as jogging makes it possible to use '*b*' to represent Bob as jogging. Ordinarily, '*b*' is simply used to represent Bob. In this special situation, it represents him as doing something. Such an act might be appropriate in answer to the question "Which doctor jogs?" The question already reveals that the person in question jogs. The 'jogs' in the answer is simply an echo of the 'jogs' in the question.

3. Negation

We now need to understand the act of using a sentence ~ *A*, where ~ *A* is obtained from *A* by the negation transformation. In dealing with $\overline{\mathcal{L}}$, I will consider '~' to be a simple, unanalyzable expression. So the act of using '~' is not itself complex. If the sentence ~ *A* is used alone, and not embedded in a larger sentence, then the negation sign might be used to indicate illocutionary force. In such a case, '~' would be a sign of rejection. Saying "~ *A*" would come to the same thing as saying "I deny that *A*." Following the lines of our earlier discussion, such an act might have this structure:

~: *A*
¦
A

Here *A* is used to perform a sentential act. This enables, by providing its material, the act of rejecting the sentential act. The negation sign is used to perform the act of rejecting *A* (the act of rejecting the act of using *A*).

When '~' is used as a sign of rejection, ~ *A* is not used to perform a propositional act. The sentence *A* is used to perform a propositional act. But '~' is used to reject that act, not to perform a further propositional act. $\overline{\mathcal{L}}$ contains no special expressions for making illocutionary force explicit. And I will not in providing a semantic account for $\overline{\mathcal{L}}$ "allow" for the force-indicating use of '~.' A person who actually spoke $\overline{\mathcal{L}}$ might use '~' to perform acts of rejection. But the semantic account for $\overline{\mathcal{L}}$ will not cover this. Let us consider how a sentence ~ *A* is used when it is used propositionally.

We might wonder whether the sentence ~ *A* could be used to perform an act like this:

~ *A*
/ \
~ *p* *A*

Here ~ *p* would be used to perform a predicative act of representing an arbitrary propositional act as false. The sentence *A* would be used to perform a propositional act. Both acts would be performed in order to represent the propositional act as false. However, such an analysis is not satisfactory. We *can* represent a propositional act as false—as when we say "Scott's statement is false." But when we use *A*, we are not representing a propositional act, we are performing one. The act performed with $\sim A$ is not a representing act. Once we perform the propositional act of using A, we don't need to represent this act. We can simply take the act to be false. The propositional act of using A is an enabling act. It enables, by providing its material, the act of taking A to be false. The propositional act of using $\sim A$ has the same general structure as the illocutionary act of rejection:

$$\begin{array}{ll} \sim: & A \\ & \vdots \\ & A \end{array}$$

The input act is a sentential act. It may be a representing act—an act of taking for. The output act is an act of taking to be: the act of taking the input to be false. Since the input act is an individual with which the language user is acquainted (by virtue of performing it), there is no need for the language user to perform a separate individual act of taking to be. The sentential act is itself sufficient to enable the predicative act of taking the sentential act to be false.

When the input to the negation transformation is a sentential act, the output does not represent. A representing act is an act of taking for. An act of taking to be is not a representing act. (A single act might be at once an act of taking to be and an act of taking for. But it is not an act of taking for by virtue of its being an act of taking to be.) Since a sentence $\sim A$ is not used to represent, we might choose to say that '$\sim$' (and $\sim A$) has no representational meaning. Instead, I will say that the representational meaning of '$\sim$' when it is used to "generate" $\sim A$ is *to present* A (the act of using A) *as false*. We might also say that a sentence $\sim A$ does not depict. However, it is technically convenient to say that $\sim A$ depicts A if A *is* false; it fails to depict otherwise.

It is interesting to consider the use of the English expression often used to provide a reading for '$\sim$.' Take the sentence 'It is false that Tom jogs.' Someone might use 'It is false that' as a single expression, and perform an act with this structure:

```
It is false that: Tom jogs.
                       ¦
                  Tom jogs
                   /     \
                Tom    x jogs
```

The prefix could be used either to perform an illocutionary act of denying that Tom jogs, or to perform an act of taking the propositional act to be false. However, the deliberate language user would not perform the act illustrated above. I think she would perform an act with this structure:

```
        It is false:  that Tom jogs.
       /         \                 \
     It   x is false     (that +) Tom jogs
                                  /     \
                               Tom    x jogs
```

In the prefix, I don't think we should regard 'It' as having an antecedent. 'It' isn't used in either the ordinary or the reflexive way. The pronoun 'It' functions like 'he' in 'He is very tall,' when this sentence is uttered in the presence of a very tall man. The tall man is not the antecedent of the pronoun 'He.' The presence of the tall man is the context that enables the pronoun 'He' to be used to refer to the tall man. In the same way, the propositional act performed with 'Tom jogs' makes 'It's referring possible by providing a target for the referring. The prefix 'It is false' is used in two ways: (1) To represent the propositional act as false, (2) To take the propositional act to be false. (Instead of (2), we could have: (2′) To reject the propositional act as false.) It is common to use sentences which describe (and represent) present experience to perform acts of taking to be that are also acts of taking for.

In the act diagramed above, the prefix act is both an act of taking for and an act of taking to be. It is the act of taking the propositional act to be false. And the act of taking the prefix for the propositional act—the act of representing the propositional act as false. (Both acts are enabled by the propositional act.) When the negation transformation in $\overline{\mathcal{L}}$ yields a sentence $\sim A$, that sentence is not used to represent (neither is its prefix). Even if A is used to perform a representing act, $\sim A$ is not. In fact, $\sim A$ *cancels* any representing done with A. But suppose A is an open predicate, containing free occurrences of individual variables. Then A is a schema rather than a sentence. Since an act performed with $\sim A$ is not a sentential act, it must represent. So both the input and the output acts of the negation transformation will represent in this case. But even when A has empty argument places, the act of using $\sim A$ will not have this structure:

```
     ~ A
    /   \
  ~ p    A
```

When a complex representing act has such a structure, the representing of the complex act simply combines the representing of the components. But suppose '[*x H*]' means *x is human*. The predicate '[*x H*]' is used to represent an arbitrary individual as human; it depicts each human. The predicate '~[*x H*]' will represent an arbitrary individual as not human. The predicate '~[*x H*]' will depict none of the same individuals as '[*x H*].' For similar reasons, the predicate ~ *A* cannot be used to perform an act with this structure:

(~ +) *A*
A

The representing and depicting of '[*x H*]' is not simply restricted to get the representing and depicting of '~[*x H*].'

Even with an open predicate, the negation transformation is associated with this structure:

~: [*x H*]
[*x H*]

The input represents an arbitrary individual as human; it depicts each human. The output act is performed with '~.' In this case it is the act of taking the sign of negation for an arbitrary individual *x* such that it is false that *x* is human. In the output we must regard the empty argument place (or places) as "belonging to" the negation sign. When dealing with radical transformations, I will explain representational meaning and depicting in two steps. First, the transformation is explained when the inputs are sentences (sentential acts). In the output act the input acts are taken to be this or that. If the output is true, it depicts a sentential act or acts. Second, when the output contains free variables (when the output act is a predicative but not a sentential act), the output act represents arbitrary individuals as such that the input acts have certain properties with respect to them. The output depicts *n*-tuples for which the output is true.

To give a set-theoretic explanation of depicting for the negation transformation, it is convenient to extend $\overline{\mathcal{L}}$ to *pseudo-languages* $\overline{\mathcal{L}}_{\mathcal{D}}$—as $\mathcal{L}$ was extended to pseudo-languages $\mathcal{L}_{\mathcal{D}}$ in the soundness proof for $\mathcal{S}$. A pseudo-language $\overline{\mathcal{L}}_{\mathcal{D}}$ is a "language" obtained from $\overline{\mathcal{L}}$ by treating individuals in $\mathcal{D}$ as names of themselves. If f is an interpreting function of $\overline{\mathcal{L}}$ for $\mathcal{D}$, then f^+ is the extension of f which assigns each individual in $\mathcal{D}$ to itself. A pseudo-predicate or a pseudo-sentence of $\overline{\mathcal{L}}_{\mathcal{D}}$ is either a predicate (sentence) of $\overline{\mathcal{L}}$, or is obtained from a predicate of $\overline{\mathcal{L}}$ by replacing occurrences of free variables by occurrences of individuals in $\mathcal{D}$. If A is a predicate (or pseudo-predicate) containing free occurrences of distinct individual variables $\alpha_1, \ldots, \alpha_n$, and $\rho_1, \ldots, \rho_n$ are individuals in $\mathcal{D}$, then $A[\alpha_1, \ldots, \alpha_n; \rho_1, \ldots, \rho_n]$ is the result of replacing the free occurrences of $\alpha_1, \ldots, \alpha_n$ by occurrences of $\rho_1, \ldots, \rho_n$ (respectively). If A is a predicate containing free occurrences of individual variable α, and ρ is an individual, then to say that $A[\alpha; \rho]$ is true amounts to the same thing as saying that A is true for ρ as value of α.

In $\overline{\mathcal{L}}_{\mathcal{D}}$, not only can an individual ρ occur in a pseudo-sentence, but so can an indexed individual ρ_{α_i}. For individuals in $\overline{\mathcal{L}}_{\mathcal{D}}$ are treated like individual constants in $\mathcal{L}$ (and $\overline{\mathcal{L}}_{\mathcal{D}}$). In dealing with $\mathcal{L}_{\mathcal{D}}$, we provided a *real* transformation to introduce an individual into a pseudo-predicate. We need a different real transformation for $\overline{\mathcal{L}}_{\mathcal{D}}$.

(*Real*) Let A be a pseudo-predicate of $\overline{\mathcal{L}}_{\mathcal{D}}$ which contains free occurrences of distinct individual variables $\alpha_1, \ldots, \alpha_n$ and no others; this is their canonical order. Let $\rho \in \mathcal{D}$.

(a) Then $\rho_{\alpha_i} A$ is obtained from ρ, A by the *real* transformation.

(b) Let all the free occurrences of α_i in A other than the first be within the scope of the first free occurrence of α_i in A. Let no constant or operator whose operative occurrence of α_i is to the left of the first free occurrence of α_i in A bind occurrences of $\overline{\alpha}_i$ to the right of the first free occurrence of α_i in A. Then A' is obtained from ρ, A be replacing the first free occurrence of α_i by ρ_{α_i}. A' is obtained by the *real* transformation.

(c) Let A contain a single free occurrence of α_i. Then A' is obtained from ρ, A by replacing the single free occurrence of α_i by ρ. A' is obtained by the *real* transformation.

The scope of an individual ρ or ρ_{α_i} is determined like the scope of an individual constant. Since individuals are not used to perform linguistic acts, there is no reason to give an account of the effect of the real transformation on representational meaning. We need to give a set-theoretic explanation of its effect on depicting. Suppose A is suited to depict m-tuples, and the jth position in these m-tuples answers to the free occurrences of α_i in A. Let $f^+(A) = V$.

(Real a) Then $f^+(\rho_{\alpha_i} A) = V' = \{< \rho, e_1, \ldots, e_{m-1}> \mid < e_1, \ldots, e_{j-1}, \rho, \ldots, e_{m-1}> \in V\}$.

(Real b, c) Then $f^+(A') = V' = \{< e_1, \ldots, e_{j-1}, \rho, e_j, \ldots, e_{m-1}> \mid < e_1, \ldots, e_{j-1}, \rho, \ldots, e_{m-1}> \in V\}$.

Now that we are considering pseudo-languages $\overline{\mathcal{L}}_{\mathcal{D}}$, we can give a set-theoretic account of depicting for the negation transformation. This also "fits" $\overline{\mathcal{L}}$, for $\overline{\mathcal{L}}$ is a sublanguage of $\overline{\mathcal{L}}_{\mathcal{D}}$.

(9a) Let $\sim A$ be obtained from A by the negation transformation. Let $f^+(A) = V$. And let $\beta_1, \ldots, \beta_m$ be the distinct individual variables, in canonical order, occurring in A. If $m = 0$, then $f^+(\sim A) = \{A\}$ if $V = \emptyset$; $f^+(\sim A) = \emptyset$ otherwise. If $m > 0$, then $f^+(\sim A) = V' = \{< e_1, \ldots, e_m > \mid f^+(\sim A[\beta_1, \ldots, \beta_m; e_1, \ldots, e_m]) = \{A[\beta_1, \ldots, \beta_m; e_1, \ldots, e_m]\}\}$.

Our treatment of negation shows certain features that are characteristic of radical operators. One is that such operators cancel the representing done with the inputs to their transformation. Some of the expressions in the inputs which depict in the inputs may no longer depict in the result of the transformation. Free variables which are found both in the input and the result will depict very different individuals. Suppose '[*x V*]' means *x is a vampire*. In '[*x V*]' the variable *x* depicts nothing. (Strictly speaking, it is the predicate which depicts or doesn't. The individuals depicted occur in positions which answer to expressions occurring in argument positions. We can informally say the expressions in argument positions depict individuals in answering positions.) In the predicate '~[*x V*],' the variable '*x*' (and the whole predicate) depicts every individual.

The infixed negation operator can be used to perform an act like the prefixed operator:

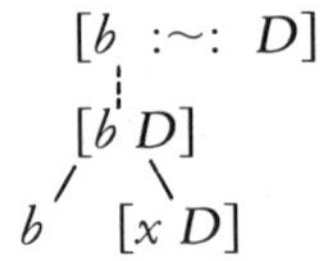

The infixed operator can also be used in the blocking role explained earlier. I previously suggested that a blocking act has this structure:

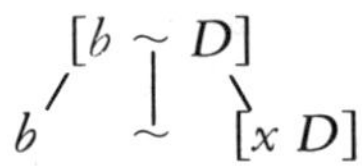

However, to make this out, there must be some act performed with '~' whose purpose is to block the representation of Bob as a doctor. There does not seem to be such an act—the act of using '~' is itself a blocking act. It also sounds awkward to say that '*b*' is used to represent Bob in order to block the representation of Bob as a doctor. The following diagram gives a more plausible analysis of the judgment of division:

$$[b :\sim: D]$$

$$b \qquad [x\ D]$$

The acts of representing Bob and representing an arbitrary individual as a doctor are enabling acts. They make possible the act of blocking the representation of Bob as a doctor. A blocking act only seems possible with a sentence. If '~' is inserted into an open predicate, it must be used like the prefixed '~.'

The account of depicting for the infixed negation is like that for the prefixed negation.

(9b) Let $[\alpha_1 \sim \phi\ \alpha_2, \ldots, \alpha_r]$ be obtained from $[\alpha_1\ \phi\ \alpha_2, \ldots, \alpha_r]$ by the negation transformation. Let $f^+[\alpha_1\ \phi\ \alpha_2, \ldots, \alpha_r] = V$. And let $\beta_1, \ldots, \beta_m$ be the distinct individual variables, in canonical order, occurring free in $[\alpha_1 \sim \phi\ \alpha_2, \ldots, \alpha_r]$. If $m = 0$, then $f^+[\alpha_1 \sim \phi\ \alpha_2, \ldots, \alpha_r] = \{[\alpha_1\ \phi\ \alpha_2, \ldots, \alpha_r]\}$ if $V = \emptyset$; $f^+[\alpha_1 \sim \phi\ \alpha_2, \ldots, \alpha_r] = \emptyset$ otherwise. If $m > 0$, then $f^+[\alpha_1 \sim \phi\ \alpha_2, \ldots, \alpha_r] = V' = \{< e_1, \ldots, e_m > \mid f^+([\alpha_1 \sim \phi\ \alpha_2, \ldots, \alpha_r]\,[\beta_1, \ldots, \beta_m; e_1, \ldots, e_m]) = \{[\alpha_1\ \phi\ \alpha_2, \ldots, \alpha_r]\,[\beta_1, \ldots, \beta_m; e_1, \ldots, e_m]\}\}$.

The picture theory of linguistic acts does not fit all linguistic acts. Since a sentence $\sim A$ is not used to perform a representing act, it is not used to picture.

$\mathcal{L}$ does not contain a 'truth' prefix. But suppose it did; let us suppose for the moment that 'τA' means *it is true that* A. Like '~,' 'τ' can be used in different ways which have the same effect. The prefix 'τ' might be used to indicate illocutionary force, marking an assertion. When 'τ' is used to indicate illocutionary force, there are two possible structures. We might have an act like this:

$$\tau\!: A$$

$$A$$

The sentential input enables the sentence's (the act's) acceptance; the prefix is used to accept the input act. The assertion might also have this structure

$$(\tau\ +)\ A$$

$$/|\backslash$$

The sentence A is used-and-accepted. There is no sentential enabling act; the prefix act serves to make explicit that the sentential act is accepted.

The prefix could be used to indicate that a sentence is taken to be true, when the taking need not be accepted. When used this way, we can have the same two (general) structures:

$$\begin{array}{rl} \text{T}: & A \\ & \vdots \\ & A \end{array}$$

In this case, the sentential act performed with *A* enables the act of taking the sentential act to be true. The prefix can also be used to give a special character to the sentential act:

$$\begin{array}{rl} (\text{T} +) & A \\ & A \end{array}$$

Here the prefix act makes explicit that the sentential act represents things as they are—as opposed to, say, representing things as the speaker would like them to be. In this context, to say that the sentence is used to represent things as they are is not to say that the sentence is true. Nor is it necessary that the person who takes the sentence to be true believe that the sentence is true. The representing or the taking must be accepted before the language user is committed. When 'T' is not used to indicate illocutionary force, the structure

$$(\text{T} +)\ A$$

would be appropriate in making a concession like this:

> It is true that Bob has no alibi for the night of the crime, but. . .

When 'T' is not used to indicate illocutionary force, and is used to perform an act like this:

$$\begin{array}{rl} (\text{T} +) & A \\ & A \end{array}$$

the act represents if the act performed with *A* represents. The prefix act simply gives a special character to the representing act. But when the prefix is used to perform an act like this:

$$\begin{array}{rl} \text{T}: & A \\ & \vdots \\ & A \end{array}$$

then the enabled act is not a representing act. It is an act of taking to be, not an act of taking for. However, if the sentential act performed with *A* represents, this representing is not "disturbed" by the truth prefix. *A*'s representing remains "in force." We will say that in this case τA represents indirectly whatever is represented by (using) *A*. (The locution for distinguishing direct from indirect representing fails at this point.) Similarly, τA depicts whatever *A* depicts.

4. Disjunction and Conjunction

A radical operator cancels, or wipes out, the representing of acts with which it is combined. A radical adjective like 'former' is used in an act like this:

```
former: barn
          ¦
        barn
```

The act of representing a barn enables the act of representing a former barn. But the act of representing a former barn eliminates the representing of a barn. A radical connective like '~' is used to perform an act like this:

```
~: [b J]
      ¦
   [b J]
```

The input represents Bob as jogging. The output does not represent; it cancels the representing of the input. We have previously classified 'v' (and 'or') as a radical operator. We must now consider how to understand (perform) the disjunction transformation. Suppose sentences *A*, *B* are both used to perform representing acts. What kind of act can we perform with [*A* v *B*]? It will not be an act with this structure:

```
   [A v B]
  /       \
A          B
```

Or this:

```
   [A v B]
  /   |   \
A  [p v q]  B
```

For [*A* v *B*] is not used to perform a complex representing act which includes or incorporates the representing done with *A*, *B*. The wedge is not a predicate. Neither is it used to give a special character to the acts performed with *A*, *B*. The representing done with *A*, *B* does not remain in force in the act performed with [*A* v *B*]. The disjunction is used to indicate that at least one of *A*, *B* is true, but it does not say which is true. The disjunctive act must have this structure:

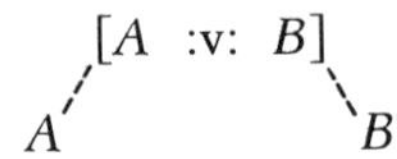

The acts performed with *A*, *B* enable the act performed with 'v.' We must now determine just what (kind of) act this is. With negation we take a single sentential act to be false. With disjunction, we are doing something which involves two acts. We might say that the two sentential acts are taken to be related in such a way that at least one is true. While this seems correct, it is an awkward way to put things. Such a relation is not very relational. I will say instead that the wedge is used to take the collection of sentential acts to be such that at least one is true.

If *A* contains n free variables and *B* contains m free variables ($n + m > 0$), then the disjunctive act is the act of taking 'v' (together with the unfilled argument places) for $n + m$ arbitrary individuals $e_1, \ldots, e_{n+m}$ such that either the predicative act performed with *A* is true for $e_1, \ldots, e_n$ or the predicative act performed with *B* is true for $e_{n+1}, \ldots, e_{n+m}$.

(10) Let [*A* v *B*] be obtained from *A*, *B* by the disjunction transformation. Let $f^+(A) = V$, $f^+(B) = W$. Let $\alpha_1, \ldots, \alpha_n$ be the distinct individual variables, in canonical order, occurring free in *A*. Let $\beta_1, \ldots, \beta_m$ be the distinct individual variables, in canonical order, occurring free in *B*. If $m = n = 0$, then $f^+[A \text{ v } B] = \{< A, B >\}$ if $V \cup W \neq \emptyset$; otherwise, $f^+[A \text{ v } B] = \emptyset$. If $n + m \neq 0$, then $f^+[A \text{ v } B] = V' = \{< d_1, \ldots, d_n, e_1, \ldots, e_m > \mid f^+([A \text{ v } B][\alpha_1, \ldots, \alpha_n, \beta_1, \ldots, \beta_m; d_1, \ldots, d_n, e_1, \ldots, e_m]) = \{< A[\alpha_1, \ldots, \alpha_n; d_1, \ldots, d_n], B[\beta_1, \ldots, \beta_m; e_1, \ldots, e_m]>\}\}$.

Conjunction is not a radical transformation. Other relations should be possible for the conjunction transformation than the relation between enabling and enabled acts. It will help us understand conjunction in $\overline{\mathscr{L}}$ if we begin by considering an English sentence in which 'and' means *and then:*

(1) Megan pushed Andrea, and Andrea fell down.

The sentential acts performed with:

(2) Megan pushed Andrea

(3) Andrea fell down

each represent. The two representing acts are combined into a complex representing act which represents the "situation" represented by (2) as prior to that represented by (3). It should be possible to use (1) to perform an act with this structure:

(4) Megan pushed Andrea, and Andrea fell down.

/ | \

Megan pushed Andrea   *p* and *q*   Andrea fell down

The sentential inputs have further structures which are not shown. The word 'and' is used to perform a predicative act; this represents arbitrary situations *p, q* as such that *p* preceded *q*. (The predicate '*p* and *q*' would more properly be described as representing precedence which is neutral between past, present, and future. The actual tenses are supplied by the component sentences.)

The structure shown in (4) seems reasonable. But there are some problems. Two separate sentential acts might be performed with this text:

(5) Megan pushed Andrea. Andrea fell down.

Even without the 'and,' (5) would be understood like (4). In (5) there is no predicate expression. In performing the two sentential acts, there seems to be no need for a predicative act (to combine the sentential acts). If the sentences are used to perform separate acts, it is most natural for these sentential acts to be assertions. These two assertions will be components of a complex act—a complex illocutionary act. In general, complex illocutionary acts do not require predicates (predicative acts) to hold them together. Suppose we have a two-premise inference from p_1, p_2 to q. Each component sentence is asserted. Each assertion is performed in order to constitute the inference—in order to reason from p_1, p_2 to q. However, each assertion is not unqualified. The premises are asserted *as supporting the conclusion*. The conclusion is asserted *as supported by the premises*. The role of the conclusion is *to be supported by the premises*. No predicate is needed, or wanted, to characterize the conclusion as the conclusion. (But words like 'so,' 'thus,' 'must,' etc. are often used to give a special, explicit character to the conclusion assertion.)

The two sentential acts performed with (5) can both be performed in order to represent (and assert) Megan's pushing Andrea as prior to Andrea's falling down. The first sentential act then represents Megan as pushing Andrea, *as earlier than what the second act represents*. The second act represents Andrea as falling down, *as later than what the first act represents*. The italicized 'as'-clauses are given by the roles of the component sentential acts in the complex assertion. No predicative act is required. Predicative acts are needed to constitute the basic illocutionary acts. Complex illocutionary acts don't require immediate predicative components.

The sentence (1):

(1) Megan pushed Andrea, and Andrea fell down.

can be used to perform an act represented in (4) above. This sentence can also be used to perform an act like that performed with (5). The two component sentences are asserted in order to constitute a complex assertion. In this case, 'and' does not function as a predicate. It has a function similar to that of 'so' or 'thus' in the conclusion of an argument—to make explicit the relation which the complex assertion represents as linking the two situations. When (1) is used like (5), the act has this structure:

(6) Megan pushed Andrea, (+ and +) Andrea fell down.
/ \
Megan pushed Andrea Andrea fell down

Sentence (1) can be used to perform such an act even when it isn't asserted. The propositional components can combine to constitute the complex propositional act without being joined by a predicative act.

Sentence (1) would naturally be used to perform an act with either structure (4) or (6). Structure (4) is associated with an act where 'and' is stressed; structure (5) with an act where it isn't. Sentence (1) can even be used this way:

(7) Megan pushed Andrea, :and: Andrea fell down.
/ \
Megan pushed Andrea Andrea fell down

The output act is an act of using 'and' to represent Andrea's falling down as subsequent to her being pushed. The word 'and' could not normally be used to represent this; the input acts constitute a special context making possible 'and's complicated representing. This structure is not typical for sentence (1). It would be appropriate in correcting someone who thought Andrea fell down before she got pushed.

In English, 'and' is not always used with the sense *and then*. In $\overline{\mathcal{L}}$, '&'

is never used with this sense. We can use '&' to connect sentences which do and which don't represent. Even when it connects two sentences used to represent, it does not give rise to a further, more complex representation. When '&' connects two representing sentences, we have two separate representing acts which don't constitute parts of a more comprehensive representing act. So '&' is not used to perform acts with this structure:

```
      [A & B]
     /   |   \
   A [p & q] B
```

The ampersand is not a predicate functor.

We can often use a conjunction like:

(8) Jorge is a philosopher and Norma is an accountant.

to achieve the same effect that can be achieved with two separate sentences:

(9) Jorge is a philosopher. Norma is an accountant.

(We can do this when the sentences are asserted.) We shall try to gain an understanding of the way that (8) (and its $\overline{\mathcal{L}}$ counterpart) is used by considering how the sentences (9) are used. When the assertion of *A* is followed by the assertion of *B*, the two sentential acts need not constitute a complex illocutionary act or be components of some more inclusive complex illocutionary act. The separate assertions *may* be components of some complex illocutionary act; the sentences (9) might be asserted in order to constitute an explanation of some fact. But they don't constitute a complex illocutionary act simply by virtue of being asserted one after the other. When *A* is asserted, followed by the assertion of *B*, the sentential act *B* can be regarded as supplementing act *A*. *A* gives some information, and *B* gives more information without "disturbing" *A*'s information. Consecutive sentential acts of this sort are *intended* to supplement one another. But the second act is not performed *in order* to supplement the first. Performing the second act *is* supplementing the first. We might say that the purpose for performing the major components of *B* (if *B* is a complex act) is *to perform sentential act B, supplementing sentential act A*. (Its supplementary role is a special character of the sentential act, though in this case the special character is not conferred by a separate act.) Acts *A*, *B* may have a common purpose so that they constitute some further act. But *A*'s act supplemented with *B*'s act does not, independently of their purposes, constitute a single intentional act.

I will recognize a new category of acts so that I can describe this situation. Act *A* supplemented with act *B* is a *composite act*. A composite act is not an intentional act. It is not a simple intentional act, and it is not a complex act defined by the purpose of its components. But a composite act can in many situations be treated as a unit. The two components of the composite act *A*-followed-by-*B* have purposes of their own (or are enabling acts), but they are intended to go together.

The components of a conjunction in $\mathcal{L}$ can be used in the same way as two separate sentences: to constitute a composite act. I will represent this by:

```
[A (+ & +) B]
/|\       /|\
```

The ampersand is used to give a special explicit character to the composite (conjunctive) act; the ampersand makes explicit the fact that the act is of this sort. Since the composite act is not a single intentional act, it cannot strictly have a property conferred on it by an intentional act. The act performed with the ampersand serves to relate the components rather than to characterize a single item. John Stuart Mill may have been thinking of some such structure as the act illustrated here when he declared that a conjunction is no more a compound sentence than a street is a compound house.

Even when *A, B* are not asserted, a sentence [*A* & *B*] can be used as illustrated (and explained) above. The sentential acts supplement each other without being components of a single intentional act. If a composite sentential act is the input to the negation transformation, the act should be represented like this:

```
~:   [A & B]
     /      \
 [A (+& +) B]
```

Each conjunct's act is independently an enabling act for the act of taking the composite act to be false. Even though the above representation is the more accurate, I might sometimes be less careful and represent the speech act structure this way:

```
~:   [A & B]
        ¦
 [A (+& +) B]
```

Predicative acts which are not sentential can also be combined to form composite (conjunctive) acts. Such composite acts will not be given special characters by subsequent transformations. They can be components of complex acts defined by the purpose of the conjuncts. They can enable subsequent acts.

The structure illustrated above is the typical way to use a conjunctive sentence occurring as a separate sentence. A conjunction can also be used to perform an act like this:

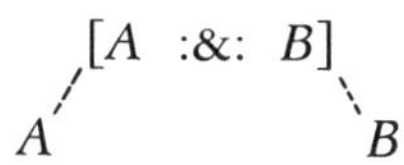

The ampersand is used to take the collection of sentences *A, B* to be such that both members are true. An act with the illustrated structure is more natural when one of *A, B* is an open predicate. If *A* contains n free variables and *B* contains m free variables ($m + n > 0$), this act would be an act of taking the collection of *A, B* for arbitrary individuals $e_1, \ldots, e_{m+n}$ such that *A* is true for $e_1, \ldots, e_n$ and *B* is true for $e_{n+1}, \ldots, e_{n+m}$.

A composite act performed with [*A* & *B*] represents what *A* represents (if anything) and what *B* represents. If *A, B* are sentences, an act:

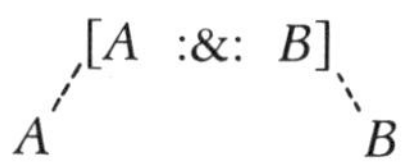

is not a representing act. The representing performed with *A* and *B* is undisturbed by the enabled act; whatever is represented by *A, B* is represented indirectly by the enabled act. But if *A, B* contain unfilled argument places, then the enabled act represents arbitrary individuals directly. The other individuals represented by *A, B* are represented indirectly. Since each part of a composite act is "autonomous," each depicts, or fails to depict, on its own. But the parts are intended to supplement one another. So the composite depicts only if both parts depict. The depicting done with [*A* & *B*] is the same whether the sentence is used to perform a composite act, or the ampersand is used to perform an act enabled by the acts of using the conjuncts. If *A* depicts n-tuples and *B* depicts m-tuples, then [*A* & *B*] depicts $(m + n)$-tuples $< d_1, \ldots, d_n, e_1, \ldots, e_m >$ such that *A* depicts $< d_1, \ldots, d_n >$ and *B* depicts $< e_1, \ldots, e_m >$. The set-theoretic description of the effect of the conjunction transformation is given with respect to f (and $\overline{\mathscr{L}}$) rather than f^+ (and $\overline{\mathscr{L}}_{\mathscr{D}}$). The account for f^+ and $\overline{\mathscr{L}}_{\mathscr{D}}$ is exactly the same, once 'f' is replaced by 'f^+.'

(11) Let [A & B] be obtained from A, B by the conjunction transformation. Let $f(A) = V$, $f(B) = W$. Let A be suited to depict n-tuples and B be suited to depict m-tuples. Then $f[A \& B] = V' = \{<d_1, \ldots, d_n, e_1, \ldots, e_m> \mid <d_1, \ldots, d_n> \in V$ and $<e_1, \ldots, e_m> \in W\}$. The positions in the $(n + m)$-tuples answer to the obvious occurrences of expressions in A, B.

5. The Horseshoe

Although I will not use the horseshoe to capture the meanings of English conditional sentences, I would like for the treatment of the horseshoe in $\overline{\mathcal{L}}$ to shed some light on English conditionals. If A, B are sentences used to represent, then a conditional 'If A, then B' might be used to perform a complex representing act which incorporates the representing of antecedent and consequent. Perhaps the conditional represents two "situations" related causally, as:

(1) If Frank struck the match, then it lit.

Frank's striking the match might be represented as the cause of the match's lighting. In this case, it seems likely that the relation between the situations is both causal and temporal. For the lighting is subsequent to the striking. Another conditional might represent situations related temporally without being related causally:

(2) If the next card is a club, then the one after that will be a spade.

But some conditionals don't represent two situations as related:

(3) If Dave got the right answer, then he guessed.

This is even clearer with conditional sentences which contain a non-representing component:

(4) If it is false that Laramie is the capital of Wyoming, then Cheyenne is the capital of Wyoming.

When a conditional sentence is used to represent two situations as causally related, the conditional sentence does not have the same meaning as a "plain" causal sentence. Sentence (1) has a different meaning from (5):

(5) The match lit because Frank struck it.

Conditional sentences which represent temporally related situations have a different meaning than "plain" representations of such relations. Sentence (2) has a different meaning from (6):

(6) The next card will be a club. The one after that will be a spade.

When a conditional sentence is used to represent, its conditional meaning is "over and above" its representing. This conditional meaning is shared with conditional sentences which are not used to constitute complex representations.

To make sense of conditional sentences, I think we should regard the use of a conditional sentence as involving two acts; the conditional transformation has two steps. (There are inputs, an intermediate step, and the output.) When a sentence 'If *A*, then *B*' is used to form a complex representation, the representing is the first step. It is the second step which introduces conditionality. I will describe the second step as the act of taking the consequent to be conditional on the antecedent. It isn't the situation represented by the consequent which is conditional on that represented by the antecedent. For the situations represented by a true conditional need not obtain. If they don't, then there are no situations to be related. And when the components of a conditional sentence do not represent, there are also no situations to be related. The second stage of the conditional transformation is the act of taking one propositional act to be conditional on another. The conditional relation that concerns us is a relation between sentential acts.

Suppose that in using the conditional sentence 'If *A*, then *B*,' the component acts are combined to constitute a complex representation. In that case the conditional act might be like this:

```
If:   A, then B
         ⋮
      A, (+ then +) B
     /               \
    A                 B
```

The sentential acts *A, B* are performed in order to represent *A*'s situation as related to *B*'s situation in a certain way. This representation enables the act of taking *B*'s representing to be conditional on *A*'s. (It might be better in this case to say that the whole complex representing act is taken to be conditional on *A*'s representing.) When *A, B* are not combined to constitute a complex representing act, I think they form a composite act. The components of this act separately enable the act of taking to be. I will represent such an act this way:

```
If:  A,  then:  B
     ¦          ¦
     A  ( + )   B
```

The '+' in parentheses is to indicate that using *A, B* together constitutes a composite act. The two acts supplement each other, and are intended to do so.

It is typical of radical operators that they are used to perform acts enabled by the inputs to their transformations. Nonradical operators can also be used in this way, but nonradical operators have other uses. If the typical use of a conditional expression is to perform acts like those represented above, this suggests that the conditional expression is radical. We previously classified the conditional expression (and the horseshoe) as nonradical, because in a conditional sentence like:

(7) If Brian sees a beetle, he will step on it.

the indefinite phrase 'a beetle' in the 'if'-clause is the antecedent of 'it' in the consequent. However, besides its typical speech act structure, the conditional expression possesses some other characteristics of radical operators. To see this, we must first consider some transformations that don't introduce radical operators. In this individual transformation:

```
      [b H y]
     /       \
    b      [x H y]
```

the predicate input depicts pairs $< \alpha, \beta >$ such that α hit β. The output depicts pairs $<$ Bob, $\beta >$ such that Bob hit β. In the pairs depicted by the output, every individual which answers to the free occurrence of '*y*' in '[*b H y*]' is also a second member of a pair depicted by the predicate input, answering to the free occurrence of '*y*.' Consider this reflexive transformation:

$$[x\ K\ (+\ x)]$$
$$[x\ K\ y]$$

The input depicts pairs < α, β > such that α killed β. The output depicts individuals α such that α killed α. But every individual depicted by the output answers to the free occurrences of '*x*' in '[*x K x*].' And every such individual is a first member of a pair depicted by the input, and answers to the free occurrence of '*x*' in the input.

The negation transformation is a radical transformation, introducing the radical operator '~.' In this instance of the negation transformation:

$$\sim\!:\ [x\ D]$$
$$[x\ D]$$

the input depicts every doctor. Every doctor answers to the free occurrence of '*x*' in the input. The output depicts individuals that aren't doctors. The individuals depicted by the output, and answering to the free occurrence of '*x*' in the output, are not among the individuals depicted by the input and answering to the free occurrence of '*x*' in the input. The disjunction transformation is also radical. In the following:

$$[[x\ J]\ :\!\mathrm{v}\!:\ [y\ S]]$$
$$[x\ J] \qquad\qquad [y\ S]$$

the left input depicts individuals that jog, and the right input depicts individuals who swim. The output depicts pairs < α, β > such that either α jogs or β swims. So the output can depict a pair < α, β > in which α doesn't jog. This α answers to the free occurrence of '*x*' in the output, but is not among the individuals depicted by '[*x J*]' and answering to the free occurrence of '*x*' in the left input.

It is characteristic of radical transformations that individuals answering to occurrences of a free variable in the output need not be individuals which answer to occurrences of the same free variable in the input. If we consider the horseshoe and our intentions for it, we can determine that it must be radical. For the predicate '[[*x J*] ⊃ [*y S*]]' should depict pairs < α, β > such that either α doesn't jog or β does swim. The predicate could depict a pair < α, β > in which α doesn't jog. This α is not depicted by '[*x J*],' which is one mark of a radical operator. We can similarly determine that the English conditional expression is radical. For whatever is the correct explanation of the (ordinary) conditional relation between propositional acts, it is clear that 'If x jogs, then y swims' will depict some pairs $< \alpha, \beta >$ in which α isn't depicted by 'x jogs.'

A conditional sentence 'If A, then B' can be used to perform an act like this:

```
If:   A,   then:  B
       ¦          ¦
       A   (+)    B
```

I will take this to be the typical structure of the conditional transformation (of the act with which the conditional transformation is associated) for $\overline{\mathcal{L}}$:

```
[A :⊃: B]
 ¦      ¦
 A (+) B]
/|\    /|\
```

An act of using a sentence $[A \supset B]$ will have the same structure as an act of using an English conditional 'If A, then B.' The important difference between the horseshoe and the ordinary conditional expression does not concern the structures of acts of using these expressions. The important difference is between the conditional relations linking antecedent and consequent. But, now, if conditional expressions are radical, how can an indefinite phrase in the 'if'-clause serve as antecedent to a pronoun in the consequent? This problem is solved by the two stages in the conditional transformation. The initial stage of the conditional transformation yields a composite act. In the second, and final, stage of the conditional transformation, the "right" part of the composite act is taken to be conditional on the "left." The output of the first stage of the conditional transformation can serve as input to pronomial transformations. This "defers" the second stage of the conditional transformation.

Consider the sentence 'If Bob sees Anne, then he will talk to her.' Let the corresponding sentence of $\overline{\mathcal{L}}$ be '$[[b_x \; S \; a_y] \supset [\bar{x} \; T \; \bar{y}]]$.' An act of using this sentence might have the following structure:

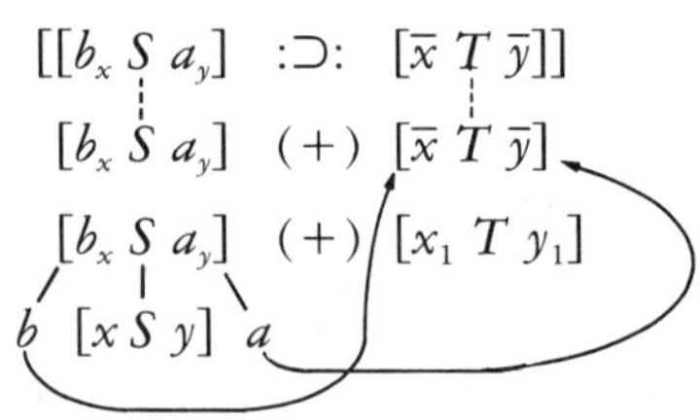

The first intermediate conditional expression is transformed into the second intermediate expression by simultaneous pronomial transformations. The only lines leading to the second intermediate expression lead to the right half. The act which constitutes the left half of the first composite act also constitutes the left half of the second composite act. (In the tree diagrams, colons and pluses indicate features of acts. We do not ordinarily think of them as expressions of $\mathcal{L}$ or $\overline{\mathcal{L}}$. But an intermediate conditional expression is an auxiliary expression of $\mathcal{L}$ and $\overline{\mathcal{L}}$, and contains '(+).' The auxiliary expression is useful for describing transformations. It is not used by speakers of the artificial languages.) The English sentence 'If Bob sees Anne, then he will talk to her' can also be used to perform an act with the structure illustrated above.

In the conditional transformation, two predicative (or sentential) acts are combined to constitute a composite act. This is marked by an intermediate conditional expression. This intermediate expression can serve as input either to pronomial transformations (which yield intermediate conditional expressions) or to the final stage of the conditional transformation—this is an act of taking the consequent-act to be conditional on the antecedent-act. The representing and depicting of the composite act's intermediate conditional expression are the same as for the conjunction transformation. We must now determine how two sentential acts are related when one is conditional on the other.

When a speaker uses an English conditional 'If *A*, then *B*,' what seems to be involved is this: Given what the speaker now knows (or currently envisages), adding the antecedent also gives the consequent. Given what the speaker knows, it won't happen that the antecedent is true and the consequent isn't. If *A* and *B* are both true, then 'If *A*, then *B*' is true. If *A* is true and *B* isn't, the conditional isn't true. If the speaker's current knowledge is incompatible with *A*, then the conditional sentence is "vacuously" true. ("If *A*, then I'm a monkey's uncle.") Otherwise (i.e., in case *A* isn't true but isn't ruled out either) the conditional sentence is true if the subjunctive conditional 'If *A* were true, then *B* would be true' is true for that speaker. If *A* is true, then 'If *A*, then *B*' has the same value for all language users. But if *A* isn't true, then the value of the conditional sentence is relative to a language user, and what he knows or envisages at that time. This makes it difficult to develop a formal account which captures the meaning of ordinary conditionals. This difficulty is compounded by the need for a successful treatment of subjunctive conditionals.

An adequate account of conditional sentences (and the acts of using them) would be too long for this book. Instead I shall introduce a different conditional relation such that every act of using a conditional sentence has the same value. With this relation, sentence *B* (the sentential act of using *B*) is conditional on *A* iff for any "way" of making *A* true, there is a corresponding way to make *B* true. (I said *any* way, not *every* way. As I understand English, 'any' admits of vacuous truth.) There is only one way to make a sentence like '[*b J*]' ("Bob jogs"), true: Bob has to jog. But '[*aM J*]' ("Some man jogs") can be made true in many ways—there is one way for each man. If *A* is suited to depict *r*-tuples and *B* is suited to depict *s*-tuples, we can describe the conditional relation by saying that for any *r*-tuple $< d_1, \ldots . d_r>$ depicted by *A*, there is an *s*-tuple $< e_1, \ldots . e_s>$ such that $< d_1, \ldots . d_r, e_1, \ldots . e_s>$ is depicted by (the intermediate conditional sentence) [*A* (+) *B*]—we could also say that $< d_1, \ldots . e_s>$ is depicted by [*A* & *B*].

Consider the conditional sentence '[[*b J*] ⊃ [*a G*]]' ("If Bob jogs, then Anne plays golf"). The intermediate conditional expression '[[*b J*] (+) [*a G*]]' represents Bob as jogging and Anne as playing golf. If Bob jogs and Anne plays golf, the intermediate expression depicts < Bob, Anne >. Suppose Bob does jog. Then '[*b J*]' depicts Bob (and nothing else). The conditional sentence is then true if '[[*b J*] (+) [*a G*]]' depicts a pair < Bob, *d* > such that '[*a G*]' depicts *d*. The only acceptable *d* would be Anne. So if Bob does jog, the conditional is true just in case Anne plays golf. If Bob doesn't jog, the sentence '[*b J*]' doesn't depict. This makes the conditional sentence vacuously true, because for *any* individual α depicted by '[*b J*],' there is a corresponding β such that < α, β > is depicted by '[[*b J*] (+) [*a G*]].'

Now consider '[[*aM J*] ⊃ [*a G*]].' The sentence '[*aM J*]' depicts each man who jogs. (We haven't yet considered depicting for the indefinite transformation, but this is how it will come out.) The conditional is true if for each man α who jogs, Anne plays golf. For then the intermediate conditional expression '[[*aM J*] (+) [*a G*]]' will depict < α, Anne > for each jogging man α. The conditional [[*aM J*] ⊃ [*aW G*]]' ("If some man jogs, then some woman plays golf") will be true if for each man who jogs, we can find a woman who plays golf (but the same woman will do for each man).

The conditional transformation is radical, though its first step is not. If *A*. *B* are sentences, then [*A* ⊃ *B*] does not represent. In case *B* *is* conditional on *A* we will say that [*A* ⊃ *B*] depicts {*B*}. If *A*. *B* contain *n* distinct free variables, then [*A* ⊃ *B*] represents *n* arbitrary individuals as such that [*A* ⊃ *B*] is true (for them). And [*A* ⊃ *B*] depicts *n*-tuples for which [*A* ⊃ *B*] is true.

Now let us give the set-theoretic account of depicting for the conditional transformation.

(12) Let *A*, *B* be predicates such that *A* is suited to depict *r*-tuples and *B* is suited to depict *s*-tuples. Then the intermediate conditional expression [*A* (+) *B*] depicts $(r + s)$-tuples $< \gamma_1, \ldots, \gamma_r, \delta_1, \ldots, \delta_s >$ such that *A* depicts $< \gamma_1, \ldots, \gamma_r >$ and *B* depicts $< \delta_1, \ldots, \delta_s >$.

If *A*, *B* are sentences, then [$A \supset B$] depicts {*B*} if for every *r*-tuple $< \gamma_1, \ldots, \gamma_r >$ which is depicted by *A*, there is an *s*-tuple $< \delta_1, \ldots, \delta_s >$ such that [*A* (+) *B*] depicts $< \gamma_1, \ldots, \gamma_r, \delta_1, \ldots, \delta_s >$. Let *A* contain free occurrences of *n* distinct individual variables $\alpha_1, \ldots, \alpha_n$ and no others; this is their canonical order. Let *B* contain free occurrences of *m* distinct individual variables $\beta_1, \ldots, \beta_m$ and no others; this is their canonical order. $(m + n > 0)$ Then $f^+[A \supset B] = V' = \{< \upsilon_1. \ldots . \upsilon_n. \mu_1, \ldots, \mu_m > \mid f^+ ([A \supset B] [\alpha_1, \ldots, \alpha_n, \beta_1, \ldots, \beta_m; \upsilon_1, \ldots, \upsilon_n, \mu_1, \ldots, \mu_m]) = \{B[\beta_1, \ldots, \beta_m; \mu_1, \ldots, \mu_m]\}\}$.

If [*A* (+) *B*] is the output of the pronomial transformation, its depicting is determined by that transformation. If [A (+) *B*] contains no free variables, then [$A \supset B$] depicts {*B*} if it is true—this is determined above. If *A*, *B* contain $n + m$ distinct free variables, then [$A \supset B$] depicts $(n + m)$-tuples determined as above.

6. Two Quantifiers

In this section I will discuss the indefinite and universal quantifiers. It seems likely that we can use our treatment of these quantifiers as a model for our treatment of others. Recall how an open predicate is used to represent. The one-place predicate '[*x J*]' can be used to represent an arbitrary individual as a jogger (as jogging). We can also say that the predicate is used to represent an arbitrary jogger. Similarly, the two-place predicate '[*x S y*]' can be used to represent a pair of arbitrary individuals as related by seeing. An open predicate is a schema; the predicative act is schematic. Schemata and schematic acts are contrasted with sentences and sentential acts that represent specific individuals. Schematic acts and expressions concern arbitrary rather than specific individuals. An open predicate is also incomplete—its gaps or free variables mark this incompleteness—and a predicative act performed with an open predicate is incomplete. When such an act is combined with individually representing acts, the predicative act serves to provide a property or relation to the individual acts. This is its role in the complex act.

Once we have names and predicates available, with the names taking the empty places of predicates, it seems a small change to allow predicates (or predicate functors) in the empty places of predicates. If this practice is allowed, it will be most convenient to allow one-place functors (common nouns) in the argument places of predicates. If we can use '[*b J*]' to represent Bob as jogging, and '[*x M*]' means *x is a man,* why not use '[*M J*]' to represent an arbitrary man as jogging? The predicate '[*x J*]' represents an arbitrary individual as jogging; this predicate is schematic. The sentence '[*b J*]' represents a specific individual as jogging; it is not schematic. If we allowed ourselves to use '[*M J*]' to represent an arbitrary man as jogging, our expression would be schematic. But it would not be incomplete.

In English, we cannot simply put a one-place predicate functor (an intransitive verb) into the argument place of a predicate. Nor can we do this with the corresponding singular common noun. (We cannot correctly say "Works jogs" or "Worker jogs.") English requires that we use a quantifier (which may be an article). But it seems that we can use the indefinite phrase to achieve the effect we intended by placing a predicate functor in an argument place. For a sentence 'Some man jogs' (or '[*aM J*]') can be used to represent an arbitrary man as jogging. And in the plural, quantifiers are not required—'Men jog' is acceptable. Indeed, I have been told that there are languages, like Polish, where an unadorned common noun can occupy the same place as a proper noun.

While the step from putting proper names in argument places to putting predicate functors, common nouns, or quantified phrases in argument places seems a small one, this step is of immense importance. This move provides language with an expressive power that would not otherwise be available. (Except by treating quantified phrases in the first-order fashion, and invariably prefixing them.) The use of schematic expressions to form sentences in which not all gaps are filled with names makes universal knowledge possible. Hobbes may have been the first theorist to appreciate this feature of language. Although his insight was not appreciated because of the general feeling that language was incidental to thought, Hobbes was right that a kind of language is what makes possible a kind of thought. But he was mistaken in thinking that a sophisticated sensory apparatus, and the ability to use one thing to represent another, are all the abilities needed for using language. Chimpanzees and gorillas may be able to combine names and predicates to perform complex linguistic acts, but this is no guarantee that they have the mental equipment needed for using quantifiers and quantified phrases. That would put them in our league.

A sentential act like this:

```
     [b J]
    /     \
   b     [x J]
```

pictures. The act of representing Bob individually has the property of being combined with the predicative act. This act with its property pictures Bob with the property of jogging (of being a jogger). A drawn or painted picture can also represent a specific individual doing this or that. But a drawing can also represent an arbitrary individual—it can represent, say, an arbitrary python digesting an arbitrary elephant. The sentence '[*a*M *J*]' pictures an arbitrary man with the property of jogging. With either drawings or words, we can distinguish definite from indefinite representing. Linguistically, definite representing can be performed with a proper name. Indefinite representing can be performed with an indefinite phrase—as well as with an open predicate. When an indefinite phrase is used in this way, it seems that the role of the indefinite article (or 'some') is to make the indefinite character explicit. This would give an act of indefinite representing with the following structure: (*a* +) *M*.

When a sentential act represents a specific individual as this or that, the act is true iff it depicts. If it is true, then the specific individual really is this or that. We can accept or reject such an act as representing things as they are. A sentence which represents an arbitrary individual as this or that is schematic. An open predicate is also schematic, but a schematic sentence (sentential act) is both schematic and complete. In a sentential act performed with '[*a*M *J*],' the act performed with '*a*M' depicts every man. The predicative act performed with '[*x J*]' depicts every jogger. And the sentential act depicts every man who jogs. The schematic sentential act is true or false; it is true iff it depicts. I.e., it is true iff some man jogs. We can also accept a schematic sentential act as representing things as they are.

If an indefinite phrase is used to represent an arbitrary individual, this representing act can be incorporated in a predicative act like this:

[*aM J*]
(*a* +)*M* [*x J*]

The indefinite phrase can also be used to give a special character to a predicative act:

[((*a* +) *M* +) *J*]
[*x J*]

It can be used to perform an act enabled by a predicative act:

[(*a* +)*M*: *J*]
[*x* *J*]

It can be used to enable an open predicate to be used to perform a sentential act:

[*aM* :*J*]
(*a* +) *M*

A representing act performed with a name or indefinite phrase is a *nominal* rather than a predicative act. When an indefinite phrase is used to represent, the nominal act is primarily the act performed with the noun or predicate functor. The indefinite article (quantifier) merely gives an explicit character to this act and does not make the representing indefinite. While a predicative act represents an individual or individuals as this or that, a nominal act represents an individual or individuals, but not *as* anything. When the predicate functor '*M*' is an ingredient of the predicate '[*x M*],' it is used to represent an arbitrary individual as a man. Used in the indefinite phrase '*aM*,' it is used to represent an arbitrary man. Even when a predicate functor is complex, like '(*Mx* ∋ [*x L aW*])' ("man who loves a woman"), the phrase '*a*(*Mx* ∋ [*x L aW*])' does not represent one thing as this or that. The phrase '*a*(*Mx* ∋ [*x L aW*])' represents *directly* a man who loves a woman. It represents *indirectly* a woman. It does not represent a man *as* loving a woman or a woman *as* being loved. The sentence '[*a*(*Mx* ∋ [*x L aW*]) *J*]' represents (directly) a man who loves a woman as jogging. It indirectly represents a woman.

There are difficulties in extending our treatment of the indefinite quantifier and the indefinite phrase to the universal quantifier and universally quantified phrase. Since the sentence '[*aM J*]' is used to represent an arbitrary man as a jogger, we might think that '[∀*M J*]' is used to represent every man as a jogger. In that case, the act of using '∀*M*' must represent every man. The act of using the expression must be the act of *taking* the expression (or its component functor) *for* every man. But it isn't clear that we can do this. A drawn picture can either be a picture of a specific individual (say, Napoleon) or a picture of a kind of individual, of an arbitrary individual of a kind (say, a nineteenth-century French officer). One drawing cannot be a picture of many individuals—i.e., if the drawing consists of one individual-representation. (A drawing of an individual like the common man is a drawing of a single abstract type. We invest that abstract type with features shared by many individuals.) Similarly, we cannot have one act which is an act of taking a single expression for different individuals. It would require different acts to take a single expression for different individuals. Nor are we representing a class or collection when we use a universal phrase.

When a quantified phrase like '∀*M*' (or 'every man') is used, the predicate functor must be used to represent an arbitrary man. One way to represent an act of using '[∀*M J*]' is as follows:

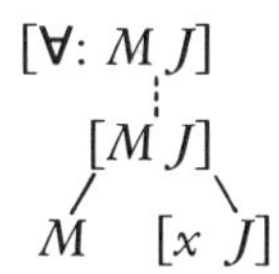

The predicate functor is used to represent an arbitrary man, the predicate to represent an arbitrary individual as jogging, both in order to represent an arbitrary man as jogging. The act of representing an arbitrary man as jogging is the output of the first stage of this universal transformation, and the input to the second stage. In the second stage, the universal quantifier is used to take the input act to be true for every man. A slightly more satisfactory representation of this transformation is the following:

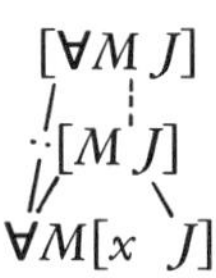

This representation reflects the fact that the quantified phrase is a syntactic unit in $\overline{\mathcal{L}}$ (and in English). The line connecting the quantified phrase to the sentence has a colon on it, indicating that the quantifier is used to perform an act enabled by the intermediate act. As an abbreviation, the line with the colon will sometimes be omitted. And when the universal transformation is part of a more comprehensive speech act structure, and I am not particularly interested it it, I will abbreviate the representation of this universal transformation even further:

$$
\begin{array}{ccc}
 & [\forall M\ J] & \\
 / & & \backslash \\
\forall M & & [x\ J]
\end{array}
$$

The unabbreviated representation of the universal transformation contains an expression, '[*M J*],' which is not an expression of $\overline{\mathcal{L}}$. This is an *intermediate quantificational expression*. It is an auxiliary expression that we shall introduce to $\overline{\mathcal{L}}$ to assist in representing speech act structure and in describing quantificational transformations. The intermediate expression is not spoken or written by language users, but this expression represents an act that language users perform. The intermediate act is a schematic act which is incomplete in a different way than a predicative act performed with an open predicate. The intermediate act contains no empty places; but English requires that a quantifier be used if there is to be a sentential act. The act of taking the intermediate act to be true for every man might better be described as the act of taking the intermediate act to be true without restriction—i.e., without any restriction as to men. Such an act of taking to be is not a representing act; it cancels the representing of the intermediate act. I will say that the output act depicts the intermediate act, if the intermediate act is true and unrestrictedly so.

The universal transformation represented above is a two-stage transformation. There is also a simpler universal transformation:

$$
\begin{array}{r}
[\forall(+\ M) :\ J] \\
\vdots\ \ \\
[x\ \ J]
\end{array}
$$

The input act represents an arbitrary individual as jogging. This act enables the output act, an act of taking the input act to be true for every man (true-for-every-man). The predicate functor is used to represent an arbitrary man; this gives a special character to the prefix act. Both transformations are exemplified in typical acts of using universal phrases. (A single act will exemplify only one transformation. Acts exemplifying either transformation are typical acts.) If the predicate functor (noun) is emphasized in using a universal phrase, then the two-stage transformation is typical. If the emphasis is on '∀' ('every') rather than the functor, then the single-stage transformation is typical. The one-stage transformation is typical of acts of using "composite" expressions like 'everything,' 'everybody,' and 'everyone.'

Universal phrases can't be used in the same ways that were previously considered for indefinite phrases. We cannot represent every man in order to represent every man as a jogger. However, indefinite phrases can be used to perform acts with the same structures as those performed with universal phrases. So we can have acts like these:

The left act involves two steps. The first represents an arbitrary man as jogging, and the second takes the first step to be true. The right act has an input which represents an arbitrary individual as jogging and is taken by the output to be true for at least one man (for an arbitrary man). Acts (1) and (2) are different from the acts of using indefinite phrases that we considered earlier:

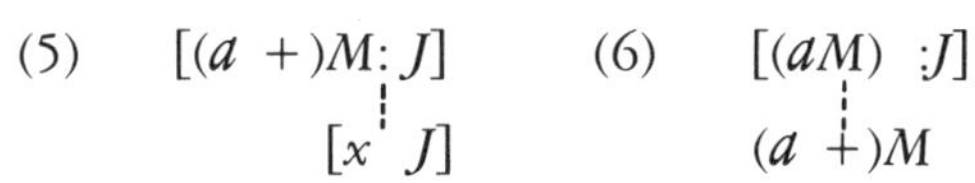

The (output) acts have different representational meanings, but the differences are not great. All of the acts represent, directly or indirectly, the same thing. There are differences between what is directly and indirectly represented and about which expressions are used to carry out the representing. In speaking, the differences between acts (1) through (6) show up in different emphases, intonations, and timings. We can also regard the different acts in terms of different situations in which they are appropriate. In acts (3) through (6), the whole indefinite phrase is used to represent an arbitrary man. We shall regard this indefinite phrase as being essentially the same as the English phrase 'some man.' In (3) through (6), the phrase 'some man' would be used with only a brief "space" between 'some' and 'man.' In (3), which is the most typical of (3) through (6), the emphasis on the indefinite phrase is about the same as the emphasis on 'jogs' (which is the "reading" for '*J*'). In (4) and (6) there is a greater emphasis on 'jogs' than on the indefinite phrase. Either (4) or (6) could occur appropriately in a situation where someone says, "Frank said that some man jokes." And Frank replies, "No. Some man jogs." The difference between (4) and (6) would concern the degree of emphasis on 'jogs,' as well as the space between 'some man' and 'jogs.' Act (6) emphasizes 'jogs' more strongly than does act (4). In (5) the indefinite phrase is emphasized more strongly than 'jogs.' Act (5) might occur when Frank says "Some man jogs," but Clare does not hear him and asks, "Who did you say jogs?" Then Frank could repeat his original sentence, emphasizing 'Some man.'

In act (2):

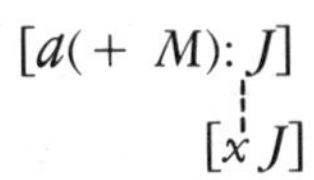

the indefinite phrase is a unit, but 'some' is emphasized more than 'man.' And the indefinite phrase is emphasized more than 'jogs.' Frank might perform act (2) in correcting the error in Delia's remark, "Frank said ten men jog." In act (1):

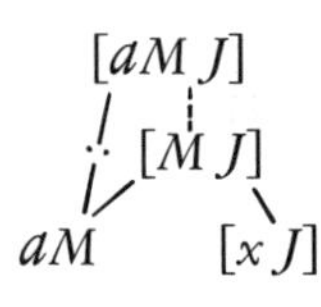

the indefinite phrase does not function as a unit. In performing act (1), there might be a slight pause between 'some' and 'man jogs.'

Acts (1) and (2) are acts of using indefinite phrases that are structurally similar to acts of using universal phrases. But the universal quantifier is a radical operator, while the indefinite quantifier is not radical. By analogy with earlier situations, there should be still more acts that can be performed with the indefinite phrase:

```
(7)    [(a + )M J]   or, preferably:    [aM J]
                                          |
           [M J]                          + [M J]
           /   \                          |/     \
          M    [x J]                    aM      [x J]
```

Here '*M*' is used to represent an arbitrary man, and '[*x J*]' is used to represent an arbitrary individual as jogging, both in order to represent an arbitrary man as jogging. The quantifier '*a*' is used to give a special character to the act of representing an arbitrary man as jogging; the special character makes explicit the schematic nature of the representing. Still another act is possible:

```
(8)    [(a(+ M) + ) J]
                  [ x J]
```

The prefix act receives a special character from (the act of using) '*M*,' and gives a special character to the act of representing an arbitrary individual as jogging. With its special character, the predicative act represents an arbitrary man as jogging. In both (1) and (7), '*M*' and '[*x J*]' are used to represent an arbitrary man as jogging. In (1), this representing act is taken to be true (for at least one man). In (7), the representing act is given a special character that makes its schematic character explicit. Acts (1) and (7) are appropriate in the same circumstances; in (1), 'some' is emphasized more than in (7). In (8), 'jogs' is emphasized at the expense of the indefinite phrase, but the difference in emphasis is less than in (2).

Chapter 12
A Semantic Account for $\overline{\mathscr{L}}$: Part 2

1. Representational Meaning

When we began considering language and linguistic acts, we noted that one sentence can have more than one speech-act syntactic structure. In natural languages, different structures are a source of ambiguity—as this is ordinarily understood. One sentence can be used to perform acts with different structures, where the acts have different inferential meanings and different truth conditions. In $\mathscr{L}$ and $\overline{\mathscr{L}}$, one sentence cannot be used to perform acts with different inferential meanings or truth conditions. But even in $\mathscr{L}$ and $\overline{\mathscr{L}}$, one sentence, when used to perform acts with different structures, will be representationally ambiguous. If we take the sentence '[*b H a*]' ("Bob hit Laura") again, we note that these acts have different representational meanings:

The left act represents Bob directly, and Laura indirectly. The right act represents Laura directly and Bob indirectly. Representational ambiguity is not ordinarily regarded as ambiguity—it is classified as a difference in emphasis, or focus, etc. The present speech act approach to language provides a unified framework for dealing with a variety of linguistic phenomena. Syntactic ambiguity is identified with different speech-act syntactic structures. So are differences in emphasis. What initially seem to be separate and unrelated phenomena are now seen to be different instances of a common phenomenon.

We originally understood different speech-act structures to be constituted by the different orders in which transformations are carried out, and the different items that get transformed. The left act above first combines '[*x H y*]' and '*a*' by the individual transformation; "next" it combines '*b*' and '[*x H a*].' The right act combines '*b*' with '[*x H y*]' to start; then it combines '[*b H y*]' with '*a*.' In these cases, we have two applications of the individual transformation, but the transformations "work" on different inputs. The sentence '[*b H aG*]' ("Bob hit a girl") can be used to perform acts where the individual transformation precedes and comes after the indefinite transformation. However, not all differences in speech act structures amount to differences in transformational order or transformational inputs. For we have seen that a single transformation can be associated with different speech act structures.

The simple sentence '[*b J*]' ("Bob jogs") is obtained from '*b*' and '[*x J*]' by the individual transformation. But this sentence can be used to perform acts having the following structures:

```
(1) [b J]              (2) [(b +) J]
    /   \
   b   [x J]                 [x J]

(3) [b: J]             (4) [b :J]
       ¦                    ¦
     [x J]                  b
```

Originally it seemed that each transformation was associated with a particular structure, so that a description of the transformation was simply an abstract description of a speech act structure. But the description of a transformation in terms of inputs and outputs is neutral with respect to the three fundamental structural relations. The inputs may be component acts whose purpose defines the output act. The inputs might enable the output, or one input might serve to give a special character to the other. This neutrality allows the same transformation to be realized by different structures. The description of a transformation is a more abstract description of a speech act structure than it first seemed.

We have seen that the fundamental structural relations are hierarchically arranged. The "highest" relation is that between component acts and the complex which they constitute, and which is defined by their purpose. In second place is the relation between an act which gives a special character to a second act and that second act. The lowest relation in the hierarchy is the relation between an enabling and an enabled act. The relations constitute a hierarchy in this respect: If a transformation can be realized by acts which exemplify a higher relation, then it can also be realized by acts exemplifying lower relations. But some transformations can only be realized by acts exemplifying lower relations. An absolute adjective like 'round' can be used in acts exemplifying all three structural relations:

```
     round barn           (round +) barn        round:  barn
       /     \                                            :
  round       barn                   barn               barn
```

But 'former' can only be used this way:

```
former:  barn
           :
         barn
```

Although a single transformation might be realized by acts which exemplify different structural relations, one or more structures will be typical for that transformation. The typical structures exemplify the highest possible structural relation. The typical act of using 'round barn' is:

```
     round barn
       /     \
  round       barn
```

The only act possible for 'former barn' is its typical act.

The typical act of using '[*b J*]' has this structure:

```
(1)  [b J]
      /  \
     b   [x J]
```

The other structures are departures from the typical structure; each gets its "point" from its contrast with the typical structure. In speaking, the different structures show up as differences in emphasis, intonation, and timing. In act (1), the typical act, the emphasis on '*b*' ('Bob') and '*J*' ('jogs') is about the same. There is neither a rising nor a falling intonation, and there is no hesitation between the two words. Act (1) is appropriate in many settings. Act (2):

[(*b* +) *J*]

[*x J*]

is appropriate when we are more concerned with the jogging than with the jogger. If Sara says something about Bob, but Neil doesn't hear her, he might say "Bob did what?" Sara's reply could appropriately exemplify the structure shown in (2). In this reply, '*J*' ('jogs') is emphasized with respect to '*b*' ('Bob'). Act (4):

[*b* :*J*]

b

also emphasizes the jogging rather than the jogger. It is appropriate in the same circumstances where (2) is appropriate. In (4), the '*J*' is emphasized more strongly than it is in (2). There would be more hesitation between the two words. In (3):

[*b*: *J*]

[*x J*]

Bob rather than jogging is the focus of attention. If Sara said that Bob jogs, but Neil couldn't make out the "Bob," he might ask her "*Who* jogs?" Sara's answer could appropriately exemplify (3).

Each transformation is associated with a typical structure or structures. An understanding of the different structural relations and their hierarchical organization enables us to understand (predict) the nontypical structures associated with a transformation, once we know the typical structures. In discussing the effect of various transformations on representational meaning, I will consider only the effect on typically structured acts. (Each different structure gives a different representational meaning.) We should note at this point that the concepts we have been using to discuss, describe, and think about representational meaning are inadequate. We have so far employed a distinction between direct and indirect representing that is legitimate, but not sufficient to adequately characterize representational meaning. For example, in both (2) and (4) above, Bob is represented as jogging, and Bob is represented indirectly. But the two acts don't have exactly the same representational meaning. I will not try to provide one here, but what is needed is a new conceptual framework for thinking and talking about representational meaning. We must either adapt old words or introduce new ones, and use them to signal the important features of representational meaning. We must clarify the relations between these important features, and between the features and the purposes that speakers try to achieve by talking. A thorough semantic account of any language will require this new framework.

Just to get some idea how complicated such an account must be, let us consider the different structures that are possible for an act of using '[*b H a*].' These acts have typical structures:

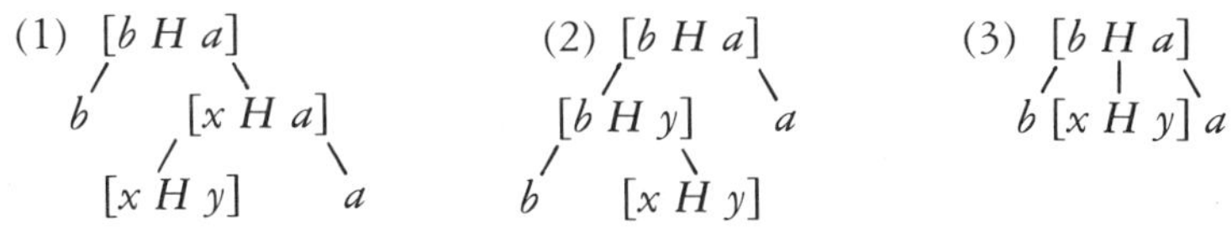

These acts have nontypical structures:

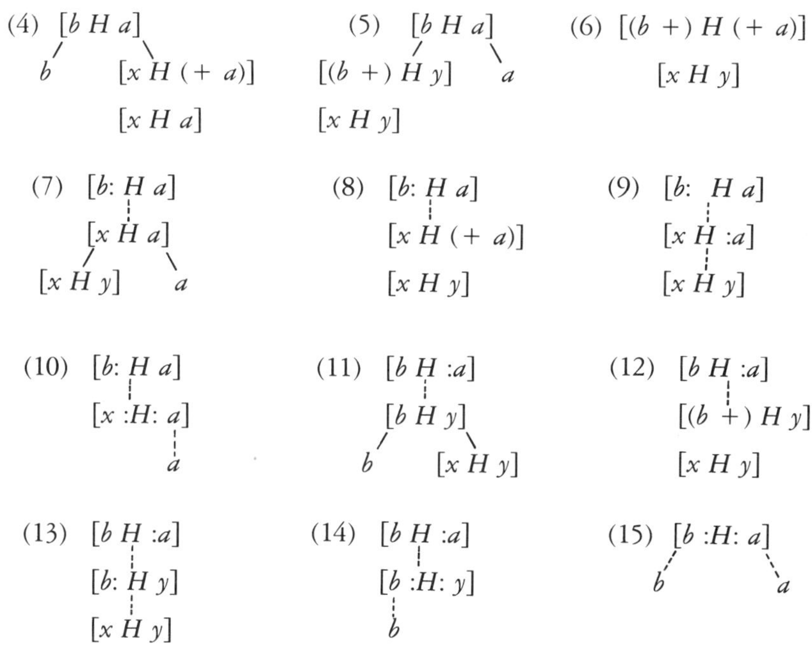

2. The Return of the Quantifiers

There are two typical acts of using a universal quantifier. They are illustrated below for the sentence '[∀*M J*].'

One act involves two steps, or stages. The other involves only one. When a sentence is used rather than an open predicate, both acts will be acts of taking another act to be of a certain kind. To accommodate the two uses of the universal quantifier, two universal transformations will be provided: ($\forall_1$) and ($\forall_2$). (From now on transformations will be labeled with symbols rather than numerals.) The transformation ($\forall_2$) is a two-step transformation. Each of these two transformations has three forms, to accommodate prefixed and infixed quantified phrases.

($\forall_1$) Let A be a predicate containing free occurrences of the distinct individual variables $\alpha_1, \ldots, \alpha_n$ and no others; this is their canonical order. Let ϕ be a one-place predicate functor which contains no free variables in common with A. And let $\beta_1, \ldots, \beta_m$ be the distinct individual variables, in canonical order, occurring free in ϕ.

(a) Then $\forall\phi\alpha_i\, A$ ($= A'$) is obtained from ϕ, A by the *first universal transformation*. The displayed occurrence of α_i and the free occurrences of α_i in A are bound occurrences in A'; they are bound by the initial occurrence of '$\forall$.' The displayed occurrence of α_i is the *operative* occurrence of α_i in the occurrence of $\forall\phi\alpha_i$ in A'.

(b) If the first free occurrence of α_i in A is within the scope of no operators in A, there is no β_j ($1 \leqslant j \leqslant m$) such that the first free occurrence of α_i in A is within the (plain) scope of an expression binding occurrences of β_j, and there is no overlined variable $\overline{\gamma}$ in A which could be bound by an antecedent in ϕ if $a\phi\alpha_i$ replaced the first free occurrence of α_i in A, then A' is obtained from ϕ, A by replacing the first free occurrence of α_i by $\forall\phi\alpha_i$. A' is obtained by the *first universal transformation*. The displayed occurrence of α_i in $\forall\phi\alpha_i$ is the operative occurrence of α_i in the occurrence of $\forall\phi\alpha_i$.

(c) If there is only one free occurrence of α_i in A, this is within the scope of no operator in A, there is no β_j ($1 \leqslant j \leqslant m$) such that the free occurrence of α_i in A is within the (plain) scope of an expression binding occurrences of β_j, and there is no overlined variable $\overline{\gamma}$ in A which could be bound by an antecedent in ϕ if $a\phi$ replaced the free occurrence of α_i in A, then A' is obtained from ϕ, A by replacing the free occurrence of α_i by $\forall\phi$. A' is obtained by the *first universal transformation.*

In (b) and (c), the universal phrase cannot be inserted if ϕ contains an expression such that $a\phi\alpha_i$ or $a\phi$ could bind occurrences of an overlined variable $\overline{\gamma}$ should the indefinite phrase be inserted. The first universal transformation inserts $\forall\phi\alpha_i$ or $\forall\phi$, not $a\phi\alpha_i$ or $a\phi$. But '$\forall$' is a radical operator, and this might prevent expressions in ϕ from binding occurrences of a variable $\overline{\gamma}$ in A. In the two-step universal transformation, occurrences of an expression in ϕ *can* bind overlined variables outside of ϕ. Since the output expression of the first universal transformation could also be obtained by the second universal transformation, we must prevent the first universal transformation taking

$$[a_x\ B\ y,\ \overline{x}]$$

to

$$[a_x\ B\ \forall(Dy \ni [b_x\ A\ y]),\ \overline{x}].$$

In the lower expression, the overlined '$\overline{x}$' would be bound by 'b,' even though this '$\overline{x}$' is bound by 'a' in the upper predicate.

If A' is a sentence, then it does not represent. This sentence depicts the predicate A if every individual labeled by ϕ is labeled by A. If $(m + n) > 0$, then A' represents $m + n$ arbitrary individuals $x_1, \ldots, x_{m+n}$ as such that every individual which has ϕ's relation to $x_1, \ldots, x_m$ has A's relation to $x_{m+1}, \ldots, x_{m+n}$. These individuals are represented directly; no individuals are represented indirectly. If $(m + n) > 0$, then A' depicts $(m + n - 1)$-tuples $< d_1, \ldots, d_{m+n-1} >$ such that $A[\alpha_1, \ldots, \alpha_{i-1}, \alpha_{i+1}, \ldots, \alpha_n; d_{m+1}, \ldots, d_{m+n-1}]$ labels every individual labeled by $\phi[\beta_1, \ldots, \beta_m; d_1, \ldots, d_m]$. The positions in these $(m + n - 1)$-tuples answer to the obvious occurrences of free variables in A'.

For the set-theoretic account of depicting, let ϕ be suited to depict r-tuples and let A be suited to depict s-tuples. The jth position in these s-tuples answers to the free occurrences of α_i in A.

($\forall_1$a) A' is $\forall\phi\alpha_i\ A$. Suppose A' is a sentence. Then $f^+(A') = \{A\}$ iff $f^+(\phi) \neq \emptyset$ and for every d_1 such that $< d_1, \ldots, d_r > \in f^+(\phi)$ for some $d_2, \ldots, d_r$, there are $e_1, \ldots, e_{s-1}$ such that $< e_1, \ldots, e_{j-1}, d_1, \ldots, e_{s-1} > \in f^+(A)$. Otherwise, $f^+(A') = \emptyset$. If A' is not a sentence, then $f^+(A') = V' = \{< d_1, \ldots, d_{m+n-1} > \mid f^+(A'[\beta_1, \ldots, \beta_m, \alpha_1, \ldots, \alpha_{i-1}, \alpha_{i+1}, \ldots, \alpha_n; d_1, \ldots, d_{m+n-1}]) = \{A[\alpha_1, \ldots, \alpha_{i-1}, \alpha_{i+1}, \ldots, \alpha_n; d_{m+1}, \ldots, d_{m+n-1}]\}\}$.

($\forall_1$b, c) A' is obtained by replacing the first (or only) free occurrence of α_i in A by $\forall\phi\alpha_i$ or $\forall\phi$. If A' is a sentence, then $f^+(A') = \{A\}$ iff $f^+(\phi) \neq \emptyset$ and for every d_1 such that $< d_1, \ldots, d_r > \in f^+(\phi)$ for some $d_2, \ldots, d_r$, there are $e_1, \ldots, e_{s-1}$ such that $< e_1, \ldots, e_{j-1}, d_1, \ldots, e_{s-1} > \in f^+(A)$. Otherwise, $f^+(A') = \emptyset$. If A' is not a sentence, then $f^+(A') = V' = \{< d_1, \ldots, d_{m+n-1} > \mid f^+(A'[\alpha_1, \ldots, \alpha_{i-1}, \beta_1, \ldots, \beta_m, \alpha_{i+1}, \ldots, \alpha_n; d_1, \ldots, d_{m+n-1}]) = \{A[\alpha_1, \ldots, \alpha_{i-1}, \alpha_{i+1}, \ldots, \alpha_n; d_1, \ldots, d_{i-1}, d_{i+m-1}, \ldots, d_{n+m-1}]\}\}$.

The second universal transformation is a two-step transformation. Other quantifiers also have two-step transformations. For many of the quantifiers, the first step of the two-step transformation is the same, so the first step will be given only once.

(Quant) Let A be a predicate containing free occurrences of the distinct individual variables $\alpha_1, \ldots, \alpha_n$ and no others; this is their canonical order. Let ϕ be a one-place predicate functor which contains no free variables in common with A. And let $\beta_1, \ldots, \beta_m$ be the distinct individual variables, in canonical order, occurring free in ϕ.

(a) Then $\phi\alpha_i A$ ($= A'$) is an *intermediate quantificational expression*. A' is obtained from ϕ, A as the *first step* of a *quantifier* transformation. The displayed occurrence of α_i and the free occurrences of α_i in A are bound occurrences in A'; they are bound by the displayed occurrence of α_i. The displayed occurrence is the *operative* occurrence of α_i in the occurrence of the indexed functor $\phi\alpha_i$.

(b) If the first free occurrence of α_i is within the scope of no operators in A, there is no β_j ($1 \leq j \leq m$) such that the first free occurrence of α_i in A is within the (plain) scope of an expression binding occurrences of β_j, and there is no overlined variable $\overline{\gamma}$ in A which could be bound by an antecedent in ϕ if $\phi\alpha_i$ replaced the first free occurrence of α_i in A, then A' is obtained from ϕ, A by replacing the first free occurrence of α_i by $\phi\alpha_i$. A' is an *intermediate quantificational expression*. A' is obtained as the *first step* of a *quantifier* transformation. The displayed occurrence of α_i in $\phi\alpha_i$ and the free occurrences of α_i in A other than the first are bound by the occurrence of α_i in $\phi\alpha_i$. The occurrence of α_i in $\phi\alpha_i$ is the *operative* occurrence of α_i in the occurrence of the indexed functor.

(c) If there is only one free occurrence of α_i in A, this is within the scope of no operator in A, there is no β_j ($1 \leq j \leq m$) such that the free occurrence of α_i in A is within the (plain) scope of an expression binding occurrences of β_j, and there is no overlined variable $\overline{\gamma}$ in A which could be bound by an antecedent in ϕ if ϕ replaced the free occurrence of α_i in A, then A' is obtained from ϕ, A by replacing the free occurrence of α_i by ϕ. A' is an *intermediate quantificational expression*. A' is obtained as the *first step* of a *quantifier* transformation.

For the first stage of the quantifier transformations, it is not convenient to give a uniform statement of the effect of this (half-)transformation on representing. I will indicate which individuals are represented, but not what they are represented as. I could say they are represented as satisfying a certain predicate; this is not enlightening in particular cases. The following intermediate expression:

$$[M\ J]$$

represents an arbitrary man as jogging. If '$[x\ K\ y]$' means x *knows* y, then

$$[(Mx \ni [x\ K\ b])\ J]$$

represents an arbitrary man who knows Bob as jogging. But

$$[(Mx \ni [x\ K\ y])\ J]$$

represents an arbitrary man who knows an arbitrary individual y, and the arbitrary individual y, as such that the man who knows y jogs. It sounds more natural to say that this intermediate quantificational expression represents an arbitrary man who knows an arbitrary individual as jogging. But that locution fails to list separately each individual that is represented directly.

(a) A' ($= \phi\alpha_i\ A$) directly represents (in this order) an arbitrary individual satisfying ϕ, arbitrary individuals $\beta_1, \ldots, \beta_m$, and arbitrary individuals $\alpha_1, \ldots, \alpha_{i-1}, \alpha_{i+1}, \ldots, \alpha_n$. A' indirectly represents all the individuals directly or indirectly represented by A or ϕ, other than the arbitrary individuals represented by A or ϕ.

(b, c) A' directly represents arbitrary individuals $\alpha_1, \ldots, \alpha_{i-1}$, an arbitrary individual satisfying ϕ, arbitrary individuals $\beta_1, \ldots, \beta_m$, and arbitrary individuals $\alpha_{i+1}, \ldots, \alpha_n$. A' indirectly represents all the individuals directly or indirectly represented by A or ϕ, other than the arbitrary individuals represented by A or ϕ.

Suppose A is suited to depict p-tuples, and ϕ is suited to depict q-tuples. Let the uth position in the p-tuples answer to the free occurrences of α_i in A.

(a) Then A' ($= \phi\alpha_i\ A$) depicts $(q + p - 1)$-tuples $< d_1, \ldots, d_q, e_1, \ldots, e_{p-1} >$ such that ϕ depicts $< d_1, \ldots, d_q >$ and A depicts $< e_1, \ldots, e_{u-1}, d_1, \ldots, e_{p-1} >$. The first position in these $(q + p - 1)$-tuples answers to the occurrence of ϕ introduced by this (half-)transformation.

(b, c) Then A' depicts $(q + p - 1)$-tuples $< e_1, \ldots, e_{u-1}, d_1, \ldots, d_q, e_u, \ldots, e_{p-1} >$ such that ϕ depicts $< d_1, \ldots, d_q >$ and A depicts $< e_1, \ldots, e_{u-1}, d_1, \ldots, e_{p-1} >$. The uth position in these $(q + p - 1)$-tuples answers to the occurrence of ϕ introduced by this (half-)transformation.

The set-theoretic statement of truth conditions (of depicting) is just like the preceding. Let $f(\phi) = W$ and $f(A) = V$.

(a) Then $f(A') = V' = \{< d_1, \ldots, d_q, e_1, \ldots, e_{p-1} > \mid < d_1, \ldots, d_q > \in W$ and $< e_1, \ldots, e_{u-1}, d_1, \ldots, e_{p-1} > \in V\}$.

(b, c) Then $f(A') = V' = \{< e_1, \ldots, e_{u-1}, d_1, \ldots, d_q, e_u, \ldots, e_{p-1} > \mid < d_1, \ldots, d_q > \in W$ and $< e_1, \ldots, e_{u-1}, d_1, \ldots, e_{p-1} > \in V\}$.

Like the intermediate expression of the conditional transformation, the intermediate expression of the quantifier transformations is able to serve as input to pronomial transformations. This explains how we can translate a sentence like:

> Every man who knows a ballerina admires her.

For the pronomial transformation takes effect before the universal quantifier does. We use our translation to perform an act like this:

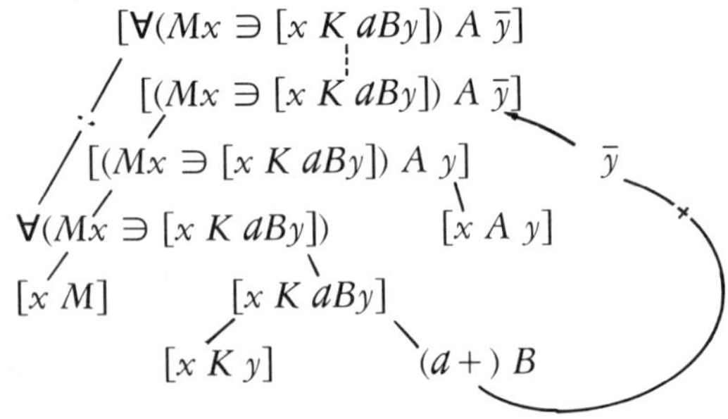

We will now complete the second universal transformation.

($\forall_2$a) Let $\phi\alpha_i A$ ($= A'$) be an intermediate quantificational expression. Then $\forall\phi\alpha_i A$ ($= A''$) is obtained from A' by the *second universal transformation* (as the *last step* of the second universal transformation). The occurrences of α_i that were bound by the occurrence of α_i (in $\phi\alpha_i$) in A' are bound in A'' by the occurrence of '$\forall$' introduced by A''. The occurrence of α_i in $\forall\phi\alpha_i$ is the *operative* occurrence of α_i in the occurrence of $\forall\phi\alpha_i$.

($\forall_2$b, c) Let A' be an intermediate quantificational expression which contains an occurrence of $\phi\alpha_i$ or ϕ in an argument position. Then A'' is obtained from A' by introducing a '$\forall$' immediately to the left of the occurrence of ϕ. A'' is obtained as the *last step* of the *second universal transformation*. If A'' is obtained by introducing '$\forall$' to the left of $\phi\alpha_i$, then the occurrences of α_i that were bound by the occurrence of α_i (in $\phi\alpha_i$) in A' are bound in A'' by the occurrence of '$\forall$' introduced in A''. The occurrence of α_i in $\forall\phi\alpha_i$ is the *operative* occurrence of α_i in the occurrence of $\forall\phi\alpha_i$.

In case A'' is a sentence, the universal quantifier is used to take the intermediate quantificational expression (the intermediate act) to be unrestrictedly true—with respect to the ϕ's. So, for example, in this act:

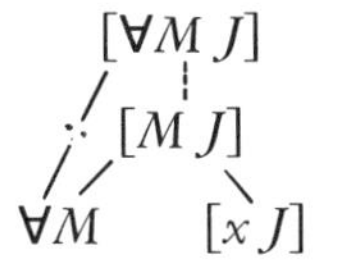

the expression '[*M J*] is taken to be true without restriction—i.e., to be true for every man. The universal quantifier is a radical operator. It cancels the representing of the intermediate expression; the sentence A'' does not represent. We will stipulate that A'' depicts A' iff A' is true for every individual labeled by ϕ.

In case A'' contains free occurrences of distinct individual variables $\gamma_1, \ldots, \gamma_r$ and no others, and this is their canonical order, A'' represents arbitrary individuals $\gamma_1, \ldots, \gamma_r$ as such that the intermediate quantificational expression A' is true for these individuals, for every individual labeled by ϕ. A'' depicts r-tuples $< d_1, \ldots, d_r>$ such that $A'[\gamma_1, \ldots, \gamma_r; d_1, \ldots, d_r]$ is true for every individual labeled by $\phi[\gamma_1, \ldots, \gamma_r; d_1, \ldots, d_r]$. ($A''$ depicts and labels the same r-tuples, if it labels any.)

The set-theoretic account of depicting is as follows.

($\forall$a) A'' is $\forall\phi\alpha_i A$. Suppose A'' is a sentence. Then $f^+(A'') = \{A'\}$ iff $f^+(\phi) \neq \emptyset$ and $f^+(\phi) \subseteq \{< d_1, \ldots, d_q> \mid < d_1, \ldots, d_q, e_1, \ldots, e_{p-1}> \in f^+(A')$ for some $e_1, \ldots, e_{p-1}\}$. Otherwise, $f^+(A'') = \emptyset$. If A'' is not a sentence, and contains free occurrences of distinct individual variables $\gamma_1, \ldots, \gamma_r$ and no others (this is their canonical order), then $f^+(A'') = V'' = \{< d_1, \ldots, d_r> \mid f^+(A''[\gamma_1, \ldots, \gamma_r; d_1, \ldots, d_r]) = \{A'[\gamma_1, \ldots, \gamma_r; d_1, \ldots, d_r]\}\}$.

($\forall$b, c) A' has an occurrence of $\phi\alpha_i$ or ϕ in an argument position, and A'' is obtained by inserting '$\forall$' to the left of ϕ. If A'' is a sentence, then $f^+(A'') = V'' = \{A'\}$ iff $f^+(\phi) \neq \emptyset$ and $f^+(\phi) \subseteq \{< d_1, \ldots, d_q> \mid < e_1, \ldots, e_{u-1}, d_1, \ldots, d_q, e_u, \ldots, e_{p-1}> \in f^+(A')$ for some $e_1, \ldots, e_{p-1}\}$. Otherwise (still in case A'' is a sentence), $f^+(A'') = \emptyset$. If A'' is not a sentence, $f^+(A'')$ is the same as in case ($\forall$a).

The indefinite quantifier can be used to perform acts having the same structures as acts performed with the universal quantifier:

(1) 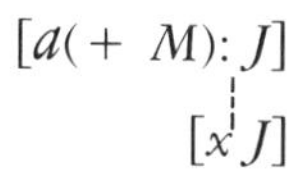

(2) 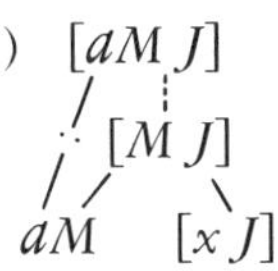

These structures are characteristic of (typical of) radical transformations. The corresponding structures that are typical for the nonradical indefinite transformations are:

(3) $[(a(+\ M)\ +)\ J]$

$[x\ J]$

(4) $[aM\ J]$

$[M\ J]$

aM $[x\ J]$

When the indefinite phrase is used to constitute a sentence, and the acts are as in (1) through (4), then the indefinite quantifier "concerns" a nonsentential schematic act. This is either a predicative act, as in (1) and (3). Or an act in which a predicate functor (noun) is used to fill the argument place of a predicate—an intermediate quantificational act. Unlike the universal phrase, the indefinite phrase can also be used like a name:

$[a\mathrm{M}\ \mathrm{J}]$

$(a\ +)M$ $[x\ J]$

In its name-like use, the indefinite quantifier concerns the predicate functor (noun) rather than a schematic act. The first uses of the indefinite quantifier (and the indefinite phrase) are *typically quantificational uses*. The only uses of the universal quantifier (and universal phrase) are typically quantificational. When the quantifiers are used with open predicates, but the acts have the structures of typically quantificational sentential acts, then the quantifiers are also used in a typically quantificational fashion.

I will begin by describing two indefinite transformations that are exactly parallel to the two universal transformations. These transformations "cover" acts in which the indefinite quantifier is used quantificationally.

(a_1) Let A be a predicate containing free occurrences of the distinct individual variables $\alpha_1, \ldots, \alpha_n$ and no others; this is their canonical order. Let ϕ be a one-place predicate functor which contains no free variables in common with A. And let $\beta_1, \ldots, \beta_m$ be the distinct individual variables, in canonical order, occurring free in ϕ.

(a) Then $a\phi\alpha_i\ A$ ($= A'$) is obtained from ϕ, A by the *first indefinite transformation*. The displayed occurrence of α_i and the free occurrences of α_i in A are bound occurrences in A'; they are bound by the initial occurrence of 'a.' The displayed occurrence of α_i is the *operative* occurrence of α_i in the occurrence of $a\phi\alpha_i$.

(b) If the first free occurrence of α_i in A is within the scope of no operators in A, there is no β_j ($1 \leq j \leq m$) such that the first free occurrence of α_i in A is within the (plain) scope of an expression binding occurrences of β_j, and there is no overlined variable $\overline{\gamma}$ in A which could be bound by an antecedent in ϕ if $a\phi\alpha_i$ replaced the first free occurrence of α_i in A, then A' is obtained from ϕ, A by replacing the first free occurrence of α_i by $a\phi\alpha_i$. A' is obtained by the *first indefinite transformation*. The displayed occurrence of α_i in $a\phi\alpha_i$ and the free occurrences of α_i in A other than the first are bound by the initial occurrence of 'a' in the occurrence of $a\phi\alpha_i$. The displayed occurrence of α_i in $a\phi\alpha_i$ is the *operative* occurrence of α_i in the occurrence of $a\phi\alpha_i$.

(c) If there is only one free occurrence of α_i in A, this is within the scope of no operator in A, there is no β_j ($1 \leq j \leq m$) such that the free occurrence of α_i in A is within the (plain) scope of an expression binding occurrences of β_j, and there is no overlined variable $\overline{\gamma}$ in A which could be bound by an antecedent in ϕ if $a\phi$ replaced the free occurrence of α_i in A, then A' is obtained from ϕ, A by replacing the free occurrence of α_i by $a\phi$. A' is obtained by the *first indefinite transformation*.

If A is a sentence, then the input to this transformation represents an arbitrary individual as satisfying A. In the output, the input's representing is "cut down"; the output act represents an arbitrary ϕ as satisfying A. The prefix act is itself complex. The predicate functor is used to (directly) represent an arbitrary ϕ; this gives a special character to the act of using the indefinite quantifier. The prefix act, in turn, gives a special character to the predicative act. The quantifier makes explicit that at least one ϕ satisfies A. The point of making this explicit may be to contrast at least one ϕ with more than one. It may be to contrast at least one ϕ with no ϕ's. ("Some guest said 'Thank you.'" (at any rate)). A' directly represents an arbitrary ϕ as satisfying A. It indirectly represents the other individuals represented by ϕ, A. If $(m + n) > 1$, then for (a_1a), A' directly represents an arbitrary ϕ, and arbitrary individuals $\beta_1, \ldots, \beta_m, \alpha_1, \ldots, \alpha_{i-1}, \alpha_{i+1}, \ldots, \alpha_n$ as such that the arbitrary ϕ satisfies A. A' indirectly represents the other individuals represented by ϕ, A. For (a_1b, c), A' directly represents arbitrary individuals $\alpha_1, \ldots, \alpha_{i-1}$, an arbitrary ϕ, and arbitrary individuals $\beta_1, \ldots, \beta_m, \alpha_{i+1}, \ldots, \alpha_n$ as such that the arbitrary ϕ satisfies A. A' indirectly represents the other individuals represented by ϕ, A.

Suppose A is suited to depict p-tuples and ϕ to depict q-tuples. Let the uth position in the p-tuples answer to the free occurrences of α_i in A. Then, (a_1a) A' ($= a\phi\alpha_i A$) depicts $(q + p - 1)$-tuples $< d_1, \ldots, d_q, e_1, \ldots, e_{p-1}>$ such that ϕ depicts $< d_1, \ldots, d_q>$ and A depicts $< e_1, \ldots, e_{u-1}, d_1, \ldots, e_{p-1}>$. The first position in these $(q + p - 1)$-tuples answers to the occurrence of $a\phi\alpha_i$ introduced by this transformation. (a_1b, c) Then A' depicts $(q + p - 1)$-tuples $< e_1, \ldots, e_{u-1}, d_1, \ldots, d_q, e_u, \ldots, e_{p-1}>$ such that ϕ depicts $< d_1, \ldots, d_q>$ and A depicts $< e_1, \ldots, e_{u-1},$

$d_1, e_u, \ldots, e_{p-1}>$. The uth position in these $(q + p - 1)$-tuples answers to the occurrence of $a\phi\alpha_i$ or $a\phi$ introduced by this transformation.

The set-theoretic statement for the first indefinite transformation is as follows.

Let $f(\phi) = W$ and $f(A) = V$. (a_1a) Then $f(A') = V' = \{< d_1, \ldots, d_q, e_1, \ldots, e_{p-1}> \mid < d_1, \ldots, d_q> \in W$ and $< e_1, \ldots, e_{u-1}, d_1, \ldots, e_{p-1}> \in V\}$. ($a_1$b, c) Then $f(A') = V' = \{< e_1, \ldots, e_{u-1}, d_1, \ldots, d_q, \ldots, e_{p-1}> \mid < d_1, \ldots, d_q> \in W$ and $< e_1, \ldots, e_{u-1}, d_1, \ldots, e_{p-1}> \in V\}$.

The second indefinite transformation has two steps. The first step is the transformation (Quant) given above. The second is as follows.

(a_2a) Let $\phi\alpha_i A$ ($= A'$) be an intermediate quantificational expression. Then $a\phi\alpha_i A$ ($= A''$) is obtained from A' by the *second indefinite transformation* (as the *last step* of the second indefinite transformation). The occurrences of α_i that were bound by the occurrence of α_i (in $\phi\alpha_i$) in A' are bound in A'' by the occurrence of 'a' introduced in A''. The occurrence of α_i in $a\phi\alpha_i$ is the *operative* occurrence of α_i in the occurrence of $a\phi\alpha_i$.

(a_2b, c) Let A' be an intermediate quantificational expression which contains an occurrence of $\phi\alpha_i$ or ϕ in an argument position. Then A'' is obtained from A' by introducing 'a' immediately to the left of ϕ. A' is obtained as the *last step* of the *second indefinite transformation*. If A'' is obtained by introducing 'a' to the left of $\phi\alpha_i$, then the occurrences of α_i that were bound by the occurrence of α_i (in $\phi\alpha_i$) in A' are bound in A'' by the occurrence of 'a' introduced in A''. The occurrence of α_i in $a\phi\alpha_i$ is the *operative* occurrence of α_i in the occurrence of $a\phi\alpha_i$.

When A'' is a sentence, and the indefinite quantifier is used to perform a typical act associated with the a_2 transformation, then the intermediate quantificational expression (act) represents an arbitrary ϕ as satisfying A. The indefinite quantifier serves to make explicit the schematic character of this act. When the quantifier is used to take the intermediate expression to be true (for at least one ϕ), then the output is not a representing act. But the representing of the intermediate act is left in place—in this case, all representing is indirect. If A'' contains free variables, and the act is typical, the representing of the intermediate and final expression is still the same. If A'' is used like this:

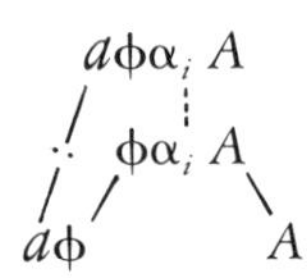

then the output directly represents arbitrary individuals $\beta_1, \ldots, \beta_m$, $\alpha_1, \ldots, \alpha_{i-1}, \alpha_{i+1}, \ldots, \alpha_n$ and indirectly represents the other individuals represented by ϕ and A. Regardless of whether or not A'' is a sentence, or is used typically, the depicting of A' and A'' are the same.

If $f(A') = V'$, then $f(A'') = V'$.

There are some transformations for which multiple applications can be performed simultaneously. As explained originally, the reflexive transformation allows free occurrences of a variable β in a predicate A to be replaced by α, which is another variable occurring free in A. But we allow the transformation to be used to simultaneously replace free occurrences of β, γ by α. Individual transformations can be combined, so that free occurrences of different variables can be simultaneously replaced by constants. We will also allow a two-step quantifier transformation to be performed simultaneously with an individual transformation. So we can have an act:

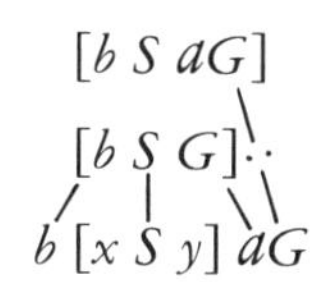

The individual-representing act serves as input into the first stage of the quantifier transformation. The one-step transformations cannot be performed simultaneously with the individual transformation. Neither can different applications of quantifier transformations, whether one-step or two-step, be performed simultaneously in $\overline{\mathcal{L}}$. On some occasions English speakers do seem to combine quantificational acts in this way, but I have seen no examples which convince me that this is an important feature of English, or that simultaneous quantifier transformations are used to say what can be said in no other way. I am ignoring simultaneous quantifier transformations because they would introduce many complications into $\overline{\mathcal{L}}$. Simultaneous transformations give rise to branching quantifiers, a subject of considerable complexity.

3. The Name-Like Use of the Indefinite Phrase

So far, we have considered name-like uses of the indefinite phrase as acts in which the whole phrase is used to represent an arbitrary individual of a kind. Such an act can be incorporated in subsequent acts in the same ways that a name can. Unlike a name, an indefinite phrase can represent more than one individual, either directly or indirectly. Consider the functor '$(Mx \ni [x\ K\ b])$' ("man who knows Bob") and the phrase '$a(Mx \ni [x\ K\ b])$.' If the functor is obtained like this:

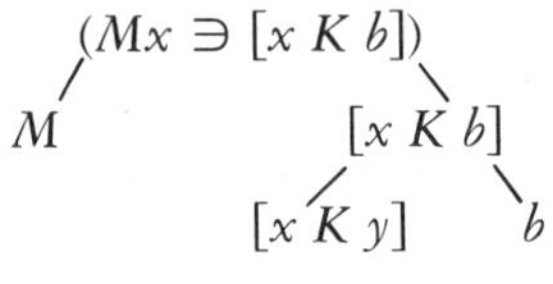

and the indefinite phrase is used in a name-like way, then the phrase directly represents an arbitrary man who knows Bob. It indirectly represents Bob. But when the phrase '$a(Mx \ni [x\ K\ y])$' is used in a name-like way, it will directly represent both an arbitrary man who knows an arbitrary individual *and* the arbitrary individual. The predicative act:

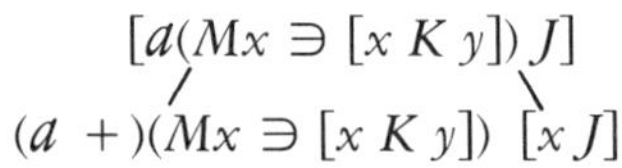

directly represents an arbitrary man who knows an arbitrary individual and the arbitrary individual as such that the arbitrary man jogs.

It is also possible to use an indefinite phrase in a name-like way to represent a specific individual. If I tell my daughter, "Some boy called you while you were out," I do not mean that at least one boy called. I may not know the boy's name, or be able to provide further identification, but I am using the indefinite phrase (the 'some'-phrase) to represent a specific individual: the boy who called at such and such a time. I am using the indefinite phrase to represent that boy indefinitely. (I don't just do this, in English, with 'some.' I could perform the same kind of act with 'A boy called you while you were out.') The name-like use of an indefinite phrase to represent a specific individual is a typical use of the indefinite phrase.

That a speaker can use an indefinite phrase to represent a specific individual when he doesn't have useful identifying information is illustrated by the sentence 'Some boy called you while you were out'; another example could be provided by Michelle's remark, "Some man rowed across the Atlantic Ocean." Michelle uses 'Some man' to represent the man she vaguely remembers reading about in a newspaper or magazine. Someone who gets his information from Michelle could use in the same sentence the indefinite phrase to represent the man Michelle told him about. A speaker can also use an indefinite phrase to represent a specific individual when he does have useful identifying information. I might tell my wife, "A girl in my class told me that I have sexy eyes." I (of course) know that girl's name, but don't use the name when my audience doesn't know the girl in question.

When someone uses an indefinite phrase to represent a specific individual, she can be mistaken in various ways. If Kathy says, "Some vampire lived in a castle in Transylvania," she may be recalling a story she read or a movie she saw. But if she is not intending to deal with fictional contexts, Kathy is mistaken. There is no vampire which Kathy's phrase depicts. It may also be the case that 'some ϕ' is used to represent a specific individual that doesn't have the property predicated of it. If Michelle says, "Some boy will call me tonight," she may be representing a particular boy who isn't going to call. It is also possible that a speaker uses 'some ϕ' to represent a particular individual, but the speaker is confusing different individuals, so that no individual answers to her use of the indefinite phrase.

It is important to distinguish the use of an indefinite phrase to represent a specific individual from the other uses of an indefinite phrase. The different uses can affect all three meanings of a sentence. In this sentence:

(1) If Michelle doesn't get a call tonight from a boy, she will be angry at him.

the way the indefinite phrase 'a boy' is used will affect the number of boys who are targets of Michelle's anger. If the 'a' in 'a boy' is used quantificationally, sentence (1) has Michelle being angry at every boy who does not call. If the indefinite phrase is used in a name-like way to represent an arbitrary boy, sentence (1) still has Michelle being angry at lots of boys. But if 'a boy' is used to represent a specific individual, then Michelle only needs to be angry at one boy—if he fails to call.

When an indefinite phrase is used in a name-like way, it may contain free variables (empty argument places). But when it is used to represent a specific individual, it cannot. A phrase used to represent a specific individual may represent more than one. If '$\mathcal{a}(Mx \ni [x\ K\ b])$' is used to represent a specific individual, then it directly represents him and indirectly represents Bob. But '$\mathcal{a}(Mx \ni [x\ K\ y])$' cannot be used to represent a specific individual. An indefinite phrase used to represent a specific individual can directly represent only that individual.

We don't need another transformation to provide for the name-like use of an indefinite phrase to represent an arbitrary individual. The first indefinite transformation (i.e., a_1) is satisfactory. So now we must recognize two typical structures which realize transformation (a_1). The typically quantificational realization is illustrated by:

$$[(a(+\ M)\ +)\ J]$$

$$[x\ J]$$

The name-like realization is:

$$[aM\ J]$$

$$(a\ +)M \qquad [x\ J]$$

The depicting of the output is the same for both kinds of acts. The representing is different, but this has been discussed at sufficient length.

I will also allow indefinite phrases to be allowed to represent specific individuals in $\mathscr{L}$. But this specific representing must be marked symbolically. Otherwise, $\mathscr{L}$ would contain sentences that are inferentially and truth-conditionally ambiguous. When an indefinite phrase is used to represent a specific individual, it will be enclosed in angular parentheses: $< a\phi >$. This is an *angular* indefinite phrase. If this phrase is indexed, the index occurs outside the parentheses: $< a\phi >\alpha$. An indefinite phrase can be enclosed in angular parentheses only if the predicate functor contains no free variables. If ϕ contains free variables, the indefinite phrase $a\phi$ cannot be used to represent a specific individual.

Two transformations are needed to account for the use of the angular indefinite phrase. These are designated ($a_{3.1}$) and ($a_{3.2}$). The first of these combines the indefinite quantifier with the predicate functor. The typical act associated with this transformation has the following structure:

$$< (a\ +)\phi >$$

$$\phi$$

Since there is unlikely to be confusion as to input and output, it is normally sufficient to represent the act this way: $< (a+)\phi >$. In such an act, the predicate functor is used to represent a particular individual. The quantifier serves to make explicit the indefinite character of the representing. The indefinite phrase can also be used this way:

$$\begin{array}{c} < a\text{:}\ \phi\ > \\ \vdots \\ \phi \end{array}$$

In the input the functor is used to represent an arbitrary ϕ. This enables the quantifier to be used to represent a particular ϕ. Such a structure would be normal for using a sentence like: That's some automobile you have there, Charlie. A transformation is needed to obtain an indefinite phrase when it is used to represent a specific individual, because the quantifier's function concerns the formation of the quantified phrase. A separate transformation not shown here could also be provided for the other name-like use of the indefinite phrase.

($a_{3.1}$) Let ϕ be a one-place predicate functor which contains no free occurrences of individual variables. Then $< a\phi >$ is obtained from ϕ by the *preliminary transformation to the third indefinite transformation*.

The angular indefinite phrase $< a\phi >$ is used to directly represent a particular individual which is ϕ. It indirectly represents other individuals represented by components of ϕ. If ϕ is suited to depict s-tuples, then $< a\phi >$ depicts those s-tuples $< d_1, \ldots, d_s >$ depicted by ϕ, in which d_1 is the individual intended by the speaker—if there is such an individual. (If there is no such individual, then $< a\phi >$ does not depict.)

It is difficult to provide a set-theoretic account of depicting for the angular indefinite phrase. The same indefinite phrase can depict different individuals on different occasions; sometimes it depicts no individual. I would like for an interpreting function f of $\overline{\mathcal{L}}$ for $\mathcal{D}$ to be redefined, so that f not only assigns individuals to names and sets to predicate functors, but f also assigns the right things to angular phrases. A function can't assign more than one value to one argument. But when an angular indefinite phrase depicts different individuals on different occasions, it is not the phrase but different acts of using it which depicts them. These different acts involve different occurrences of the phrase. I will accommodate occurrences by understanding angular parentheses to be equipped with numerical subscripts:

$$<\quad >_1, <\quad >_2, \ldots$$

The subscript will normally be omitted, but it is an official part of the angular phrase. This requires that ($a_{3.1}$) be reformulated so that it takes ϕ to $< a\phi >_m$ for some numeral m. We can now describe the set-theoretic depicting.

($a_{3.1}$) Let ϕ be suited to depict s-tuples. Let $f(\phi) = V$. And let $< a\phi >_m$ be an angular indefinite phrase. Then either f assigns $\emptyset$ to $< a\phi >_m$, or else there is a $d \in \mathcal{D}$ such that $f< a\phi >_m = \{< d, e_1, \ldots, e_{s-1}> \mid < d, e_1, \ldots, e_{s-1}> \in V\}$.

($a_{3.2}$) Let $< a\phi >_m$ be an angular indefinite phrase. Let A be a predicate which contains free occurrences of the distinct individual variables $\alpha_1, \ldots, \alpha_n$ and no others; this is their canonical order.

(a) Then $< a\phi >_m\alpha_i\ A\ (= A')$ is obtained from $< a\phi >_m, A$ by the *third indefinite transformation*. The displayed occurrence of α_i and the free occurrences of α_i in A are bound occurrences in A'; they are bound by the initial occurrence of 'a.' The displayed occurrence of α_i is the *operative* occurrence of α_i in the occurrence of $< a\phi >_m\alpha_i$.

(b) If the first free occurrence of α_i in A is within the scope of no operators in A, and there is no overlined variable $\overline{\gamma}$ in A that could be bound by an antecedent in ϕ if $< a\phi >_m\alpha_i$ replaced the first free occurrence of α_i in A, then A' is obtained from $< a\phi >_m, A$ by replacing the first free occurrence of α_i by $< a\phi >_m\alpha_i$. A' is obtained by the *third indefinite transformation*. The displayed occurrence of α_i in $< a\phi >_m\alpha_i$ and the free occurrences of α_i in A other than the first are bound by the initial occurrence of 'a' in the occurrence of $< a\phi >_m\alpha_i$. The displayed occurrence of α_i is the *operative* occurrence of α_i in the occurrence of $< a\phi >_m\alpha_i$.

(c) If there is only one free occurrence of α_i in A, this is within the scope of no operator in A, and there is no overlined variable $\overline{\gamma}$ in A which could be bound by an antecedent in ϕ if $< a\phi >_m$ replaced the free occurrence of α_i in A, then A' is obtained from $< a\phi >_m, A$ by replacing the free occurrence of α_i by $< a\phi >_m$. A' is obtained by the *third indefinite transformation*.

Even though an angular indefinite phrase functions like a name, scope considerations are important. For an indefinite phrase may fail to depict, while, in $\mathcal{L}$, names cannot fail to depict. Suppose '[x V]' means x *is a vampire*, and '[x U]' means x *is upstairs*. Then

(2) $\sim[< aV > U]$

is true, but

(3) $< aV > x \sim[x\ U]$

is false.

If A' is a sentence, then A' directly represents a particular ϕ as satisfying A. If A' contains free variables, then A' directly represents a particular

ϕ and arbitrary individuals. Suppose ϕ is suited to depict s-tuples, A is suited to depict r-tuples, and the uth position in these r-tuples answers to the free occurrences of α_i in A. Then (a) $< a\phi >_m\alpha_i\, A$ depicts $(s + r - 1)$-tuples $< d_1, \ldots, d_s, e_1, \ldots, e_{r-1}>$ such that $< a\phi >_m$ depicts $< d_1, \ldots, d_s>$ and A depicts $< e_1, \ldots, e_{u-1}, d_1, e_u, \ldots, e_{r-1}>$. The first position in these $(s + r - 1)$-tuples *answers to* the occurrence of $< a\phi >_m\alpha_i$. (b, c) A' depicts $(s + r - 1)$-tuples $< e_1, \ldots, e_{u-1}, d_1, \ldots, d_s, \ldots, e_{r-1}>$ such that $< a\phi >_m$ depicts $< d_1, \ldots, d_s>$ and A depicts $< e_1, \ldots, e_{u-1}, d_1, e_u, \ldots, e_{r-1}>$. The uth position in these $(s + r - 1)$-tuples *answers to* the occurrence of $< a\phi >_m\alpha_i$ or $< a\phi >_m$.

The set-theoretic account is similar.

($a_{3.2}$) Let $f< a\phi >_m = W$, $f(A) = V$. (a) Then $f(A') = V' = \{< d_1, \ldots, d_s, e_1, \ldots, e_{r-1}> \mid < d_1, \ldots, d_s> \in W$ and $< e_1, \ldots, e_{u-1}, d_1, \ldots, e_{r-1}> \in V\}$. (b, c) Then $f(A') = V' = \{< e_1, \ldots, e_{u-1}, d_1, \ldots, d_s, e_u, \ldots, e_{r-1}> \mid < d_1, \ldots, d_s> \in W$ and $< e_1, \ldots, e_{u-1}, d_1, \ldots, e_{r-1}> \in V\}$.

4. The Quantifiers 'Λ' and 'η'

The quantifiers 'Λ' and 'η' each have two transformations. The first is a one-step and the second a two-step transformation. The statements of these transformations will not be supplied here because they are exactly parallel to the statements for the universal transformations. Both 'Λ' and 'η' are radical operators. Their transformations cancel the representing of the inputs. If the output to either transformation is a sentence, the output act does not represent; it is an act of taking the input to be this or that. If the output contains n free variables, then it represents n arbitrary individuals as appropriately qualified. If the outputs are sentences, and true, their depicting is the same as the corresponding sentential outputs of the universal transformations. If the outputs are open predicates, they depict suitable n-tuples.

Suppose '[x V]' means *x is a vampire* and '[x J]' means *x jogs*. Then the sentence '[ΛV J]' is true, because any vampire is a jogger. (Remember, I use 'any' so that it yields sentences which admit of vacuous truth.) This sentence can be used in either of the following ways:

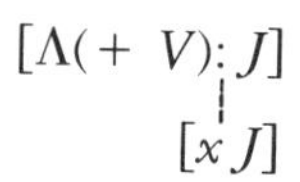

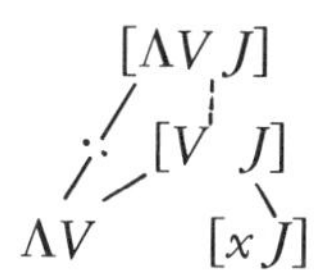

The left act takes the act of representing an arbitrary individual as jogging to be true for every—in the mathematical sense—vampire. The right act first represents an arbitrary vampire as jogging, then takes this representing to be true for any individual it depicts. The sentence '$[\eta V J]$' is also true. It can be used to perform acts with similar structures to those shown above.

The set-theoretic accounts of the tranformations are given below. For the first transformations, let ϕ be suited to depict *r*-tuples and *A* be suited to depict *s*-tuples. The *u*th position in these *s*-tuples answers to the free occurrences of α_i in *A*.

(Λ_1a) A' is $\Lambda\phi\alpha_i A$. Suppose A' is a sentence. Then $f^+(A') = \{A\}$ iff for any d_1 such that $< d_1, d_2, \ldots, d_r> \in f^+(\phi)$ for some $d_2, \ldots, d_r$, there are $e_1, \ldots, e_{s-1}$ such that $< e_1, \ldots, e_{u-1}, d_1, e_u, \ldots, e_{s-1}> \in f^+(A)$. Otherwise, $f^+(A) = \emptyset$. If A' is not a sentence, then $f^+(A') = V' = \{< d_1, \ldots, d_{m+n-1}> \mid f^+(A'[\beta_1, \ldots, \beta_m, \alpha_1, \ldots, \alpha_{i-1}, \alpha_{i+1}, \ldots, \alpha_n; d_1, \ldots, d_{m+n-1}]) = \{A[\alpha_1, \ldots, \alpha_{i-1}\ \alpha_{i+1} \ldots, \alpha_n;\ d_{m+1}, \ldots,\ d_{m+n}]\}\}$.

(Λ_1b, c) A' is obtained by replacing the first (or only) free occurrence of α_i in *A* by $\Lambda\phi\alpha_i$ or $\Lambda\phi$. If A' is a sentence, then $f^+(A') = \{A\}$ iff for any d_1 such that $< d_1, d_2, \ldots, d_r> \in f^+(\phi)$ for some $d_2, \ldots, d_r$, there are $e_1, \ldots, e_{s-1}$ such that $< e_1, \ldots, e_{u-1}, d_1, \ldots, e_s> \in f^+(A)$. Otherwise, $f^+(A') = \emptyset$. If A' is not a sentence, then $f^+(A') = V' = \{< d_1, \ldots, d_{m+n-1}> \mid f^+(A'[\alpha_1, \ldots, \alpha_{i-1}, \beta_1, \ldots, \beta_m, \alpha_{i+1}, \ldots, \alpha_n; d_1, \ldots, d_{m+n-1}]) = \{A[\alpha_1, \ldots, \alpha_{i-1}, \alpha_{i+1}, \ldots, \alpha_n; d_1, \ldots, d_{i-1}, d_{i+m-1}, \ldots, d_{m+n-1}]\}\}$.

(η_1a) A' is $\eta\phi\alpha_i A$. Suppose A' is a sentence. Then $f^+(A) = \{A\}$ iff there is no d_1 such that $< d_1, d_2, \ldots, d_r> \in f^+(\phi)$ for some $d_2, \ldots, d_r$, and $< e_1, \ldots, e_{u-1}, d_1, \ldots, e_{s-1}> \in f^+(A)$ for some $e_1, \ldots, e_{s-1}$. Otherwise, $f^+(A') = \emptyset$. If A' is not a sentence, then $f^+(A') = V' = \{< d_1, \ldots, d_{m+n-1}> \mid f^+(A'[\beta_1, \ldots, \beta_m, \alpha_1, \ldots, \alpha_{i-1}, \alpha_{i+1}, \ldots, \alpha_n; d_1, \ldots, d_{m+n-1}]) = \{A[\alpha_1, \ldots, \alpha_{i-1}, \alpha_{i+1}, \ldots, \alpha_n; d_{m+1}, \ldots, d_{m+n-1}]\}\}$.

(η_1b, c) A' is obtained by replacing the first (or only) free occurrence of α_i in *A* by $\eta\phi\alpha_i$ or $\eta\phi$. If A' is a sentence, then $f^+(A') = \{A\}$ iff there is no d_1 such that $< d_1, d_2, \ldots, d_r> \in f^+(\phi)$ for some $d_2, \ldots, d_r$, and $< e_1, \ldots, e_{u-1}, d_1, \ldots, e_{s-1}> \in f^+(A)$ for some $e_1, \ldots, e_{s-1}$. Otherwise, $f^+(A') = \emptyset$. If A' is not a sentence, then $f^+(A') = V' = \{< d_1, \ldots, d_{m+n-1}> \mid f^+(A'[\alpha_1, \ldots, \alpha_{i-1}, \beta_1, \ldots, \beta_m, \alpha_{i+1}, \ldots, \alpha_n; d_1, \ldots, d_{m+n-1}]) = \{A[\alpha_1, \ldots, \alpha_{i-1}, \alpha_{i+1}, \ldots, \alpha_n; d_1, \ldots, d_{i-1}, d_{i+m-1}, \ldots, d_{m+n-1}]\}\}$.

For the second transformations, let ϕ be suited to depict *r*-tuples and A' to depict *s*-tuples. Let the *u*th position in these *s*-tuples answer to the occurrence of $\phi\alpha_i$ or ϕ in A'.

(Λ_2a) A' is $\phi\alpha_i A$. If A'' is a sentence, then $f^+(A'') = \{A'\}$ iff $f^+(\phi) \subseteq \{< d_1, \ldots, d_r > \mid < d_1, \ldots, d_r, d_{r+1}, \ldots, d_s > \in f^+(A')$ for some $d_{r+1}, \ldots, d_s\}$. Otherwise, $f^+(A'') = \emptyset$. If A'' is not a sentence, and contains free occurrences of p distinct individual variables $\gamma_1, \ldots, \gamma_p$ and no others (this is their canonical order), then $f^+(A'') = V'' = \{< d_1, \ldots, d_p > \mid f^+(A''[\gamma_1, \ldots, \gamma_p; d_1, \ldots, d_p]) = \{A'[\gamma_1, \ldots, \gamma_p; d_1, \ldots, d_p]\}\}$.

(Λ_2b, c) A' has an occurrence of $\phi\alpha_i$ or ϕ in an argument position, and A'' is obtained by inserting 'Λ' to the left of ϕ. If A'' is a sentence, then $f^+(A'') = \{A'\}$ iff $f^+(\phi) \subseteq \{< d_u, \ldots, d_{u+r-1} > \mid < d_1, \ldots, d_u, \ldots, d_s > \in f^+(A')$ for some $d_1, \ldots, d_{u-1}, d_{u+r}, \ldots, d_s\}$. Otherwise, $f^+(A'') = \emptyset$. If A'' is not a sentence, $f^+(A'')$ is as in case (Λ_2a).

(η_2a) A' is $\phi\alpha_i A$. If A'' is a sentence, then $f^+(A'') = \{A'\}$ iff $f^+(\phi) \cap \{< d_1, \ldots, d_r > \mid < d_1, \ldots, d_r, \ldots, d_s > \in f^+(A')$ for some $d_{r+1}, \ldots, d_s\} = \emptyset$. Otherwise, $f^+(A'') = \emptyset$. If A'' is not a sentence, and contains free occurrences of p distinct individual variables $\gamma_1, \ldots, \gamma_p$ and no others (this is their canonical order), then $f^+(A'') = V'' = \{< d_1, \ldots, d_p > \mid f^+(A''[\gamma_1, \ldots, \gamma_p; d_1, \ldots, d_p]) = \{A'[\gamma_1, \ldots, \gamma_p; d_1, \ldots, d_p]\}\}$.

(η_2b, c) A' has an occurrence of $\phi\alpha_i$ or ϕ in an argument position, and A'' is obtained by inserting 'η' to the left of ϕ. If A'' is a sentence, then $f^+(A'') = \{A'\}$ iff $f^+(\phi) \cap \{< d_u, \ldots, d_{u+r-1} > \mid < d_1, \ldots, d_u, \ldots, d_s > \in f^+(A')$ for some $d_1, \ldots, d_{u-1}, d_{u+r}, \ldots, d_s\} = \emptyset$. Otherwise, $f^+(A'') = \emptyset$. If A'' is not a sentence, then $f^+(A'')$ is as in case (η_2a).

5. The Definite Phrase

A definite phrase can either be used in a typically quantificational fashion or like a name. When the definite article is used like a quantifier, there are two typical acts. Consider the $\overline{\mathcal{L}}$-translation of 'The neighbor of Bob's who owns a German shepherd is unfriendly': $[\iota(Px \ni [[x\ N\ b]\ \&\ [x\ O\ aG]])\ U]$. The definite quantifier might be involved in a two-step transformation:

$$[\iota(Px \ni [[x\ N\ b]\ \&\ [x\ O\ aG]])\ \ U]$$

$$[(Px \ni [[x\ N\ b]\ \&\ [x\ O\ aG]])\ U]$$

$$\iota(Px \ni [[x\ N\ b\ \&\ [x\ O\ aG]]) \qquad [x\ U]$$

The intermediate act represents an arbitrary neighbor who owns a German shepherd as being unfriendly. The definite quantifier gives a special character to this act so that it represents the one and only neighbor who owns a German shepherd as being unfriendly. The special character indicates that the intermediate act is true for a single individual. The definite quantifier can also be used in a one-step transformation. Let '[ιM M c]' be 'The Mayor married Clare.' This can be used:

$$[(\iota(+\ M)+)\ M\ c]$$

$$[x\ M\ c]$$

The predicate input represents an arbitrary individual as marrying Clare. This is given a special character so that it represents the Mayor as marrying Clare. The special character emphasizes the uniqueness of the Mayor. ('The' is emphasized more than 'Mayor.') The two typical quantificational acts for the nonradical definite quantifier have the same structures as the typical quantificational acts for the indefinite quantifier. The first two definite transformations are exactly parallel to the first two indefinite transformations, and will be omitted here.

It is easy enough to determine the representing and depicting associated with the first two definite transformations. No statements will be provided. The set-theoretic statements are as follows.

(ι_1) Let A' be obtained from ϕ, A by the first definite transformation. Let A be suited to depict p-tuples and ϕ to depict q-tuples. In the p-tuples, the uth position answers to the free occurrences of α_i (this is the variable affected by the definite quantifier). Let $f(\phi) = W$, $f(A) = V$.

(a) Then A' is $\iota\phi\alpha_i A$. $f(A') = V' = \{<d_1, \ldots, d_q, e_1, \ldots, e_{p-1}> \mid <d_1, \ldots, d_q> \in W, <e_1, \ldots, e_{u-1}, d_1, e_u, \ldots, e_{p-1}> \in V$, and for every $<m_1, \ldots, m_q> \in W, m_1 = d_1\}$.

(b, c) Then $f(A') = V' = \{<e_1, \ldots, e_{u-1}, d_1, \ldots, d_q, \ldots, e_{p-1}> \mid <d_1, \ldots, d_q> \in W, <e_1, \ldots, e_{u-1}, d_1, \ldots, e_{p-1}> \in V$, and for every $<m_1, \ldots, \mathrm{m}_q> \in \mathrm{W}, \mathrm{m}_1 = \mathrm{d}_1\}$.

(ι_2) Let A'' be obtained from A' by the second definite transformation. Let A' be suited to depict p-tuples and ϕ to depict q-tuples. In the p-tuples, let the uth position answer to the occurrence of $\phi\alpha_i$ or ϕ that is prefixed with 'ι' to obtain A''. Let $f(\phi) = W$ and $f(A') = V'$.

(a) Then $f(A'') = V'' = \{<d_1, \ldots, d_q, \ldots, d_s> \mid <d_1, \ldots, d_s> \in V'$ and for every $<m_1, \ldots, m_q> \in W, m_1 = d_1\}$.

(b, c) Then $f(A'') = V'' = \{<d_1, \ldots, d_u, \ldots, d_s> \mid <d_1, \ldots, d_s> \in V'$ and for every $<m_1, \ldots, m_q> \in W, m_1 = d_u\}$.

Although a definite article can be used quantificationally, it is much more common for definite phrases to be used like names. The earlier sentence about Bob's unfriendly neighbor might be used like this:

$$
\begin{array}{ll}
 & [\iota\, (Px \ni [[x\ N\ b]\ \&\ [x\ O\ aG]])\ U] \\
 & \quad / \qquad\qquad\qquad\qquad\qquad\qquad \backslash \\
(\iota\ +) & (Px \ni [[x\ N\ b]\ \&\ [x\ O\ aG]]) \quad [x\ U]
\end{array}
$$

The predicate functor '$(Px \ni [[x\ N\ b]\ \&\ [x\ O\ aG]])$' is used to represent the neighbor with the German shepherd. The definite quantifier is used to give a special character to this representing act, so that it is explicit that there is only one such neighbor. The sentence could also be used like this:

$$
\begin{array}{ll}
 & [\iota\, (Px \ni [[x\ N\ b]\ \&\ [x\ O\ aG]]) \quad U] \\
 & \quad / \qquad\qquad\qquad\qquad\qquad\qquad\quad \backslash \\
\iota: & (Px \ni [[x\ N\ b]\ \&\ [x\ O\ aG]]) \quad [x\ U] \\
 & \qquad\qquad\qquad \vdots \\
 & (Px \ni [[x\ N\ b]\ \&\ [x\ O\ aG]])
\end{array}
$$

The predicate functor is used to represent an arbitrary neighbor who owns a German shepherd. This enables the definite quantifier to be used to represent the only neighbor who owns a German shepherd.

It might be thought that when a definite phrase is used in a name-like way, the phrase will always represent a specific individual. This is not the case. A definite phrase with a free variable (an empty argument position) can be used in a name-like way. Let the $\mathcal{L}$-translation of 'The owner of every dog must buy a license' be: $\forall Dy\ [\iota(Px \ni [x\ O\ y])\ B\ aL]$. The sentence might be used this way:

$$
\begin{array}{ll}
\forall Dy: & [\iota\, (Px \ni [x\ O\ y])\ B\ aL] \\
 & \qquad\qquad\quad \vdots \\
 & [\iota\, (Px \ni [x\ O\ y])\ B\ aL] \\
 & \quad / \qquad\qquad\qquad\quad \backslash \\
(\iota\ +) & (Px \ni [x\ O\ y]) \qquad [x\ B\ aL]
\end{array}
$$

The definite phrase represents an arbitrary person x and an arbitrary individual y, in such a relation that the person is the one and only person that owns y. The definite phrase does not represent them *as* related in such a way; it is characteristic of predicative acts to represent individuals as related. (This is *our* characteristic way of *describing* predicative acts.) The definite phrase represents the individuals *in* their relation. The definite phrase represents both the person x and the individual y *directly*.

In $\overline{\mathcal{L}}$, if a definite phrase contains no free variables, and it is used in a name-like way, then the phrase must be used to represent a specific individual. And the definite phrase will directly represent only that individual. A definite phrase used to represent a specific individual will be enclosed in angular parentheses: $< \iota\phi >$. This is like the notation for indefinite phrases used to represent specific individuals, except for one feature. The "official" angular parentheses for indefinite phrases are equipped with numerical subscripts: $< a\phi >_m$. When definite phrases are enclosed in angular parentheses, numerical subscripts are not required. All occurrences of one angular definite phrase will represent the same individual.

In $\overline{\mathcal{L}}$, a definite phrase without free variables will directly represent just one individual, when used in a name-like way. $\overline{\mathcal{L}}$ is simpler than English at this point. $\overline{\mathcal{L}}$ has not been provided with transformations that take nominal acts to nominal acts. There is, for example, no transformation that takes '$\iota(Px \ni [x\ O\ y])$' to '$\iota(Px \ni [x\ O\ aD])$.' Such transformations are required if we are to give an adequate account of English. Providing such transformations would make it possible for one definite phrase, with no free variables, to directly represent two individuals when used in a name-like way. These transformations will not be introduced to $\overline{\mathcal{L}}$. They are more appropriate in a language which has a greater variety of noun (nominal) phrases. To introduce such transformations, we would need to duplicate most existing transformations. For the transformations that have been provided for $\mathcal{L}$ and $\overline{\mathcal{L}}$ are "predicative" transformations; at least one input is a predicate, and the output is a predicate (or sentence). The individual transformation, for example, can take the name 'b' and the predicate '$[x\ D]$' to the predicate (and sentence) '$[b\ D]$.' A nominal individual transformation might take 'b' and the functor '$(Px \ni [x\ K\ y])$' to '$(Px \ni [x\ K\ b])$.'

The third definite transformation has a preliminary part ($\iota_{3.1}$) and a "main" part ($\iota_{3.2}$). This transformation need not be stated, because its two parts, except for the subscripts on the angular parentheses, are parallel to the third indefinite transformation's two parts. When a definite phrase contains free variables and is used in a name-like way, its use is "covered" by the first definite transformation (which can be typically realized by either of two structures). When the name-like definite phrase contains no free variables, it must be enclosed in angular parentheses. Its use comes under ($\iota_{3.1}$) and ($\iota_{3.2}$).

The set-theoretic statement of depicting for the third definite transformations is below.

($\iota_{3.1}$) Let ϕ be suited to depict p-tuples. Let $f(\phi) = V$. And let $< \iota\phi >$ be a name-like definite phrase. Then $f< \iota\phi > = V' = \{< d_1, \ldots, d_p> \mid < d_1, \ldots, d_p> \in V$ and for every $< m_1, \ldots, m_p> \in V$, $m_1 = d_1\}$.

($\iota_{3.2}$) Let A' be obtained from $< \iota\phi >$, A by the third definite transformation. Let ϕ be suited to depict p-tuples and A to depict q-tuples. Let the uth position in the q-tuples answer to the free occurrences of α_i in A. And let $f< \iota\phi > = W$, $f(A) = V$.

(a) Then $f(A') = V' = \{< d_1, \ldots, d_p, e_1, \ldots, e_{q-1}> \mid < d_1, \ldots, d_p> \in W$ and $< e_1, \ldots, e_{u-1}, d_1, e_u, \ldots, e_{q-1}> \in V\}$.

(b, c) Then $f(A') = V' = \{< e_1, \ldots, e_{u-1}, d_1, \ldots, d_p, \ldots, e_{q-1}> \mid < d_1, \ldots, d_p> \in W$ and $< e_1, \ldots, e_{u-1}, d_1, \ldots, e_{q-1}> \in V\}$.

The fact that a definite phrase can be used in both a quantificational and a name-like way shows that neither Frege nor Russell was "right" about definite phrases. Of course, neither man was concerned with the structures of linguistic intentional acts. But Russell, in effect, maintained that definite phrases are always used in a quantificational way, and Frege held that they are always used in a name-like fashion. Frege does not appear to have considered definite phrases which contain free variables, for he treated definite phrases as if they always directly represented just one individual. However, Frege seems to have been more nearly right than Russell, for most uses of definite phrases are name-like. Russell appears right, at least for a language like $\overline{\mathcal{L}}$, in thinking that whenever a sentence containing a definite phrase is used, there is an inferentially equivalent sentence in which the definite phrase is used quantificationally. I.e., we could convey whatever information we wish if we always used definite phrases quantificationally. Frege and Russell were both wrong in thinking that there can be only one use of an expression like a definite phrase.

6. The Unique Quantifier

I have been regarding '$\mathcal{O}$' as a nonradical operator. This seems to be an error. It is not easy, however, to find clear English examples which demonstrate that 'only' is radical. The sentence:

> (1) Only John will ask a girl to the dance, and she will turn him down.

can be used to perform different kinds of acts. Some of them are legitimate. If 'a girl' is used in a name-like way, then sentence (1) is acceptable. It is also acceptable if the indefinite transformation is performed "later" than the unique transformation. But if the unique transformation is performed later, I think (1) is anomalous. In that case, I want to ask who "she" is. I feel the same way about this sentence:

(2) Only Barb owns a book, and she hasn't read it.

These examples aren't clear enough to make the radical character of 'only' obvious. But in developing a semantic account, it proved impossible to deal with '𝕆' in a way similar to that in which '*𝕒*' and 'ι' were treated. The sentence:

(3) Only Bob likes a girl.

does not represent Bob and an arbitrary girl as such that Bob likes the girl and no one else does. Sentence (3) says that Bob is the only one who likes *any* girl.

The unique quantifier is a radical operator. Let '*c*' name Scott, and '[*x Y*]' mean *x said "Thank you"* (on some specified occasion). There are two typical acts of using the sentence '[𝕆*c Y*].' There are two unique transformations. The sentence might be used to perform an act like this:

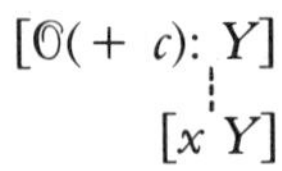

The input act represents an arbitrary individual as saying "Thank you" on the occasion in question. The act performed with the prefix is an act of taking the input act to be true for only Scott; that is, for Scott and no one else. This negative character may be responsible for the unique quantifier's being radical. The second act that can be performed with the sentence involves two steps; the first is an ordinary predicative or sentential act.

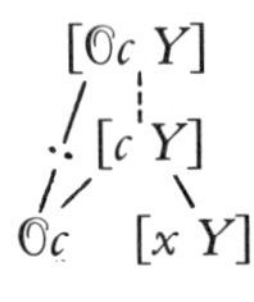

The intermediate act represents Scott as saying "Thank you." This enables the output act: taking the intermediate act to be such that nothing other than Scott satisfies the predicate '[*Y*].'

($𝕆_1$) Let *A* be a predicate containing free occurrences of the distinct individual variables $\alpha_1, \ldots, \alpha_n$ and no others; this is their canonical order. Let β be an individual constant.

(a) Then $\mathbb{O}\beta_{\alpha_i} A$ (= A') is obtained from β, A by the *first unique transformation*. The subscripted occurrence of α_i and the free occurrences of α_i in A are bound occurrences in A'; they are bound by the initial occurrence of '$\mathbb{O}$.' The subscripted occurrence of α_i is the *operative* occurrence of α_i in $\mathbb{O}\beta_{\alpha_i}$.

(b) Let the first free occurrence of α_i in A be within the scope of no operator in A. Then A' is obtained from β, A by replacing the first free occurrence of α_i by $\mathbb{O}\beta_{\alpha_i}$. A' is obtained by the *first unique transformation*. The subscripted occurrence of α_i and the free occurrences of α_i in A other than the first are bound in A' by the occurrence of '$\mathbb{O}$' in the occurrence of $\mathbb{O}\beta_{\alpha_i}$. The subscripted occurrence of α_i is the *operative* occurrence of α_i in the occurrence of $\mathbb{O}\beta_{\alpha_i}$.

(c) Let A contain a single free occurrence of α_i. Let this occurrence of α_i be within the scope of no operator in A. Then A' is obtained from β, A by replacing the free occurrence of α_i by $\mathbb{O}\beta$. A' is obtained by the *first unique transformation*.

If A' is a sentence, it does not represent. Otherwise, it represents $n - 1$ arbitrary individuals. Let β depict d. If A' is a sentence, then A' depicts A if A is true for d and nothing else. If A' contains free variables, then A' depicts $(n - 1)$-tuples $<e_1, \ldots, e_{n-1}>$ such that $A[\alpha_1, \ldots, \alpha_{i-1}, \alpha_{i+1}, \ldots, \alpha_n; e_1, \ldots, e_{n-1}]$ is true for d and nothing else.

($\mathbb{O}_1$) Let $f^+(A) = V$, $f^+(\beta) = d$. Let A be suited to depict m-tuples in which the jth position answers to the free occurrences of α_i in A. If A' is a sentence, then $f^+(A') = \{A\}$ iff for every m-tuple $< e_1, \ldots, e_m> \in V$, $e_j = d$. Otherwise, $f^+(A') = \emptyset$. If A' is not a sentence, then $f^+(A') = V' = \{< e_1, \ldots, e_{n-1}> \mid f^+(A'[\alpha_1, \ldots, \alpha_{i-1}, \alpha_{i+1}, \ldots, \alpha_n; e_1, \ldots, e_{n-1}]) = \{A[\alpha_1, \ldots, \alpha_{i-1}, \alpha_{i+1}, \ldots, \alpha_n; e_1, \ldots, e_{n-1}]\}\}$.

The second unique transformation corresponds to a two-step act structure. But the transformation does not have two steps, for the output of the first stage would be an ordinary predicate.

($\mathbb{O}_2$) Let A be a predicate containing an occurrence of β_α or β which is not part of a quantified phrase $\mathbb{O}\beta_\alpha$ or $\mathbb{O}\beta$. Let the occurrence of β_α or β be within the scope of no operator in A. Then A' is obtained from A by the *second unique transformation* by inserting '$\mathbb{O}$' immediately to the left of β. The occurrences of α that were previously bound by α are now bound by the occurrence of '$\mathbb{O}$.' If '$\mathbb{O}$' is inserted immediately to the left of β_α, the subscripted occurrence of α is the *operative* occurrence of α in the occurrence of $\mathbb{O}\beta_\alpha$.

If A' is a sentence, it does not represent. If it contains n distinct free variables, it (directly) represents n arbitrary individuals. Let δ be an individual variable not occurring in A. Let A'' be obtained from A by replacing the occurrence of β_α and all the occurrences of α bound by the occurrence of β by δ, or by replacing the occurrence of β by δ. Let β depict d. Then if A' is a sentence, A' depicts A iff A'' is true for d and nothing else. If A' contains free occurrences of distinct individual variables $\gamma_1, \ldots, \gamma_n$ and no others (this is their canonical order), then A' depicts n-tuples $< e_1, \ldots, e_n >$ such that $A'[\gamma_1, \ldots, \gamma_n; e_1, \ldots, e_n]$ depicts $A[\gamma_1, \ldots, \gamma_n; e_1, \ldots, e_n]$.

$(\mathfrak{C}_2)$ Let $f^+(A'') = V$, $f^+(\beta) = d$. Let A be suited to depict m-tuples in which the jth position answers to the occurrence of β_α or β in A. If A' is a sentence, then $f^+(A') = \{A\}$ iff for every m-tuple $< e_1, \ldots, e_m > \in V$, $e_j = d$. Otherwise, $f^+(A') = \emptyset$. (And $f^+(A') = \emptyset$ if $V = \emptyset$.) If A' is not a sentence, then $f^+(A') = \{< e_1, \ldots, e_n > \mid f^+(A'[\gamma_1, \ldots, \gamma_n; e_1, \ldots, e_n]) = \{A[\gamma_1, \ldots, \gamma_n; e_1, \ldots, e_n]\}\}$.

7. Passive Voice and Relative Clauses

There isn't much to say about the passive voice operator with respect to speech act structure. The transformation which takes a predicate functor ϕ to $\breve{\phi}$ does not normally correspond to one or more related speech acts. It is conceivable that someone might use the sentence '$[a\ \breve{H}\ b]$' ("Laura was hit by Bob") this way:

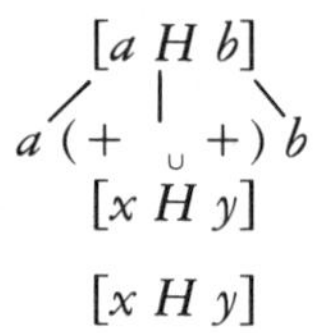

The predicate '$[x\ H\ y]$' is used to represent arbitrary individuals x, y such that x hit y. The passive voice operator serves to give a special character to this predicative act so that it represents arbitrary individuals x, y such that x was hit by y. This predicative act is an immediate component of the sentential act. The sentence could also be used like this:

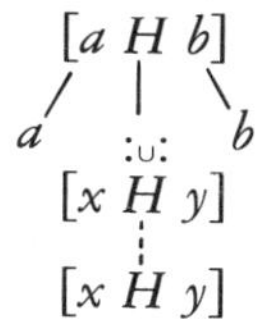

In this case the act of representing arbitrary individuals *x, y* as such that *x* hit *y* enables the act of using the passive voice operator to represent arbitrary individuals *x, y* as such that *x* was hit by *y*.

Acts with the structures represented above are highly unlikely. An active voice predicative act would not normally be performed as input to a transformation yielding a passive voice predicative act. An act of using a predicate like '[$x\ \overset{\cup}{H}\ y$]' would normally be a simple intentional act, not enabled by some other act. The "total" structure of an act of using '[*a H b*]' might be like this:

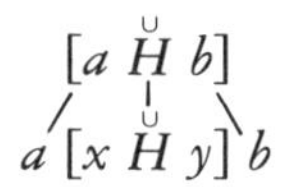

There is no speech act of using '*H*' or '[*x H y*]' which is preliminary to the act of using '[$x\ \overset{\cup}{H}\ y$].'

If α, β are distinct individual variables, and ψ is a two-place functor, then [$\alpha\ \overset{\cup}{\psi}\ \beta$] represents arbitrary individuals α, β as such that β has ψ's relation to α. This predicate depicts pairs $< d, e >$ such that [$\alpha\ \psi\ \beta$] depicts $< e, d >$.

(Passive Voice) If ψ is a two place predicate functor and $f(\psi) = V$, then $f(\overset{\cup}{\psi}) = V' = \{< d, e > \mid < e, d > \in V\}$.

To provide an account of the speech acts associated with the relative clause transformation, we must depart somewhat from our practice of modeling the acts of using expressions of $\overline{\mathcal{L}}$ on the acts of using corresponding English expressions. In $\overline{\mathcal{L}}$, a single predicate functor ϕ can be used to perform a predicative act when it is part of a predicate [$x\ \phi$], and to perform a nominal act when it is part of a quantified phrase like $a\phi$. (A nominal act is not the same as a name-like act. A nominal act is an act typically performed with a *noun*. But a name-like act is one kind of nominal act.) There are no English expressions which play such dual roles. A predicative act performed with [$x\ \phi$] is understood on the model of acts performed with English predicates, like '*x* jogs.' A nominal act performed with ϕ as part of $a\phi$ is understood on the model of acts performed with English nouns, like an act performed with 'jogger' in the phrase 'some jogger.' In a predicative act performed with $[x\ \phi]$ an arbitrary individual is represented *as* something or other. (If ϕ is complex, there may be more than one arbitrary individual represented as related in some way.) In a non-name-like nominal act performed with $a\phi$, ϕ is used to represent an arbitrary individual of a kind. But it is not represented *as* anything. In a name-like act performed with $< a\phi >$, the phrase is used to represent a specific individual of the kind; again it is not represented as anything. If ϕ is complex, a nominal act performed with ϕ may represent an n-tuple rather than an individual, but the representing will not be predicative. If '$[x\ M]$' means *x is a man,* and '$[x\ M\ y]$' means *x is married to y*, then a nominal act performed with '$(Mx \ni [x\ M\ y])$' represents an arbitrary man married to an arbitrary individual y, and the arbitrary individual y. Neither is represented *as* married to the other, since that is the characterization of a predicative act.

In $\mathcal{L}$, the relative clause transformation produces a predicate functor. The predicate functor can be used either predicatively or nominally. In English, relative clauses are used nominally. There are no relative-clause-like English expressions which typically function in a predicative fashion. The act of using a nominal relative clause will be modeled on the act of using its English translation. The act of using a predicative relative clause will be one that would be appropriate for actual users of $\mathcal{L}$. There are two relative clause transformations.

($\ni$) Let ϕ be a one-place predicate functor containing free occurrences of distinct individual variables $\beta_1, \ldots, \beta_m$ and no others; this is their canonical order. Let A be a predicate which contains no free individual variables in common with ϕ. Let $\alpha_1, \ldots, \alpha_n$ $(n > 0)$ be the distinct individual variables, in canonical order, occurring free in A.

($\ni_1$) Let γ be an individual variable which does not occur free in A or in ϕ, unless γ is α_i. Then $[\gamma\ (\phi\alpha_i \ni A)]$ $(= A')$ is obtained from $[\gamma\ \phi]$, A by the *predicative relative clause transformation*. The occurrence of α_i indexing ϕ and the free occurrences of α_i in A are bound occurrences in A'; they are bound by the occurrence of '$\ni$.' The indexing occurrence of α_i is the *operative* occurrence of α_i in the occurrence of the predicate functor.

The typical act associated with ($\ni_1$) has this structure:

$[\gamma\ (\phi\alpha_i \ni A)]$
/ \
$[\gamma\ \phi]$ A

Both inputs are representing acts; they are performed in order to constitute a complex representing, predicative, act. The predicate $[\gamma\ (\phi\alpha_i \ni$

$A)]$ is used to directly represent arbitrary individuals $\gamma, \beta_1, \ldots, \beta_m, \alpha_1, \ldots, \alpha_{i-1}, \alpha_{i+1}, \ldots, \alpha_n$ as whatever. Let $[\gamma\ \phi]$ be suited to depict s-tuples, and A be suited to depict r-tuples. Let the uth position in these r-tuples answer to the free occurrences of α_i in A. Then $[\gamma\ (\phi\alpha_i \ni A)]$ depicts $(r + s - 1)$-tuples $< d_1, \ldots, d_s, e_1, \ldots, e_{r-1}>$ such that $[\gamma\ \phi]$ depicts $< d_1, \ldots, d_s>$ and A depicts $< e_1, \ldots, e_{u-1}, d_1, e_u, \ldots, e_s>$. The first position in these $(r + s - 1)$-tuples answers to the initial occurrence of γ in $[\gamma\ (\phi\alpha_i \ni A)]$. The other positions answer to the obviously appropriate occurrences of expressions in A'.

($\ni_2$) Then $(\phi\alpha_i \ni A)$ ($= A'$) is obtained from ϕ, A by the *nominal relative clause transformation*. The occurrence of α_i indexing ϕ and the free occurrences of α_i in A are bound occurrences in A'; they are bound by the occurrence of '$\ni$.' The indexing occurrence of α_i is the *operative* occurrence of α_i in the occurrence of $(\phi\alpha_i \ni A)$.

The typical act associated with ($\ni_2$) has this structure:

```
   (φα_i ∋ A)
    /      \
   φ        A
```

The nominal act and the predicative act are both performed in order to perform a nominal representing act. The predicate functor $(\phi\alpha_i \ni A)$ is used to directly represent an arbitrary individual satisfying ϕ, arbitrary individuals $\beta_1, \ldots, \beta_m$, and arbitrary individuals $\alpha_1, \ldots, \alpha_{i-1}, \alpha_{i+1}, \ldots, \alpha_n$. The predicate functor indirectly represents the other individuals represented by ϕ and A. Let ϕ be suited to depict s-tuples and A to depict r-tuples. Let the uth position in these r-tuples answer to the free occurrences of α_i in A. Then $(\phi\alpha_i \ni A)$ depicts $(r + s - 1)$-tuples $< d_1, \ldots, d_s, e_1, \ldots, e_{r-1}>$. The first position in these $(r + s - 1)$-tuples answers to the occurrence of ϕ (or $\phi\alpha_i$) in $(\phi\alpha_i \ni A)$. The other positions answer to the obviously appropriate occurrences of expressions in A'.

The same set-theoretic statement works for both transformations.

($\ni$) Let $f(\phi) = W$, $f(A) = V$. Then $f(A') = V' = \{< d_1, \ldots, d_s, e_1, \ldots, e_{r-1}> \mid < d_1, \ldots, d_s> \in W$ and $< e_1, \ldots, e_{u-1}, d_1, e_u, \ldots, e_{r-1}> \in V\}$.

8. Pronomial Transformations

We can reduce the number of pronomial transformations for $\overline{\mathcal{L}}$ to two. The first transformation covers those cases where the antecedent is a name or a quantified phrase used to represent a specific individual. The second covers the cases where the antecedent is an indefinite or a definite phrase, not used to represent a specific individual. To understand the first transformation, it is important to understand the difference between depicting and labeling for an angular quantified phrase. An individual constant α depicts and labels the same individual. But an angular phrase $< a\phi >$ or $< \iota\phi >$ may depict n-tuples. If it does, the first position in these n-tuples answers to the occurrence of the whole phrase; and the same individual occupies the first position in every n-tuple depicted by an angular phrase. The angular phrase labels the individual which occupies first place in the depicted n-tuples, though it may not label any individual.

(Pro_1) Let A be a predicate, intermediate quantificational expression, or an intermediate conditional expression. Let μ be one of:

(i) an indexed constant α_β,
(ii) an indexed unique phrase $\mathbb{O}\alpha_\beta$,
(iii) an indexed angular indefinite phrase $< a\phi >_m\beta$,
(iv) an indexed angular definite phrase $< \iota\phi > \beta$.

(In every case, the indexing variable is β.) Let A contain an occurrence, the *selected occurrence*, of μ. Let $\gamma_1, \ldots, \gamma_n$ be the distinct individual variables, in canonical order, occurring free in A. Let every free occurrence of γ_i in A be within the extended scope of the selected occurrence of μ. Let no free occurrence of γ_i in A be at a place where an occurrence of $\overline{\beta}$ could be bound by an operator or constant other than the occurrence of the operator or constant in the selected occurrence of μ. Then A' is obtained from μ, A by replacing the free occurrences of γ_i by $\overline{\beta}$. A' is obtained by the *first pronomial transformation*. The occurrences of $\overline{\beta}$ introduced by this transformation are bound by the occurrence of the operator or constant in the selected occurrence of μ. (If A is an intermediate conditional expression, then so is A'. If A is an intermediate quantificational expression, then so is A'.)

Suppose A is a predicate, intermediate quantificational expression, or intermediate conditional expression that represents $\rho_1, \ldots, \rho_r$ as ψ. Suppose ρ_j is the arbitrary individual γ_i. Then A' represents $\rho_1, \ldots, \rho_{j-1}$, the individual represented by μ, $\rho_{j+1}, \ldots, \rho_r$ as ψ. Suppose A is suited to depict s-tuples, in which the kth position answers to the free occurrences of γ_i in A. And suppose μ labels e. Then A' depicts those s-tuples $< d_1, \ldots, d_s >$ depicted by A, in which $d_k = e$. The kth position in these s-tuples answers to the occurrences of $\overline{\beta}$ introduced by this transformation.

Let $f(A) = V$. Let $f(\mu) = e$ or $f(\mu) = \{< e, m_1, \ldots, m_t> \mid \ldots\}$. Then $f(A') = V' = \{< d_1, \ldots, d_s> \mid < d_1, \ldots, d_s> \in V \text{ and } d_k = e\}$.

Consider the sentence 'If Rosemary sees a golden eagle, she will be pleased.' This sentence might be translated by the following: $[[a_x\ SaG] \supset [\bar{x}\ P]]$. This could be used to perform an act having the structure illustrated below:

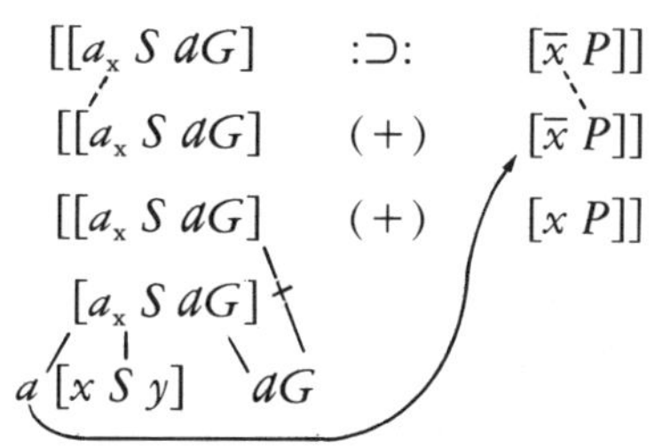

The first intermediate conditional expression represents Rosemary seeing a golden eagle—normally this would be used to represent the seeing as in the future. It also represents an arbitrary individual as being pleased in the future. If it depicts at all, this first intermediate expression depicts triples $<$ Rosemary, β, γ $>$ where β is a golden eagle Rosemary sees (or will see) and γ is an individual who will be pleased. The second intermediate conditional expression represents Rosemary seeing a golden eagle and Rosemary as being pleased in the future. If it depicts, this act depicts triples $<$ Rosemary, β, Rosemary $>$, where β is a golden eagle that Rosemary sees (or will see). The final conditional act takes the act representing Rosemary as being pleased to be conditional on the act which represents Rosemary and the golden eagle as related by seeing. The consequent act *is* conditional on the antecedent act if for any pair $<$ Rosemary, golden eagle $>$ depicted by the antecedent act, there is the individual Rosemary such that $<$ Rosemary, golden eagle, Rosemary $>$ is depicted by the second intermediate conditional expression (act).

The following English sentence:

Bob asked only Anne to the dance, and she turned him down.

might be translated this way in $\overline{\mathcal{L}}$: $[[b_x\ A\ ©a_y]\ \&\ [\bar{y}\ D\ \bar{x}]]$. This could be used to perform an act with the structure illustrated here:

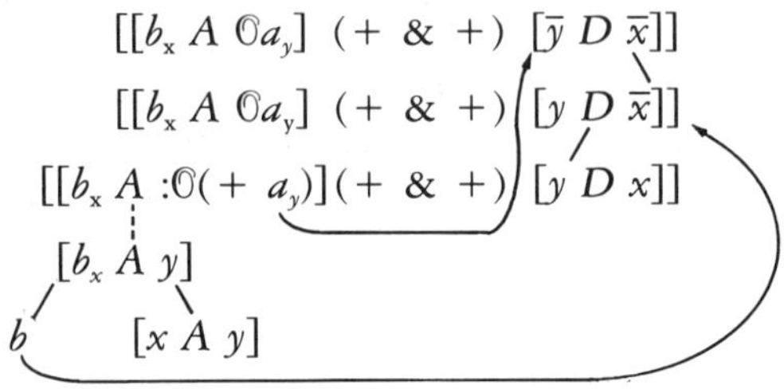

Suppose Bob did ask only Anne to the dance. Then '$[[b_x\ A\ \copyright a_y]\ \&\ [y\ D\ x]]$' depicts pairs < *d, e* > such that *d* is an individual who turned down *e*'s invitation to the dance. If Bob did not ask Anne, if Bob asked others than Anne, or if no one's invitation to the dance was turned down, then this predicate does not depict. If Bob asked only Anne to the dance, the predicate '$[[b_x\ A\ \copyright a_y]\ \&\ [y\ D\ \bar{x}]]$' depicts pairs < *d*, Bob > such that *d* turned down Bob's invitation to the dance. If the sentence '$[[b_x\ A\ \copyright a_y]\ \&\ [\bar{y}\ D\ \bar{x}]]$' depicts, it depicts < Anne, Bob >.

We will allow different applications of pronomial transformations to be performed simultaneously. So the sentence could be used like this:

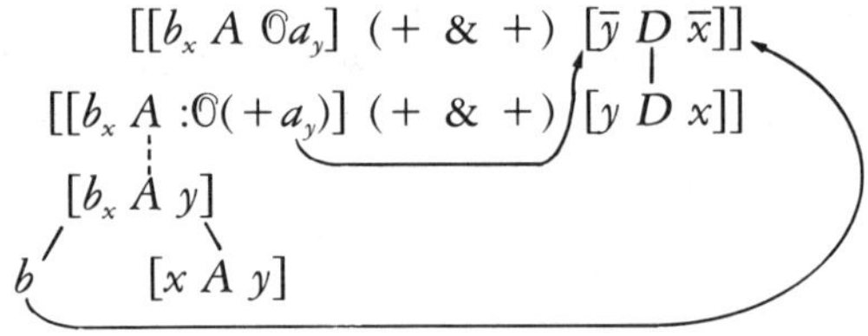

(Pro_2) Let *A* be a predicate, intermediate quantificational expression, or an intermediate conditional expression which contains an occurrence, *the selected occurrence,* of $a\phi\beta$ or $\iota\phi\beta$. Let $\gamma_1, \ldots, \gamma_n$ be the distinct individual variables, in canonical order, occurring free in *A*. Let every free occurrence of γ_i in *A* be to the right of the operative occurrence of β in the selected occurrence of the quantified phrase. Let no free occurrence of γ_i in *A* be at a place where an occurrence of $\bar{\beta}$ could be bound by an operator or constant other than the (first) occurrence of the quantifier in the selected occurrence of the quantified phrase. And let the selected occurrence of $a\phi\beta$ or $\iota\phi\beta$ be within the scope of no radical operator. Then A' is obtained from the quantified phrase and *A* by replacing every free occurrence of γ_i by $\bar{\beta}$. A' is obtained by the *second pronomial transformation*. The occurrences of $\bar{\beta}$ that are introduced by this transformation are bound by the occurrence of the quantifier in the selected occurrence of the quantified phrase.

Suppose A is a predicate, intermediate quantificational expression, or an intermediate conditional expression. And suppose A represents $\rho_1, \ldots, \rho_r$ as ψ. Let ρ_j be the arbitrary individual satisfying ϕ which corresponds to the selected occurrence of $a\phi\beta$ or $\iota\phi\beta$. Let ρ_k be the arbitrary individual which corresponds to the free occurrences of γ_i. Then A' represents $\rho_1, \ldots, \rho_{k-1}, \rho_j, \rho_{k+1}, \ldots, \rho_r$ as ψ. Let A be suited to depict s-tuples, in which the uth position answers to the selected occurrence of $a\phi\beta$ or $\iota\phi\beta$, and the vth position answers to the free occurrences of γ_i. Then A' depicts those s-tuples $< d_1, \ldots, d_s >$ which are depicted by A, in which $d_u = d_v$. The vth position in these s-tuples answers to the occurrences of $\overline{\beta}$ introduced by this transformation.

Let $f(A) = V$. Then $f(A') = V' = \{< d_1, \ldots, d_s > \mid < d_1, \ldots, d_s > \in V \text{ and } d_u = d_v\}$.

Consider this sentence of $\overline{\mathcal{L}}$: $[[aMx\ K\ aBy] \supset [\overline{x}\ A\ \overline{y}]]$. ("If a man knows a ballerina, then he admires her.") This can be used to perform an act like the following:

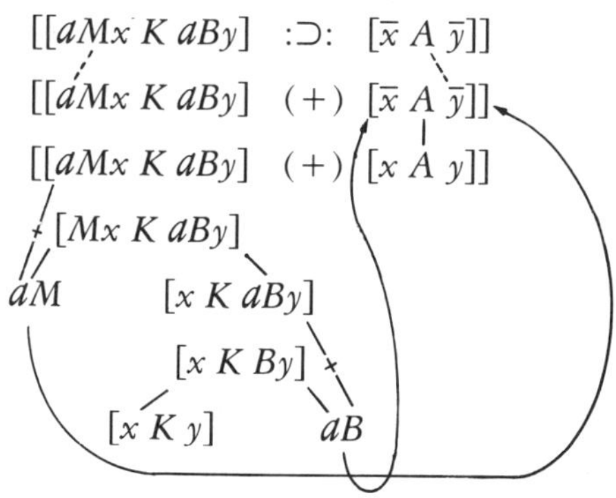

The last intermediate act is correct iff for any pair $< d, e >$ depicted by '$[aMx\ K\ aBy]$,' there is a pair $< m, n >$ such that $< d, e, m, n >$ is depicted by '$[[aMx\ K\ aBy]\ (+)\ [\overline{x}\ A\ \overline{y}]]$.' But in this case, m must $= d$, n must $= e$. So the conditional sentence is true if for any pair $< d, e >$ such that d is a man, e is a ballerina, and d knows e, the intermediate expression '$[[aMx\ K\ aBy]\ (+)\ [\overline{x}\ A\ \overline{y}]]$' depicts $< d, e, d\ e >$. It is not difficult to determine that the following sentence has the same truth conditions as the above conditional sentence: $[\Lambda\ (Mx \ni [x\ K\ aBy])\ A\ \overline{y}]$.

9. Speech Act Structures

Now that we have given a thorough account of the transformations of $\overline{\mathcal{L}}$ and the speech act structures associated with them, it is possible to raise some questions about the value of the present approach. It might be argued that a language can be adequately described in a way that is independent of intentional acts. A language can only be "realized," or employed, through the medium of linguistic acts. But linguistic acts are merely the vessels into which language is poured. We can see the difference between a language with its features and acts with their features in the phenomena where a single expression is employed in different acts with different structures, and where a single transformation is realized by acts having different structures. Expressions and possibly transformations are linguistic; intentional acts are something else. But if language is independent of intentional acts and their features, then theories of syntax and semantics should be formulated in linguistic terms, not in terms of speech acts.

No one can seriously suppose that a language containing words, phrases, and sentences exists prior to the linguistic acts that employ the language. But someone might think that nonlinguistic abstract entities like concepts and propositions are prior to linguistic acts. In such a view, concepts and propositions have features of their own; propositions have structures. Since there are more abstract entities, and kinds of them, than there are kinds of acts, different kinds of entities may be expressed by one kind of act or act structure. This is no reason to think the entities have an important feature in common. It may also happen that one abstract item gets expressed by different kinds of act. The same concept, for example, might be expressed by a verb, a noun, and an adjective.

Someone who holds that such abstract entities are prior to and independent of linguistic acts can attack the claim that there is an important connection between the three kinds of adjectives and the three fundamental structural relations. No one can deny that there is a nice "fit" between the two triples. But in the view being considered, the three relations don't explain the three kinds of adjectives. (Neither do the adjectives explain the relations.) It is simply a convenient coincidence that there are three relations to express the three kinds of concepts that correspond to adjectives. The proponent of these abstract entities can even admit that, if the relation between an enabling and an enabled act was not available to adjectives, we would be unable to employ radical adjectives. The loss of one of the other fundamental relations would leave us with all three kinds of adjectives. Some abstract items may require certain kinds of acts for their expression; in many cases, the connection between abstract entity and act (or act structure) is arbitrary.

The abstract-entities-first proponent can also deny that differences in emphasis are a special case of the same general phenomena as differences in syntactic structure. It can be admitted that different act structures serve to express different syntactic structures, and provide different emphases to acts of using a single expression. But the fact that one feature of acts is used to convey two features of language is no reason to think the linguistic features are basically the same. In fact, syntactic structure can be identified by means of transformations. But one transformation can be realized by a variety of act structures—these provide different emphases for expressions with the same syntactic structure.

I believe that no one can take seriously the claim that languages are prior to and independent of intentional acts. And I am not sympathetic to the view that abstract items like concepts and propositions are prior to and independent of linguistic acts. I believe the abstract items are simply postulated. They are intended but fail to provide explanations for language and various linguistic phenomena (including intentional phenomena), because they are simply abstract versions of the linguistic items they are alleged to explain. When the linguistic items are explained by abstract versions of themselves, the abstract items are left in need of explanation.

My view is that linguistic acts are the fundamental linguistic reality. We don't use these acts to realize or express an independent language, or to express prior abstract entities. We do use linguistic acts to represent, and to perform a variety of other tasks. Linguistic expressions are instruments which find their meanings in linguistic acts.

There are only three fundamental structural relations. These are exemplified by acts which have a much greater variety than that provided by relations and structures. Very different acts can exemplify the same structures. In some cases the similarity of structures may not be important to us. There is nothing about this situation that is peculiar to linguistic acts. An act of fastening two boards together may enable a further constructive act, and an act of turning on lights may enable an act of reading. The constructing situation has not got much in common with the reading situation. But the structural similarity is real; in some cases it might be important.

When different acts, or act structures, are used to express the same concept, the different acts (structures) are used to perform the same task. There is nothing specially linguistic about this situation either. Consider the act or activity of fastening two boards together. A great variety of component acts and act structures are possible. We can use glue, or screws, or nails. Even with nails, there are many different ways to proceed. No one would postulate an abstract item—fastening two boards together—and attribute to it a status prior to and independent of the various acts. In this case, the fastening is the purpose or goal of the constructive acts. There is a sense in which its purpose or goal is prior to an act; but it is not independent of the act. Apart from the case where different acts have the same goal is the case where different acts are of the same general kind, but not the same specific kind. Two acts may be representing acts, but represent differently. Two very different acts might both be acts of splashing water. Being able to bring them under a general heading does not show that the general heading or its feature is prior to and independent of the acts.

Consider the connection between the three fundamental structural relations and the three kinds of adjectives. Do the three relations explain the three kinds of adjectives? It seems odd to speak of an explanation in this case. It is as if someone asked whether the fact that triangles have three angles explains the fact that they have three sides. The two facts are very nearly the same fact. Even if they aren't quite the same (who can count facts?), they are close enough that talk about explanation seems out of place. An adjective of one kind is constituted an adjective of that kind by the structure of a typical act of using the adjective. Besides the typical structure of an adjectival act, an adjective associated with a higher structure can also be used in acts exemplifying lower structures. The typical act of using 'round barn' has this structure:

```
   round barn
     /    \
 round     barn
```

The phrase can also be used in these ways:

```
(round +) barn        round: barn
                             :
          barn               barn
```

But the possibility of using the adjective in nontypical acts is determined by the typical use. When an adjective is used atypically, its representational meaning is derived from the representational meaning of the typical use.

The different classes of adjectives are constituted by the different structural relations that their typical uses exemplify, but they correspond to different kinds of features they are used to represent. Absolute adjectives represent objects which have an "independent and autonomous" feature. (They represent objects with the features, not the features.) In a noun phrase, the adjectives give a feature to the associated nominal act, so that the total act represents an object with the feature. (The noun phrase represents an object *with* a feature, *not* an object *as* having a feature.) A relative adjective doesn't represent on its own. It *merely* contributes a feature to the nominal act, so that that act represents an object with a "comparative" feature—as opposed to an independent and autonomous feature. A radical adjective, by itself, represents an object with a feature. This feature can only be understood with respect to objects of a kind. It is "parasitic" rather than independent and autonomous or comparative. The different features to which the different kinds of adjectives correspond may be abstract, but they are not quasi-linguistic like concepts and propositions. The different kinds of features don't explain the different kinds of adjectives, but they "call for" them.

Finally, let us consider whether the phenomenon of emphasis—which we might better call *giving prominence*—is a special case of the same general phenomena as the different syntactic structures of a single sentence. The answer must be "Yes." Syntactic structure *is* speech act structure; there is nothing more to it. But different specific structures can be instances of the same general structure. Syntactic structure is identified in terms of transformations; these are understood with respect to the typical acts which realize them. Different speech act structures associated with the same transformation are not considered to be different syntactic structures, but they are instances of the same phenomena that constitute those structures. When different specific structures are used to realize the same transformation with the same expressions, the different specific acts are of the same general kind.

Bibliography and References

1. Gottlob Frege. "On Sense and Reference," *Translations from the Philosophical Writings of Gottlob Frege*, pp. 56–78.
2. Bertrand Russell. "On Denoting," *Logic and Knowledge*, pp. 39–56.

Chapter 13
More Heuristic Models

1. The Cognitive Map

We have now developed a fairly detailed account of systems of language. Consisting of expressions and experiences, a system of language has a conceptual structure. It is organized by inferential relations and relations of analogy. A system of language is an example of what I call a heuristic model. Such a model is not a genuine entity, but we can better understand language and linguistic activity if we think of and talk about this model as if it were real. The reality behind it contains people who use language and have linguistic dispositions and skills. These people constitute a linguistic community which endures through time.

I will now describe a new heuristic model; in some respects it is an extension of the system of language. A person's *cognitive map* consists of those sentences which she is readily disposed to accept or reject, either as representing things as they are or as used to perform acts of taking linguistic acts to be this or that, together with the experiences she has and accepts. By limiting the cognitive map to one's ready dispositions, I am leaving out the sentences that would be accepted or rejected on the basis of considerable thought. But the concept of a ready disposition is vague. I cannot specify with any precision just how ready a person must be to accept a sentence in order for that sentence to belong to her cognitive map.

A cognitive map is constituted by the linguistic expressions of a person's knowledge and beliefs, together with her experience. I am calling this a map because a person uses it to deal with the world, to find her way around in the world. A cognitive map has two parts: The positive part consists in the sentences that are (would be) accepted and the experiences that are accepted. The negative part consists in the sentences that are rejected. It is also possible to reject an experience, as when we see that something looks blue but recognize that it isn't blue. In talking about the cognitive map we ordinarily focus on the positive part. But the negative part is essential to the map.

Jerrold Katz has sometimes suggested that we think of people as containing both a dictionary and an encyclopedia in their heads. The dictionary is roughly analogous to a system of language, and the encyclopedia to a cognitive map. But dictionaries and encyclopedias are misleading with respect to my heuristic models. Katz thinks of these (the two books in each person's head) as separate. In fact a system of language provides the framework for a cognitive map. It contains experiences, actual and possible, and expressions: sentences we accept and are disposed to accept, sentences we reject and are disposed to reject, and sentences which we are disposed neither to accept or reject. Like a filled-in, or actualized, portion of the system of language, the cognitive map contains sentences which belong to the propositional subsystem of language (it contains sentences which we would accept or reject as representing what is the case, or sentences which we can use to perform acts of taking to be that we would accept or reject). The cognitive map contains experiences we actually have and accept.

The knowledge and beliefs in the cognitive map should not be thought of as extralinguistic (Katz's model suggests this). The system of language is just a framework which a person must have certain knowledge to possess. This knowledge is not constitutive of the system; it belongs to the cognitive map, which contains both linguistic and extralinguistic knowledge and beliefs.

A person's cognitive map changes over time. She acquires new knowledge and beliefs. She has new experiences. She also forgets things and changes her mind. At a given time, the experience a person is having and accepts belongs to her cognitive map. The experience a person has just had (and accepted) has enough presence to belong to her cognitive map. But what about more remote past experiences? How can they be incorporated in the cognitive map? Past experiences are no longer being experienced. Nor can we be readily disposed to reexperience and accept them. We might say that past experiences are present in the form of memory, but this isn't very enlightening. It is more helpful to say that past experiences are available in the form of sentences about the past that a person is readily disposed to accept or reject, and in the form of images that a person is disposed to accept or reject as representing past experiences.

2. Supplemented Systems of Language

Even though the cognitive map is within the framework of the system of language, this map adds something to the system of language. (A person's cognitive map adds something to his system of language.) A *supplemented system of language* is a plain system of language together with (supplemented by) a cognitive map. (The system and the cognitive map must belong to the same person.)

The purely linguistic meaning of an expression is explained with respect to the plain system of language. The inferential meaning of the expression links the expression to other expressions and to experiences. These links are based on commitments to accept or reject which connect sentences containing the given expression to other sentences and experiences. The representational meaning of an expression is based on inferential links to expressions and experiences, on relations of analogy, and on the structure of the expression. Representational and inferential meaning come down to the place an expression occupies in the plain system of language. As well as occupying a place in the plain system of language, an expression occupies a place in a person's supplemented system of language.

It is possible that, for a given person, an expression might acquire an extralinguistic meaning that is as well entrenched as its linguistic meaning. Let us consider a far-fetched example. Suppose that John, in his dealings with mathematicians, has found them all to be devious. (I.e., all of the mathematicians whom John knows are devious.) Because of this, John has come to believe that every mathematician, without exception, is devious. As far as John is concerned, being devious is an essential feature of mathematicians. John's belief about mathematicians has the same status for John as other beliefs "incorporated" in his plain system of language. In such a case we can describe John's belief that mathematicians are devious as primarily inferential. While John is readily disposed to accept the sentence 'Mathematicians are devious,' the inferences he draws from being a mathematician to being devious require no supplemental premises. Once John learns that Nick is a mathematician, he distrusts Nick. The inference from 'Nick is a mathematician' to 'Nick is devious' is immediate. In terms of John's own practice, the move from 'Nick is a mathematician' to 'Nick is devious' has the same status as the move from the same premise to 'Nick studies abstract objects.' It is characteristic of knowledge which "transcribes" relations constituting the plain system of language that it is primarily inferential in this sense. However, John's understanding of 'mathematician' is not part of the purely linguistic meaning of the word, and he knows that it isn't. For his understanding is not shared by other members of the linguistic community. His understanding has the right status, for John, to constitute part of the linguistic meaning of 'mathematician.' If his understanding were common to other members of the linguistic community, it would be part of the meaning.

John's belief about mathematicians has a peculiar status. Like all his beliefs, it belongs to his cognitive map and his supplemented system of language. But this belief has some things in common with analytic beliefs (beliefs stated by analytic sentences). Analytic sentences "transcribe" features of the system of language. The sentence 'Anything that is blue is colored' is analytic—we can recognize the truth of this sentence on the basis of recognizing the inferential relations between 'blue' and 'colored.' While 'Any mathematician is devious' is not analytic, it is still a kind of "transcription" of John's inferential dispositions. This example gives us reason to amend the description given above of a supplemented system of language. A person's supplemented system of language is constituted by his plain system of language, by relations based on his other well entrenched inferential dispositions, and by his cognitive map.

An extralinguistic belief need not be so well entrenched in order to affect the way an expression is understood. So long as a person accepts or rejects sentence *A*, or is readily disposed to do so, his commitment relations between sentences will be affected. Suppose *A* and *B* together entail *C*, but that neither entails *C* on its own. If John accepts *A*, then his further acceptance of *B* will commit him to accepting *C*. For John, who has accepted *A* but hasn't made up his mind about *B* (or *C*), it is *B* that carries with it the commitment to accept *C*. In the plain system of language, we find plain semantic features like entailment and incompatibility. In the supplemented system I will speak of the enthymematic versions of the plain relations. For John, *B* enthymematically entails *C*. (Ordinarily, if *P* plainly entails *Q*, then *P* also enthymematically entails *Q*.) Every plain feature has an enthymematic counterpart, but there isn't much interest in some of them. For example, any sentence that a person is readily disposed to accept is enthymematically analytic for that person. The various meanings of an expression are to be explained with respect to the plain system or systems of language. I will not use the word 'meaning' in connection with a supplemented system of language. Instead

I will speak of the *import* or the *significance* that an expression has for a person, when I am concerned with the expression's place in a supplemented system of language. For John, the import of 'mathematician' is considerably different from the meaning of the word. (The meaning of a word is part, but only part, of its significance.)

When we consider the role of context in determining the significance of an expression, we are really concerned with the difference between a supplemented and a plain system of language. The context in which a sentence is uttered is part of the users' present experiences, or else the context involves extra-linguistic knowledge of present conditions. I can use 'he' to refer to a present person, where the pronoun has no linguistic antecedent, because our supplemented systems of language allow me to do this and my audience to understand me. Similarly, when a person in 1947 used 'the Pope' to refer to the then current pope, it required supplemented systems of language to identify the intended individual as Pius XII.

3. Purely Proper Names

The "bulk" of the significance of most expressions consists in their purely linguistic meanings. But it is possible to find expressions whose purely linguistic meanings are less important than their extralinguistic significance. It is even possible for a significant expression to have no purely linguistic meaning. This possibility is most often realized by names. A *purely proper name* is a name (proper noun) which has no purely linguistic meaning. Its whole significance is determined by the supplemental part of a supplemented system of language. Not all names are purely proper, but many are. I will construe individual constants in $\mathscr{L}$, $\overline{\mathscr{L}}$, and other extensions of $\mathscr{L}$ as purely proper names.

Purely proper names are genuine expressions of a language. They do possess some properly linguistic features. The fact that an expression is a proper name is a linguistic (grammatical) fact about the expression. It is a linguistic fact that a proper name is used to represent a specific individual. For a purely proper name, it is not a linguistic matter which specific individual is represented.

The individual represented by a purely proper name is ordinarily determined by a person's cognitive map. For Phil, a certain name may be used to represent an individual he has experienced. For George, the same name represents an individual he has not experienced, but that individual is related in specific ways to individuals he has experienced. The expression might name the mother of a person George knows or an individual that he has heard about or read about. (Hearing and reading are experiences.) For the person who uses a proper name and knows what he is doing, there must be some connection between the named individual and individuals he has experienced. The person who uses a name and knows what he is doing must be able to supply information which approximately identifies the named individual.

A person's knowledge and beliefs characterize his use of a purely proper name. People whose relevant knowledge and beliefs are different will use the same name in different ways. These people can succeed in labeling (or depicting) the same individual with a given name, so long as their relevant knowledge and beliefs are substantially correct. Purely proper names don't have meanings, because I am using 'meaning' in such a way that an expression's meaning is derived from a plain system of language. A purely proper name has an inferential significance and a representational significance. If I am told that Isaac Newton is buried in Westminster Abbey, I can infer that a great scientist is buried in Westminster Abbey. For one of my fundamental beliefs about Isaac Newton is that he was (is?) a great scientist. When an expression has a purely linguistic meaning, then, with respect to that meaning, its inferential meaning is prior to its representational meaning. The inferential and analogical links between the expression, other expressions, and experience enable us to represent with that expression. A predicate typically has a purely linguistic meaning. But purely proper names have no such meanings. It is conceivable for a purely proper name to have an inferential significance that is prior to its representational significance. We can make up a story about John and some purely proper name that is analogous to our story about John and 'mathematician.' But it is typical of purely proper names that their representational significance is primary. Their representing depends on extralinguistic knowledge and beliefs that don't have a primarily inferential status. To know how to take a purely proper name, we must situate the name on our cognitive map. We use a given name to represent the individual that is *A, B, C,* etc. Once we can represent that individual, our identifying knowledge of the individual supports inferences concerning that individual.

Let us compare the present view to some other views about purely proper names. (These are ordinarily described more simply as views about proper names. But in my terminology, a proper name might have a properly linguistic meaning. A purely proper name is a proper name which has no linguistic meaning.) Frege claimed that names have meanings, for otherwise he could not see how a given name gets tied to a specific individual. He did not recognize the distinction between a plain and a supplemented system of language, or between meaning and significance. Armed with that distinction, we can allow a purely proper name to have significance without meaning. This is sufficient to satisfy Frege's legitimate reasons for requiring names to have meanings. It avoids the problems that his own view encounters. (E.g., how is it that different people successfully use the same name, even though they don't understand it in the same way?)

John Stuart Mill claimed that purely proper names have no meanings. I have agreed with him about that, so long as we restrict 'meaning' to the properly linguistic. But Mill had nothing of interest to say about extralinguistic significance. Mill's account, like Frege's, is partially correct; it needs to be supplemented. Since the present view incorporates features essential to both Frege's and Mill's views, it is a kind of compromise position that holds the middle ground between the two extremes. This is exactly how John Searle describes his own view of proper names. Let us consider his view, to see if the present view is merely a disguised version of his.

Searle claims that names have meanings. But the meaning of a purely proper name is not like the meaning of some other kind of expression. Among those who hold that names have meanings, it is common to think that the meaning of a name is like a definite description—or that it is like the meaning of a definite description. Searle denies this. He holds that the meaning of a name is like a cluster, or group, of definite descriptions—or like a cluster of meanings of definite descriptions. The cluster is such that different elements of it serve to identify the same individual. Different people who are able to use the name can know different members of the cluster. Some members of the cluster can be mistaken; in that case, the remaining members outweigh the mistaken members, and they serve to correctly identify the named individual. Searle regards his view as a compromise because on the one hand he holds that names have meanings. And, on the other, he holds that the meanings of names are not like the meanings of other expressions. In Searle's view, the meaning of a name has a certain variability. This allows different people to know different things and still understand the name.

Searle doesn't clearly explain the status of the cluster of descriptions associated with a name. Is the association a matter of language, or could it be regarded as extralinguistic? Searle neither recognizes nor discusses the distinction between linguistic and extralinguistic associations. But he would apparently say that the association is a matter of language, for he holds that some sentences containing (purely proper) names are analytic, where their analyticity depends on specific elements of their clusters. (Not only is 'Aristotle was an individual' analytic, but so is 'Aristotle was a philosopher.') This view that the cluster of descriptions is associated with a name as a matter of language places Searle's view nearer to Frege's than to Mill's. Searle's view differs from my own not because it involves clusters—my view might be described in those terms—but because it fails to distinguish plain from supplemented systems of language. The cluster of identifying expressions is associated with a purely proper name by a supplemented system of language, not by a plain system. The fact that Searle seems unaware of the difference between these two systems makes it possible to consider the present view of names as an improved version of Searle's view.

Kripke has criticized Searle for confusing the meaning of a name with the way that the name's reference is fixed. We often use definite descriptions to fix the reference of a name. This doesn't give the meaning (or part of it) of a purely proper name, for purely proper names don't have meanings—at least, they don't have meanings that are adequate for identifying the named individual. We can see the difference between the meaning of a name and descriptions associated with a name when we reflect on the fact that all, or almost all, of the descriptions that a person associates with a name can be mistaken. But, in spite of this, the person can understand the name and use it to label the right individual. When we aren't introducing a name (and fixing its reference), we use identifying descriptions to explain to someone what we believe about the named individual. What links our use of the name to the right individual is a causal chain leading from the situation where the individual got its name to us. The individual was given its name in some fashion or other. The givers of the name "passed" the name along to others, who passed it to still others. When we use a name, we are exploiting the chain linking us to the author of the name. It is the chain that produces reference, regardless of whether we have correct identifying information about the named individual.

We can consider my view to be a variant of Searle's, once we locate his clusters in supplemented rather than plain systems of language. But in so far as Kripke is understood to be rejecting the view that there is a meaning (adequate to identify the individual) associated with a name as a matter of language, his view is also compatible with mine. For Kripke agrees that different people will associate different identifying information with a name, and that this is not "as a matter of language." But even though my variant of Searle's view is more nearly compatible with Kripke's view—or more nearly untouched by Kripke's criticisms, for

Kripke denies that he is presenting a theory of his own—there are still some differences. Mine and Kripke's view disagree about the way to describe certain errors. So long as people using names have the relevant true beliefs, and they use the names in a correct manner, there is no basis for preferring one view over the other. Consideration of various errors can help us to understand how the views differ, and whether one is more satisfactory than the other.

I will follow tradition in these matters, and make up different stories about Aristotle. Among the beliefs that educated people have about Aristotle are these: (i) Aristotle was a pupil of Plato; in fact, Aristotle was Plato's most outstanding pupil. (ii) Aristotle was the teacher of Alexander the Great. (iii) Aristotle was the person who wrote or was otherwise responsible for the works in philosophy that are attributed to Aristotle. (iv) Aristotle was the person who is historically and causally connected to our current use of the name 'Aristotle.' We may suppose that 'Aristotle' is a purely proper name, and that people use the above and other beliefs to determine who it is they are talking about in using 'Aristotle.'

(1) Our first story is that in ancient Athens there was a very stupid man named Aristotle. As a kind of joke, some of his more clever contemporaries began to attribute important intellectual achievements to Aristotle. In fact, this very stupid Aristotle never studied anything with anyone—certainly not with Plato. He never wrote or dictated any works in philosophy. He had no connection with Alexander the Great. And the various works in philosophy were due to a variety of authors. By a bizarre set of circumstances, the joke about Aristotle came to be taken seriously by subsequent generations, including our own. Given this story, what are to say about one of our contemporaries who makes a statement about Aristotle? Suppose she says, "Aristotle was a brilliant logician." Just who, in fact, is she talking about? In the present view, and Kripke's, she is mistaken. Searle would apparently say that she is not talking about anyone. For most of her beliefs about Aristotle are incorrect, which renders her statement empty. (I am not positive that Searle would say she is talking of no one, for he uses different Aristotle stories than I do. What I have heard Searle say is that Aristotle could not possibly turn out to be a fishmonger in New Jersey.) It is not yet clear how my variation on Searle's view should describe her error. But it seems that Kripke should hold that she is talking about the ancient idiot. For the idiot is the one who is historically, causally connected to our present use of 'Aristotle'—whether we know it or not.

Before we consider what is the right way to describe our friend's error, let us situate this problem within the present theoretical framework. We have characterized the problem as one of determining who our friend's remark is about. This is not sufficiently precise. There are different senses in which a sentence (a sentential act) can be about an individual. In talking about "aboutness," we might be concerned with an intentional relation like denoting or representing. We might also be concerned with a real relation like labeling or depicting. When someone uses a purely proper name to perform an act of individual-representing, the representing act performed is essentially determined by her knowledge and beliefs. For we can represent mythical, fictional, and impossible individuals as well as real ones. But when we ask about labeling and depicting we are concerned to know which individual in the world corresponds to an expression that is used—to the act of using that expression. Since we can represent Aristotle whether he is real or not, and the Aristotle we represent is the Aristotle of our beliefs, our problem does not concern representing. We are trying to determine who is labeled and depicted when our friend uses 'Aristotle.' Is the ancient Athenian idiot depicted, is no one depicted, or is there some third candidate?

Before we decide what to say about our first story we will consider some other stories. (2) This time, Aristotle did study with Plato and did write (or dictate) the philosophy, but he didn't teach Alexander. Someone else, not named Aristotle, taught Alexander. Now suppose that Professor H, an historian, says the following:

> Aristotle taught syllogistic logic to Alexander. This gave Alexander the desire to conquer the world.

Story (2) now subdivides into two stories. (2a) We tell Professor H the facts about Aristotle and Alexander. Professor H replies, "Well it doesn't matter. I am trying to explain Alexander's behavior. Whoever was his tutor taught him syllogistic logic. That let to Alexander's desire." (2b) This time, when we tell Professor H the facts, he replies, "That spoils my hypothesis. I thought the philosopher Aristotle would very likely have taught logic to Alexander. And that would explain Alexander's desire."

It is important to realize that in both stories, Professor H's original remarks involve a mistake. In one case, the mistake is aptly called a background error. In the other, the mistake is in the foreground. In story (2a), Professor H is most concerned with Alexander's tutor. He thinks Aristotle was that tutor, and this belief is false. In case (2a), Professor H is depicting Alexander's tutor. The significance of a purely proper name is determined by a person's beliefs about the named individual.

Some of these beliefs are more important than others. Some may be correct and others incorrect. The representing act is determined by all beliefs, whether correct or not. In the case of depicting (and labeling) some beliefs can override others. If an unimportant belief is wrong but the important beliefs are right, they determine which individual is depicted. The ranking of these beliefs is not fixed once and for all. A speaker's intentions on a given occasion can determine that, on this occasion, a particular belief is more important than another. As I am understanding story (2a), Professor H's belief that Aristotle taught Alexander is crucial for the occasion in question. Professor H thinks that Aristotle taught Alexander, but he is depicting whoever taught Alexander. The situation is different in (2b). In that story Professor H is depicting the philosopher Aristotle.

(3) Now let us change (2) so that Aristotle studied with Plato, wrote philosophy, and didn't teach Alexander. No one taught Alexander. He never had a tutor. Professor H makes the same remarks in this story as in (2). Since no one taught Alexander, Professor H can't be depicting whoever did. Let us suppose that, as in (2a), Professor H intended to depict whoever taught Alexander. It was of only incidental interest that that teacher was the philosopher Aristotle. Now we must decide who the professor depicted in using 'Aristotle.' In this case our choice seems underdetermined by the situation. We understand this situation well enough; our problem is to come up with a description of it. We have a choice between saying that the professor depicted no one, and saying that he depicted the philosopher Aristotle. It is to some extent arbitrary which choice we make, though I believe most people would find it most natural to say he depicted the philosopher.

When someone uses a purely proper name, three factors interact to determine what individual (if any) is depicted:

(i) The speaker's knowledge and beliefs.
(ii) The speaker's intentions on that occasion.
(iii) The way the world is.

When the speaker's knowledge and beliefs contain no mistakes, there is no problem in determining what individual is depicted. If some beliefs are mistaken, then the various factors must be weighed to determine who or what is depicted. It isn't conceivable that all of the speaker's beliefs are mistaken. And I'm not sure it makes sense to suppose that most of the speaker's beliefs can be mistaken, because I don't know how to count beliefs. Discussions of a speaker's beliefs about an individual he is trying to depict usually concentrate on beliefs that seem striking or interesting. Hardly anyone mentions the belief that there is a historic, causal chain linking the current use of a name to the bearer of the name. This is not because there is no such belief; it seems rather that the belief goes without saying. In weighing the factors to determine who or what a mistaken speaker is depicting, we don't have to consider the situation in which all his beliefs are wrong. We don't have to insist that he doesn't know who or what he is talking about. This doesn't mean we will always be able to determine which individual is being depicted. 'Depict' is a vague term. Cases can arise where there are reasons for saying that α is depicted and reasons for saying that β is depicted (or that nothing is depicted), but there is no basis for choosing between the alternatives. We could redefine 'depict' in such a case, but this solves the problem by making a decision, not by finding something out. There are many problem cases for which it isn't important that they be decided one way or another. One mistake underlying the Searle-Kripke dispute is the belief that the same analysis (the same weighting of factors) must be applied whenever a given speaker uses a given name. In fact, the intentions of a speaker on a given occasion are often crucial. (But even so, the world can defeat his intentions by failing to provide them with targets.)

In story (1), we haven't been given enough information to determine who our friend labeled. In story (1a), the speaker is a student of logic. She is concerned with the brilliance and the historical importance of the pseudo-Aristotle's logical writings. In this story, the speaker is not depicting the ancient Athenian idiot, she is instead depicting the author of the logical writings. In story (1b), the speaker is concerned with the author of all the philosophical writings. Her statement is motivated, not by considering the logical writings, but by considering the logical reasoning in all of the writings. In this story, there is no one person associated with the philosophy for her to depict. Here it is somewhat arbitrary whether we say that the speaker labeled the ancient idiot, or that she labeled no one. But I find it slightly more natural to follow Searle and say that she is not depicting anyone.

Kripke seems to have it in mind that the way a given purely proper name gets connected with a specific individual is through a historic, causal chain. Stated generally, this is certainly true. But the chain need not always take us back to an individual whose name was the source of the one we use. In the (1) story (stories), there are a variety of chains tying our 'Aristotle' to different people. The ancient idiot wouldn't have first claim to our attention.

4. More of the Same

A fictional or mythical individual can have a purely proper name. Such a name can't be used to depict, because only real individuals can be depicted. But fictional and mythical individuals have sufficient status that some sentences about them are true and others are false. We can use names to represent these individuals; the named individuals can be identified entirely by extralinguistic information. Both 'Sherlock Holmes' and 'James Bond' appear to be purely proper names.

It may not be clear why most names of fictional characters are purely proper. For if all the people who are in a position to use a name have the same knowledge and beliefs about the named individual, the common knowledge and beliefs should provide a meaning for the name. Remember John who believes that all mathematicians are devious. As far as John goes, being devious has the right status to be part of the meaning of 'mathematician.' If the rest of the language-using community agreed with John, being devious would be part of the meaning of 'mathematician.' With a fictional individual, the information needed to use and understand the individual's name is provided by the stories in which the individual figures. If the same character occurs in many stories, then readers of different stories may know different things about the individual. The knowledge and beliefs about the named individual would not be shared by all those in a position to use the name. But if a certain character figures in only one story, it seems that anyone who is able to use the name of that character will identify the character in the same way. Why doesn't that identifying knowledge constitute the meaning of the character's name? That the character figures in just one story doesn't guarantee that everyone who can use the name understands it in the same way. A reader might not finish the story, but still be able to use the character's name. That reader would not know the same things as a reader who had finished the story. Still another reader might start reading in the middle of the story, and learn who the character is without having read the passage in which the character is officially introduced. However, even if there is some "official" information shared by all those who are able to correctly use the name of the fictional character, this is not sufficient to make that information the linguistic meaning of the name. For a name to have a meaning, the shared beliefs must transcribe inferential relations in the system of language.

If a simple expression (i.e., an expression used to perform simple intentional acts) has a linguistic meaning, then its inferential meaning is prior to its representational meaning. The expression must belong to the plain system of language. It represents by virtue of its place in that system. The expression's relations to other expressions and to experience make the expression suitable for representing whatever it does represent. (A complex expression—one used to perform complex acts—has its meaning partly determined by its structure. The meaning of the complex is due to the meanings of its components and to its structure. With many complex expressions, it will not make clear sense to say that one of the inferential meaning and the representational meaning is prior to the other.) The inferential meaning of an expression or act of using the expression shows up in dispositions to perform certain acts, and in actual performances of these acts. If being ϕ entails being ψ, then a speaker who says that α is ϕ should be disposed to admit (to infer) that α is ψ. His disposition to accept the inference is activated by his claiming that α is ϕ. He should also be disposed to reject the sentence characterizing α as θ, if being θ is incompatible with being ϕ. A person might use ϕ without being aware of all its inferential connections—without having all of the appropriate dispositions. But the inferential meaning of a simple expression must come down to the inferential dispositions of the educated or other authoritative members of the linguistic community. (The inferential meaning of a complex expression may not be fully grounded in inferential dispositions. Combining the inferential meanings of the component expressions may be a difficult deductive task.) When a simple expression has a linguistic meaning, its inferential meaning is prior to its representational meaning. The inferential dispositions associated with that expression are dispositions to perform immediate inferences. The inference from [α ϕ] to [α ψ] does not depend on supplemental premises.

When a name is used to represent a specific individual, the act of using the name will activate inferential dispositions. This is true whether or not the name has a linguistic meaning. If it does have a linguistic meaning, then some of the inferential dispositions are associated with the system of language. The inferences which "discharge" these dispositions are immediate. If the language user also has extralinguistic knowledge and beliefs about the named individual, then using the name will also activate inferential dispositions not associated with the name's inferential meaning. These may be dispositions to make enthymematic inferences, since they depend on unstated supplemental premises. If a name has no linguistic meaning, the inferential dispositions activated by using the name will depend on extralinguistic knowledge and beliefs. The inferences may still be immediate. They might depend on knowledge not shared by the linguistic community. But this knowledge can be so well-entrenched for a particular person that she is disposed to make immediate inferences. Perhaps the speaker has extralinguistic knowledge that α and β are the same individual. She may be disposed to immediately infer that β is ϕ on hearing that α is ϕ. Or she may deeply believe that α is ψ. If her belief has an inferential status (i.e., her belief is now simply the transcription of her inferential dispositions), she can immediately infer that γ is ψ once she learns that γ is α. The inferential dispositions associated with a name need not be immediate. In that case they are dispositions to perform enthymematic inferences. The language user must recall what she knows and believes about the named individual before she can make the inferences. For a name to have an adequate linguistic meaning, there must be official information needed to use the name correctly. This information must be sufficient to identify the individual. And the information must have a primarily inferential status: sentences giving the information simply transcribe inferential connections (inferential dispositions). Most names of fictional characters do not have this status.

A name is associated with inferential dispositions. There is also another kind of disposition associated with the use of a name. I will call these *dispositions to identify*. They are dispositions to supply information about the named individual. This does not mean that the language user is disposed to supply information to her audience. She may intend to deceive her audience. She is disposed to supply the information, to come up with the information, for herself. Inferential dispositions are dispositions to make moves. The inferential moves may be associated with either the plain or the supplemented system of language. Identifying dispositions are dispositions to supply information. These are associated with a person's cognitive map. Even sentences which transcribe inferential connections belong to a cognitive map rather than the plain system of language, which contains expressions, including sentences, and experiences that are structured and related in various ways to constitute the system. The plain system of language contains sentences, but their acceptance or rejection is not a feature of the system—not even for those sentences which state essential features of the system.

When we use a name to represent a specific individual, our dispositions to identify are given more prominence than our inferential dispositions. The naming act "picks out," or represents, a specific individual. Doing this allows the individual to be characterized. The role of a naming act in the complex acts or enabled acts we have considered makes identification of the named individual the central concern. This is in contrast to predicative acts. When we represent an arbitrary individual as ϕ, we are not so interested in identifying ϕ's. We do have, and activate, such dispositions. But the role of predicative acts is to provide a character to individual acts—so that we can represent individuals as characterized. The characterizing is understood in terms of inferential connections. If a name has no meaning, its inferential connections are supported by (extralinguistic) knowledge and beliefs about the named individual. These are the "content" of dispositions to identify. Since dispositions to identify are more prominent than inferential dispositions in a naming act, it is natural for a name to have no meaning. (At least, to have no meaning sufficient to identify the named individual.) With a predicative act, where inferential dispositions are more prominent, it is natural for inferential meaning to be prior to representational meaning and representational significance. Much identifying information will simply transcribe inferential connections (dispositions).

If a name has a linguistic meaning, then some identifying information associated with the name simply transcribes inferential connections of the plain system of language. Certain inferences from sentences containing the name will be immediate, discharging dispositions associated with the linguistic meaning of the name. We would expect a name with a meaning to be used for more acts than acts of representing the named individual. We might use it as a predicate functor, or in predicates. If α has a meaning, it should be common to say of an individual that it is like α. We might also say of something else that it is an α. ("He's a Napoleon." "He's another Hitler.") A name with a meaning would easily be transformed into an adjective. (Satanic, Dionysian.) There is a range of names from the purely proper to the other extreme (totally improper?). A name might have a linguistic meaning that is not sufficient for identifying the named individual. To use the name to represent a specific individual, we must rely on extralinguistic information. Such a name would "authorize" immediate inferences to certain predicates. But no conjunction of predicates would support an immediate inference to the name. (E.g., there might be an immediate inference from 'That man is Socrates' or 'That man is like Socrates' to 'That man is wise.' But there would be no collection of properties or predicates whose possession or satisfaction would lead us to immediately infer that an individual is Socrates.) Some examples of names which are not now purely proper are the following: Santa Claus, Aphrodite, Earth, Satan.

It is common for names to have no meanings. This is not so common for predicate functors, nouns, and predicates, but it does happen. If a predicate has no meaning (or a meaning that is insufficient for determining its proper use), then extralinguistic information is needed to support the inferential connections (dispositions) associated with correct use of the predicate. This information (knowledge, beliefs) may have a primarily inferential status, or it may support enthymematic inferences. Since inferential dispositions are more prominent than identifying dispositions for a predicative act, we expect that at least some of the extralinguistic information will have a primarily inferential status. There might be a predicate which, to begin with, has no linguistic meaning, but after a time certain "official" information becomes needed to use the predicate correctly, and this information comes to have a primarily inferential status for those who understand and use the expression. When this happens, the predicate has acquired a linguistic meaning.

A predicate like '[is French]' is a candidate for one whose proper use depends on extralinguistic information. If 'France' were a purely proper name, then '[is French]' would have no linguistic meaning. Even in that case, it is likely that the belief that if a person is French then that person is from France would have a purely inferential status. The inference from 'Jean Pierre is French' to 'Jean Pierre is from France' would be immediate. It isn't now true that 'France' is a purely proper name, though I don't know whether the linguistic meaning of 'France' is sufficient to identify France. (I don't know whether 'France' is totally improper.) If it is sufficient, then '[is French]' has an (adequate) linguistic meaning.

There have been some claims that expressions for natural kinds (cats, dogs, oak trees) are like purely proper names. The theorists making these claims have not been working within the present framework. Translating their claims to our framework, the claims amount to this: either natural kind expressions have no purely linguistic meanings or else their meanings are not sufficient to determine what they represent. Either they have significance but not meanings, or their significance repairs the shortcomings of their meanings, and outweighs their meanings. This is highly unlikely. Expressions for familiar natural kinds are in most adults' vocabularies. It is to be expected that a person would immediately infer from something's being a cat that it is likely to hunt mice and birds. One doesn't first have to consult her internal encyclopedia's entry for cats to know that they will look a certain way and act in certain ways. If the significance of natural kind terms is primarily inferential, and the linguistic community agrees about this inferential significance, then this significance constitutes the linguistic meanings of natural kind expressions. The principal reason for trying to make natural kind expressions like purely proper names is that if these expressions have linguistic meanings, their meanings can incorporate factual errors. Such factual errors would allegedly prevent us from using language in the ways we actually do use language. One of Putnam's examples is supplied by the story in which cats are really Martian robots. If 'cat' has a meaning, then it is surely analytic that cats are mammals. In Putnam's story, the sentence 'Cats are mammals' would be both analytic and false. Again, if natural kind expressions have purely linguistic meanings, their inferential meanings serve to determine which individuals are depicted when we use the expressions. But even if cats are Martian robots, we have surely all along been using 'cat' to depict these robots.

In the present account of analyticity, nothing prevents an analytic sentence from being false. To understand how we can use a word like 'cat' to depict objects which don't satisfy the linguistic criteria associated with the word, we need only realize that 'criteria' is plural. A given expression will have more than one purely linguistic criterion for determining what it represents and depicts. Like criteria associated with names, these criteria are weighted; some are more important than others. There are many expressions which have other than purely verbal criteria. The criteria associated with familiar natural kind expressions include certain kinds of experiences. To be a cat, an animal must look a certain way, observably behave in certain ways, etc. The observable criteria associated with 'cat' outweigh the theoretical criteria. The Martian robots are still cats, even though they are very different from what we thought. (However, if cats are Martian robots, a person's intention on a given occasion when he uses 'cat' may prevent him from depicting those robots. He may be talking about whatever animals have the attributes theoretically associated with 'cat.')

5. Jobs

When someone uses an expression to perform a representing act, her act has both inferential and representational significance. If the expression has a linguistic meaning, its inferential meaning is prior to its representational meaning. But even when an expression has a linguistic meaning, extralinguistic knowledge and beliefs will affect acts of using the expression. The extralinguistic knowledge and beliefs show up in the inferential and identifying dispositions associated with acts of using the expression.

With a predicative act inferential dispositions are more prominent than identifying dispositions. A predicative act provides a character to acts it is combined with. In this act:

```
   [b D]
   /   \
  b   [x D]
```

the act of representing Bob is given the character *being combined with the act of representing an arbitrary individual as a doctor.* The individual act, with its character, represents Bob as a doctor. The character provided to the individual act is not simply the character *being combined with a certain inscription*. The character conferred by the predicative act is chiefly due to the inferential dispositions associated with this act. The relations tying the predicate to other expressions and to experience suit the predicate to represent an individual as a doctor rather than something else.

When a name is used to represent a specific individual, dispositions to identify are more prominent than inferential dispositions. This is true not just for acts of using a name, but for *nominal acts* in general. These acts include using a name to represent a specific individual or using a description to represent a specific individual. An act of using a predicate functor or common noun (noun phrase) to represent an arbitrary individual of a kind is also nominal if it isn't a predicative act. A nominal act picks out, represents, a specific individual or an individual of a kind. The dispositions to identify are dispositions to supply information about that individual or kind of individual. The role of a nominal act in a complex act is to be characterized—so that the specific individual or individual of a kind can be represented as this or that.

A person's linguistic acts are informed not just by the ability to use language, but also by the knowledge and beliefs incorporated in a person's cognitive map. If Jesse and Brian have different beliefs about dogs, then they perform specifically different kinds of acts when they use 'dog' to represent a dog. Two people with different knowledge and beliefs about Richard Nixon perform specifically different kinds of act when they use 'Richard Nixon' to represent Richard Nixon. Someone who uses an expression to perform a nominal or a predicative act uses the expression (an instrument) in a specific instrumental manner. These manners are what distinguish a person's use of 'dog' from her use of 'cat,' or her use of names for different people: Jesse uses 'dog' in one instrumental manner when he represents a dog; Brian uses 'dog' in a different instrumental manner.

Let us consider instrumental manners of using expressions more carefully, and ask just what they consist in. When we use an expression to represent, the structure of the representing act is an important feature of the manner in which the representing expression is used. We have already considered speech act structures in some detail. Apart from speech act structure, the key notion for understanding the instrumental manner of using a representing expression is *disposition*. If a speaker uses an expression and thinks about what she is doing (she is not parroting the expression, or reciting a rote formula), certain dispositions are *activated*. (These dispositions are brought nearer to being discharged.) The most important of these are inferential dispositions and identifying dispositions. The speaker must be ready to make and to admit certain inferences based on the expressions she uses. She must also be prepared to come up with information about the individuals she represents.

Consider a name, say 'Napoleon,' that Jean Pierre knows how to use. When he is not using the name or thinking about Napoleon, he has dispositions to identify Napoleon in such and such ways. To discharge these dispositions would require some effort on his part. He must give some thought to the matter, and try to recall what he knows and believes about Napoleon. When Jean Pierre uses the name 'Napoleon' in a thoughtful way, he is more nearly ready to supply identifying information, and *he is aware of being in this position*. The instrumental manner of using a representing expression involves the self-conscious activation of various dispositions to make inferences and supply information.

When Katherine uses an expression to denote or represent, the specific kind of act she performs depends on (1) the linguistic meaning of the expression, if it has one and Katherine knows it, and (2) her extralinguistic understanding, including the information she has about the represented individuals. Because of (2), different people won't very often perform the same specific kind of representing act. But Mary's representing act can be generically the same as Katherine's if the two acts are informed by the same linguistic meanings. The more beliefs Mary shares with Katherine about the represented items, the more similar will be their representing acts. Ordinarily, but not always, generically similar representing acts are sufficient to make communication possible, and to enable one person to report the beliefs and statements of someone else.

We saw earlier that the speaker's intentions on a given occasion can determine which individual he depicts. It is important to consider intentions with respect to real relations like labeling and depicting. It is not so important for denoting and representing—except for those intentions which define complex acts of representing. Which kind of representing act Katherine performs depends on all her beliefs (etc.), not just on the true ones. The speaker's intentions on a given occasion can determine that some beliefs are more important than others. This doesn't make two representing acts to be specifically different kinds; two acts of the same kind can have different purposes.

When a speaker uses a given expression to perform a representing act, which specific kind of act she performs depends on the expression she uses. Even if α and β are synonyms, an act of using α is specifically different from an act of using β. If the speaker thinks that α and γ represent the same individual or kind of individual, but the linguistic meaning of α is different from that of γ, the acts of using α and γ are specifically different. The two representing acts do not activate the same specific dispositions. When we consider the kind of denoting or representing act performed by someone with expression α, but abstract from the fact that α is used, and also abstract from whether an inferential or identifying disposition is based on linguistic meaning or extralinguistic information, we are considering what I shall call a denoting *job* or a representing *job*. If the speaker believes that ϕ's and ψ's coincide, then she uses the predicates [x ϕ] and [x ψ] to perform the same representing job and the same denoting job, even though neither of [α ϕ], [α ψ] entail the other. If Katherine uses 'dog' twice to represent an arbitrary dog, then she has used 'dog' twice to perform the same representing job. If Katherine mistakenly believes that dogs and canines coincide (that all dogs are canines and all canines are dogs), then she can also use 'canine' to perform this representing job. One person can use several expressions to perform the same representing or denoting job, but it is unusual when two people can perform the same representing or denoting job.

With a name there is no difference between representing and denoting. The denoting job that Jean Pierre performs with 'Napoleon' is the same as the representing job he performs with this expression. (If Jean Pierre believes that some other expression is also a name for Napoleon, then he can perform the same job with that expression that he can with 'Napoleon'.) In a simple nominal act, there is still no difference between representing and denoting. If [x ϕ] is an atomic predicate, then the denoting job performed with this predicate is *denoting an arbitrary* ϕ. If Jack believes that the ϕ's and ψ's coincide, then he performs the same denoting job with both [x ϕ] and [x ψ]. He also performs the same representing job with the two predicates. But the representing job is *representing an arbitrary individual as* ϕ (or *as* ψ). When some argument places are filled in a predicate, two predicates might be used to perform the same denoting job without performing the same representing job. Suppose '[x P]' means *x is a prince*, and we are understanding a prince to be a king's son. Let '[x K]' be *x is a king*, and '[x S y]' be *x is a son of y*. Then for anyone who understands them, '[x P]' and '[x S aK]' can be used to perform the same denoting job. But they cannot (at least, not by the deliberate language user) be used to perform the same representing job. For '[*x P*]' is used to represent (directly) an arbitrary individual as a prince; as so used, it does not represent indirectly. But '[*x S aK*]' will be used to directly represent an arbitrary individual as a king's son; it will either directly or indirectly represent an arbitrary king.

In modern times, logicians and philosophers have made many attempts to explain synonymy. These have not been successful, for a variety of reasons. One difficulty has been the absence of an adequate theoretical framework for conceiving of and investigating language. A second has been the belief that there is a single, well-defined concept of synonymy. In fact, there are several candidates for synonymy relations—there are several kinds of synonymy. Expressions which have the same inferential meaning are equivalent; equivalence is one kind of synonymy. Equivalent expressions need not have the same representational meaning but expressions with the same representational meaning will be equivalent. Having the same representational meaning is a second kind of synonymy. The predicates:

[*x P*] [*x S aK*]

are inferentially synonymous but not representationally synonymous. Once we consider representational meaning, we can distinguish various degrees, or kinds, or representational synonymy. Full representational synonymy between expressions requires that acts of using the expressions have the same structure, and that components also be representationally synonymous. Weaker synonymy relations can settle for less. As well as representational synonymy we could consider denotational synonymy, which would occur for two predicates if, as a matter of language, they denote the same thing or *n*-tuple. There is no end to the different synonymy relations we might consider, but we must have definite goals to achieve before we can decide which of those relations are the important ones.

As well as synonymy relations based on linguistic meanings, we can consider analogous relations based on significance—enthymematic synonymy relations. It seems odd to call such relations synonymy relations, but if we don't, a sentence which contains a purely proper name can't be synonymous to any sentence, not even to itself. This has become a serious problem for those who take propositions seriously. It leads philosophers like Plantinga to deny that there are purely proper names in my sense—and to invent rather preposterous meanings for what seem to be purely proper names. From the present perspective, a purely proper name hasn't got a linguistic meaning, and a sentence containing a purely proper name hasn't got a complete sentential, linguistic, meaning. But proper names are significant. So are sentences that contain them.

The problem of determining when two expression are used to perform the same, or approximately the same, denoting or referring job has not ordinarily been associated with synonymy. In recent philosophy it comes to the fore as the problems of accurately reporting someone's beliefs (hopes, desires, etc.), and of accurately paraphrasing someone's statements. Some of these problems can be solved by developing systems of modal logic, and getting clear about the scopes of modal operators. (Modal operators have scopes in systems of modal logic, but not in English.) Many problems cannot be solved this way. When another person makes mistakes that we don't, or we know things that he doesn't, we can find it difficult to report his beliefs or paraphrase his statements. It can even happen that there are no sentences we can use to do an adequate job—though we can both understand and explain what is going on. The failure so far to solve these problems is in considerable part due to the failure to understand how a person's knowledge and beliefs affect his linguistic acts, or how the same words, with the same meanings, can be used by different people to perform specifically different kinds of acts. Another source of difficulty is the failure to realize that in reporting someone else's beliefs, we often choose expressions that reflect our audience's knowledge and beliefs, rather than our subject's.

6. Referring

When we accept or reject a sentence, we commit ourselves to accepting or rejecting other sentences, to having or not having certain experiences. Even where we aren't using language (aren't performing linguistic acts), we are disposed to accept or reject various sentences, and we are committed to accepting or rejecting various sentences. When we use a name, we may be committed to the existence of the named object. This means that we are committed to accepting sentences which attribute existence to this object. (We will also be committed to rejecting other sentences, and, possibly, to having or not having various experiences.) Someone might be committed to the existence of an object without realizing it. Most of us are disposed to accept mathematical sentences which commit us to the existence of very large prime numbers that we know nothing about. When a person is committed to the existence of an object, and he is readily disposed to accept sentences which attribute existence to that object, I will say that he is *self-consciously committed* to the existence of that object (self-consciously committed to accepting the existence of that object). Self-conscious commitment is primarily a matter of dispositions. But if the occasion arises, these dispositions will be discharged. Ordinarily, when a person uses a name to represent an object whose existence he is self-consciously committed to accept, the person is not prepared to call into question the existence of the named individual. If he rejects a sentence which contains such a name, the sentence's shortcomings are not allowed to include the nonexistence of the named individual.

When a speaker uses a name for an object, and he is self-consciously committed to the existence of that object, his commitment may "show up" in dispositions to publicly accept sentences which attribute existence to the object. They need not always show up in this way. He might be considering a hypothetical situation in which the individual in question does not exist. Someone might suppose there were no planet Jupiter, to see what difference this would make to the orbits of the other planets. Or a religious believer in a group of nonbelievers might wish to pass himself off as a nonbeliever—he is disposed not to (publicly) accept sentences attributing existence to God. I need terminology to describe the situation in which a speaker is disposed to publicly accept sentences attributing existence to an object. It is not sufficient to be able to talk about self-conscious commitment. I will say that the speaker or other language user is *disposed to acknowledge* the existence of a certain object. A person who is self-consciously committed to the existence of a certain object may not be disposed to acknowledge the existence of that object. The opposite can also happen. A person might be disposed to acknowledge the existence of an object when he isn't self-consciously committed to the existence of that object. A nonbeliever may pass himself off as a religious believer, and be disposed to acknowledge the existence of God.

I have been speaking of existence in the real world. But someone can have analogous commitments and dispositions with respect to fictional and mythical individuals. As well as being committed to the existence of Chicago, I can be committed to a suitable fictional status for Sherlock Holmes. I *am* committed to his having such a status, but I deny any such status to Sherlock Holmes' wife. In what follows, I will speak of a self-conscious commitment to and of the disposition to acknowledge the existence *or other suitable status* of an individual.

When a person uses a name to represent an individual, and the person is disposed to acknowledge the existence or other suitable status of the named individual, then that person has performed a *referring* act. A referring act is one kind of linguistic act. But referring is also an intentional relation. For a speaker can refer to an individual whether the individual exists or not. A speaker might refer to Chicago. A speaker might also refer to Camelot, mistakenly believing Camelot to have been a real place. A speaker can refer to Sherlock Holmes, correctly believing him to be a fictional character, or he might think he is naming an individual with fictional status, when the individual does not have even that much status. The speaker might, for example, use 'Monica Holmes' to refer to the wife of Sherlock Holmes.

My use of 'refer' is at odds with the use or uses of other philosophers and theorists of language. There is not some one phenomenon, referring, about which we disagree. Instead we disagree about which real phenomenon deserves to be called referring. In recent philosophical writing, it is most common to use 'refer,' 'referring,' etc. for an act that involves audience participation (a consummated act in my terminology), and for a real relation linking the act (and the expression) to an individual in the world. If 'refer' is understood in that way, we cannot refer to an individual that doesn't exist. It is commonly held that a speaker who attempts to refer but doesn't succeed does not make any statement either; at the very least, anything he says about a nonexistent individual will fail to be true or false. I already have at my disposal the words 'label' and 'depict'; these indicate real relations between linguistic acts and objects in the world. I have no need of a real relation referring. More importantly, the problems and the phenomena that have been associated with referring as understood by other philosophers can be resolved and explained in terms of my kind of referring.

In using 'refer' as I do, I am continuing my practice of giving existing expressions new meanings. It is not only ordinary expressions and ordinary meanings that get changed. I also alter the technical meanings of expressions. The reason that I can't adopt standard terminology with standard meanings is that doing so would force me to "carve up" the phenomena being studied in a way I find unsatisfactory. I disagree with standard views as to what phenomena should be considered together and what should be considered separately. Technical terms with the meanings I assign them mark what I take to be the proper dividing lines—the "joints" of reality. For example, I don't find it helpful to focus on those referring acts where there is audience participation or where there is genuinely an external object. I give a similar account of cases where there is and cases where there isn't an external object.

The conventional philosophical understanding of 'refer' has a success requirement: the referent must exist. In the present understanding of 'refer,' there is also a success requirement. Using a name to represent a specific individual is not sufficient for referring. The language user must be disposed to acknowledge the existence or other suitable status of the referred-to individual. In English, there is no expression, gesture, or tone of voice which conventionally indicates that the speaker is referring. Referring is primarily a matter of dispositions. If the disposition to acknowledge is discharged, the speaker will actually assert that the individual in question exists. This makes clear that he is referring when he names the individual. There are also many kinds of things a speaker can say about an individual which will make it clear that the speaker believes the individual exists. Because a name is customarily used to refer, when someone uses a name, he is presumed to be referring. Only special provisos or special circumstances cancel this presumption.

A name is ordinarily used to refer. Whatever I say about, for example, Napoleon, I am not willing to consider it a possibility that he doesn't (didn't) exist. However, not every use of a name constitutes a referring act. Consider an imaginary country where there is an official list of names to be given to children. No child may be given a name not on the list. No two people can have the same name. The list is very long; there is no guarantee that all of its names will be used. Suppose 'Drimfilda' is on the list, but hasn't yet been used. Someone might say, "If Drimfilda is a boy, everyone will make fun of him." The speaker need not be disposed to acknowledge that someone will eventually be named Drimfilda. (And she is not mentioning the expression 'Drimfilda.') She is using 'Drimfilda' to represent Drimfilda, but she isn't referring to Drimfilda. Another case of using a name to represent but not refer would be the following. A friend might tell me, "You criticized Gregory Schum severely last night." And I could reply, "I never heard of Gregory Schum; I was talking about George Schumaker." My friend referred to Gregory Schum, but I did not. I merely represented (and denoted) Gregory Schum individually. A final example of a nonreferring use of a name is a case of using a name for a fictional character outside of a fictional context (a fiction-discussing context). I might correct someone's error by saying, "Sam Spade was never elected to public office in California." I have not referred to Sam Spade. To refer to an individual, I must be disposed to acknowledge that the individual has a status which is appropriate in the given context.

A sincere referring act is based on the belief that a certain individual exists, but it doesn't take much by way of belief to support a referring act. Suppose I hear someone talking about some person about whom I know nothing. I can start talking about that person too, and I can refer to him, for I have nothing against there being such an individual. I am willing to accept on the speaker's authority that the individual exists. In this case, my referring is parasitic on the speaker's referring. I can only identify the individual in question as the individual to whom the speaker was referring.

7. Referring With Other Expressions

A name is used to represent a specific individual. We can represent a specific individual when there is no such individual, because representing-a-specific-individual is one kind of representing act. Representing is not a real relation between expressions (acts) and extralinguistic items. A person can represent a specific individual when she believes the individual to have a certain status; she can believe that the individual is real, or fictional, or mythical. A person can also represent a specific individual when she doesn't believe that it has an appropriate status. If Carol corrects Ben's error by saying, "There is no Monica Holmes," she has used 'Monica Holmes' to perform an act of representing a specific individual, the individual who Ben thinks is married to Sherlock Holmes.

When a name is used to represent a specific individual, and the language user is disposed to acknowledge the existence or other suitable status of that individual, then the language user has performed a referring act. (For the act to count as referring, his disposition must be a ready disposition.) A name is not the only expression that can be used to represent a specific individual. Both indefinite and definite phrases can be used in this way. It is common for the representational significance of a name to be prior to its inferential significance. The name is used to represent an individual that is identified by what the language user knows and believes. The knowledge and beliefs support inferences involving the name. When an indefinite phrase is used to represent a specific individual, that phrase has an inferential meaning, but the inferential meaning is not sufficient to determine which individual is represented. The speaker's extralinguistic information will determine what individual he is representing. So an indefinite phrase used to represent a specific individual will have a representational significance which is prior to its inferential significance. With a definite phrase, either inferential meaning or representational significance may be prior, depending on what the language user knows and believes about what he uses the phrase for.

The most common use of a name or of an indefinite phrase used to represent a specific individual is the referring use. A speaker who uses an indefinite phrase to represent a specific individual must have something in mind which determines just which individual is represented. What he has in mind is presumably sufficient to commit him to the existence or other suitable status of the represented individual. And if he uses the indefinite phrase to represent a specific individual, then he is presumably disposed to acknowledge the existence or other suitable status of that individual. An indefinite phrase used to represent a specific individual is most commonly used to refer, but such a phrase might be used in a nonreferring way if the represented individual has a status, but not one suited to the context. If Don says, "Some vampire did not really terrorize London in the nineteenth century," he can be using 'some vampire' to represent a vampire in a particular movie. He is not referring to that vampire, because the context is a real-world one, and Don is not disposed to acknowledge the existence of the vampire. A definite phrase used to represent a specific individual can be used in both referring and nonreferring ways. If I (truly) say, "Jean Teissier is not the present king of France," I have used 'the present king of France' to represent the present king of France. But I am not disposed to acknowledge the existence of the present king of France.

$\mathscr{L}$ and $\overline{\mathscr{L}}$ are not suited to exploring the difference between the referring and nonreferring uses of names. For it is a constitutive principle of these languages that every individual constant labels (and depicts) a real individual. Our treatment of $\mathscr{L}$ and $\overline{\mathscr{L}}$ presupposes both that every use of a name is a referring use, and that the speaker's disposition to acknowledge the existence of the represented object is always correct—for every referring act performed with a name labels a real individual. To clarify the difference between referring and nonreferring uses of names, we need to consider another extension of $\mathscr{L}$.

The treatment of angular definite and indefinite phrases in $\overline{\mathscr{L}}$ is more satisfactory. Because these phrases don't always label individuals, the language user can perform referring and nonreferring acts with them. They allow the language user to refer, and be mistaken about the existence of the represented individual. However, even with angular phrases, $\overline{\mathscr{L}}$ is not well-suited for exploring referring. For in $\overline{\mathscr{L}}$ we have no way to determine whether or not an angular phrase is being used to refer.

8. Presupposition

At least two kinds of presupposition are important for understanding linguistic acts. These two kinds need to be disentangled from one another.

In the first sense, a propositional act which contains a noncancelled predicative representing act presupposes that the predicative representing is satisfied. (What is noncancelled is the representing of the predicative act.) For example, suppose that Rosemary asks "Who hit Laura?" She is told, "Bob hit Laura." The following represents a natural structure for the reply:

```
        Bob hit Laura.
        /           \
     Bob         x hit Laura
                  /        \
             x hit y       Laura
```

The component '*x* hit Laura' represents an arbitrary individual as hitting Laura. This representing is not cancelled in the propositional act. So the answer presupposes that something hit Laura. (The question also presupposes that someone hit Laura. I am not now concerned with that presupposition.)

We can compare the above act to an act represented by:

```
        Bob did not hit Laura.
        /                \
     Bob         x :did not: hit Laura
                      ¦
                 x hit Laura
                  /       \
          x hit y         Laura
```

In the course of performing this sentential act, the predicate '*x* hit Laura' is used to represent an arbitrary individual as hitting Laura. This representing is cancelled by the negation transformation. So the sentential act does not presuppose that something hit Laura.

I am not sure that it is desirable to use the word 'presupposition' for this first kind of presupposition. Given the present theory, with its terminology, we already have the resources to describe the situations in question. Radical operators, or radical transformations, cancel the representing of inputs to transformations. We can distinguish cases where representing is cancelled from cases where it isn't without speaking of presuppositions. If we call noncancelled representations presuppositions, we are only introducing additional terminology for what we can already describe without inconvenience. I will call the next kind of presupposition *existential presupposition*. To understand this, we must take another look at referring.

When someone uses a name to represent a specific individual, the specific individual is identified for the language user by her knowledge and beliefs. When she uses a name in a thoughtful way, the language user activates her dispositions to identify the named individual—these are dispositions to come up with identifying information. To determine which individual is labeled by a name used on a given occasion, we must consider the language user's knowledge and beliefs, her intentions, and the way the world is. Her intentions on the occasion in question determine how her knowledge and beliefs about the named individual are to be weighted. They determine which of her beliefs are on that occasion most important for identifying the named individual. In a general way, a person is committed to accepting those sentences she believes. In fact, dispositional belief is defined as the ready disposition to accept. A person is committed to accepting those sentences she is readily disposed to accept. She is committed to accepting the consequences of the sentences she is readily disposed to accept, though she may not realize that she is thus committed. A person's beliefs, her dispositions to accept, are weighted; she believes some things more strongly than others. However, the weighting of beliefs does not concern only their relative strengths. On a certain occasion, certain beliefs may be heavily weighted. This does not mean that they are believed more strongly on that occasion. A belief that is weighted heavily on a given occasion is one that is particularly important for a given project or purpose on that occasion, but a deeply held belief that is irrelevant to the given project will not be weighted heavily on that occasion. A belief which is not accepted with full confidence may be crucial for a given project or purpose. With respect to that project or purpose, the person does not consider the possibility that the belief is mistaken; she weights it heavily. An ancient mariner who believed, with some hesitation, that the Earth is round, might have undertaken the project of circumnavigating the Earth. The belief that the Earth is round would have been weighted heavily on that occasion, with respect to that project.

On an occasion where someone uses a name, certain beliefs about the named individual may be heavily weighted. Her using the name on that occasion strongly commits the language user to those beliefs. Because if the beliefs are incorrect, the use of the name is undermined. This situation can be illustrated by the earlier story about the historian who, concerned with Alexander the Great, talks about Aristotle. On that occasion, the belief that Aristotle taught Alexander is heavily weighted. I will say that the use of the name *carries with it* the commitment to the beliefs that are heavily weighted on that occasion. If those beliefs are mistaken, then so are the statements about the named individual. Suppose α names β, and our speaker is in a situation where her use of α carries with it a commitment to β's being ϕ. In such a situation, if the speaker were to use α to deny that β is ϕ, then she would have contradicted herself. The sentence $\sim[\alpha\ \phi]$ is not contradictory. It might be possible for someone to use this sentence to say something true. But sentences are not the primary bearers of truth and falsity; sentential acts are. Neither are sentences the primary bearers of contradiction. On the occasion described, the speaker's use of α in asserting $\sim[\alpha\ \phi]$ commits her to accepting $[\alpha\ \phi]$. She is not so committed by the inferential meanings of the expressions involved; it is her intentions on that occasion that commit her. Her act of asserting $\sim[\alpha\ \phi]$ is contradictory, but not obviously so as it would be if she asserted $[[\alpha\ \phi]\ \&\ \sim[\alpha\ \phi]]$.

When a speaker uses a name on a given occasion, the use of the name carries with it the commitment to certain beliefs about the named object. And when a speaker uses a name (or indefinite phrase or definite phrase) to refer, her use of the name carries with it the commitment to the existence of the named individual. Just as the use of a name activates dispositions to identify the named individual in various ways, so the referring use activates dispositions to acknowledge the existence of the named individual. The commitment to (publicly) accept the existence of the named individual is carried by the referring use of the name. So if α names β, and the speaker uses α to deny that β exists (or that β has whatever status is suitable), then her sentential act is contradictory. The sentence itself is not contradictory. It may be possible for someone to use that sentence to say what is true. But the speaker who uses α to refer, while denying that β exists, has performed a contradictory sentential act.

When a speaker uses a name or other expression to refer, then whatever she says *existentially presupposes* that the named object exists (or has whatever status is suitable). If the speaker uses a name to refer, and the named object does not exist, then the speaker is mistaken. The exact nature of her mistake needs to be determined. If we follow Frege, we would say that a sentence (sentential act) which contains a referring expression for which there is no referent is neither true nor false. Frege could not have known about the view presented here, and so did not develop his account within the present framework. But from our perspective we might describe Frege as holding that every serious use of a name or definite description is a referring use. A serious use is one where we are talking about the real world as opposed to fictional or mythical contexts. When α is used to refer, but there is no real individual labeled by α, then a sentence [α ϕ] causes certain problems. The sentence cannot be true. But if it is false, then its denial should be true. If we use ~[α ϕ] for the denial, and α is still used to refer, this sentence cannot be true either. Frege thought it essential that every sentence have a denial, and that if either the sentence or its denial is true or false, then the other member of the pair has the opposite value. Because of this, he held that a sentence with an unsatisfied existential presupposition is neither true nor false. We might give up the belief that every sentence has a denial, or that a sentence and its denial have opposite values, if they have any values. Or we might give up the belief that ~[α ϕ] is the denial of [α ϕ]. Frege did not consider the first two possibilities. He did consider the third; but he regarded as absurd the proposal that the denial of [α ϕ] is: Either ~[α ϕ] or 'α' does not label any individual.

To know whether Frege is right, we must determine what is the right or the best way to understand a negating expression. A negating expression is sometimes used to perform an illocutionary act of rejection, but this use is not important to the issue under consideration. Just as we can reject a sentence we believe to be false, so we can also reject a sentence we believe to be neither true nor false. We want to understand the use of '~' when ~*A* is used to perform a propositional act. We have previously analyzed such an act as having the following structure:

~: *A*
⋮
A

The negating expression '~' is used to take the sentential act to be false. So now the question we need to answer is this: What is it for a sentence (sentential act) to be false? Historically, considerable attention has been given to the question of what truth consists in—whether this is correspondence to reality or something else. Different versions of a correspondence theory and alternatives to correspondence theories have been developed. So far as I know, there are no analogous discussions of falsity, and what it consists in. The absence of such discussions is puzzling. The problem is important, and the answer is not obvious. Many people probably think the answer *is* obvious: A sentence of the right sort (for which questions of truth and falsity are appropriate) is false just in case it isn't true. This answer has two drawbacks: (1) It renders unintelligible discussions of whether there are significant sentences (of the right sort) which are neither true nor false. (2) It has the effect of taking negation to be more fundamental than falsity.

If a false sentence is one that isn't true, then if α is used to refer but labels nothing, both [α ϕ] and ~[α ϕ] will be false. So if a false sentence is one that isn't true, Frege's view about sentences with unsatisfied existential presuppositions is mistaken. This, by itself, is not a terrible consequence. We are trying to determine *if* Frege is right. We haven't determined *that* he is. However, if a false sentence is one that isn't true, then the proposal that some sentences of the right sort are neither true nor false is unintelligible. A person who makes such a proposal is simply confused about the concept of falsity (he doesn't have an adequate grasp of the concept). For anyone who understands what falsity is, the proposal that some suitable sentences are neither true nor false makes no sense. However, discussions of this issue don't seem to be unintelligible. (Though no proponent of the view that some sentences are neither true nor false has explained what falsity is.)

If we explain what it is for a sentence to be false by saying that a sentence is false if it is not true, then we are using negation ('not') to explain falsity. This appears to be a reductive definition. Falsity is reduced to negation and truth. Sometimes we explain an expression in an artificial language by means of an expression in the metalanguage. We might, for example, explain '&' in $\mathcal{L}$ by means of 'and' in English. This is not a reductive explanation; we are explaining one *and* by another. This might be a sign that we are taking conjunction as a fundamental concept. When we explain falsity by means of negation, we are not regarding falsity as fundamental. We do seem to be regarding negation as fundamental. Accounts taking negation as fundamental in this way must provide some objective counterpart to negative expressions. Such accounts are typically driven to admit negative extralinguistic items of some sort. The negative items might be negative facts or states of affairs. They might also be negative properties like that of *not being blue*.

I find it implausible that there are negative extralinguistic items. Negative properties have some suitable status, but I find implausible that they are fundamental and irreducible. Since I also find it intelligible that a significant sentence might be neither true nor false, I need a different understanding of falsity. My conception comes to this: A sentence is false if, and only if, it is incompatible with true sentences. This makes incompatibility a fundamental relation; the new conception also requires that people be able to recognize some cases of incompatibility. These don't seem to be problems. There is nothing objectionable about an incompatibility which is fundamental and irreducible. Incompatibility links linguistic items (linguistic acts). Recognizing it as fundamental does not commit us to accepting extralinguistic items like negative facts, states of affairs, or fundamental, irreducible, negative properties. Truth and incompatibility are more fundamental than falsity. But negation is explained in terms of falsity. When we negate a sentence, we *mean* that the sentence is false.

We can extend this account of falsity to hold that a sentence is false if it either is incompatible with true sentences or is quasi-incompatible with correct (propositional) experiences—or with a combination of sentences and experiences. (A limited language might lack the resources to adequately describe certain experiences. A sentence might be quasi-incompatible with an experience when the sentence is not incompatible with any sentence—of the language—describing the experience.) In the present conception, the truth of sentences representing "situations" in the world is absolute. Their truth depends on the world's being as represented. But falsity is relative to a language (or to a system of language, which includes experience). The truth of some sentences which are used to perform acts of taking other acts to be this or that can also be relative to a language. (Just as the falsity of A is relative to language L, so the truth of $\sim A$ will be relative to L.) We might have a sentence A in a language L which isn't true. But L possesses no true sentences with which A is incompatible. So, in L, A is neither true nor false. But there might be an extension L^+ of L which contains true sentences with which A is incompatible. In L, sentence A is neither true nor false; in L^+, A is false.

Suppose α is a name occurring in sentence A, α is used to represent β, and β does not exist. Suppose someone uses A, and in using A, refers with α. This use of A commits the speaker to accepting the sentence 'α exists.' The commitment is not a matter of language, but depends on the speaker's intentions and dispositions in using α. But entailment has been defined in terms of commitment, so the speaker's use of A entails the sentence 'α exists.' There are presumably true sentences which are incompatible with 'α exists.' This means that there are true sentences which are incompatible with the speaker's act of using A. So his act of using A is false. But for the same reasons, an act of using $\sim A$ (or 'It is false that A') will be false—so long as α is used to refer. *The commitment carried with a referring act overrides anything that is said in the sentence.* This phenomenon reveals an essential limitation on negating expressions. *When a language contains referring expressions which do not label any individuals, there cannot be an expression '$\sim$' such that $\sim A$ is true whenever A is false.* (Some paradoxical sentences are like sentences that contain referring expressions. A paradoxical sentence A and its negation $\sim A$ can both be false.)

When a referring act is performed in the course of using sentence A, but the referring act does not label, then the sentential act performed with *A* will be false. An act performed with ~ *A* will also be false, if the component expression is still used to refer. In this case the speaker's act is false, but he cannot truly say so. However, we can say so, and truly. For we can use ~ *A* to deny his sentential act, but without ourselves performing the referring act. We can further explain his error by saying 'α does not exist'—again, without performing a referring act. The limitation on negating expressions does not prevent us from understanding what is going on, or from saying what we want to say.

When we use an expression to represent a specific individual, and are disposed to acknowledge that the individual exists, we have performed a referring act. We can also use a predicate functor or common noun in a situation where we are (readily) disposed to acknowledge the existence of appropriate objects. We can use, and normally do use, the expressions:

any man
some girl
every child
no dog

in such a way that our use carries commitments to there being men, girls, children, and dogs. These are additional cases of existential presupposition.

Bibliography and References

1. Gottlob Frege. "On Sense and Reference."
2. Jerrold Katz. *Propositional Structure and Illocutionary Force, A Study of the Contribution of Sentence Meaning to Speech Acts.*
3. Saul A. Kripke, "Naming and Necessity."
4. Alvin Plantinga. "The Boethian Compromise," *American Philosophical Quarterly* 15 (1978): pp. 129–138.
5. Hilary Putnam. "It Ain't Necessarily So," *Readings in the Philosophy of Language*, edited by Jay F. Rosenberg and Charles Travis, pp. 52–62. Englewood Cliffs, New Jersey: Prentice-Hall, Inc., 1971.
6. John R. Searle. *Speech Acts, An Essay in the Philosophy of Language.*

Chapter 14
The Language ($(\mathscr{L})$)

1. Some Differences Between Referring and Nonreferring Uses

Because the language $(\mathscr{L})$ is not a further development of $\overline{\mathscr{L}}$, we will in $(\mathscr{L})$ drop the unique quantifier and overlined variables that were introduced in $\overline{\mathscr{L}}$. But to get $(\mathscr{L})$, we are not returning to $\mathscr{L}$ and starting over. We can regard the language $(\mathscr{L})$ as being obtained from a sublanguage of $\overline{\mathscr{L}}$. Most transformations that were developed for $\overline{\mathscr{L}}$ are retained for $(\mathscr{L})$. These require some changes. We must drop the various clauses which involve extended scopes and overlined variables and make other changes that will be noted later. As well as the statements of the transformations, we will retain the accounts given of representational meaning, depicting, and speech act structure.

When $\mathscr{L}$ was first presented, a variable transformation was given. No speech act structure is associated with this transformation; it introduces a notational change which does not involve speech acts. The variable in the input which is replaced in the output is not spoken or written by the language user. Such variables are a convenience for describing syntactic structure, not for using the language. The variable transformation will be retained for describing the syntax of $\overline{\mathscr{L}}$ and $(\mathscr{L})$. It has no semantic effects. The transformations of $\overline{\mathscr{L}}$ that are more-or-less the same for $(\mathscr{L})$ are:

the variable transformation
the reflexive transformation

the connective transformations
the quantifier transformations
the passive voice transformation
the relative clause transformation

The language ($\mathcal{L}$) is being developed so that we can get a better understanding of existential presupposition. We want to use ($\mathcal{L}$) to investigate referring, and to determine just what are the differences between an act of using an expression to refer, and an act of using that expression to represent a specific individual without referring to an individual. With respect to individual constants, in ($\mathcal{L}$) we must allow individual constants which don't label individuals and introduce some notation to distinguish referring from nonreferring uses. If α is an individual constant, the sign that α is used to refer will be our enclosing α in parentheses: (α). An *enclosed constant* is only used to refer; an unenclosed constant is not used to refer. Similarly, *enclosed angular phrases* are referring expressions: $(< a\phi >_m)$, $(< \iota\phi >)$. *Any indexing variables go outside the parentheses:* $(\alpha)_\beta$ $(< a\phi >_m)\beta$, $(< \iota\phi >)\beta$.

The referring and nonreferring uses of a name are two different kinds of act. These different kinds of act are not marked notationally in English. To study the difference between these two kinds of act, we have introduced a notational distinction in ($\mathcal{L}$). When someone uses ($\mathcal{L}$), her act of using an enclosed constant (α) is not a complex act. We don't have one act of using α, and a distinct act of using the parentheses. Similarly, the act of using the parentheses is not a distinct act in an act of using an enclosed angular phrase. However, the act of using (α) is an act with a special character. When a language user uses either α or (α), she is using the expression to represent a specific individual. Her act of using (α) to represent a specific individual has a special character provided by the parentheses. (When one act has a special character, it doesn't always take a distinct act to give this character. Victor's act of turning the radio on softly had a special character not provided by a distinct act.) The special character indicates that the writer (speaker) is disposed to acknowledge the existence of the individual labeled by the enclosed expression.

When a speaker or writer addresses an audience, the speaker (writer) performs linguistic acts. If her audience understands her, the audience performs similar acts with her expressions. But when the writer uses (α) to refer, her audience may not be disposed to acknowledge the existence of an individual labeled by α. How can the audience use the writer's expression to understand the writer, if the audience is unwilling to accept the commitments that go with using (α)? This is not a serious problem.

Suppose a speaker says, "I assert *A*," where 'I assert' is used to accept the sentential act *A*—i.e., his act has this structure:

$$\begin{array}{rl} \text{I assert:} & A \\ & \vdots \\ & A \end{array}$$

The audience can understand the speaker without accepting *A*. The speaker and his audience use *A* to perform the same kind of sentential act. For the speaker, this sentential act enables the illocutionary act performed with the prefix. (Different act structures are possible for 'I assert *A*' than the one shown here.) The audience might even use the prefix to perform an act with this structure:

$$\begin{array}{rl} \text{I assert:} & A \\ & \vdots \\ & A \end{array}$$

But the audience is not asserting or accepting *A*. The audience is using the prefix to take *A* to be asserted (and accepted) by the speaker. The audience accepts its own act of taking to be without accepting *A*. Similarly, when the writer uses (α) to refer, her audience can use (α) to represent a specific individual. The audience also takes (and accepts this) the speaker to be disposed to acknowledge the existence of the individual α labels. The enclosing parentheses only carry a commitment for the language producer, not for her audience.

If the distinction between referring and nonreferring names is to have any point, we must allow names that don't label. This changes the kind of interpreting functions we deal with in the set-theoretic account. An interpreting function of f of ($\mathcal{L}$) for $\mathcal{D}$ will assign individuals in $\mathcal{D}$ to 0 or more of the individual constants of ($\mathcal{L}$). If a constant α does not depict an individual, then α is an *empty name*. No change is needed in the treatment of angular indefinite phrases. Even in $\overline{\mathcal{L}}$ it was possible for a phrase $< a\phi >_m$ to have no individual (or n-tuple) assigned to it. If α is a constant and is assigned value ρ by f, we will write '$f(\alpha) = \rho$' to indicate this. The parentheses around α "come with" 'f'. If, instead, we wish to consider the value that f assigns to (α)—which will be the same as the value assigned to α—we will write: $f[(\alpha)] = \rho$. Since names don't have to depict (label), it is no longer necessary to restrict our attention to nonempty domains. For ($\mathcal{L}$), the domain $\mathcal{D}$ may be empty or nonempty.

Now that we have empty names in ($\mathcal{L}$), it is important to understand that we are not dealing with fictional or mythical individuals. That subject is too complicated for the present book. If a name has no individual assigned to it, we must not regard it as the name of a fictional or mythical individual. The situation is instead like the imaginary country which contains an official list of names to be given to children. All names must be chosen from the list, but there is no requirement that all names on the list be used. A sentence which contains an empty name is like a sentence which contains a name that is never chosen.

Now let us consider the differences between a sentence containing α and a similar sentence containing (α). Suppose we have two sentences: $[\alpha\ \phi]$, $[(\alpha)\ \phi]$. If α labels some individual, these two sentences should have the same value. They are both true if α's individual is ϕ. They are false if α's individual isn't ϕ. Suppose α is an empty name. Any sentence which contains (α) presupposes that α labels a real individual. So any sentence which contains (α) will be false. $[(\alpha)\ \phi]$ will be false. But what about $[\alpha\ \phi]$? Could such a sentence be true when α is empty?

Suppose that $[x\ \phi]$ means something like *x is unreal.* We want to know if $[\alpha\ \phi]$ will be true when α is empty. It can be misleading in this case to consult our "intuitions" about corresponding English sentences. Sentences like:

(1) Dracula is unreal.
(2) Dracula does not exist.
(3) Dracula is fictitious.

are all legitimate. They are all true. But these sentences are about an individual who has a certain status—a fictional, possibly a mythical, status. Sentences (1) and (2) deny that Dracula, who has some status, has the status of a real object. The third sentence assigns Dracula his correct status. The situation with these sentences is analogous to a situation where we say of some object which *is* yellow that it isn't blue. A colored object might be yellow, or blue, or green, etc. An object which has some status or other might be real, or fictitious, or mythical, etc. (The fictitious and mythical could be further subdivided.) It can be true of an individual with one status that it hasn't got some other. It can't be true of any individual that it has no status at all—having no status is a contradictory status. However, not much is required to give an individual some status. A fictional individual gets its status by someone's telling a story. (I hope that no one expected me to locate fictional individuals in possible worlds.) In making up examples of mistakes of various kinds, I have been telling stories. When I told a story about a person who mistakenly thought Sherlock Holmes' wife is named Monica, I gave that person a status. We can talk about him, refer to him. That person had in mind a story in which Sherlock Holmes was married, to Monica. His story gives a status to Monica Holmes, so that we can even refer to her. But we must not confuse her status with the Conan Doyle-conferred status of Sherlock Holmes.

In ($\mathscr{L}$) we are not considering individuals which have a different status than real. An empty name does not represent or depict a fictitious or mythical individual. So in ($\mathscr{L}$), if [x ϕ] means *x is unreal*, this predicate can only be used to attribute a contradictory status to an individual. Regardless of whether α is empty, the sentence [α ϕ] will contradict every sentence. Since it will contradict every true sentence, it must be false. Regardless of what ϕ means, a predicate [x ϕ] will be used to represent an individual as something. It might represent an individual as something impossible, or as something an individual could be, but that nothing happens *to* be. Or it might represent an individual as something which some things really are. But in ($\mathscr{L}$), any individual which is something, must exist. A sentence [α ϕ] entails 'α exists'—i.e., [α T]. Since ($\mathscr{L}$) is not really a language that people use, we cannot investigate ($\mathscr{L}$) to determine if ($\mathscr{L}$) contains true sentences with which [α T] is incompatible when α is empty. We will simply stipulate that ($\mathscr{L}$) is sufficiently rich that any sentence [α ϕ] with an empty name α is false. This means that when α is empty, both [α ϕ] and [(α) ϕ] are false. The referring use of a name or of enclosed and unenclosed angular phrases doesn't seem to make much difference with a relatively simple sentence. In a sentence [α_1 ϕ α_2, . . . , α_n], the value will be unchanged if we replace α_i by (α_i). (Here each α_i is either a name or an angular phrase.)

With respect to truth and falsity, there is no difference between a sentence [α ϕ] and a sentence [(α) ϕ]. But we might wonder if it is appropriate to use [α ϕ]. If someone asserts [α ϕ], he is committed to the existence of α's individual, and this commitment is obvious. So in asserting [α ϕ], a language user is making the same commitment that can be made with [(α) ϕ]. But this sentence is the one designed for the job; the language user should have asserted [(α) ϕ]. However, there is a difference between [α ϕ] and [(α) ϕ] when they are components of larger sentences. There is also a difference between these two when they are *supposed* rather than asserted. Asserting a sentence is an illocutionary act; so is supposing a sentence (supposing that a sentence is true). Supposing [α ϕ] is different in important respects from supposing [(α) ϕ]. If we suppose [α ϕ], we are supposing both that α labels an individual and that that individual is ϕ (has ϕ's property). If our supposition leads to a contradiction, then we can reject [α ϕ]. We may want to deny that α's individual exists. If we suppose [(α) ϕ], we are not supposing that α labels an individual. Our referring act overrides our supposition. We are committing ourselves to the existence of α's individual; we are supposing that α's individual is ϕ. If this supposition leads to a contradiction, we will reject [(α) ϕ]. But we must not deny that α's individual exists. A referring act is similar in several respects to an illocutionary act. It carries the same kinds of commitments. But one illocutionary act cannot be "performed on" another. We cannot assert an assertion or a rejection. Although we can, of course, reject what someone else asserts, we cannot reject an assertion or a referring act. And we cannot suppose a referring act.

Now let us consider the difference between [α ϕ] and [(α) ϕ] when they occur as parts of a larger sentence. Let us compare the sentences ~[α ϕ] and ~[(α) ϕ]. If α labels an individual, these two sentences will have the same value. Suppose α does not label an individual. In this case, any sentence which contains (α) will be false. So ~[(α) ϕ] is false. But we have said that [α ϕ] will be false when α does not label. In that case, ~[α ϕ] will be true. Both [(α) ϕ] and ~[(α) ϕ] are false. This is due to the nature of referring. We do not want to have both [α ϕ] and ~[α ϕ] false. However, there are some problems with the sentence ~[α ϕ]. This can be used to perform two different acts:

(4) 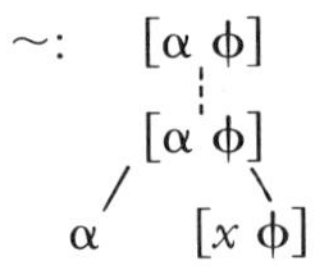

(5) 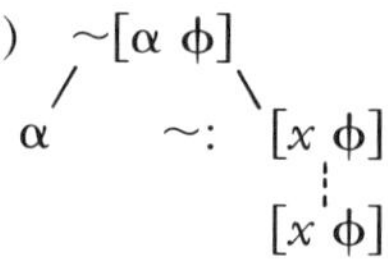

When we said that ~[α ϕ] should be true, we were thinking about structure (4). In (4) the sentential act enables the act of taking the sentential act to be false. The sentential act *is* false. So the act of taking [α ϕ] to be false is true. But in (5), the predicate ~[x ϕ] represents an individual as not being ϕ. The sentential act in (5) represents α's individual as not being ϕ. But α hasn't got an individual. It isn't true that α's individual is ϕ. It isn't true that α's individual is not-ϕ. Sentential act (5) entails that α's individual exists. So sentential act (5) is false.

The sentence ~[α ϕ] is ambiguous. More than representationally ambiguous, it is also inferentially and truth conditionally ambiguous. The language ($\mathscr{L}$) would lose much of its value if it were allowed to contain such ambiguous sentences. I will get around this problem by taking a step which I avoided earlier. In ($\mathscr{L}$), to prevent (5) from being a legitimate structure, an unenclosed individual constant will be counted as an operator. For one operator cannot be inserted within the scope of another. Instead of (5), we can only perform this act:

```
(6)  α_x   ~[x φ]
     /         \
    α        ~: [x φ]
                  ¦
                [x φ]
```

The sentence $\alpha_x \sim[x\ \phi]$ is false if α is an empty name. But $\sim[\alpha\ \phi]$ is true. For now (4) represents the only act of using this sentence. No changes are needed in the transformations for unenclosed angular phrases, for we have always treated the quantifiers as operators.

With a referring expression there is no important difference between $(\alpha)_x \sim[x\ \phi]$ and $\sim[(\alpha)\ \phi]$. The commitment to α's individual overrides anything that is said in the sentence; it does not matter at what point in the speech act structure the referring expression enters. The same is true for referring definite and indefinite phrases. There is no important difference between $(< a\psi >_m)_x \sim[x\ \phi]$ and $\sim[(< a\psi >_m)\ \phi]$, or between $(< \iota\psi >)x \sim[x\ \phi]$ and $\sim[(< \iota\psi >)\ \phi]$. We can now see the extent to which the earlier treatment of individual constants presupposed that individual constants are only used to refer. The individual transformation allowed "moves" that are characteristic of referring expressions. These expressions can be inserted within the scopes of operators; operators can be inserted within their "scopes." Even though the earlier individual transformation treated constants as referring expressions, we were not faced with the oddity of two sentences A, $\sim A$ both being false. For our treatment also presupposed that every referring expression labels an individual.

2. The New Transformations

We need to introduce a *referential* transformation to ($\mathcal{L}$). This combines a referring expression with a predicate. The referential transformation is very similar to the individual transformation of $\overline{\mathcal{L}}$ (and $\mathcal{L}$). In ($\mathcal{L}$) an unenclosed constant α is an operator. But the referring expression (α) is not an operator. With an operator, scope is important. With a referring expression, scope isn't important. We also want to prevent the quantifiers in enclosed angular phrases from "counting" when we have restrictions that involve the scopes of operators. We will accomplish this by stipulating that in an enclosed quantified phrase $(< a\phi >_m)$ or $(< \iota\phi >)$, the scope of the quantifier extends no further than the enclosing parentheses.

(*Refer*) Let A be a predicate that contains free occurrences of distinct individual variables $\beta_1, \ldots, \beta_m$ and no others; this is their canonical order. Let μ be one of:

(i) an individual constant α;
(ii) an angular indefinite phrase $< a\phi >_m$;
(iii) an angular definite phrase $< \iota\phi >$.

If μ is α, let $(\mu)\beta_i$ be $(\alpha)_{\beta_i}$. If μ is $< a\phi >_m$ or $< \iota\phi >$, then $(\mu)\beta_i$ is $(< a\phi >_m)\beta_i$ or $(< \iota\phi >)\beta_i$.

(a) Then $(\mu)\beta_i\ A\ (= A')$ is obtained from μ, A by the *referential transformation*. The indexing occurrence of β_i and the free occurrences of β_i in A are bound occurrences in A'; they are bound by the occurrence of (μ). The indexing occurrence of β_i is the *operative* occurrence of β_i in the occurrence of $(\mu)\beta_i$. A' *existentially presupposes* that (μ) depicts. A' also *existentially presupposes* whatever is existentially presupposed by A or by μ.

(b) Let every free occurrence of β_i in A other than the first be within the scope of the first free occurrence of β_i. Then A' is obtained from μ, A by replacing the first free occurrence of β_i by $(\mu)\beta_i$. A' is obtained by the *referential transformation*. The indexing occurrence of β_i in $(\mu)\beta_i$ and the free occurrences of β_i in A other than the first are bound by the occurrence of (μ) in the occurrence of $(\mu)\beta_i$ in A'. The indexing occurrence of β_i is the *operative* occurrence of β_i in the occurrence of $(\mu)\beta_i$. A' *existentially presupposes* that (μ) depicts. A' also *existentially presupposes* whatever is existentially presupposed by A or μ.

(c) If A contains a single free occurrence of β_i, then A' is obtained from μ, A by replacing the free occurrence of β_i by (μ). A' is obtained by the *referential transformation*. A' *existentially presupposes* that (μ) depicts. A' also *existentially presupposes* whatever is existentially presupposed by A or μ.

A referring expression is not affected by being within the scope of an operator. So clauses (b) and (c) do not require that the first or only free occurrence of β_i in A be within the scope of no operator. When a referring expression binds variables, it is the whole expression that does this, not a component like 'ι.' The referential transformation introduces an existential presupposition. It also preserves the existential presuppositions of its components. Of course, an individual constant α has no existential presuppositions. But an angular phrase like '$< \iota(Px \ni [x\ L\ (< \iota K >)]) >$' can have an existential presupposition. *The statement of every transformation of ($\mathcal{L}$) must be equipped with a sentence saying that the output existentially presupposes whatever is existentially presupposed by the inputs.*

If A' is $(\mu)\beta_i A$, then A' (directly) represents the individual labeled by μ, and arbitrary individuals $\beta_1, \ldots, \beta_{i-1}, \beta_{i+1}, \ldots, \beta_m$ as this or that. If A' is obtained by (b) or (c), then A' represents arbitrary individuals $\beta_1, \ldots, \beta_{i-1}$, the individual labeled by μ, and arbitrary individuals $\beta_{i+1}, \ldots, \beta_m$. Let A be suited to depict s-tuples in which the uth position answers to the free occurrences of β_i in A. And let μ be suited to depict r-tuples. (a) Then A' $(= (\mu)\beta_i A)$ depicts $(r + s - 1)$-tuples $< d_1, \ldots, d_r, e_1, \ldots, e_{s-1}>$ such that μ depicts $< d_1, \ldots, d_r>$ and A depicts $< e_1, \ldots, e_{u-1}, d_1, \ldots, e_{s-1}>$. The first position in these $(r + s - 1)$-tuples *answers to* the occurrence of $(\mu)\beta_i$ introduced by this transformation. (b, c) Then A' depicts $(r + s - 1)$-tuples $< e_1, \ldots, e_{u-1}, d_1, \ldots, d_r, e_u, \ldots, e_{s-1}>$ such that μ depicts $< d_1, \ldots, d_r>$ and A depicts $< e_1, \ldots, e_{u-1}, d_1, \ldots, e_{s-1}>$. The uth position in these $(r + s - 1)$-tuples *answers to* the occurrence of $(\mu)\beta_i$ or (μ) introduced by this transformation.

The account of representing and depicting for the referential transformation is like that for the individual transformation, third indefinite transformation, and third definite transformation of $\overline{\mathscr{L}}$. The main difference between the referential transformation and these earlier transformations does not involve representing or depicting. It is that the referential transformation introduces an existential presupposition. An expression containing an occurrence of (μ) (or $(\mu)\beta_i$) presupposes that μ depicts. This amounts to same thing as presupposing that μ labels a single individual. This presupposition is *satisfied* if μ does label exactly one individual.

The set-theoretic account of depicting is like the account of depicting above. If μ is an individual constant α, let $W = \{f(\alpha)\}$. If μ is an angular phrase, let $f(\mu) = W$. And let $f(A) = V$. (a) Then $f(A') = V' = \{< d_1, \ldots, d_r, e_1, \ldots, e_{s-1}> \mid < d_1, \ldots, d_r> \in W \text{ and } < e_1, \ldots, e_{u-1}, d_1, \ldots, e_{s-1}> \in V\}$. (b, c) Then $f(A') = V' = \{< e_1, \ldots, e_{u-1}, d_1, \ldots, d_r, e_u, \ldots, e_{s-1}> \mid < d_1, \ldots, d_r> \in W \text{ and } < e_1, \ldots, e_{u-1}, d_1, \ldots, e_{s-1}> \in V\}$.

If 'c' names Claude, and '$[x\ K]$' means *x is presently king of France*, then '$\sim[(c)\ K]$' is true. So is '$\sim[(c) = < \iota K >]$.' (The sentences '$\sim[c\ K]$' and '$\sim[c = < \iota K >]$' are also true.) The sentence '$\sim[(c) = (< \iota K >)]$' is false, since it presupposes that there is a present king of France. The sentence '$[(c) = (< \iota K >)]$' is also false. Both sentences also presuppose that Claude is real, but he *is*.

A new individual transformation is needed, now that unenclosed constants are operators of ($\mathscr{L}$). (But they aren't *radical* operators.)

(*Indiv*) Let A be a predicate containing free occurrences of distinct individual variables $\beta_1, \ldots, \beta_m$ and no others; this is their canonical order.

(a) Then $\alpha_{\beta_i} A$ $(= A')$ is obtained from α, A by the *individual trans-*

formation. The indexing occurrence of β_i and the free occurrences of β_i in A are bound occurrences in A'. They are bound by the initial occurrence of α. The indexing occurrence of β_i is the *operative* occurrence of β_i in the occurrence of α_{β_i}. Every occurrence to the right of the initial occurrence of α in α_{β_i} A is within the scope of this occurrence of α. A' *existentially presupposes* whatever is existentially presupposed by A.

(b) If the first free occurrence of β_i in A is within the scope of no operator in A, then A' is obtained from α, A by replacing the first free occurrence of β_i by α_{β_i}. A' is obtained by the *individual transformation*. The subscripted occurrence of β_i and the free occurrences of β_i in A other than the first are bound by the occurrence of α (in α_{β_i}) in A'. Every expression to the right of the occurrence of α introduced by this transformation is within the scope of the occurrence of α. The subscripted occurrence of β_i is the *operative* occurrence of β_i in the occurrence of α_{β_i}. A' *existentially presupposes* whatever is existentially presupposed by A.

(c) If there is only one free occurrence of β_i in A, and this is within the scope of no operator in A, then A' is obtained from α, A by replacing the free occurrence of β_i by α. A' is obtained by the *individual transformation*. Every expression occurring to the right of α is within the scope of this occurrence of α. A' *existentially presupposes* whatever is existentially presupposed by A.

In (a), A' represents the individual named by α and arbitrary individuals $\beta_1, \ldots, \beta_{i-1}, \beta_{i+1}, \ldots, \beta_m$ as whatever. In (b) and (c), A' represents arbitrary individuals $\beta_1, \ldots, \beta_{i-1}$, the individual named by α, and arbitrary individuals $\beta_{i+1}, \ldots, \beta_m$ as whatever. Let A be suited to depict n-tuples in which the jth position answers to the free occurrences of β_i in A. Then (a) A' ($= \alpha_{\beta_i}$ A) depicts n-tuples $< d_1, \ldots, d_n >$ such that $< d_2, \ldots, d_j, d_1, d_{j+1}, \ldots, d_n >$ is depicted by A and d_1 is depicted (labeled) by α. The first position in these n-tuples answers to the occurrence of α (of α_{β_i}) introduced by this transformation. (b, c) A' depicts those n-tuples $< d_1, \ldots, d_n >$ depicted by A in which d_j is depicted by α. The jth position in these n-tuples answers to the occurrence of α (or α_{β_i}) introduced by this transformation.

Let $f(A) = V$. (a) Then $f(A') = V' = \{< d_1, \ldots, d_n > \mid < d_2, \ldots, d_j, d_1, d_{j+1}, \ldots, d_n > \in V \text{ and } f(\alpha) = d_1\}$. (b, c) Then $f(A') = V' = \{< d_1, \ldots, d_n > \mid < d_1, \ldots, d_n > \in V \text{ and } f(\alpha) = d_j\}$.

If we extend $(\mathcal{L})$ to pseudo-languages $(\mathcal{L})_{\mathcal{D}}$, we need a real transformation to allow for combining individuals of $\mathcal{D}$ with predicates. The real transformation for $\overline{\mathcal{L}}_{\mathcal{D}}$ does not need changing. That transformation treated individuals in $\mathcal{D}$ like individual constants of $\overline{\mathcal{L}}$. We have changed our treatment of individual constants in ($\mathcal{L}$). But the earlier treatment is still appropriate for individuals in $\mathcal{D}$. An individual cannot fail to "correspond" to itself. The real transformation of $\mathcal{T}_{\mathcal{D}}$ only needs to be changed (i) to delete restrictions involving overlined variables, and (ii) to incorporate a provision to insure that existential presuppositions are preserved.

3. Some Other Changes

We must change the statement of the negation transformation which inserts '$\sim$' into a predicate. Before, a predicate $[\alpha_1\ \phi\ \alpha_2, \ldots, \alpha_n]$ could be taken to $[\alpha_1 \sim \phi\ \alpha_2, \ldots, \alpha_n]$ so long as α_1 was either a variable or an individual constant. We must now insist that α_1 be a variable or a referring expression.

Every transformation preserves existential presuppositions. The referential transformation introduces existential presuppositions. Let us consider what happens when a predicate (or sentence) has an existential presupposition that isn't satisfied. This will not affect the representing of the predicate, but it does affect the depicting. If the referential transformation combines (μ) and A to obtain A', and μ fails to depict, then A' won't depict either. ($f(A') = \emptyset$) We must insure, for all transformations, that if an input has an unsatisfied existential presupposition, the output does not depict. This is not a problem for transformations which aren't radical. With a nonradical transformation, what is depicted by the output is also depicted by an input. So if an input does not depict—as an input with an unsatisfied presupposition would not—then the output does not depict. With radical transformations, the output can depict what isn't depicted by an input.

Let '$[x\ K\ y]$' means *x knew y*, and '$[x\ M]$' mean *x is (was) an author of Principia Mathematica*. The angular phrase '$< \iota M >$' can be used to represent the author of *Principia Mathematica*. This phrase does not depict, because *Principia Mathematica* did not have a single author. The predicate '$[x\ K < \iota M >]$' is *suited* to depict pairs $< d, e >$ such that d is an individual, d knew e, and e was the author of *Principia Mathematica*. There are no such pairs; the predicate does not depict. But this predicate has no existential presuppositions. If we input this predicate to the negation transformation, the output will be: $\sim[x\ K < \iota M >]$. This output depicts every individual α which is not labeled by the input. The output depicts every individual. The predicate '$[x\ K\ (< \iota M >)]$,' like '$[x\ K < \iota M >]$,' does not depict. But '$[x\ K\ (< \iota M >)]$' has an existential presupposition; it presupposes that *Principia Mathematica* had exactly one author. If we input this predicate to the negation transformation, we obtain '$\sim[x\ K\ (< \iota M >)]$.' If we leave our earlier account of the negation transformation unchanged, this predicate will also depict every individual. But this result isn't wanted. Every predicate with an unsatisfied existential presupposition must fail to depict.

We must change our earlier account of depicting for the negation transformation to one that reads like this: If $\sim A$ is a sentence, then $\sim A$ depicts A if A is false, UNLESS A has an existential presupposition that is not satisfied. If A has an unsatisfied presupposition, then $\sim A$ does not depict. If $\sim A$ contains free occurrences of distinct individual variables $\beta_1, \ldots, \beta_m$ and no others (this is their canonical order), then $\sim A$ depicts those m-tuples that are not labeled by A, UNLESS A has an unsatisfied existential presupposition. If A has an unsatisfied presupposition, then $\sim A$ does not depict.

Each radical transformation must be altered in a similar way (except the universal transformation, which does not require a separate clause for unsatisfied presuppositions.) Doing this insures that every sentence with an unsatisfied presupposition will come out false.

The introduction of referring expressions and the referential transformation to ($\mathcal{L}$) produces sentences that can't appropriately be used by everyone. If A is a sentence without existential presuppositions, then anyone can use A to say something true. The sentence $[A \supset A]$ will be true; its use is unproblematic for any speaker. However, if A contains a referring expression (α), and α does not label an individual, then no sentence (of ($\mathcal{L}$)) that contains A will be true. Someone who believes that α labels an individual can appropriately assert $[A \supset A]$. What he says is false. If we do not believe that α labels an individual, we cannot appropriately either write or speak A. If we assert $[A \supset A]$, we commit ourselves to the existence of α's individual. If we know or believe that α does not label an individual, we cannot use $\sim A$ to say that A is false. But if A' results from A by replacing the '(α)'s in A by α's, we can assert $\sim A'$. We can also assert: $\sim[\alpha\ T]$. (But we can *never* truly assert a sentence: $[\beta \sim T]$.)

($\mathcal{L}$) also contains sentences that no rational person can use. No matter what '$[x\ F]$' means, the functor '$(Fx \ni \sim[x\ F])$' represents an (arbitrary) impossible individual—an F that isn't F. So '$<\iota(Fx \ni \sim[x\ F])>$' can be used to represent a specific individual. It represents *the* F that isn't F. We shall describe this angular phrase as representing the impossible individual. (There is no impossible individual. We can represent-the-impossible-individual.) A person who wrote or spoke a sentence containing '$(<\iota(Fx \ni \sim[x\ F])>)$' would commit herself to the existence of the one and only F that isn't F. In $(\mathscr{L})$, we indicate that x exists by writing (claiming) '$[x\ T]$.' So the sentence '$[(<\iota(Fx \ni {\sim}[x\ F])>)\ T]$' says and presupposes that the angular phrase labels an individual. The sentence says and presupposes that the impossible individual exists. The contradictory sentence '${\sim}[(<\iota(Fx \ni {\sim}[x\ F])>)\ T]$' says it is false that the impossible individual exists and also presupposes that the impossible individual does exist. If we want to deny that the impossible individual exists (or assert that it is false that the impossible individual exists), we should use this sentence: ${\sim}[<\iota(Fx \ni {\sim}[x\ F])>\ T]$. (We must not try to say it this way: $[<\iota(Fx \ni {\sim}[x\ F])> {\sim}\ T]$.)

Not all names in $(\mathscr{L})$ label individuals. The presence (or possibility) of empty names changes the standing of certain sentences. A sentence like '$[a\ T]$' no longer has an "axiomatic" status in $(\mathscr{L})$. When 'a' is empty, the sentence is false. But if 'a' is empty, then '${\sim}[a\ T]$' is true. (Both '$a_x\ {\sim}[x\ T]$' and '$[a\ {\sim}\ T]$' will be false in this case.) However, if ρ is a member of a domain $\mathscr{D}$, the pseudo-sentence $[\rho\ T]$ (in the pseudo-language $(\mathscr{L})_{\mathscr{D}}$) retains an "axiomatic" status. An existing individual cannot fail to be an existing individual. Sentences like '$[a = a]$' also lose their axiomatic status in $(\mathscr{L})$. If 'a' is empty, then '$[a = a]$' and '$[a_x = x]$' are false.

In dealing with $\mathscr{L}$ and $\mathscr{T}$, we required that domains $\mathscr{D}$ be nonempty. We might regard this as an existential presupposition of our accounts of $\mathscr{L}$ and $\mathscr{T}$. This is also an existential presupposition of standard logical languages. We have abandoned this presupposition for $(\mathscr{L})$, as a kind of "extension" of our decision to allow empty names. Our opening the door to the empty domain deprives the following sentences of the status of logical truths:

$$
\begin{array}{l}
[\forall T\ T] \\
[\mathit{a}T\ T] \\
\forall Tx\ [x = x] \\
\mathit{a}Tx\ [x = x]
\end{array}
$$

However, the following are still logical truths:

$$
\begin{array}{l}
[\Lambda T\ T] \\
\Lambda Tx\ [x = x]
\end{array}
$$

In the empty domain, even the following are true (but not logically so):

$$
\begin{array}{l}
[\eta T\ T] \\
\eta Tx\ [x = x]
\end{array}
$$

For the empty domain, no sentence $\forall\phi\alpha$ *A* or *a*$\phi\alpha$ *A* will be true. In contrast, every sentence $\Lambda\phi\alpha$ *A* and $\eta\phi\alpha$ *A* will be true—so long as neither ϕ nor *A* contains a referring expression.

4. More Existential Presuppositions

When a person performs a referring act, she uses an expression to represent a specific individual, and she is readily disposed to acknowledge the existence or other suitable status of the represented individual. It is also possible to use a quantified phrase like $\forall\phi$, $\Lambda\phi$, $\eta\phi$, *a*ϕ, or $\iota\phi$, and to be readily disposed to acknowledge the existence of ϕ's. A nominal act of using ϕ can carry with it a commitment to there being ϕ's. It is not similarly the case that a predicative act of using [*x* ϕ] will carry with it a commitment to there being ϕ's. A person might be committed to this, and be readily disposed to acknowledge that there are ϕ's. But a predicative act normally exploits inferential connections in providing a representation. To represent an arbitrary individual as ϕ is primarily to be disposed to make some inferences and shun others. (This is the instrumental manner of using the predicate.) When we use the predicate, we understand what it is to be ϕ in terms of these inferences. Our understanding of the predicate (predicative act) is not much affected by our either believing or not believing that there are ϕ's. With a nominal act we are normally representing an individual located with respect to our knowledge and beliefs—our cognitive map. This knowledge may be at least in part a "transcription" of inferential connections, but it is primary for determining which individual is represented. In this case, it makes more difference than in the predicative case whether our cognitive map includes the belief that there are ϕ's. It is also the case that the presupposition of a nominal act has more interest than any presupposition of a predicative act, because of the effect this presupposition has on our understanding of falsity. If we deny a sentence [(α) ϕ], it is clear that what is wrong with the sentence is not allowed to include the nonexistence of α's individual—in contrast to our denying [α ϕ]. Similarly, if we deny $\forall\phi\alpha$ *A*, but presuppose that there are ϕ's, then some ϕ must not satisfy *A*. (Without the presupposition, the denial would mean either that some ϕ doesn't satisfy *A* or that there are no ϕ's.) However, if we deny [α ϕ] (or [(α) ϕ]), and presuppose that there are ϕ's, this presupposition in no way affects our understanding of what is wrong with the sentence.

Just as I have introduced a special notation in ($\mathscr{L}$) to mark referring acts, so I will also introduce a special notation for a writer's use of a quantified phrase $Q\phi$ when she is readily disposed to acknowledge that there are ϕ's. Such a use carries with it a commitment to there being ϕ's. I will adapt the notation used for referring expressions to obtain *enclosed quantified phrases*:

$(\forall\phi)$	$(\forall\phi)\alpha$
$(\Lambda\phi)$	$(\Lambda\phi)\alpha$
$(\eta\phi)$	$(\eta\phi)\alpha$
$(a\phi)$	$(a\phi)\alpha$
$(\iota\phi)$	$(\iota\phi)\alpha$

In an enclosed quantified phrase, *the functor* ϕ *must not contain free variables*. An enclosed quantified phrase will not be used together with angular expressions; i.e., we will not allow expressions: $<(a\phi)>_m$, $<(\iota\phi)>$. (We already have enclosed angular phrases, but those are referring expressions.)

There is no convenient expression for acts performed with enclosed quantified phrases. ('Referring acts' is a convenient expression for acts performed with enclosed constants.) I will call these *presumptive* quantificational acts. An enclosed quantified phrase is a *presumptive* expression. We need presumptive quantificational transformations which are counterparts to the quantificational transformations. The presumptive transformations are exactly parallel to the plain transformations, and will not be stated here. (The statements of the presumptive transformations are slightly simpler, because of the fact that ϕ does not contain free variables.) The quantifier in a presumptive expression *does* count as an operator in the predicate to which it is introduced. A quantifier has the same scope whether or not it is enclosed.

The representing is the same for plain and presumptive transformations, but the depicting is not quite the same. Any predicate A' containing an enclosed quantified phrase $(Q\phi)$ will fail to depict if ϕ fails to depict. Suppose '$[x\ V]$' means *x is a vampire*, and '$[x\ C]$' means *x lives in Chicago*. Then '$[\eta V\ C]$' is true, but '$[(\eta V)\ C]$' is false. The second sentence does, and the first does not, presuppose that there are vampires. If A' is the output of a presumptive transformation which introduces $(Q\phi)$, then A' existentially presupposes that ϕ depicts. This presupposition is *satisfied* if ϕ depicts.

In ordinary talking and writing, most uses of quantified phrases are uses which have existential presuppositions. We don't very often talk about vampires and unicorns outside of logic classes. We don't very often use quantified phrases when we aren't sure if their nouns label objects. It seems likely that an understanding of presumptive phrases and presumptive transformations is more important for understanding normal acts of using natural-language expressions than the understanding of plain quantified phrases and their transformations. As far as syllogistic logic goes, this claim makes classical Aristotelian logic more important than syllogistic logic given a "Boolean" interpretation.

When it occurs in a sentence, but is not within the scope of another operator, a presumptive phrase can often be replaced by a plain phrase without affecting the truth or falsity of the sentence. Let '[x C]' mean *x is a cat,* '[x B]' mean *x is disposed to hunt birds*, and '[x V]' mean *x is a vampire*. Then the sentences '[$\forall C$ B]' and '[$(\forall C)$ B]' have the same value—presumably truth. The sentences '[$\forall V$ B]' and [$(\forall V)$ B]' have the same value; they are both false. Similarly it makes no difference as far as truth and falsity go whether we say '[aC B]' or '[(aC) B].' (There is a difference between plain and presumptive universal or particular phrases when they occur within the scope of a radical operator.) With the mathematical and negative quantifiers, there is a difference between the plain and the presumptive phrase even when they don't occur within the scope of an operator. The sentence '[ηV B]' is true, while '[(ηV) B]' is false. And '[ΛV B] is true though '[(ΛV) B]' is false.

It is interesting to note that the difference between '$\forall$' and 'Λ' "disappears" when these quantifiers occur in presumptive phrases. Both '[$(\forall F)$ G]' and '[(ΛF) G]' imply '[(aF) G]' (they also imply '[aF G]'). Both '$\sim$[$(\forall F)G$]' and '$\sim$[(ΛF) G]' imply '[(aF) $\sim$ G].' Two sentences $\forall\phi\alpha$ A and $\Lambda\phi\alpha$ A are not equivalent. But $(\forall\phi)\alpha$ A and $(\Lambda\phi)\alpha$ A are equivalent. This equivalence raises the possibility that in ordinary English, 'every' might not have two meanings. Perhaps the mathematical meaning of 'every' is the real meaning, and what I have been calling the ordinary meaning is really nothing more than the presumptive use of the quantified phrase. So the difference between the two meanings of 'every' would be the difference between $\Lambda\phi$ and $(\Lambda\phi)$. I will leave this as an open problem, though I think there are really two meanings involved. (There are $\Lambda\phi$, $\forall\phi$, and $(\Lambda\phi)$—or the equivalent $(\forall\phi)$.)

Earlier I said that the treatment of $\mathcal{L}$ and $\overline{\mathcal{L}}$ existentially presupposed that the domains $\mathcal{D}$ are not empty. One way to reflect such a presupposition in $(\mathcal{L})$ is by using enclosed phrases when 'T' is involved: $(\forall T)$, (ΛT), (ηT), (aT). A sentence containing one of these phrases presupposes that '[x T]' depicts—i.e., it presupposes that the domain is not empty. The present treatment of $(\mathcal{L})$ does not presuppose that any predicate depicts. The treatment of $\mathcal{L}$ and $\overline{\mathcal{L}}$ did not presuppose that every predicate depicts. It did presuppose that 'T' depicts. If we had continued that treatment for $(\mathcal{L})$, there would then have been no difference between a quantified phrase 'QT' and a quantified phrase '(QT).'

5. Inferential Meaning

In studying $\mathcal{L}$, I developed a deductive system $\mathcal{S}$. This system provides an account of the inferential meanings of the logical expressions in $\mathcal{L}$. In studying $\overline{\mathcal{L}}$, I did not alter $\mathcal{S}$ to obtain a system $\overline{\mathcal{S}}$. But it will not be difficult to develop $\overline{\mathcal{S}}$. Neither will it be an interesting task to develop $\overline{\mathcal{S}}$. What is interesting about pronouns in their ordinary use primarily involves representational meaning and truth conditions. The task of developing a deductive system seems both routine and mechanical. I am not going to develop a system $(\mathcal{S})$ for the language $(\mathcal{L})$ either. My omission is in no way due to this task's being either easy or uninteresting. To develop $(\mathcal{S})$ will be both fascinating and difficult. But developing this system must be part of another book-length project.

The deductive system $\mathcal{S}$ of chapter eight is not sound for $(\mathcal{L})$. Perhaps the most obvious problems concern the rules = Introduction and T Introduction. We no longer presuppose that every individual constant depicts, so we cannot simply introduce a sentence '$[a = a]$' or '$[a\ T]$.' These problems are easy enough to fix.
We can adopt a rule = Introduction like this:

$$\frac{[\alpha\ T]}{[\alpha = \alpha]}$$

or for β an individual variable:

$$\frac{[\alpha\ T]}{[\alpha_\beta = \beta]}$$

We can adopt a T Introduction rule like this:

$$\frac{\alpha_\beta\ A}{[\alpha\ T]}$$

Other problems that can be fixed without much trouble involve the insertion and extraction rules for quantifiers. The following inference sequence:

$$[a\ F\ \Lambda G]\ /\ \Lambda Gy\ [a\ F\ y]$$

is valid, but the reverse sequence:

$$\Lambda Gy\ [a\ F\ y]\ /\ [a\ F\ \Lambda G]$$

is not valid. (If neither '*a*' nor '*G*' depicts, the premise will be true. In that case, the conclusion will be false.) With referring expressions, both:

$$[(a)\ F\ \Lambda G]\ /\ \Lambda Gy\ [(a)\ F\ y]$$
$$\Lambda Gy\ [(a)\ F\ y]\ /\ [(a)\ F\ \Lambda G]$$

are valid.

A serious problem with $\mathscr{S}$ which isn't easy to fix is associated with the hypothetical nature of natural-deduction proofs. A hypothesis that contains a referring expression or a presumptive expression has a noncancelable existential presupposition. The presupposition is not hypothetical. Consider the referring expression '$(<\iota(Fx \ni {\sim}[x\ F])>)$,' which represents the impossible individual. If we begin a subproof with this hypothesis:

(1) $[(<\iota(Fx \ni {\sim}[x\ F])>)\ T]$

we should, if our rules are adequate, be able to deduce the following conclusion:

(2) ${\sim}[(<\iota(Fx \ni {\sim}[x\ F])>)\ T]$

Our derived rule of ~ Introduction would allow us to cancel the hypothesis and keep the conclusion. So (2) would be a theorem. But (1) is deducible from (2). So the system would be inconsistent.

To solve these problems (and, incidentally, to solve some logical paradoxes), we must invent and investigate a subject that I want to be called *illocutionary logic*. I propose to extend language ($\mathscr{L}$) to il($\mathscr{L}$)o for carrying out this task. The deductive system for il($\mathscr{L}$)o will contain both hypothetical and "absolute" proofs. In studying the language and its system, we will determine the right ways to reason with various kinds of expressions, including referring and presumptive expressions. We will determine the right ways to establish various kinds of result. But that project is deferred until another time.

Chapter 15
Odds and End

1. Lexical Transformations

In developing the present account of speech-act syntactic structure, we have focused attention on the deliberate language user, who performs as many distinct acts as possible in using a complex expression. In normal speech, a person might use a complex expression to perform a simple intentional (linguistic) act—even though the deliberate language user would use that expression and its components to perform an act with some structure. (In this context, we are not counting an act like the following:

$$\begin{array}{rl} \sim: & A \\ & \vdots \\ & A \end{array}$$

as simple. The act performed with '$\sim$' does not have act components. But this act is structured, intentionally. The negating act is a complex act without components; the enabling act is enough like a component that we don't want to classify an enabled act as simple.) The normal speaker is able to simplify the deliberate speaker's acts when a certain complex expression occurs frequently, or a certain kind of complex expression occurs frequently.

As an example of normal simplification, consider the following instance of the first universal transformation:

[∀(+ *P*): *J*]
⋮
[*x* *J*]

The predicative input represents an arbitrary individual as jogging. This enables the output act, which is performed with the quantified phrase '∀*P*.' The quantified phrase is used to take the predicative act to be true for every person. The act performed with the quantified phrase is itself complex. The functor '*P*' is used to represent an arbitrary person. This gives a special character to the act of using the universal quantifier. The special character accounts for the predicative act's being taken to be true for every person as opposed to every something else. The quantified phrase is one that would occur frequently. It corresponds to the English expressions 'everyone' and 'everybody.' The phrase '∀*P*' would normally be used to perform an act of taking to be that does not have a structure of its own:

[∀*P*: *J*]
⋮
[*x* *J*]

This quantificational act does not count as a simple act in the present context, since it is an act enabled by the predicative input. But this structure is simpl*er* than the act performed by the deliberate language user. When '∀*P*' is used like one expression, it is used to perform a quantified-phrase act with a special character. The special character is furnished by the expression '*P*,' but this character is not conferred by a distinct intentional act.

Another example of simplification is furnished by adjective-noun combinations which occur frequently, like 'green grass' or 'red blood.' The deliberate language user will perform an act like this:

green grass
/ \
green grass

The normal speaker will very often use 'green grass' to perform an act without structure.

There are some complex expressions which we couldn't accuse even the deliberate language user of using to perform complex acts. It seems that *nobody* would perform a complex act with a predicate like '[*x* *F* *y*].'

The passive voice transformation simply does not correspond to a speech act structure. However, there is a systematic relation between '[*x F y*]' and '[*x* $\overset{\cup}{F}$ *y*],' between '$\overset{\cup}{F}$' and '*F*.' I will describe this relation by saying that '[*x* $\overset{\cup}{F}$ *y*]' is obtained from '[*x F y*],' and '$\overset{\cup}{F}$' from '*F*,' by a *lexical transformation*. A lexical transformation is a functional relation which takes one or more input expressions to an output expression. The various meanings of the output expression are functions of the meanings of the input expressions. A lexical transformation is being opposed to a speech act transformation, whose statement is an abstract description of a speech act structure. The statement of a lexical transformation explains expressions which are not outputs of speech act transformations. I believe that the passive voice is a strictly lexical transformation.

But some transformations are both speech act and lexical transformations. The earlier examples illustrate transformations that are speech act transformations on certain occasions and lexical transformations on others. The adjectival transformation which combines 'green' with 'grass' is a speech act transformation for a person who performs an act with this structure:

```
    green grass
      /     \
  green      grass
```

The combining transformation is lexical for the person who uses 'green grass' to perform a simple intentional act. (The expressions could be combined in a speech act transformation at one time, and in a lexical transformation at another, in acts performed by the same person. If we are contrasting green grass with grass of some other color, the speech act transformation would be normal. If we are using 'green grass' in a situation where the 'green' seems redundant, the lexical transformation might be expected.) The quantificational example mentioned above is not a case of a speech act and a lexical transformation. For we have not recognized a separate transformation for combining a quantifier with a noun (predicate functor). We could have done this. The combining transformation would be a preliminary transformation to the first universal transformation. Had we organized the syntactic account that way, there would be speech act and lexical transformations combining a quantifier with a predicate functor. As it stands, the combining of '$\forall$' with ϕ is incorporated in the first universal transformation. The lexical transformation gives an expression $\forall\phi$ which combines with a predicate A in a slightly different transformation than the first universal transformation.

The difference between speech act and lexical transformations does not concern some formal characteristic of the transformations, nor does it show up in descriptions of the inputs and outputs of these transformations. The difference concerns the way that the language user employs the expression "yielded" by the transformation. Strictly speaking, it isn't correct that the same transformation is sometimes a lexical and sometimes a speech act transformation. Instead, some lexical and speech act transformations correspond so closely to one another that the same abstract description may fit both.

When a speech act transformation corresponds closely to a lexical transformation, the latter transformation derives from the former, which is more fundamental. An understanding of the speech act transformation is sufficient to yield an understanding of the lexical transformation, but an account of a lexical transformation won't explain the speech act structures associated with the speech act transformation. However, many lexical transformations do not correspond closely to speech act transformations; the passive voice transformation is one of them. So is the transformation that turns a verb like 'works' (or 'to work') into the noun 'worker.' In the syntactic account of a language, it is necessary to include strictly lexical transformation, as the passive voice transformation was included in the syntactic accounts of $\mathscr{L}$, $\overline{\mathscr{L}}$, and ($\mathscr{L}$). Although lexical transformations play an auxiliary role in a syntactic account, they must be explained, for their outputs serve as inputs to speech act transformations, which are primary.

2. The Broadest System of Language

In this book I have developed artificial languages to model features of natural languages, especially English. I have not been concerned with an entire natural language, but have restricted my attention to the propositional subsystem of a natural language: to those sentences used to perform propositional acts, the components of those sentences, and propositionally structured experience. The artificial languages have shed light on only a small number of features of the propositional subsystem. Much work remains to be done to understand even the propositional subsystem of a natural language. In this section I will briefly consider what more there is to a system of language than its propositional subsystem.

Earlier I indicated that there are different modalities of accepting and rejecting sentences (sentential acts). If A represents, to *simply* accept A is to accept A as representing things as they are. But suppose A does not represent. Suppose A is $\sim B$. Then in using A, I take B to be false.

Accepting *A* is accepting *B*'s being false as the way things are. I can accept a sentential act as representing things as they are, or accept it as the way things are. I can also accept or reject a representing *A* as representing things as I would like them to be. I can accept a nonrepresenting *A* as being the way I would like things to be (I accept *B*'s being false as what I would like to be the case). I can accept *A* as representing things as I hope they will be, or as I am obligated to make them be. The modalities of accepting and rejecting are fundamental. They are not derivative from something "deeper." Suppose I accept the sentence 'Arabs and Jews are friends' as representing what I would like to be the case. There is not some more fundamental state of liking Arabs and Jews to be friends which supports my acceptance. My liking for Arabs and Jews to be friends *is* my accepting the sentence 'Arabs and Jews are friends' under the modality of what I would like to be the case. (The liking is more accurately identified with my ready disposition to accept some such sentence under the indicated modality.)

When I accept a sentence under a modality, we must not think that I am taking the sentence (sentential act) to be this or that. As well as accepting the sentence 'Arabs and Jews are friends' as what I would like to be the case, I *can* take the sentential act to be one which represents what I would like to be the case. (And I can accept this act of taking to be.) But this sentential act of taking to be is derivative from my modal acceptance. My act of taking to be is true only if I am readily disposed to accept the sentence as representing what I would like to be the case. Those who misconstrue intentional relations as real relations with abstract relata will misunderstand the various modalities of accepting and rejecting. In the present view, we must understand that when George accepts *A* and also accepts *B*, we don't have one relation linking George to two propositions. We have two specifically different but generically similar acts of accepting. When George would like for *A* to be the case and for *B* to be the case, there are not two instances of the relation *liking to be the case*. There are two specifically different acts (or dispositions to acts) of accepting-as-what-he-would-like-to-be-the-case.

We can expand the propositional subsystem of language by introducing the different modalities of accepting and rejecting. This expansion does not enrich the vocabulary of the propositional subsystem. It does enrich the inferential structure of the propositional subsystem. The propositional subsystem is structured by inferential relations derived from commitment. But this is the commitment to accept or reject a sentence as representing, or being, things as they are. The various modalities of accepting and rejecting generate commitments to accept and reject under the modalities. The propositional subsystem is basic, and the commitment relations involving the other modalities are not very different from the commitment relations of the propositional subsystem. But there are some differences.

The *enriched propositional subsystem* is the propositional subsystem enriched with the inferential structure generated by the various modalities of accepting and rejecting. To this enriched subsystem, we might introduce expressions for making explicit the modalities of accepting and rejecting. We might introduce modal operators:

> I would like it to be the case (that)
> I hope (that)
> I believe (that)
> I am obligated to make it the case (that)

When these expressions are conceived as modal operators, they are used to perform acts like the act of taking a sentential act A to be an act representing what I would like to be the case. The modal operators will be used to perform acts of taking to be which are accepted (rejected) as simply being the case. Conceived as modal operators, these expressions (and their acts) already belong to the propositional subsystem of language. The enriched propositional subsystem is not further enriched by adding these expressions. The expressions used as modal operators might also be used to indicate illocutionary force. Asserting a sentence is accepting (or pretending to accept) a sentence as representing what is the case. If we accept a sentence under a different modality, we have a different illocutionary act.

The different illocutionary acts corresponding to the different modalities are not usually recognized. In the case of assertion, we have the word 'assert' and the prefix 'I assert.' This prefix is normally used to perform an illocutionary act, in an act like this:

I assert: that A
¦
(that +) A

or to make explicit the illocutionary force of a sentential act like this:

(I assert +) that A

(that +) A

The prefix is not normally used as a modal operator. For it seems pointless to assert that I assert *A*; though I might want to deny that I assert *A*. The plain assertion of *A* might also be done with one of:

> I believe that *A*
> I am convinced that *A*
> I know that A

As well as being used to indicate illocutionary force, the prefixes 'I believe,' 'I am convinced that,' and 'I know that' can be used as modal operators. While there is some understanding of their roles as modal operators, there is almost no appreciation of the fact that these expressions can be used to indicate illocutionary force. The same is true of expressions like 'I hope,' 'I am obligated to make it the case,' 'I would like it to be the case,' etc. For these prefixes, there is no word analogous to 'assert' that can be used to perform what everyone would easily recognize to be a distinctive form of illocutionary act.

When the modal operators are used to indicate illocutionary force, we have further enlarged the enriched propositional subsystem. For a (sub)system of language is determined by a set of sentences and their component expressions, experience, the inferential structure linking expressions and experiences, and the structures of acts of using complex expressions. (We either think of one expression as having a set of structures associated with it, or we think of the expressions as "equipped" with structures, so that the same expression can occur more than once as an element of the subsystem. In that case the elements are structured expressions.) By allowing the additional acts (and structures) performed with illocutionary-force-indicating expressions, we expand the enriched propositional subsystem. Once we allow modal operators to be used to perform illocutionary acts and to make illocutionary force explicit, we might as well add other expressions for indicating illocutionary force. We not only use language to accept and reject sentences, we also use language to get things done. We ask questions, make requests, give commands, and make promises. The vocabulary of the enriched propositional subsystem is being expanded with expressions like:

> I assert (that)
> I promise (that)
> I command (that)

The components of these prefixes already belong to our vocabulary. But these first-person forms are used to perform illocutionary acts and make illocutionary force explicit.

When the enriched propositional subsystem (of a natural language) is further enriched with expressions, and their acts, for indicating illocutionary force, the result is the *minimal illocutionary subsystem*. This subsystem does not contain interrogative or imperative sentences like these:

> What time is it?
> Shut the door.

It does contain sentences like these:

> I request that you tell me the time.
> I command that you shut the door.

Expressions in English that are used to indicate illocutionary force are representing expressions. When I make an assertion by saying "I assert that *A*," I have represented myself as asserting. I might use the prefix to make the assertion, performing an act like this:

```
 I assert:  that A
 /     \      \
I   x assert (that +) A
```

In the prefix act, if I am deliberate, I represent myself as asserting. In representing myself as asserting, I *am* asserting *A*—enabled by the sentential act. I might also use the prefix to make explicit that I am asserting *A* in performing the sentential act:

```
 (I assert +) that A
 /      \
I    x assert    (that +) A
```

I still represent myself as asserting, which representing act gives a special, explicit, character to the sentential act. Even when an illocutionary "operator" is used by the speaker to indicate illocutionary force, it is typically used to represent. The same expressions are normally used to describe illocutionary acts, though this usually does not involve the first person and the present tense. (I describe myself as having asserted *A*, without presently asserting *A*, when I say, "I asserted *A*.") And when the speaker uses an illocutionary operator to indicate the force of his utterance, his audience will typically use that operator to represent him as performing a certain kind of illocutionary act—without using the operator to perform the speaker's kind of act.

We can imagine a language where illocutionary-force-indicating expressions employ different symbols than other expressions. In a written language, we might use '$\vdash$' for assertion and '$\dashv$' for denial. If such expressions were used, a speaker or writer would no longer represent himself in using an illocutionary operator. His audience will presumably use these operators to perform representing acts—to represent the speaker as performing an act of a certain kind. Such a language would be awkward, since different symbols must be used to perform and to describe illocutionary acts. A speaker (writer) in such a language would not use an illocutionary operator to represent or depict. But the expression has an official role: to perform a certain kind of act and to enable the audience to understand what kind of act is performed. Even a representing illocutionary operator is used in this role, in addition to its representing. A new semantic concept is need to accommodate this "dimension."

The vocabulary of the minimal illocutionary subsystem, including its complex expressions, is contained in the vocabulary of the propositional subsystem. But the minimal illocutionary subsystem also contains:

> An enriched inferential structure;
> Different illocutionary acts and their structures.

The minimal illocutionary subsystem is still far removed from a system of language which constitutes a natural language. For natural languages not only contain sentences designed for performing a narrow range of (nonassertive) illocutionary acts. In the minimal illocutionary subsystem we have these sentences (and the associated acts and structures):

> I assert that Denver is in Colorado.
> I promise that I will wash the dishes tonight.
> I am sorry that I bumped you.
> I hope that there will be peace on Earth.
> This is an order: you will shut the door.

In these sentences, there is a neat division between an illocutionary "operator" and a sentence (sentential act) on which this operator "works." As well as containing sentences with two such distinct parts, a natural language contains sentences that combine propositional representing and illocutionary-force indicating in such a way that the distinct jobs can't be assigned to distinct expressions. Consider the sentence 'What time is it?'

This sentence is used to perform the illocutionary act of *asking* what time it is. The sentence 'It is nine o'clock' might be used to perform an act like this:

```
          It is nine o'clock.
           /              \
(It +) is y          nine o'clock
```

In the predicative act, 'It' is used to represent the present time. The predicative act represents an arbitrary individual as being the present time; the sentential act represents nine o'clock as being the present time. Some questions consist of incomplete propositional acts—the addressee is requested to complete them. The question 'What time is it?' might be used like this:

```
            What time is it?
             /            \
What (+ time)        x is (+ it)
```

The predicative input represents an arbitrary individual as being the present time. The expression 'What time' represents the present time. 'time' is used to give an explicit temporal character to the representing, since the addressee cannot tell from 'it' that the speaker is representing the present time (the present moment?). The question represents an arbitrary time as the present time. The form of the question, and its intonation, will indicate the illocutionary force; this is "mixed together" with its schematic propositional "content" to perform an act requesting the addressee to represent the present time specifically.

The *illocutionary system* of language is obtained from the minimal illocutionary subsystem by adding sentences whose form indicates (typical) illocutionary force. This includes sentences like:

What time is it?
Shut the door!
Please pass the salt.
Would that there were peace on Earth!

The illocutionary system also contains expression (and their structures) used to perform illocutionary acts which do not represent or present their propositional content. This includes expressions like:

I agree.

Watch out!
Hurrah!

The illocutionary system comes close to being the total system of language. But it falls short of the total system. To understand this, it is helpful to recall some of the later Wittgenstein's language games. Let us make up one of our own. Suppose there is a game in which different players occupy different positions. For each new position that a person occupies, there is a different word that must be uttered. Failure to produce the word, or producing the wrong word, penalizes the player. These words belong to our language; acts of uttering them play roles in the game. The words have no representational meaning; they do not indicate illocutionary force. (The words could be used to represent in a derivative fashion. They would undoubtedly be used to describe particular instances of the game.) I am reluctant to say that the game words are meaningful or significant. Instead I will say that they are *intelligible.* An expression is intelligible with respect to a certain form of activity in which acts of using the expression play an "official" role. The total system of language consists of all intelligible expressions, together with experience, the inferential structure, and the structures of acts of using the expressions.

Meaning and significance are special cases of intelligibility. So an expression can be intelligible without being significant, but can't be significant and not intelligible. A meaningful expression has both an inferential and a representational meaning; significant expressions are inferentially and representationally significant. In English, expression used to indicate illocutionary force are also used to represent; they have inferential meanings. These expressions also have a semantic dimension that isn't part of their meaning. In this dimension, they are intelligible but not meaningful. They are intelligible with respect to the activity of indicating illocutionary force.

3. A New Division of Experience

In English, the expressions used to indicate illocutionary force are both meaningful and intelligible. We could develop a language in which the force-indicating expressions are intelligible without being meaningful—at least from the standpoint of the speaker or writer. (When illocutionary force is indicated by form, and not by an expression, as with interrogative sentences, we might describe that form as being intelligible but not meaningful.) An expression which is intelligible is so with respect to some form of activity. (A form of activity is much the same as one of

Wittgenstein's forms of life.) The game-playing expressions mentioned earlier are intelligible with respect to the activity of playing the game; the intelligibility of each expression consists of its role in the game. In a general way, every expression in a language is intelligible with respect to the activity of using language. While this is true, it is not enlightening. There are many linguistic activities, and they must be described narrowly and specifically if we are to explain particular expressions. In addition, many linguistic activities are parts of larger activities, not properly described as linguistic. The linguistic acts constitute only a small portion of the game-playing activity. To understand a linguistic activity, it is often important to situate it in a larger context.

Let us consider the intelligibility of expressions used to indicate illocutionary force. And let us ignore their meaningful dimension: their use to represent the speaker, and their inferential roles. Apart from the meaningfulness, in what does their intelligibility consist? An illocutionary-force-indicating expression is used to perform illocutionary acts, and to make clear the force of these acts. It would frequently be impossible to perform the acts unless their forces were explicit. Many illocutionary acts are essentially consummated acts that cannot take place unless the audience understands what is going on. (A nonconsummated command is no command at all.) In this connection, it seems that illocutionary-force-indicating expressions are important for a speaker's communicating with his audience. These expressions make clear what the speaker is doing—they make clear what is the force of his utterance. In the game example, the expressions were intelligible with respect to a larger, not strictly linguistic, activity. With illocutionary operators, their larger activity is linguistic. They are intelligible with respect to successful linguistic communication. We can subdivide the activity of verbal communication into different classes. (Perhaps we could use Searle's concept *direction of fit* for this.) One class might contain acts of commanding, requesting, and praying. Another could contain asserting, hypothesizing, suggesting, etc. Some force-indicating expressions might be intelligible with respect to a single subform of the activity of verbal communication. Others might be intelligible with respect to more than one—this would be determined by the fineness of our subdivisions.

Let us consider expressions which are significant or meaningful. With respect to what are they intelligible? Significant expressions are used to represent or to take some linguistic act to be this or that. These expressions are closely tied to experience. We must remember that experience is not something that happens to us. It is something we do, a form of activity. Expressions which are significant are intelligible with respect to experience. Meaningful expressions are used to organize experience, to constitute its propositional structure. Meaningful expressions are used to represent experience and to represent things which we understand through their relations to experience.

We have previously distinguished three levels of experience. The first is preverbal and preconceptual; the second and third involve conceptual organization. Now I want to make a new division that admits two kinds of experience. These kinds cut across the three levels. The first kind of experience is *perception*, which includes what we experience through sensation. We perceive external objects and (some of) their features. We perceive our own bodies and their features. Perception is intimately tied to second-level experience, but perceptual experience is also structured by third-level concepts. We can perceive that this is an object of a certain kind. We can perceive that *A* causes *B*. Expressions significant with respect to perception include expressions for ordinary physical objects and their sensible features. This class contains expressions for objects that are related causally, modally, and by analogy to objects we perceive. An expression which is significant with respect to perception need not label objects we can perceive, but to understand the expression, and to represent with it, we must know how the represented objects are related to objects we do perceive.

Perception is part of our mental life. Perceiving things is a way of being aware of things, of thinking about them. Perception is also a kind of experience. Other areas of our mental lives do not count as experience—if we merely think about an object, we are not experiencing that object. If we imagine an object, feel love or hate for an object, or if we feel desire or fear for an object, we are not (we need not be) experiencing the object.

But there are important similarities between perception and other areas of our mental lives, the most important of which concern the fact that when we perceive an object, we are not making (mental) contact with the object. We can perceive an object when the object is present. We might have a qualitatively identical perceptual "experience" when the object is absent. (In such a case, we would probably believe that the object is present.) We can similarly imagine or think about real or fictional objects that aren't present—we can desire or fear absent and nonexistent objects. We can say of other mental acts (excepting perceptual acts) which don't make contact with their objects, that they are intentional acts, and generate intentional relations. (E.g., the intentional relations *thinking about, imagining, desiring*, and *fearing*.) In first-level perception, we don't perform intentional acts. We do perform acts, but they aren't intentional because we are not aware of what we are doing. I believe that first-level perception involves neural states and events, and I have proposed to understand first-level acts involving neural states and events on the model of (intentional) acts of taking to be. "Interpreting" neural states and events is taking them to be external objects and events. It is because we aren't consciously aware of the neural items that we aren't performing intentional acts in first-level perception. (If we could become consciously aware of the neural states and events, and we used them to perform intentional acts, then the acts would be acts of taking for. We would take the neural items for external objects and events.)

We don't normally consider first-level perception to "generate" intentional relations. For first-level perception isn't intentional; it doesn't involve acts of taking for (most intentional relations that we notice are generated by acts that involve representing). However, first-level perception does involve intentional relations—if we consider it the essential feature of an intentional relation that an individual can have an intentional relation to an object that "isn't there." Consider two qualitatively identical first-level perceptions. The first experience is caused by light reflected from a table striking the subject's eyes and producing neural events which culminate in the subject's seeing the table (as whatever). But this is first-level experience, so the subject is not aware that the seen object is a table. In the second "experience," the subject has the same neural events and states as in the first. This time the neural phenomena are produced by electrical stimuli applied through electrodes implanted in the subject's brain. The subject interprets these phenomena the same way as in the first experience, making whatever response is appropriate on seeing a table. These are not two experiences of seeing a table. Seeing is a real relation, not an intentional relation. No one can see a table that is not there to be seen. To see a table, the subject must suitably interpret neural phenomena that are actually produced by a table. But we could introduce an expression ψ for an intentional relation "behind" seeing. If we had such an expression, we could say that the subject ψ's a table in both cases, but only sees a table in the first case.

Introducing a new terminology for intentional relations behind first-level perception could be confusing, for we currently use the same terms for both first-level and higher-level perception. My dog sees the table and so do I; we both hear the same sounds. But the intentional relation behind first-level perception is different from the intentional relation behind higher-level perception. Second and third-level perception are intentional. First-level perception interprets neural phenomena. Higher-level perception further interprets neural phenomena by intentionally taking it to be this and that—without there being distinct moments such that we first interpret the neural phenomena, and then take this to be something or other. Higher-level experience is essentially propositional and judgmental. We take things to be the case. We accept this taking to be. In third-level experience, we might interpret this neural phenomenon to be a distinct individual, which act enables us to take the individual to be a table. If I turn out to be mistaken—either the individual isn't a table or there is no individual at all—then I will say I thought I saw a table. The intentional relation behind higher-level perception is *thinking I perceive*, so long as this is understood in such a way that when I really perceive I also think I perceive.

When I see that there is a table before me, there must be a table before me which causes the neural phenomena I take to be a table. Even though we normally misconceive that is going on when we perceive, perception involves real relations between perceivers and objects. I really do see a table, in spite of the fact that I take neural phenomena to be the table. Taking (and accepting this) appropriately caused neural phenomena to be a table is what seeing the table *is*. The present view is a mixture of representationalism and direct realism. We really do see real external objects, by way of "operating" on neural intermediaries. Although the neural phenomena are intermediaries which correspond to external objects, we do not perceive these intermediaries. The mistake of most representationalist theories is holding that we perceive the intermediate entities and infer the external objects. In fact, we take the intermediate entities to be the external objects, without being consciously aware of the intermediate entities as they are in themselves.

Not all experience is perceptual, we are also aware of our mental lives. We are aware of intentional acts and their features. We know when we are acting; we often know why. We know when we are imagining or thinking, and what we are thinking about. We are aware that we are perceiving. The experience of our mental and intentional lives is *reflection*. In reflection, unlike perception, we actually do "make contact" with the objects of experience. An experience of an intentional act, or an experience of thinking, is an experience of the real thing. In first-level reflection, we are not operating on neural phenomena which we take to be this or that. We are instead *acquainted* with the intentional phenomena. This does not mean we are aware of everything which these phenomena involve. For intentional acts surely involve neural states and events; but we are not consciously aware of them. Since we are acquainted with intentional acts in first-level reflection, there is no need in higher-level reflection to perform acts of taking the first-level items to be distinct individuals. Acquaintance with an intentional act is sufficient to enable acts of taking the intentional act to be this or that. One of the first philosophers to understand the difference between perception and reflection, Descartes, thought it appropriate to gain some understanding of reflection before tackling the external world.

Expressions for different kinds of mental act and activity, for different kinds of intentional act and activity, and for the various features of such acts are intelligible and meaningful with respect to reflection. However, not every expression significant with respect to perception represents an object or feature we can perceive, and not every expression significant with respect to reflection represents an object we can experience in reflection. We might, for example, introduce an expression which labels those physical objects Jane thought about last week. The expression would be used to represent objects that can be perceived, but the expression itself would not be significant with respect to perception. A more important expression is 'picture.' A picture is a physical object, but to be a picture it must be intended to be used to represent. This makes 'picture' significant with respect to reflection. 'True,' 'truth,' 'false,' and 'falsity,' as well as other metalinguistic expressions like 'entail,' or 'incompatible,' are significant (and meaningful) with respect to reflection.

Some expressions are meaningful with respect to perception alone. These include expressions for sensible qualities, for familiar physical objects, and for spatial relations and geometric features. Some expressions are meaningful with respect to reflection alone. These include expressions for mental acts, for intentional acts and intentional phenomena. Still other expressions are meaningful with respect to both perception and reflection. Such expressions as 'same,' 'different,' 'similar,' 'exists,' 'part,' 'individual,' and 'event' belong to this class. This tripartite classification scheme recalls Descartes' account of simple ideas. (In the *Regulae*, he called these simple *natures*.) Some simple ideas are of mental features, some are of physical features, and some simple ideas represent both mental and physical features. Descartes believed that all the ideas we need to understand and explain the world are either simple ideas or are obtained by "manipulating" simple ideas.

Descartes thought we have a fixed and finite fund of simple ideas and that the important simple ideas are innate. (Once we understand that ideas are skills for recognizing instances of things of a kind, and skills for representing things of a kind, it no longer seems crazy to hold that there are innate ideas. That view seems crazy only when ideas are understood to be images.) Descartes' belief in the fixed and finite number of simple ideas justified his deductive conception of knowledge, for anything we are capable of understanding, anything we are even capable of thinking about, must be conceivable with ideas obtained from our basic stock. (It is part of Descartes' view that God has supplied us with those simple ideas that are needed for understanding the world we live in.) By exploring simple ideas, their relations to one another, and the combinations that are possible, we can through conceptual analysis discover what things are possible and necessary. If we observe some phenomena that we wish to understand, we search for combinations of simple ideas which represent objects that would behave in the observed ways. We try to perform experiments to eliminate unsatisfactory hypotheses. If we are left with two or more equally successful explanations of the phenomena in question, we are free to adopt any of them.

Hume retained the view that we have a basic stock of simple ideas from which all thinking is derived. He did not regard these as innate, but thought they are supplied by sensation. Although Hume agreed with Descartes that the stock of simple ideas available to us limits thought and knowledge, he did not base a deductive conception of knowledge on this view. Because the basic ideas he recognized weren't ideas of objects and their qualities, but were ideas of qualities that don't depend on objects, Hume believed only mathematical knowledge could be obtained in deductive fashion. For Hume, empirical knowledge is obtained by observing which of the large number of possible combinations of simple ideas actually obtain.

Even Kant accepted Descartes' claim that we have a stock of basic ideas (concepts) to work with, and that all thought and knowledge (and experience) are constrained by this limited stock. These views were conceived with respect to mental items (ideas, concepts) rather than expressions, but they imposed restrictions on language, since a significant representing expression must express an idea (or a concept). For these views, it is out of the question that someone could introduce an entirely new concept, one not explicable in terms of our basic stock of given concepts. However, this is just what we can do. Our doing this is illustrated over and over again in the history of science. We do not start with a few fundamental concepts or expressions, and explain all the rest in terms of them. In the present conception, the linguistic system is fundamental; an expression's meaning is traced to its place in the system. This conception does not require a small foundation. New expressions, expressing new concepts, can be developed by developing new linguistic systems. These will be extensions of, or modifications to, a present system. They won't be reducible to that present system.

4. Identity and Difference

Some expressions are closely associated with grammatical categories. Consider the category of expressions used to represent a specific individual. This includes names, indefinite descriptions, and definite descriptions. Let us call these *referring expressions.* They aren't always used to refer when they are used to represent a specific individual, but they are the kind of expressions that are used to refer. To use a referring expression, we must understand what it is to encounter the same individual twice, and to represent the same individual twice. We couldn't understand what it is to be concerned with the same individual on different occasions if we didn't understand what it is for individuals to be different. The concepts of identity and difference, and expressions for these concepts, are associated with the category of referring expressions. The two concepts are equally fundamental; we don't define difference by negating identity. For a sentence '[*a* = *b*]' to be false, it must be incompatible with true sentences. It is false if the true sentences include '*a* is different from *b*,' or sentences which entail that *a* is different from *b*. (The sentence '[*a* = *b*]' might also be quasi-incompatible with our recognition that *a* is different from *b*.)

Expressions for identity and difference are meaningful with respect to perception and reflection. For we must be able both to identify and distinguish perceived individuals, and to identify and distinguish objects encountered in reflection. But there is a sense in which expressions for identity and difference are primarily significant with respect to the activity of using referring expressions. In first-level experience, we experience an individual as qualified, or individuals as related. We don't have concepts of the quality or relation (if we did, our experience wouldn't be first-level), but the first-level experience of a quality or relation provides the basis for our introducing a concept. Before we had concepts, we could experience an object as red, or two objects as next to each other. These experiences enable us to introduce expressions (and their concepts) 'red,' and 'is next to.' It does not seem possible that someone in his first-level experience could experience an individual as the same as itself, or experience two individuals as different. There is no first-level experience which "calls for" or supports the concepts of identity and difference. The acquisition of these concepts is instead concurrent with our learning to use referring expressions. For we can't use referring expressions without possessing the concepts of identity and difference. We can't possess the concepts unless we can use referring expressions.

It is conceivable that someone could get the hang of using referring expressions without having words like 'same,' 'identical,' or 'different' in his vocabulary. Explicitly talking about these concepts, or objects that fall under them, is slightly more sophisticated than simply using referring expressions. (It isn't much more sophisticated. The person who can refer but not discuss the issue of whether two individuals are the same can't say very much.) There is an important sense in which the person who can perform referring acts can recognize and judge about identity and difference, even without being able to use words which express these concepts. For we can be disposed to use two or more names interchangeably, or to reuse a name that we have used before, and *be aware of this disposition*. Not only can we be disposed, but we can actually do these things, and recognize that we are doing them. We can also be disposed to refrain from using a name in a given situation, or to refrain from using two names interchangeably. We can reject a sentence which contains the wrong name for an individual we are concerned with. The fact that a person could "possess" the concepts of identity and difference without having words for them could easily lead someone to claim that these concepts are innate. A more plausible explanation is that they are acquired when we learn to refer. Most concepts are acquired when we learn to use expressions for them, but certain fundamental concepts can be acquired in the absence of the relevant words. An important result of this is that, without having the expression '=' in her vocabulary, Michelle can in effect believe that [$a = b$], and she can be committed to accept the consequences of '[$a = b$],' because she is committed to using 'a' and 'b' interchangeably. It might also happen that our speaker possesses an expression for identity but no expression for difference. Her "virtual" beliefs can lead her to reject '[$a = b$],' not because the sentence is incompatible with other sentences that she accepts, but because it is ruled out by the belief incorporated in her disposition to not use 'a' and 'b' interchangeably.

5. Logical Expressions

I think it is characteristic of distinctively logical expressions to be associated with a grammatical category, as expressions for identity and difference are associated with the category of referring expressions. So distinctively logical expressions will express concepts that are necessarily acquired when we learn to use expressions belonging to the associated category. Let us consider some other categories, to see what expressions and concepts (if any) are associated with them.

We shall begin with the category of predicate functors (or the categories of common nouns and intransitive verbs); we could as well consider the category of predicates. The concepts of similarity and difference are associated with these categories, but this is a different difference than we considered in the preceding section. The expressions 'similar' and 'different' are not generally considered to be logical expressions; these expressions are not ordinarily investigated in logic. In fact, it doesn't seem useful to study either these expressions or the related concepts. (But an expression might be a distinctively logical expression without being an expression worth studying.) Similarity and difference are always in a certain respect. If we considered plain similarity, then every individual α is similar to every individual β. With plain difference, every two individuals are different. Ordinary predicates mark similarity in various respects. α is similar to β in respect *F* iff both [α *F*] and [β *F*]. α is different from β in respect *F* iff either [α *F*] and ~[β *F*] or ~[α *F*] and [β *F*]. The ability to employ predicate functors and predicates gives the ability to deal with similarity and difference. It is no saving to write '[α *S*{*F*} β]' ("α is similar in respect *F* to β") rather than '[[α *F*] & [β *F*]].' In logic we deal with similarity and difference when we deal with predicates and predication.

Adding the words 'similar' and 'different' (different in a respect) to our vocabulary does not increase our expressive capabilities as 'identical' and 'different' would. However, we might carry out a comprehensive study of similarity in general and difference in general by allowing ourselves to quantify over predicate functors. To indicate that α and β are similar in some respect or other, we can write: (∃*f*)[[α *f*] & [β *f*]]. From the present perspective, a higher-order language will be distinctively logical, designed to explore the logical concepts of similarity and difference. Let us consider the difference between ordinary quantifiers and quantified phrases and higher-order quantifiers and quantified phrases. In first-order languages, in $\mathscr{L}$, $\overline{\mathscr{L}}$, and ($\mathscr{L}$), and in English, when a quantifier is used quantificationally to yield a sentence, it is used either to take a schematic expression (act) to be true for every, no, some, etc. individual, or to give a special character to a schematic act so that it represents an arbitrary or specific individual as this or that. When quantified phrases are used in name-like ways, they are used to represent an arbitrary or specific individual. Ordinary quantification is not basically substitutional; it is concerned with individuals, not with expressions representing individuals. (We can, however, provide a substitutional statement of the truth conditions associated with ordinary quantified phrases. For example, the sentence '[*a**M* *J*]' is true iff there is a name α in our language or some extension of it such that '[[α *M*] & [α *J*]]' is true.) Ordinary quantifiers can be used for both concrete and abstract individuals. We can talk about every person, any triangle, no property, some relation, or the even prime number. When we use quantified phrases to talk about abstract individuals, our quantifiers do not thereby become higher-order. In fact, there is no natural higher-order version of $\mathscr{L}$, $\overline{\mathscr{L}}$, or ($\mathscr{L}$) in which the quantified phrases are used to represent extralinguistic entities. English does not contain higher-order quantified phrases which represent properties, relations, etc. Someone who thought that ordinary nouns, predicate functors, and predicates are names (or like names) of properties and relations might be inclined to construe higher-order quantified phrases as concerned with some property, every relation, etc. But a noun like 'man' does not name humanity. The predicate '[*is red*]' does not name redness. Nouns and predicates are used to represent individuals: an arbitrary individual of a kind, or an arbitrary individual as this or that. In a higher-order version of one of our artificial languages, the quantifiers should be construed substitutionally. A sentence '(∃*f*)[[α *f*] & [β *f*]]' would not *mean* that α and β have a property in common. (It would *entail* that they do.) The sentence is understood as saying that some one-place predicate functor can be combined with both α and β to form a true sentence. The functor need not already belong to the language. The quantified sentence will be true if the language now contains an appropriate functor; it will we true if an appropriate functor can be introduced into the language (which yields an extension of the current language).

Now consider the category of sentences. It is likely that there is a large number of concepts associated with this category in such a way that the ability to use sentences as we do requires that we possess those concepts. It is a fundamental feature of the category of sentences that some sentences are used to represent. Even the functioning of sentences that aren't used to represent depends on the representing sentences. If *A* is a sentence used to represent, the basic modes of accepting and rejecting *A* are accepting and rejecting *A* as representing things as they are. To be able to use a sentence to represent, we must understand what it is for things to be as the sentence represents. But a representing sentence is true if things are as it represents. The concept of truth for representing sentences is a fundamental concept associated with the category of sentences. When a sentence *A* is used in such a way that some component is used to take other components to be this or that, it is essential that the user understand what it is for the other components to be this or that. Such a sentence is true if the other components are what they are taken to be. For example, $\sim B$ is true if B is false, $[A \vee B]$ is true if the collection of A, B is such that at least one member is true. The truth of a representing sentence is different from the truth of a sentence in which the "main" expression is used to perform an act of taking to be. But both concepts of truth are fundamental concepts associated with the category of sentences. Truth is a logical concept; expressions used to indicate that a sentence is true are logical expressions. To use sentences, we must know what it is for a sentence to be true, even if we don't possess a word for truth. To use sentences, we must also understand entailment and incompatibility. So these are logical concepts. If a sentence is false just in case it is incompatible with true sentences, then falsity is a logical concept. Expressions which are used to take a sentence to be false are logical expressions. So '$\sim$' and 'not' are logical expressions.

Expressions for disjunction are logical expressions, because they are used to take a collection of sentences to be such that at least one member is true. An expression for conjunction can be used to take a collection of sentences to be such that each member is true. In this use, the expression would be a logical expression. But the typical use of a sign of conjunction is to provide a special character to acts, making it explicit that they supplement each other. The use of sentences to supplement each other in this way is fundamental to the category of sentences. Even when used typically, expressions for conjunction are logical expressions. It is also an essential feature of our use of sentences that we can take one sentence (sentential act) to be conditional on another. To use sentences as we do, we must understand the conditional relation. This would make conditional expressions logical expressions. But someone might object to this argument to support the claim that conditionality is a logical concept. They might contend that we can equally well claim it to be essential to our use of sentences that we use sentences to attribute colors to things. But that the concept of color-attribution should be counted a logical concept is absurd. It is true that it is essential to our linguistic practice that we attribute colors to things, but color-attribution is more properly linked to predicates than to sentences (which are a proper subclass of predicates). Even when we consider predicates, we don't want to say that the concept of representing an individual as colored is a logical concept. It is an essential fact about us and the world we live in that we experience objects as colored, and we use (some) predicates to represent objects as colored. But it is not a fundamental fact about predicates as such that some predicates are used to represent objects as colored. Only some predicates are color predicates. If the concept of representing an individual as colored were logical, then the class of color predicates would constitute a distinct grammatical (sub)category of expressions. The concept of representing an individual as colored would be associated with that category. But I will adopt as a rule the principle that a grammatical category can be further subdivided into grammatical categories only if distinctive speech act structures are associated with each subcategory. (There are three grammatical categories of adjectives; these cannot be further subdivided to provide additional grammatical categories.) We can subdivide the category of predicates into grammatical categories of intentional and nonintentional predicates, but we cannot make the case that color predicates constitute a grammatical category.

The category of sentences is a grammatical category that can be subdivided to yield other grammatical categories. Understanding the conditional relation is essential to our use of sentences, but conditional expressions are used to perform acts having distinctive structures. So we can regard conditional sentences as constituting a grammatical subcategory of the category of sentences. Conditional expressions express concepts whose understanding is fundamental for using expressions in this grammatical subcategory. The conditional expressions of English are logical expressions, as are their watered-down versions incorporated in our artificial languages.

Our system of language has a modal structure. It not only contains experiences we do have and expressions for representing them. It also contains experiences we might have and sentences which represent what is possible, both in the sense of what might be true for all we know, and in the sense of what is now open—waiting to be decided. To understand the system of language it is necessary to understand its modal structure. We must, for example, understand how doing one thing opens certain possibilities while doing something else opens others. To use our language, we must understand various concepts of necessity and possibility, expressions for which are logical expressions. As well as modalities of possibility and necessity, I have spoken of modalities of accepting and rejecting sentences. We can accept a sentence as representing what is the case, or as representing what we are obligated to make be the case. The different modalities of accepting and rejecting are primarily associated with various illocutionary acts. But we can also introduce modal operators to express these modalities. Such operators will be additional logical expressions.

Quantifiers, used quantificationally, are associated with predicates and with intermediate quantificational acts. I suggested earlier that it might be possible for a person (or chimpanzee) to use names and predicates without being able to use quantifiers. However, it is essential to *our* use of language that it includes quantifiers. The concept of a predicate's being true of some individual or other, or of an intermediate act's being true, are fundamental and logical concepts. Every typically quantificational act, when it yields a sentence, involves a predicative or intermediate act's being true (for every, no, some, etc. individual). The concepts of being true, being unrestrictedly true, never true, true for an individual of a kind, true for every individual of a kind, etc. are logical concepts with logical expressions. Even when quantified phrases are used in a name-like way, quantifiers are logical expressions, for they serve to mark the use of a functor (noun) to represent an arbitrary or specific individual. These uses of functors are characteristic uses of expressions in their category. We must understand what it is to represent an arbitrary or specific individual if we are to understand and use such expressions.

In the present view, for any distinctive class of expressions constituting what we take to be a grammatical category, we can expect to find fundamental concepts and logical expressions associated with that category. Symbols for identity and (individual) differences are logical expressions. Our connectives and quantifiers are logical expressions. So are higher-order (substitutional) quantifiers. Other concepts associated with sentences (e.g., analyticity) are modal notions—modal expressions are logical. Expressions indicating tense constitute a grammatical category and give rise to a logical theory. We might also expect to find plurality logics, adjectival logics, and adverbial logics: a wide range of subjects is open to logical investigation.

Now I want to consider how the new understanding of distinctively logical expressions ties in with what we know about logical expressions. I had thought it was an important feature of logical expressions that we could explain their meanings by giving their (real world) truth conditions. This contrasts logical expressions with expressions like color words. We might give truth conditions for color words in terms of wave lengths of light; this would not give the meanings of color expressions. But any explanation of the truth conditions of the truth-functional 'and' will enable us to determine the meaning of this expression. I no longer think this is such an important feature of logical expressions, because it also characterizes nonlogical expressions; some logical expressions might not possess it.

We learn to use many expressions by learning to label and depict with them. We subsequently distinguish the meanings of the expressions from the things we label with the expressions. So there are lots of expressions whose meanings we learn via their truth conditions. For those expressions for which we can provide truth conditions without giving their meanings (like color words), we must have extralinguistic information about the represented objects. When we give this kind of truth conditions, we are situating the expressions in a supplemented system of language. The fundamental character of logical expressions rules out the possibility of our obtaining extralinguistic identifying information for most of them. For example, we can't imagine an extralinguistic criterion of truth—a way to determine which sentences are true that does not enable us to understand 'true,' 'truth,' etc. There must be many nonlogical expressions for which we don't have extralinguistic identification criteria, and with respect to logical temporal expressions, it is conceivable (but not likely) that some radiation phenomena might enable us to give truth conditions that are of no help in determining meaning.

Another more important feature of logical expressions is their intimate connection with inference. Of course, not only logical expressions have inferential meanings; every meaningful expression has an intimate connection with inference via its inferential meaning. To understand how logical expressions can have an even more intimate connection with inference, we must distinguish two kinds of inferences. In an *ordinary* (valid deductive) inference, we have premises which characterize objects (either positively or negatively), and a conclusion which characterizes objects; the validity of the inference depends on relations between the relevant characteristics (and between their expressions). An inference from 'α is scarlet' to 'α is red' is an ordinary inference, depending for its validity on scarlet's being a shade of red. An inference from 'α is red' to 'α isn't green' is also ordinary. So is an inference from 'It is true that Albany is the capital of New York' to 'It isn't false that Albany is the capital of New York.'

In an *extraordinary* inference, we have a premise (or premises) which characterize a linguistic act. This characterization authorizes a certain performance of the linguistic act, which performance is or is contained in the inference's conclusion. If we use a sentence $\sim A$ this way:

$$\begin{array}{l} \sim\!: A \\ \quad\ \vdots \\ \quad\ A \end{array}$$

we have used A to perform a sentential act. This enables our using '$\sim$' to take the sentential act to be false—our doing this *characterizes* the sentential act as false. (Characterizing an object α as ϕ is more general than representing α as ϕ. We can characterize α as ϕ by representing α as ϕ. We can also do it by taking α to be ϕ.) The premise which characterizes A as false authorizes a conclusion which consists in rejecting

A. A move from accepting ~ *A* to rejecting *A* is an extraordinary inference. The sentence 'It is true that Albany is the capital of New York' might be used like this:

It is true: that Albany is the capital of New York.
(that +) Albany is the capital of New York

Here the prefix is used to take the sentential act to be true. The sentence can also be used like this:

(It is true +) that Albany is the capital of New York.
(that +) Albany is the capital of New York.

In this act, the prefix is used to give a special character to the sentential act. The special character makes explicit that the sentential act has the character of a true sentential act. Having this character is either representing things as they are or being performed with an expression used to take things to be what they are. We can accept the sentential act with its special character; making explicit that a sentential act has a certain character is also a way of characterizing an act. If we characterize a sentential act as true, and accept this characterization, this authorizes our accepting the sentential act. So an inference from 'It is true that Albany is the capital of New York' to 'Albany is the capital of New York' is an extraordinary inference. Similarly, a move from premises [*A* v *B*], ~ *A* to conclusion *B* is an extraordinary inference. A move from the same premises to 'It is true that *B*' is an ordinary inference.

A move from a premise which performs an act to a conclusion which characterizes the act is also an extraordinary inference. So a move from rejecting *A* to accepting ~ *A* is extraordinary. So is the inference from 'Albany is the capital of New York' to 'It is true that Albany is the capital of New York.' Or from *A* to [*A* v *B*]. In an extraordinary inference, we don't just proceed from an act to a description of it, or vice versa. Consider the inference from 'It is true that Albany is the capital of New York' to 'Albany is the capital of New York.' The premise characterizes the sentential act performed with 'Albany is the capital of New York.' But for the inference to be an inference, the premise must be accepted (or supposed). The conclusion consists in a sentential act. What is important is not simply that this act is performed, but that the conclusion is accepted. (Accepting the premise justifies accepting the conclusion.) Accepting the premise which characterizes the sentential act authorizes us to accept the conclusion, which in this case consists of the characterized act. In a move from [A v B], ~ A to B, both premises characterize sentential acts. Accepting the premises authorizes us to perform and accept an act which is among those characterized by the premises. The important feature of an extraordinary inference is that it takes us from accepting an act or acts which characterize other acts to accepting a conclusion which employs an act characterized in the premises—or vice versa. The intimate connection of logical expressions with inference consists in the fact that logical expressions figure in extraordinary as well as ordinary inferences. Their inferential meanings involve both kinds of inferences. In contrast to the inferential meaning of a word like 'blue.'

The relation of logical expressions to extraordinary inferences is clear for connectives. The rules for connectives in system $\mathcal{S}$ characterize the connectives by their roles in extraordinary inferences. Consider the quantifiers. A sentence '[∀*M J*]' can be used this way:

[∀(+ *M*): J]
⋮
[*x J*]

The quantified phrase is used to take the predicative act to be true for every man. The predicative act is characterized as being true for every man. We can also say that the acts performed with '*M*' and '[*x J*]' are characterized as such that everything depicted by the first is also depicted by the second. Accepting this sentence authorizes an inference from a sentence '[α *M*]' to '[α *J*]' for any α. (We can be authorized not only to accept sentences (as true) but also to accept inferences (as valid).) We might represent the extraordinary inference from '[∀*M J*]' to the inference this way:

$$[\forall M\ J]\ /\ \frac{[\alpha\ M]}{[\alpha\ J]}$$

An inference from premises '[∀*M J*],' '[α *M*]' to the conclusion '[α *J*]' is also extraordinary. Only one of the premises characterizes linguistic acts. This together with the second premise authorizes the conclusion which performs but doesn't characterize a linguistic act. An inference from '[α *M*],' '[α *J*]' to '[*a*M *J*]' is also an extraordinary inference.

The connection between expressions for identity and extraordinary inferences is harder to detect than with other logical expressions. For if we use the predicate '[$x = y$]' to represent arbitrary individuals as related by identity, we do not seem to be characterizing linguistic acts. However, if we construe '=' on the model of 'is' in English, then identity predicates will not normally be used to represent pairs. We will not have acts with these structures:

```
   [α = β]              [α = β]                       [α = β]
   /  |  \              /      \                      /      \
 α [x = y] β           α      [x = β]           [α = y]       β
                              /     \            /    \
                          [x = y]    β          α    [x = y]
```

The most typical use of '=' will be as the 'is' of predication. Typical acts of using '$[b = aD]$' ("Bob is a doctor") might have these structures:

```
(1) [b = aD]                         (2) [b = aD]
    /      \                             /      \
   b     [x = (+ a(+ D))]               b     [x = (+ a +) D]
                                              [x = (+ D)]

(3) [b = aD]
    /      \
   b     [x = (+ (a +)D)]
```

In (1) and (2), the indefinite quantifier is used quantificationally. In (1) the indefinite phrase gives a special character to the predicative act so that it represents an arbitrary individual as a doctor. The use of 'D' gives a special character to the quantified phrase. In (2), the predicate functor 'D' is used to give a special character to the predicate so that it represents an arbitrary individual as a doctor. The quantifier gives a special character to this intermediate quantificational act, making explicit its schematic character. In (3), the quantified phrase is used in a name-like fashion. The predicative act still represents an arbitrary individual as a doctor. Similarly, the sentence '$[c = < \iota M >]$' ("Chuck is the mayor") might be used like this:

```
(4) [c = < ιM >]
    /          \
   c      [x = (+ < ιM >)]
```

The predicate '$[x = y]$' is like intentional predicates in that it is not used to represent arbitrary individuals x, y as related. It is used to determinably represent an arbitrary individual x as anything at all (as existing?). Expressions which go in to second argument position serve to give a special determinate character to the predicative act. So that the predicate then represents an arbitrary individual x as something determinate (e.g., a doctor, the mayor).

When '=' is used for the 'is' of identity between two referring expressions, the act will typically have this structure:

$$\begin{array}{ccc} & [\alpha :=: \beta] & \\ \diagup & & \diagdown \\ \alpha & & \beta \end{array}$$

The sign '=' is used to take the two enabling acts to label a single individual—i.e., to be such that there is one individual that they both label. In this case, the identity sentence is used to characterize acts. If we accept this characterization, we are authorized to use α and β interchangeably in a variety of contexts.

We can also consider a real relation of identity between individuals—i.e., a real relation linking every individual to itself and nothing else. We can use '=' or some other symbol to represent individuals related by real identity. But our understanding of this relation derives from our understanding what it is to represent a single individual more than once (which also requires us to understand what it is to represent more than one individual with more than one act). The concept of the real relation of identity owes its claim to being a logical concept to its close ties to the concept of using one or more expressions to represent one object. The inferential role of the expression for real identity will be understood on the model of that for the expression used to represent related acts.

The discussion of extraordinary inferences enables us to understand a further feature of logical expressions. Any valid inference can be turned into a logically valid inference by adding analytic premises constructed with logical (and other) expressions. The inference:

> Some cat is black.
> So some feline is black.

is turned into:

> Every cat is a feline.
> Some cat is black.
> So some feline is black.

The analytic premise 'Every cat is a feline' contains the logical expressions 'Every,' 'is,' and 'a.' In using this premise we might take the act representing an arbitrary cat as a feline to be unrestrictedly true:

```
        Every cat is a feline.
        |            :
        ·· cat is a feline
        |    /          \
      Every cat    is (+ (a +) feline)
```

We might take the predicative act to be true for every cat:

```
Every (+ cat): is a feline
                      :
             x is (+ (a +) feline)
```

In either case we have characterized the acts of using 'cat' and 'is a feline' as such that whatever is depicted by the first is depicted by the second. This authorizes us to (extraordinarily) infer 'α is a feline' from 'α is a cat' for any individual α. The second premise tells us that some black individual is a cat. The authorization of the first premise combined with the second premise yields the conclusion. Logic is the study of semantic features associated with logical form, which is grammatical form plus logical expressions. Logical expressions are used to characterize expressions in various grammatical categories. The added analytic premises can turn ordinary inferences into extraordinary inferences; they characterize linguistic acts in ways which authorize the drawing of the conclusion.

Bibliography and References

1. Rene Descartes. *The Philosophical Works of Descartes.*
2. David Hume. *An Inquiry Concerning Human Understanding.* Indianapolis, Indiana: The Bobbs-Merrill Company, Inc., 1955.
3. Immanuel Kant. *Critique of Pure Reason.*
4. Ludwig Wittgenstein. *Philosophical Investigations.* New York: The MacMillan Company, 1953.

Index